T0350488

Handbook of Research on Enterprise Systems

Jatinder N.D. Gupta
The University of Alabama in Huntsville, USA

Sushil K. Sharma
Ball State University, USA

Mohammad Abdur Rashid
Massey University, New Zealand

INFORMATION SCIENCE REFERENCE

Hershey · New York

Director of Editorial Content: Kristin Klinger
Director of Production: Jennifer Neidig
Managing Editor: Jamie Snavely
Assistant Managing Editor: Carole Coulson
Typesetter: Jeff Ash
Cover Design: Lisa Tosheff
Printed at: Yurchak Printing Inc.

Published in the United States of America by
        Information Science Reference (an imprint of IGI Global)
        701 E. Chocolate Avenue, Suite 200
        Hershey PA 17033
        Tel: 717-533-8845
        Fax: 717-533-8661
        E-mail: cust@igi-global.com
        Web site: http://www.igi-global.com

and in the United Kingdom by
        Information Science Reference (an imprint of IGI Global)
        3 Henrietta Street
        Covent Garden
        London WC2E 8LU
        Tel: 44 20 7240 0856
        Fax: 44 20 7379 0609
        Web site: http://www.eurospanbookstore.com

Library of Congress Cataloging-in-Publication Data

Handbook of research on enterprise systems / Jatinder N.D. Gupta, Sushil K. Sharma, and Mohammad Abdur Rashid, editors.

        p. cm.

Includes bibliographical references and index.

Summary: "This book Systems addresses the field of enterprise systems covering progressive technologies, leading theories, and advanced applications"--Provided by publisher.

ISBN 978-1-59904-859-8 (hbk.) -- ISBN 978-1-59904-860-4 (ebook)

1. Management information systems. 2. Information technology--Management. I. Gupta, Jatinder N. D. II. Rashid, Mohammad A. III. Sharma, Sushil K.

HD30.213.H354 2009

658.4'038011--dc22

                            2008031502

British Cataloguing in Publication Data
A Cataloguing in Publication record for this book is available from the British Library.

Editorial Advisory Board

List of Contributors

Table of Contents

Section I
Enterprise Systems: Technologies, Solutions, and Strategic Perspectives

Section IV
Enterprise Systems: Implementations and Applications

Section V
Enterprise Systems: ERP and Beyond

Detailed Table of Contents

Section I
Enterprise Systems: Technologies, Solutions, and Strategic Perspectives

Section I of this handbook starts with the growing importance of increasing agility in the organization and then focuses understanding the technologies available to develop and deploy Enterprise Systems (ES) in organizations. In the current global and competitive business environment, it is essential to be flexible and agile simultaneously. Appropriate design and alignment of enterprise systems with business strategies can enable a business to create a competitive advantage in the global markets, at least in the short-term. Various chapters in this section discuss the technologies for enterprise systems' integration, solutions such as SAP Business Blueprint, and the strategic perspective of implementing and using enterprise systems for providing sustained competitive advantage.

The first chapter of this handbook presents a holistic approach for Enterprise Agility and explains why the term "enterprise agility" has been adopted for characterizing this capability. Furthermore, it provides a holistic approach for analyzing enterprise agility that is based on a viewpoint-oriented Enterprise Architecture. The ultimate purpose of this chapter is to provide the means for researchers to explore enterprise agility in a systematic way and to identify a number of important issues regarding the attainment of such capability.

Chapter II

This chapter discusses the concepts behind SAP Business Blueprint. It views the ERP solution as an integral component of the design process. It argues that the modernized approach for SAP Business Blueprint may be driven by the technical configuration of the solution landscape; hence the layout and foundation for the organizational design are set from the start. The chapter concludes that such an integrated environment simplifies the enterprise design process during SAP implementation and facilitates the transition, support, and maintenance of the new enterprise environment.

Chapter III

This chapter introduces the key aspects of Free/Open Source Enterprise Resources Planning systems (FOS-ERP). The chapter highlights (a) the differences between FOS-ERP and their proprietary equivalents (P-ERP) in terms of business models, selection, customization, evolution and maintenance; and (b) the challenges and opportunities that they offer to adopters, vendors, researchers, and individual collaborators. The chapter also identifies the challenges and opportunities that the open source enterprise systems offer to stakeholders and developer communities.

Chapter IV

The chapter discusses the Business Process Modeling (BPM) concepts and evolving modeling standards and technologies that have the potential to dramatically change the nature of phases of the systems development life cycle (SDLC). Although the notation is still in working draft format, this chapter suggests that the system architects and designers should consider incorporating the concepts of BPM into their current and future systems analysis and design procedures.

Chapter V

This chapter discusses the Enterprise Resource Planning system's effects and strategic perspectives in organizations. The focus of the chapter is on how information technology and ERP, together, facilitate in aligning the business to achieve excellent productivity. Because the ERP systems are large and complex, taking years to implement, the inclusion of today's strategic choices into the enterprise systems may significantly constrain future action. By the time the implementation of an ERP system is completed, the strategic context of the firm may have changed. Therefore, this chapter explores various ways by which an ERP system can provide sustained competitive advantage.

Chapter VI

Gary P. Moynihan, The University of Alabama, USA

This chapter describes an Executive Information Systems (EIS) as a software system designed to support the informational needs of senior management. The EIS is characterized by an easy to use and maintainable graphical user interface; integrated capabilities for data access, analysis, and control; analysis and report generation across multiple files; and on-request "drill down" capability. By understanding the concept and functionality of traditional executive information systems, readers will be able to better understand how EIS has adapted to meet the requirements of senior management in an enterprise system environment.

Section II
Enterprise Systems: Risks, Performance, and Business Value

Section II discusses the risk and performance issues related to enterprise systems. Business operations are composed of a collection of business processes. The enterprise system is an approach to integrate business processes people, applications and systems; in essence integrating the business, for business transformation and business value creation. Studies have proven that integration is not only a key reason for the adoption of Service Oriented Architecture (SOA) but also for improving business value. However, in doing so, it is important to assess the risk of implementing enterprise systems and the performance gains that can be achieved. Further, it is important to consider integration in a wider concept, including the entire supply chain and the customer relationships. Various chapters in this section are devoted to the discussion of relevant topics to enable the reader to understand the relationship between risks, performance, and business value while developing, implementing and deploying integrated enterprise systems.

Chapter VII

Joseph Bradley, University of Idaho, USA

As ERP systems have proven difficult and costly to implement, organizations must consider the risks and rewards of embarking on complex and time consuming implementation projects. Therefore, this chapter describes the reasons for the firms to adopt Enterprise Resource Planning systems, identifies the benefits firms seek, discusses various risks firms face as they adopt these systems, and suggests ways firms can manage these risks. It also discusses some well publicized ERP failures, risk management tools, and future trends in ERP implementation. The chapter suggests that while organizations will continue to adopt ERP as a strategic necessity to remain competitive in their industry, few, if any, will gain any sustainable competitive advantage by adopting ERP.

This chapter contends that ERP investments may contribute to the achievement of improved business performance and examines the conditions under which this contribution occurs. The findings presented in this chapter also suggest that, while in the long-run the pervasive diffusion of standardized software may decrease its strategic value, in the short-run early ERP adopters can profit from a window of opportunity to obtain above average returns.

This chapter deals with the enterprise information system's administrative and execution context as a component of the application software development process. It is argued that while the application software lifecycle considers the functionality of a given collection of components within the context of a consumer's requirements definition, it frequently overlooks the application integration requirement within the context of the enterprise environment. The chapter illustrates the potential impact of these considerations on the acceptance and application of enterprise systems.

This chapter explores a model of transforming ES data into knowledge and results by comparing two case studies that examine the impact of enterprise systems information on organizational functions and processes leading to realization of business value. A qualitative research methodology is used to explore how firms can leverage ES technologies to realize improved business value. These findings suggsest that the ongoing transformation of an organization to extract value from data, distribute results from analysis, apply knowledge, and establish decisions for strategic organizational benefits will lead the path towards business success.

This chapter discusses two popular initiatives of supply chain management (SCM) and customer relationship management (CRM). SCM focuses on optimizing the materials, information, services, and financial flows through a supply network. CRM focuses on marketing, sales, and customer service, and aims to maximize the value of customer relationships. The chapter highlights some lessons learned in the SCM-CRM implementation.

Chapter XII

Euripidis Loukis, University of the Aegean, Greece
Ioakim Sapounas, University of the Aegean, Greece
Konstantinos Aivalis, ICAP, Greece

This chapter discusses the alignment of enterprise systems with business strategy and its impact on the business value that enterprise systems generate. It reports the results of an empirical investigation conducted by the authors to ascertain the impact of enterprise systems' strategic alignment on business performance. The chapter provides guidelines to help researchers and practitioners to incorporate the strategic alignment of enterprise systems in their research and practice respectively.

Section III
Enterprise Systems: Small, Medium, and Large Organizations

The initial developments in enterprise systems in the form of enterprise resource planning (ERP) systems concentrated on their deployment in large business firms. However, in the modern competitive landscape, it is essential to apply these systems in small to medium enterprises. ERP requirements, investments, and challenges for small and medium enterprises (SMEs) are different from large organizations. Skeptics argue that heavy investments in ERP implementation in SMEs may not bear the same fruits as large organizations. It is thought that SMEs may take a great deal of time, money, and effort to understand the business processes restructuring and technology, and may never effectively customize enterprise systems due to nature of its small and medium size. The chapters in Section III of this handbook discuss the issues related to the development, implementation, and use of enterprise systems in SMEs. The final chapter in this section explores the impact of organization size on the benefits of enterprise systems.

Chapter XIII

Sanjay Mathrani, Massey University, New Zealand
Mohammad A. Rashid, Massey University, New Zealand
Dennis Viehland, Massey University, New Zealand

The purpose of this chapter is to gain insights into what is a typical case of enterprise systems (ES) implementation and to understand how current implementations in the SME sector differ from the earlier implementations in the large enterprise sector through a perspective of ES vendors, ES consultants, and IT research firms in a NZ context. The chapter further discusses the implications for practice in the implementation processes, implementation models, and organizational contexts.

Chapter XIV

Kerstin Fink, University of Innsbruck, Austria
Christian Ploder, University of Innsbruck, Austria

This chapter investigates the use of knowledge processes and knowledge methods for SMEs. The learning objectives of this chapter are to assess the role of knowledge management and knowledge processes in SMEs. Based on the results of several empirical studies, an integration concept for knowledge processes, knowledge methods, and knowledge software tools for SMEs is introduced. In concluding their chapter, the authors propose a three-dimensional theoretical framework for successful knowledge diffusion in SMEs.

Chapter XV

Tobias Schoenherr, Michigan State University, USA
Ditmar Hilpert, Reutlingen University, Germany
Ashok K. Soni, Indiana University, USA
M.A. Venkataramanan, Indiana University, USA
Vincent A. Mabert, Indiana University, USA

This chapter discusses the challenges and issues faced in implementing integrated enterprise systems in small and medium sized enterprises (SMEs). Using the observations from eight SMEs in the German manufacturing sector, the study provides valuable insights towards understanding ES implementations and their peculiarities in the German manufacturing sector. Results reported in this chapter suggest that further exploration of these topics, preferably related to the experiences of companies in regions and countries other than North America and Germany will be useful.

Chapter XVI

Darshana Sedera, Queensland University of Technology, Australia

This chapter explores the proposition that the size of the organization (e.g. medium, large) may contribute to the differences in benefits received from enterprise systems. The alleged differences in organizational performance are empirically measured using a previously validated model, using four dimensions employing data gathered from 310 respondents representing 27 organizations. Results from this study indicate that organization size undoubtedly has a strong influence on the benefits received from the enterprise system.

Section IV
Enterprise Systems: Implementations and Applications

The implementation and application of enterprise systems is a complex technical and organizational process. Lack of understanding of the issues involved in successful application development and implementation is responsible for many enterprise system failures in practice. However, utilizing appropriate implementation and application development methodologies, tools, and techniques can significantly increase the chances of success in beneficial use of enterprise systems. Various chapters in this Section IV of this handbook discuss the issues involved and the possible approaches that can be taken for application development and successful implementation of enterprise systems in various industrial sectors.

Chapter XVII

Joseph Bradley, University of Idaho, USA

This chapter examines what ERP implementation projects involve, what the best of breed strategy is, when it is used, and what advantage adopting companies seek. Utilizing examples of best of breed implementations, differences in critical success factors in "vanilla" and best of breed projects are identified, and future trends in the best of breed strategy are suggested. The chapter argues that the best of breed strategy offers firms the opportunity to maintain or create competitive advantage based on unique business processes while "Vanilla" ERP implementations may result in all competitors adopting the same business processes leaving no firm with any advantage.

Chapter XVIII

Ganesh Vaidyanathan, Indiana University, USA

This chapter discusses ERP implementation procedure using the SAP implementation. ERP implementations in recent years have raised a number of questions regarding its success. Many companies regard ERP as their one and only savior, and many others despise that ERP as a single-system that has brought them to their knees. Regardless, many more companies, small to medium size companies in particular, are beginning to invest in ERP. An industrial practitioner from such small to medium companies needs to understand how to implement ERP. This chapter provides the necessary tools and background for the industrial practitioner to implement not only ERP systems but implement the next generation of enterprise applications as well.

Chapter XIX

Călin Gurău, GSCM – Montpellier Business School, France

This chapter discusses the importance of business modeling for implementing e-CRM systems. The introduction of e-business models requires the adaptation of the Marketing Information System to the specific characteristics of the online environment. Considering the specific requirements of this adaptation and re-structuring marketing information system, this chapter presents the advantages of the Eriksson-Penker Business Extensions of the Unifying Modeling Language (UML), and exemplifies their use for modeling the Marketing Information System during the implementation of an interactive e-CRM approach.

Chapter XX

Albert Boonstra, University of Groningen, The Netherlands

This chapter describes and analyzes how ES implementation within a hospital affects the interests of stakeholders and which specific problems may arise as a result. It uses the evidence from a case study to reveal important dimensions of the organizational change issues related to ES implementation within hospitals. The author suggests that an understanding the possible impact of ES on particular stakeholder interests may help project managers and others to manage ES implementation within hospitals in a more effective way.

Chapter XXI

S. Padmanaban, Pune, India

This chapter discusses the experience from two projects on designing to deploying ERP systems for two different organizations engaged in education and construction. Reporting on various processes, practices, techniques, and methods employed through the projects, and the lessons learnt from them, the chapter argues that time has come for designing and deploying industry-neutral generic ERP systems cost effectively. It proposes that through a combination of appropriate technologies, innovative tools, techniques and strategies, highly adoptive and customizable ERP systems can be designed and deployed at affordable costs and within reasonable timeframes.

Chapter XXII

Mateja Podlogar, University of Maribor, Slovenia
Katalin Ternai, Corvinus University of Budapest, Hungary

This chapter introduces the ERP systems, their complexity, and especially their integration in higher education as a significant challenge for many institutions. Information society paradigm, globalization, and the rapidly changing environment affect both the contents and the organization of higher education. In the always-conservative academic world, the organizational structure is very hierarchical and the knowledge transfer is fragmented. This chapter illustrates a way to develop training programs in higher education on an integrated ERP platform from a regional perspective.

Section V
Enterprise Systems: ERP and Beyond

ERP is already the mainstay of present business applications. The next generation enterprise applications will focus on supply chain management, customer relationship management for collaborative decision-making while encompassing more domains of business and other public organizations. Also, the drivers for future enterprises would be applications with open and flexible architectures. Thus the enterprise architecture will move towards service-oriented architecture (SOA) and will include a wider range of applications and scope of enterprise systems. Various chapters in the final section of this handbook discuss these aspects and look beyond ERP to suggest a wider scope and role for enterprise systems including e-government and knowledge distribution.

Chapter XXIII

Valentin Nicolescu, Technische Universität München, Germany
Holger Wittges, Technische Universität München, Germany
Helmut Krcmar, Technische Universität München, Germany

This chapter provides an overview of past and present development in technical platforms of ERP systems and their use in enterprises. Taking into consideration the two layers of application and technology, the chapter presents the classical scenario of an ERP system as a monolithic application block. The chapter highlights how ERP is shifting towards more flexible architecture like the service-oriented architecture (SOA) in modern companies. The chapter not only discusses the historical development of ERP system landscapes but also presents its application and technology view.

Chapter XXIV

This chapter discusses the evolution of ERP and salient features of ERP II including the disruptive technologies which will help reengineer ERP systems rapidly. The results of an international survey pertaining to the embedding of intelligence in the modern day ERP are also presented. The common causes for the failure of ERP implementation are included to shed light on aspects which are of utmost importance to ERP implementation. The example of placing order remotely over Internet by a sales clerk sitting away from the factory forms a part of this chapter to benefit the readers in better understanding the functioning of an ERP system.

Chapter XXV

The chapter introduces the essence of ERP in Government as a tool for integration of government functions which provides the basis for citizen services. It discusses the challenges faced in modernization of government "businesses" and the strategies available for ERP implementation. Acknowledging the basis of Enterprise Resource Planning (ERP) solutions as integration of functions which capture basic data through transactions to support critical administrative functions such as budgeting and financial management, revenue management, supply chain management and human resources management, the author argues that Enterprise solutions (ES) today go beyond ERP to automate citizen-facing processes.

Chapter XXVI

This chapter empirically tests eleven of the most common user-focused identity management frameworks that are emerging, and their associated technologies. The chapter also discusses issues and challenges with domain-centric identity management paradigm and presents unique value propositions of user-focused frameworks. The chapter does provide a comprehensive and cohesive coverage of common user-focused identity management frameworks. The chapter provides useful insights and understanding to users, technologists, and systems and security managers about frameworks and associated technologies relating to user-focused identity management. The authors suggest that a user-focused approach to identity management is a very promising way to improve the user experience and the security of online interactions that are often necessary in the deployment of enterprise systems.

Chapter XXVII
Ramón Brena, Tecnologico de Monterrey, Mexico
Gabriel Valerio, Tecnologico de Monterrey, Mexico
Jose-Luis Aguirre, Tecnologico de Monterrey, Mexico

The chapter provides a review of advanced information technologies (IT) being proposed for supporting knowledge distribution processes. Even though they are not mainstream technologies nowadays, they are expected to materialize in future generations of IT for knowledge distribution. The chapter suggests that knowledge management (KM) strategies refinement is an essential issue, which is currently being explored by researchers and practitioners.

Preface

Advances in computing and communication technologies have profoundly accelerated the development and deployment of complex Enterprise Systems (ES) in small, medium, and large enterprises seeking organizational improvements and business benefits. These systems are helping organizations reduce working capital requirements such as cash and inventory, and improve customer service by reducing cycle time and increasing service levels thus increasing companies' operational effectiveness. In fact, Enterprise Systems have evolved to become the information backbones of the organizations. This backbone has been further expanded to supply chain optimization, customer relationship management, data warehousing, and many other management intelligence systems. The implementation of such complex information systems in industries and organizations is considered as one of the most important developments in corporate use of information technology.

Enterprise Resource Planning (ERP) is now being hailed as a foundation for the integration of organization-wide information systems. ERP systems link together entire organization's operations such as accounting, finance, human resources, manufacturing, distribution, and so forth. Moreover, they also connect the organization to its customers and suppliers through the different stages of the product or the process life cycle. ERP is a part of the larger set of technology and operations driven systems, called Enterprise Systems that aim at integrating the entire enterprise and even a set of enterprises. The literature on ERP success and/or failure is inconclusive. While some analysts report positive impacts and outcomes of ERP application, others have revealed ERP failures. One of the reasons behind these different views lies in the multidimensionality of the concept of success and the difficulty of developing a single success/failure measurement.

This *Handbook of Research on Enterprise Systems* aims to encompass the most comprehensive source of coverage related to the past, present, and emerging directions of Enterprise Systems in their broadest scope and role in the organizations. Topics included in this handbook provide a broad basis for understanding the issues, technologies, theories, applications, opportunities, and challenges being faced by researchers and organizations today, in their quest for Enterprise Systems development, implementation, management, and vision for the future.

To create such a handbook of research on Enterprise Systems, we decided to launch this project where researchers from all over the world were invited to contribute. The primary objective of this project was to assemble as much research coverage related to the Enterprise Systems as possible. The idea behind this project was to gather the latest information on Enterprise Systems from researchers worldwide. Therefore, in order to provide the best balanced coverage of concepts and issues related to the selected topics of this handbook, researchers from around the world were asked to submit proposals describing their proposed coverage and the contribution of such coverage to the handbook. All proposals were carefully reviewed by the editors in light of their suitability as well as the researchers' record of similar work in the area of the proposed topics.

The goal was to assemble the best minds in the Enterprise Systems field to contribute to the handbook. Upon the receipt of full chapter submissions, each submission was forwarded to expert external reviewers on a double-blind, peer review basis. Only submissions with strong and favourable reviews were chosen as chapters for this handbook. In many cases, submissions were sent back for several revisions prior to final acceptance. As a result, this handbook includes 27 chapters highlighting concepts, issues, emerging technologies, and applications of enterprise systems. All entries are written by knowledgeable, distinguished scholars from well-known academia and prominent research institutions around the world. The authors who have contributed to this book are well known Enterprise Systems experts who have been doing research on various aspects of Enterprise Systems for several years and have tried to present their work in most lucid and simple words. It is hoped that readers will find it easy to understand and implement some of suggested approached.

This handbook is organized into five broad sections for cohesive and comprehensive presentation of a variety of topics related to the Enterprise Systems. A brief description of each section, followed by coverage of the various chapters in each section, is provided below.

Section I, Enterprise Systems: Technologies, Solutions, and Strategic Perspectives, begins with the growing importance of increasing "enterprise agility" in the organization with the understanding of the technologies available to develop and deploy Enterprise Systems (ES) in organizations. In the current global and competitive business environment, it is essential to be flexible and agile simultaneously. The six chapters in this section discuss the technologies, solutions, and strategic perspective of implementing and using enterprise systems and the tools available to analyze and evaluate proposed solutions. These research-based discussions include topics such as the means for researchers to explore enterprise agility in a systematic way and identify a number of important issues regarding the attainment of such capability, the concepts behind SAP Business Blueprint as an integrated environment that simplifies the enterprise design process, the key aspects of Free/Open Source Enterprise Resources Planning systems (FOS-ERP), Business Process Modeling (BPM) concepts and evolving modelling standards and technologies for enterprise systems' integration, how information technology, and ERP together facilitate in aligning the business and the role and place of executive information systems in the evolution of enterprise systems.

Section II, Enterprise Systems: Risks, Performance, and Business Value, discusses risk and performance issues related to enterprise systems. Business operations are composed of a collection of business processes. An enterprise system is an approach to integrate business processes, people, applications, and systems; in essence integrating the business, for business transformation and business value creation. Studies have proven that integration is not only a key reason for the adoption of Service Oriented Architecture (SOA) but also for improving business value. However, such a wider scope and holistic view of enterprise systems creates high level of complexity which leads to increased levels of risk and issues concerning their performance and business value. Therefore, it is important to assess the risk of implementing enterprise systems and the performance gains that can be achieved. Further, it is important to consider integration in a wider concept, including the entire supply chain and the customer relationships. The six chapters in this section are devoted to the discussion of relevant topics to enable the readers to understand the relationship between risks, performance, and business value while developing, implementing, and deploying integrated enterprise systems. The chapters in this section discuss the alignment of enterprise systems with business strategy and its impact on the business value that enterprise systems generate, the potential of integrating SCM and CRM, ERP investment and achievement of improved business performance, the potential impact of the consideration of enterprise information systems' administrative and execution context as a component of the application software development process.

Section III, Enterprise Systems: Small, Medium, and Large Organizations, is devoted to the ERP implementations in small, medium, and large organizations. The initial developments in enterprise systems in the form of enterprise resource planning (ERP) systems concentrated on their deployment in large business firms. However, in the modern competitive landscape, the ERP solutions have received favourable response from corporate as well as small and medium enterprises (SMEs). Many SMEs are implementing ERP initiatives for enhancing their inventory management, cash management and thereby trigger the overall efficiency of the enterprise. ERP requirements, investments and challenges for small and medium enterprises (SMEs) are different from large organizations. Sceptics argue that heavy investments in ERP implementation in SMEs may not bear the same fruits as large organizations. It is felt that SMEs may take a great deal of time, money and effort for them to understand the business processes restructuring and technology and may never effectively customize enterprise systems due to nature of its small and medium size. The first three chapters in this section discuss the issues related to the development, implementation, and use of enterprise systems in SMEs. The final chapter in this section explores the impact of organization size on the benefits of enterprise systems.

Section IV, Enterprise Systems: Implementation and Applications, deals with the approaches, frameworks, methods, tools, and technologies that are used in ES implementation and applications. Usually, companies have silos of information making retrieving and exchanging disparate corporate data often a complex and time consuming process. ERP systems are used to consolidate the desperate resources into an integrated database for seamless exchange and retrieval of information. Integrated information helps in enhancing enterprise performance and increase business value. However, lack of understanding of the issues involved in successful application development and implementation of enterprise systems is responsible for many enterprise system failures in practice. Utilizing appropriate implementation and application development methodologies, tools, and techniques can significantly increase the chances of success in beneficial use of enterprise systems. Six chapters in this section discuss the issues involved and the possible approaches that can be taken for application development and successful implementation of enterprise systems in various industrial sectors.

Section V of this handbook deals with the topic of **ERP and Beyond**. The boundaries of the enterprise have shifted and now extend to customers and suppliers who are outside the organization. The next generation enterprise applications will focus on supply chain management, customer relationship management for collaborative decision-making, all while encompassing more domains of business and other public organizations. Also, the drivers for future enterprises would be applications with open and flexible architectures. Thus the enterprise architecture will move towards service-oriented architecture (SOA) and will include a wider range of applications and scope of enterprise systems. Five chapters in this final section of the handbook describe state-of-the-art developments in Enterprise Systems and look beyond ERP to suggest a wider scope and role for Enterprise Systems including e-government and knowledge distribution. The authors having contributions in this section also suggest guidelines to emerging frameworks and next generation IT for knowledge distribution in enterprises.

This handbook is edited to cover a wide range of topics that are considered at the core of research and development of enterprise systems and applications. The coverage of this Handbook of Research on Enterprise Systems provides a reference resource for enterprise systems researchers both from industry and academia and professionals in obtaining a greater understanding of the concepts, issues, problems, trends, challenges, and opportunities related to this field of study. It is hoped that the diverse and comprehensive coverage of Enterprise Systems in this handbook will contribute to a better understanding of the research focuss and trends towards future developments in this evolving field of study. It is our sincere hope that this publication, with its great amount of information, will assist the enterprise systems researchers, faculty members, graduate students, and organizational decision makers in enhancing their understanding of the current and emerging issues in enterprise systems. Furthermore, we hope that the contributions included in this handbook will be instrumental in the expansion of the body of knowledge in this vast field.

Jatinder N. D. Gupta
The University of Alabama in Huntsville, USA

Sushil K. Sharma
Ball State University, USA

Mohammad Abdur Rashid
Massey University, New Zealand

Acknowledgment

This handbook would not have been possible without the cooperation and assistance of many people: the authors, reviewers, our colleagues, and the staff at IGI Global. The editors would like to thank Mehdi Khosrow-Pour for inviting us to produce this handbook, Jan Travers for managing this project, Kristin Roth and Julia Mosemann Assistant Managing Development Editors for answering our questions and keeping us on schedule. Many of the authors of the chapters in this book also served as reviewers of other chapters, and so we are doubly appreciative of their contributions. We would like to thank the members of the International Editorial Advisory Board for their cooperation, suggestions and help in organizing and reviewing chapters. We also acknowledge our respective universities for supporting us for this project. Finally, the editors wish to acknowledge their families for their support throughout the project.

Jatinder N. D. Gupta
The University of Alabama in Huntsville, USA

Sushil K. Sharma
Ball State University, USA

Mohammad Abdur Rashid
Massey University, New Zealand

About the Editors

Jatinder (Jeet) N. D. Gupta is currently Eminent Scholar of Management of Technology, professor of Management Information Systems, Industrial and Systems Engineering and Engineering Management at the University of Alabama in Huntsville, Huntsville, Alabama. Most recently, he was professor of Management, Information and Communication Sciences, and Industry and Technology at Ball State University, Muncie, Indiana. He holds a PhD in industrial engineering (with specialization in production management and information systems) from Texas Tech University. Co-author of a textbook in Operations Research, Dr. Gupta serves on the editorial boards of several national and international journals. Recipient of the Outstanding Faculty and Outstanding Researcher awards from Ball State University, he has published numerous papers in such journals as *Journal of Management Information Systems*, *International Journal of Information Management*, *Operations Research*, *INFORMS Journal of Computing*, *Annals of Operations Research*, *Journal of Scheduling*, and *Mathematics of Operations Research*. More recently, he served as a co-editor of several special issues including the *Neural Networks in Business* of *Computers and Operations Research*, *Semiconductor Wafer Production*, Special Issue of *Production Planning and Control*, and *Design, Building and Evaluation of Intelligent Decision Making Support Systems:* Special Issue of *Journal of Decision Systems*. He co-edited several books that include the *Handbook of Research on Information Assurance and Security* and *Creating Knowledge-based Healthcare Organizations* published by Idea Group Publishing. He is also the coeditor of the book: *Managing E-Business* published by Heidelberg Press, Heidelberg, Australia and the book: *Intelligent Decision-making Support Systems*, published by Springer. His current research interests include information security, e-commerce, supply chain management, enterprise systems, information and decision technologies, scheduling, planning and control, organizational learning and effectiveness, systems education, knowledge management, and enterprise integration. Dr. Gupta has held elected and appointed positions in several academic and professional societies including the Association for Information Systems, Production and Operations Management Society (POMS), the Decision Sciences Institute (DSI), and the Information Resources Management Association (IRMA).

Sushil K. Sharma is currently professor and Department Chair of Information Systems and Operations Management at Ball State University, Muncie, Indiana, USA. He co-edited five books that include the *Handbook of Research on Information Assurance and Security* and *Creating Knowledge-based Healthcare Organizations* published by Idea Group Publishing. He is also the coeditor of the book: *Managing E-Business* published by Heidelberg Press, Heidelberg, Australia. Dr. Sharma has authored over 100 refereed research papers in many peer-reviewed national and international MIS and management journals, conferences proceedings and books. He serves on editorial boards of several national and international journals and has also edited special issues. He is the founding editor-in-chief of the *International Journal of E-Adoption*. His primary teaching and research interests are in e-commerce, computer-mediated communications, community and social informatics, information systems security, e-government, ERP systems, database management systems, cluster computing, web services, and knowledge management. He has a wide consulting experience in information systems and e-commerce and has served as an advisor and consultant to several government and private organizations including projects funded by the World Bank.

Mohammad Abdur Rashid is a senior lecturer of Computer, Information and Communications Engineering at Massey University, New Zealand. Prior to his current position he served as an associate professor of Dhaka University, as a senior lecturer of University Brunei Darussalam and also as an associate professor of Computer and Information Engineering and Deputy Dean of the Faculty of Engineering at the International Islamic University, Malaysia. He received MScEng degree in electronics engineering specializing in engineering cybernetics systems from the Technical University of Wroclaw in 1978 and PhD from the University of Strathclyde, UK in 1986. Dr. Rashid is a co-author of *Enterprise Resource Planning: Global Opportunities and Challenges*. He has publications in international journals and conferences covering his areas of research. His research interests are multimedia communication networks, embedded systems design, network protocols and performance studies, mobile wireless multimedia communication and ERP systems.

Section I
Enterprise Systems:
Technologies, Solutions, and Strategic Perspectives

Chapter I
A Holistic Approach for Enterprise Agility

Nancy Alexopoulou
University of Athens, Greece

Panagiotis Kanellis
University of Athens, Greece

Mara Nikolaidou
University of Athens, Greece

Drakoulis Martakos
University of Athens, Greece

ABSTRACT

Efficient response to change, both upon expected and unpredicted contingencies, is a critical character-istic for modern enterprises. This chapter presents the various ways this feature has been addressed in the literature and explains why the term "enterprise agility" has been adopted for characterizing this capability. Furthermore, it provides a holistic approach for analyzing enterprise agility that is based on an introduced viewpoint-oriented Enterprise Architecture. The ultimate target is to provide the means for researchers to explore enterprise agility in a systematic way and identify a number of important issues regarding the attainment of such capability.

INTRODUCTION

Nowadays, organizations operate in highly turbu-lent environments having to cope with a frenetic pace of change (Rockart et al, 1996). Globalization and continual technological evolution are the main drivers of this turbulence. Other change factors include political issues, deregulation, consolida-tion in the business network, etc. (Oosterhout et al. 2006). As firms continuously sense opportunities for competitive action in their product-market spaces, it is agility which underlies firms' success in continuously enhancing and redefining their value creation in highly dynamic environments (Sambamurthy et al., 2003).

Indeed, agility has been recognized as a key characteristic of a modern enterprise. It has been therefore the concern of a plethora of researchers who have identified that agility is of a polymorphous nature and cannot easily be attained. To explore the concept of enterprise agility taking into consideration all necessary aspects, we propose an approach that is based on a viewpoint-oriented *Enterprise Architecture*. The term *Enterprise Architecture* as employed in this chapter is in contrast to enterprise architecture as perceived by IFEAD (http://www.enterprise-architecture. info/ifead%20about.htm) or Zachman framework (Zachman, 2004) where IT is considered the focus of attention. Our approach treats all perspectives, for example people, business process and information systems, as of equal importance. This is necessary for a proper examination of enterprise agility, as any partial approach will not be able to identify all the parameters necessary for an enterprise to be deemed agile.

Through this viewpoint-oriented architecture and the proposed approach, we provide a structured method for a holistic analysis of enterprise agility, aiming at helping researchers to identify issues or requirements for the attainment of agility. This chapter provides such an analysis through which a number of important agility issues are identified.

The chapter is structured as follows: First a literature review is provided which leads to the deduction of useful conclusions regarding agility. Then, the viewpoint-oriented Enterprise Architecture and the proposed approach are presented. The following two sections demonstrate the approach. The last section wraps up the chapter with some concluding remarks.

LITERATURE REVIEW

Enterprises able to respond efficiently to change are characterized by different terms in the literature, such as *flexible organizations, agile enterprises, adaptive enterprises, sense-and-respond enterprises*, and less often, *intelligent enterprises*.

The term *flexible organization* is introduced by Leeuw and Volberda (Leeuw and Volberda, 1996) who describe organizational flexibility through synonyms such as *mobility, responsiveness, agility, suppleness* and *litheness*. Based on system control theory, they have developed a definition for organizational flexibility according to which *"flexibility is the degree to which an organization possesses a variety of actual and potential procedures, and the rapidity by which it can implement these procedures, in order to increase the control capability of the management and improve the organization and the environment"*. Evans (Evans, 1991) denotes that flexibility is the ability to do something other than what was originally intended, emphasizing thus the ability to respond to unforeseen changes as well. Evans characterizes flexibility as a polymorphous concept and analyses it by relating it to other similar concepts, most notably *adaptability, agility, versatility, resilience* and *malleability*. Evans distinguishes two types of flexibility in terms of intention, namely *offensive* and *defensive flexibility*, and two types in respect to time, namely *ex ante* and *ex post flexibility*. Offensive flexibility concerns creating and seizing an initiative, while defensive means guarding against predatory moves or correcting past mistakes. Ex ante flexibility involves in advance preparation for future transformations, while ex post concerns adjustments that take place after a triggering episode has occurred. Golden and Powel (Golden and Powel, 2004) define flexibility as the capacity to adapt and specify four flexibility dimensions; *temporal, intention, range* and *focus*. The first denotes how long it takes for an organization to adapt and the second indicates whether the adaptation is proactive or reactive. Range denotes the options an organization has for expected as well as unpredicted changes. The distinction between flexibility for expected changes and flexibility for unforeseen changes has been also addressed by Carlsson (Carlsson, 1989). Lastly, focus specifies whether the flexibility is internal or external with regard to enterprise boundaries.

The term *agile enterprise* has been extensively used by Dove (Dove, 2005a) to characterize firms in terms of *knowledge management, value proposition skills* and *response ability*. Knowledge management concerns the timely awareness that a change should be made, both in a reactive and proactive manner. Value proposition skills regard the ability to effectively select the most appropriate among competing response alternatives. Response ability refers to the modification of business processes in real time. Response ability, besides change proficiency, requires a system response architecture structured as reconfigurable systems of reusable modules in a scalable framework, and an efficient change management process. Dove et al. (Dove et al., 1996) have defined four change proficiency metrics, namely *time, cost, robustness* and *scope*. Time and cost are self-explanatory. Robustness measures the quality of the change process. Scope indicates how much change can be accommodated. The term *agile enterprise* has been also used by Kubil and Nadhan (Kubil and Nadhan, 2005) and Henbury (Henbury, 1996).

The term *adaptive enterprise*, and more specifically *adaptive complex enterprise*, is introduced by Desai (Desai, 2005). Desai is influenced by systems theory, and in particular from complexity theory. Complexity theory is based on relationships, patterns and iterations and specifies that the universe is full of systems which are complex and constantly adapting to their environment; hence complex adaptive systems. Haeckel (Haeckel, 1995; Haeckel, 1999) also suggests managing organizations as complex adaptive systems. Based on systems theory, he introduces the *sense-and-*

respond enterprise to distinguish a modern organization model from that of the more traditional make-and-sell model. According to Haeckel, the behavior of sense-and-respond organizations can be represented by a four-phase adaptive loop; first, sense change in their environment and internal states, second, interpret this change in the context of their experiences, aims and capabilities, filtering opportunities from threats, third, decide how to respond and fourth, act according to their decisions. Haeckel believes that through the adaptive loop process, sense-and-respond firms can cope with rapid change in an uncertain environment. Haeckel (Haeckel, 1999) relates agility to the sense-and-respond enterprise, based on the two dimensions suggested by this model. More specifically, following this dual perspective, a firm's agility can be distinguished to *sensing agility* and *response agility*. He defines sensing agility as a firm's capacity to rapidly discover and interpret the market opportunities through its information systems. Response agility relates to the organizational capability to effectively transform knowledge into action in response to the environmental signals. The terms *adaptive complex enterprise* and *sense-and-respond enterprise* are also used by Ramanathan (Ramanathan, 2005) to characterize firms that have embraced change and learned to operate in varying circumstances. Jeng et al. (Jeng et al., 2005) and Evgeniou (Evgeniou, 2002) have employed the term *adaptive enterprise* in a similar fashion.

In contrast to the aforementioned terms, the term *intelligent enterprise* occurs much more rarely in the literature. However, it has been also used to denote an enterprise that has the ability to easily evolve, following the changes of its ecosystem. Delic and Dayal (Delic and Dayal, 2003) claim that an intelligent enterprise is one that can behave like a biological system morphing into new forms whenever imposed by environmental changes, and bearing the characteristics of agility and adaptability. To achieve this, the enterprise should be able to sense its environment, understand the situation, exhibit learning behavior and create a feasible and effective plan to execute.

Our literature review reveals that the need for a new kind of enterprises able to cope with environments that are intensely competitive, highly turbulent and continuously innovative has been widely addressed, even though there is no standardized or common term to characterize them. Most prevailing terms are based on the concepts of *flexibility*, *adaptability* and *agility*. However, there is confusion regarding the relation among these concepts. Some researchers consider them synonyms or almost synonyms (Leeuw and Volberda, 1996; Evans, 1991). Others specify a dependency relationship between them. Evgeniou (Evgeniou, 2002), for instance, deems flexibility as a prerequisite for an adaptive enterprise. Dove (Dove, 2005b) on the other hand, differentiates flexibility from agility by stating that the former refers to the ability to respond to expected changes while the latter concerns unforeseen changes as well. This is in contrast to other researchers who employ the term flexibility both for expected as well as unforeseen contingencies (Evans, 1991; Carlsson, 1989).

Furthermore, there is apparently an overlap among different research approaches. For example, offensive and defensive flexibility defined by Evans (1991) correspond to active and passive flexibility respectively, specified in Leeuw and Volberda (1996). Likewise, knowledge management, value proposition and response ability introduced by Dove (Dove, 2005a) are very close to the interactive loop stages suggested by Haeckel (Haeckel, 1999). In particular, knowledge management corresponds to sensing and interpretation, value proposition maps to decision, and response ability corresponds to action. Temporal and intention dimensions of flexibility defined by Evans (Evans, 1991) are also stated in Golden and Powel (2004).

It should be noted that most researchers, although using different terms, they have recognized that the ability alone to adapt quickly and easily to change does not adequately delineate the profile of the enterprise that can thrive in highly dynamic environments. Therefore, they have extended the meaning of either flexible or adaptive or agile enterprise to include the capability to analyze information effectively and sense environmental changes in a timely manner, and make not only reactive but even proactive movements based on efficient decision-making. Thus, they have designated a manifold interpretation to these terms.

In the remaining of this chapter, the term *agile enterprise* is adopted, as we regard that the meaning of the words flexibility and adaptability is narrowed to the ability to change. According to Oxford Advanced Genie Dictionary, the terms *flexibility* and *adaptability* are synonyms and mean the ability to change to suit new conditions or situations. In the same dictionary, the term *agility* is defined as the ability to move quickly and easily. As such, agility is a more appropriate word because it incorporates also the meaning of rapidity - a very important aspect. For example, a company may adapt to new market conditions in 10 years. This may render the company adaptable but by no way agile, as its response to change is far from fast. In addition, the word agility may be used in a broader sense to denote not only efficient response to change but also the ability for proactive movements in advantageous positions, implying not only responding to change but even causing change.

ENTERPRISE ARCHITECTURE

The attainment of an agile enterprise is a difficult issue. It requires effective knowledge management and learning capacity through data collection and analysis. It involves efficient decision making and quick deployment of a rigorous solution in response to environmental signals, enabled by flexible information systems. Therefore, agility as a property should characterize all aspects of a firm, such as employees, information, business processes, technology, etc. Consider for example an enterprise that has developed a 'super agile' IT infrastructure. Such an infrastructure has no value at all if personnel are unable to understand and adjust themselves to new circumstances. Likewise, efficient response to change will not be feasible if the necessary applications exist but the fast and effective communication between stakeholders is hindered due to an inflexible organizational structure. Consequently, an enterprise is agile only if it exhibits agility at any level from any perspective.

As already mentioned, to explore the concept of enterprise agility taking into consideration all necessary aspects, we propose an approach that is based on a viewpoint-oriented *Enterprise Architecture*, which treats all organizational perspectives as of equal importance. IEEE's Recommendation Practice for Architectural Description of Software-Intensive Systems (IEEE 1471-2000) proposes that an *architecture* is a collection of *viewpoints*, i.e. architectural descriptions that concern each individual *stakeholder*. Each viewpoint is associated with a specific *view*. A view is a representation of a whole system from the perspective of a related set of concerns. This approach has been adopted by various initiatives (Zachman, 1999; ISO/IEC & ITU-T). The Open Distributed Processing Reference Model (RM-ODP), for example, is a conceptual framework established by ISO (ISO/IEC & ITU-T) for the specification of large-scale distributed systems. RM-ODP integrates aspects related to the distribution, interoperation and portability of distributed systems, in such a way that network/hardware infrastructure is transparent to the user. RM-ODP manages system internal complexity through the "separation of concerns", addressing specific problems appearing during system development, from five generic and complementary viewpoints (namely *Enterprise*, *Information*, *Computational*, *Engineering* and *Technology*).

Figure 1. A viewpoint-oriented enterprise architecture

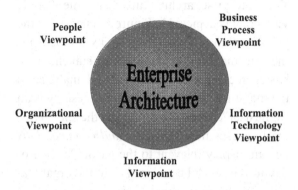

Similarly, IEEE recommendation can be applied in order to specify a viewpoint-oriented Enterprise Architecture. The introduced Enterprise Architecture, as presented in Figure 1, is considered from five distinct viewpoints, namely *people*, *organizational*, *business process*, *information technology* and *information*.

The identification of different viewpoints facilitates the procedure of agility analysis as it is easier through the 'separation of concerns' to focus on certain issues associated with a specific viewpoint. However, as these viewpoints are interrelated, analyzing enterprise agility by merely considering each view in isolation does not suffice. What is additionally required is the examination of view interrelations, resulting in the 'integration of concerns'. As such, our analysis approach includes two phases:

1. *Separation of concerns*: implications for enterprise agility are identified for each different view.
2. *Integration of concerns*: implications for enterprise agility are identified from the interrelation between views.

In the remaining of this section, we present the enterprise architecture from each separate viewpoint.

People View

The enterprise architecture from the People viewpoint is depicted in Figure 2. The role of the people within an entrepreneurial environment, i.e. the information systems users or stakeholders, has been extensively examined and analyzed in the literature. If what is deemed necessary is an "agile user", he may be defined by the *knowledge* that he posses, the *competence and technical skills* he can display relevant to the particular line of day-to-day work he undertakes in the organization plus the *culture* that he has.

Knowledge refers to a 'dictionary' of solutions to problems that he has to propose in a multitude of situations and the certainty that he has that these solutions will each time provide a satisfactory result. Although knowledge requires – and is the result – of extensive experience, competencies and skills are just the toolset needed to carry out the range of specific tasks that he is accountable for. Culture permeates a user's worldview and hence informs his actions as it is a set of beliefs and assumptions regarding the possible ways each activity should be performed.

Figure 2. Enterprise architecture from the people viewpoint

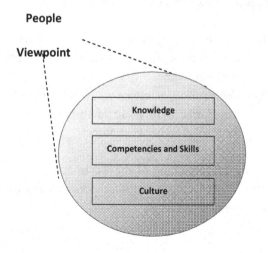

Organizational View

The enterprise personnel operate in accordance with the organizational structure of the enterprise. Thus, every employee has a specific *role* in the company (e.g. manager, secretary, etc.) and a specific relation to other employees based on the role *hierarchy* (e.g. the general director is senior to the director of every department). In addition, every employee acts according to the company's *policies*, which are a set of rules defined by the company, governing its operations, as well as its employees' actions. Lastly, the organizational structure includes also the division of the enterprise into specific *units*. The elements of the organizational structure as presented in Figure 3, are interrelated. Indeed, regarding roles and role hierarchy, their relation is self-evident. Moreover, both, roles and their hierarchy are usually associated with specific policies. Policies may also be defined regarding the organization and collaboration between units. Units may be associated with specific roles (e.g., the inventory manager is the one who is in charge of the Inventory department; in this case unit represents a department).

Information View

Information is the most valuable asset of a modern enterprise. The enterprise architecture from the Information viewpoint is depicted in Figure 4. A fundamental component of information is its *structure*, i.e. grammar and syntax. *Content* can be generated using structure. Content is characterized by *semantics*, which is the meaning that content conveys based on various parameters such as context, for example, or the person that interprets it. As such, the same content may have multiple meanings.

The U.S. Office of Management and Budget (OMB) defines information as any communication or representation of knowledge such as facts, data or opinions, in any medium or form, including textual, graphic, numerical, narrative or audiovisual

Figure 3. Enterprise architecture from the organizational viewpoint

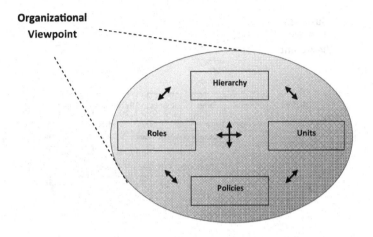

forms (OMB A-130). Therefore, representation and communication aspects are also included in the information building block stack. The double arrow between them shown in Figure 4 implies that there is a two-way dependency between representation and communication aspects. Indeed, in case of a graphical representation for example, information cannot be easily communicated by word of mouth. A printed form would be more appropriate in such a case.

Business Processes View

Business processes constitute the heart of an enterprise. Presley et al. (Presley et al., 1993) define an enterprise as a collection of enterprise activities organized into a set of business processes, which cooperate to produce desired enterprise results. Enterprise business processes may span multiple corporations because apart from internal operations they may also include business-to-business transactions.

Figure 4. Enterprise architecture from the information viewpoint

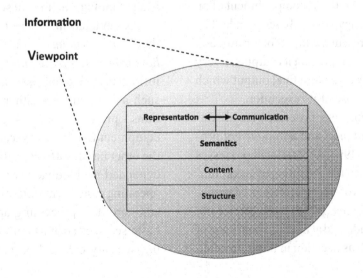

Figure 5. Enterprise architecture from the business process viewpoint

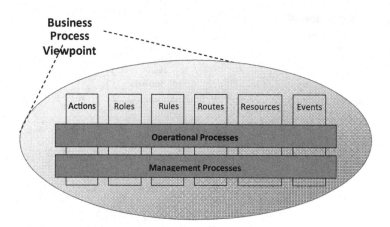

Figure 5 presents the basic entities involved in a business process description in a technology/methodology-neutral manner. As depicted in Figure 5, a business process includes a set of *actions* which, as mentioned above, may regard internal operations or business-to-business transactions. Each action may be hierarchically decomposed to sub-actions. Actions are executed by actors (users, systems, etc.) that take over specific *roles*. The sequence and execution of actions are governed by *events* which play the role of control signals, and *rules* which specify different paths of actions i.e. *routes*. During the execution of an action, each operational process both uses and produces *resources*. Resources involve anything which is necessary for the accomplishment of an action such as data, devices, and even people. The resources used represent the inputs of the process, while those produced represent its outputs. Every business process always has a final output which constitutes the purpose of its execution.

Additionally, business processes are distinguished into *operational* and *management* processes (Davenport, 1993). Operational processes are those that embody the execution of tasks comprising the activities of an organization. Management processes refer not only to those carried out by managers or conducted at management level of organizations, such as decision making. Instead,

they are associated with information handling, coordination, and control procedures, ensuring the efficiency and effectiveness of primary operations, which are the focus of operational processes. As such, management processes are usually carried out by humans who are aided by decision support systems, while operational processes may be partly or fully automated.

Information Technology View

Nowadays, the operation of most enterprises is extensively based on Information Technology (IT). Figure 6 presents in a layered fashion the elements that compose the IT of an enterprise. Again, this is a technology-neutral description.

As depicted in Figure 6, the lowest layer is the *IT infrastructure*, which is distinguished into *hardware* and *software infrastructure*. Hardware infrastructure comprises all physical devices, such as computers - either servers or workstations - printers, scanners, etc., and the network equipment like switches, cables, routers, etc. On the other hand, software infrastructure, which is depended on hardware infrastructure, includes operating systems, middleware, network protocols and core data-processing applications, offering basic services such as communication, messaging, security, etc. Such basic services provided by

Figure 6. Enterprise architecture from the information technology viewpoint

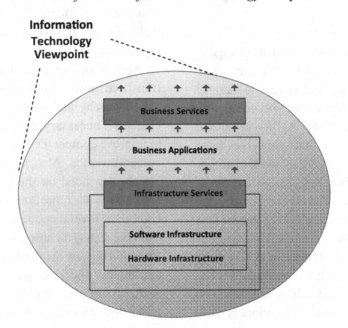

both software and hardware are common to all enterprises independently of their type. Through these services, which are characterized as *infrastructure services*, IT infrastructure provides the foundation to enable present and future *business applications* (Duncan and Bogucki, 1995). Business applications (e.g. CRM, ERP, etc.) along with the *business services* they provide, constitute the top layer. As opposed to infrastructure services, business services are enterprise-specific. Business services can be regarded as the crossing point between Business Process and Information Technology views, as business processes utilize for their implementation business services offered by IT.

Obviously, a service-oriented approach for the description of IT view is in consistency with the current trend which suggests a Service-Oriented Architecture (SOA) for IT. SOA is an architectural style whose goal is to achieve loose coupling among interacting services (IFEAD, 2007). A *service* is a unit of work done by a *service provider* to achieve desired end results for a *service consumer*. Both provider and consumer are roles played by organizational units as well as software agents on behalf of their owners.

EXAMINING ENTERPRISE AGILITY IMPLICATIONS THROUGH THE SEPARATION OF CONCERNS

In this section, the implications of agility will be examined separately for each view. Through this analysis, several agility research issues will be outlined in regard to each view. These issues are summarized in Table 1 at the end of this section. More specifically, cells that have identical row and column names include issues that can be deduced from the first phase (separation of concerns) while the others include issues that can be deduced from the second phase (integration of concerns).

Agility Implications from the People Viewpoint

People are wary of change. As such, change is not easily instigated and one of the key challenges facing any change initiative is to manage the stress and the problems that will come with the change (Hammer, 1990). Agility in human IT infrastructure implies that employees have adopted the perspective that they work in an unstable environment where any change may occur at anytime, and that they have the competency and skills, the knowledge and culture to accept first and then cope with change efficiently. Organizations must search and examine or devise ways to implant a culture which not only accepts but assigns to change a value emphasizing its necessity regarding an organization's evolutionary path. In the same vein, organizations must seek ways to manage the corporate knowledge efficiently. In other words, to define, design and implement the mechanisms to collect, store and disseminate the knowledge that is produced daily and is one of the main survival tools of the post-modern organization.

In a dynamic environment, it is critical for the employees to operate having adopted the perspective that they work in an unstable environment where any change may occur at anytime. This means that agility in human IT infrastructure is a matter not only of the aforementioned skills and knowledge but also of a specific mentality.

Agility Implications from the Organizational Viewpoint

An enterprise, in order to be deemed agile, should be always willing to adjust its organizational structure, if market demands prove its function inefficient. Agility of organizational structure though, is often hindered due to conflicts arising from the established relationships in the existing hierarchy. It should be realized however that agility in the organizational structure is critical for the overall enterprise agility. The way an enterprise is organised, affects the efficiency of decision making, as well as of activity coordination and execution.

Agility in the organizational structure is translated into the willingness to reconsider roles, role hierarchy and policies and to move on to changes if necessary, even radical ones, in order to improve company's operation and ensure thus competitiveness. Also, a company's operation is largely depended on the way departments collaborate, as it is quite common that an enterprise comprises several cooperating departments. For example, it may include a department responsible for acquiring raw material, another for production and another one for dispatching the products. As such, an agile enterprise should exhibit agility in the organization of the interdepartmental collaboration.

Developing an agile organizational structure is indeed a critical issue for the attainment of enterprise agility. The typical pyramid-like hierarchy, for example, exhibits less agility, since the functions and skills are distributed among departments (Fernandes and Duarte, 2005). In addition, coordination becomes difficult, as each of these departments has internal aims, which may create interdepartmental conflicts. As a result, clients' needs cannot be satisfied efficiently and with quality. However, as mentioned earlier, agile enterprises are oriented towards clients' needs and not internal interests. Process-oriented organization seems more appropriate for agile enterprises, since in such an organization all the necessary functions are embodied in the corresponding business processes that cross department boundaries and have the same objectives with the client's ones (Hammer, 1996). Such an organization however may need to be combined possibly with new roles and policies in order to ensure agility.

It should be noted that the organizational structure should facilitate the development of a business environment that is supportive of change but on the other hand it should ensure the required stability so that chaos can be avoided.

Agility Implications from the Information Viewpoint

Agility in the information domain concerns first of all its communication aspects. More specifically, agility in information denotes the efficient diffusion of information among stakeholders, as well as the easy discovery, at any time, of the required information. Also, the ability to represent the same information in different forms should be supported in order to be more easily understood by different target groups. Such capabilities lead to better control of activities and facilitate sensing agility through the knowledge acquired from the exploitation of information.

However, to facilitate knowledge management and value proposition (Dove, 2005a), the efficient acquirement of information does not suffice. It should be additionally ensured that information is of high quality. Quality of information is specified in terms of accuracy, timeliness, coverage and relevancy (Sanjay et al. 2004). Only if information is of high quality, can its meaning (denoted by the *Semantics* element in Figure 4) be deemed reliable and hence valuable.

Agility Implications from the Business Process Viewpoint

The ability to respond rapidly to changing marketing opportunities by utilizing agile business processes is a key attribute of an agile enterprise (Goldman et al. 1995). Enterprise agility from the business process perspective means that the enterprise is able to adjust its processes easily, in a timely and cost-effective manner, and efficiently execute them, in order to meet new market demands. This presupposes flexibility to modify the *business process definition*. The business process definition is the formal and precise description of the elements composing a business process such as those presented in Figure 5. As such, the business process definition should be agile itself, allowing even the radical change of the business process characterized by Davenport (Davenport, 1993) as *process innovation*. Currently, there are several approaches for business process definition using various modeling techniques, aiming at the attainment of agility (Bhat and Deshmukh, 2005, Lin and Orlowska, 2005, Ramanathan, 2005).

Modifying business processes easily implies high performance in their execution through their continual improvement, as well as their constant alignment with the objectives they are meant to satisfy. In an agile enterprise, a business process always reflects business objectives in a consistent manner. This presupposes a methodology or technique that will enable efficient analysis of all necessary parameters (strategic, market, customer-specific, etc.) which should be taken into consideration for the generation of a consistent business process definition.

Based on the Business Process View as presented in Figure 5, we argue that agility in the business process definition means the ability to

- add new actions or delete actions that are no longer necessary,
- change process sequence by rearranging, eliminating or inserting routes,
- redefine roles in order for example to reflect changes in the organizational structure,
- modify rules so as to apply, for example, new regulations or new policies adopted by the company,
- handle events to ensure smooth flow of the business process,
- use alternative resources if those specified initially are not available, as well as map resources to roles in an ad hoc manner, as may be imposed by unexpected conditions.

The achievement of maximum agility however implies that the modifications mentioned above can take place at run time as well, i.e. while a business process instance is being executed. Shui-Guang et al. (ShuiGuang et al., 2004) proposed such a method. According to this method, a business process is composed of *general activities*, which are predefined in detail at design time and *flexible activities,* which are like a "black box", representing an undetermined sub-process without detailed specification at build time. In other words, flexible activities encapsulate the uncertain sub-process at run time. At run time, depending on current circumstances, a flexible activity can be replaced by a concrete sub-process composed of selected activities from existing or newly added activities (constituting a pool of activities), based on selection and composition constraints.

The above pool of activities implies the ability to change a business process at run time upon an expected event for which a relative activity exists in the pool. The ability to change a business process at run time upon an unpredicted event reflects the highest grade of agility, as depicted in Figure 7. On the other hand, the lowest grade corresponds to the ability to change a business process at build time upon an expected event. The other two cases (run time modification upon expected events and build time modifications upon unexpected events) are regarded of equivalent agility as the former has the parameter of runtime while the second has the parameter of unexpected. Obviously the greatest challenge is the implementation of *super agile* business processes.

Especially for management processes, agility has different implications. It basically means the capacity to sense environmental changes and make the right decisions at the right time. As such, management processes are mainly related to *sensing agility* which denotes a firm's capacity to rapidly discover and interpret the market opportunities, in order to make not only reactive but also proactive movements and gain thus competitive advantage (Haeckel, 1999).

Agility Implications from Information Technology Viewpoint

IT agility is a critical factor for the success of corporation during periods of intense change, especially if agility in IT infrastructure acts as a foundation for overall IT flexibility (Davenport and Linder, 1994). The attainment of high IT flexibility presupposes a common IT infrastructure rather than separate IT platforms and services for separate business activities (Keen 1991, Rockart et al. 1996). In other words all information systems of a company should share a common IT infrastructure to enable high flexibility.

As presented in Figure 6, the IT view is service-oriented. As such, we argue that an agile IT is able to always offer the required services.

Figure 7. Scaling agility in business processes

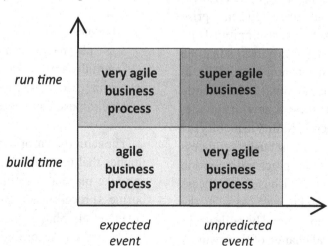

The ability to provide the required services at any time entails that new applications offering the desired services can be quickly and easily embodied into the existing infrastructure in a plug and play fashion. This in turn, implies that IT infrastructure has been deployed as a set of reusable and reconfigurable modules. Furthermore, the software and hardware infrastructure should provide for scalability as new applications are added and more users employ infrastructure resources. Reusability, reconfigurability and scalability have been identified by Dove (Dove, 2005b) as the three basic IT infrastructure principles with respect to agility.

Currently there are a number of emerging technologies promising agility like MDA, Business Process Management Systems, Grid Computing and others. Each of these technologies has a different target though, so the issue is how such technologies could be combined for the development of an agile IT bearing the characteristics of reusability, reconfigurability and scalability.

Table 1. Enterprise agility issues derived from separation of concerns

Viewpoint	Issues
People	- How can the stress and the problems that will come with the change be managed? - What is the profile of an agile employee?
Organizational	- What is the optimum organization in terms of roles, hierarchical relations, policies and units for maximum agility in the enterprise operation? - How can the balance between stability and agility be achieved?
Information	- How can efficient communication of information be ensured? - How can high information quality be ensured?
Business Process	- What methodology should be followed to efficiently analyze all necessary parameters in order to produce a business process definition that will reflect business objectives in a consistentt manner? - How can changes be supported both at build and run time? - How can unpredicted changes be accommodated? - How can events be interpreted correctly to maximize sensing ability with regard to business opportunities?
Information Technology	- How can existing technologies be combined for the development of an agile IT? - Is service oriented architecture suitable for the attainment of agility?

EXAMINING ENTERPRISE AGILITY IMPLICATIONS THROUGH THE INTEGRATION OF CONCERNS

As explained previously, approaching enterprise agility by considering each view in isolation does not suffice. As viewpoints are interrelated, it is those interrelationships that must be examined and analyzed. By doing so, the complexity of the issues at hand is unearthed; a necessary first step to a true understanding of enterprise agility. Due to space limitations though, we examine only agility implications derived from the relation between IT and Business Processes views. However, examples of issues derived from the rest view interrelations are included in Table 2 below.

Agility Implications Derived from the Relation between IT and Business Process Views

Business processes are becoming more and more interlinked with IT. As such, agility in the former presupposes the existence of agility in the second. It is true that IT has been characterised as fundamental in enabling the redesign of business processes (Broadbent et al., 1999; Davenport, 1993). It should be stressed however that while IT is a potential enabler of business process change, it may also constitute a potential constraint or inhibitor (Grover et al., 1993). This is particularly true when the firm's IT infrastructure is inappropriate or inflexible (Brancheau et al., 1996) due to the existence of incompatible systems constructed to serve local needs. Such systems cannot easily achieve the level of seamless interoperability required, putting thus limits on both process change and process integration. On the other hand, a tight integration among systems serving a specific business process may also constrain business process redesign, since even a small modification to the business process may require a great effort usually translated into time and money.

Moreover such an infrastructure is frequently the outcome of significant investments. As a result, firms cannot easily replace these systems with new ones that will satisfy the new requirements. Besides, in intensely dynamic environments the frequency of change is sometimes so high that systems become obsolete before even their implementation is finished.

Obviously, agility in IT in terms of efficient business process integration and redesign dictates an appropriate architecture of IT infrastructure that is process-oriented so that IT can play an enabling role. An emerging technology enabling a process-oriented IT infrastructure is *Business Process Management* (BPM). BPM is the descendant of Workflow Management Systems (WFMC 2002). While business process management supports the main concepts of workflow, it bears however broader capabilities, supporting the flexible management of dynamic business change. For the achievement of true agility, BPM technology should be combined with agile business process modeling techniques as those mentioned earlier.

The above discussion concerns mainly operational processes. However, IT infrastructure has implications for both operational and management processes (Mooney et al., 1996). Management processes are augmented by improved availability and communication of information, decision support systems, data warehouses and data mining systems. These technologies mainly contribute to sensing agility which, as explained earlier, denotes a firm's capacity to rapidly discover and interpret the market opportunities, in order to make not only reactive but also proactive movements and gain thus competitive advantage (Haeckel, 1999). As a result, effectively utilizing and embedding such technologies into the existing IT infrastructure so as to ensure agility in management processes, constitutes a significant issue for the overall enterprise agility.

Table 2. Enterprise agility issues derived from integration of concerns

	People	Organizational	Information	Business Process
Organizational	- How can an organizational structure facilitating people exhibit innovative energy be developed? - How can employees be made receptive to continual organizational changes?			
Information	- How can a collaborative working environment based on sincere business relationships that will facilitate information communication be ensured?	- How an enterprise should be organized in order to facilitate efficient diffusion of information?		
Business Process	- What kind of training methods should be applied to help employees become adaptable to business process changes? - How can methodologies be developed for business process transformation that consider also cultural issues such as norms and attitudes exhibited by the people involved in the process?	- What are the characteristics of an organizational environment that fosters business process modification efforts?	- How can information flow turbulence be managed in agile business processes? - How can it be ensured that there will always be sufficient information to support a potential business process adjustment?	
Information Technology	- What are the requirements for IT so that it can exhibit a high degree of usability in a dynamic environment? - What training methods could help employees to become agile in using new technologies?	- How can seamless alignment between business and IT be achieved? - Can organizational policies be formalized through an appropriate modelling language so as to increase efficiency in policy modification?	- How can IT infrastructure ensure high information quality and quick information diffusion at the same time? - How can it be ensured that IT is always aware of the information that goes around the enterprise? - How can ensure information preservation be realized?	- What kind of IT architecture can facilitate business process integration without inhibiting at the same time business process redesign? - What are the restrictions imposed by IT to business process agility? - How can agile business process modelling methods be aligned with process-oriented technologies? - How can decision support technologies be embedded into the existing IT infrastructure so as to facilitate sensing agility?

CONCLUSION

Evidently the realization of an agile enterprise is a tough matter raising multiple research issues. Such issues can be more efficiently identified through a structured approach as the one presented in the chapter, which is based on a viewpoint-oriented enterprise architecture that ensures a holistic analysis of enterprise agility. Based on our analysis of agility through the enterprise architecture viewpoints, we identified a number of research directions which exemplify a fruitful area for further applied and theoretical work.

REFERENCES

Bhat, M. J., & Deshmukh, N. (2005). Methods for Modeling Flexibility in Business Processes. *Sixth Workshop on Business Process Modeling, Development, and Support (BPMDS'05)*. Porto, Portugal June 13-14.

Brancheau, J. C., Janz, B. D., & Wetherbe, J. C. (1996). Key Issues in Information Systems Management: 1994-95 SIM Delphi Results. *MIS Quarterly, 20*(2), 225-242.

Broadbent, M., Weill, P., & Clair St., D. (1999). The Implications of Information Technology Infrastructure for Business Process Redesign. *MIS Quarterly, 23*(2), 159-182.

Carlsson, B. (1989). Flexibility and the Theory of the Firm. *International Journal of Industrial Organization, 7*, 179-203.

Davenport, T.H. (1993). *Process Innovation Reengineering Work Through Information Technology*. Boston, MA: Harvard Business School Press.

Davenport, T., & Linder, J. (1994). Information Management Infrastructure: The New Competitive Weapon. *Proceedings of the 27th Annual Hawaii International Conference on Systems Sciences, IEEE*, 1994, 885-899.

Delic, A. K., & Dayal, U. (2003). The Rise of the Intelligent Enterprise. *Virtual Strategist, 3*(45).

Desai, A. (2005). Adaptive Complex Enterprises. *Communications of the ACM, 48*(5), 32-35.

Dove, R. (2005a). Agile Enterprise Cornerstones: Knowledge, Values and Response Ability. *IFIP 8.6 Keynote*, Atlanta, May 2005.

Dove, R. (2005b). Fundamental Principles for Agile Systems Engineering. *2005 Conference on Systems Engineering Research (CSER)*, Stevens Institute of Technology, Hoboken, NJ, March 2005.

Dove, R., Benson, S., & Hartman, S. (1996). A Structured Assessment System for Groups Analyzing Agility. *Fifth National Agility Conference*, Agility Forum, Boston, March 1996.

Duncan & Bogucki, N. (1995). Capturing Flexibility of Information Technology Infrastructure: A Study of Resource Characteristics and Their Measure. *Journal of Management Information Systems, 12*(2), 37-57.

Evans, J. S. (1991). Strategic Flexibility for High Technology Manoeuvres: A Conceptual Framework. *Journal of Management Studies, 28*(1), 69-89.

Evgeniou, T. (2002). Building the Adaptive Enterprise. *Information Strategies For Successful Management of Complex, Global Corporations in Times of Change*. INSEAD June 2002.

Fernandes, M. J., & Duarte, J. F. (2005). A reference framework for process-oriented software development organizations. *Software Systems Model, 4*, 94-105.

Golden, W., & Powel, P. (2004). Inter-organizational Information Systems as Enablers of Organizational Flexibility. *Technology Analysis & Strategic Management, 16*(3), 299-325.

Goldman, S. L., Nagel, R. N., & Preiss, K. (1995). *Agile Competitors and Virtual Organizations*. New York:Van Nostrand Reinhold.

Grover, V., Teng, J. T. C., & Fiedler, K. D. (1993). Information Technology Enabled Business Process Redesign: An Integrated Planning Framework. *OMEGA International Journal of Management Science, 21*(4), 433-447.

Hammer, M. (1990). Reengineering Work. Don't Automate, Obliterate. *Harvard Business Review,* 104-112.

Haeckel, S. H. (1995). Adaptive Enterprise Design: The Sense-and-Respond Model. *Planning Review, 23*(3), pp. 6-42.

Haeckel, S. H. (1999). *Adaptive Enterprise: Creating and Leading Sense-and-Respond Organizations.* Harvard Business School Press, Boston 1999.

Hammer, M. (1996). *Beyond Reengineering: How the Process-Centered Organization Is Changing Our Work and Our Lives.* Harper Collins.

Henbury, C. (1996). *Agile Enterprise/Next Generation Manufacturing Enterprise.* http://ourworld. compuserve.com/homepages/chesire_henbury/agility.htm

Jeng, J-J., Chang, H., & Bhaskaran, K. (2005). On Architecting Business Performance Management Grid for Adaptive Enterprises. *Proceedings of the 2005 Symposium on Applications and the Internet (SAINT' 2005),* IEEE.

IFEAD (Institute for Enterprise Architecture Developments) (2007). *EA & Services Oriented Enterprise (SOE) / Service Oriented Architecture (SOA) and Service Oriented Computing (SOC) IFEAD.* http://www.enterprise-architecture.info/EA_Services-Oriented-Enterprise.htm

ISO/IEC & ITU-T: Information technology – Open Distributed Processing – Part 1 – Overview – ISO/IEC 10746-1 | ITU-T Recommendation X.901

Keen, P. G. W. (1991). *Shaping the Future: Business Design through Information Technology.* Boston: Harvard Business School Press, 1991.

Kubil Rolf and Nadhan E. G. (2005). Banking on a Service-Oriented Architecture. EDS

Leeuw, A., & Volberda, H. W. (1996). On the Concept of Flexibility: A Dual Control Perspective. Omega. *International Journal of Management Science, 24*(2), 121-139.

Lin, J. Y. C., & Orlowska, M. E. (2005). Partial completion of activity in business process specification. *Proceedings of IRMA 2005,* San Diego, CA, USA, pp.186-189.

Mooney, G. J., Gurbaxani, V., & Kraemer, L. K. (1996). A Process Oriented Framework for Assessing the Business Value of Information Technology. *The DATA BASE for Advances in Information Systems, 27*(2), 68-81.

OMB A-130: US Office of Management & Budget (1996). *Memorandum for Heads of Executive Departments and Establishments: Management of Federal Information Resources.*

Oosterhout, van M., Waarts, E, & Hillegersberg, van J. (2006). Change factors requiring agility and implications for IT. *European Journal of Information Systems, 15,* 132-145.

Presley, A. R., Huff, B. L., & Liles, D. H. (1993). A Comprehensive Enterprise Model for Small Manufacturers. *Proceedings of the 2nd Industrial Engineering Research Conference,* 430-434. Institute of Industrial Engineers, Atlanta, Georgia.

Pyke, J. (2005). *BPM in Context: Now and in the Future.* The Process Factory Ltd. www.bptrends.com

Ramanathan, J. (2005). Fractal Architecture for the Adaptive Complex Enterprise. *Communications of the ACM, 48*(5), 51-57.

Rockart, F. J., Earl J. M., & Ross, W. J. (1996). Eight Imperatives for the New IT Organization. *Sloan Management Review, 38*(1), 43-54.

Sambamurthy, V., Bharadwaj, A., & Grover, V. (2003). Shaping Agility through Digital Options:

Reconceptualizing the Role of Information Technology in Contemporary Firms. *MIS Quarterly, 27*(2), 237-263.

Sanjay, G., Arvind, M., & Omar, El S. (2004). Coordinating for Flexibility in e-Business Supply Chains. *Journal of Management Information Systems, 21*(3), 7-45.

ShuiGuang, D., Zhen, Y., ZhaoHui, W., & LiCan, H. (2004). Enhancement of Workflow Flexibility by Composing Activities at Run-time. *Proceedings of the 2004 ACM Symposium on Applied Computing*, 667-673.

Zachman, J. (2004). *Enterprise Architecture and Legacy Systems.* http://members.ozemail.com.au/~visible/ papers/zachman1.htm

Zachman, A. J. (1999). A Framework for Information Systems Architecture. *IBM Systems Journal, 31*(3), 445 –470.

WFMC (Workflow Management Coalition) (2002). *Workflow: An introduction.*

KEY TERMS

Adaptability: The ability to change to suit new conditions or situations.

Agile Enterprise: The enterprise that can efficiently respond to change both upon expected and unpredicted contingencies as well as cause change in a proactive manner to gain competitive advantage.

Agility: The ability to move quickly and easily.

Architecture: A collection of descriptions that concern each individual stakeholder.

Business Process Viewpoint: The enterprise perspective referring to business processes comprising actions, roles, rules, routes, resources and events.

Enterprise Architecture: The description of all the perspectives of an enterprise, i.e. organizational structure, personnel, information, business processes and information technology along with their interrelations.

Flexibility: The ability to change to suit new conditions or situations.

Information Technology Viewpoint: The enterprise perspective referring to information technology comprising IT infrastructure and business applications along with the provided services.

Information Viewpoint: The enterprise perspective referring to information aspects comprising representation, communication, semantics, content and structure.

Organizational Viewpoint: The enterprise perspective referring to organizational structure comprising roles, policies, hierarchy and units.

People Viewpoint: The enterprise perspective referring to people characteristics, i.e. knowledge, competencies, skills and culture.

View: A representation of the whole system from the perspective of a related set of concerns.

Viewpoint: The perspective from which a view is taken. It serves a specific category of system stakeholders.

Chapter II
What is SAP Business Blueprint?

Hossana H. Aberra
Enterprise Integration, Inc., USA

ABSTRACT

SAP Business Blueprint is a vital part of SAP implementation exercise. A well-defined business blueprint may set the foundation for successful implementation of the subsequent SAP implementation phases; provided that the necessary project success factors are in position. This chapter clarifies some of the concepts behind SAP Business Blueprint. It explains and views the ERP solution as an integral component of the design process. It outlines different aspects of SAP business blueprinting from technical infrastructure enablement, while setting the solution landscape, to the details of business process definition. It points out how the SAP Solution Manager facilitates (business process) architecture-driven implementation through tight integration with ARIS Business Architect for NetWeaver. It details ways of moving toward Service Oriented Architecture (SOA) utilizing Enterprise Services, and an approach for generating Business Process Execution Language (BPEL) models using Web Services Description Language (WSDL) imported objects for analysis.

INTRODUCTION

In the past, it was implied that the task of SAP Business Blueprinting may be conducted independently of the solution landscape. The solution landscape was set and configured after the Business Blueprinting phase of the SAP implementation lifecycle, that is, during the Realization (Configuration & Testing) phase. In a sense, the design was independent of the solution landscape. This approach may also be considered as the pre-SAP Solution Manager practice.

After the introduction of SAP Solution Manager in January 2002 (Oswald, 2002), the solution landscape became an integral component of the Project Prep and Business Blueprint phases.

The SAP Solution Manager is a complete solution lifecycle management tool that facilitates SAP implementation, as well (Prior, Hommel & Vonkarey, n.d.). Assessment and design of the enterprise is one of the major activities accomplished during the Business Blueprinting phase. While some still favor using the tools and methodologies prior to Solution Manager, such approach may also force reassessment of the enterprise during the Realization Phase.

The following discussion focuses on three areas on the enterprise pyramid (see Figure 1): enterprise architecture, applications and services. Strategic, Communication and Technical Infrastructure levels are outside of the scope of this discussion.

This chapter discusses that the modernized approach for SAP Business Blueprint may be driven by the technical configuration of the solution landscape, hence the layout and foundation for the organizational design are set from the start. The discussion also covers the challenge of pre-developed enterprise architectures that reflect semi-system enabled enterprises as enterprises move toward a fully modernized environment. It points out how the SAP Solution Manager facilitates (business process) architecture-driven implementation through the tight integration with ARIS Business Architect for NetWeaver, as well as describes how to move toward Service Oriented Architecture (SOA) utilizing Enterprise Services, and how to develop complete and consistent architecture traceability up to the strategic level.

BACKGROUND

The SAP Business Blueprint phase includes a number of activities, events, milestones, and deliverables as described in the Accelerated SAP (ASAP) Roadmap (2005), generally classified as having overall project management significance. The Business Blueprint is the output (or product) of the project design tasks as they are managed in

Figure 1. Enterprise pyramid (Source: Adopted from mySAP Business Suite: Service Provisioning, Enterprise Service-Oriented Architecture, 2006, p. 7)

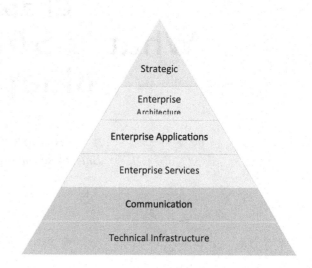

the appropriate tools – the SAP Solution Manager and ARIS Business Architect for SAP NetWeaver. These tools support architecture-driven implementation through a tight integration of the solution (SAP) and the enterprise architecture (ARIS).

While enterprise services design is not part of the SAP Business Blueprinting phase, the phase may be a viable starting point. With that in mind, the topic is addressed in the following section.

SAP BUSINESS BLUEPRINT

A comprehensive approach to the SAP Business Blueprinting is necessary to design a solution that accurately reflects the enterprise landscape. This implies that the Business Blueprint to include the solution landscape configuration and to support Enterprise Services development. Such an approach makes the design of the enterprise operation and the solution landscape fully complementary.

To support this notion, the topic of SAP Business Blueprinting will be discussed in terms of enterprise architecture, application and services.

A Business Blueprint process can be applied based on the guidelines provided by SAP; however, this chapter discusses the development of Business Blueprint from a practical SAP implementation project perspective.

Enterprise Architecture

SAP Business Blueprint is derived through an iterative definition of the business process and technical requirements for a specified project using the SAP Solution Manager and ARIS Business Architect for NetWeaver. The Business Blueprint also refers to determining the contents on the solution and business process architecture repository. The phase begins after Project Preparation on the SAP implementation lifecycle and ends prior to the Realization (Configuration) phase (Feuring, 2005). Therefore, it is important to note that nothing is built during the Business Blueprint phase. The plan (i.e., the completed Business Blueprint) describes a completely configured SAP solution, including all interface and security requirements. During the Realization phase, the customer and the implementation consultants, working together, "realize" the plan that is defined by the completed Business Blueprint.

The SAP Solution Manager is critical for generating content for the solution architecture. Three key elements are required in order to create Business Scenarios for a project on the Solution Manager. For each Business Scenario scope, SAP Solution Manager creates a corresponding Organization Unit, Master Data, and Business Scenarios structure (SAP Library, 2005). These three elements defined during the blueprinting phase set the foundation for accurately aligning the SAP solution to the enterprise business processes.

A high-level solution architecture content generation process includes (Business Process Modeling, 2006):

a. Creating a project in the SAP Solution Manager;

b. Selecting cross-functional business processes from predefined Business Scenarios in the SAP Solution Manager;

c. Synchronizing the SAP Solution Manager project content to the solution architecture repository in ARIS Business Architect for NetWeaver;

d. Further developing the business processes using the ARIS Business Architect for NetWeaver; and

e. Synchronizing solution architecture content from the ARIS business process repository to the SAP Solution Manager.

The Solution Manager controls both the SAP part of the solution as well as those business processes that are not enabled by the SAP software (SAP Solution Manager, 2002). This step is less critical if the enterprise enables all of its business processes in the SAP product suite, but that is seldom (if ever) the case.

In reality, a number of activities have to be accomplished to ensure that the Business Blueprint, on the solution side, and the architecture side comply with applicable rules and regulations. Most organizations must be compliant with some larger regulatory environment, from Sarbanes-Oxley to one of the many public sector compliance requirements. Thus, the somewhat simplified SAP guidelines fall short of addressing the compliance requirements as they apply to existing architecture development and implementation guidelines.

For example, SAP recommends using the SAP Solution Composer as a starting point to pick suitable business scenarios from the SAP Business Process Repository (BPR ST-ICO150) inside the SAP Solution Manager (Business Process Modeling, 2006). The predefined business processes serve as the basis for the "to-be" business processes to be realized in the SAP solution. Thus the existing processes may be forced to fit (align) to the predefined business processes. This approach is known to work in some private sector organizations, but in large and complex institutions, these "to-be" processes are problematic. These "to-be" processes may not "fit" within the "as-is" scenarios (in customer terms) that are bound by systems which may not be replaced by the SAP solution. This alignment requires considerable additional modeling and analysis outside of the solution architecture. Further alignment of the end-to-end business processes to the SAP solution's predefined business processes is required to develop a new "to-be" scenario, as well as a "transition" architecture that "fits" organizational requirements.

In some organizations, architecture development starts without tight integration with a live solution. Some solution architecture may contain proprietary concepts, standards, structures, and semantics that can be described using any acceptable architecture frameworks. Thus the "as-is" architecture, which may also serve as the compliance architecture, matures faster. As the SAP implementation begins, a new "as-is" (a redocumentation) is captured during the SAP Level 1 and 2 blueprinting workshops. This makes it even more cumbersome to maintain a repository that captures a matured "as-is" architecture in addition to the new workshop "as-is" models, the predefined solution architecture, and the "to-be" architectures.

Unfortunately, compliance takes time. Concurrent development of the "to-be" architecture from a combination of the "as-is" and the solution architecture could be time-consuming. To fully realize the benefits of enterprise architecture, the architecture repository must be designed to enable multi-purpose analysis by incorporating the different "flavors" of the business processes in a single architecture repository, as well. Such analysis includes the different patterns of the SAP Scenarios to the Processes. For every SAP Scenario, there could be one or more processes performed, which could be mapped into a pattern. Such analysis in turn makes each instance on the pattern a unique instance. For instance, for Sales

Order Processing and Third Party Order Processing (SAP Scenarios) and Credit Management (SAP Process), there could be Credit Management in Sales Order Processing; Credit Management in Third Party Order Processing, etc. Such relationship-based analysis could be performed to evaluate the state of the "to-be" enterprise operation.

In addition, relationship-based architecture analysis supports communication with the general user community by providing clarity on the system capabilities. For instance, often when stating a scope, statements may be made implying a process (like Credit Management) that resides within the scope of an SAP project. Such notion may be too vague for setting organizational touch points and boundaries. Instead, it may be important to articulate the scope in reference to the result of an architecture analysis. Thus, for instance, it may be possible to state that Credit Management in Sales Order Processing is within the scope of SAP project. While this may be one example of an architecture analysis, a number of analysis schemes may be derived based on the core solution architecture content to help better understand the enterprise.

Nevertheless, the enterprise depiction process is critical and must be comprehensive because the SAP solution must completely align with the non-SAP business processes in a complex organization with many systems enabling the landscape. If the SAP software enables only a portion of an organization, the Business Blueprint must define how the "to-be" SAP processes align with the "as-is" business processes that fall outside of the SAP solution. Otherwise, the organization cannot efficiently execute the cross-functional business processes that flow across SAP and non-SAP solution components.

The subsequent section discusses the details of the SAP solution landscape configuration, including the delineation of the system organization in terms of structure and units, as well as the determination of master data.

Enterprise Application: SAP Solution Landscape Configuration

Some of the terms used in this section are summarized and adopted from various definitions posted on the line SAP Help Portal (SAP Library, 2005). Refer to the Terms and Definitions section for more information.

System Organization

Organization in SAP implies two distinct sets of expressions: one referring to a system configuration structure, and another, to organizational units. In SAP, a system configuration structure defines the financial and logistical operational structures while configuring the solution. It is defined in terms of company code for financials, plant for logistics, and sales area for sales and distributions. System configuration structures are derived from the reporting hierarchy and roles of units in terms of production, procurement, maintenance and material planning, selling, and purchasing power. Selecting a suitable SAP organization structure is an intricate analysis process.

An organizational unit in SAP implies to the organizational (org) roles of units in terms of responsibilities for the associated costs. On the other hand, a traditional organization unit structure usually reflects a hierarchy and authority rather than financial obligations. Hence, an org unit in SAP is derived from creating a cost-controlling area. Both system organization structure and organization unit will be discussed in the next section.

System Organization Structure

An organizational structure defines an enterprise, reflecting its focus. The structure defines, at a minimum, information flows and financial roll-ups hierarchy for reporting and control. In order to set-up the SAP software, the organization must ensure that its structure will be enabled by the SAP software solution. The system organization model reflects the degree of centralization across an enterprise. For instance, an enterprise with one company code, controlling area, and funds management area is considered highly centralized. Decentralization for such enterprise begins at the profit, cost, and business center levels. Conversely, an enterprise with multiple company codes mimics a highly decentralized enterprise, even though each entity may have, to a certain degree, identical controlling and funds management area.

If the SAP solution is fragmented, it may be impossible to truly align the software with enterprise information flows and reporting structure, forcing an artificial Business-to-Business (B2B) e-commerce solution inside of the enterprise.

Similarly, for logistics, organizational structure is configured through the purchasing power of plants. The purchasing organization unit divides an enterprise according to the purchasing requirements. Unlike the financial system organizational structure, the logistics system organizational structure determines the degree of cross-organizational business process harmonization for activities such as inter-plant planning and transfers. As an example, a purchasing organization may have one or more plants that are further sub-organized to multiple storage locations containing warehouses. Such structure simplifies business processes largely among the plants. Conversely, multiple purchasing orgs with individual plants increase the complexity of business procedures among the plants.

The sales area ties the products and services offered within an enterprise with the corresponding financial transactions. The sales area consists of a sales org, distribution channel, and division. When defining an enterprise on SAP, a sales org is assigned to one company code, as well as one plant. However, multiple sales orgs may also be assigned to a plant. Distribution channel(s)--product/service outlet vehicles--and division(s)--product/service sellers--are designated to one or more sales orgs. The assignment of a sales org to a plant provides transparency to the activities within a plant, including warehouse inventories and services. One organizational entity that is not tied to any of the org structures discussed above but has important relationships with sales and distribution is a shipping point. Shipping points are simply stated schedule and process shipments.

As discussed previously, defining a system organization structure has a greater operational implication on an enterprise, unless outlined diligently. This is because, once configured, it is hard to go back and undo the company structure unless the system is re-installed.

Organizational Unit

An organizational unit in SAP takes a slightly different approach than the traditional functional job classification used by most organizations. An organization unit could be a plant, cost center, distribution channel, project team, group, etc. with a responsibility over cost. SAP maintains each organization unit's information, such as account assignment, cost distribution, address, work schedule, and quota planning, based on functional requirement, allocation criteria, physical location, and responsibility for cost. Examples of an organizational unit are sales area, receiving point, shipping point, storage bin, and loading point.

How is the organization structure on the Human Resources (Personnel) side linked to organization units defined per cost centers? SAP's enterprise organization supports such relationship by assigning cost and profit centers to traditional organization structures. Thus, it provides a comprehensive view of the enterprise by roles and responsibilities, costs and revenues.

Ultimately, each user is then given a role in and assigned to an organizational unit, and this must be defined and documented in the Business Blueprint. SAP's scheme for assigning roles and authorizations applies a three-tiered approach for granting access to transactions and task delegation

(Accelerated SAP, 2005). The ASAP Implementation Roadmap (2005) strongly recommends that the three-tier approach be followed and if possible, only Tier 3: Specific job access authorization be given to users. This reduces the complexity of assigning user roles and authorization. Still, the assignment of roles and authorization is a complex process, and SAP does not provide adequate tools to enable it. ARIS may be used to manage the roles and authorizations, since it provides a methodology for maintaining tight configuration management control over those assignments.

Master Data Component

Master data is part of each Business Scenario scoped on the SAP Solution Manager. Rather than addressing master data as it applies to the scoped scenarios, its significance may be viewed in terms of the importance to the overall project. A properly sourced and identified data should be linked directly to the enterprise architecture, as the data is the information that fuels the enterprise (Dr. Carsten Svensson, personal communication, February 7, 2007).

Master data are identified, inventoried, and targeted for data conversion as part of the Business Blueprint. Master data are key variables that are relatively constant. These data may change, but infrequently. Master data could include business partner records, product conditions, master records, material information, material classification, charts of accounts, cost centers, fund centers, customer material information, etc. Data conversion requires that all necessary master data be migrated from legacy sources and loaded into the SAP production database. This can be efficiently accomplished using Extract, Transform, and Load methods and tools, but this approach cannot alleviate problems of improperly identified (i.e., sourced) or missing data on the system side.

The SAP solution requires high quality master data, and since the solution is enabled by a consolidated production database, there is a low tolerance for data gaps. Therefore, significant pre-analysis is required to assess master data readiness for any SAP project. The Master Data essentially becomes a critical element in applying Enterprise Services to SOA.

What are the Contents of SAP Business Blueprint on the Architecture and Solution Side?

The contents of SAP Business Blueprint on the solution side is thus the details of the SAP solution landscape configuration, system organization structure, organization units, and master data with the supporting documentation. On the architecture side reside the details of the business scenarios, including business process, process steps, and transactions.

For documentation purposes, the solution landscape configuration information can be stored in the SAP Solution Manager and may be translated into architecture framework in the enterprise architecture repository.

The enterprise architecture repository may contain various types of models that depict the enterprise business process. For instance, the business process can be displayed using the Extended Event-Driven Process Chain (eEPC) model type in ARIS. The process (represented via SAP function object) on an eEPC may be assigned directly to the SAP process step using the Function Allocation Diagram (FAD) model type. This model also depicts the details of organizational units, master data entities, and transactions. Figure 2 portrays an eEPC and FAD models representing the SAP process and process step, and their tie with the SAP Solution Manager. Other relevant objects could be displayed using the FAD, including interfaces, Key Performance Indicators (KPIs), or any additional information that may be relevant for planning purposes. The Business Blueprint architecture products can then be used to further analyze and optimize the enterprise business processes, support enterprise-wide governance, and manage process performance once the solution is deployed.

Figure 2. SAP solution manager and ARIS business architect for NetWeaver: eEPC and FAD models representing an SAP process and process step, and their tie with SAP solution manager

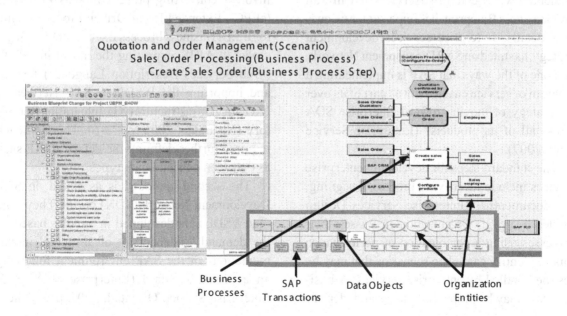

Upon launching of the SAP solution, users are able to execute a transaction from the solution architecture side on ARIS to SAP. Such tight integration of the architecture and the solution facilitates transition to the new "to-be" business processes, as well as user training and acceptance.

Properly documented Business Blueprint is the core of a larger implementation plan. It may be important for projects to have a complete Business Blueprint phase prior to entering the subsequent SAP phase. Many projects move forward with an incomplete Business Blueprint and a promise to "catch up" during the ASAP Realization phase. The "catch up" seldom occurs and it is possible to have an incomplete Business Blueprint, which may significantly reduce the scope upon implementation or lead to failure.

Furthermore, architecture-driven implementation reduces implementation cycle-time and facilitates future project upgrades; hence good documentation is an absolute requirement. It is a good business practice to document solution information, so that it may be continually reused for maintenance over the solution lifecycle.

Enterprise Services

To identify where enterprise services fit within an SAP Business Blueprint, it is important to discuss their details. Enterprise services development strategy, as stated on SAP Development Network, "are one of the ways that SAP is implementing a program of service enablement as part of its over all strategy of moving toward enterprise SOA across all of its products" (Enterprise Service Wiki, 2007).

The standard steps for developing enterprise services include identifying process, designing, and documenting (Enterprise Services Design Guide, 2005, p. 21). Organizations may assess their processes using a combination of performance data to identify candidate scenarios that may be best be handled by enterprise services. A business case may be proposed to asses and identify

the scenarios based on "high-execution time" or "high-execution cost" (2005). Performance data for enterprises that are blueprinting may be computed based on information provided from manual and legacy system processes, or there may be documented performance matrix using frameworks such as Six Sigma or the Supply Chain Council Reference (SCOR) model.

Once the process or a set of processes is identified, SAP's Enterprise Services Design Guide (2005) outlines three approaches for designing enterprise services (pp. 21-23). Level 1 is the design of a single enterprise service such as assembling information across many systems for a particular process. Level 2 is to develop a set of enterprise services to address a group of processes; in this case, each service may be analyzed when executed individually and collectively. And Level 3 is to develop large scale enterprise services to enable multiple enterprises.

For the purpose of this discussion, numerous tests were conducted to assess the intricacy of enterprise services and to explore ways of developing architecture models that depict enterprise services framework.

There are two approaches for developing enterprise services. The first approach in a nutshell involves converting process models known as (eEPC - Extended Event-Driven Process Chain) to BPEL (Business Process Execution Language) model in ARIS, exporting the model in WSDL (Web Services Description Language) format, and importing the WSDL to SAP NetWeaver Exchange Infrastructure (XI), Integration Repository (Natarajan, 2006, pp. 3-6). This approach requires further defining the details in XI, such as data elements and data types.

The second approach is as stated on SAP Development Network (SDN) portal. They state that WSDLs are developed in bundles based on the demand "independent of an actual implementation" of the SAP environment following an accepted standard (Enterprise SOA, p. 5; Enterprise Service-Oriented, 2005, p. 3). These services may be then be integrated on the SAP NetWeaver XI Integration Repository for testing and implementation.

A list of WSDL Enterprise Service bundles in XML are listed on SDN. Those services cover different areas such as SAP ERP 2005, SAP SCM, SAP SRM, and various Industries. Therefore, the other option is to import the WSDL directly to ARIS Business Architect for NetWeaver and then further analyze and integrate the imported content in the existing architecture repository.

When importing WSDL into ARIS, a folder structure containing the enterprise service objects is created (Figure 3). A large number of objects are created after importing the contents of the enterprise services bundle into ARIS. Among the imported objects are Port Type, Service Operation, Message Type, Message Data Type, Global Data Type, and Core Component Technical Specification (CCTS) Core Data Type, marked "Imported" on Figure 4. The figure shows the structure, object type and relationship of the Enterprise Service

objects. The Service Interface, which is equivalent to Process Interface object in ARIS, depicts an enterprise function such as Manage Sales Order, i.e. an operational activity within an organization enabled by the enterprise service bundle.

It is then possible to auto-generate a BPEL model (BPEL allocation or BPEL process model) using WSDL imported objects and further develop analysis models such as SAP integration process (XI) model in ARIS.

The Process Component is equivalent to a scenario on SAP Solution Manager. A Business Object in a simple term is a form. Business Objects help trigger the execution of a set of functions or simply facilitate information entry and presentation. A Business Object and Business Object Node may be inherent to the solution (mySAP Business Suite: Service Provisioning, 2006, p. 43). For instance, SAP SRM Enterprise Service bundle enables Supplier Order Collaboration in SRM service bundle, having Sales Order Processing in SRM process component, Sales Order

Figure 3. ARIS business architect for NetWeaver, folder structure after importing predefined WSDLs

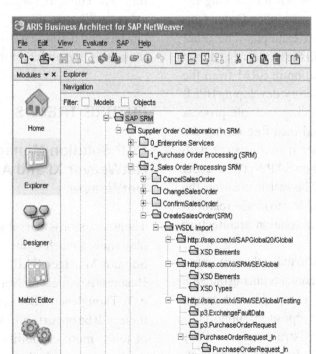

Figure 4. Entities of service interface and business object models (Source: mySAP Business Suite: Service Provisioning, Enterprise Service-Oriented Architecture, p. 42)

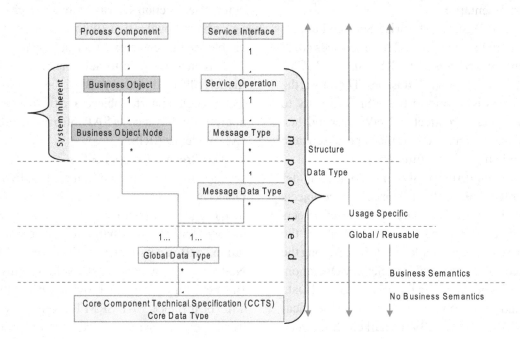

business object, and Create Sales Order service (Figure 5).

Enterprise Services Wiki (2007) also describes how the process steps flow when executing the business process within a Supplier Order Collaboration in SRM as an example. The other alternative is to identify all the models that depict Supplier Order Collaboration in SRM from the solution architecture repository, developing BPEL process model by referencing multiple process models, as applicable, and then fine-tuning the BEPL model to make sure it is consistent with the process flow depicted on SAP NetWeaver XI Integration Repository. The rest is creating the appropriate assignment (object to model relationship hierarchy) within the solution architecture repository.

How is it then possible to make the maximum use of enterprise services contents during the SAP Business Blueprinting? A comprehensive design of the solution architecture repository supports architecture coherency - a well structured repository that not only supports the SAP Business Blueprint-

ing, but also enterprise services, as organizations move towards SOA. Ultimately, the imported data would be consistently reused across the repository. The contents can be analyzed for different purposes like grouping the data into information clusters and defining it in relation to other objects in the solution architecture repository.

FUTURE TRENDS

SAP Solution Manager, SAP NetWeaver XI and ARIS for NetWeaver

The assumption is that subsequent product releases may show a much tighter integration of the SAP Solution Manager, SAP NetWeaver XI and ARIS Business Architect for NetWeaver (Pezzini, 2007, p. 3). Though both IDS-Scheer and SAP state that there will be opportunities for further integration of tools, more capabilities may be revealed as products are available for release.

Figure 5. Object to model relationships, enterprise services

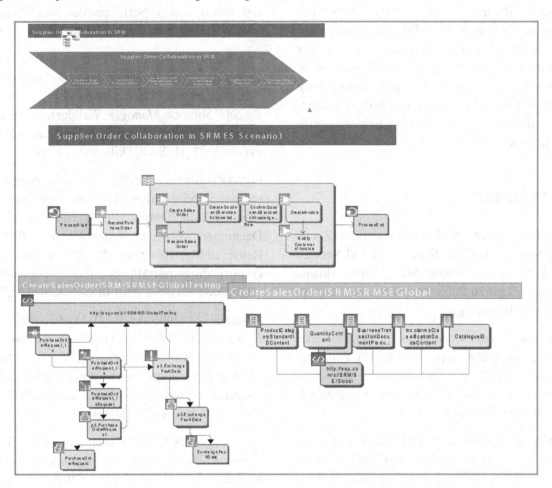

Enterprise Services

Currently, there is no single product that supports design, development, documentation, and execution of enterprise services. To assess the level of effort required for enabling enterprise services, a clearly defined migration plan may be necessary. What could be achieved now and in the future may be driven by new technology developments. A realistic plan may pave the way for integrating capabilities as opportunity avails, not only to address the business process pain-points, but also all business processes that support the entire enterprise operation.

CONCLUSION

SAP Business Blueprint phase is the phase where the operational foundation is set. The modernized approach to develop the SAP Business Blueprint products may be viewed as one that embraces the enterprise architecture, application, and services. A comprehensive SAP Business Blueprint product consists of the tools to configure, define, synchronize, integrate, and analyze the solution blueprint. Good implementation practice requires careful planning and disciplined execution. The approach discussed makes use of the ARIS Business Architect for NetWeaver, SAP Solution Manager and pre-defined enterprise services that provide the pre-conditions to develop a well-documented and managed SAP Business Blueprint. That is, SAP Business Blueprint supports the solution landscape configuration, as well as the development of the "as-is", solution, and enterprise services architecture. Such an integrated environment simplifies the enterprise design process during SAP implementation, and facilitates the transition, support and maintenance of the new enterprise environment.

REFERENCE

Accelerated SAP (ASAP). Implementation Roadmap Version 3.0. (2005, September). SAP Service Marketplace, SAP Solution Manager, Downloads. Retrieved June 26, 2006, from <http://service.sap.com/solutionmanager>

Business Process Modeling with ARIS for SAP NetWeaver. (2006, September 12-15). *Proceedings of SAP TECHED '06 Conference*. Retrieved September 22, 2006 from <http://www.sapteched.com/06/usa/home.htm>

Enterprise Service Wiki. (2007, June (Last Edited)) SAP Developer Network (SDN). Website <https://www.sdn.sap.com/irj/sdn/wiki?path=/display/ESpackages/Home>

Enterprise Service-Oriented Architecture, Sales Order Processing, mySAP SRM 2005 (SRM Server 5.5). (2005). SAP Developer Network (SDN). Enterprise Services Documentation, Download. Retrieved May 2006 from <https://www.sdn.sap.com/irj/sdn/go/portal/prtroot/docs/webcontent/uuid/c0cd8360-3b74-2910-0fae-dcceed7328e7>

Enterprise Services Design Guide. (2005). *SAP Developer Network (SDN)*. Retrieved May 2007 from <https://www.sdn.sap.com/irj/servlet/prt/portal/prtroot/docs/library/uuid/943e83e5-0601-0010-acb5-b16258f5f20a >

Enterprise SOA and Business Process Platform FAQ. (n.d.). *SAP Developer Network (SDN)*. Retrieved February 19, 2007 from <https://www.sdn.sap.com/irj/sdn/go/portal/prtroot/docs/library/uuid/3071ab59-8faa-2910-cd81-da9e20b629ed>

Feuring, N. & Streibert, T. (2005, November 3-4). *Proceedings of SAP Skills Conference, Business-Process Oriented Life-Cycle Management with the SAP Solution Manager*. Walldorf, Germany. Website <http://www.sap.com/community/pub/events/2005_11_SAP_Skills/index.epx>

mySAP Business Suite: Service Provisioning, Enterprise Service-Oriented Architecture, mySAP Business Suite 2004 and 2005, Version 2.0. (2006, December). *SAP Developer Network (SDN)*. Retrieved May 2006 from <https://www.sdn.sap.com/irj/sdn/go/portal/prtroot/docs/webcontent/uuid/c0cd8360-3b74-2910-0fae-dcceed7328e7>

Natarajan, S. (2006, April 24). *Model a Business Process in ARIS for SAP NetWeaver and Import BPEL in Exchange Infrastructure*. Retrieved May 25, 2007 from <https://www.sdn.sap.com/irj/sdn/go/portal/prtroot/docs/library/uuid/3c58e011-0b01-0010-1e88-b42e01bb961a>

Oswald, G. (2002, May 13). *Optimum Life, SAP's Solution Management Strategy*. SAP INFO. Retrieved June 18, 2007, from <http://www.sap.info/INT/int/index/Category-12613c61affe7a5bc-int/0/ >

Pezzini, M. (2007, April 10). *Q&A: Shedding Light on SAP NetWeaver XI's Road Map and Strategic Role*. [Research ID Number G00147081]. Gartner, p. 3.

Prior, Hommel & Vonkarey. (n.d.). *SAP Solution Manager Webcast: Managing System Complexity and End-to-End System Support*. Retrieved on September 26, 2006 from <http://www.sap.com/community/pub/events/2005_06_28/index.epx?logonStatusCheck=0>

SAP Library: SAP Solution Manager 3.2 SP09. (2005, September). SAP Help Portal. Retrieved September 2005 from <https://help.sap.com/>.

SAP Solution Manager, Release 220. (2002). *SAP Service Marketplace, SAP Solution Manager, Downloads.* Retrieved October 2005, from <http://service.sap.com/solutionmanager>

KEY TERMS

SAP Business Blueprint:

Business Blueprint contents and objective is detailed documentation of the results gathered during requirements workshops…documents the business process requirements of the company… better understand how the company intends to run its business within the SAP System.

Business Blueprint development process project team gathers requirements and conducts conceptual design of the solution.

Business Blueprint technical content documents the business processes...to implement…create a project structure in which relevant business scenarios, business processes and process steps are organized in a hierarchical structure…project documentation…(Extracted Source: ASAP Implementation Roadmap, 2006).

SAP System Organization Structure Components:

Company is a unit for which legal financial statements are created, while a **Company Code** is a legal entity within a company having external financial reporting obligation. There could be one or more company codes for a company. Normally each company code within a company uses the same chart of accounts.

Funds Management area is a unit for disbursement of funds, while a controlling area is where costs and revenues are collected. Then follow profit, cost, and business centers, which are used for internal purpose for creating balance sheets and income statements.

Plant is a production or a service providing entity. It could be referred as a storage location, shipping point, or work center. A plant may also have a warehouse for managing materials. Warehouse in a plant allows segregation of materials by storage bins. (Adapted from: ASAP Implementation Roadmap, 2006).

Enterprise Services are "a standards-based way of encapsulating enterprise functionality and exposing it as a reusable business service that can be combined with other services to meet new requirements. Enterprise services, defined by SAP and its partners and customers, can be assembled together to compose new applications or enable new business processes." (Source: Enterprise Services Wiki, Service Oriented Architecture)

Service-Oriented Architecture (SOA) is a style of software architecture that uses services as the fundamental building blocks. SOA "A software architecture that supports the design, development, identification, and consumption of standardized services across the enterprise, thereby improving reusability of software components and creating agility in responding to change." (Source: industry term.) (Source: SDN Enterprise Services Wiki, Service Oriented Architecture)

Service-Orientation describes an architecture that uses loosely coupled services to support the requirements of business processes and users. SOA is a design for linking business and computational resources (principally organizations, applications and data) on demand to achieve the desired results for service consumers (which can be end users or other services). A paradigm for organizing and utilizing distributed capabilities that may be under the control of different ownership domains. It provides a uniform means to offer, discover, interact with and use capabilities to produce desired effects consistent with measurable preconditions and expectations. (Source: OASIS (the Organization for the Advancement of Structured Information Standards)).

Chapter III
Free and Open Source Enterprise Resources Planning

Rogerio Atem de Carvalho
Federal Center for Technological Education of Campos, Brazil

ABSTRACT

This chapter introduces the key aspects of Free/Open Source Enterprise Resources Planning systems (FOS-ERP). Starting by related work carried out by researchers and practitioners, it argues in favor of the growing acceptance of this category of enterprise systems while showing how this subject is not yet well explored, especially by researchers. The goals of this chapter are to highlight the differences between FOS-ERP and their proprietary equivalents (P-ERP) in terms of business models, selection, customization, and evolution; and showing the challenges and opportunities that they offer to adopters, vendors, researchers, and individual collaborators. Therefore, this chapter tries to broaden the discussion around the FOS-ERP subject, currently focused only in cost aspects, bringing more attention to other aspects and pointing out their innovative potential.

INTRODUCTION

Free/Open Source[1] ERP (FOS-ERP) systems are gaining a growing acceptance and consequently improving their market share. According to a recent market study, FOS-ERP related services would hit about US$ 36 billion by 2008 (LeClaire, 2006). The reasons for this phenomenon are basically two: lower costs and free access to application's source code. On the cost side, they impose reduced or no investment in licensing in general. On the access to code side stands the perception that if customization is inevitable, why not adopt a solution that exposes its code to the client company, which can freely adapt the system to its needs? Maybe this second reason is more complex and much less studied and is addressed in many topics later in the chapter.

Given this raising on FOS-ERP deployment, and the relative small number of references to this subject, instead of simply comparing functionalities of various different solutions, this chapter aims to a) present tendencies on open source software in general and open source enterprise systems that directly influence on FOS-ERP, b) highlight the differences between FOS-ERP and proprietary ERP (P-ERP) in terms of business models, selection, customization and maintenance, and c) identify the challenges and opportunities that they offer to stakeholders and developer communities.

RELATED WORK

While increasing in market importance, FOS-ERP is still poorly analyzed by academy, where large quantities of articles put their research efforts on P-ERP deployment, project management, and economic aspects (Botta-Genoulaz, Millet & Grabot, 2005). Research on FOS-ERP software is rather deficient, and, therefore, a series of relevant aspects of FOS-ERP, which differentiate them from P-ERP, are still not well understood. As an example of this situation, a research conducted on the FOS-ERP evaluation subject, has shown how evaluating FOS-ERP brings more concerns than evaluating P-ERP (De Carvalho, 2006). One indication that FOS-ERP seems to be another situation where technology has outstripped the conceptual hawsers, is the fact that, according to Kim and Boldyreff (Kim & Boldyreff, 2005), "by September 2005 only one paper about Open Source ERP (Smets-Solanes & De Carvalho, 2003) has been published in the whole of ACM and IEEE Computer Society journals and proceedings, whereas more numerous articles have been published in non-academic industrial trade magazines." Although nowadays more research work has been done on FOS-ERP, this subject is still a new one, with many topics to be explored and tendencies to be confirmed, since the number of adopters and the operation times are still small in relation to the P-ERP figures. In fact,

FOS-ERP is a barely explored research subject. As said before, the first academic paper on this specific subject was Smets-Solanes & De Carvalho (2003); the first paper on evaluating FOS-ERP is De Carvalho (2006); and the first international event on FOS-ERP was held in Vienna, Austria, also in 2006[2]. These facts show how FOS-ERP is a young research area, with relatively very little academic effort put on it until now.

However, some good work on related topics can be found. Currently the most in-depth analysis of the economic impact of Free/Open Source Software (FOSS) in enterprise systems was the one conducted by Dreiling and colleagues (Dreiling, Klaus, Rosemann & Wyssusek, 2005). The authors argue that "standards that supposedly open development by ensuring interoperability tend to be interpreted by enterprise systems global players according to their interest". The authors follow this reasoning showing the deeper consequences of this: "[global players interests] might be incongruent with the interests of the software industry at large, those of users organizations, and may also have effects on local and national economies." And more: "despite control of interfaces and standards by few software developers, even integration of the information infrastructure of one single company with one brand of enterprise system cannot be consolidated over time [citing many other authors]." On the open standards subject, they conclude, "software engineering principles and open standards are necessary but not sufficient condition for enterprise software development becoming less constrained by the politics of global players, responsive to user interests, and for ensuring a healthy software industry that can cater for regional market."

On the innovation side, Dreiling and colleagues state that many economists agree to the point of dominant companies – like the ERP global players – are less disposed to respond to articulated customer requirements, and monopolies as well oligopolies tend to stifle product and service innovation. Furthermore, "controlling architectures by means of proprietary software and open standards in the enterprise application industry appears to actually preclude innovation that could be of benefit for many users of enterprise systems", which includes less developed economies. This seems to be a serious problem, since adapting is a crucial point to ERP, which by nature must be adapted to the adopter needs. This conclusion reinforces a positive consequence of the freedom of manipulating the source code by itself in FOS-ERP: if the vendor changes its contract terms, the client company is not locked in to a particular solution supplier (Kooch, 2004). Additionally, can two competing companies derive a strategic differential using the same ERP? Although this problem can also happen with FOS-ERP, it seems to be bigger for P-ERP, since, due to the tightly control over source code, adaptations are limited to parameterization or high-cost functionality changes through Application Program Interfaces (APIs) or proprietary languages, restricting real differentiation and raising customization costs (De Carvalho, 2006). Therefore, if the fact that integration among processes can by itself becomes a source of competitive advantage (Caulliraux, Proença & Prado, 2000), this can be extrapolated to the possibility of changing source code to drive an even better advantage.

If on one hand FOS-ERP can foster innovation and give more power to adopters, on the other some important questions are yet to be answered, given that this type of FOSS is still a newcomer to the enterprise systems landscape. Even some enthusiasts recognize that FOS-ERP vendors service level have much to improve and gain experience, while in contrast, P-ERP have a mature network of consulting partners and a long history of success and failures (Serrano & Sarrieri, 2006). In fact, evaluating FOS-ERP for instance is a subject with only a few works on it. Herzog (2006) presents a very comprehensive approach that identifies three different methods for implementing a FOS-ERP solution - select a package, develop one by itself, and integrate best

of breed solutions – and five criteria for evaluating alternatives: functional fit, flexibility, support, continuity, and maturity. This method introduces the interesting possibility, not yet well explored in practice, of integrating solutions from different vendors through Enterprise Application Integration (EAI) techniques. A successful case study on mixing P-ERP solutions is described by Alshawi and colleagues (Alshawi, Themistocleous & Almadani, 2004) – but the literature lacks examples on doing the same with FOS-ERP.

De Carvalho (2006) also presents an FOS-ERP evaluation method, named PIRCS, that holds some similarity with Herzog's[3], however stressing more on risk evaluation, given the strategic nature of ERP. In fact, according to Caulliraux and colleagues (Caulliraux, Proença & Prado, 2000) ERP is strategic, given that "it is a major commitment of money, and thus with long range implications even if only from a financial point of view", and ERP systems are also important not only as a tangible asset, but "as a catalyst through their implementation in the formation of intangible assets and the company's self-knowledge." Aiming to include risk considerations, the PIRCS method seeks to identify weaknesses in the FOS-ERP's development environment during its evaluation process phases. These phases name the process, and are summarized as Prepare the evaluation process, Identify the alternatives, Rate alternatives' attributes, Compare alternatives' results, and Select the one that best fits the adopter needs.

Also related to the strategic nature of ERP, during PIRCS' Preparation phase, the adopter must define its strategic positioning in relation to the product, behaving as a simple *consumer*, only getting the solution from the vendor, or becoming a *prosumer* (Xu, 2003), by mixing passively purchasing commodity parts of the system with actively developing or customizing strategic ones by itself. Of course, choosing how to behave is not a simple decision in these cases, since it involves a series of demands like expertise on the FOS-ERP platform and architecture, dealing with the developer community – which can mean managing demands of disparate stakeholders (West & O'Mahony, 2005), and allocating resources for development. It is a question of weighting the direct and indirect gains of developing parts of the system with the shortcomings of doing so.

Many other subjects related to open software in general that affect FOS-ERP should be addressed to better understand their dynamics. Crowston and Howison (2006) assess the health of Open Source communities as a way of helping checking if an FOSS is suitable for the adopter or contributor needs – this kind of assessment can be one of the tools to check a specific FOS-ERP project maturity. Assessing FOS-ERP communities means understanding other organizations' behavior towards the project: since ERP in general are not for individual use, contributors most of times are companies' employees, not free-lancers. Hence, to understand the differences between this and other types of open software, it is necessary to understand how commercially sponsored and community built FOSS projects behave. According to West and O'Mahony (2005), one of the key moments of commercial FOSS is the start-up phase: when the project code is opened, "an infant community is presented with a large complex system that may be harder to decipher", thus the FOS-ERP creator may have to wait until contributions from other firms become viable and also advantageous - the main economic incentive for firm participation is the emancipation from the price and license conditions imposed by large software companies (Wang and Chen, 2005), but the potential for doing such substitution must be only latent in the project. The same type of incentive is identified by Riehle (2007), who stats that solution providers can take advantage from open source software "because they increase profits through direct costs savings and the ability to reach more customers through improved pricing flexibility". Other aspect on the vendor side identified by these authors is that opening the code can reduce the costs on software test-

ing and Research & Development tasks. These advantages are stimulating a better market acceptance, according to a Zinnov (2006) study, which, among other things, shows figures on the raising of venture capitalism participation and the higher penetration in the US enterprise systems market by open source solutions. Furthermore, Goth (2005) affirms that the open software market is on a "second wave" towards enterprise software, and that FOSS business models are finally ready for facing this new market challenge. These two last references points to a general improvement on the relation between FOSS communities and enterprise systems users.

Despite the differences, FOS-ERP and P-ERP certainly have one thing in common: both have a company behind their deployment activities. Although there exist FOS-ERP maintained almost solely by communities formed basically by individuals, like GNU Enterprise, it seems that only company-sponsored FOS-ERP, such as Compiere, ERP5, OpenMFG, and SQL Ledger, are really successful. In other words, FOS-ERP are typically of the *commercial open source* kind, which "a for-profit entity owns and develops", according to Riehle (2007) classification. The next topics show how FOS-ERP differs from P-ERP, present opportunities and challenges that this kind of software offer to developers and adopters, and finally drawn some conclusions on the subject.

DIFFERENCES BETWEEN FOS-ERP AND P-ERP

The fact that FOS-ERP expose their code forces vendors and adopters processes to accommodate the consequence that customization and maintenance can be done by other than the vendor. This fact means that the adopter is free to choose the participation level of the vendor in the different phases of the ERP life cycle – meaning that, at some extent, vendor participation can be also customized[4]. Analyzing the differences between open source and proprietary ERP depend on side of the commercial relation the organization is: adopter or vendor.

Differences for the Adopter

Selecting an ERP for adoption is a complex process, because, besides the size of the task, it is an important enterprise component that impacts the adopter organization in financial and in self-knowledge terms. Therefore, it is important to use a framework to understand how open source alternatives can impact this kind of project.

The Generalized Enterprise Reference Architecture and Methodology (GERAM) is a well-known standard that provides a description of all elements recommended in enterprise engineering and a collection of tools and methods to perform enterprise design and change with success (IFIP – IFAC, 1999), providing a template life cycle to analyze FOS-ERP selection, deployment, and evolution. GERAM defines seven life-cycle phases for any enterprise entity that are pertinent during its life. These phases, presented on Figure 1, can be summarized as follows:

a. **Identification:** identifies the particular enterprise entity in terms of its domain and environment.
b. **Concept:** conceptualizes an entity's mission, vision, values, strategies, and objectives.
c. **Requirements:** comprise a set of human, process, and technology oriented aspects and activities needed to describe the operational requirements of the enterprise.
d. **Design:** models the enterprise entity and helps to understand the system functionalities.
e. **Implementation:** the design is transformed into real components. After tested and approved the system is released into operation.
f. **Operation:** is the actual use of the system, and includes user feedback that can drive to a new entity life cycle.

Figure 1. GERAM life cycle phases. The design phase is subdivided into preliminary and detailed design.

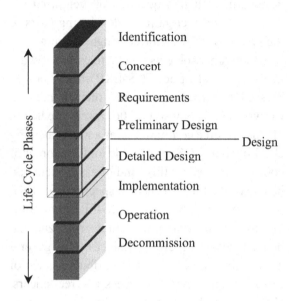

g. **Decommission:** represents the disposal of parts of the whole entity, after its successful use.

Except for *decommission* and *identification*, which are not influenced by licensing models, these phases can be used to better understand how FOS-ERP differs from P-ERP, providing key aspects for evaluating alternatives and successively refining objectives, requirements and models, as next subtopics address.

Concept

During this phase, high-level objectives are established, such as the acquisition strategy, preliminary time and cost baselines, and the expected impact of ERP adoption. In the case of FOS-ERP, the level of involvement of the adopter in development can be established. In other words, at this point the adopter can start considering the possibility of actively contributing to an open source project, becoming a *prosumer*. Of course, this decision will be possible only during the more advanced phases, when the adopter better knows the solution requisites and the decision alternatives.

Requirements and Preliminary Design

Taking as a principle that most software development (and customization) today is done through interactive and incremental life cycles, it can be considered that there is no clear borderline between the requirements and preliminary design phases and between the detailed design and implementation phases, thus they are considered together in this analysis.

The requirements phase deals with system's functional and non-functional requirements. The adopter may model some main business processes – part of the Preliminary Design – as a way to check how the alternatives fit to them. At this point FOS-ERP starts to differ more from P-ERP. Evaluating P-ERP involves comparing alternatives under the light of functionality, Total Cost of Ownership (TCO), and technological criteria. For FOS-ERP these criteria and others related specifically to FOSS must be also taken into account – remembering that even if the implementation represents a smaller financial impact, in terms of a company's self-knowledge it can assume a much bigger importance, since it holds not only a inventory of records and procedures, but also how those records and procedures are realized in technological form – through source code.

In other words, a FOS-ERP can have a smaller financial impact but a much bigger knowledge and innovation impact. Although P-ERP are also highly parameterized, and adaptable through APIs and/or dedicated programming languages, the access to the source code in FOS-ERP can drive much better exploration of the ERP's capabilities, thus allowing a better implementation of differentiated solutions.

From this standpoint, the strategic positioning of an adopter in relation to a FOS-ERP seems to be of greatest importance, given the possibility of deriving competitive advantage from the source code. Therefore, the adopter must decide to behave as a simple *consumer*, only getting the solution from the vendor, or become a *prosumer*, by mixing passively purchasing commodity parts of the system with actively developing strategic ones by itself. Thus it is clear that when an adopter considers FOS-ERP as an alternative, it should also consider developing parts of it to fit its requirements – taking into account that, as said before, this kind of positioning involves allocating managerial and technical resources for development tasks in a FOSS environment.

Detailed Design and Implementation

The detailed design phase focus on refining models, and is associated to business process modeling and parameter identification and value definition. The implementation phase concentrates on validating, integrating modules, and releasing its modules for initial use.

If the adopter decided to participate actively in the selected FOS-ERP project, deeper design decisions are involved, such as creating entire new modules or extending the basic framework. A consequence of assuming a more active role is to invest more human and financial resources for learning the FOS-ERP platform and framework, developing and maintaining parts of it, and managing the relationship with the project community. In that case, customization and maintenance contracts must define responsibilities of each part on the deployment process. For instance, what the vendor should do if the adopter finds a bug in the original code, written by the first, which is being adapted by the second? What is the priority that the vendor must follow for correcting this bug? Actually, is the vendor responsible for correcting this bug, since for this part the adopter decided to take advantage of the solution's free license, therefore exempting the vendor of responsibility for the bug?

The adopter has the option of assuming different grades of involvement for each phase. For ordinary modules, like payroll, the adopter can let the vendor do the work. However, for strategic modules, where the adopter believes that it holds competitive advantage in the related business processes, it can take an active role from detailed design to implementation and maintenance, to be sure that the business knowledge, or at least the more precious details that keep the competitive advantage, will be kept in the adopter company. In that situation the vendor is limited to act as a kind of advisor to the adopter. One can think that it is possible to keep secrecy on parts of the system by properly contracting a P-ERP vendor, which is true, but the adopter will become dependent of the vendor in a strategic part of the system. Becoming dependent means to wait for other vendor's priorities or pay a high price to become *the* priority when changes are needed. Even if the P-ERP adopter decides to develop these high-strategic parts, it will have to deal with licensing costs anyway.

A very interesting point is the openness of parts customized for and sponsored by a specific adopter. Maybe the adopter doesn't want to become a developer at all – which is most likely to happen, but it still wants to keep some tailored parts of the system in secret. In these cases, the vendor must adapt the licensing terms for its solution, so that general openness of the code is guaranteed, while some client-sponsored customized parts can be kept closed[5].

Operation

During the operation phase the resources of the entity are managed and controlled so as to carry out the processes necessary for the entity to fulfill its mission. Deviations from goals and objectives or feedbacks from the environment may lead to requests for change; therefore during this phase system maintenance and evolution occur. During operation the adopter can decide at any moment, unless contractual clauses hinders, to shift to another vendor or to assume the system's maintenance by itself. Minor changes can also be conducted by the own adopter or even by community individuals that may help on specific matters.

As a conclusive remark on the differences of FOS-ERP on the adopter side, experience has shown that most of the times the adopter will not get involved on customization or even maintenance tasks. Still, FOS-ERP can be a good choice, since it reduces vendor dependency. Moreover, the openness of code on FOS-ERP also makes adapting it to specific needs easier, thus reducing costs in customization and further evolution of the software. In other words, the central points to consider are cost reduction and freedom of choice. Last but not least, as a general rule, FOS-ERP also rely on other open technologies. For instance, while most P-ERP systems export and import data to and from MS-Office, FOS-ERP, like ERP5, interact with the also free Open Office. The same is truth for databases and operational systems – thus reducing licensing costs on ERP supportive software too.

Differences for the Vendor

The FOS-ERP vendor business models are a consequence of the customer's freedom of choice and of the general open source market characteristics. Like in other types of FOSS, if on one hand vendors benefit from the community improvements and testing work, on the other hand they face the competition of this community when dealing with deployment and maintenance. In fact, as previously shown, even an adopter can become a competitor, at some extent of course. It is important to note that there are three types of vendor: the original system creator, its partners, and free-lance vendors. In the case of partners, a formal, most of times contractual, agreement is set between them and the system creator. This agreement involves some responsibilities to the partner, in special, following creator's deployment practices, communicating new business generated by the system, opening the source code of new and improved parts of the system, and helping in development tasks managed by the creator. Free-lance vendors are free of these obligations, and as a consequence, have no special treatment by the creator, that expects that the free-lancer at least open the code of its own system improvements, following the general FOSS code of ethics[6].

Following the common reasoning about FOSS pricing, FOS-ERP vendors can take advantage from open source software because, according to Riehle (2007), FOSS "increase profits through direct costs savings and the ability to reach more customers through improved pricing flexibility", as shown on Figure 2.

Figure 2 shows a situation that maybe is more applicable to partners and free-lance vendors of FOS-ERP, which can switch from more expensive proprietary software to less expensive open source

software, thus potentially increasing their profit margin. The creator organization must know how to manage the community around the project, finding prospective partners, hiring individuals that become highly productive on the project whenever possible, and even trying to transform free-lancers into partners. Like their proprietary counterparts, FOS-ERP needs a network of partners that can help on deployment projects where the creator has no conditions to be the main contractor, and finding new markets and customers for the system. However, gathering contributors for a starting FOS-ERP project can be a hard task. As said before, ERP users are organizations, not individuals, and therefore the creator must learn how to attract partner firms that are willing to contributing to the project without becoming competitors. As a main conclusion, FOS-ERP vendors must fight hard to form a community around the project and to retain customers. This seems to be a big difference between the open and proprietary licensing models, since the risk of the vendor loose a client after deployment is

Figure 2. Sales margins and number of customers; (a) The lower price limit determines the customers the system integrator takes on; (b) Switching from closed source software to open source software can result in more customers and higher profits (Source: Riehle, 2007, with permission)

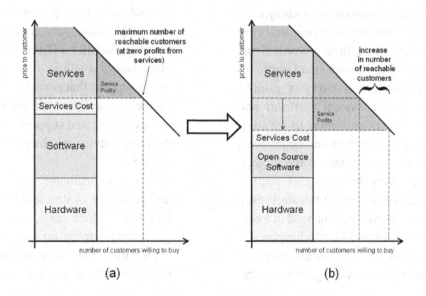

(a)   (b)

almost inexistent in the current P-ERP dominated market landscape, where global players dictate market rules in practice.

The differences between FOS-ERP and P-ERP can led to a shift from the vendor-dominated perspective of P-ERP to a more customer-driven FOS-ERP perspective. These differences in conducting selection, adoption, and selling also bring a series of opportunities and challenges for both vendors and adopters, which are addressed in the following topics.

OPPORTUNITIES AND CHALLENGES

FOS-ERP offer a series of opportunities for actors that are currently out or ill inserted into the ERP market. These opportunities come together with a series of challenges, as listed below.

For smaller consulting firms:

a. *Opportunities:* P-ERP vendors generally impose high costs and a rigid set of rules for firms that desire to enter their partner network, raising the difficulties for smaller firms to become players in this market. In contrast, smaller consulting firms can enter the FOS-ERP market in an incremental way, increasing their commitment to a project as new business opportunities appear and bring more financial income. In other words, firms can start contributing with small improvements to the project as a way of gaining knowledge on the system platform and framework, and, as customers to the solution appears, more money can be invested on a growing commitment to the project. Additionally, with the raising of venture capitalism investment on FOSS startups, a smaller firm can even get financed in a way that would be very unlikely to happen if it worked on top of a P-ERP solution, given the restrictions imposed by the global players.

b. *Challenges:* If on one hand it is easier to enter the market, on the other it is harder to retain clients: a broader consultancy basis empowers the demand side, making customers more demanding.

Keeping quality level among a heterogeneous network of consulting services providers is also a major challenge. FOS-ERP in general lack certification and quality assurance programs that guarantee service levels to clients. Moreover, FOS-ERP skeptics argue that few reliable consulting firms have experience on implementing them. But exactly those programs keep smaller consulting firms way from P-ERP, pushing them towards FOS-ERP. For a small consulting firm, a possible solution to this deadlock is to start with smaller, less demanding projects, and then go towards bigger ones, as the deployment processes and related activities gain maturity. This maturity will become the competitive advantage of the firm on a high competitive FOS-ERP market.

For smaller adopters:

a. *Opportunities:* lower costs open new opportunities for Small and Medium Enterprises (SME) to become ERP adopters. With globalization, small firms suffer more and more with competition, and when they try to modernize their processes, they hit the wall of global players' high costs, or have to adopt smaller off-the-shelf (and also proprietary) solutions that ties them to a single supplier that normally doesn't have a partner network. In contrast, FOS-ERP are less expensive and support can be found in different ways, including individuals and other SME.

This is also truth for local governments and countries in development in general. FOS-ERP reduce costs, thus helping local governments focus on their core business – directly taking care of citizens – and reducing technological dependency from global players. In fact, FOSS in general is an opportunity for countries in development to shift from buyers to players in the software industry (Ouédraogo, 2005).

b. *Challenges*: lower costs can also mean that adopters have to deal with lower service levels, then stressing the necessity of carefully evaluating FOS-ERP options and the maturity of their supportive services. Actually, as said before, consulting certification is yet on the early stages for FOS-ERP, thus quality of service must be carefully addressed during contract negotiation.

For researchers:

a. *Opportunities:* The author has been contributing to a FOS-ERP project[7] since its conception. During this time it was possible to know deeply, and sometimes take part of, all the process that compose an ERP solution, from conception and development, to business models, deployment, operation and maintenance, and evolution. This is a really good opportunity, since most research papers on ERP are related to deployment and operation, given that P-ERP companies don't usually open their projects' internals for researchers. Smaller research groups can find their way in this area by getting associated to a FOS-ERP project, and contributing to specific parts of it.

b. *Challenges[8]*: If on one hand the openness of FOS-ERP may give researchers more information on their internal features and development processes, on the other hand it is harder to get information from a distributed set of partners that sometimes carry informal agreements. Social and economical aspects, like reward structures, must be taken into account to understand the dynamics of FOS-ERP, like in every FOSS, bringing more components to be analyzed.

For individuals:

a. *Opportunities:* FOS-ERP represent an unique opportunity for an individual to install an ERP framework and understand its internals. It is the chance of participating in a big software development project without being an employee of a big company (Spinellis, 2006). Also, the developer can incrementally gain knowledge of the system, and get free support from the community, without the necessary investment on the P-ERP high cost training and certification programs. In that way an individual can improve his/her employability without investing too much money on courses, books and certifications. In the future, these advantages can make more free-lance developers enter FOS-ERP communities, currently formed mostly by companies' employees.

b. *Challenges:* learning the internals of a FOSS in general means to spend considerable time in understanding system architecture, design decisions, and specific features. Moreover, FOS-ERP in special currently lack books and courseware in general to help accelerating the learning process, and many times the individual must count on Web sites, mailing lists, discussion forums, and the good will of community members to acquire deeper knowledge on the framework.

CONCLUSION

In this chapter Free/Open Source ERP particularities, opportunities and challenges were briefly presented. It is important to note that this type of software inherits all advantages and shortcomings of open source software in general and have some more of both. As a matter of fact, FOS-ERP two main advantages are both directly related to FOSS: lower TCO given the reduced or non-existent licensing costs - including of supportive software, like spreadsheets, databases, networking and operational systems; and the possibility of having direct access to the source code whenever is needed.

Nevertheless, despite the growing interest on this subject, it still has many topics to be explored by researchers and practitioners, given the short period of time that passed since this kind of software appeared in the market and the relatively small number of users, which indicates that the list of opportunities and challenges aforesaid is a reflection of current tendencies that must be confirmed and better scrutinized as new deployments occur. For instance, currently there are no research figures on FOS-ERP success rates. In other words, in this arena, it is necessary that more data on deployment, customization, operation, and evolution become available so that *tendencies* may be confirmed and can become *facts* and *figures*.

Hence, as a relatively new kind of software, FOS-ERP has a potential to be realized, but many questions about it are yet to be answered. Nevertheless, their growing commercial acceptance is a fact, and their lower costs, easier adaptation, and potentially more competitive supplier market can slowly force a shift in the ERP market from the current vendor perspective to a customer perspective.

REFERENCES

Alshawi, S., Themistocleous, M., & Almadani, R. (2004). Integrating diverse ERP systems: A case study. *The Journal of Enterprise Information Management*, 17(6). Emerald Group Publishing Limited, pp.454-462.

Botta-Genoulaz, V., Millet, P.-A., & Grabot, B. A. (2005). Survey on the recent research literature on ERP systems. *Computers in Industry*, 56, 510-522.

Caulliraux, H. M., Proença, A., & Prado, C. A. S. (2000). ERP Systems from a Strategic Perspec-

tive. *Sixth International Conference on Industrial Engineering and Operations Management*, Niteroi, Brazil.

Crowston, K., & Howison, J. (2006). Assessing the Health of Open Source Communities. *IEEE Computer*, May, 89-91.

De Carvalho, R. A. (2006). Issues on Evaluating Free/Open Source ERP Systems. *Research and Practical Issues of Enterprise Information Systems*, 667-676. Springer-Verlag

Dreiling, A., Klaus, H., Rosemann, M., & Wyssusek, B. (2005). Open Source Enterprise Systems: Towards a Viable Alternative. *38th Annual Hawaii International Conference on System Sciences*, Hawaii.

Goth, G. (2005). Open Source Business Models: Ready for Prime Time. *IEEE Software*, November/December, pp 98-100.

Herzog, T. (2006). *A Comparison of Open Source ERP Systems*. Master thesis, Vienna University of Economics and Business Administration, Vienna, Austria.

IFIP – IFAC Task Force on Architectures for Enterprise Integration. (1999). *GERAM: Generalized Enterprise Reference Architecture and Methodology, 31*

Kim, H., & Boldyreff, C. (2005). Open Source ERP for SME. *Third International Conference on Manufacturing Research*, Cranfield, U.K.

Kooch, C. (February 01, 2004). *Open-Source ERP Gains Users*; http://www.cio.com/archive/020104/tl_open.html

LeClaire, J. (December 30, 2006). *Open Source, BI and ERP: The Perfect Match?*; http://www.linuxinsider.com/story/LjdZlB0x0j04cM/Open-Source-BI-and-ERP-The-Perfect-Match.xhtml

Ouédraogo, L-D. (2005). *Policies of United Nations System Organizations Towards the Use of Open Source Software (OSS) in the Secretariats*. Geneva, 43p.

Riehle, D. (2007). The Economic Motivation of Open Source Software: Stakeholder Perspectives. *IEEE Computer*, *40*(4), 25-32.

Serrano N., & Sarrieri, J. M. (2006). Open Source ERPs: A New Alternative for an Old Need. *IEEE Software*, May/June, 94-97.

Smets-Solanes, J., & De Carvalho, R. A. (2003). ERP5: A Next-Generation, Open-Source ERP Architecture. *IEEE IT Professional*, *5*(4), 38–44.

Spinellis, D. (2006). Open Source and Professional Advancement. *IEEE Software*, September/October, 70-71.

Wang, F-R. He, D., & Chen, J. (2005). Motivations of Individuals and Firms Participating in Open Source Communities. *Fourth International Conference on Machine Learning and Cybernetics*, 309-314.

West, J., & O'Mahony, S. (2005). Contrasting Community Building in Sponsored and Community Founded Open Source Projects. *38th Annual Hawaii International Conference on System Sciences*, Hawaii.

Xu, N. (2003). *An Exploratory Study of Open Source Software Based on Public Archives.* Master Thesis, John Molson School of Business, Concordia University, Montreal, Canada.

Zinnov Research and Consulting. (2006). *Penetration of Open Source in US Enterprise software market – An Overview.* 37.

KEY TERMS

ERP: Enterprise Resources Planning, a kind of software which main goal is to integrate all data and processes of an organization into a unified system.

ERP Business Models: Broad range of informal and formal models that are used by a vendor to make profit from an ERP system deployment, customization, and maintenance.

ERP Evaluation: Process of selecting an ERP package, among various alternatives and in accordance to business processes, information, technology, and strategic requirements.

Free Software: According to the Free Software Foundation, is a Software that gives to the user the freedom to run the program for any purpose, study how the program works and adapt it to his/her needs, redistribute copies, improve the program, and release his/her improvements to the public, so that the whole community benefits.

Free/Open Source ERP: ERP systems that are released as Free Software or Open Source Software.

Free/Open Source Software Adopter Types: According to Xu (2003) it is possible to classify a software user company in accordance to its positioning in relation to a FOSS:

- Consumer: a passive role where the adopter will just use the software as it is, with no intention or capability of modifying or distributing the codes.
- Prosumer: an active role where the adopter will report bugs, submit feature requests, post messages to lists. A more capable Prosumer will also provide bug fixes, patches, and new features.
- Profitor: a passive role where the adopter will not participate in the development process but simply will use the software as a source of profits.
- Partner: an active role where the adopter will actively participate in the whole open source development process for the purpose of earning profits.

Open Source Software: According to the Open Source Initiative, licenses must meet ten conditions in order to be considered open source licenses:

1. The software can be freely given away or sold.
2. The source code must either be included or freely obtainable.
3. Redistribution of modifications must be allowed.
4. Licenses may require that modifications be redistributed only as patches.
5. No Discrimination Against Persons or Groups.
6. No Discrimination Against Fields of Endeavor.
7. The rights attached to the program must apply to all to whom the program is redistributed without the need for execution of an additional license by those parties.
8. The program cannot be licensed only as part of a larger distribution.
9. The license cannot insist that any other software it is distributed with must also be open source.
10. License Must Be Technology-Neutral

The official definition of Open Source Software is very close to the definition of Free Software, however, it allows in practice more restrictive licenses, creating a category of "semi-free" software.

ENDNOTES

[1] The precise definitions of Free Software and Open Source Software are on the chapter's Key Terms list. Although there are differences between them – the Free Software Movement has also some political connotations for instance - for the goals of this work the two terms will be treated as synonyms.

[2] The IFIP First International Workshop on Free/Open Source Enterprise Information Systems/ERP, held during the First IFIP TC8 International Conference on Research and Practical Issues of Enterprise Information Systems – CONFENIS 2006.

[3] Despite the fact that these methods hold some similarities, they were developed without having knowledge of each other and were published in a very close range of time: Carvalho's method was published in April and Herzog's in June, 2006.

[4] This is a generic assumption, since in practice the vendor can impose specific license terms that keep the software open, but constrain deployment to terms that keep vendor control on it.

[5] Although this seems to be nonsense in FOSS terms, it is a common real life situation in FOS-ERP. In fact, the author knows a case where an adopter company sponsored the whole development of an FOS-ERP during a three-year period, without becoming a *prosumer*, and keeping only a specific algorithm, related to its product pricing schedule, in secret. The original license had to be changed to fit this customer demand.

[6] In practice, this return from free-lancers doesn't happen all the times.

[7] ERP5 http://www.erp5.com

[8] The author considers that these challenges represent, in fact, new research opportunities.

Chapter IV
The Changing Nature of Business Process Modeling:
Implications for Enterprise Systems Integration

Brian H. Cameron
The Pennsylvania State University, USA

ABSTRACT

Business process modeling (BPM) is a topic that is generating much interest in the information technology (IT) industry today. Business analysts, process designers, system architects, software engineers, and systems consultants must understand the foundational concepts behind BPM and evolving modeling standards and technologies that have the potential to dramatically change the nature of phases of the systems development life cycle (SDLC). Pareto's 80/20 rule, as applied to the SDLC, is in the process of being drastically altered. In the past, approximately 20 % of the SDLC was spent on analysis and design activities with the remaining 80 % spent on systems development and implementation (Weske, Goesmann, Holten, & Striemer, 1999). Today, with the introduction of the Business Process Management Initiative (BPMI), Web services, and the services-oriented architecture (SOA), the enterprise SDLC paradigm is poised for a dramatic shift. In this new paradigm, approximately 80 % of the SDLC is spent on analysis and design activities with the remaining 20 % spent of systems development and implementation. Once referred to as workflow and process automation, business process modeling (BPM) has evolved into a suite of interrelated components providing significant business value. Emerging BPM technologies will be the primary vehicle by which current application portfolios transition to service-oriented architectures and Web services (Aversano, & Canfora, 2002). Business Process Management Initiative's Business Process Modeling Notation (BPMN) subgroup is currently finalizing a standardized notation for business process modeling. Although the notation is still in working draft format, system architects and designers should consider incorporating the concepts of BPM into their current and future systems analysis and design procedures.

INTRODUCTION

Adaptive organizations want to be able to rapidly modify their business processes to changes in their business climate including competitive, market, economic, industry, regulatory/compliance, or other factors. Meanwhile, enterprise architects within IT organizations have long dreamed of a repository for models that are interconnected and extend to support application delivery. No single tool exists that enables enterprise architects to connect the dots between high-level models geared toward a business audience and executable code to instantiate the vision (Carlis, & Maguire, 2000).

BPM is both a business concept and an emerging technology. The concept is to establish goals, define a strategy, and set objectives for improving particular operational processes that have significant impact on corporate performance. It does not imply re-engineering all business processes; rather the focus is on business processes that directly affect some metric of corporate success. Business performance management and measurement emphasize using metrics beyond financial ones to guide business process management strategies (Delphi, 2001). Metrics related to customer value or loyalty are examples. Business process modeling is becoming the central point of organization for many systems. BPM as a concept is not new; multiple process management methodologies such as Six Sigma and Lean Manufacturing have existed for years. However new BPM technologies are fueling a renewed interest in process thinking (Ettlinger, 2002). New BPM technologies promise business modelers and managers a visual dashboard to manage and adjust, in real time, human and machine resources, as well as information being consumed as work progresses.

The business and IT worlds are taking more strategic and holistic views of IT and how it supports the business. IT strategy, business process improvement, and IT architecture are experiencing a renaissance. Enterprise architects have tackled the technical architecture effectively.

Now, enterprise architects are looking to expand their efforts into the business architecture space. Enterprise business architecture is the expression of the enterprise's key business strategies and their impact on business functions and processes (Adhikari, 2002b). Business architecture efforts in most organizations are limited to thematic project-level initiatives. Thematic business architecture artifacts generally fail to evolve once the projects are complete because little perceived value exists for keeping business architecture content alive. However, emerging standards show promise in keeping business architecture and associated artifacts alive to serve as key business strategy enablers.

The IT world is moving more toward a model of integrating pieces or components, versus building from scratch (Adhikari, 2002a). Organizations are looking to strategically optimize, automate, and integrate key processes to provide seamless service to more demanding customers in a multi-channel world. To do this effectively, systems must be integrated at the process level as well as the data level. Integrating systems at the process level has been a challenge which, when unmet, leads to data duplication and inconsistency and functional overlap (i.e., inefficient processes/processing) (Reingruber & Gregory, 1994). Many organizations are embarking on process improvement exercises to increase organizational efficiency or effectiveness.

These efforts go by many names, including industrial engineering, ISO certification, Six Sigma, enterprise business architecture (EBA), business process improvement (BPI), business process re-engineering (BPR), and lean thinking, to name a few. Most of these techniques involve visual modeling to capture the current state and validate improved future-state design. Several notations exist for visual process modeling (e.g., event-driven process chains (EPCs), IDEF, American National Standards Institute (ANSI)); however, a new standard (BPMN) is emerging that promises to allow extension of visual models into executable script or source code (BPMI.org Releases.., 2005). Although reminiscent of the promises of computer-aided software engineering (CASE) technologies, advances in the fields of mathematics and computer science make the "model to execute" vision more viable. While notations and methods for process modeling and improvement within the business are mature and notations and methods for application delivery within IT are mature, business and IT process models and methods fail to align well with one another (Adhikari, 2002b).

BPMN is mapped to Business Process Modeling Language (BPML) and Business Process Execution Language for Web Services (BPEL-4WS), thus any models created in a manner that is closely aligned with BPMN will automate more rapidly (Ewalt, 2002). Business Process Query Language (BPQL) has been put forth by the Business Process Management Initiative to process repositories as SQL is to data repositories. Although currently in draft state, several concepts presented in BPMN should be considered for immediate adoption. First and foremost is agreement on a standard notation and principles for process modeling. A plethora of software vendors are incorporating support for BPML and BPEL4WS. Modeling technologies are beginning to incorporate BPMN notation because it supports both BPML and BPEL4WS.

Technical models (e.g., UML, entity relationship diagrams) are being married with more business-oriented approaches (e.g., swim-lane diagrams, BPMN) to graphically narrow the business/IT alignment divide. The outcome of these efforts is to incorporate, at a minimum, a recommended set of common guidelines into all modeling efforts organizationally and interorganizationally (i.e., process integration with trading partners). Organizations are moving to standardize on an approach to process/business modeling and select common tools to support disparate but related improvement and change initiatives.

Software tools have long been used to automate tasks and reduce manual interactions. Thus, it is important to distinguish business processes from IT applications. A business process is a sequence of activities performed by people and machines necessary to produce a desired result (Adhikari, 2002b). It is initiated by the arrival of work (such as a phone call, faxed order, or timing event) which triggers the sequence of operational activities. An application is a logical grouping of tasks automated by a computer with the objective of reducing or augmenting human interactions. Thus, an application is a subset of the tasks of a business process. Many human-centric activities of a business process have largely been unautomated (though some organizations use workflow automation to manage electronic work queues).

A business process management suite (BPMS) is a new development environment that enables business users to collaborate with IT professionals in the design and development of optimized business processes (not applications), thus reducing the communication gap between business and IT. Ideally a business process management suite supports a business process modeling environment that is shared by business analysts, process engineers, IT architects and programmers. The modeling surface or palette exposes different capabilities to support each of these roles. Unlike earlier code-generating tools, the modeling environment creates XML metadata that describes how application functionality and information and human activities should interact and be instantiated at runtime.

The new runtime engines interpret the metadata at runtime (Mangan & Sadiq, 2002). Increasingly, vendors are endorsing Business Process Execution Language (BPEL) as the standard process description language. Thus, changing a business process requires changing the graphical model, regenerating the metadata and redeploying process instances. This is a much simpler and faster approach to changing how work gets done. This faster rate of change to operational best practices and the ability to change activities dynamically are what make an organization adaptive. An adaptive organization can adjust its operational business processes in near real time to capitalize on opportunities, avoid threats, and maximize corporate performance.

MODELING MADNESS: A BRIEF HISTORY

Modeling has been taught in a variety of forms for years in university curriculums. Models have long been a part of many technical curriculums, traditionally leveraging ANSI standard flow charts. The technology field leveraged this approach to communicate logic flow prior to creation of machine executable code. Some readers may remember those flimsy green flowchart templates provided by IBM. As business and technology continued to evolve, so too did the field of modeling. Modeling tools were introduced to technology-enable modeling. Spreadsheets were introduced as well. To business purists, modeling became synonymous with financial modeling - a series of spreadsheets with what-if scenarios. To the IT world, modeling became synonymous with a host of visual techniques, including the following:

- Entity relationship diagrams
- ANSI standard flowcharts
- Process models
- Data flow diagrams
- Unified Modeling Language (UML) diagrams (activity, class, etc.)
- Network diagrams
- CRUD (create, read, update, and delete) matrices
- Integrated Definition (IDEF) charts
- Engineering Process Control (EPC) charts

Models have been used as a mechanism to communicate a complex ecosystem. Business-oriented modeling approaches tend to focus on productivity and quality metrics (e.g., processing time, wait time, cycle time, cost, setup time, outputs, defects). IT-oriented modeling approaches have properties that tend to focus on logic, business rules, and data elements. Differences in modeling notations and rules around modeling have suboptimized the benefits of visual modeling. A group of leading modeling tool vendors has joined forces to develop a common notation for business process modeling (BPMN) that can do much to optimize the potential of visual modeling (BPMI. org Releases.., 2005). This group is leveraging collective best practices of its organizations and currently has published Version 9 of its notation (www.bpmi.org).

Although currently in working draft stage, some of its leading practices can and should be incorporated into all courses that utilize modeling. There should be an expectation that visual business models help expose characteristics of the underlying business process. For example, a business process related to entering purchase orders should be able to expose the underlying user interface for all data entry points of the process, as well as expose the underlying data tables related to the transaction. At a higher level of abstraction, the business models should be linked to entity-relationship diagrams as well, which highlight the overall table structure.

A technique for process modeling popularized in the 1990s with the business process re-engineering (BPR) rage, swim-lane diagrams, are near universally accepted among all who model. Often referred to as UML activity diagrams with lanes, the line-of-visibility method/technique (i.e., LOVEM - IBM's process modeling methodology), or Rummler-Brache swim-lane diagrams, this modeling technique graphically denotes responsibility for work with vertical or horizontal lanes (i.e., lines of demarcation). BPMN also incorporates the notion of pools, which can contain lanes, to relate external entities. This is extremely important when moving toward a world of linking and automating processes with customers and suppliers (Aversano & Canfora, 2002). Incorporating pools and lanes enables responsibility to be recognized throughout the extended enterprise. When appropriate, visual modeling must incorporate lanes and pools to clearly bound business areas and define or articulate ownership and responsibility.

UML is maintaining its popularity as the modeling language of choice for software development. Object Management Group's (OMG's) Model Driven Architecture (MDA) is gaining traction, with the release of UML 2.0. However, UML was originally designed by technical people for technical people. OMG recognizes that UML does not provide a facility that actively addresses the needs of IT business modelers (Sadiq, Orlowska, Sadiq, & Foulger, 2004). OMG is currently considering BPMI's Business Process Modeling Notation (BPMN) to fill this void. A merger, alliance, or convergence of the modeling standards efforts of OMG with those of BPMI would be a major advance for enterprise architecture. Joining BPMN with UML would do much to minimize redundant questioning by IT organizations during the system development life cycle.

One of the strengths of BPMN, and the languages it supports, is the ability to support more ambiguity. Beyond process triggers and end states, events have been undermodeled by BPM teams. Processes have events and triggers. BPMN distinguishes among beginning, intermediate, and ending events, as well as, events start, interrupt, and end the flow of the process. Often, intermediate event information is buried in symbol properties or text annotations (BPMI.org Releases.., 2005). BPMN provides for several types of events and the current event types are more comprehensive than most, if not all, modeling notations. For example, one of the challenges with prior modeling notations and workflow systems is their inability to effectively contend with exceptions. An BPMN error event symbol assists with meeting this challenge. A

compensate event exists to mirror roll-forward and roll-back conditions (i.e., two-phase commits). This is another event type that exists in the real world and has posed an artistic challenge to the modeling community.

A distinction must be made between modeling and drawing business processes. Modeling requires adherence to guidelines when depicting a process ecosystem graphically. By adhering to appropriate guidelines, process models can be used for simulation, refinement of existing processes, automation, and integration (Smith & Fingar, 2003a). Unless tied to a rigorous methodology or technology (e.g., workflow system), modelers have much discretion in modeling process flows. BPMN formalizes process flow gates to enable consistent modeling of forks, joins, and decisions. The notation's standardization of these process patterns is elegant in its simplicity and is gaining wide acceptance.

BPMN AND UML

UML, conceived in 1996, was designed to provide a common modeling language to support software development. It was adopted and refined by OMG and 21 member companies. Since its inception, it has become the de facto standard for visual software development, spawning a host of new products to increase developer productivity and augmenting the functionality of existing modeling tools. As UML and XMI (i.e., XML Metadata Interchange, a standard enabling UML model interchange) advanced, interoperability was made practical among tools traditionally used for business process modeling/enterprise architecture and those used for visual development environments (Carlson, 2001). Further advances in UML enabled modeling of more complex software systems.

UML, however, failed to provide the simplicity needed by non-IT business modelers. At best, a UML activity diagram could be created with swim lanes to provide the functional equivalence of swim-lane diagrams; however, adhering to UML standards might be overly burdensome to business modelers. OMG recognizes this and is currently moving up the stack to provide the appropriate level of standardized modeling language to enable business modelers to perform their needed tasks without undue effort. BPMN has been mapped to the UML standard (Torchiano & Bruno, 2003).

BPMN was developed to provide a common modeling notation to support a common process modeling language. At the outset, BPMN was designed to appeal to both IT and non-IT modelers of business processes. BPMN is gaining rapid acceptance; leading modeling-tool vendors support or plan to support BPMN (Smith & Fingar, 2004). This feat is accomplished by providing simple swim-lane diagramming ability to non-IT modelers and enabling the subsequent addition of technical detail to the same models as notational properties (i.e., the gory details are hidden from the non-technical audiences within the tool).

If BPMN is accepted into UML, even in part, BPMI's efforts will be further legitimized. At present, much flux exists in the process modeling language space. Two languages, BPML and BPEL4WS, were viewed as competitors running a head-and-neck race for market acceptance. However, the broader vision of BPMI is to have a common modeling notation that generates a process modeling language that can be stored in a process management system, used to manage automated process change within and between organizations . If OMG adopts BPMN, even in part, the likelihood of BPMN as the notational support for BPEL4WS dramatically increases.

Long has been the vision of a modeled enterprise that maintains linkages from the conceptual business leaders to the operations. However, due to lack of standards and insufficient tool support, this vision has remained out of sight until now. As developers adopt service-oriented architectures, they will continue to rely on UML. As enterprise architecture continues to evolve to include enterprise business architecture, enterprise architecture modeling will expand to include business modeling. If BPMN is incorporated into UML, simple business process models can rapidly be extended to generate BPML, BPEL4WS, or additional UML diagrams to extend down the MDA stack (Frankel, 2003). The vision of an enterprise repository of accurate models becomes reality as UML and MDA enable automation with insurance against technology obsolescence.

A NEW PARADIGM FOR PROCESS MODELING

With the introduction of BPMI, Web services, and the services-oriented architecture (SOA), the enterprise SDLC paradigm is poised for a dramatic shift. An SOA is dynamic, general-purpose, extensible, federated interoperability architecture. Designing for SOA involves thinking of the parts of a given system as a set of relatively autonomous services, each of which is (potentially) independently managed and implemented and they are linked together with a set of agreements and protocols into a federated structure (Clark, Fletcher, Hanson, Irani, & Thelin, 2002). A composite application (i.e., based on SOA principles) is made of relatively autonomous services, each of which is (potentially) independently managed and implemented. These services are linked together with a set of agreements and protocols into a federated structure. For enterprise application architects and developers, composite applications will be based on the SOA principles of dynamic, extensible, and federated interoperability and will be enabled by XML-based technologies such as Web services (Shegalov, Gillmann, & Weikum, 2001).

Mobile calculi, process algebras, and pi calculus are forms of mathematics are of great importance to lines of business, IT professionals, and business architects. Process algebra and pi calculus are ushering in a new wave of process modeling and management systems. Pi calculus systems are evolving to become the new wave of software infrastructure to manage business processes (Smith & Fingar, 2003b). These systems are being front-ended by BPMN. Enterprise business architects are embracing BPMN because it brings life and longevity to their modeling exercises.

Pi calculus systems are becoming prevalent, supported by BPMN. With the advent of third-generation languages (3GLs), application developers adopted a paradigm that was procedural and deterministic. This paradigm can be expressed with a form of mathematics known as lambda calculus. 3GLs tended to be sequential in nature, lending themselves to rigid codification of business activity. Pi calculus, providing a paradigm that is parallel, non-deterministic, and tolerant of change and ambiguity, enables systems to more closely resemble real life. Pi calculus enables systems to treat "things" as processes and relationships. It changes the programming paradigm from procedural and deterministic to one of inter-related processes (Smith & Fingar, 2003b).

This shift in thinking enables relationships and processes to be automated in a manner that more closely resembles natural workflow (and in fact, how computers work at the machine level). Ironically, computers, at the machine level, are well suited for a pi calculus paradigm; machine language, which manipulates operands within a computer's memory location based on the operator selected, atomically resembles a pi calculus paradigm (Smith & Fingar, 2004). BPML is a pi calculus-based standard text language to define and automate processes developed by the Business Process Management Initiative. BPEL4WS a pi calculus-based standard language for automating business processes as Web services. This standard was jointly developed by Microsoft and IBM.

Enterprise Business Architecture (EBA) is a creative process of future-state design of business processes, functions, and organizations. Business architects rely heavily on visual modeling to refine future-state design. Selected future-state business design must be implemented, which usually includes a certain degree of automation. One of the challenges of EBA has always been keeping models alive through the system development life cycle (including maintenance and enhancement) (Smith, 2003). However, with BPMN, keeping the models current is critical to keeping the underlying BPMS functioning. Also with BPMN, the underlying pi supports simulation, an art returning to popularity within businesses.

The Business Process Management Initiative (BPMI) formed a subgroup to develop a notation to front-end its pi calculus-based language, BPML. The BPMN subgroup recognized three important things. First, modeling notations needed to exist that were interpretable to business audiences and could subsequently be used by solution delivery specialists; the BPMN subgroup chose a tiered approach, with the first tier resembling swim-lane diagrams. Second, a more detailed visual modeling notation needed to exist for system delivery; BPMN's tiered approach maps the swim-lane-like business process modeling notation to a more precise technical notation. Third, the BPMN subgroup recognized that BPML and BPEL4WS could merge/converge or coexist, or BPML could be replaced by BPEL4WS; the BPMI proactively chose to map its visual notation to both BPML and BPEL4WS. Business architects and technologists can design models with the top-tier notation with business leaders, easily passing the baton to delivery specialists after a decision to proceed is made with little or no rework (Delphi, 2001). BPMN enables changing of the visual notation per audience without losing the requisite values/properties/attributes necessary to extend to executable process language. This critical functionality was lacking or less robust in previous attempts to standardize on a notation-to-execute modeling approach (Smith & Fingar, 2003a).

The shift from the use of business process automation technology as a departmental workflow tool to that of an enterprise change agents requires a planned approach for implementing processes centered on enterprise business strategy. Using this new paradigm, and associated technologies, to orchestrate and execute these processes enables organizations to move beyond simple automation to business process optimization. Workflow, process automation, and business process management tools and technologies will evolve into fully integrated BPM suites in the near future. BPM suites will be the primary vehicle by which current application portfolios are transitioned to service-oriented architectures. Emerging BPM suites will include the following integrated components (Smith & Fingar, 2004):

- *Process modeling:* This component provides a graphical tool for modeling business processes in the "as is" and "to be" states. Models can also be tailored to depict best practices for exception handling or be pre-packaged to reflect vertical industry-specific needs. The visual representation used (e.g., swim lane diagrams, UML models) increasingly must enable a business user (not a developer) to model the process from a business perspective, not a programming perspective.

- *Process improvement methodology:* Aligning the enterprise business strategy with a process improvement program is a critical success factor for process improvement. Many modeling tools have incorporated support for business-oriented improvement methodologies (e.g., Six Sigma, Lean Thinking, business process integration and management, balanced scorecards).

- *Process orchestration engine:* A process orchestration engine (POE) takes runtime instructions from a process model. These engines have been fairly proprietary to date. Many are migrating to support emerging description and execution standards (e.g., BPML, BPEL4WS), yet few of these are commercially available. Engines must

understand the modeling language and be able to track the progress of a process (in other words, manage state). State management directly impacts how long-running the process can be managed.

- *Integration servers:* These tools bind the abstracted business process to the data, documents, business logic, messages, and events needed by the process. Adapters connect the Integration server under the orchestration engine controller to structured data and logic in the underlying applications, unstructured data from the content management environment, search terms from a taxonomy library, and messages/events from message queue managers.

- *Process monitoring and analysis:* Products in this category are some of the newest, thus there is significant variation in their capabilities. The primary function of these tools is to enable the analysis of live data as it moves through the process. There are two aspects to this real-time activity monitoring and analysis; 1) analysis of the process itself for optimal design (completeness and bottlenecks); and 2) monitoring of the performance of the operational process for predefined key performance indicators (KPIs) and notifying users of out-of-tolerance limits. This provides the opportunity to define and initiate corrective actions, including transactions.

- *Process simulation/optimization:* These tools are used to simulate the business process through multiple options, discovering bottlenecks and creating alternatives. Allowing the analytics captured above to be used as input into the simulation creates a more efficient process (via both design and runtime feedback). Some products allow a process to be simulated against production conditions to provide feedback.

PROCESS MODELING CHALLENGES

Many organizations are seeking new methods for developing software and system automation. The convergence of Web services (promising universal connectivity) and model-driven development and architectures (promising technology-neutral system development) paints a compelling vision of the future of systems design and development. This future will be process-oriented, with systems created by using a process model to direct the interaction of various systems and human actors. The systems will be accessible, since their functions are exposed as services, and the process engine will be sophisticated enough to capture all the semantics of the business process at various levels (O'riordan, 2002).

Currently, most organizations use business process automation in discrete areas, primarily as part of their integration environments. Leading organizations will enable process development across organizational boundaries, but most will struggle with the business (rather than technological) issues associated with these activities. The process model is becoming a standard part of the developer toolkit and standards-based engines will shortly replace proprietary ones. Many organizations have this future vision, particularly those that are adopting service-oriented architectures. However, IT organizations struggle with how to advance this vision incrementally, due to the many challenges of the interim states.

The first roadblock organizations encounter on the path toward business process management is its basic value proposition. Although many projects using BPM tools have shown significant value (in terms of ROI), much of that value comes from the automation of manual processes. These processes, typically those that span organizational boundaries, involve manual touches to information and manual decision making that are not tracked through the formal automation systems embodied in the enterprise applications. The simplest means of creating value in this circumstance is to use process automation to automate these manual processes and their interfaces to enterprise applications and systems (Sharp & Mcdermott, 2001). This is useful, since it creates automation for manual tasks, and often will significantly reduce the costs and errors inherent in those tasks. However, the scope of this automation is clearly not the complete process, but only that portion of it that is reflected in these manual steps.

Even in this limited scope case, there can be significant challenges. The manual processes often are developed to address exceptions and inconsistencies in the formalized processes embodied in the enterprise application portfolio. These processes often are either incomplete as implemented, or the business activities have changed yet the process assumptions on which the enterprise systems are based have not. In either case, one finds a situation where the manual parts of the process often are undefined or do not have clear rules, roles, or responsibilities. They may even contradict logic that is embodied in the formal systems. The BPM exercise will highlight the weaknesses for interaction in the existing model (Ettlinger, 2002). Furthermore, many of the manual parts of the process will retain manual components, since they primarily focus on exception handling.

Compounding this issue is the challenge of the ownership and stewardship of business processes. Unless an organization has taken an aggressive, process-oriented view toward its business, there often is a tremendous amount of confusion about process definition and ownership (Adhikari, 2002b). Because the processes whose automation can provide the most value often span functional areas, there are usually no individuals with responsibility for the overall process. Instead, we have functional managers, each with individual responsibility for the subprocess performed by their areas. Effectively automating these processes requires the creation of new channels of communication as well as new decision processes to enable the organizations involved to reach an agreement on how to handle the processes.

Another issue affecting the achievement of this vision is that Web services are not complete. Although substantial progress is being made regarding the standards for and interoperability of Web services, the practical use of Web services within corporations is in its early stages (Charfi & Mezini, 2004). The universal connectivity that is required to link a process execution engine with the various actors and systems in the environment requires a substantial investment in integration technologies, and the minimal integration among various components in the infrastructure demands a substantial investment in the software platform. There is little doubt that creating business process models, deriving application code from those business models, and monitoring such models can create the right level of organizational linkage between IT and business executives. The problem is that much of this is an afterthought in a world that contains a collection of ERR best-in-class, and legacy applications that are either unmodeled or modeled with multiple tools.

CONCLUSION

Business process modeling is quickly becoming the central point of organization for many systems. Model-driven development frameworks are quickly becoming the preferred platform for service-oriented architecture, Web services composite application design, development, and deployment (Smith & Fingar, 2004). Business-user-oriented modeling environments enable businesspeople to model the process as if it were an assembly line of swappable components (tasks) that can be reordered to achieve various results. A business process management suite exposes these components as XML Web services. Business Process Modeling Notation (BPMN) will offer a common standard for enterprise process model-

ing that has the potential to make the "model to execute" vision more viable. Business analysts, process designers, system architects, software engineers, and systems consultants that utilize process modeling should begin their evaluation and adoption of emerging business process management suites that utilize BPMN.

These IT professionals must understand foundational BPM concepts as well as the emerging technologies and standards that enable these concepts. With this foundation, they will be able to better assess the importance of business agility, better perform business process performance analysis, and model business process and systems in a manner that expedites development. More than technology, becoming an adaptive organization requires leadership and change management. The cross-boundary characteristic of BPM initiatives creates a unique opportunity for the leaders of the initiatives to become the enterprise change agents.

Corporations are beginning the transformation to a process culture and the implementation of business process management methodologies and technologies (Smith, 2003). The first steps can be problematic and political, even within organizations that have already committed to transforming to a process culture. Organizations are looking to strategically optimize, automate, and integrate key processes to provide seamless service to more demanding customers in a multi-channel world. To do this effectively, systems must be integrated at the process level as well as the data level (Simsion, 2000). This environment requires system architects, consultants, analysts, integrators, and developers that have an organizational perspective and a diversified set of skills.

REFERENCES

Adhikari, R. (2002a, May). 10 Rules For Modeling Business Processes. *DMReview.* Retrieved From Http://Adtmag.Com/Article.Asp?Id=6300

Adhikari, R. (2002b, May). Putting The Business In Business Process Modeling. *DMReview.* Retrieved From Http://Adtmag.Com/Article. Asp?Id=6323

Aversano, L., & Canfora, G. (2002). Process and Workflow Management: Introducing Eservices in Business Process Models. *Proceedings of the 14th International Conference on Software Engineering And Knowledge Engineering.*

BPMI.Org. Releases Business Process Modeling Notation (BPMN) Version 1.0. Retrieved April 5, 2005 from Http://Xml.Coverpages.Org/Ni2003-08-29-A.Html

Carlis, J., & Maguire, J. (2000). *Mastering Data Modeling: A User Driven Approach (1st Ed.).* Addison- Wesley.

Carlson, D. (2001). *Modeling XML Applications With UML.* Addison Wesley.

Charfi, A., & Mezini, M. (2004). Service composition: Hybrid Web service composition: Business processes meet business rules. *Proceedings of the 2nd international conference on Service oriented computing.*

Clark, M., Fletcher, P., Hanson, J. J., Irani, R., & Thelin, J. (2002). *Web Services Business Strategies and Architectures.* Wrox Press.

Delphi. (2001). *In Process: The Changing Role of Business Process Management in Today's Economy.* Retrieved From Http://Www.Ie.Psu. Edu/Advisoryboards/Sse/Articles/A4bd42eb1. Delphi-Ip-Oct2001.Pdf

Ettlinger, B. (2002, March 5). The Future of Data Modeling. *DMReview.* Retrieved From Http://Www.Dmreview.Com/Article_Sub. Cfm?Articleid=4840

Ewalt, D. W., (2002, December 12). *BPML Promises Business Revolution.* Retrieved From Http:// Www.Computing.Co.Uk/Analysis/1137556

Frankel, D. S. (2003). *Model Driven Architecture: Applying MDA To Enterprise Computing.* Wiley.

Mangan, P., & Sadiq, S. (2002). On Building Workflow Models for Flexible Processes. *Australian Computer Science Communications, Proceedings of the Thirteenth Australasian Conference on Database Technologies - 5,* 24(2)

O'riordan, D. (2002. April 10). Business Process Standards for Web Services: The Candidates. *Web Services Architect.* Retrieved From Http://Www. Webservicesarchitect.Com/Content/Articles/ Oriordan01.Asp

Reingruber, M. C., & Gregory, W. W. (1994). *The Data Modeling Handbook: A Best Practice Approach to Building Quality Data Models.* Wiley And Sons.

Sadiq, S., Orlowska, M., Sadiq, W., & Foulger C. (2004). Data Flow and Validation in Workflow Modeling. *Proceedings of the Fifteenth Conference on Australasian Database, 27.*

Sharp, A., & Mcdermott, P. (2001). *Workflow Modeling: Tools for Process Improvement and Application Development.* Norwood,Ma: Artech House.

Shegalov, G., Gillmann, M., & Weikum, M. (2001). XML-Enabled Workflow Management for E-Services Across Heterogeneous Platforms. *The VLDB Journal — The International Journal On Very Large Data Bases,* 10(1).

Simsion, G. (2000). *Data Modeling Essentials: A Comprehensive Guide to Data Analysis, Design, and Innovation (2nd Ed.).* Coriolis Group Books.

Smith, H. (2003, September 22). *Business Process Management 101.* Retrieved From Http://Www. Ebizq.Net/Topics/Bpm/Features/2830.Html

Smith, H., & Fingar, P. (2003a). *Business Process Management (BPM): The Third Wave (1st Ed.).* Meghan-Kiffer Press.

Smith, H., & Fingar, P. (2003b). *Workflow Is Just A Pi Process.* Retrieved From Http://Www. Fairdene.Com/Picalculus/Workflow-Is-Just-A-Pi-Process.Pdf

Smith, H., & Fingar, P. (2004, February 1). *BPM Is Not About People, Culture And Change. It's About Technology.* Retrieved From Http://Www.Avoka. Com/Bpm/Bpm_Articles_Dynamic.Shtml

Torchiano, M., & Bruno, G. (2003). Article Abstracts With Full Text Online: Enterprise Modeling By Means Of UML Instance Models. *ACM Sigsoft Software Engineering Notes,* Volume 28 Issue 2.

Weske, M., Goesmann, T., Holten, R., & Striemer, R. (1999) A Reference Model for Workflow Application Development Processes. *ACM Sigsoft Software Engineering Notes , Proceedings of the International Joint Conference on Work Activities Coordination and Collaboration,* Volume 24 Issue 2.

Chapter V
Enterprise Resource Planning Systems:
Effects and Strategic Perspectives in Organizations

Alok Mishra
Atilim University, Turkey

ABSTRACT

In the age of globalization, organizations all over the world are giving more significance to strategy and planning to get an edge in the competition. This chapter discusses the Enterprise Resource Planning (ERP) systems effects and strategic perspectives in organizations. These are significant how information technology and ERP together facilitate in aligning the business in such a way so that it should lead to excellent productivity. It further explores in what ways effects of ERP system in organizations can provide sustained competitive advantage.

INTRODUCTION

Enterprise Resource Planning (ERP) software is one of the fastest growing segments of business computing today (Luo and Strong, 2004) and ERPs are one of the most significant business software investments being made in this new era (Beard and Sumner, 2004). Davenport (1998) has declared that 'the business worlds's embrace of enterprise systems may in fact be the most important development in the corporate use of information technology in the 1990's. Mabert et al. (2001) noted that industry reports suggests as many as 30,000 companies worldwide have implemented ERP systems. According to a report by Advanced Manufacturing Research, the ERP software market is expected to grow from $ 21 billion in 2002 to $ 31 billion in 2006 and the entire enterprise applications market which includes Customer Relationship Management and Supply Chain Management software will top $ 70 billion (AM Research, 2002). Further, AMR Research has projected as much as $ 10 billion in global investments in ERP (as cited in Kalling, 2003). The ERP market is projected to grow from a current $15 billion to $ 50 billion in the next five years and to reach $ 1 trillion by 2010 (Bingi et al., 1999). ERP systems offer the advantage of providing organizations with a single, integrated software system linking the core business activities such as oprations, manufacturing, sales, accounting, human resources, and inventory control (Lee and Lee, 2000; Newell et al., 2003; Shanks and Seddon, 2000). According to Brown and Vessey (2003) this integrated perspective may be the first true organization-wide view available to management. According to Lee and Myers (2004) much of the literature on ERP implementation suggests that ERP systems should support the strategic objectives of the organization. They observed that some ERP vendors tend to assume that implementing their products is a straightforward translation from strategy to IT-enabled business processes.

ERP helps organizations to meet the challenges of globalization with a comprehensive, integrated application suite that includes next-generation analytics, human capital management, financials, operations, and corporate services. With support for industry-specific best practices, ERP helps organizations improve productivity, sense and respond to market changes, and implement new business strategies to develop and maintain a competitive edge. ERP is designed to help businesses succeed in the global marketplace by supporting international legal and financial compliance issues and enabling organizations to adapt internal operations and business processes to meet country-specific needs. As a result, organizations can focus on improving productivity and serving their customers instead of struggling to ensure they are in compliance with business and legal requirements around the world. Companies that automate and streamline workflows across multiple sites (including suppliers, partners, and manufacturing sites) produced 66% more im-

provement in reducing total time from order to delivery, according to Aberdeen's 2007 study of the role of ERP in globalization. Those companies that coordinate and collaborate between multiple sites, operating as a vertically integrated organization, have achieved more than a 10% gain in global market share. The majority of companies studied (79%) view global markets as a growth opportunity, but of those companies, half are also feeling pressures to reduce costs (Jutras, 2007). Those companies that coordinate and collaborate between multiple sites, operating as a vertically integrated organization, have achieved more than a 10% gain in global market share (Marketwire, 2007).

INFORMATION TECHNOLOGY AND STRATEGIES

Inspite of lots of literature and guidance available less than 10% of strategies effectively formulated are effectively executed (Kaplan and Norton, 1996). Mintzberg (1992) defined strategy as " a plan –some sort of consciously intended course of action, a guideline (or set of guidelines) to deal with a situation. He further tried to define strategy from the perspectives of being a plan, a ploy, a position, a pattern, and a perspective (Ikavalko, and Aaltonen, 2001). Michael Porter's (1996) definition of strategy focuses more on the outcome, "the creation of a unique and valuable position, involving a different set of activities". He believes that a strategy is a way an organization seeks to achieve its vision and mission and that a successful strategy allows a company to capture and sustain a competitive advantage. Porter's (1985) value chain methodology identified five key forces that impact on an organization's competitive position:

- The bargaining power of suppliers;
- The bargaining power of buyer;

- The threat of new entrants;
- The threat of substitute products; and
- Rivalry among existing organizations.

He believed that the impact of these forces could be influenced by strategies that focused on low cost provider and on product differentiation. These strategies determine how various discrete activities are performed to add value and eventually a competitive advantage. An organization's activities can be categorised into primary activities that can directly add value and supporting activities. These interrelated activities make up Porter's Value Chain. One of the supporting activities he identified was the technology development. Porter and Miller (1985) proposed an information intensity matrix to assist in identifying where information technology could be used strategically in the Value Chain. Later on Somogyi and Galliers (1987) supported this by identifying how information technology could be used to assist organizations to accomplish competitive advantage in the various focuses across the Value Chain. During last two decades organizations have already identified the significance of information technology in achievement of strategic objectives. Scott Morton (1991) identified five interrelated factors (Structure, Strategy, Technology, Management Processes, Individual & Roles) that influence the attainment of strategic objectives. One of these factors was information technology. A recent survey of more than 300 CEO's and CIO's identified the alignment of IT and business strategy as their number one priority (Beal, 2003). Tallon and Kraemer (2003) in a survey of 63 companies found there was significant value gained from the alignment of these strategies. Broadbent and Weill (1993) define this IT-business alignment as the extent to which business strategies were enabled, supported, and stimulated by information strategies. Teo and King (1997) proposed four different scenarios or degrees of integration between the business and IT strategies. These included:

- **Administrative integration:** Where there is little relationship between the business and IT strategy.
- **Sequential integration:** Where the business strategy is developed in firstly in isolation to the IT strategy. The IT strategy is then developed to support the business strategy.
- **Reciprocal integration:** This is where a reciprocal and interdependent relationship exists between both strategies. The IT strategy is used to support the influence business strategy.
- **Full integration:** Occurs when both strategies are developed concurrently in an integrated manner.

This increased need for closer alignment has resulted in companies focussing on Strategic Information Systems Planning (SISP) and the development of methodologies to support this (Pant and Hsu, 1995; Hackney et al, 2000). Hackney et al. (2000) identified the assumptions which underlie SISP and discuss their validity. According to them main assumption are:

- Business srategies must exist as a precursor to SISP,
- Business strategies are different from IT,
- IT and Business strategies can be aligned.

They further argue that as business strategies evolve, it is often difficult for IT strategies to respond.

ERP AND CORPORATE STRATEGIES

ERP systems are widely adopted in a diverse range of organizations and define the business model on which they operate. For many organizations they were relieved that ERP system could help them define a business srategy and provide the

IT infrastructure to support it (Davenport, 2000). Hackney et al. (2000) believe that ERP systems can provide a "dynamic stability" to the alignment of business and IT strategies. These systems can provide a stable predictable environment of which their usage can evolve in accordance with a company's business strategy. Brancheau et al. (1996) observed that alignment of an informaion system (IS) with the strategic goals and operational objectives of an organization has been an important issue through the 1980s and 1990s. ERP research has exlpored how these types of systems contribute value to an organization (Markus and Tanis, 1999; Ross and Vitale, 2000; Somers and Nelson, 2001), as well as how they should be integrated with already-existing IT resources (Hayman, 2000). Large and small organization's continue to invest between $ 300,000 and hundreds of millions of dollars in ERP software and accompanying hardware (Markus, 1999). Different business justifications, including improved productivity, reduced costs, greater operational efficiency, enhanced customer relationship management, and better supply chain management (Brown and Vessey, 2003; Mabert et al, 2001). Finally, for the return on investment in ERP systems to be achieved, these systems should yield a strategic advantage. Kalling (2003) argues whether ERP systems provide a competitive advantage. Current perceptions of ERP systems, as evidenced in trade publications and the academic literature, emphasize their role in enhancing economic efficiency and improving financial performance (Dillard and Yuthas, 2006).

Beard and Sumner (2004) observed that regarding competitive advantage one challenge is that ERP systems impose a 'common systems' approach by establishing a common set of applications supporting business operations. Successful implementation of an ERP system requires re-engineering business processes to better align with the ERP software, so that the common systems approach is imposed (Brown and Vessey, 2003; Dahlen and Elfsson, 1999). This 'common' stru-

cture approach allows for faster implementation of the ERP system because there are fewer customized pieces to the software and the limited customization means that it will be simpler to upgrade the ERP software as new versions and features emerge over time (Beard and Sumner, 2004). Another challenge related with accomplishing a competitive advantage through ERP is the significant complexity of the implementation and integration process as it often takes several years to fully implement the ERP system. This includes integrating ERP with already-existing IS and accomplishing the related reengineering of the organization (Beard and Sumner, 2004). It is time consuming process to refine the alignment of organization to the ERP system and to more fully leverage the opportunities offered by the ERP system .

As ERP provides both tangible and intangible benefits, many organizations consider them as essential information system infrastructure to be competitive in today's business world and provide a foundation for future growth. A recent survey of 800 top U.S. companies showed that ERP systems accounted for 43% of these companies budgets (Somer & Nelson, 2001). The market segment of ERP systems varies considerably from industry to industry. According to Computer Economics Inc. Report 76% of manufacturers, 35% of insurance and health companies, and 24% of Federal Government agencies already have an ERP system or are in the process of installing one (Stedman, 1999). The global market for ERP software, which was $ 16.6 billion in 1998, is expected to have had 300 billion dollars spent over last decade (Carlino, 1999). There are number of vendors of ERP systems in the market although major one is SAP with approximately 56% of the market. In Australia 9 out of the top 12 IT users were SAP customers and 45% of the total list were also SAP users (BRW, 2002). Growth in ERP systems is due to several factors for example; the need to streamline and improve business processes, better manage information system expenditure, competitive pressures to become a low cost producer, increased responsiveness to customers and their needs, integrate business processes, provide a common platform and better data visibility, and as a strategic tool for the move towards e-commerce (Davenport et al. 2003; Markus et al., 2001; Somer et al., 2001).

ERP SYSTEM AND STRATEGIC ADVANTAGE

Davenport (2000) believes that ERP systems by their very nature impact on a organization's strategy, organization and culture. Mabert et al. (2001) report that companies view the standardization and integration of business processes across the enterprise as a key benefit. As one of the executives mentioned 'ERP is the digital nerve system that connects the processes across the organization and transmits the impact of an event happening in one part to the rest accurately' (Mabert et al. , 2001). Regarding tangible benefits, the companies often observed reported lower inventories, shorter delivery cycles, and shorter financial closing cycles although, the ERP system did not lead to reductions in work force or savings in operational costs in the short term (Beard and Sumner, 2004). According to Davenport (2000) cycle time reduction (e.g. cost and time reductions in key business processes), faster information transactions (e.g. faster credit checks), better financial management (e.g. shorter financial closing cycle, improved management reporting), and laying the ground work for electronic commerce (e.g. providing the back office functions for Web-based product ordering, tracking, and delivery processes), as well as a better understanding of key business processes and decision rules are general benefits of ERP systems. Laughlin (1999) suggests that the business justification for ERP includes both hard dollar savings (e.g. reductions in procurement cost, inventory, transportation, increased manufacturing throughput, and productivity) and

soft dollar savings (e.g. revenue growth, margin enhancement, and sales improvements). Interestingly both Mabert et al. (2001) and Laughlin (1999) observed that there is no evidence of ERP providing headcount reduction.

When an ERP works well it can 'speed up business processes, reduce costs, increase selling opportunities, improve quality and customer satisfaction, and measure results continuously (Piturro, 1999). Regarding business benefits of ERP, managers mention many productivity enhancements, including the ability to calculate new prices instantly, more accurate cost comparisons among different facilities, better electronic data interchange with vendors and suppliers, improved forecasting, and the elimination of bottlenecks and duplicative procedures (Plotkin, 1999). Other benefits deal with eliminating the redundancies associated with leagcy systems (Beard and Sumner, 2004). For example, at Owens Corning, there were 200 legacy systems, most running in isolation from one another. Eastman Kodak had 2600 different software applications (Palaniswamy and Frank, 2000). Organizations with ERP systems have made improvements in cross functional coordination and business performance (Oliver, 1999).

According to Markus et al. (2000) larger value of ERP is measured when the organization captures actual business results (for example reduced inventory costs), but these results don't occur until the phase in which the systems have already been successfully implemented and integrated into business operations-in referred by Markus et al. (2000) as 'onward and upward phase'- a stage three evolution. Holland and Light (2001) also support that the business benefits of ERP occur in a 'third stage' of evolution, during which innovative business processes are thoroughly implemented. As observed by Beard and Sumner (2004) that ERP may not necessarily directly provide organizations with a competitive advantage through reduction of these organizations cost below or by increasing these organizations' revenues above what would have been the case if these systems had not been implemented. They further argued that the advantages mentioned are largely value-added measures, such as increased information, faster processing, more timely and accurate transactions, and better decision-making.

CONCLUSION AND FUTURE TRENDS

ERP systems are increasingly popular IT platform that are being installed to assist organizations in better capturing, managing, and distributing organization-wide operational data to decision makers throughout the organization (Beard and Sumner, 2004). They further discussed that

Table 1. Benefits of ERP

Company	Business benefits	Source
Fujitsu	90% reduction in cycle time for quotation from 20 to 2 days 50% reduction in financial closing times from 10 to 5 days	Jensen and Johnson (1999)
Boeing	Simplification of processes	Jensen and Johnson (1999)
Pacific coast feather company	Inventory reduction; improved Customer service	Jensen and Johnson (1999)
IBM storage products company	Time for checking customer credit upon receiving an order was reduced from 15 to 20 minutes to instantaneously Responses to customer billing inquiries occurred in real time (vs. 15-20min) Entering pricing data into the system took 5 min. where it took 8 days beforehand Shipping repair and replacement was done in 3 days, compared to as many as 44 days	Jensen and Johnson (1999)
Earthgrains	On-time product delivery rate increased to 99% Operating margins improved from 2.4% to 3.9%	Bingi et al. (1999)
Par industries	Delivery performance improved from 80% on-time to more than 95%; Lead times to customers were reduced from 6 to 2 weeks Repair parts were reduced from 2 weeks to 2 days; Work-in-process inventory dropped almost 60% Life of a shop order dropped from weeks to hours	Bingi et al. (1999)

continued on following page

Table 1. continued

Owens corning	Inventory levels were reduced significantly Lot sizes and machine allocations more efficient Growth in inter-facility coordination	Palaniswami & Frank (2000)
Viskase	Reductions in lead time and inventory Reduction in headcount Integration of information Decision-making times are reduced significantly Production-based decisions are tied to sales-based decisions in a timely manner	Palaniswami & Frank (2000)
Diebold	Real-time access to data across the organization Better control of manufacturing processes	Palaniswami & Frank (2000)
Valenite	Lower levels of inventory Improved customer satisfaction Faster, more accurate order processing Accurate and timely financial information	Palaniswami & Frank (2000)
Leeson	Reduction in paperwork related to order processing Ability of end-users to gain access to information Improved accuracy of financial and inventory transactions Improved currency of manufacturing databases	Palaniswami & Frank (2000)

sustainable competitive advantage with an ERP system, important characteristics that will create sustained competitive advantage and reengineering the organization without disrupting or destroying the characterisctics that gave it a competitive advantage are further research areas to know more about effects and strategic advantages of ERP. These may be include empirical, qualitative or both the approaches in the organization. Comparison of ERP implementation effects and strategic advantages in two organizations may be an interesting area. Regarding limitation and concern as observed by Lee and Myers (2004) is

that ERP systems are so large and complex and take years to implement, the inclusion of today's strategic choices into the enterprise systems may significantly constrain future action. By the time the implementation of an ERP system is finished, the strategic context of the firm may have changed.

REFERENCES

AMR Research, (2002). AMR Research predicts enterprise applications market will reach $ 70 billion in 2006. *AMR Research*. Online available at www. amrresearch.com

Beal, B. (2003). The priority that persists. Retrieved November, 2003, from SearchCIO.com Web site: http://searchcio.techtarget.com/originalContent/0,29142,sid19_gci932246;00.html

Beard, J. W., & Sumner, M. (2004). Seeking strategic advantage in the post-net era: viewing ERP systems from the resource based perspective. *Journal of strategic Information Systems, 13*(2004), 129-150.

Bingi, P., Sharma, M., & Godla, J. (1999). Critical issues affecting ERP implementation. *Information System Management, 16*(3), 7-14.

Brancheau, J. C., Janz, B. D., & Wetherbe, J. C. (1996). Key issues in information system management: 1994-95 SIM Delphi results. *MIS Quarterly, 20*(2), 225-242.

Broadbent, M., & Weill, P. (1993). Improving business and information strategy alignment: learning from the banking industry. *IBM Systems Journal, 32*(1), 162-179.

Brown, C. V., & Vessey, I. (2003). Managing the next wave of enterprise systems: Leveraging lessons from ERP. *MIS Quarterly Executive, 2*(1), 65-77.

Carlino, J. (1999). AMR Research Unveils Report on Enterprise Application Spending and Penetration, at www.amrresearch.com/press/files/99823. asp accessed July 2001.

Communications of the ACM, 2000

Dahlen, C., & Elfsson, J. (1999). *An analysis of the current and future ERP market- with a focus on Sweden.* http://www.pdu.se/xjobb.pdf (accessed April 24, 2003)

Davenport, T., Harris, J., & Cantrell, S. (2003). *Enterprise Systems Revisited: The Director's Cut.* Accenture.

Davenport, T. (2000). *Mission Critical – Realizing the Promise of Enterprise Systems*. Boston, MA: Harvard Business School Press

Davenport, T. (1998) Putting the enterprise into the enterprise system. *Harvard Business Review, 76*(4), 121-131.

Dillard, J. F., & Yuthas, K. (2006) Enterprise Resource Planning Systems and Communicative Actions. *Critical Perspectives on Accounting, 17*, (2-3), 202-223.

Hackney, R., Burn, J., & Dhillon, G. (2000). Challenging Assumptions for Strategic Informations Systems Planning: Theoretical Perspectives. *Communications of the Association for Information Systems, 3*(9).

Hayman, L. (2000). ERP in the Internet economy. *Information System Frontiers, 2*, 137-139.

Holland, C., & Light, B. (2001) A Stage maturity model for enterprise resource planning use. *Databse for Advances in Information Systems, 35*(2), 34-45.

Ikavalko, H., & Aaltonen, P. (2001). Middle Managers' Role in Strategy Implementation – Middle Managers View. *In the proceedings of 17th EGOS Colloquium*, Lyon France.

Jensen, R., & Johnson, R. (1999) The enterprise resource planning system as a strategic solution. *Information Strategy, 15*(4), 28-33.

Jutras, C. (2007) *The Role of ERP in Globalization* available at http://www.aberdeen.com/summary/report/benchmark/RA_ERPRoleinGlobalization_CJ_3906.asp

Kaplan, R., & Norton, D. P. (1996) Using the balance score-card as a strategic management system. *Harvard Business Review*, Jan/Feb, 75-85.

Kalling, T. (2003) ERP systems and the strategic management processes that lead to competitive advantage. *Information Resources Management Journal, 16*(4), 46-67.

Laughlin, S. P. (1999) An ERP game plan. *Journal of Business Strategy, 20*(1), 32-37.

Lee, J. C., & Myers, M. D. (2004). Dominant actors, political agendas, and strategic shifts over time: a critical ethonography of an enterprise systems implementation. *Journal of Strategic Information Systems, 13*(2004), 355-374.

Luo, W., & Strong, D. M.(2004). A Framework for evaluating ERP implementation choices. *IEEE Transactions on Engineering Management, 51*(3), 3222-333.

Mabert, V. A., Soni, A., & venkataramanan, M. A. (2001). Enterprise resource planning: Common myths versus evolving reality. *Business Horizons, 44*(3), 69-76.

Marketwire (2007). Thinking Global? *Don't Lose Sight of Profitable Growth* available http://www.marketwire.com/mw/release_html_b1?release_id=224493

Markus, L., Petrie, D., & Axline, S., (2001). Bucking The Trends, What the Future May Hold For ERP Packages, in Shanks, Seddon and Willcocks (Eds.) *Enterprise Systems: ERP, Implementation and Effectiveness*, Cambridge University Press.

Markus, M. L., & Tanis, C. (1999). The enterprise systems experience- from adoption to success, In: Zmud, R.W., (Ed.), *Framing the Domains of IT Research: Glimpsing the Future Through the Past, Piinaflex Educational Resources*, Cincinnati, OH.

Markus, M. L. (1999)Keynote address: Conceptual challenges in contemporary IS research. *Proceedings of the Australasian Conference on Information Systems (ACIS)*, New Zeland, pp.1-5.

Mintzberg, H. (1992). Five Ps for Strategy. In the Strategy Process, H Mintberg and JB Quinn (eds.). Englewood Cliffs, NJ: Prentice –Hall

Oliver, R. (1999). ERP is dead, long live ERP. *Management Review 88*(10), 12-13.

Palaniswami, R., & Frank, T., (2000). Enhancing manufacturing performance with ERP systems. *Information Systems Management, 17*(3), 43-55.

Pant, S., & Hsu, C. (1995) Strategic Information Systems: A Review. *In the proceedings of the 1995 IRMA conference*, Atlanta, Georgia.

Piturro, M. (1999). How midsize companies are buying ERP. *Journal of Accountancy, 188*(3), 41-48.

Plotkin, H. (1999). ERP: How to make them work. *Harvard Management Updat,e* March, 3-4.

Porter, M. (1996). What is Strategy? *Harvard Business Review*, November-December.

Porter, M. (1985). *Competitive Advantage: Creating and Sustaining Superior Performance*. New York: Free Press,

Porter, M., & Miller, V. (1985). How Information Gives You Competitive Advantage. *Harvard Business Review, 63*, 4.

Ross, J. W., & Vitale, M. R. (2000). The ERP Revolution: Surviving vs. Thriving. *Information System Frontiers. 2*, 233-241.

Lee, Z., & Lee, J. (2000). An ERP implementation case study from a knowledge transfer perspective. *Journal of Information Technology, 15*, 281-288.

Newell, S., Haung, J. C., Galliers, R. D. , & Pan, S. L. (2003). Implementing enterprise resource planning and knowledge management system in tandem: Fostering efficiency and innovation complementarity. *Information and Organization, 13*, 25-52.

Scott, M. (1991). *The Corporation of the 1990s: Information Technology and Organizational Transformation*. Oxford University Press, Cambridge.

Shanks, G., & Seddon, P. (2000). Editorial. *Journal of Information Technology, 15*, 243-244.

Somer, T., & Nelson, K. (2001). The impact of Critical Success Factors across the Stages of Enterprise Resource Planning System Implementations. *Proceedings of the 34th Hawaii International Conference on System Sciences*, 2001, HICSS.

Somogyi, E., & Galliers, R. (1987). *Towards Strategic Information Systems*. Cambridge: Abacus Press.

Stedman, C. (1999). What's next for ERP? *Computerworld*, 33(33).

Tallon, P., & Kraemer, K. (2003). *Investigating the relationship between Strategic Alignment and IT Business value: The Discovery of a Paradox, Relationship Between Strategic Alignment and IT Business Value*. Idea Group Publishing, Hershey USA.

Teo, T., & King, W. (1997). Integration between business planning and information systems planning: an evolutionary contingency perspective. *Journal of Management Information Systems, 14*.

KEY TERMS

Business Benefits:

- Also known as: business benefits of ERP
- Similar to: Combined tangible and intangible benefits to organizations due to ERP implementation
- Associated in the manuscript with: Effects and benefits of ERP implementation

Business Processes:

- Also known as: IT-enabled business processes
- Similar to: integration of business processes
- Associated in the manuscript with: business processes to better align with the ERP software

Competitive Advantage:

- Also known as: Organization's sustains profits that exceed the average said to possess competitive advantage
- Similar to: A competitive advantage is an advantage over competitiors by offering consumers greater value either by means of lower prices or by providing greater benefits
- Associated in the manuscript with: competitive advantage through ERP

ERP:

- Also known as: Enterprise Resource Planning
- Similar to: systems attempt to integrate all data and processes of an organization into a unified system
- Associated in the manuscript with: Effects and Strategic Perspectives in Organizations

Global:

- Also known as: globalization
- Similar to: Multinational Organizations, Organizations distributed at international level
- Associated in the manuscript with: global market for ERP software, global marketplace

Integrated:

- Also known as: Combining different functional aspects of the organization
- Similar to: integrated application suite
- Associated in the manuscript with: integrated software system linking the core business activities such as oprations, manufacturing, sales, accounting, human resources, and inventory control

Chapter VI
An Overview of Executive Information Systems

Gary P. Moynihan
The University of Alabama, USA

ABSTRACT

An executive information system (EIS) is a software system designed to support the informational needs of senior management. The EIS is characterized by an easy to use and maintainable graphical user interface; integrated capabilities for data access, analysis, and control; analysis and report generation across multiple files; and on-request "drill down" capability. Most existing management information systems provide an enormous quantity of detailed status reports. However, they lack the capability of providing summarized levels of information, in an appropriate format, for higher levels of management. This problem has continued despite the emergence of enterprise resource planning systems. By understanding the concept and functionality of traditional executive information systems, readers will also be able to better understand how EIS has adapted to meet the requirements of senior management in an enterprise system environment.

INTRODUCTION

Executives are upper-level managers who exert a strong influence on the direction and activities of the entire organization (e.g. McLeod and Schell, 2001). An executive information system (EIS) is a computer-based system designed to support the unique informational needs of these very senior managers. These systems are designed to simplify the user's interface with the computer, facilitate retrieval and manipulation of data from different sources, and display results in a single presentation. Finally, executive information systems provide the capability to highlight exceptions, and explore data at progressively lower levels of detail.

The concept of the executive information system can be traced to 1982, when Rockart and

Treacy introduced this term to describe an emerging category of information systems. They noted that there are four critical components to the EIS concept. First, there is the *Executive,* the human element in the EIS environment. The executive requires timely information, quick inquiry response, and systemic ease of use. *Information* supports both critical success factor analysis and leading indicators of potential problems. The third component is the *System* architecture that encompasses linkages to the relevant, and the processing of this data into critical information. The final component is the *Organizational* structure that manages the databases and systems, and maintains information security. All four components must be integrated for the EIS to be successful.

To do this, an EIS combines two complimentary approaches. According to McNurlin and Sprague (2002), "at its heart, an EIS should filter, extract, and compress a broad range of up-to-date internal and external information. It should call attention to variances from plan and also monitor and highlight critical success factors of the individual executive user" (p. 386). This perspective defines an EIS as a structured reporting system to meet the unique needs of executive management. The second fundamental approach of the EIS, as identified by McNurlin and Sprague (2002), is as a human communications support, such that. "the managers make requests, give instructions, and ask questions to selected members of this network to get people going on the desired action" (p. 387). Alter (2002) confirms this by emphasizing the networks of internal and external contacts used to gather information about specific issues of current importance, as opposed to only utilizing formalized information systems.

The terms executive information system and executive support system (ESS) are often used interchangeably (e.g. Laudon and Laudon, 1998). Other authors make a distinction between the two, based upon the fundamental approach used or emphasized. For example, based on Rockart and DeLong's (1988) original discussion, Turban and Aronson (2001) further define an executive support system as "a comprehensive support system that goes beyond EIS to include communication, office automation, analysis support, and business intelligence" (p. 308). An important feature, especially to upper-level management, is access to external data. Thus, where core EIS functionality focuses on the processing and presentation of information, an ESS implies other communications support capabilities more oriented toward the second fundamental EIS approach mentioned above. These communications support capabilities may include e-mail, office automation functions like electronic calendars, and linkages to stock market news and industry trends.

Further, EISs were initially developed to support a small set of high-level executives within an organization. These systems normally served up to 10 or 15 senior executives. The success of these initial implementations has led to an expansion of these systems to support mid-level managers with cross-functional information needs. This type of system served up to sixty executives and managers, and has been termed an "extended EIS" In some cases, EIS, have been adapted to the entire organization (McLeod and Schell, 2001). Rockart and DeLong (1988) first observed this migration. For this paper, the term "executive information systems" will be used across this spectrum of applications and levels of use, with consideration of how the EIS concept has evolved in the process.

BACKGROUND

Historically, the traditional management information systems (MIS) within a company have been developed independently of each other. These systems typically supported marketing, manufacturing, distribution, personnel, accounting, order entry, inventory control, and purchasing. They are used to support organizational planning and control, and are capable of producing both summary and very detailed reports. Senior managers have typically tried to utilize these MIS reports to identify exceptions and trends that require management attention. However, in attempting to assimilate outputs beyond the limited functional areas, MIS systems are frequently deficient in supporting the company-wide perspective required by executive decision-makers. Although these MIS systems may be subsequently interfaced, there was no true integration. There is a wide variety of screens and reports provided. Each system focuses on individual areas of concern, and each may have its own format under separate security access. Timliness of the resulting information may vary based on the specific system execution and the data that it uses. These reports frequently take the form of an endless stream of computer print-outs or online reports, which the executive has little or no time to review. There is a limited capability of providing summarized levels of information, in an appropriate format, for higher levels of management. Even when the reams of data are condensed and summarized, relevant information is frequently difficult to extract or understand. Too often decisions were a reaction to an event that has already occurred.

Briefing books, sometimes referred to as management reporting systems (MRS), were an early effort to address these problems by automating data acquisition from a wide variety of corporate systems and databases, and providing online output in the form of fixed-format reports (e.g. Laudon and Laudon, 1998). The purpose of a MRS was to integrate, select, and reduce raw data to valuable information; create and distribute finished quality reports and charts; and to ensure reporting of consistent information across the corporation. Management reporting systems tended to be MIS-based transaction systems linked to a presentation manager interface. These levels represent the major functional components of the MRS, where the transaction system tracks the status of operations and reports performance relative to plan based on data accessed from the

appropriate data source. The presentation manager provides the formatted executive information in the form of reports to the user, as well as a means of system access and inquiry. Thus, they only addressed the earliest phases of decision-making (i.e. isolating problems and raising questions). The information output was considered to be restrictive and inflexible.

Review of the literature has noted considerable work on the development of decision rules and computer-based support systems to aid in entire decision-making process. Decision support systems (DSS) are software systems that utilize sophisticated algorithmic approaches to solve problems. Within the DSS, the data processor (i.e. the database management system) controls the access and update of data from external files and datasources. The modelbase contains the specific analytical methods used for processing the accessed data. Although decision support systems were originally intended to serve the needs of upper management, they became to tools of analysts and lower-level managers. A further evolution was needed to better meet executive needs. As noted in Figure 1, the integration of DSS capabilities within the MRS framework led to the emergence of the true executive information system.

Insertion of the DSS level into this framework provides a means whereby users can better develop their plans, specify what activities should take place, and better organize the operational information for executive inquiry. For example, Turban and Aronson (2002) describe a pharmaceutical company's product managers utilizing an EIS-based DSS module to predict the end-of-month order status. Similarly, the commercially-available DecisionWeb EIS software provides ad-hoc analysis for determining trends and variances. As noted in Figure 1, this DSS integration may be executed either by using the presentation manager as a selection interface, or automatic access from the source database(s). The results of the DSS analysis are then formatted through the presentation manager for display to the user.

Figure 1. Executive information system architecture

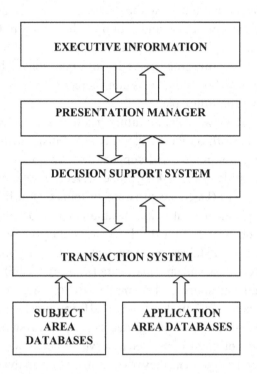

Although, DSS and EIS capabilities were initially considered to be separate and distinct, as reported in the literature, Alter (2002) noted an accelerating trend during the 1990s towards their integration. This is frequently expressed through the use of a spreadsheet facility.

Executive Requirements

Considerable research has been conducted on the informational needs and decision making processes used by executives. Watson et al. (1993) provided a comprehensive survey of the available research at that time. Executives' busy schedules preclude either long training sessions or long uninterrupted time for system use. Systems must be intuitive and easy to use, with very quick response. They must allow "environmental scanning" by accessing and integrates a broad range of internal and external data, and support management by exception by highlighting potential problems

and tracking critical data. The EIS should store aggregated data for rapid access, efficiently index and retrieve information, and sort screen data according to user defined criteria. Although earlier research focused on large corporations, Walters et al. (2003) confirmed that executives in smaller manufacturing companies also shared these same requirements. Perhaps the most important aspect is that an EIS must meet the information needs of the executive user. Determining precisely what information should be included in the system continues to be a major topic of research in this area (e.g. Rainer and Watson, 1995; Walstrom and Wilson, 1997).

The literature particularly notes executives' reliance on critical success factors (CSFs). Critical success factors consist of a relatively small number of easily identified operational goals that are believed to ensure the success of an organization. These CSFs may be derived by the industry, the specific firm, the manager, and the broader business environment. For example, McLeod and Schell (2001) identify "styling, an efficient dealer network, and tight control of manufacturing cost" as critical success factors within the automobile industry (P. 332). Rockart and Treacy (1982) argued that the information requirements of an organization, and particularly of that organization's executives, are shaped by these critical success factors. The CSFs then determine a smaller data set on which resulting information systems can focus to best meet the executives' requirements.

The EIS is subsequently utilized to monitor each of the CSFs according to five categories of information (Turban and Aronson, 2001). Key problem narratives are reports that highlight overall performance, major problems, and the potential underlying reasons for these problems. Associated narrative explanations are often linked to supporting tables and graphs. Highlight charts display summary information based on the user's indicated perspective and judgment. Since they are personalized to the user's concerns, they visually highlight the performance status of priority areas versus respective CSFs. Key factors provide specific measures of CSFs, referred to as key performance indicators (KPIs). These corporate-level displays usually employ management by exception to investigate measures of CSFs identified as problems, or potential problems, on the highlight chart. Typical key performance indicators include profitability measures, financial ratios, turnover rate, sales growth, market share, and demographic data. Detailed KPI responsibility reports indicate the detailed performance of or business areas critical to the success of the organization.

Functionality

Consistent with these defined executive user requirements, an EIS promotes a proactive anticipatory style of management by which problem indicators are closely monitored based on their CSFs, and timely corrective action implemented prior to serious problem occurrence. This type of system may be further defined by having the following characteristics:

1. An easy to use and maintainable graphical user interface.
2. Integrated capabilities for data access, analysis, and control.
3. Analysis and report generation across multiple data sources.
4. On-request "drill down" capability to lower levels of detail.
5. Depiction of organizational critical success factors.
6. Functionality for decision support, ad-hoc queries and what-if analysis.
7. Sophisticated tools for system navigation.
8. Data analysis features.
9. Advanced report generation.
10. Access to a variety of external data sources.

The resulting combination of capabilities provides a powerful tool for senior management. They can navigate through data hierarchies, view data from different dimensions, analyze it, and create reports tailored to their specific informational needs.

As noted by Laudon and Laudon (1998), most EIS systems provide "colorful presentations and pictorial menus that can be learned intuitively, with variances and exceptions highlighted in color" (p. 611). Users frequently access data and make selections via touch screen, keyboard, or mouse. Navigation to deeper levels of detail may be conducted based on their own selections, or by following pre-defined paths. The screen displays frequently incorporate management by exception by comparing the planned (or budgeted) performance with the actual performance of an operation. Accordingly, the executive's attention is focused on exceptions to standards. Significant exceptions (i.e. those beyond a pre-identified threshold) are automatically identified by the EIS and highlighted (or otherwise brought to the executive user's attention. This saves significant time in sifting through the data for exception conditions.

This last capability allows the pointing and clicking on a specific data field for which the user desires an additional level of detail. As a result, the components of that data field are then displayed. EIS systems have a top-level menu, often referred to as an "executive dashboard" or "executive scorecard" (Liang and Miranda, 2001). The intent of the dashboard is to provide a single-screen display of relevant and critical business metrics and/or statuses, frequently featuring stoplight indicators. It is configured with a "hotspot" button at the intersection of the reporting categories and the organization identifiers, indicating the appropriate status. (See Figure 2.) Red, yellow, and green lights are indicated based on comparison to preset thresholds, where green indicates a nominal condition, yellow indicates a warning, and red identifies performance outside of the pre-established boundaries. (Some EIS systems also provide audio signals to alert the executive to arriving information.) White indicates that no information is currently available. The colors thus allow the user to prioritize his actions, and address potential problems requiring immediate attention. This enables more efficient and effective decision-making.

Clicking on any of these stoplights allows drill down to the desired level of reporting, in order to indicate the source of any problems. (See Figure 3.) This concept allows users at various managerial to see data details relevant to their position and viewing responsibility. For example, the dashboard may provide a set of KPIs (e.g. revenue forecasts, gross profit, or inventory levels) with drill-down capabilities for each KPI monitored (Bose, 2006).Users at lower levels can view data details specific to their individual business function, while users at higher levels can view summaries across multiple functions. All levels are able to track data across multiple months. Drill-down capability exists for visibility to even further levels of detail.

An EIS normally includes tools for modeling and analysis within its DSS layer. These frequently include built-in functions for statistical (e.g. trending, regression, and Monte Carlo analysis) and financial models (such as profitability analysis, marginal utility, and benefit-cost analysis). Other functions may include goal-seeking (i.e. specify the values for the output data and the system will determine the required value of the input variable) and forecasting models. This may be deployed through the use Excel or similar spreadsheet program linkages in order to create graphic comparisons (e.g. by time period; by product: by region; or by price range). Costlier systems include more sophisticated specialty analysis built-in programs as part of their on-line analytical processing (OLAP) capabilities. OLAP supports decision-making based on analysis of multi-dimensional aggregated (i.e. summary) data. Examples of these include Pilot Software's Decision Support Suite, Informix's MetaCube Product Suite, and Cognos' PowerPlay. To aid in the decision-making process, interactive support functions are normally available which allow

Figure 2. Example top-level selection matrix

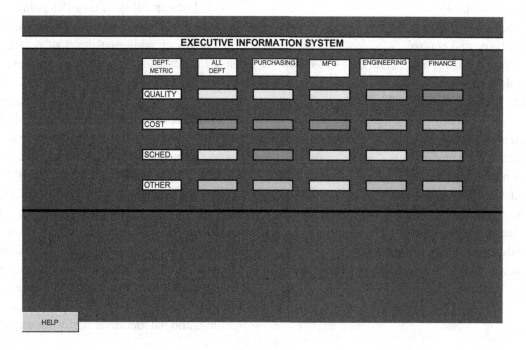

Figure 3. Sample subordinate display

STANDARD SCORE CARD FOR THE MONTH	MAY'07				
	FABRICATION	ASSEMBLY	PAINTING	INSPECTION	TEST
1 Management Responsibility					
2 Quality System					
3 Internal Quality Audit					
4 Training					
5 Financial Considerations to Quality Systems					
6 Product Safety					
Z1 Corporate Strategy					
7 Contract Review, Quality in Marketing					
8 Design Control					
9 Process Planning					
10 Document and Data Control					
11 Purchasing					
12 Control of Customer - Supplied Products					
13 Product Identification and Traceability					
14 Inspection and Testing					
15 Process Control					
16 Control of Inspection, Measuring and Test Equipment					
17 Control of Nonconforming Product					
18 Corrective and Preventive Action					
19 Handling, Storage, Packing, Preservation and Delivery					
20 Control of Quality Records					
21 Servicing					
22 Statistical Method					

the user to initiate ad hoc queries and "what-if" analysis. What-if analysis is a particularly useful tool for managers, whereby they can project the effect of modifications to the input data or other parameters will have on a resulting decision.

Construction of an EIS implies the need for a security system that will control access to sensitive information. The EIS, its data and software, must be protected at all times from unauthorized access. Accepted backup and recovery procedures need to be incorporated. Additional security features also need to be incorporated that will restrict access to data and information outside a specific user's organization and/or subordinate offices. Multi-level security for data access needs to be established for any EIS that is used by multiple executives. In addition to prohibiting access to the system by unauthorized personnel, the security system must be multi-level in nature, to restrict access within a variety of classifications (Moynihan, 1993b). The security system should also be as transparent as possible to the executive user. Multiple levels of user-input passwords should be avoided Most senior managers prefer "one-button" access to

their systems. Security supports the integrity of the data by ensuring that the data cannot be tampered with, viewed by outside parties, or that the data cannot be lost. The security feature enforces the drill-down functionality such that users at various levels of the organization see data details relevant to their position and viewing responsibility. Users at the lowest levels view data details specific to their functional area, while users at higher levels initially view summaries across subordinate organizations, but can drill-down for visibility to further levels of detail. There are several strategies in addressing this problem. Some organizations adopt a multi-level security system utilizing the capabilities of an EIS application development software. An alternate approach utilizes a multi-level, centralized database system to support data having different classifications and users having different clearances.

Development Approach

The EIS can be coded directly using a conventional programming language, analogous to any decision support system. Accepted DSS development methodology identifies four primary phases: data acquisition, system design, system construction, and verification and validation. During the data acquisition phase, the key concepts, relationships and sources are identified. One major purpose of the general system design phase is to establish the overall definitions and descriptions of the proposed system. This is represented through the development of a requirements definition (RD) document. Laudon and Laudon (1998) provide a series of recommended steps for determining EIS requirements:

1. Identify a set of issue-generating critical events.
2. Obtain, from the executive, his assessment of the impact of the critical events on his goals and determine a set of critical issues.
3. Determine three to five indicators which can be used to track each critical issue.
4. Obtain, from the executive, a list of potential information sources for the indicators.
5. Identify exception heuristics for each indicator.

During the subsequent detailed design phase, the acquired data and candidate mathematical models is organized within the RD context. This may provoke further investigation into supporting models and data. A functional system design document is then developed identifying the overall system architecture, processing considerations, and definition of displays and reports. The identified requirements and functionality can be utilized for software selection. The general design is then "fine-tuned" to map to the capabilities of the software. This step precedes actual programming of the EIS system. Upon completion of the system's construction, a thorough verification and validation is conducted. Traditional software engineering techniques, i.e., using a set of predetermined tests, are generally used to verify the integrity of the system. The validation process establishes that the system's functionality addresses the original engineering problem and the user's needs.

Because executive's needs may change rapidly, some developers recommend utilizing prototyping, also referred to as rapid, application development, to develop an EIS. In this approach, a series of preliminary working versions, each having progressively more functionality, are constructed for demonstration and evaluation. Due to the executive user's expectations, developers must be certain that the system will work before demonstrating it to the user. Each stage of the prototype must have an intuitive user interface, i.e. one that the executive can learn very rapidly.

Alternatively, a commercial off-the-shelf (COTS) product can be utilized. While early EIS systems were programmed exclusively using internal company resources, by the mid-1980s Comshare and Pilot Software introduced the first COTS development products (Watson and Carte, 2000). A COTS product is not an EIS per se, but rather a set of software tools with which to construct an EIS. They generally include the capability for constructing standard executive information features, such as picture menus, icons, hotspots, key performance indicators, and drill-down. Utilization of a COTS diminishes EIS development cost due to the availability of such product-specific data manipulation tools. The literature review indicates that subsequent maintenance costs for a COT-based system would be substantially less than in-house development (e.g. Watson et al., 1993). A variety of such EIS application software shells are now commercially available, which allow customization to individual company needs.

Executive information systems tend to be unique in that the implementation (and even post-implementation) issues often overshadow the actual system development. According to Rockart and Delong (1988), "the fragmented nature of executive work, the high degree of environmental uncertainty at this level of the organization, and the political ramifications of providing top management with more and better information, as well as other factors, make implementing EIS a special challenge" (p. 158). While data management may not be considered to be a significant problem when an EIS prototype is first installed, the practical barriers to providing executives with the data that they need can be a major road block post-implementation. As such, the system developers must contend with a number of issues relating to data availability, ownership, infrastructure, integrity, integration and management (Moynihan, 1993b). Once the EIS application goes online, the data owners are responsible for insuring the accuracy of the data. If the data are too old, too detailed, or too summary, or simply wrong, the executives may make the wrong decisions. Procedures need to be instituted in order to insure that the appropriate data are collected on time, refreshed when necessary, consolidated where applicable, and made available in the appropriate format. An underlying problem with traditional data management is the difficulty of integrating data originally designed to meet the needs of isolated applications. This problem of decentralized development has lead to discrepancies in data definitions, data redundancy, and synchronization problems. The resulting lack of accessible, quality data often limits executive access to information, and hinders system maintenance (Moynihan, 1993b).

Rather than providing direct linkage to source data, one approach to EIS construction recommends the establishment of a separate EIS database. As noted by McNurlin and Sprague (2002), there is concern that the executive would need too much detailed knowledge to access, interpret, and use the raw source data. Instead, the desired data should be extracted from these data sources, formatted and incorporated into the EIS database. This information should be organized into a hierarchical fashion such that highlights are indicated in the top layer. Most raw data sources contain mostly current data, with little historical

context. In order to be able to identify trends, the EIS database needs to incorporate time series data. Further, the executives need to track external sources of information. An EIS that accesses internet-based sources gives executives a greatly improved ability to assess competitive conditions. Conversely, this access has its limitations; i.e. internet-based sources may be of questionable accuracy and reliability. Those data definitions that are closely defined and controlled in an EIS, are not controlled in these external internet sources. This may lead to confusion as outside information is merged with the well-defined EIS database (McNurlin and Sprague, 2002).

It is also to be noted that, as executive user personnel, become familiar with an EIS and its capabilities, these users inevitably begin to identify new system "requirements". Sometimes, this occurs before the system is even formally implemented. This user community is used to getting its own way. Despite the flexibility inherent in most EIS systems, some of these requests may involve modifications well beyond those originally specified in the design. Some requests are relatively easy to accommodate, others are not (e.g. those requiring the establishment of a new database). The fact that users are discovering increasing potential for the system is beneficial and should be encouraged. However, the introduction of major modifications too early can result in an unforeseen, yet interrelated, impact elsewhere in the EIS. Therefore a strict policy should be established as early as possible, regarding the type and extent of changes that are permitted before implementation, and how post-implementation modifications will be handled. The subsequent addition of numerous enhancements can degrade system efficiency. Judgment must be applied in order to balance system capabilities versus response rate. Rapid response is considered vital to the executive user.

TRADITIONAL EIS APPLICATIONS

A variety of executive information system applications have been developed for private industry. By necessity, very large corporations were among the first to realize the advantages that an EIS could provide. One such representative example is Conoco's EIS (Belcher and Watson, 1993). Senior management was interviewed regarding their specific needs, and statistics tabulated on utilization of specific software applications. The system was designed and constructed by in-house staff with a heavy emphasis on the use of financial and refining capacity models. The completed EIS has continued to grow in usage and capability, including 75 decision support applications which were used in some form by over 4,000 Conoco employees throughout the world (Belcher and Watson, 1993). The cited benefits of the system included increased productivity, improved decision-making, and cost savings.

Pratt and Whitney's Commercial Engine Business purchased Commander, a commercial EIS software package from Comshare, to view metrics on customer service and jet engine product performance (Laudon and Laudon 1998). The Commander software shell was customized to track critical quality and reliability measures (e.g. parts availability, spares inventories, and delivery statuses) for each engine model by the specific customer. As with many such COTS shells, Commander has graphics facilities, exception reporting/ variance highlighting and an easy-to-use system navigation capability. The resulting EIS was used to provide drill down capabilities to determine the reasons for specific engine repairs, and where quality improvements should be implemented. The system was initially utilized by approximately 25 executives, but was planned for significantly expanded use (Laudon and Laudon, 1998). Pizza Uno, a food service chain, similarly employed the Pilot Software OLAP-based (Online Analytical Processing) shell to integrate its existing corporate intranets

(Turban and Aronson, 2001). The resulting EIS was characterized by a user-friendly graphical user interface and an ability to conduct multidimensional analyses across different product lines. For example, marketing executives utilized the system to measure the results of test marketing a new menu and how it relates to labor and other costs (Turban and Aronson, 2001).

A number of EIS systems have also been applied to the government environment. One of the first was an EIS developed for the New York State Office of General Services beginning in 1988. With a budget of $500 M and over 4000 employees, the agency needed to consolidate and integrate its data and information on the "design, construction, and maintenance of state buildings, food and laundry services to both correctional facilities and health-related institutions, statewide vehicle management, and centralized printing" (Laudon and Laudon, 1998, p. 612). The system provided conventional EIS capabilities of status monitoring, comparison of budgets to actuals, and financial estimates, with drill-down to view details in any category. The EIS was fielded on a set of networked PCs linked to the agency's mainframe computer.

Another early public sector system was the center-wide EIS for NASA's Marshall Space Flight Center (MSFC). Prior to this effort, there were a variety of Program Office and functional directorate systems. In March 1992, the MSFC Center Director appointed a steering committee and working group to begin efforts toward a center-wide EIS (Moynihan, 1993a). The resulting system linked existing communication networks to support both Windows-based and MacIntosh-based workstations then used at the Center, with the capability to also support a planned UNIX-based platform. Based on an analysis of MSFC executive user requirements, the HOLOS EIS application shell was purchased. HOLOS provided a comprehensive set of tools for constructing standard EIS features, such as picture menus, icons, hotspots, key performance indicators and drill-down. The software also allowed multi-dimensional modeling with associated calculations, statistical analysis, regression, and financial- and time-based functions (Moynihan, 1993a).

Watson and Carte (2000) completed a comprehensive survey on the use of EISs in the federal government environment. Among the organizations they cited include the Internal Revenue Service, the Government Printing Office, Department of Commerce, Department of Defense, and the General Services Administration. Liang and Miranda (2001) note that non-federal public sector EIS applications remain limited but are anticipated to grow. Among the state and city governments they cite with active EIS development projects are: Utah, Texas, San Francisco, Albuquerque, and Philadelphia. Recently, the State of Minnesota Department of Finance has pursued the development of an executive information system. The purpose of the system is to permit executive users to access pre-defined views of data stored on legacy state information systems. Conventional EIS capabilities (e.g. graphical and tabular formats, drill-down, and exception reporting) have been implemented in conjunction with Web-based access (Liang and Miranda, 2001). Planned development would increase user flexibility and functionality with the ability to develop what-if analyses, cost projections, and scenario sharing/update.

RELEVANCE TO ENTERPRISE SYSTEMS

The advent, and subsequent adoption, of enterprise resource planning systems would appear to have addressed much of the underlying rationale for EIS development. As noted by Umble et al. (2003), ERP provides the twin benefits of integrating the information processing of many departments in order to create a coordinated corporate response, and creating a consistent, common set of databases. It may also include integration with the information systems of other companies. These overall enterprise systems accumulate all transaction data from sales, purchasing, manufacturing, and other business functions, then provide coordinated and integrated reporting of this data. This solves such traditional EIS development problems of disparate databases and conflicting data definitions. However, senior management may still be inundated with status report output from the enterprise system. The primary mission of the traditional EIS still remains in the ERP environment: to extract, filter, compress and track critical executive information (e.g. Liang and Miranda, 2001; Walters et al., 2003).

As noted by Bose (2006), "managing enterprise performance is an important, yet difficult process due to its complexity. The process involves monitoring the strategic focus of the enterprise, whose performance is measured from the analysis of data generated from a wide range of interrelated business activities performed at different levels within the enterprise" (p. 43). Effective management thus requires an understanding of how each discrete business action affects the entire organization. Conventional ERP provides snapshots of organizational performance but do not adequately support continuous planning activities increasingly necessary for enterprise management. EIS has evolved to become a complementary component to ERP systems.

As suggested by McLeod Schell (2001), Figure 3 depicts how enterprise systems provide the foundation for various business area systems (e.g. manufacturing information systems, and financial information systems). One aspect of the enterprise system is to gather and distribute data to all of the business processes within the organization. At the top of this architecture resides the executive information system. Executives and managers still need to make decisions based on data within this framework. Thus, the EIS provides an overlay to the ERP system such that it the processes enterprise data into decision-making information for senior management.

Figure 4. EIS within the enterprise system framework

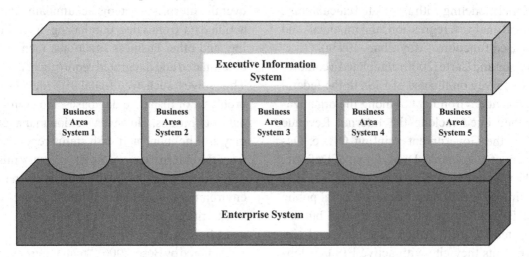

During the late 1990's, the independent EIS concept described previously began to be integrated with more cost-effective enterprise-based systems. Martinek and Szikova (2005) have discussed such an extended system to support printed circuit board production in Europe. Umble et al (2003) detail a successful implementation at Huck International, Inc. during 1998 and 1999. Huck purchased the Baan ERP system to replace a legacy MRPII hosted on HP3000hardware platform at ten international sites. In addition to the expected personnel reductions, cost of information processing, better inventory and order control, and improved cash management, the capabilities for improved management decision-making were identified and added as an enhancement to the system.

This type of integration serves to better leverage existing ERP capabilities. For this reason, EIS has begun to transform into an acronym for enterprise information systems. This connotes an organization-wide system that provides consistent and integrated managerial information from a company point of view. Different users across the enterprise can utilize the system for different purposes, as well as serving the purposes of top executives. Increasingly DSS and traditional EIS capabilities are routinely added to commercially-

available ERP software products. In the SAP ERP software package, these capabilities are referred to as "strategic enterprise management systems" (Turban and Aronson, 2001).

FUTURE DIRECTIONS

As the EIS concept has expanded and adapted to serve more levels of management utilizing enterprise systems and databases, the term executive information system has begun to lose its relevance. Data warehouse products can provide data in user-friendly, graphics-oriented query systems, consistent with EIS requirements. These data warehouses also provide filtered enterprise-wide data. The traditional linkage of an EIS to multiple subject area databases, or specific applications databases, is being replaced by a data warehouse interface. Further, information delivery via the corporate internet is evolving into Web-enabled support systems to better access internet-based information. For example, the SAS Institute includes this internet support function in its Enterprise Software Suite. Vendors are increasingly beginning to use the term enterprise information system, or "business intelligence" (BI), to reflect this emerging role of EIS (Negash and Gray,

2003). With the advances in data warehousing and Web-networks, the traditional independent EIS is continuing to evolve into the concept of the enterprise (or corporate) portal for business intelligence purposes. This portal concept is intended to better integrate internal company applications with a variety of external applications available via the internet.

Ease of use has always been a primary requirement for executive information systems. Traditionally, this has inferred an intuitive graphical user interface. To further improve the user interface, software vendors have begun to provide capabilities to quickly customize the EIS for the specific executive user through the inclusion of a toolbox option for analytical and graphical objects (Turban and Aronson, 2001). This allows easy customization capabilities. Pilot Decision Suite and Comshare's DecisionWeb provide two examples of this emerging capability.

However, "ease of use" is also beginning to imply that the system has sufficient intelligence to automate some (if not all) aspects of the process. Although EISs are effective in monitoring present status, they can neither interpret nor explain. This necessitates a combining of EIS functionality with artificial intelligence capabilities. As these intelligent EIS system expand, the task of drill-down will be progressively automated. By querying a "Why" function, the executive will initiate an intelligent agent to conduct the drill-down and ascertain the answer. This will depict the logic stream to locate and evaluate the significance of key indicators influenced the results. Simple trending or comparisons can already be determined by such agents, with automatic alerts provided based on comparison to a threshold value. Turban and Aronson (2001) report on such a deployment of EIS-based intelligent agents for improved environmental scanning, i.e. to monitor specific websites for relevant news and pricing data. The collected data will then be routed for quantitative analysis by DSS components of the EIS. Results will be customized for each executive, and communicated as an e-mail alert.

As an extension of the ESS aspect, it has been proposed that linkages be established to groupware to facilitate communication among executives to solve common problems. (Groupware refers to collaborative software and technologies beyond e-mail or videoconferencing. Lotus Notes is a common example.) Other authors have proposed architectures for distributed intelligent EISs composed of an integrated framework of intelligent agents, expert systems, neural networks and conventional DSS to support the executive decision-making process. For example, Bose (2006) discusses such a framework as the basis for business intelligence-based enterprise performance management.

CONCLUSION

Much of the value of executive information systems come from their flexibility. Executives are free to determine the problems that they need to address, using the system as an extension of their own thinking process. The most apparent benefits of EIS are their ability to analyze, compare, and highlight trends, frequently through the use of graphics. EIS becomes a reality when executives access vital information, analyze trends with integrated diagnostics, and can model multiple alternatives. To be truly successful, the EIS system components must require a minimal level of support, offer a fast development cycle, and are responsive and adaptable to the changing needs of executives.

The progressive incorporation of EIS capabilities, within the enterprise system, reduces the quantity of data that an executive must filter while dramatically increasing the quality of the information output. Future applications of intelligent EIS will automatically incorporate explanations, analyses, and forecasts that will further enhance the executive's understanding of this output. They will anticipate potential business problems by examining leading indicators and alerting users to future possibilities, as well as suggesting strategies and solutions when provided specific constraints.

REFERENCES

Alter, S. (2002). *Information Systems: Foundation of E-Business* (4th ed.). Upper Saddle River, NJ: Prentice Hall.

Belcher, L. W., & Watson, H.J. (1993). Assessing the value of Conoco's EIS. *MIS Quarterly.* *17*(9), 239-253.

Bose, R. (2006). Understanding management data systems for enterprise performance management. *Information Management and Data Systems*, *106*(1), 43-54.

Laudon, K. C., & Laudon, J. P. (1998). *Management Information Systems: New Approaches to Organization & Technology (5th ed.)* Upper Saddle River, NJ: Prentice Hall.

Liang, L. Y., & Miranda, R. (2001). Dashboards and scorecards: executive information systems for the public sector. *Government Finance Review, 17*(6), 14-19.

Marteinek, P., & Szikora, B. (2005). Integrated enterprise resource planning system. *In 28th International Seminar on Electronics Technology* (pp. 417-421). IEEE.

McLeod, R., & Schell, G. (2002). *Management Information Systems* (8th ed.). Upper Saddle River, NJ: Prentice Hall.

McNurlin, B. C., & Sprague, R. H. (2002). *Information Systems in Practice* (5th ed.). Upper Saddle River, NJ: Prentice Hall.

Moynihan, G. P. (1993a). Development of an executive information system for Marshall Space Flight Center. In B.Y. Kang & J.U. Choi (Eds.) *Proceedings of the Second International Conference of the Decision Sciences Institute, Vol. 2, Managing the Global Economy: A Decision Sciences Perspective* (pp. 606-608), Seoul, Korea: Sungrim Press.

Moynihan, G. P. (1993b). An executive information system: Planning for post-implementation at NASA. *Journal of Systems Management, 44*(7), 8-31.

Negash, S., & Gray, P. (2003). Business intelligence. In *9th American Conference on Information Systems* (pp. 3190-3199).

Rainer, R. K., & Watson, H. J. (1995). The keys to executive information systems success. *Journal of Management Information Systems, 12*(2), 83-98.

Rockart, J. F., & DeLong, D. W. (1988). *Executive Support Systems: The Emergence of Top Management Computer Use.* Homewood, IL: Down Jones-Irwin.

Rockart, J. F., & Treacy, M. E. (1982). The CEO goes on-line. *Harvard Business Review, 60*(1), 84-88.

Turban, E., & Aronson, J. (2001). *Decision Support Systems and Intelligent Systems.* Upper Saddle River, NJ: Prentice Hall.

Umble, E. J., Haft, R. R., & Umble, M. M. (2003). Enterprise resource planning: implementation procedures and critical success factors. *European Journal of Operational Research*, 146(2), 241-257.

Walstrom, K. A., & Wilson, R. L. (1997). An examination of executive information system (EIS) users. *Information and Management, 32*(1), 75-83.

Walters, B. A., Jiang, J. J., & Klein, G. (2003). Strategic information and strategic decision making: the EIS/CEO interface in smaller manufacturing companies. *Information and Management, 40*(6), 487-495.

Watson, H., Rainer, R. K., & Koh, C. (1993). Executive information systems: a framework for development and a survey of current practices. *MIS Quarterly, 17*(3), 13-29.

Watson, H. J., & Carte, T. A. (2000). Executive information systems in government organizations. *Public Productivity and Management Review, 23*(3), 371-382.

KEY TERMS

Critical Success Factors (CSFs): A relatively small number of easily identified operational goals that are believed to ensure the success of an organization.

Drill Down Capability: EIS capability to display details of summary-level information by allowing the pointing and clicking on a specific data field for which the user desires an additional level of detail. As a result, the components of that data field are then displayed

Enterprise Information System: The linkage of EIS and ERP to provide an organization-wide system that provides consistent and integrated managerial information from a company point of view.

Executive Dashboard (also referred to as executive scorecard): Top-level EIS screen that provides a single-screen display of relevant and critical business metrics and/or statuses.

Executive Information System (EIS): Computer-based system designed to support the informational needs of senior management.

Executive Support System (ESS): Often synonymous with executive information system, it connotes an expansion of basic EIS functionality to include extended communication support often through inclusion of office automation and external data access.

Key Performance Indicators (KPIs): Specific measures of critical success factors.

Management Reporting System (MRS): Early effort to address executive requirements by automating data acquisition from a wide variety of corporate systems and databases, and providing online output in the form of fixed-format reports.

Section II
Enterprise Systems:
Risks, Performance, and Business Value

Chapter VII
Enterprise Resource Planning System Risks and Rewards

Joseph Bradley
University of Idaho, USA

ABSTRACT

Enterprise Resource Planning systems have proven difficult and costly to implement. Organizations must consider the risks and rewards of embarking on complex and time consuming implementation projects. This chapter explores why firms adopt ERP systems, identifies the benefits firms seek, discusses the various risks firms face as they adopt these systems, and suggests ways firms can manage these risks.

INTRODUCTION

As global business markets become increasingly competitive, firms look to technology to manage and improve their performance. Timely and accurate information is a key to gaining performance efficiency. Many firms have implemented Enterprise Resource Planning systems ("ERP") to meet these objectives. ERP systems are complex, off-the-shelf software packages that claim to meet the information needs of organizations. These systems replace hard to maintain solutions created by IS departments or older off-the-shelf packages that often provided only piecemeal solutions to an organization's information needs. ERP systems evolved in the early 1990s from material requirements planning systems ("MRP") and manufacturing resources planning systems ("MRP II"). MRP dealt with material planning and control. MRP II dealt with scheduling and planning a firm's manufacturing resources. ERP systems serve the entire enterprise, not just manufacturing and inventory control as with its predecessors. ERP integrates information for the entire organization in a single database. But ERP implementations are often complex and experience serious problems (Liang et al., 2007; Xue et al., 2005). Failures, abandoned projects and general dissatisfaction have been well publicized in the business press. ERP systems are "expensive and difficult to implement, often imposing their own logic on a company's strategy and existing culture (Pozzebon, 2000, p. 1015)." Muscatello and Parente (2006) cite ERP failure rates to be as high as 50%.

BACKGROUND

Three characteristics distinguish ERP implementations from other IT projects (Somers, Ragowsky, Nelson, & Stern, 2001).

- ERP systems are "profoundly complex pieces of software, and installing them requires large investments of money, time and expertise (Davenport, 1998, p. 122)."
- Software packages may require changes in business processes and procedure, may induce customization, and leave the implementing firm dependent on a vendor for support and updates (Lucas, Walton, & Ginsberg, 1988).
- The adopting firm is usually required to reengineer its business processes. As a result, the project must be managed as a broad program of organizational change rather than a software implementation (Markus & Tanis, 2000; Somers et al., 2001).

Despite these risks, global firms were spending $10 billion on ERP software and another $10 billion on consultants to implement the systems in the late 1990s (Davenport, 1998). An AMR study expected firms to spend $47 billion on ERP packages in 2001 (Cotteleer, 2002). Large sums are still being spent on ERP implementation projects. A Forrester survey found that ERP and enterprise applications remained "the top IT spending priority for 2005 (Hamerman & Wang, 2006)." A summer 2005 survey of members of the Society for Information Management (SIM) showed that ERP is among the top six application concerns of its members (Luftman et al., 2006). Hunter and Lippert (2007) forecast the ERP market to reach $US 1 trillion by 2010.

This article discusses the benefits firms expect to realize by adopting ERP systems, why some firms do not adopt these systems, risks associated with ERP implementation, some well publicized ERP failures, risk management tools and future trends in ERP implementation.

BENEFITS; WHY DO FIRMS ADOPT ERP?

Firms adopt ERP systems for both technical and business reasons. Technical reasons include: reducing systems operating costs, solving specific problems, such as Y2K, accommodating increased system capacity, and solving maintenance problems with legacy systems. Business reasons may include: presenting a single face to the customer, quoting realistic delivery times, accommodating business growth, improvement of business processes, standardization of data, reduction of inventory carrying costs, and elimination of delays in filling orders (Markus & Tanis, 2000).

The rapid growth of the commercial market for ERP is attributed to the following factors (Watson & Schneider, 1999):

- Use of the popular client/server platform,
- Can be used as an enabler for reengineering projects,
- Y2K compliant,
- Marketed to CEO's and CFO's as "strategic solutions" rather than as transaction processing software, and
- A way to outsource a significant part of the IS function.

Advantages of ERP systems include (Rashid, Hossain, & Patrick, 2002):

- Reliable information access by using a single database.
- Avoiding multiple data entries, reducing cost and improving accuracy.
- Delivery and cycle time reduction minimizing delays in reporting.
- Cost reduction including time saving and improved controls.
- Easy adaptability with business process options based on best practices easy to adapt.
- Improved scalability.
- Improved maintenance with long-term vendor contracts.
- Global outreach with extensions to modules such as CRM and SCM.
- E-commerce and e-business capabilities.

An example of a decision to adopt an ERP system is provided by Geneva Pharmaceuticals, a manufacturer of generic drugs. Faced with eroding margins and continuing price pressure, the existing systems were proving inadequate. Data shared across business units had to be re-keyed resulting in frequent errors. Data was locked in "functional silos" and did not support new processes. Geneva adopted ERP to solve the following problems (Bhattacherjee, 2000, p. 12):

- Implement best practices in business processes,
- Integrate data across business units (hence reduce re-keying and maintenance costs),
- Enforce data standardization (to reduce software maintenance costs),
- Integrate well with new technologies or systems of acquired companies,
- Provide scalability with growing product and customer base, and
- Be Y2K (year 2000) compliant.

A survey of Fortune 1000 firms identified organizational changes following ERP implementations, including (Jones & Young, 2006):

- Greater collaboration among functional areas in divisions,
- Reorganization of processes,
- Greater integration of processes across the organization,
- Reduced silo behavior within divisions of the organization,
- Reduced costs of operations,
- Reduced silo behaviors across the organization,
- Greater collaboration across divisions of the organization, and
- Greater integration of processes within divisions.

In addition, Jones and Young (2006) found people have a better view of the big picture, utilize more teamwork, and are more receptive to change.

Shang and Seddons (2000) developed a comprehensive framework for classifying benefits of ERP systems. They identified five major classifications of benefits: operational, managerial, strategic, IT infrastructure and organizational. Components of the Shang & Seddons framework are listed below.

Operational benefits include cost reduction, cycle time reduction, productivity improvement, quality improvement and customer services improvement.

Managerial benefits which accrue from ERP centralized data base and build in analytic tools include better resource management, improved decision making and planning, and performance improvement.

Strategic benefits include support of business growth, support of business alliances, building business innovations, building cost leadership, generating product differentiation, building external linkages with supply chain partners. An example of supporting business growth is the case of Smith Bits and Services. An Oracle ERP system enabled this manufacturer and distributor of drilling bits and related products and services to absorb 32 acquisitions in a 24 month period, something that would have been impossible with its legacy software (Bradley, 2004).

IT infrastructure benefits include building business flexibility, IT cost reduction, and increased IT infrastructure capability. A benefit of the ERP implementation at MI Drilling, a Houston based energy services company, was to make IT costs more scaleable and less subject to the necessity of layoff and hiring cycles as demand for the company's products fluctuated (Bradley, 2004).

Organizational benefits include support of organizational changes, facilitation of business learning, empowerment, and building of common visions.

The timing of benefits from ERP implementation may be delayed for some time after the implementation. Nicolaou (2004) cites a Benchmarking Partners report that indicates "synergies of people, process, and technology" reach their peak 9 to 24 months after implementation following periods of productivity decline and skills development. Hunton et al. (2003) found that financial performance differed little between ERP adopting firms and non adopters until two years after adoption of ERP. Shang and Seddons (2002) found ERP operational, managerial, strategic, IT infrastructure and organizational benefits were realized 2-3 years after implementation.

With the identification of the prospective benefits of ERP, why have some firms not adopted ERP?

WHY DO FIRMS NOT ADOPT ERP?

Markus and Tanis (2000) identified three very broad categories of reasons why firms that oth-erwise have all or some of the reasons to adopt ERP systems, do not adopt it or only adopt ERP in part. These firms may adopt only certain modules and rely on legacy systems or new custom systems for their needs. Other firms may begin an implementation only to discontinue it for a variety of reasons. The reason for this non-adoption or partial adoption can be categorized as follows:

1. Lack of feature-function fit,
2. Company growth, strategic flexibility and decentralized decision-making, and
3. Availability of alternatives to increase systems integration.

Lack of feature-function fit may be due to the design of most ERP for discrete manufacturing. Many companies have specialized processes common to their industry, which may not be solved by the best practices embedded in ERP systems. The various modules may not fully support process manufacturing industries, such as food processing and paper manufacturing, project industries, such as aerospace, or industries that manufacture products with dimensionality, such as clothing or footwear (Markus & Tanis, 2000). Although as the ERP market becomes saturated, vendors are designing packages for industries that were previously viewed as too complex.

Companies concerned with maintaining rapid growth rates, those needing strategic flexibility and those without a top down decision making style may be non-adopters or partial adopters of ERP systems. Dell Computer Corp. planned full implementation of SAP R/3 but discontinued the implementation after installing the human resource module. Dell's CIO expressed concern with the software's ability to keep pace with Dell's extraordinary growth rate. Visio, a software company subsequently acquired by Microsoft, expressed concern with the ability of SAP to handle the frequent changes it required to its sales analysis and commission requirements (Markus & Tanis, 2000, p. 29).

The experiences of Dell and Visio focus on the need for efficiency and flexibility in dealing with the external environment and internal processes. In a stable environment, mechanistic structures are appropriate consisting of "high degrees of standardization, formalization, specialization and hierarchy (Newell, Huang, Galliers, & Pan, 2003)." In a dynamic environment, organic structures are needed to enable organizations to be flexible to change products, processes and structures. In these organizations low levels of standardization, formalization, specialization and hierarchy are most appropriate. ERP may maximize organizational efficiency at the cost of flexibility (Newell et al., 2003). The result may be an inability to respond quickly to changes in the environment, reducing the firm's competitiveness.

Organizational culture may also be a factor in non-adoption or partial adoption of ERP systems. Kraft Foods Inc. was highly decentralized but slowly moving to a one-company philosophy. ERP was regarded as culturally inappropriate with this strategy (Markus & Tanis, 2000).

Lean enterprises succeed "as a growth strategy for increasing sales by trimming the company's product delivery system into a competitive weapon (Bradford & Mayfield, 2001)." Lean enterprises have difficulty using ERP systems due to the lack of flexibility. "ERP creates many nonvalue-added transactions by making companies track every activity and material price in the factory. This is counter to Lean philosophy, which aims at speeding up and smoothing production (Bradford & Mayfield, 2001, p. 30)."

Alternatives to ERP systems include data warehousing technologies that integrate data from source systems for query and analysis. These systems, sometimes described as "poor man's ERP," are limited by the quality of the underlying source systems (Markus & Tanis, 2000). In 1993 Great Atlantic & Pacific Tea Company, Inc. completed a supply chain and business process infrastructure based on a "robust data warehousing capacity for category management and other grocery-specific functionality (Retek, 2003)."

Other problems identified with implementation of ERP include time, expense, vendor dependence, and complexity.

RISKS ASSOCIATED WITH ERP IMPLEMENTATION

Implementing ERP can be a risky proposition for firms. Brown and Vessey (2003) observe "although failures to deliver projects on time and within budget were an old IT story, enterprise systems held even higher risks - they could be a 'bet-our-company' type of failure (Brown & Vessey, 2003, p. 65)."

Markus (2000) proposes 10 categories of IT related risks, all of which would apply to ERP systems:

Financial risk	Non-use, underuse, misuse risk
Technical risk	Internal abuse
Project risk	External risk
Political risk	Competitive risk
Contingency risk	Reputational risks

"IT-related risk includes anything related to IT that could have significant negative effects on the business or its environment from the perspective of an executive investing in IT (Markus, 2000)."

Some firms may be averse to the risks an ERP implementation can create. Scott (2003) discusses some of the risks identified by Markus (2000). He describes project risks, information systems risks, organizational risks, and external risks in ERP implementations.

Project risks stem from the customization of purchased packages and the difficulty of interfacing with legacy systems. When firms believe their business process are unique, they may customize ERP software instead of adopting best practices imbedded in a standard implementation. Data conversion can also be a problem when firms do not clean up their data before embarking on a project. After implementing SAP, Halliburton reported that inventory accuracy stood at less than 80% (Anderson, 2003). Project leadership, limiting project scope, avoiding customization, and a phased implementation (rollout) can minimize this risk (Scott, 2003).

Information systems risks arise from system performance problems. ERP systems may be poorly configured or the hardware may need upgrading. Another risk arises when the use of multiple vendors creates the need for multiple interfaces. Multiple vendors contributed to the problems in the Hershey Food Corporation implementation. Information systems risks can be minimized by avoiding customization, use of data warehousing for reports and queries and avoiding multivendor implementations (Scott, 2003).

Organizational risks of a bad ERP implementation can impact the firm's operating profits. Customer deliveries can be delayed putting customer relationships at risk. Impacts can be with customers, financial performance, or internal business objectives. Organizational risks can be minimized with training and strong leadership, which assures that sufficient resources are allocated to the project and inspires employees who may resist the implementation (Scott, 2003).

External risks center on litigation associated with the implementation. Firms with implementation problems may sue consultants and/or ERP vendors. Overbilling by consultants and use of incompetent trainees have been sources of litigation (Scott, 2003). Gore-Tex claims its consultant promised expert staff and delivered incompetent trainees. Managing consultants by specifying goals and individual competence of consultants can minimize this risk (MacDonald, 1999).

Political risk occurs "if a dominant coalition attempts to use the ERP package as a means by which to impose its views on other functional areas" (O'Gorman, 2004, p. 25). A case study at an international energy supplies company, where the ERP implementation was dominated by the financial management of the business, left the sup-

ply chain management function without the tools they believed they needed (Bradley, 2005).

A survey of members of the Chinese Enterprise Resource Planning Society identified the top ten ERP risk factors as follows (Huang, Chang, Li, & Lin, 2004):

- Lack of senior management commitment to the project,
- Ineffective communication with users,
- Insufficient training of end-users,
- Failure to get user support,
- Lack of effective project management methodology,
- Attempting to build bridges to legacy applications,
- Conflicts between user departments,
- The composition of project team members,
- Fail to redesign business processes, and
- Unclear/misunderstanding changing requirements.

Competitive Advantage. Another reason for non-adoption may be that a standard software package available to all potential purchasers may reduce a firm's competitive advantage. A resource-based view of the firm assumes that the individual firm's unique collection of resources and capabilities are a potential source of competitive advantage. Capabilities leading to competitive advantage may be embedded in current business processes.

To create competitive advantage such capabilities must be valuable, rare, costly to imitate and non-substitutable. "Valuable and rare organizational resource can only be sources of *sustained* competitive advantage if firms that do not possess these resources cannot readily obtain them" (Barney, 1991, p. 107). An off-the-shelf ERP package may be costly, but would not be rare or costly to imitate. Adoption of ERP packages based on "best practices" may cause the loss of the unique and valuable advantage imbedded in current business processes. A case study showed that:

...the introduction of SAP-specific business routines can threaten established core, enabling and supplemental capabilities and related knowledge sets. The integration of SAP's embedded business routines and reporting functionality contributed to the creation of (a) highly rigid reporting structures; (b) inflexible managerial decision-making routines; and (c) reduced autonomy on the factory floor... (Butler & Pyke, 2004, pp. 167-8).

WELL PUBLICIZED FAILURES AND PROBLEMS

Numerous descriptions of ERP failures have appeared in the business press. The experience of serious problems at many well run, well-financed firms may be enough to discourage some firms from beginning an ERP implementation.

Hershey Foods embarked on an ERP investment in mid-1996 to solve its Y2K problems and improve its ability to perform just-in-time store deliveries to its customers (Severance & Passino, 2002). After spending $112 million on an ERP project, Hershey Foods Corporation was unable to fill Halloween candy orders in October 1999, resulting in a 19% drop in third quarter profits (Stedman, 1999). As a result of Hershey's problems its stock price fell by a third and the firm lost market share to Mars and Nestle (Severance & Passino, 2002). Hershey estimates it suffered a 3% permanent decrease in market share from this experience (Sutton, 2003).

Nike's ERP implementation is included in a listing of "infamous failures in IT project management" (Nelson, 2007). Major ERP related inventory problems at Nike resulted in a profit drop of $100 million in the 3rd quarter of 2000.

A study by the PA Consulting Group found that "92% of companies are dissatisfied with results achieved to date from their ERP implementation and only 8% achieved a positive improvement in their performance ("ERP Implementation Disappoints Companies," 2000)."

Davenport (1998) identifies several unsuccessful implementation efforts:

- Fox-Meyer Drug claims that an ERP system led to its bankruptcy.
- Mobil Europe spent hundreds of millions on ERP, but abandoned the project when a merger partner objected.
- Dell found that its ERP system did not support its new decentralized management style.
- Applied Materials gave up on its ERP implementation when it became overwhelmed with the organizational changes it required.

ERP success stories receive much less publicity.

MANAGING RISKS

ERP vendors have tried to overcome the concern of potential clients by developing tools to assess and manage risks associated with ERP implementation. Risk management as a process should (Zafiropoulos, Metaxiotis, & Askounis, 2005):

- Identify the context and criteria of the risk
- Identify the risks
- Determine the significance of each risk
- Identify, select and implement risk management options
- Monitor and review the corrective options

These risk management systems allow project managers to make more realistic cost and time estimates to help avoid problems during implementation. Zafiropoulos et al. (2005) found that the use of a generic risk management tool they developed provided a structured way to assess risks, better integrated the use of consultants, improved communications between consultants and the project manager, led to more realistic time planning, and reduced the impact of problems when they occurred since the problems were expected and part of the project planning.

CRITICAL SUCCESS FACTORS

Practitioners and academics have attempted to reduce the risk of ERP projects and improve the ability of firms to successfully implement ERP by identifying the factors critical to implementation success. Critical Success Factors (CSFs) are defined as "the few key areas of activity in which favorable results are absolutely necessary for a particular manager to reach his goals" (Bullen & Rockart, 1981, p. 383).

Nah (2001) reviewed ten articles written by academics and practitioners between 1998 and 2000 discussing "What are the key critical factors for ERP implementation success?" These articles discussed eleven critical success factors listed in Table 1 together with the number of articles discussing each of the factors. Nah did not distinguish whether empirical research, case studies or other methods determined the factors mentioned.

Brown and Vessey (2003) identify five critical success factors based on case studies of a dozen ERP implementations. The five factors are:

- Top management is engaged, not just involved
- Project leaders are veterans and team members are decision makers
- Third parties fill gaps in expertise and transfer their knowledge
- Change management goes hand-in-hand with project management
- A satisficing mindset prevails.

Bradley (2005, 2004) examined ten CSFs proposed in IT and ERP literature in a multiple case study of eight implementation projects and identified three factors related to successful project but not to unsuccessful projects.

- Choosing the right full-time project manager
- Quantity and quality of training
- Project champions

ERP risks will likely be reduced by following these and other CSF factors examined by practitioners and academic researchers (Pinto and Slevin, 1987; Laughlin, 1999).

FUTURE TRENDS

The Gartner Group coined the term "ERP II" to describe a shift in ERP from an enterprise information base to moving information across the supply chain ("Taking the Pulse of ERP," 2001). New risks and challenges will be faced by organizations opening up information systems to supply chain partners. Supply chain partners could be potential competitors or pass information to existing competitors. Resolving trust issues will be a key factor in the advancement of ERP II. Gartner does not expect to see ERP II systems fully deployed before 2005 ("Taking the Pulse of ERP," 2001).

Davenport and Brooks (2004) discuss the need for both infrastructural and strategic capabilities in the organization. ERP or Enterprise Systems provide core functionality but are expensive and time consuming to implement. "These infrastructural capabilities provide very little in the way of real business value (p. 13)." These systems do not provide "short-term cost savings or other competitive advantage (p. 13)." In contrast, SCM applications provide "strategic, competitively-oriented capabilities (p. 13)" which can reduce inventories and improve customer service. Firms beginning to build infrastructure with ERP systems may run out of time and money, neglecting the strategic supply chain management systems (Davenport & Brooks, 2004).

Along with the benefits describe above, ERP II brings significant new risks. Most Interorga-

Table 1. Nah's critical success factors (Adapted from Nah et al., 2001)

Critical Factor	No of articles mentioning
ERP teamwork and composition • ERP project should be the teams top priority • The teams workload should be manageable • Incentives for successful implementation	8
Change management program and culture • A culture of shared values is conducive to success	7
Top management support • Align with strategic business goals • Tie management bonuses to project success • Top management priority	6
Business plan and vision • Tie project to specific business model	6
BPR and minimum customization • Willingness to change business to fit software • Software should not be modified	6
Effective communications • Management of communications, education and expectations critical	5
Project management • Individual or group should be given responsibility for success • Plan with well-defined tasks and accurate estimation of effort	5
Software development, testing and trouble shooting • Appropriate choice of system functionality and links to legacy systems • Work with vendors and consultants to resolve software problems	5
Monitoring and evaluation of performance • Measurement against completion dates • Monitoring through milestones and targets • Management needs information on effect of project on business processes	5
Project champion • Oversee entire life cycle of project • High level executive sponsor • Business leader should be in charge	4
Appropriate business and IT legacy systems • Stable and successful business setting is essential	2

nizational communication involves web services. Swart et al. (2007) identify some of these risks by interviews with vendors, consultants and CIOs. Using a supply chain partnership model, risks are identified.

• Once a supply chain partner has access to a system the partner could explore other data. Security features tend to be added on, rather than built into these systems.

• Few organizations plan for the dissolution of a partnership and how to remove an organization.

• Companies tend not to invest in the resources necessary to protect their data. Conversely, if they do invest it may send a message to the partner that they are not trusted, impacting the partnership in other way.

• Once partner access is added, from a network security view the IT systems are merged into a unified system enabling participant organizations access to the system.

Another trend in ERP systems is that small and mid-sized enterprises ("SMEs") will become leading adopters of ERP system as the large company market becomes saturated. Vendors are developing less expensive versions of their software to appeal to the SME market.

CONCLUSION

ERP implementation projects continue to present risks to adopting organizations. Continuing ERP spending demonstrates that most organizations have concluded that the benefits resulting from such implementations outweigh the substantial risks and cost of ERP systems. Perhaps the risks of not adopting ERP are determined to be greater than the risks faced by adopters. The prospect of extending ERP beyond organizational boundaries to supply chain partners makes ERP even more attractive and possibly more risky. Organizations will continue to adopt ERP as a strategic necessity to remain competitive in their industry, but few, if any, will gain any sustainable competitive advantage by adopting ERP.

REFERENCES

Anderson, A. (2003). *When Closeness Counts*. Retrieved Dec. 23, 2003, from http://www.datasweep.com/ds/2003/article_2003.asp?page_id=newsln_002print

Barney, J. (1991). Firm resources and sustained competitive advantage. *Journal of Management, 17*(1), 99-120.

Bhattacherjee, A. (2000). Beginning SAP R/3 Implementation at Geneva Pharmaceuticals. *Communications of the Association for Information Systems, 4*(2).

Bradford, M., & Mayfield, T. (2001). Does ERP Fit in a LEAN World? *Strategic Finance, 82*(11), 28-34.

Bradley, J (2004). *Enterprise Resource Planning Success: A Management Theory Approach to Critical Success Factors*. Doctoral Dissertation, Claremont Graduate University, UMI No. 3139266.

Bradley, J. (2005). Are all critical success factors created equal? In *Proceedings of the 11th Americas' Conference on Information Systems,* Atlanta (pp. 2152-2159). Omaha, NE: Association for Information Systems.

Brown, C. V., & Vessey, I. (2003). Managing the Next Wave of Enterprise Systems: Leveraging Lessons from ERP. *MIS Quarterly Executive, 2*(1), 65-77.

Bullen, C. V., & Rockart, J. F. (1981, June). Appendix: *A primer on critical success factors*. In Rockart, J. F., & Bullen, C.V. (Eds.), The Rise of Managerial Computing, 383-423. Homewood, IL. Dow-Jones-Irwin.

Butler, T., & Pyke, A. (2004). Examining the influence of ERP systems on firm-specific knowledge assets and capabilities. In F. Adam & D. Sammon (Eds.), The enterprise resource planning decade: Lessons learned and issues for the future (pp. 167-206), Hershey, PA: Idea Group Publishing.

Cotteleer, M. J. (2002). *An Empirical Study of Operational Performance Convergence Following Enterprise-IT Implementation* (Working Paper No. 03-011): Harvard Business School.

Davenport, T. H. (1998). Putting the Enterprise into the Enterprise System. *Harvard Business Review, 76*(4, July-August), 121-131.

Davenport, T. H., & Brooks, J. D. (2004). Enterprise Systems and the Supply Chain. *Journal of Enterprise Information Management, 17*(1), 8-19.

Drucker, P. F. (1973). Management: Tasks, Responsibilities, Practices (Harper Colophon 1985 Ed.). New York: Harper Row.

ERP Implementation Disappoints Companies. (2000, August 31). *Australian Banking & Finance, 9,* 8.

Hall, D., & Hulett, D. (2002). *Universal Risk Project: Final Report, February 2002.* Milford, NH: PMI Risk SIG.

Hamerman, P., & Wang, R. (2006). ERP: Still a Challenge after All These Years, Enterprise Applications, Jan 29, 2006, p. 1-2 Downloaded on Sept. 25, 2006 from http://www.networkcomputing.com/gswelcome/showArticle.jhtml?articleID=177104905.

Huang, S.-M., Chang, I.-C., Li, S.-H., & Lin, M.-T. (2004). Assessing risk in ERP projects: identify and prioritize the factors. *Industrial Management & Data Systems, 104*(8/9), 681-688.

Hunter, M. G., & Lippert, S. K. (2007). *Critical Success Factors of ERP Implementation.* Paper presented at the Information Resources Management Conference, Vancouver, BC, Canada.

Hunton, J. E., Lippincott, B., & Reck, J. L. (2003). Enterprise resource planning systems: comparing firm performance of adopters and nonadopters. *International Journal of Enterprise Information Systems,* 4(2003), 165-184.

Jones, M. C., & Young, R. (2006). ERP Usage in Practice. *Information Resources Management Journal, 19*(1), 23-42.

Liang, H., Saraf, N., Hu, Q., & Xue, Y. (2007). Assimilation of enterprise systems: The effect of institutional pressures and the mediating role of top management, *MIS Quarterly,* 31(1), 59-87.

Lucas, H. C., Jr., Walton, E. J., & Ginsberg, M. J. (1988). Implementing Packaged Software. *MIS Quarterly*(December 1988), 537-549.

Luftman, J., Kempaiah, R., & Nash, E. (2006). Key issues for IT executives 2005. *MIS Quarterly Executive, 5*(2), 81-99.

MacDonald, E. (1999, Nov. 2). W. L. Gore Alleges PeopleSoft, Deloitte Botched a Costly Software Installation. *The Wall Street Journal,* 14.

Markus, M. L., & Tanis, C. (2000). The Enterprise Experience - From Adoption to Success. In R. W. Zmud (Ed.), *Framing the Domains of IT Research: Projecting the Future through the Past.* Cincinnati, OH: Pinnaflex Educational Resources, Inc.

Muscatello, J. R., & Parente, D. H. (2006). Enterprise Resource Planning (ERP): A Postimplementation Cross-Case Analysis. *Information Resources Management Journal,* 19(3), 61-80.

Nah, F. F.-H., Lau, J. L.-S., & Kuang, J. (2001). Critical Factors for Successful Implementation of Enterprise Systems. *Business Process Management, 7*(3), 285-296.

Nelson, R. R. (2007). IT Project Management: Infamous Failures, Classic Mistakes and Best Practices. *MIS Quarterly Executive,* 6(2), 67-78.

Newell, S., Huang, J. C., Galliers, R. D., & Pan, S. L. (2003). Implementing enterprise resource planning and knowledge management systems in tandem: fostering efficiency and innovation complementarity. *Information and Organization, 13,* 25-52.

Nicolaou, A. I. (2004). Quality of postimplementation review for enterprise resource planning systems. *International Journal of Accounting Information Systems, 5*(2004), 25-49.

O'Gorman, B. (2004). The road to ERP: Has industry learned or revolved back to the start? In F. Adams & D. Sammon (Eds.), *The enterprise resource planning decade: Lessons learned and issues for the future* (pp. 22-46). Hershey, PA: Idea Group Publishing.

Pozzebon, M. (2000). *Combining a Structuration Approach with a Behavioral-Based Model to Investigate ERP Usage.* Paper presented at the AMCIS 2000, Long Beach, CA.

Rashid, M. A., Hossain, L., & Patrick, J. D. (2002). The Evolution of ERP Systems: A Historical Perspective. In F. F.-H. Nah (Ed.), *Enterprise Resource Planning Solutions & Management* (pp. 35-50). Hershey, PA: IRM Press.

Retek (2003). *A&P Completes Supply Chain/Business Process Initiative: IBM and Retek Deliver Enterprise Merchandising Solutions.* Retrieved March 13, 2004, from http://www.retek.com/press/press.asp?id/id=507

Scott, J. (2003). What risks does an organization face from an ERP implementation? In D. R. Laube & R. F. Zammuto (Eds.), *Business Driven Information Technology: Answers to 100 Critical Questions for Every Manager* (pp. 274-278). Stanford: Stanford Business Books.

Severance, D. G., & Passino, J. (2002). *Making I/T Work.* San Francisco: Jossey-Bass.

Shang, S., & Seddon, P (2000). A Comprehensive Framework for Classifying the Benefits of ERP Systems. Proceedings of the Americas' Conference for Information Systems. Long Beach, CA, 1005-14.

Shang, S., & Seddon, P.B. (2002). Assessing and managing the benefits of enterprise systems: the business manager's perspective. *Information Systems Journal*, 12, 271-299.

Somers, T. M., Ragowsky, A. A., Nelson, K. G., & Stern, M. (2001). *Exploring Critical Success Factors across the Enterprise Systems Experience Cycle: An Empirical Study* (Working Paper). Detroit, Michigan: Wayne State University.

Stedman, C. (1999, November 1). Failed ERP Gamble Haunts Hershey: Candy maker bites off more than it can chew and 'Kisses' big Halloween sales goodbye. *Computer World,* 1.

Swart, R.S., Marshall, B.A., Olsen, D.H., & Erbacher, R. (2007). ERP II System Vulnerabilities and Threats: An Exploratory Study. In M. Khosrow-Pour (ed.), Managing Worldwide Operations and Communications with Information Technology, (pp. 925-8). Hershey, PA: IGI Global.

Sutton, S. (2003). Keynote Address, AIS Educator Meeting. Copper Mountain, CO.

Taking the Pulse of ERP. (2001). *Modern Materials Handling, 56*(2), 44-51.

Watson, E. E., & Schneider, H. (1999). Using ERP in Education. *Communications of the Association for Information Systems, 1*, Article 9.

Xue, Y., Liang, H., Boulton, W.R., & Snyder, C. A. (2005). ERP implementation failures in China: Case studies with implications for ERP vendors. *International Journal of Production Economics*, 97(3), 279-295.

Zafiropoulos, I., Metaxiotis, K., & Askounis, D. (2005). Dynamic risk management systems for modeling, optimal adaption and implementation of an ERP system. *Information Management & Computer Security, 13*(2/3), 212-234.

KEY TERMS

Critical Success Factors (CSFs): Bullen and Rockart (1981) define critical success factors (CSFs) as "the few key areas of activity in which favorable results are absolutely necessary for a particular manager to reach his goals." Successful managers must focus their scarcest resource, their time, "on those things that make a difference between success and failure" (p. 389). The concept of critical success factors is consistent with a Drucker (1973) statement: "One has to control by controlling a few developments which can have significant impact on performance and results."

Enterprise Resource Planning Systems (ERP): An off-the-shelf accounting-oriented information system that meets the information needs of most organizations. A complex and expensive information tool to meet the needs of an organization to procure, process and deliver customer goods or services in a timely, predictable manner.

ERP II: Gartner group coined this expression to describe opening up ERP systems beyond the enterprise level to exchange information with supply chain partners. ERP II extends beyond the four-walls of the business to trading partners. ERP II includes supply chain management (SCM) applications, customer relationship management (CRM) applications, and e-commerce applications. ERP II is also referred to as extended enterprise systems.

IT-Related Risk: This risk includes "anything related to IT that could have significant negative effects on the business or its environment from the perspective of an executive investing in IT". (Markus, 2000).

Legacy Systems: Transaction processing systems that are designed to perform specific tasks. These systems usually involve only a single functional area a business and are not integrated. Many legacy systems become outdated as business needs change and the hardware and software available in the market place improved.

Material Requirements Planning Systems (MRP): Processes that use bills of materials, inventory data and a master productions schedule to time phase material requirement, releasing inventory purchases in a manner that reduces inventory investment yet meets customer requirements.

Manufacturing Resources Planning (MRPII): Extends MRP by addressing all resources in addition to inventory. MRPII links material requirements planning with capacity requirements planning avoiding over and under shop loading typical with MRP.

Risks: "A risk is a future event that may or may not occur. The probability of the future event occurring must be greater than 0% and less than 100%. The consequences of the future event must be unexpected or unplanned for" (Hall & Hulett, 2002).

Risk Management: A system designed to avoid "problems during a project, which can lead to deviation from project goals, timetables, and cost estimations (Zafiropoulos et al., 2005).

Chapter VIII
ERP–Driven Performance Changes and Process Isomorphism

Andrea Masini
London Business School, UK

ABSTRACT

After observing that the pervasiveness of IT may soon render it strategically irrelevant, management scholars have recently questioned the value of information technology. This chapter challenges the above view, contends that ERP investments may contribute to the achievement of improved business performance, and examines the conditions under which this contribution occurs. The panel analysis of a sample of SAP R/3 adopters provides several insights. First, it suggests that the ERP exerts a generalized positive impact on both productivity and profitability. Second, the results confirm that the widespread diffusion of best practices embedded in the software may limit the ability of firms to use ERP to effectively differentiate from competitors. However, they also suggest that, whilst in the long run the pervasive diffusion of standardized software may decrease its strategic value, in the short run early ERP adopters can profit from a window of opportunity to obtain above average returns.

INTRODUCTION

The rising level of competitiveness and the high degree of market turbulence of most industries induces business organizations to increase their investments in information technology (IT) to improve the efficiency and responsiveness of operations. Enterprise Resource Planning (ERP[1]) applications represent perhaps the most relevant example of this trend. ERP has become prevalent over the last few years, particularly in the manufacturing sector (Scott and Shepherd, 2002). Investments in this technology continue to grow steadily in all major markets. Compound annual growth rates for 2005 ranged from 5.2% for the Europe, Middle East and Africa market (EMEA) to 11.8% for the Asia-Pacific region (Pang and Eschinger, 2006).

While highly complex, risky, and often characterized by difficult implementations, ERP applications have a clear appeal: they generate internal operations benefits and help firms improve their competitiveness. Yet, in spite of their pervasive diffusion, the benefits of ERP are still uncertain (Vemuri and Palvia, 2006). The scale of ERP projects suggests that ERP deployment should have a significant and measurable effect on firm performance (Hitt et al., 2002). However, there is conflicting empirical evidence regarding the benefits of ERP investments (Hayes et al., 2001; Poston and Grabski, 2001; Hitt et al., 2002; Cotteleer and Bendoly, 2006; Wieder et al., 2006). A significant amount of heterogeneity also exists across firms, as large and mostly unexplained performance differences have been observed across ERP adopters (Mabert et al., 2003; Umble et al., 2003).

Although management scholars and practitioners have dedicated a significant amount of attention to study enterprise systems, several gaps still remain in the literature. First, whilst most studies have sought to establish whether a link exists between ERP adoption and performance, few scholars have analyzed the conditions under which this link occurs. One important aspect that has been often neglected is the issue of adoption timing. As a result of the increasing uncertainty and of the high cost of ERP implementation, most companies prefer to defer their ERP projects and wait for newer and less complex versions of the software. Yet, deferring implementation is also risky because it causes delays in the realization of operational improvements. Very little research has been conducted to shed light on this trade-off and help managers in making this decision.

A second important aspect that has been overlooked is the extent to which the pervasive diffusion of standardized business process templates embedded in the ERP software may reduce the ability of firms to differentiate from competitors. Some scholars have indeed questioned the strategic value of IT, arguing that as the technology can be easily imitated, it does not bring any long-term competitive advantage (Carr, 2003). A few anecdotal examples have been used to support this claim. However, to our knowledge, very few studies have provided sound empirically grounded evidence for this hypothesis.

Finally, with the relevant exception of Hitt et al. (2002), most empirical studies seeking to establish a link between ERP and performance were based on cross-section analyses. A cross-section model enables the researcher to verify whether such a link exists at a particular point in time. Yet, it does not allow for the analysis of the long-term implications of the phenomenon investigated. In the case of ERP systems, which often exert their benefits several years after implementation, this is clearly a limitation.

These observations constitute the point of departure for our study. We use a panel data analysis to shed further light on the relationship between ERP adoption and performance. The study has three specific objectives: i) to quantify the average impact of ES investments on both productivity and profitability; ii) to examine whether the timing of adoption affects this impact; iii) to examine whether the widespread diffusion of best practices embedded in the software creates business process isomorphism and presents risks for the achievement of long-term competitive advantage.

The remainder of this chapter is organized as follows. In section 2 we provide some background on Enterprise Systems. In section 3 we develop three sets of testable research hypotheses. In section 4 we describe the data and the econometric approach used to test the hypotheses. In sections 5 we present and discuss the results of our analysis. Finally, in section 6 we discuss the implications and some limitations of our study, and we identify some avenues for future research.

BACKGROUND

Enterprise Systems are one of the most representative information technology innovations appeared on the market in the past few years. They are large computer systems that – through a common database - integrate different application programs in many (possibly all) functions of the firm: accounting, sales, manufacturing, finance and human resource management.

Besides the important technical benefits they produce (increase of accuracy, homogeneity and timeliness of information within the organization), these systems also help organizations create business process competences. These competences are generated primarily during the implementation of the system, through various mechanisms: the redesign of processes in various functional areas, the customization of the software, or the integration of the business knowledge of internal business experts with the technical skills of external IT consultants (Hitt et al., 2002).

IT managers, software vendors, and information systems consultants provide numerous recipes for maximizing the success of ERP implementations. Yet, these recipes are often inconsistent. Some suggest that ERP should be considered as a strategic resource and therefore managed in-house, because implementation projects require process re-engineering efforts that facilitate the development of core process competences. Others stress that these benefits are minimal and that these projects should be outsourced to minimize costs (Ettlie et al., 2005). By the same token, some organizations report having successfully profited from ERP projects, streamlining business processes and promoting organizational changes (Davenport, 2000). Others argue that this strategy is potentially dangerous, because it combines the technical uncertainty of large IT projects with the organizational uncertainty of change-management programs.

Regardless of the specific implementation strategy adopted, ERP systems have the distinc-tive characteristic of becoming catalysts for business process re-engineering programs. This property is due to the fact that Enterprise Systems are organized around "best practices" or "reference models". These are generic built-in process templates contained in the software library that suggest an organization what the optimal process configuration and the most efficient resource allocation scheme(s) should be for the execution of a particular task. As a consequence of this particular structure, a firm that adopts an enterprise system is forced to analyze its business model, to map and codify its processes and, possibly, to re-configure them (either to eliminate possible bottlenecks that have emerged or simply to better match the process templates contained in the software library). This architectural reorganization is de facto a major business re-engineering process and one of the causes of the performance changes observed after the adoption of the system. It is also – as we will argue – a potential source of strategic risks because it may reduce the ability of an organization to differentiate its processes from those of its competitors.

IMPACT OF ERP ON BUSINESS PERFORMANCE

Direct Impact of ERP on Productivity and Profitability

Enterprise systems can impact business performance through various mechanisms. They can affect productivity by reducing operating costs. For instance, the centralization of IT applications and the replacement of fragmented legacy systems with a single integrated application can help firms reduce the time spent in planning, developing and maintaining and using the systems. The automation of business processes can help manufacturing companies decrease their production and distribution costs. ERP can also reduce infrastructure and capital costs and improve information quality, thereby promoting operational efficiency and management effectiveness (Salmela, 1997; Gupta and Kohli, 2006).

ERP can also exert an impact on revenue generating activities. For instance, it can leverage organizational competitiveness, by improving the way in which strategically valuable information is produced, shared and managed across functions and locations (Gupta and Kohli, 2006). Also, the increased interoperability across functions allows for faster new product development processes, while the ability to disseminate timely and accurate information translates into an improved capacity to match demand changes and better communication with customers (Davenport, 2000). Consistently with this view and with previous studies on the productivity and profitability impact of enterprise systems (Hitt et al., 2002) we propose therefore the following hypotheses:

- Hypothesis 1a: The adoption of ERP adoption exerts a positive impact on productivity
- Hypothesis 1b: The adoption of ERP adoption exerts a positive impact on profitability

The Role of Adoption Timing

Management scholars have recently observed that the pervasiveness of IT may soon render it strategically irrelevant (Carr, 2003). A direct consequence of this observation is that, in order to minimize the risk of starting costly projects that yield limited and uncertain returns, firms should postpone the adoption of IT innovations until the technology becomes sufficiently commoditized and well understood. This argument applies well to the case of enterprise systems, which are characterized by long and extremely expensive implementation projects. Yet, both the academic literature and some anecdotal examples demonstrate that a few organizations have been able to achieve significant advantages after adopting an

aggressive (i.e. innovative) stance with respect to ES adoption.

As a matter of fact, there are arguments for and against the occurrence of first mover advantages in ERP adoption. On the one hand, there are real efficiency gains from the ERP implementation because the system is a business process optimizer. Clearly, early adopters can enjoy these benefits for a longer period of time. Furthermore, early adoption can be a signal to the market. It can effectively differentiate companies with high quality processes from competitors and generate additional demand for firms that pursue this strategy. If early adopters meet customer expectations, reputation and trust increase even more, and further differentiate adopters from non-adopters in a self-reinforcing process similar to the one described in a Spence signaling model (Mas-Colell et al., 1995).

On the other hand, companies that defer ERP implementation may enjoy other types of benefits. The literature has noted the occurrence of important performance dips after ERP adoption (McAfee, 1999). As the number of ERP implementations increases, the technology becomes collectively better understood: ERP vendors may release newer and simpler versions of the software, while IT consultants devise more effective implementation strategies. As a result, late adopters typically face less risky and less expensive ERP projects. The combined effect of these benefits should reduce the magnitude and the duration of the performance dips usually observed after implementation.

We argue that the benefits associated with a deferred implementation are not large enough to offset the delays in the realization of the operational benefits produced by a late ERP adoption. Accordingly, we propose the following hypotheses:

- Hypothesis 2a: The positive effect of ERP on productivity is larger for early adopters than for late adopters

- Hypothesis 2b: The positive effect of ERP on profitability is larger for early adopters than for late adopters

Business Process Isomorphism and Decreasing Heterogeneity in Performance

In his often cited Harvard Business Review article, Nicolas Carr questioned the value of information technology as a strategic resource and suggested that the widespread diffusion of systems that can be easily imitated does not lead to the achievement of long term sustained advantage (Carr, 2003). This risk is particularly important in the case of enterprise systems because of the particular nature of the technology. The implementation of ERP usually forces the adopters to reengineer their business processes according to the templates embedded in the software (so-called "best practices"). The market for enterprise systems is extremely concentrated, with the five largest vendors enjoying more than 70% of the overall market in 2005 (Shepherd, et al., 2005). Clearly, the pervasive diffusion of a specific type of enterprise system from the same vendor generates business process isomorphism and reduces heterogeneity across firms. As a result, ERP adopters may not be able to rely on their business processes to effectively differentiate from their competitors. Therefore, even if on average ERP adoption is expected to exert a positive impact on performance, we expect post-ERP adoption performance to be converging among adopters as the number of adoptions increases. We propose therefore the following hypotheses:

- Hypothesis 3a: Differences in productivity across firms tend to decrease over time as the number of ERP adoptions increase
- Hypothesis 3b: Differences in profitability across firms tend to decrease over time as the number of ERP adoptions increase

METHODOLOGY AND ANALYTICAL ISSUES

Model Specification

Impact of ERP and ERP Adoption Timing on Performance

To test hypotheses 1-3 above, we examined the impact of ERP on two performance measures: productivity and profitability. Following Hitt et al.(2002), we employed two approaches to assess the impact on productivity. The first approach was based on the Cobb-Douglas production function, which relates value added (VA) to capital (K) and labor cost (L) through an exponential function: $VA = cK^\beta L^\alpha$. To estimate the effect of ERP adoption on productivity, we first linearized the Cobb Douglas function by taking log transformations on both sides and then added appropriate control and dummy variables as displayed in eq. 1:

$$(1)$$

$$ln(VA_{it}) = \beta_0 + \beta_1 ln(K_{it}) + \beta_2 ln(L_{it}) + \beta_3 ERP_{it} + \beta_4 rank_{it} + \sum_j \beta_j control_{jit} + \varepsilon$$

A first dummy variable, ERP_{it}, was introduced to reflect whether a company had or had not adopted an ERP at time t. Extant research has suggested that the impact of ERP on firm performance does not become evident until the system becomes fully operational (Hitt et al. 2002). In the ERP jargon this event is denoted by a specific date in the system life cycle: the ERP live date. Accordingly, we used this date to construct the dummy variable that indicates ERP adoption. At any given year t, and for any company i the dummy ERP_{it} was set equal to 0 if the company i's live date was smaller or equal than t and it was set equal to 0 otherwise.

To test whether the time of adoption created any first-adopter advantage we constructed a second dummy variable, $rank_{it}$, which indicates the year in which company i adopted the software relative to the other companies in the sample ($rank_{it} = 1$, 2, 3, etc... if company i adopted R/3 in the first, second, third... year of observation). We finally added year and industry dummies to control for differences in industries and for changes in the economic cycle[2]. The coefficient β_3 in eq. 1 was used to assess the impact of ERP adoption on firm output, whereas the coefficient β_4 indicated the impact of adoption timing.

In addition to the production function approach, we also analyzed the effect of ERP productivity by examining changes in revenue per employee. We regressed revenue against the number of employees, the ERP adoption dummy, the adoption timing dummy and the usual year and industry control variables (eq. 2). The impact of ERP adoption and ERP adoption timing on performance is indicated by the coefficients β_2 and β_3.

$$(2)$$
$$ln(\ Revenue_{it}\ ) = \beta_0 + \beta_1\ ln(\ Employees_{it}\ ) + \beta_2 ERP_{it} + \beta_3 rank_{it} + \sum_j \beta_j control_{jit} + \varepsilon$$

A second set of models was used to assess the impact of ERP on business profitability. The IS literature traditionally used ratios such as return on asset (ROA) and/or return on equity (ROE) as dependent variables to assess this impact (Hitt and Brynjolfsson, 1996). Hitt et al.(2002) proposed a slightly modified version of this approach, arguing that using the log of the numerator (profit before taxes) as dependent variable and the log of the denominator (total assets or equity) as independent variables allows for a more flexible model specification. Similarly to what discussed in the case of eq. 1 and eq. 2, this approach also allows for the incorporation of price deflation through year dummies. Following this approach, we used therefore the model specifications represented in eq. 3 and eq. 4 (for ROA and ROE, respectively). As usual, the coefficient β_2 and β_3 reflect the im-

pact of ERP adoption and ERP adoption timing on the two profitability measures.

$$(3)$$
$$ln(\ profit_{it}\ ) = \beta_0 + \beta_1\ ln(\ equity_{it}\ ) + \beta_2 ERP_{it} + \beta_3 rank_{it} + \sum_j \beta_j control_{jit} + \varepsilon$$

$$(4)$$
$$ln(\ profit_{it}\ ) = \beta_0 + \beta_1\ ln(\ assets_{it}\ ) + \beta_2 ERP_{it} + \beta_3 rank_{it} + \sum_j \beta_j control_{jit} + \varepsilon$$

Studies in this area have mostly used pooled OLS as estimation method. Yet, pooled OLS is inadequate to address firm heterogeneity and endogeneity issues, because it assumes there is neither serial correlation nor correlation between the error term and the regressors. This may cause inconsistent coefficient estimates. For example, firms with superior IT management tend to adopt ERP earlier. At the same time superior IT management may also contribute to improve performance as well. When this is the case, endogeneity issue arises because IT management quality is not observed and it is implicitly accounted for in the error term.

To avoid this problem, we estimated eq. 1-4 using a fixed effect model with a single error component structure $\varepsilon_{it} = \alpha_i + \eta_{it}$ (where η_{it} is iid). This approach takes effectively into account the above issue (a Hausman specification test rejected the random effect model and confirmed the potential endogeneity problem).

Business Process Isomorphism

A thorny problem in the evaluation of changes in performance differences occurring after ERP adoption is the measurement of performance heterogeneity. As sample variance is not a good measure (it is sensitive to outliers and to the measurement unit employed), we used an approach derived from the method developed by Dess and Beard (1984) to measure environmental turbulence.

We initially focused on the restricted sample of ERP adopters with the objective to examine whether the performance differences among these firms changed over time. For every performance measure of interest, we first conducted a cross sectional analysis. In each year t we estimated the model:

$$ln(PRN_i) = \beta_0 + \beta_1 ln(PRD_i) + \sum_j \beta_j control_j + \varepsilon$$

where PRN and PRD are the numerator and the denominator of the performance ratio of interest (Revenue per employee, ROA or ROE). A first performance heterogeneity measure *Perf_heterogeneity_1* was created by dividing the standard error of the coefficient estimate β_1 in the cross-section regression by the mean of the dependent variable, i.e.: *Perf_heterogeneity_1= StandErr(β_1)/Mean(PRN)*. In the second step we conducted a longitudinal analysis and estimated the model represented in eq. 5. The coefficient γ_1 was used to examine changes in performance heterogeneity and to test hypothesis 3.

$$\tag{5} Perf\_heterogeneity\_1_t = \gamma_0 + \gamma_1 year + \varepsilon$$

The above approach assumes that a large part of the remaining variance in firm performance is due to ERP adoption, which may not be necessarily true. To address this issue and relax this assumption we applied a slightly modified version of the above method to the pooled sample, which included both adopters and non adopters. The presence of non adopters required the use of an ERP adoption dummy. This approach examines therefore how the contribution of ERP adoption to changes in performance changes over time. Accordingly, the cross sectional analysis was based on the following model:

$$ln(PRN_i) = \beta_0 + \beta_1 ln(PRD_i) + \beta_2 ERP_i + \sum_j \beta_j control_j + \varepsilon$$

where ERP_i is the usual dummy variable that reflects ERP adoption. A second performance heterogeneity measure was constructed by dividing the standard error of the coefficient estimate β_2 in the cross-section regression by the mean of the dependent variable, i.e.: *Perf_heterogeneity_2 = StandErr(β_2)/Mean(PRN)*. Finally, as in the restricted sample case, we estimated the longitudinal model displayed in eq. 6. As usual we used the coefficient γ_1 to assess changes in performance heterogeneity.

$$\tag{6} Perf\_heterogeneity\_2_t = \gamma_0 + \gamma_1 year + \varepsilon$$

Sample Selection and Data Collection

The panel for this study was obtained by combining a sample of ERP adopters and a control sample of non-adopters. The sample of ERP adopters included 174 small and medium companies operating in Italy that implemented SAP R/3 between 1994 and 2002 in the manufacturing and in the consumer products sectors (table 1). The data set, obtained from SAP, included information about the client, as well as the ERP project start date and live date. This information was integrated with financial data obtained from public sources (AMADEUS).

The window 1994-2002 was chosen because it covered the entire diffusion process of a specific release of SAP R/3 in the country examined. The ERP adoption pattern for the companies in the sample followed the well documented S-shaped curve: no adoptions were registered in 1994; only 7 companies adopted the software in 1995; the number of adopters increased to reach a maximum of 48 in 1999 and gradually fell to reach a mini-

Table 1. The sample of ERP adopters

Industry sector	N	%
Manufacture of fabricated metal products, except machinery and equipment	30	17.2%
Manufacture of furniture	15	8.6%
Manufacture of other transport equipment	12	6.9%
Recycling	11	6.3%
Manufacture of wood and wood products except furniture	7	4.0%
Manufacture of machinery and equipment	6	3.4%
Manufacture of motor vehicles	6	3.4%
Manufacture of office machinery and computers	5	2.9%
Manufacture of radio, television and communication equipment and apparatus	5	2.9%
Manufacture of basic metals	4	2.3%
Wholesale trade and commission trade	4	2.3%
Other	69	39.7%
Total	174	100.0%

mum of 1 in 2002. The data base of ERP adopters was then matched with a control sample of 174 non-adopters selected randomly from a population of companies of similar size that operated in the same country. Table 2 displays descriptive statistics and Pearson correlations coefficients for the pooled sample for all the variables used in the various econometric models.

RESULTS

Impact of ERP and ERP Adoption Timing on Productivity and Profitability

Table 3 presents the results of fixed effect estimates for models (1)-(4). The models are all significant at the .01 level and have high explanatory power. All coefficient estimates are also significant at the .01 level. The results provide strong support for hypotheses 1 and 2. The coefficient of the ERP adoption dummy is consistently positive and significant at the .01 level in all the models tested. This suggests that the adoption of ERP contributes to generate productivity and profitabil-

ity increases. The result is consistent with earlier studies on ERP that used a similar methodology (Hitt et al., 2002). Conversely, the ERP adoption timing variable is significant at the .01 level, but it is negative in all models. This suggests that the adoption timing has also a strong impact on the ability of firms to generate benefits from their ERP investments and provides strong support for hypothesis 2. The learning effects and the reduced performance dip associated with late ERP adoption were outweighed by the delays in the realization of operational benefits as early ERP adopters clearly enjoyed greater benefits than late adopters.

The coefficients of models (1)-(4) can also be used to calculate the point in the observation window after which the adoption of ERP started generating negative returns. The production function model in eq. 1 can be used as an illustrative example. The coefficient estimates for the ERP adoption dummy and for the ERP adoption timing (column 1 in table 3) show that the effect of ERP adoption on ln(value added) can be written as ERP adoption*(0.39-0.23*ln(ERP adoption timing)). As $0.39-0.23*ln(6)<0<0.39-0.23*ln(5)$, firms that adopted an ERP in or after the 6th year

Table 2. Pearson Bivariate correlations and descriptive statistics (data refer to the year of ERP implementation)

	Mean	Std.	1	2	3	4	5	6	7	8
ERP adoption	0.36	0.48	-							
Value added	9.94	1.99	0.48	-						
Capital	8.59	2.57	0.41***	0.83***	-					
Labor cost	9.24	2.02	0.47***	0.97***	0.79***	-				
Revenue	11.24	1.89	0.45***	0.91***	0.74***	0.87***	-			
N. of employees	5.60	1.93	0.45***	0.93***	0.76***	0.95***	0.82***	-		
Profit before tax	8.10	2.25	0.47***	0.88***	0.74***	0.81***	0.81***	0.77***	-	
Assets	11.26	2.02	0.46***	0.93***	0.87***	0.88***	0.88***	0.84***	0.83***	-
Equity	9.75	2.33	0.45***	0.91***	0.89***	0.85***	0.81***	0.82***	0.87***	0.91***

Table 3. Panel data analysis with fixed effects: impact of ERP adoption and ERP adoption timing on productivity and profitability

	Value added		Revenue		Pre-tax profit		Pre-tax profit	
	Parameter Estimate	St. Error	Parameter Estimate	St. Error	Parameter Estimate	St. Error	Parameter Estimate	St. Error
Capital	0.09***	0.02						
Labor	0.83***	0.02						
N. of Employees			0.63***	0.02				
Assets					0.96***	17.56		
Equity							0.84***	17.07
ERP	0.39***	0.13	0.80***	0.23	1.46***	4.01	1.36***	3.76
ERP adoption timing	-0.23***	0.08	-0.49***	0.14	-1.04***	-4.21	-0.93***	-3.83
F	10.99***		68.53***		8.24***		4.68***	
R^2	0.99		0.99		0.99		0.99	
N	1917		1935		1674		1665	

* Significant at the .1 level. ** Significant at the .05 level. ***Significant at the .01 level.

of our observation window (i.e. after 1999) had a lower productivity compared to firms that adopted the system earlier. A similar analysis can be repeated for models 2, 3 and 4 and provides similar results.

Business Process Isomorphism

Table 4 displays the results of the longitudinal models used to examine the evolution of performance heterogeneity over time. The regression results are consistent across all models. The coefficients γ_l in eq. 5 and eq. 6 are negative and significant at the .01 level in all models tested, both in the pooled sample and in the restricted sample. The results of the restricted sample analysis indicate that performance differences among ERP adopters have actually decreased during the period of observation. The results of the pooled sample analysis suggest that the contribution of ERP adoption to increases in performance has also decreased over time. Altogether the two sets of models provide strong support for hypothesis 3. As ERP systems are becoming increasingly commoditized, the widespread diffusion of the standardized process templates embedded in the software reduces differences among firms and tends to generate business process isomorphism at the industry level. As a consequence, relying on solely on ERP for achieving competitive advantage becomes progressively more difficult with an increase in the number of adoptions.

Analysis of Adoption Drivers

To rule out the possibility that the above results cold be affected by a self-selection bias, i.e. by the fact that ERP adopters could be already the most profitable companies before implementing the software, we conducted several additional tests. As a first step, we examined the impact of profitability on the survival time T_i. For the generic firm i, the survival time T_i was defined

as the time elapsed between the year in which R/3 was first released to the market (alike to a "birth") and the year in which company i adopted the system (alike to a "death"). To estimate the model we used a Cox-proportional hazard model, which controls for data censoring and allows for time-repeated measurements without imposing a specific form for the underlying survivor function. We run several versions of the model, using firm's profitability and lagged profitability (from T-1 to T-3) both jointly and individually as explanatory variables and revenue or number of employees as controls for firm size.

All the models analyzed were consistent. Table 5 reports the results of a general model in which all the profitability variables are introduced simultaneously. The results suggest that, after controlling for firm size, the impact of profitability on survival time is not significant. It is also worth noting that larger firms were likely to adopt an ERP system earlier than small firms, at least within the time window examined (1994-2002). This observation is in line with anecdotal evidence, as the first generation of enterprise systems was primarily targeted to the market of medium and large firms.

Overall, the analysis suggests that – at least in the time window examined - the decision to adopt an enterprise system was driven more by idiosyncratic and technical factors (solving the Year 2000 problem, upgrading the IT infrastructure) or by internal process optimization needs (improving business process performance, supporting growth) than by the financial health of the organizations in the years prior to adoption. This confirms that the observed performance differences between adopters and non-adopters were actually driven by the operational improvements generated by the implementation of the software rather than by other contingent factors.

Table 4. Cross-section and longitudinal analyses: impact of ERP adoption on performance heterogeneity

POOLED SAMPLE

	Cross-section analysis: productivity Dependent variable: Revenue Independent variable: N. of Employees **Longitudinal analysis:** Dep. Variable: St.Err. of coeff. Estim. of Employees		Cross-section analysis: ROA Dependent variable: Profit before tax Independent variable: Assets **Longitudinal analysis:** Dep. Variable: St.Err. of coeff. estimate of Assets		Cross-section analysis: ROE Dependent variable: Profit before tax Independent variable: Equity **Longitudinal analysis:** Dep. Variable: St.Err. of coeff. estimate of Equity	
	Parameter Estimate	St. Error	Parameter Estimate	St. Error	Parameter Estimate	St. Error
Year	-0.007 **	0.003	-0.012 ***	0.004	-0.01 ***	0.004
F	6.68 **		8.24 **		7.56 **	
R²	0.53		0.58		0.56	
N	9		9		9	

RESTRICTED SAMPLE (ERP ADOPTERS ONLY)

	Cross-section analysis: productivity Dependent variable: Revenue Independent variable: N. of Employees, ERP **Longitudinal analysis:** Dep. Variable: St.error of coeff. estimate of ERP		Cross-section analysis: ROA Dependent variable: Profit before tax Independent variable: Assets, ERP **Longitudinal analysis:** Dep. Variable: St.error of coeff. estimate of ERP		Cross-section analysis: ROE Dependent variable: Profit before tax Independent variable: Equity, ERP **Longitudinal analysis:** Dep. Variable: St.error of coeff. estimate of ERP	
	Parameter Estimate	St. Error	Parameter Estimate	St. Error	Parameter Estimate	St. Error
Year	-0.001 ***	<0.001	-0.001 ***	<0.001	-0.001 ***	<0.001
F	8.75 **		10.05 ***		9.85 ***	
R²	0.66		0.72		0.70	
N	9		9		9	

*Significant at the .1 level. ** Significant at the .05 level. ***Significant at the .01 level.*

CONCLUSIONS, LIMITATIONS AND FUTURE RESEARCH

In this chapter we have shed some light on the relationship between ERP and business performance. The panel data analysis of a sample of Italian manufacturing companies that adopted SAP R/3 between 1994 and 2002 provided several interesting insights.

First, the analysis confirmed the results of previous research in this area and suggested that the adoption of ERP exerts a positive effect on both productivity and profitability (ROA and ROE). Second, the results indicated the existence of a window of opportunity for adopting ERP. This is suggested by the fact that early adopters exhibit higher performance than late adopters and by the fact that the contribution of ERP adoption to performance improvements decreases as the number of adoptions increases. Finally the study clearly indicated that the widespread diffusion of a technology that embeds standard process templates decreases process heterogeneity and tends to level out performance differences among firms.

This result questions the role of ERP as a strategic tool. The pervasive diffusion of best practices may reduce the possibility that firms are able to use this technology to create strategic operational advantages in the long run. Yet, the results also suggest that in the short term there exist some windows of opportunities during which early adopters can obtain important productivity and profitability advantages from their ERP investments. While in the long run the massive adoption of enterprise solutions tends to level out performance differences (high-performing companies become better, and low-performing companies improve even more), the analysis clearly showed that early adopters enjoy higher returns than later adopters. This suggests the existence of strong first-mover advantage effects.

Our study makes several contributions. A first set of contributions is theoretical. The chapter contributes to the literature on the "IT paradox" by shedding additional light on the relationship between ERP investments and performance. It also clarifies the role of adoption timing in this process, which had been somewhat overlooked in the literature. A second set of contributions is methodological. We proposed the use of a fixed-effect model as a correct econometric approach to estimate the panel data equations. We also devised a general method to measure changes in performance heterogeneity over time which overcomes the limitations of traditional variance-based measures. A third contribution is managerial. By quantifying the benefits of ERP as well as by identifying the conditions under which it may no longer guarantee the achievement

Table 5. Hazard model: analysis of ERP adoption drivers

Analysis of Maximum Likelihood Estimates					
Variable	Parameter Estimate	Standard Error	Chi-Square	Pr > ChiSq	Hazard Ratio
Revenue	0.02	0.01	5.75	0.02	1.02
Profit	0.30	1.27	0.06	0.81	1.35
Profit_1	1.15	1.59	0.52	0.47	3.16
Profit_2	0.24	1.41	0.03	0.86	1.27
Profit_3	-0.87	1.12	0.60	0.44	0.42
-2LL	470.65				
χ^2	5.19				

of competitive advantage, the chapter provides useful insights to firms that are investing or aim to invest in this technology.

Our results should be viewed in the context of some limitations. First, the target population of this study was narrowly defined to include a reasonably homogeneous set of firms that had purchased their ERP systems from a specific vendor and operated in a specific country. While a restrictive sampling approach enhances confidence that the findings are indeed a result of the hypothesized relationships, it may limit the generalizability of the research. Second, our study focused on the first and second generations of ERP systems, which are mainly aimed at streamlining internal business processes. With the advent of the network economy, organizations increasingly invest in IT to streamline processes not just within their own boundaries but especially across the value chain. This new generation of systems has greater complexity and a wider reach. As a consequence, it is likely to have a far greater impact on performance. These observations point toward several avenues for future research. These pertain to the extension of our analysis to other industries, to other geographical regions and, especially, to other IT technologies.

ACKNOWLEDGMENT

The author would like to thank Xiaorui Luo for his invaluable help in the preparation of this manuscript.

REFERENCES

Carr, N. G. (2003). IT Doesn't Matter. *Harvard Business Review*, 81(5), 41-49.

Cotteleer, M. J., & E. Bendoly (2006). Order Lead-Time Improvement Following Enterprise Information Technology Implementation: An Empirical Study. *MIS Quarterly* 30(3), 643-660.

Davenport, T. H. (2000). *Mission Critical: Realizing the Promise of Enterprise Systems*. Harvard Business School Press, Cambridge, MA.

Dess, G. G., & Beard, D. W. (1984). Dimensions of Organizational Task Environments. *Administrative Science Quarterly, 29*(1), 52-73.

Ettlie, J. E., Perotti, V. J., Joseph, D. A., & Cotteleer, M. J. (2005). Strategic Predictors of Successful Enterprise System Deployment. *International Journal of Operations & Production Management,* 25(9/10), 953.

Gupta, M., & Kohli, A. (2006). Enterprise resource planning systems and its implications for operations function. *Technovation, 26*, 687-696.

Hayes, D. C., Hunton, J. E., & Reck, J. L. (2001). Market Reactions to ERP Implementation Announcements. Journal *of Information Systems, 15*(1), 3-18.

Hitt, L. M., & Brynjolfsson, E. (1996). Productivity, business profitability, and consumer surplus: Three different measures of information technology value. *MIS Quarterly* 20(2), 121-142.

Hitt, L. M., Wu, D. J., & Xiaoge, Z. (2002). Investment in Enterprise Resource Planning: Business Impact and Productivity Measures. *Journal of Management Information Systems, 19*(1), 71-98.

Mabert, V. A., Soni, A. & Venkataramanan, M. A. (2003). Enterprise Resource Planning: Managing the Implementation Process. *European Journal of Operational Research, 146*(2), 302-314.

Mas-Colell, A. & Whinston, M. D. (1995). *Microeconomic Theory*. New York, Oxford University Press.

McAfee, A. (2002). The impact of enterprise technology adoption on operational performance: an empirical investigation. *Production and Operations Management, 11*(1), 33-53.

Pang, C. & Eschinger, C. (2006). *Forecast: ERP*

Software, EMEA, 2005-2010 Update. Gartner Report.

Poston, R. & Grabski, S. (2001). Financial Impacts of Enterprise Resource Planning Implementations. *International Journal of Accounting Information,* 2, 271-294.

Salmela, H. (1997), From information systems quality to sustainable business quality, *Information and Software Technology,* 39, 819-825.

Scott, F. & Shepherd, J. (2002). *The Steady Stream of ERP Investments.* AMR Research Outlook, August 26.

Shepherd, J., Locke, B., D'Aquila, M., & Carter, K. (2005). *The Enterprise Resource Planning Report, 2004-2009.* AMR Research Report.

Umble, E. J., Haft, R. R. & Umble, M. M. (2003). Enterprise Resource Planning: Implementation Procedures and Critical Success Factors. *European Journal of Operational Research, 146*(2), 241-257.

Vemuri, V. K. & Palvia, S. C. (2006). Improvement in Operational Efficiency Due to ERP Systems Implementation: Truth or Myth? *Information Resources Management Journal, 19*(2), 18-36.

Wieder, B., Booth, P., Matolczy, Z. P., & Ossimitz, M.-L. (2006). The Impact of ERP Systems on Firm and Business Process Performance. *Journal of Enterprise Information Management, 19*(1), 13-29.

KEY TERMS

Best Practice: Generic process template built in the ERP software that suggests what the optimal process configuration and the most efficient resource allocation scheme(s) should be for the execution of a particular task.

Business Process Isomorphism: Phenomenon whereby organizations tend to display similar business processes. It can be associated with the adoption of similar software packages containing similar process templates.

Business Process Reengineering (BPR): Activity consisting in rationalizing and streamlining business processes, often associated with the implementation of an Enterprise System

Live Date: Date that identifies the beginning of the operational phase of the ERP software. After the live date the organization starts using the ERP (or a significant part of it) to support its operations.

Panel Data: Panel data are data where multiple cases (e.g. firms) are observed over multiple time periods. The data contain two kinds of information: the cross-sectional information reflected in the differences between case, and the time-series information reflected in the changes within subjects over time. Panel data offers several advantages compared to cross-sectional or time-series data as the researcher can exploit these different types of information.

Performance Dip: Phenomenon often observed after the implementation of an ERP system whereby the organization adopting the system experiences a decrease in process and/or organizational performance immediately after the live and then increases performance above the initial level several weeks or months after the dip.

ENDNOTES

1   In the reminder of the paper we use intercgangably the terms Enterpise Resource Planning (ERP) and Enterprise Systems (ES).

2   Another important advantage of this approach is that the year dummies incorporated into the model can take effectively into account the effect of price deflation.

Chapter IX
Application Integration within the Enterprise Context

Ronda R. Henning
Harris Corporation, USA

ABSTRACT

The application software life cycle considers the functionality of a given collection of components within the context of a consumer's requirements definition. One set of requirements that are frequently overlooked are the requirements for application integration within the context of the enterprise environment. If an application creates vulnerabilities for other applications, is an administrative nightmare to maintain, or does not consider the security context required for execution; the application may not fulfill the intended requirements. This chapter addresses the question of the consideration of the enterprise information system's administrative and execution context as a component of the application software development process. The potential impact these considerations have on the acceptance of an application by the application's user community is presented, with illustrations of some representative problem areas for the reader's consideration.

INTRODUCTION

During the software application development life cycle the primary emphasis is on fulfilling the user's functional requirements. For example, if an enterprise specifies a transaction based service that is initiated in response to a user request, the software development team takes great care in defining the format and contents of a transaction, the initiation logic, and the criteria for completion. The primary emphasis is placed upon application functionality, user and process interaction, and system verification. These processes are used to measure the success or failure of the application development team in meeting the user's expectations.

Beyond the basic software development processes, however, there are implicit requirements that require integration of an application within the enterprise's operational infrastructure. An application that is deployed on an independent server, with unlimited bandwidth, and its own user interface is a relative rarity in the current enterprise computing environment.

To address the fact that various applications may share a processing infrastructure, the concept of a technical reference model has been developed. Technical reference models provide a blueprint for the coexistence of applications within a given enterprise. However, a technical reference model may not address all the integration issues that can be anticipated in during the integration of a new application with the existing infrastructure. An enterprise may support a specific user authentication process that relies upon digital certificates and directory services. If the development team does not have access to these capabilities, the application may not execute correctly when placed in the enterprise infrastructure.

BACKGROUND

The focus of the application development life cycle is the satisfaction of the functional requirements that must be fulfilled to address the user's vision. Applications are developed in response to perceived user needs, or requirements. They collect, process, and present information from one or more sources to the user in a specified format. The application is tasked with collecting the information, providing analytical or presentation functions, and interacting with either the user or other applications as required. The development process ensures that the application addresses the requirements as specified, and that these requirements are traceable and correctly allocated to various component elements of the application.

Few applications exist as independent entities that do not integrate with the other applications within an enterprise. Provisioning is defined as "a preparatory step in anticipation of some need" (Microsoft, 2003). In the case of an enterprise application, this preparatory step is the integration of the application with the enterprise's information technology infrastructure. This infrastructure includes the network, servers, and other software applications. The enterprise user or subscriber must also be made known to the application. For example, Xuan Shi (2006) defines a provisioning context in which the application is responsible for providing:

- A valid user name and authentication mechanism
- The data source used in the application
- Using the combination to find the data requested.

An application can only perform as expected if it has an ability to communicate within the enterprise to find its data, determine the authenticity of its users, and process the information requests. If an application cannot access and exercise the enterprise infrastructure, then it cannot function successfully within the enterprise's information processing context.

ADDRESSING THE ENTERPRISE CONTEXT

The provisioning process facilitates enterprise application integration and verification activities. Provisioning should be the final step in the application integration planning process. Well executed, the enterprise infrastructure will be transparent to an application's users. Poorly accomplished, enterprise context integration activities can result in a cost and schedule nightmare. If additional network capacity, hardware, or software licenses are required, these must be acquired through the corporate procurement processes. The project may not have the budgetary reserve to address these issues if they are not considered during the early design phases of a project.

Further, if access privileges are not correctly established and testing during integration, user information access will become a nightmare. Access controls will not be deployed on a least privilege basis, but on the basis of what is expedient to gain a working application environment. This may not be good security practice, but it does accomplish project implementation schedule goals. It may also leave the organization vulnerable to malicious code or information piracy.

Considering the provisioning process during the system development process forces the developer to consider the constraints on the application environment while there is still time to adapt the design to them. Ignoring the enterprise context ensures additional complications and may require last minute corrective measures to integrate the application with the enterprise computing environment. To maintain flexibility and enforce an enterprise's architecture standards, provisioning

issues must be addressed throughout the development process.

Provisioning extends from the network infrastructure, to the hardware platform, the supporting software environment, the applications, and the user. With the integration of physical security systems into the information technology infrastructure (Alliance for Enterprise Security Risk Management, 2006), provisioning becomes a cradle-to-grave user function that is part of the user's employment lifecycle within an enterprise.

Figure 1 illustrates this activity flow.

Decomposing the Enterprise Context

Yuri Pikover and John Drake (2006) presents a comprehensive set of checklists to ensure that an application developer addresses the contextual constraints a given enterprise infrastructure may place upon an application. These checklists provide an audit template that can be used to validate a provisioning process. This model is adapted in Figure 2, and described in the following paragraphs.

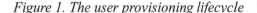

Figure 1. The user provisioning lifecycle

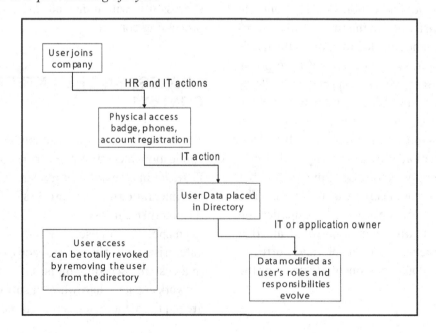

A development assumption that an enterprise has sufficient network bandwidth and processing power to address a given application's communications requirements may not be a prudent act. Applications may require large volumes of data originating from multiple sources, all of which require network capacity to migrate the eventual result to the target client system. The network management team usually maintains a margin of excess capacity to accommodate new applications and occasional peak traffic loads. However, there is no guarantee that an existing network infrastructure can accommodate increased traffic loads without coordination with the network infrastructure maintenance personnel.

An additional consideration is the backup and recovery infrastructure required for continuity of operations. If an application is critical to the organization's operation, it should be integrated into the organizational contingency management plan. An application developer that assumes all transactions are written to recovery logs may have to make alternate arrangements if the operations team has a policy to limit transaction log size. Data replication and backups during off peak hours may not be possible if network capacity is not in place to support these operations.

Figure 2. A five-tiered model for enterprise provisioning

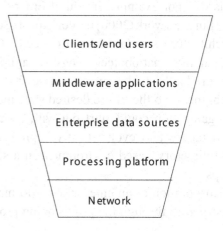

Clients/end users

Middleware applications

Enterprise data sources

Processing platform

Network

Measurement of network bandwidth requirements both from the client and the processing infrastructure perspective should be accomplished during the system development process. Projected bandwidth calculations should be compared to actual network traffic generated by an application, or the application subscribers may be faced with unacceptable network performance. That is other applications may pay a performance penalty for a network traffic intensive application if there is contention for network resources. Advance coordination with the network team allows them to plan sufficient network capacity, establish bandwidth management parameters and projected rate limits for specific applications.

Platform provisioning activities focus on the processing power, memory, and disk sizing associated with the server hosting the application. Development platforms usually support excess resource capacities to facilitate the development and debugging process. If an application will be installed on a shared production platform, it may develop resource contention issues. Memory or disk space may be at a premium, or a given suite of network protocols may not be installed on a given device.

If an application expects to have unlimited access to data from diverse sources, there may be contention and conflict in resource access. Queries that are compute intensive may execute flawlessly and quickly in a development lab, but have unacceptable response times in the production environment. In these cases, live data trials can be applied to optimize resource allocations and access requirements. For example, an application that routinely accesses a remote server may benefit from a shadow server being established locally. Both network bandwidth and user performance may be more satisfactory if the data was moved closer to the end user.

Application processing priorities may need to be established. An application that has no resource contention in an isolated development environment may be constantly waiting for responses when faced with competition and contention among other applications. In this situation, priorities and pre-emption strategies may have to be considered. If every user considers his processing requests the highest priority need within the organization, the information technologist has to apply prioritization across the enterprise to address the needs of all user requests.

A step in the provisioning process that may be missed is the configuration of middleware services, the supporting software that facilitates the application. With the emergence of services-oriented architecture (SOA) development paradigms, there may be several layers of software utilities and supporting applications that are required to execute a given application. A key consideration in using software utilities and services is software usage licensing. Developers may underestimate the number of concurrent licenses which are required to support a given application, or a utility may be used by many applications and exhaust the supply of license keys. This can lead to resource contention issues, licensing noncompliance, or locked out user accounts.

An application is usually installed within an operational network infrastructure, the issues associated with that integration are corrected, and the application is never touched again. The subscribers or users of an application may have frequent account or privilege modifications based on personnel activities such as hiring, terminations, and promotions. When a subscriber moves to an alternate role in an enterprise, the access privileges or authentication requirements associated with that role may also change. Access rights have to be modified and propagated throughout the enterprise. These activities can be greatly facilitated with provisioning software products.

A subscriber's identification and authentication credentials must be updated when they expire. For example, if a password is changed, or a digital certificate has been revoked, the user's authentication data has also been changed. Updating account information is a relatively simple task in a small

enterprise, but when business is conducted on a global scale changes must be propagated rapidly and efficiently. Beyond account revocation, as users move throughout the enterprise their access rights may change as well. These changes must be reflected across the enterprise in a timely fashion, or the user will not be able to accomplish the required tasks. Privileged roles provide application users with the capability to modify corporate databases. These capabilities can subvert the integrity of corporate data. For example, sales figures can be modified and executive decisions made based on faulty information.

When an application spans multiple enterprises, it is possible that the management hierarchy is not uniform among the cooperating enterprises. For example, a vice president may have financial responsibilities in one division, but a vice president in another division may not have financial control. The application development team should be sensitive to such organizational distinctions and have an infrastructure in place with the flexibility to map subscriber roles and responsibilities across diverse organizational management hierarchies.

Additional Benefits of Enterprise Context Integration

Consideration of the enterprise information context in the provisioning process can be used to enforce conformance to enterprise architecture standards. For example, in Murat Erder's and Pierre Pureur's work (2006) the concept of a series of architecture standards is introduced. Over time, an information technology organization could gradually evolve an enterprise from the current model to the future desired state model. An organization could start out with a simple user database and evolve to a comprehensive X.500 directory based environment in a series of steps.

Incorporation of an enterprise's information infrastructure through the provisioning process allows an organization to enforce policy standards in a uniform and efficient manner. If a corporation determines that data can be accessed remotely, but only during business hours when the help desk can provide technical support, that policy can be readily enforced with a directory based solution. Users with a remote access attribute can have the access hours modified to reflect the corporation's business hours. Similarly, an enterprise might choose to enforce a policy that particular databases may only be accessed at a corporate facility. Such location-based policies can be established and enforced with a centralized user management infrastructure. Consideration of such constraints during the application development process can allow the developer to focus on the application's core functionality and minimize duplication of system service functions.

FUTURE TRENDS

The provisioning of an enterprise application is gradually becoming a more automated process. As infrastructures grow and incorporate more location-based technologies, it becomes more difficult to ensure that all applications understand the current enterprise context. Promising technologies include active networks and autonomous provisioning languages.

Active Networks

Active, or aware networks, react and adapt to dynamic changes in the enterprise infrastructure. In this context, the network management function monitors bandwidth consumption, potential security issues, and access violations, adapting the network posture if required. Francine Krief (2004) states the four functions of an aware network are:

1.   Self-configuration – configuration of components

2.   Self-optimization – seeking to improve performance and effectiveness
3.   Self-healing – detection, diagnosis, and repairing hardware and software problems
4.   Self-protection – protecting the system from attacks or cascading failures by anticipation of the network's response.

For example, if a given user is consuming high percentages of the network's available bandwidth, an active network will adjust the user's bandwidth allocation according to a specified quality of service (Krief, 2004).

In the increasingly network centric information environment, an application must establish the user's resource allocations and is responsible for enforcement of enterprise governance constraints on the user's environment. Within the enterprise context, the application developer should verify the bandwidth, privileges, and performance utilization factors as part of the development life cycle.

Standardization of Protocols and Processes

There are two emerging provisioning standards that are gaining a foothold in the marketplace:

1.   The Service Provisioning Markup Language (SPML), and
2.   The J2EE provisioning environment.

The Service Provisioning Markup Language standard (OASIS, 2006) is being promulgated by the Organization for the Advancement of Structured Information Standards (OASIS) Provisioning Services Technical Committee (PSTC). SPML defines an XML-based framework for exchanging user, resource, and service provisioning information. The Technical Committee specification is an end-to-end, open, provisioning specification that includes the following components:

- Active Digital Profile (ADPr)
- eXtensible Resource Provisioning Management (XRPM)
- Information Technology Markup Language (ITML)

SPML is an "overlay" language, in that it expects to work in conjunction with a Lightweight Directory Access Protocol (LDAP) metadata model (Internet Engineering Task Force, 1997). SPML defines a set of formatted request/response structures and the legal attribute/value pairs that comprise the query/response format. It expects that each end user will have a standard X.509 Distinguished Name, and that some sort of digital trust relationship exists between the requesting authority and the provisioning service provider (Internet Engineering Task Force, 1999). An overview of SPML interaction is provided in Figure 3.

The SPML standard is now at version 2.0. SPML has been adopted by several integrated solution vendors such as Computer Associates and IBM as a method of providing transparent interoperability in heterogeneous enterprise environments. An SPML compliant application accommodates registration and configuration of user accounts in response to an authorized request. This capability will become increasingly necessary as service oriented architectures become more commonplace.

For Java based applications, the J2EE Client Provisioning Specification (Sun Microsystems, 2003) serves the same purpose as SPML, but it is specific to the J2EE application development environment. The Java language is very popular, and by defining a set of standard libraries for client provisioning, third party software applications are more readily created and integrated into existing Java based environments. Figure 4 illustrates the J2EE Client Provisioning Specification architecture.

In the J2EE model, a provisioning API provides the interface to the provisioning application, which, in turn, accesses the enterprise services that provide essential provisioning information. In this regard, it is very similar to SPML, but it is a Java based architectural instantiation instead of XML.

Enterprise infrastructure vendors such as IBM, Computer Associates, and Sun Microsystems all support products that facilitate middleware and user provisioning. These products provide a centralized user interface for account registra-

Figure 3. SPML interaction overview

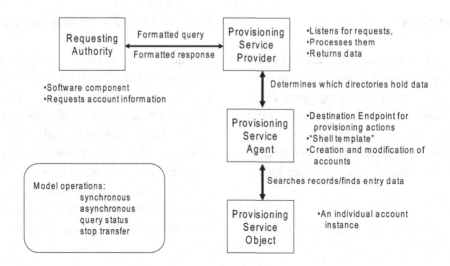

Figure 4. J2EE client provisioning

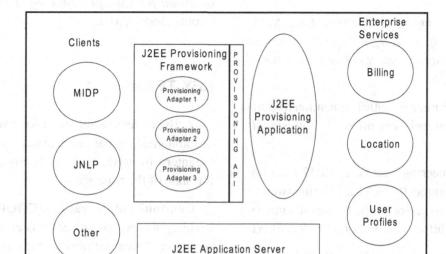

tion, maintenance, and privilege management functions. In most cases, these applications also provide a recovery and propagation capability to ensure change management is effectively accomplished throughout the enterprise.

Consultancies such as Gartner frequently survey the commercial marketplace (Witty, Ant, and Wagner, 2006) to determine standard features and emerging trends. If an enterprise has adopted an infrastructure management paradigm and tool suite, the integration capabilities of the tool suite are also used to facilitate adaptation of new applications to the enterprise's processing context.

CONCLUSION

Integration of the application within the constraints of the enterprise's processing context is an often overlooked aspect of system development. Without careful early consideration, performance modeling and possibly simulation, an application environment may not meet user expectations. An application that requires additional expenditures for improved performance creates hidden costs for the enterprise. The final application integration process proceeds in a more orderly fashion when the contextual constraints of the enterprise environment are considered throughout the development process. The choice, like so many others in system development, is simple: invest resources and pay attention to the enterprise's operating constraints early, or invest more heavily in later program phases when time and resources are at a premium.

FOR MORE INFORMATION

The latest data on the Service Provisioning Markup Language, SPML, is available from OASIS at www.oasis-open.org.

For information on the J2EE provisioning environment, visit www.sun.com.

For general guidance on user provisioning, the National Institute of Standards and Technology, (NIST), maintains a security best practices web site at www.csrc.nist.gov.

REFERENCES

Alliance for Enterprise Security Risk Management (2006). *Convergent security risks in physical security systems and it infrastructures.* Alexandria, VA.

Erder, M., & Pureur, P. (2006). Transitional architectures for enterprise evolution. *IT Professional, 8*(3), 10-17.

Internet Engineering Task Force (IETF). (1997). Request for comment (RFC) 2251, the lightweight directory access protocol, v3. Retrieved January 7, 2007 from http://www.ietf.org/rfc/rfc2251.txt

Internet Engineering Task Force (IETF). (1999). Request for comment (RFC) 2459, Internet x.509 public key infrastructure certificate and CRL profile. Retrieved January 7, 2007, from http://www.ietf.org/rfc/rfc2459.txt

Krief, F. (2004). Self-aware management of IP networks with QoS guarantees. -*International Journal of Network Management, 14* (July 2004), 351-364.

Microsoft. (2003). Encarta dictionary, Microsoft Press.

Organization for the Advancement of Structured Information Standards (OASIS). (2006). OASIS service provisioning markup language (SPML) v2 -- DSML v2 profile.

Pikover, Y., &. Drake, J. (2006). *Security provisioning: Managing access in extended enterprises.* Chicago, IL.

Shi, X. (2006). Sharing service semantics using SOAP-based and REST Web services. *IT Professional, 8*(2), 18 - 24.

Sun Microsystems. (2003, 6 October 2003). Java specification request: J2EE client provisioning specification. Retrieved January 7, 2007, 2007, from http://web1.jcp.org/en/jsr/detail?id=124

Witty, R.. J., Ant, A., & Wagner, R. (2006). *Magic quadrant for user provisioning, 1h06.* Gartner Group, Boston, MA.

KEY TERMS

Active or Aware Network: A network capable of autonomous dynamic adaptation to changes in the enterprise network architecture or the processing state of the network

Continuity of Operations (COOP): The processes, policies, and procedures described in the contingency management plan to ensure a given enterprise can continue to function in the event of a catastrophic or minor disruption of service.

Enterprise Context: The totality of the information technology infrastructure supporting a given organization's information processing functions, services, and applications.

Management Hierarchy: The chain of decision making within a given enterprise or business

Middleware: The supporting software components that enable application functions, but are not a component of the application itself. Middleware is transparent to the application user.

Provisioning: Configuration of a network, platform, software, or application to support the integration of additional functionality or components.

Service Provisioning Markup Language: An XML-based language to facilitate the provisioning of information services.

User or Subscriber Provisioning: Configuration of a specified user or group of users system attributes to support the integration of additional functionality or components.

Chapter X
The Impact of Enterprise Systems on Business Value

Sanjay Mathrani
Massey University, New Zealand

Mohammad A. Rashid
Massey University, New Zealand

Dennis Viehland
Massey University, New Zealand

ABSTRACT

A significant investment in resources is required for implementation of integrated enterprise systems as technology solutions while the effectiveness of these systems to achieve business value remains unclear and empirically largely unexplored. Enterprise systems integrate and automate business processes, but unarguably, the real business value can only be achieved from improvements through the transformation of enterprise systems data into knowledge by applying analytic and decision making processes. This study explores a model of transforming ES data into knowledge and results by comparing two case studies that examine the impact of enterprise systems information on organizational functions and processes leading to realization of business value.

INTRODUCTION

The implementation of enterprise systems has been considered the most important development in corporate use of information technology (Davenport, 1995, 1998; Davenport & Prusak, 1998;

Deloitte, 1998). Enterprise systems (ES) broadly include all enterprise-wide systems. These include enterprise resource planning (ERP) systems or any extended modules such as supply chain management (SCM) or customer relationship management (CRM) systems. However, despite a few dramatic successes, many organizations still fail to realize the benefits while incurring huge costs and schedule overruns (Dalal, Kamath, Kolarik, & Sivaraman, 2004). It has been estimated that half of all ES implementations fail to achieve the desired results (Jarra, Al-Mudimigh, & Zairi, 2000). In most cases enterprise systems are implemented to improve organizational effectiveness (Davenport, 1998, 2000; Marcus & Tanis, 2000). These software applications connect and manage information flows across complex organizations, allowing managers to make decisions based on information that accurately reflects the current state of their business (Davenport, Harris, & Cantrell, 2002).

These systems are implemented to bring about definite business benefits that justify the investment. Truly significant return on investment (ROI) comes from the process improvements that ES supports and not just from improved information access. In most implementations, ES software alone makes marginal improvement in business performance. If organizations continue to follow the same pre-ES business processes after implementation, they can expect the same or possibly worse performance. ES software can, however, enable and support many new and improved processes, but not without the organization deciding what those processes are and committing to them. Positive ROI can come from changing the way business was performed in the past to more streamlined, faster and lower cost processes that better serve the needs of the customer and, if that is done well, the organization will be a winner (Donovan, 2003).

The focus of this paper is to better understand the effectiveness of enterprise systems technology in an organizational setting. A qualitative research methodology is used to explore how firms can leverage ES technologies to realize improved business value. Field studies were conducted in two large manufacturing organizations in India that have implemented ESs, in order to understand their experience in achieving growth by leveraging

data from their ES investment. Semi-structured interviews were conducted with senior managers of the two organizations between January 2005 and February 2006. The empirical data were integrated and analysed to formulate inferences presented in this paper. Both organizations had aggressive growth plans with an objective to achieve better penetration capability into the competitive market by improving their operations. Both organizations had implemented ES for at least three years and so were in their mature phase of implementation. One organization had achieved considerable success from their ES implementation whereas the other had achieved little success. The two cases are compared to identify reasons for their levels of success.

BUSINESS BENEFITS

The justification for adopting ES centres on anticipated business benefits from the ES. To receive benefit from an ES, there must be no misunderstanding of what it is about, its usability, and, even more importantly, organizational decision makers must have the background and temperament for this type of decision making coupled with the right quality of information (Donovan, 1998). Many researchers have evaluated benefits from ES investments (Cooke & Peterson, 1998; Davenport et al., 2002; Deloitte, 1998; Donovan, 1998, 2001; Hedman & Borell, 2002; Ittner & Larcker, 2003; Shang & Seddon, 2000; Yang & Seddon, 2004). These studies have found that ES's are designed to help manage organizational resources in an integrated manner. Furthermore, the level of integration that is promoted across functions in an enterprise closely relates to the primary benefits that are expected as a result of their implementation. After adoption, improved business performance should produce both operational and strategic benefits (Irving, 1999; Jenson & Johnson, 2002; Nicolaou, 2004).

A study of 85 global companies (Deloitte, 1998) found tangible benefits (e.g. cost savings, faster processing) and intangible benefits (e.g., improved information visibility, new/improved processes, and improved customer responsiveness) from ES implementation. In a survey of 163 large firms (Davenport et al., 2002) key benefits realized by organizations adopting ES included better management decision making, improved customer service and retention, ease of expansion/growth, increased flexibility, faster and more accurate transactions, cost reduction, and increased revenue. There have also been some studies on organizational benefits resulting from overlapping implementation of knowledge management (KM) and ES in organizational settings (e.g., Newell, Huang, Galliers, & Pan, 2003; Baskerville, Pawlowski, & McLean, 2000; Bendoly, 2002). However, this paper focuses on the impact of ES on realizing business value through the process of ES data transformation into knowledge by applying analytic and decision-making processes. This study attempts to establish the link between data, decisions, and actions, its impact on functional and business processes, and their outcomes.

TURNING ES DATA INTO ES KNOWLEDGE

A model conceptualized and used by Davenport (2000) and his team of researchers for turning ES data into ES knowledge is shown in figure 1. The model comprises three major steps. The first is the context. This includes the factors that must be present for transformation of ES data into knowledge and results. The second is transformation of ES data into knowledge which takes place when the data are actually analyzed and then used to support a business decision. The third are the outcomes which are the events that change as a result of the analysis and implementation of the

decisions made. As Davenport's model shows, the process of ES data transformation into knowledge leads into organizational changes. The most basic potential outcome of this process is the changes in behaviors of individual managers, employees, customers, suppliers, and all stakeholders in the value chain. Another outcome from the decisions or the behavioral changes may be new initiatives to bring about improvements in business or make changes in existing projects. The results of decisions can also include process changes – determining that an existing process is not working effectively can lead to changes in the existing process or design and implementation of an entirely new process. The ultimate results of all these activities are the business benefits which lead to positive financial impacts for the organization. "Decisions lead to new behaviors, new initiatives, and processes, which do not matter unless they improve the bottom line and the return to share holders" (Davenport, 2000) p. 225). It may be difficult to draw a direct chain of influence from prerequisites to transformation to non-financial outcomes to financial results, but establishing that linkage should be the objective of an organization that invests effort and resources in ES data transformation (Davenport, 2000) and is the focus of this study.

The two case studies are presented next and the discussion follows Davenport's model- context, transformation, and outcomes for both cases as shown in Figure 1.

CASE STUDY 1

Company Overview

Growel Limited[1] is a U.S. $1 billion forging manufacturing company and is one of the world's largest manufacturers and exporters of automotive engine and suspension components. It has the world's largest single-location forging capacity and one of the most technologically advanced commercial forge shops in the world. Growel has been a publicly traded company whose stock has appreciated more than 200 percent since March 2004. With manufacturing facilities in India and Germany, the company manufactures a wide range of forgings and machined components for the automotive, diesel engine, railway, earthmoving, cement, sugar, steel, coal, ship building, and oilfield industries. An ISO 9001:2000, ISO/TS 16949:2002 accredited company, Growel is internationally reputed for its cutting edge technology, established quality processes, and capabilities to meet the exacting standards of the most demanding customers in the world. Growel Limited is a global corporation with world class engineering capabilities, state-of-the-art manufacturing facilities, and a global customer base that includes General Motors, Toyota, Ford, Daimler Chrysler, Honda, Renault, Volvo, Caterpillar – Perkins, and several others. It is the largest manufacturer of axle components for heavy trucks and has a 35% global market share, with a 10% global market share in engine components. The following sections discuss how Growel leveraged knowledge-driven technologies

to improve business dynamics with considerable success. The discussion follows Davenport's model – context, transformation, outcomes – as shown in Figure 1.

Context: Strategic

Growel's journey towards becoming an international e-business began in the late 1990's. The company wanted to grow exports, widen its global footprint, secure new customers, become the world's largest manufacturer of axle components, and be a key global provider of engine components. To achieve these goals, Growel planned to double its manufacturing capacity by implementing a major capacity expansion program. However, this involved large investments and risks. The company had to resort to major cost controls, improve operational efficiencies and optimize its business processes to counter the adverse financial effects of the major investments. Senior managers in the company decided to pursue a strategy of operational excellence. The company historically lacked integration between its order-to-cash, shipping, and accounts receivable processes. There

Figure 1. A model of how ES data are transformed into knowledge and results

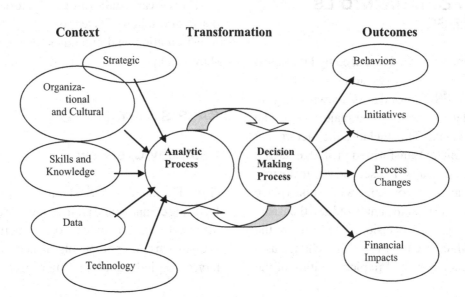

were disputes on invoices and purchase orders relating to price and terms of business. There was a lack of visibility into finished goods inventory and overall accuracy of inventory was poor. Visibility of material requirements and inventory throughout the value chain was inadequate and did not provide decision support at all stages of operations.

The company had not integrated the design and development practices with the operational systems; therefore the time lag between development and marketing of products was large and resulted in poor customer service and dissatisfaction. The pre-production approval process was another aspect which required attention. The company needed the ability to interactively participate with its customers at the early stages of product development and avoid rework at a later stage. The product forecasting process also required improvements. Managers only discovered that they had a shortage of manufacturing capacity when the line ran out. On the sales side, management had limited visibility of who its most and least profitable customers and products were. They also did not have information on whether they were buying in the most cost effective manner. The management team recognized what types of decisions had to be made to support their strategic objectives but could not utilize the available operational data.

Context: Organizational and Cultural

A company is as good as its people and Growel has the advantage of having a highly qualified and motivated manpower base. Since its inception, Growel has attached great significance to "people power" and considers its employees as important assets. With interactive communications at all levels, Growel continues to provide a congenial and peaceful working atmosphere to its employees. In the process of ES implementation, the organizational and cultural elements were aligned to support the use of transaction data at Growel. The compensation system was also changed to reward sales people for sales volume and profit to include a fixed and variable component of pay. The company created a friendly atmosphere within the organization which fostered orientation to change. The organization also adopted a data-oriented culture and encouraged employees to use data to support any business decision.

Context: Skills and Knowledge

Growel has always had a high quality, motivated work force. The company employs about two thousand workmen of which over four hundred are engineers with a high ability to learn and implement modern manufacturing methods using high tech equipment. The company provides extensive training both in house and externally, including overseas exposure. Within the group of knowledge workers and analysts, the skills include detailed knowledge of the organization's underlying business processes. They possess extensive skills for interpreting the SAP data, including understanding how key elements relate and their limitations for analysis. They also have a thorough working knowledge of several analytic and data presentation software packages, along with strong interpersonal skills to train and support end users.

Context: Data

Issues of data quality were less at Growel, where transaction data captured in the SAP system were created internally based on all transactions from sales orders to shipping invoices. Monitoring and updating of data was a regular feature at Growel and the transaction data was made available in a timely fashion to support decision making.

Context: Technology

Growel had historically been using a home-grown legacy system which provided disparate information which lacked proper integration and utilization. However, this lack of operational data to support decision making changed with the implementation of SAP's R/3 in 2000-01. The modules implemented were finance, sales and distribution, materials management, production management, and human resources. The company now had unprecedented visibility into its operations and customer base. SAP business intelligence tools were extensively used to extract, analyze, and develop adhoc reports.

Transformation

The transformation process at Growel was a result of putting knowledge-leveraging activities into action. How this happened is explained next. The value creation process was initially described in detail to gain an in-depth understanding of where and how Growel adds value for its customers. A critical success factor framework for each functional area was developed and a strong linkage between departmental performance indicators and top-level metrics for gauging the effectiveness of company strategy was put in place. Task groups within each functional area translated the general framework into team-specific programs to leverage innovations for achieving strategic goals and plans.

The model was shared with all the relevant team players. Descriptive indicators of the improvement and corrective-action plans were identified to facilitate decision making. The implementation plans for these decisions to achieve the desired results along with the steps to create the results were identified. Forms were designed to describe these plans and their measures. The indicators were documented choosing the reference for benchmarking and external validation along the time-line. The analytical process was the means by which ES data became knowledge. The SAP data, required for each of the indicators were identified, extracted, and interpreted, to create useful information for monitoring the progress for achieving the objectives. The signals and messages coming from each indicator were analyzed and evaluated to support decision-making. The decision-making process was based on high-quality, well-analyzed ES data on a multitude of factors. Some key areas where ES data were utilized for improvements were customer and product profitability analysis, price/volume analysis, market and customer segment analysis, sales forecasting and operations planning analysis. All actions likely to improve the likelihood that the result will be coherent with the strategic intent were identified, evaluated, and implemented.

Outcomes: Changing Behaviors

One of the major outcomes from the initiatives described above was changing behaviors. Improved information sharing, transparency, and openness with customers, suppliers, employees, and all stakeholders resulted in improved interpersonal and business relations. Having easy access to invoice and purchase order data enabled Growel to improve price synchronization with customers and suppliers. The earlier disputes on invoices and purchase orders relating to price and terms of business diminished. The online visibility of demand and supplies with customers and suppliers through the integrated supply chain management (SCM) system led to less volatility in sudden spurts of demand which existed earlier. This resulted in more streamlined supplies and a dramatic change in customer and supplier behavior since Growel could react better to change orders now and was able to be more flexible in the manufacturing environment.

Outcomes: New Initiatives

The ability to analyze customer and product profitability lead to a new initiative of value engineering to improve or change the design to make the product more profitable. Unprofitable products and customers were identified and the division's existing unprofitable product lines were replaced by more profitable new product lines. New initiatives towards implementing just-in-time inventory systems were undertaken, which decreased inventory costs substantially.

Outcomes: Process Changes

Growel recognized that the SAP data created opportunities for redesigning some business processes which could create entirely new sets of decisions. Growel is moving at full speed to re-design some business processes and build e-commerce applications with SAP as a backbone for their legacy systems and other collaborative software like SCM (Supply Chain Management) and PLM (Product Lifecycle Management). SAP provides capabilities such as CRP (Capacity Resource Planning), and BPR (Business Process Re-engineering) which offer powerful links within the entire value chain from customers to suppliers. The company has set up an integrated supply chain management system which enables real-time visibility of material requirements and inventory throughout the value chain and provides decision support at all stages of operations. With a majority of the company's suppliers receiving supply chain data, the company has a real-time total demand management system in place. A virtual private marketplace has been created for Growel through which the company engages in e-procurement and reverse auctions. The company has already started selling scrap online.

In a development that will substantially reduce product development time and bring the company closer to its customer, Growel is in the process of implementing a Collaborative Product Commerce

(CPC) module. CPC will enable the company to work online with its customers to design and develop products and share information and knowledge with the customers. This will reduce product development time and costs and, more importantly, forge close ties with the customers from early stages of product development.

CASE STUDY 2

Company Overview

Primemover[2] is a multi-faceted engineering enterprise. Established in 1859, Primemover is one of India's leading and well-diversified engineering companies with a US$500 million turnover. The company's core competencies are in diesel/petrol engines, power generating sets (gensets), agricultural and construction equipment. The business operations of the company are divided into various business groups strategically structured to ensure maximum focus on each business area and yet retain a unique synergy in the operations. The business groups are power generation, agricultural equipment, light engines, and infrastructure equipment. Primemover has six manufacturing plants located at several locations in India. The company has an extensive sales and service network manned by a highly skilled and dedicated workforce.

The power generation group of Primemover designs and manufactures diesel engines and gensets for industry sectors such as power, oil and gas, construction, earthmoving, and transportation and supplies to various countries all over the world. The unit employs about 1,200 people. Originally Primemover only manufactured diesel engines. In 1993 the company collaborated with a German company to include gensets in order to extend its range of products, to develop a more complete supply capability to the engine manufacturing industry, and to position the company for long-term growth. Both product ranges served as solution providers for their customers, provided products with a large-range of kva and hp ratings. The synergies created by the integration of the two product ranges enabled better designs and product offerings. Specifically, customers had more effective, one-stop access to a comprehensive range of products as well as simplified commercial relationships. By enabling improved service to customers, the integration of the two product lines enhanced the market position of the power generation group of Primemover. However, the company realized that it would face challenges to ensure its profitable growth in the long term.

Context: Strategic

Primemover was one of the few companies that were full-line supplier of the entire product range in industry markets however; the company was facing growing challenges. Despite increased demand resulting from a healthy growing market, greater competition in its core markets and high operating costs could inhibit the achievement of financial returns expected from its operations. Primemover had to overcome the competition, and leverage the new opportunities to ensure profitable growth for the future. To compete effectively, Primemover needed to improve its supply chain performance and cost; the business processes of the two product lines were not performing at the levels necessary to grow profitably in the emerging competitive environment. The time frames required to commit to delivery of finished goods to customers were not competitive; customer order handling and service processes were complex; operations were not sufficiently flexible to enable rapid response to shifting demand; market share was not growing rapidly; and inventory-carrying costs and other expenses inhibited achievement of adequate financial returns. These challenges were compounded by the fact that 60% of Primemover diesel engine and genset parts were externally sourced and there were long lead times for products such as pistons from Germany and turbochargers from UK. Forecast accuracy was low, inventory data and related information were inaccurate. Thus, key goals for Primemover included enhancing its ability to respond to customer requirements, improving market share, and reducing costs throughout the operation. Primemover determined that it must improve its supply chain planning and execution capabilities to improve its operations in order to achieve better penetration capability into the competitive market, which was their prime objective.

Context: Organizational and Cultural

Primemover has an overall employee base of about three thousand employees and has a change-oriented organizational culture. Primemover enjoys the enviable reputation of being one of the few corporates that has successfully maintained harmonious human relations year after year and the credit for this goes to all its employees who have always been open to and welcomed change. The organization structure is collaborative and the compensation system is aligned to achieving goals.

Context: Skills and Knowledge

Out of the three thousand workmen Primemover employs, over five hundred are qualified engineers having technical and commercial expertise. The company has hired mostly skilled workmen in the last fifteen years. The company has been providing on-going training and development to upgrade the skills and knowledge of its employees including knowledge of the organization's underlying business processes.

Context: Data

Quality of data was not an area of focus for Primemover prior to ES implementation. The maintenance of data records was not consistent and discrepancies were often encountered in the data records. There was a lack of discipline in updating transactions in the warehouse which would lead to stock and other data discrepancies. This lack of accuracy and currency of information led to data integrity issues amongst employees. The tools for data extraction were also inadequate. Availability of transactional data and information was an issue. Data extracts could not be made easily available and in time to support decision making.

Context: Technology

Primemover realized a need to couple its execution systems with a new class of supply chain planning software to address its requirements in the future. After considering various software solutions and determining the business strategy, the company selected SAP R/3 to be the foundation of the planning system for its integrated operations. Primemover had historically been using an internally-developed system which provided disparate information that lacked proper integration and utilization. However, the situation changed with the implementation of SAP's R/3 in 2000-01. The company implemented financial, sales and distribution, production management, human resources along with Web-enabled supply chain management systems. Primemover now had better visibility into its operations and customer base. Standard reports from SAP and Microsoft's Excel were used to analyze and report data.

Transformation

The transformation process at Primemover was based on the information from the SAP system. The available SAP data were utilized, interpreted, and analyzed in various areas of operations to support decision-making for achieving the company's strategic objectives. Standard reports from the SAP system were used and evaluated on a regular basis to support decision-making. Many of these reports were transformed into Excel spreadsheets to facilitate application of analytical processes. The decision-making process was based on well-analyzed ES data on a multitude of factors.

However the organization's business strategy needed more alignment into departmental and divisional strategies. The definition of information critical to the success of the organization was missing. This was evident by a remark from one of the interviewees when he said "there was a lot of confusion on what is to be achieved, which data needs to be analysed, where it is to be applied and to achieve what results". The analytical and decision-making process was based on ES data which were not very accurate. There was a lack of timely availability of data extracts to support analytical decision making and the link between data, decisions, and actions was missing. Some key areas where ES data were utilized for improvements were market and sales forecasting and operations planning analysis, theory of constraints in manufacturing analysis, raw material cost analysis, inventory analysis, activity-based costing, and process efficiency analysis.

Outcomes: Changing Behaviors

As a result of implementing an ES, the attitude of customers, suppliers, employees, and all stakeholders improved but did not reach the levels expected since inaccuracies were still present in the historical data. The online visibility of demand and supplies with customers and suppliers through the integrated SCM system reduced the number of out-of-inventory events, but did not achieve the reduction and streamlining of inventories anticipated. The lead times could not be reduced substantially and delivery performance improved marginally. The supply issues from vendors and customers continued and dramatic overall improvement in behaviors was not achieved.

Outcomes: New Initiatives

With some ability to analyze demand and with the information now visible, the company implemented the following changes to its supply chain processes. Primemover analyzed its various market and customer segments, determined the service requirements for these segments, and classified products according to volume and variability of demand. Primemover established monthly sales-forecasting and operations-planning meetings where the supply-and-demand plans were formally reviewed; performance of locally produced and imported product was considered; exceptions and unique requirements were brought up for discussion; and market intelligence and longer-term constraints in material and production were factored into plans.

Outcomes: Process Changes

In order to shorten lead times, reduce inventory, and increase throughput, Primemover employed a "theory of constraints" model, establishing processes to identify critical material and capacity constraints – and to optimize these constraints in its manufacturing operations on an ongoing basis. As operations of the two product lines were unified, customer account numbers were merged; SKUs were combined; and the number of warehouses was reduced from five to three. These consolidations required considerable revamping of numbering schemes and physical storage strategies. Warehouse consolidation was coupled with improved policies associated with material movement, virtually eliminating the need to transfer material between locations once received. Due to better tracking of material and a substantial reduction of the need to move material multiple times, costs for damaged and lost material declined from 1.60% to 0.78% of sales. Also, strategically significant and measurable improvements to inventory, cost, and customer service were achieved.

Forecast accuracy improved as the company gained experience with sales forecasting and operations planning. The new processes also gave visibility into material requirements for scheduled orders and further facilitated procurement planning. Primemover had earlier been placing large, irregular orders monthly or bimonthly with its suppliers but is now placing regular weekly orders, improving its suppliers' abilities to plan and thereby improving Primemover's negotiating position. The store manager at Primemover remarked that the suppliers and customers were now giving "fewer headaches" with the new system. Primemover's customers are also able to plan better due to the company's improved forecasts. Resolution of manufacturing constraints has improved production throughput by 20%. Daily cycle counting has enabled inventory accuracy to advance from 52% to more than 80%, which has facilitated a reduction in the levels of raw materials and finished goods. Finally, many employees are undertaking what-if analyses with the range of available data, further improving planning and execution across the supply chain. Primemover has chosen to integrate related product lines, establish supply chain channels to match supply-and-demand streams, and resolve constraints in its manufacturing network. The company recognizes that its process designs are not static and that its business and enabling systems will continue to evolve in line with market demands. Ongoing achievements in cost reductions and customer service improvements have enabled Primemover to make continual improvements in market position, premium pricing opportunities, and financial return.

RESULTS AND FINANCIAL IMPACTS

Growel has surpassed the last full year's total revenue and exports in the first nine months. Today, Growel has achieved the distinguished position as the largest manufacturer of axle components for heavy trucks world wide and one of the key global players for engine components. Primemover has improved over last year's total revenue and exports (as shown in table 2). However, Primemover has not fully achieved the anticipated objectives and results. Primemover had an expectation that the inventory levels would reduce by 60-70% and cost efficiency would also improve by 40-50% however, reduction in inventory levels achieved was only 40% and improvement in cost efficiency also was only 20%. Another expectation of Primemover was that the human resources would become highly motivated as an end result but the motivation expected was not seen. Although, improvement in the areas of on-time delivery and time taken for new product development, was achieved as anticipated. On the financial side, improvement expectation in the bottom line, profit after tax, was 20% by both Growel and Primemover. An improvement of only 9% was finally achieved by Primemover whereas Growel achieved 26%.

DISCUSSION

These cases illustrated Davenport's conceptual framework (Figure 1) of how business benefits are achieved from ES data transformation into ES knowledge highlighting the effectiveness of enterprise systems in the two organizations. The overall business benefits including the financial results obtained in Growel's case surpassed those of Primemover. The reasons attributed to this are given in the following section.

Growel and Primemover both had a business strategy and had identified their business objectives however; the business strategy in Growel's case was clearly articulated and aligned. Growel worked out their value creation process and identified the critical areas that required attention and improvement. They understood the key drivers and had the means to influence those drivers and measure them. Growel was able to translate their business strategy into departmental or divisional strategies. They knew what was to be achieved, which data needed analysis, its area of application, and expected outcomes. Primemover had identified their key business objectives however,

Table 1. Key successes achieved by Growel and Primemover

Growel	Primemover
1.Product development time - Decreased to around three weeks as compared to six months earlier; this closely matches industry benchmarks	1.Product development time - Decreased to around two months compared to three months earlier; this closely matches industry benchmarks
2.On-time delivery - Increased to 98% on-time	2.On-time delivery - Increased to 85% on-time
3. Inventory - Reduced by 80%	3. Inventory - Reduced by 40%
4. Cost efficiency - Increased by 60%	4. Cost efficiency - Increased by 20%
5. Relationship management - Much improved relations with customers and suppliers	5. Relationship management - Some improved relations with customers and suppliers
6. Human resources - Highly motivated	6. Human resources – Motivated

Table 2. Financial outcomes of Growel and Primemover as on March 31, 2005

Growel	Primemover
1.Total revenues - Increased by 47%	1.Total revenues - Increased by 24%
2.Exports - Increased by 76%; contributes 48% of total revenue	2.Exports - Increased by 15%; contributes 8% of total revenue
3. Profit before tax - Increased by 37%	3. Profit before tax - Increased by 15%
4. Profit after tax - Increased by 26%	4. Profit after tax - Increased by 9%

the definition of information critical to the success of the organization was lacking. Primemover could not create the link between departmental performance indicators and top-level metrics for gauging the effectiveness of the company strategy. Managers had data from their ES investment but could not leverage it to maximize realization of benefits and achieve their business strategies.

Growel understood the complexity of problems requiring analytic support. More complex issues, requiring sophisticated modeling and data analysis, are better served when analysts and decision makers are closely linked which was the case in Growel. The quality of management reviews also improved at Growel because executives became much more reliant on numbers in explaining their performance. Issues of data quality did not exist at Growel. Monitoring and updating of data was a regular feature and the transaction data were made available in a timely fashion to support decision making. In the case of Primemover, the lack of discipline in updating transactions in the warehouse led to data discrepancies and data integrity issues amongst employees. Data extracts could not be made in time to support decision making. The analytical and decision-making process was based on ES data which were unclean and inaccurate and the link between data, decisions, and actions was lacking.

Growel had streamlined their supply chain and achieved a major change in customer and supplier behavior since Growel could react better to change orders and was able to be more flexible in the manufacturing environment. However, in the case of Primemover the online visibility of demand and supplies with customers and suppliers reduced the number of out-of-inventory events, but did not achieve the reduction and streamlining of inventories anticipated. The lead times could not be reduced substantially and delivery performance improved marginally. Their data management was inconsistent coupled with a lack of clarity on the information required to drive their strategy which were the reasons they could not achieve their full potential and anticipated objectives.

CONCLUSION

This study has examined the effectiveness of enterprise systems on organizational functions and processes for realizing business value. It has highlighted that business results follow in a culture where the business strategy is clearly articulated and defined. The organization works out their value creation process identifying the critical areas that require attention and improvement. They understand the key drivers and have the means to influence those drivers and measure them. They translate their business strategy into departmental or divisional strategies, know what is to be achieved, which data needed analysis, its area of application, and expected outcomes. The organization has a culture that supports decision makers who have the definition of the information critical to the success of the enterprise and the means to achieve it by linking data, decisions, and actions. And, for achieving all of this, the organization must possess the necessary expertise and skills in the usability of ES and its information. Quality of data plays a vital role.

In order to succeed in today's competitive world, businesses must shift their focus from improving efficiencies to increasing effectiveness. Integrated access to pertinent information captured by ES must be available so that effective decisions can be made towards successfully implementing strategies, optimizing business performance, and adding value for customers. Knowledge is a key factor in this process. Success or failure is often attributed to enterprise systems or their implementation process. However, it is evident from this study that enterprise systems provide a platform of functionalities and information to an organization. The ability of an organization to extract value from data, distribute results from analysis, apply knowledge, and establish decisions for strategic organizational benefits will lead the path towards business success which would eventually emerge from the process of ongoing transformations over a period of time.

REFERENCES

Baskerville, R., Pawlowski, S., & McLean, E. (2000). Enterprise resource planning and organizational knowledge: patterns of convergence and divergence. *Paper presented at the International Conference on Information Systems, Proceedings of the 21st International Conference on Information Systems*, Brisbane, Australia, p. 396-406.

Bendoly. (2002). Theory and Support for Process Frameworks of Knowledge Discovery and Data Mining from ERP Systems. *Information and Management, 40*(7), August 2002.

Cooke, D. P., & Peterson, W. J. (1998). *SAP implementation: Strategies and Results* (No. 1217-98-RR). New York.

Dalal, N. P., Kamath, M., Kolarik, W. J., & Sivaraman, E. (2004). Toward an integrated approach for modeling Enterprise processes. *Communications of the ACM, 47*, 83-87.

Davenport, T. H. (1995). *SAP: Big Change Comes in Big Packages*, from http://www.cio.com/archive/101595_davenpor.html

Davenport, T. H. (1998). Putting the enterprise into the enterprise system. *Sloan Management Review, July-August*, 121-131.

Davenport, T. H. (2000). Transforming the Practice of Management with Enterprise Systems. In *Mission Critical* (p. 203-235). Boston: Harvard Business School Press.

Davenport, T. H., Harris, J. G., & Cantrell, S. (2002). *The Return of Enterprise Systems: The Director's Cut*: Accenture Institute for Strategic Change.

Davenport, T. H., & Prusak, L. (1998). Working Knowledge. *Boston, Harvard Business School Press*.

Deloitte, C. (1998). *ERP's Second Wave-Maximizing the Value of ERP-Enabled Processes*. New York: Deloitte Consulting, ISBN 1-892383-42-X.

Donovan, M. (1998). *There is no magic in ERP software: It's in preparation of the process and people*. Retrieved September 8, 2/7/2002, from http://wwwrmdonovan.com/pdf/perfor_98_9.pdf

Donovan, M. (2001). *Successful ERP Implementation the first time*. Retrieved July 25, 2001, from www.mdonovan.com/pdf/perfor8.pdf

Donovan, M. (2003). *Why the Controversy over ROI from ERP?*, from www.refresher.com/archives19.html

Hedman, J., & Borell, A. (2002). The impact of Enterprise Resource Planning Systems on Organizational Effectiveness: An Artifact Evaluation. In F. F.-H. Nah (Ed.), *Enterprise Resource Planning Solutions & Management* (p. 125-142). Hershey, London: IRM Press.

Ittner, C. D., & Larcker, D. F. (2003). Coming Up Short on Nonfinancial Performance Measurement. *Harvard Business Review, 81*(11), 88-95.

Jarra, Y. F., Al-Mudimigh, A., & Zairi, M. (2000). ERP Implementation Critical Success Factors - The Role and Impact of Business Process Management. *IEEE & ICMIT, 02/2000*, 122-127.

Markus, M., & Tanis, C. (2000). The Enterprise Systems Experience - From Adoption to Success. In R. W. Zmud (Ed.), *In Framing the Domains of IT Research Glimpsing the Future Through the Past* (pp. 173-207). Cincinnati: Pinnaflex Educational Resources, Cincinnati, USA.

Newell, S., Huang, J. C., Galliers, R. D., & Pan, S. L. (2003). Implementing enterprise resource planning and knowledge management systems in tandem: fostering efficiency and innovation complementarity. *Information and Organization, 13*, 25-52.

Shang, S., & Seddon, P. (2000, August 10-13). A Comprehensive Framework for Classifying the Benefits of ERP Systems. *Paper presented at the 6th America's Conference on Information Systems*, Long Beach, California.

Yang, S., & Seddon, P. B. (2004). Benefits and Key Success Factors from Enterprise Systems Implementations: Lessons from Sapphire 2003. *Paper presented at the 35th Australasian Conference in Information Systems*, Hobart, Australia.

KEY TERMS

Business Process Re-Engineering (BPR): Rethinking and redesign of business processes to achieve performance improvements in terms of overall cost, quality and service of the business.

Conceptual Framework: A basic conceptual structure built from a set of concepts to outline possible courses of action or to present a preferred approach to solve a complex research problem.

Customer Relationship Management (CRM): Software systems that help companies to acquire knowledge about customers and deploy strategic information systems to optimize revenue, profitability and customer satisfaction.

Enterprise Resource Planning (ERP): Software systems for business management that integrates functional areas such as planning, manufacturing, sales, marketing, distribution, accounting, finances, human resource management, project management, inventory management, service and maintenance, transportation, and e-business.

Knowledge Management (KM): The creation, organization, sharing, and flow of knowledge within and among organizations.

Return on Investment (ROI): A performance measurement used to evaluate the efficiency of an investment. ROI is calculated as the annual financial benefit (return) after an investment minus the cost of the investment divided by the cost of the investment the result being expressed as a percentage or a ratio.

Supply Chain Management (SCM): Software systems for procurement of materials, transformation of the materials into products, and distribution of products to customers, allowing the enterprise to anticipate demand and deliver the right product to the right place at the right time at the lowest possible cost to satisfy its customers.

ENDNOTES

[1] A pseudonym. The name was chosen to symbolize growth.

[2] A pseudonym. The name was chosen to symbolize power.

Chapter XI
The Right Path to SCM–CRM Integration

Charlotte H. Mason
University of Georgia, USA

Aleda V. Roth
Clemson University, USA

ABSTRACT

Growing competitive pressures and escalating customer demands have led businesses to sophisticated information technology to manage costs and enhance revenues. Two popular initiatives are supply chain management (SCM) and customer relationship management (CRM). SCM focuses on optimizing the materials, information, services, and financial flows through a supply network. CRM focuses on marketing, sales, and customer service, and aims to maximize the value of customer relationships. Furthermore, the real potential lies in the integration of SCM and CRM. Disconnected implementations can result in IT "silos" with redundancies in hardware, software and staff, breaks in the information chain, and disappointing performance. There are different paths to integration. The right path depends on the organization's relative maturity on 6 key factors: 1) interconnectivity, 2) interoperability of systems' functionality, 3) information integrity, 4) interorganizational competence, 5) intellectual capital, and 6) innovative capability.

INTRODUCTION

Since the early 1990s, the number and varieties of software categories available to firms have skyrocketed. Due to advances in other information, process, and communication technologies (IPCT), and especially those related to the Internet, managers have far greater choices and expanded functionality for running their businesses than ever before. Of these, software for coordinating enterprise-wide supply and demand is among the most prominent. On the supply side, Supply Chain

Management (SCM) systems may employ enterprise resource planning (ERP) software to boost enterprise efficiency, improve decision-making by providing greater visibility into operations, and promote collaboration via information sharing. On the demand side, Customer Relationship Management (CRM) offers the opportunity to gain more information in real time about current and prospective customers, providing functionality for contact management, sales force automation, and customer service. A recent survey by the Yankee Group reveals that external applications – those aimed at enhancing customer and supplier relationships – are growing at a much faster rate than internally focused applications (Westervelt, 2004). Furthermore, companies are increasingly focused on integrating technologies.

For some firms, the SCM and CRM software solutions delivered at least partially on their promises, whereas for others the results were less than anticipated. Despite significant investments in resources, most companies were not prepared for the implementation hurdles. During the first wave of their infusion into businesses, in which individual SCM and/or CRM software modules were generally treated as separate installations, the integration with existing legacy systems proved most troublesome. The Standish Group (1995) reported that the average cost overrun was 178 percent of budget; and the implementation schedules exceed 230 percent of plan. Estimates of implementation failures of CRM ranged from 55 - 75 percent according to the Meta Group (Johnson, 2004). From a survey of 162 senior managers conducted by Bain and Co. (Cook and Hagey, 2003), researchers concluded that SCM– which was long touted as an avenue to control costs, reduce risks, and increase service performance– was mismanaged by most companies. While executives in charge of supply-chain management recognized the importance of the supply chain, many had yet to realize its potential. Interestingly, 86 percent said supply-chain performance was a priority, but two-thirds said their companies failed to track

the performance of their internal supply chains outside their corporations.

Recent evidence is more encouraging. In a survey of primarily large, established, business-to-business U.S. firms, Ramaswami, Bhargava, and Srivastava (2004) found that both CRM and SCM processes have positive and significant associations with the financial performance of firms. Rosenzweig, Roth, and Dean (2003) reported that the intensity of supply chain integration led to improved capabilities. Roth, Cattani, and Froehle (2008) empirically showed that the fundamentals of supply chain management were prerequisites to global competence; and Stratman and Roth (2008) linked ERP competence to business performance. However, many companies found that the payoff from implementing only one side of the equation was not enough (Koudal and Lavieri, 2003). In response, some are calling for a "consumer driven supply chain" (IBM, 2004) that represents a shift from traditional supply chains that focus on maximizing internal systems to end-to-end systems. These systems are highly collaborative, integrated throughout the enterprise, and emphasize more focus on the ultimate impact on the consumer. Similarly, Deloitte Consulting refers to firms who have effectively linked SCM with CRM as having a 'digital loyalty network.'

Despite its potential, integrating SCM and CRM processes has proven to be a major challenge that few have tried or accomplished (Bartholomew, 2004; Koudal and Lavieri, 2003), as steep organizational changes are often necessary – from literally revamping entire business processes, to reorganization, to aggressively developing the people competencies not only to use, but also to leverage the new systems for competitive advantage. Unfortunately, the prevailing notions of how best to achieve the 'optimal' level of integration – the right path, so to speak – is not well understood. In this chapter, we describe how firms can successfully take advantage of 'integrated' SCM and CRM functionalities. We propose a classification of the SCM-CRM integration paths in terms of business processes, technology functionality, and people competence. We will discuss the conditions that make successful integration possible, as well as those that may put obstacles in the way.

THE VALUE OF CUSTOMER RELATIONSHIP MANAGEMENT SOLUTIONS

The customer-centric orientation views customers as key assets of the firm that seeks to build a portfolio of the 'right' customers. Relationships with these customers must be developed and then effectively and efficiently managed. The fundamental principle of Customer Relationship Management (CRM) is to leverage customer data to build profitable relationships by optimizing the value delivered to and realized from each customer. CRM is not a technology, but it is made possible by technology that allows a business to integrate, analyze, and act upon large volumes of customer data. Successful CRM applications must start with a business strategy, which in turn drives changes in business processes that are made possible by information technology.

Many early CRM software products and implementations started out as 'point' solutions – ones designed for a specific function such as sales force automation or campaign management. This led to a proliferation of CRM tools, each with its own unlinked customer file. Businesses are increasingly realizing that a "360° view" or "single view of the customer" with all customer-related data in a single data warehouse is a key factor for enterprise-wide CRM success. This "single version of the truth" consolidates all bits of information about the customer, including purchases, channel preferences, demographic and psychographic data, payment history, marketing contacts, service records, complaints or inquiries, and other communications with the company (see Figure 1). CRM solutions integrate and apply this customer information to all aspects of the business including but not limited to marketing, sales, and customer service that *touch* the customer.

Where Does CRM Provide Value?

CRM is prevalent across many industries, but has been most aggressively adopted in the financial and services sectors, including banks, credit cards, airlines, hotels, and retailers. A 2002 study by

Figure 1. A single 360° view of the customer integrates all customer information

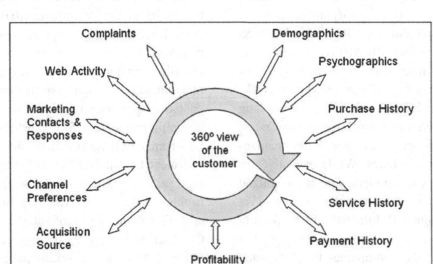

Forrester Research reported that nearly half of financial and business services firms had CRM solutions completely or partially rolled out, with another 40 percent piloting or actively considering CRM solutions. More recently, Bain's 2007 Management Tools and Trends survey showed that CRM is second only to Strategic Planning in usage, with 84 percent of surveyed firms reporting using CRM.

CRM solutions are typically split into two areas: operational CRM and analytical CRM. Operational CRM includes the customer-facing applications that focus on managing customer interactions. Analytical CRM supports and aids decision-making with a range of tools from simple spreadsheet analyses to sophisticated data mining. Operational CRM and analytical CRM support each other in a feedback loop (Chan, 2005). Operational CRM captures critical data for input into analytical analyses. Insights into customers' behaviors obtained from analytical CRM are then tied into operational CRM solutions. The most common CRM applications focus on sales, marketing, or customer service processes.

- **Sales force automation (SFA):** Regarded as the foundation of CRM tools (Ross, 2005), sales force automation is designed to help salespeople acquire and retain customers, and manage their accounts. Key components of SFA solutions include lead distribution and tracking, contact management, sales process management, pipeline management, sales forecasting tools, and automated generation of quotes and orders.
- **Customer interaction center applications:** The most prevalent of the applications focusing on customer service and support are call center applications, which aid call routing and assignment, queue management, call tracking, entitlement processing, problem resolution, and performance measurement.

- **Marketing automation:** Marketing automation uses information technology to automate the marketing process and get the right message to the right person at the right time using the right media. Marketing automation encompasses analytics to segment customers and target campaigns, campaign management to execute marketing campaigns including personalization, and detailed response tracking.

Benefits of CRM

New classes of customer-centric metrics are used to measure and monitor CRM initiatives. These include customer profitability and lifetime value, share of customer or share of wallet, retention or attrition rates, customer satisfaction, loyalty, up-sell and cross-sell rates, and cost to serve. Common benefits of successful customer relationship management initiatives include the following:

- **Increased revenues:** A larger share of customer wallet and increased revenues can result from increased usage or purchases of the products and services customers already use or increased revenues from sales of additional or higher-margin products and services. Additionally, satisfied loyal customers may be less price sensitive, so fewer price promotions are needed to drive sales.
- **Improved customer loyalty and retention:** Satisfied customers often stay longer, are less likely to churn, are less likely to consider taking their business elsewhere, and more likely to generate referrals of desirable new prospects. These result in a reduced need to solicit new customers and lower new customer recruiting costs.
- **Reduced costs of serving customers:** Predictive modeling to better target marketing communications can produce significant reductions in unproductive advertising

and marketing campaign costs. Initiatives to move customers from higher cost (e.g., phone) to lower cost (e.g., Internet) channels can realize significant cost savings.

- **Improved resource allocation:** Knowing which customers are highly profitable, which are marginally profitable, which are unprofitable, and which have upside profit potential allows firms to better to allocate marketing and customer service resources.

- **Improved product portfolio:** Through capture and analysis of interactive customer feedback, the portfolio of products can be better tailored to customers' needs and desires.

Bottom line results achieved from CRM initiatives vary widely depending, in large part, on how well the people-process-technology triangle is implemented. Successful implementations demonstrate that substantial returns are possible: by focusing attention on its most profitable business customers, a plastics company boosted revenues in excess of 400 percent while cutting its customer base nine-fold. A pharmaceutical company using CRM techniques to target customers realized a 30 percent increase in sales and a 25 percent increase in market share. A major financial services firm realized substantial increases in average customer balances and a 50 percent reduction in customer attrition. In telecommunications, CRM tests have increased customer profitability by 37.5 percent and reduced churn from 37 percent to 18.8 percent. More generally, in a 2003 survey of CEOs, PricewaterhouseCoopers' Trendsetter Barometer found that companies with programs focused on customer expansion, retention, and profitability saw revenues increase 46 percent faster than peers.

THE VALUE OF SUPPLY CHAIN MANAGEMENT SOLUTIONS

Over the past decade, coinciding with progress in CRM, many companies discovered that new information, process, and communication technologies (IPCTs) allowed them to simultaneously reduce costs and compete more effectively in different markets through better management of their supply chain networks (see Figure 2). SCM is an approach to managing a complex range of

Figure 2. Supply chain network flows

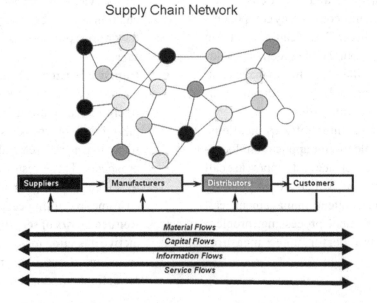

business activities that are associated with the coordination of supply network entities, channels, and resources for the effective delivery of value-added products and services to customers. At the heart of SCM is the optimization of material, information, financial and service flows through a supply network to effectively coordinate business activities that are geographically dispersed.

Because SCM focuses on the operational and strategic processes of the entire network of business entities that transform inputs (e.g., raw materials and information) into value-added, finished products and services for end customers, it enables firms to integrate, leverage, and monitor the continual flows throughout the chain. They also enable knowledge flows among business entities (Rosenzweig and Roth, 2007); and opportunities for global marketplaces, including emerging markets (Zhao, Flynn and Roth, 2006). Supply chains exist in both service and manufacturing organizations, but many are a combination of both types. Usually the activities in early stages of a supply chain are manufacturing-oriented (e.g., weaving fabric or assembling cars) and the latter stages are service-oriented (e.g., retailing apparel, logistics, or managing a car dealership). Service processes often occur at the interfaces between firms in the supply chain to coordinate information flows and logistics from customers. Frequently service businesses have their own supply chain characteristics and supply chain configurations (see for example Oliveira and Roth, 2008).

Unlike CRM, which tends to be more service-oriented, most of the published SCM articles deal with product-oriented supply chains, although the complexity of the supply chain network may vary considerably from firm to firm and industry to industry. Many companies are employing enterprise resource planning (ERP) models, such as SAP and Peoplesoft, to coordinate their supply chain network. Such coordination is a major driver in the widespread implementation of ERP systems in both manufacturing and services.

Where Does SCM Provide Value?

Vanguard companies are creatively exploiting supply chain thinking and systems to enhance their competitive position. Their organizational mindsets have moved beyond managing their supply chains for solely streamlining operations and trimming costs towards dynamic competitive capability creation. Immediately upon implementing a new real-time data collection system simultaneously with its new enterprise resources planning (ERP) system, Oki Data Americas, a Mt. Laurel, New Jersey-based manufacturer of computer printers and fax machines, increased sales by $6 million in the first month. A central objective of Oki Data's deployment of its ERP solution was to be able to handle increased business, but a surprise benefit was the more efficient flow of bar-coded data passing into the system that stemmed from the deployment of a manufacturing and warehouse execution software package. Information system retooling with ERP at Palm cut by one-third (or 48 hours) the time it took to receive information and pass that information to manufacturing and receive confirmation (Baljko, 2003).

Fully integrated CRM-SCM solutions enable advanced planning and scheduling, which gives users the ability to monitor actual supply chain process plans, simulate scenarios, assess impacts, and quickly respond to customer queries or changes. Agility has an inherent footprint with sourcing. Agile companies characteristically have distributed supply chains and a high velocity of engineering change or product changes. Dupont's savings were estimated to be $7 million through network purchasing, where its ERP system provided the common foundation for all sites to share information (Young 1999). Thus, by seamlessly linking their key customers and partners into their supply chains, supply chain exemplars are:

- Becoming more adaptive and agile.
- Improving responsiveness to customers needs.

- Providing more cost-efficient delivery options for their product, service, capital, and information flows.

In today's dynamic, clockspeed competitive environments, anecdotal, and ad-hoc decision making won't make the grade for long term survival. Just as supply chain innovators, such as Wal-Mart and Dell Computer, carved out their place at the table in the business-to-business (B2B) arena during the past decade, new players are constantly emerging with new supply chain optimizing technologies. While still few in number, several can operate effectively in virtual space. These players are not only "technology-savvy" companies, such as Amazon.com and Cisco, but also some prominent, well-established players in the automotive, chemicals, packaged goods, and services sectors.

The future appears extremely bright for those intelligent enterprises that can evolve and dynamically provide extraordinary value to customers from leveraging their supply chains for new product development, to marketing and sales, to manufacturing and distribution, to end-of life activities, such as remanufacturing and reverse logistics. Over the next few years, those firms that can remove excess costs and assets from their supply chains while simultaneously improving their own internal resources, building inimitable customer services, and improving customer responsiveness will delight customers and outperform competitors.

The most promising SCM approaches focus on:

- The development of robust supply chain strategies for integrating sales, manufacturing, distribution, customer services, and account transactions.
- Understanding economic and other trade-offs in optimizing internal processes, systems, and resources for the enterprise and across the supply chain globally, and

monitoring the relevant performance criteria.
- Cost-modeling and decision-aiding tools for "what if" scenario planning used in designing and evaluating supply chain entities.
- Building enterprise information systems to improve visibility from the suppliers' suppliers to the customers' customers.
- The transfer and use of advanced information and process technologies in manufacturing and services among supply chain entities.

Potential Benefits of SCM

SCM is evolving as a core competency for competing in the 21st century. It offers new business models for firms seeking to go beyond providing excellent service at competitive rates. Other benefits include:

- Reducing total delivered costs and time-to-volume for new products,
- Enhancing visibility, quality, and flexibility,
- Meeting the increasing and changing demands of their customers,
- Improving end-of-life and sustainable environmental practices, and
- Becoming an agile and learning organization.

But the magnitude and nature of these benefits vary greatly for companies that are in different evolutionary phases. Firms that are more inward-oriented tend to emphasize improving logistics and focus on cutting both order-cycle times and transit times. Taking days and dollars out of the supply chain is viewed as one of the first key competitive advantages of supply chains. It is not uncommon to see 25-40 percent reductions in inventory and 25-30 percent improvements in customer service levels as a result of a successful ERP implementation. Companies, that understand the value of supply-chain management, such as

Home Depot, are working twice as efficiently as those with less mastery. Yet firms must manage their extended supply chains in order to achieve the total delivered costs, increased responsiveness, and accelerated time-to-market that arise from better forecasting, stock utilization, information, and standardized processes.

Mastery of the next level of supply chain management through B2B yields greater and different economies of scope. Not only can companies realize benefits of efficient movement of goods and services; they can also benefit from changes in the solution space that make collaboration possible. For example, they can scale up design workgroups across a company's entire supply chain, quickly and affordably. Managing supply chains in the B2B arena enables companies to take full advantage of competitive capabilities from design through the manufacturing process.

Finally, SCM makes it possible to achieve strategic agility at the most sophisticated and revolutionary business-entity-to-entity levels: those of the virtual enterprise. The benefits are the ability to deliver the right product to the right customer at the right time at the right cost, and in the process to adapt and learn fast. At this level, all supply chain virtual partners have the potential to win, with real-time information access, streamlined order-to-cash processes, reduced processing and integration costs, and economies of knowledge.

INTEGRATING CRM AND SCM SOLUTIONS

Why Integrate CRM AND SCM?

The answer to this question is deceptively simple: *Integration of CRM and SCM enables companies to close the enormous gaps between supply and demand processes.* While both CRM and SCM can provide significant strategic benefits and cost savings, the full benefits can only be

realized by integrating the two. By automating back-office processing and design functions and cutting costs through more efficient order-entry systems, inventory management, logistics and production management, most SCM solutions are largely either functional or intra-enterprise-oriented. In contrast, CRM solutions focus on the customer-facing and revenue-generating aspects of the business.

A best-of-class CRM implementation, which can identify individual customers and communicate to them with tailored messages and offers, perhaps cross-selling additional products, is of limited value if the supply chain is not able to deliver the goods in a timely manner and at a reasonable cost. Similarly, a best-of-class SCM implementation that is not paired with accurate and timely knowledge of customers' needs is just a more efficient way of delivering a suboptimal end product.

Ultimately, the customer is at the end of the supply chain. The supply chain needs information collected from customer-facing touch points to make for efficient production scheduling. In return, CRM initiatives need an effective supply chain to deliver in accord with customer expectations. In summary, as stated by Min and Mentzer (2000), CRM and SCM are "inextricably intertwined." (p. 782)

Levels of Integration

The four main levels of integration between SCM and CRM are nonintegrated point solutions, limited or functional integration, intra-enterprise integration, and inter-enterprise integration (see Figure 3). With nonintegrated solutions, a business has different application programs, each operating largely as a silo. For example, within the CRM arena, a retailer's website may not be integrated with their call center for phone orders. In the next level of integration, all CRM modules are integrated and all SCM modules are integrated. The third level of integration links the demand-side CRM applications with the supply-side SCM applications within the same line of business or company; this reflects cross-functional integration within the business. The final level integrates CRM and SCM solutions that cross line-of-business or firm boundaries

Benefits of Integration

Benefits of SCM-CRM integration can be quantitative or qualitative. Quantitative benefits can be measured in hard numbers, whereas qualitative benefits can only be measured using 'soft' criteria. Increased demand and revenues and reduced costs for staff, transaction, or materials result in quantifiable, tangible benefits. Intangible benefits may include improved agility, stronger competitive position, and technical consistency.

Specific tangible benefits from traditional SCM-CRM integration include the following:

- **Reduced redundancy** in systems and staff as a result of fewer manual 'hand-offs' needed.
- **Consistent data** across functions so that, for example, a customer-facing call center application operates from the same product availability information as the manufacturing plants and distribution centers.
- **Improved response time** resulting from an unbroken chain of information and automated transaction processing across both demand- and supply-side applications.

When the CRM 'generate demand' activities and the SCM 'fulfill demand' activities are properly implemented and integrated, each one enhances the other. Far-reaching, but less tangible synergies are possible with CRM and SCM integration. These include:

- Operational synergies due to shared resources and overlapping processes.
- Financial synergies due to reduced capital risks.
- Organizational synergies result in higher quality management, and reduced asymmetric information and visibility.
- Marketplace synergies arise from better coordination and responsiveness.

Together these four types of synergies are self reinforcing, and they yield long-term financial gains from delivering increased customer value (which CRM applications can provide) while simultaneously improving the supply base from new product development through end-of-cycle practices (which SCM applications can provide).

Growing empirical evidence supports the benefits of CRM–SCM integration. In 2001, Deloitte interviewed executives at nearly 250 major consumer companies in 28 countries and concluded that consumer companies with integrated systems are two to five times more likely to achieve superior performance in sales, market share, customer service, and other key measures – and much more likely to generate higher shareholder returns

Figure 3. Levels of SCM-CRM integration

Level 1 Non-integrated	Level 2 Functional Integration	Level 3 Intra-Enterprise Integration	Level 4 Inter-Enterprise Integration
Point SCM Solutions	Integrated SCM Solution	Integrated SCM-CRM Solution	Business-to-business SCM-CRM integration
Point CRM Solutions	Integrated CRM Solution		

(CRMDaily.com, May 21, 2001). A key finding in a 2002 updated study by Deloitte Research is that companies that have effectively tied together their customer relationship management and supply chain applications – a process that lets them link service levels to profitability of individual customers–are 81 percent more profitable than those that don't (Smith, 2002).

Bartholomew (2004) reports that although few firms have made CRM and SCM systems connect, those who have–including furniture maker Herman Miller, Inc. and industrial controls and instrument manufacturer F. W. Murphy Co.–are significantly more profitable. Evidence from analysis of case studies led Heikklila (2002) to propose that supply chains should start from the customer end to yield the maximum benefit. Empirical results from a cross-section of large U.S. firms found that benefits from CRM applications are greater when CRM-generated information is integrated with supply chain partners (Mithas, Krishnan, and Fornell, 2005). Based on an international sample spanning Asia, Europe, North and South America, Frohlich and Westbrook (2001) found that firms with the widest 'arc' of integration including both suppliers and customers had the strongest performance along a diverse set of measures including customer service, quality, cost, market share, and firm profitability. Conversely, they also found that weak links between suppliers and customers appeared to hurt performance, a finding corroborated by Rosenzweig et al. (2003).

Challenges of Integration

Advancing to higher levels of CRM-SCM integration presents significant technical and organizational challenges.

Technical Challenges

Level 2 B2B solutions generally require firms to substitute automation for labor in order to integrate back-office transactions and logistics processes, including order processing, inventory management, payables and receivables, and production scheduling. Advancing to higher levels of CRM–SCM integration often necessitates a broader role particularly for automation and decision support tools, which help to improve workers' productivity and enhance their abilities. Online transaction processing (OLTP) and logistics process are core competencies of traditional SCM suppliers, while the tools for integrated customer support and collaborative product and process design are a less mature, emerging competence.

In the CRM realm, solutions are more externally focused and draw on ever-changing customer information (sometimes in real-time) to guide sales, marketing, and customer service decisions. Decision-support systems (DSS) tools, including online analytical processing (OLAP), queries, data analysis, and data mining, extract information from the customer data. The information used and analysis needed for CRM applications vary over time depending on the user, the market environment, and the business strategy. Yet the traditional IT and data warehousing solutions, which are best suited for an OLTP environment (core to SCM solutions) are different from those best suited for a DSS environment (core to CRM solutions). These differences highlight the challenges of technical integration.

Not only do the role, nature, and complexity of technology change with levels of integration, but also the complexity of decision-making. Take the evolution of manufacturing systems, for example. Simply put, materials requirements planning (MRP) is a level 2 integration system in which requirements are taken from customers or internally developed forecasts, and are compared to on-hand inventories in order to calculate what must be produced and ordered from suppliers, offset by the estimated lead times. MRP logic of "what do I need, what do I have on hand, and what do I need to get and when?" is the backbone of today's ERP systems. Yet, as depicted, the complexity of managing the diversity of technology choices has grown exponentially.

Similar levels of complexity appear with evolving CRM solutions, so the combined integration with SCM may appear to be technologically daunting. Managers typically encounter additional technical problems:

- Mission-critical data and applications are on legacy systems.
- Proprietary and varied turnkey applications are not easy to access across platforms.
- A proliferation of hardware and software systems and platforms that are incompatible.
- A hodgepodge of networking equipment, policies, documentation, and communication protocols.
- Geographically dispersed and locally operated sites.

Organizational Challenges

One of the first organizational challenges faced in CRM-SCM integration is bridging the difference in the languages and cultures of the various entities to be integrated, as is readily gleaned from observations of marketing and operations functions in companies. Such diversity is greatly accentuated by the fourth level of integration across enterprises.

Even more severe are the structural mismatches between organizational and people competencies required for integration. Technology continues to grow exponentially and businesses struggle to keep pace with organizational skills and managerial know-how aptitudes.

PATHS TO INTEGRATION

The scope, time to implementation, and cost of a fully integrated platform can be considerable. Customers with immediate needs for solutions are often not willing to wait for the major players to deliver the goods. Swift moving, smaller vendors that lack the full suites of integration, but deliver in smaller packages that 'bolt-on' to current systems, are rampant. One downside of the bolt-ons is that they do not necessarily interface with other technologies in place; and remediation and system updates can cause costly disruptions enterprise-wide, as the domino effects from tweaking can be pervasive and have unknown consequences. Other companies are opting for 'home grown' solutions. One immediate consequence of this, of course, is that companies may not have the expertise they need at the start--they don't know what they don't know. So what is the right path?

Key Factors in CRM-SCM Integration

There are multiple paths to integration. Clearly, there are no simple solutions for choosing the right path, but there are six key success factors, each strategic, as companies move to higher and higher levels of CRM-SCM integration maturity. At the heart of integration are what we call the 6 I's to CRM-SCM integration: 1) *Interconnectivity*, 2) *Interoperability of systems*, 3) *Information integrity*, 4) *Interorganizational competence*, 5) *Intellectual capital,* and 6) *Innovative capability*. The paths given in Figure 4 represent different levels of entity maturity.

1. **Interconnectivity:** At the most basic level, there must be technical connectivity among the integrating entities. In other words, the operating systems of all entities must have the means to "talk to each other" consistently and routinely. In the simplest integration, interconnectivity may take the form of telephone and fax. Further integration requires more complex automation through traditional electronic data interchange (EDI) up to more advanced IPCT applications where available information is visible. However, a first order condition is that there

be accessibility and systems reliability for *all* integrating entities. Increasingly, robust and well-designed mobile applications are enabling modules to communicate on wireless and disconnected modes.

2. **Information integrity:** Information accuracy and completeness is necessary for integration. The levels of detail and aggregation may vary, however, as will the real-time availability of the information. These will

be a function of business decision-making relevance related to the degree of integration intensity.

3. **Interoperability of systems:** Next in importance is interoperability. The ease of use by all integrating parties is essential, as is having equivalent system functionality. Here portals, web servers, and data warehouses may perform the functions that users expect – integration via hyperlinks, presentation

Figure 4. Maturity paths for CRM-SCM integration

Key Success Factors	Stage 1 Non Integrated	Stage 2 Functional	Stage 3 Intra-Enterprise	Stage 4 Inter-Enterprise
Interconnectivity	Minimal			High
Technical Accessibility Visibility	Few or no common platforms			Common cross-enterprise platforms
Information Integrity				
Accuracy, Completeness Timeliness Relevance	Myopic 'local view'			360 degree view
System Interoperability	Moderate			High
Usability Functionality				
Interorganizational Competencies	Local competencies			Overlapping competencies
Process People skills Technology				
Intellectual Capital				
Codification Learning Adaptation	Functional expertise			Business expertise
Innovative Capability				
Creativity Anticipation Proactiveness Agility	Reactive			Proactive

of content, and hyperlinks to resources. Take for example Invensys Manufacturing Solutions (IMS) Unit, based in Herndon, Virginia. IMS has developed interoperability technology software that helps define and manage the execution layer that integrates with other plant and enterprise management applications from Invensys, as well as third-party applications. There are several facets to its interoperability, namely, a common user environment; event management and reporting; configurable, standard response to detected events; and the ability to leverage data from manufacturing data sources and providers. Paul LeMert, director of strategic marketing for IMS, likens better connectivity of plant-floor data with other levels to "synchronizing the two workflows by having current islands of automation and islands of information working in concert" (Schultz, 2003).

4. **Interorganizational competence:** Interorganizational competencies are the skills, operational practices, and integrating mechanisms needed for linking entities (for an organizational competency assessment tool, see Stratman and Roth, 2002a, 2002b, and 2008 and Masini and Van Wasshenove, 2008). CRM-SCM integration is a strategic business decision. As integration intensity increases, the degree of overlapping processes, the level of people competencies and technological prowess will rise (McAfee, 2002; Robey, Ross, and Boudreau, 2002). The threshold level of integration will be established by the weakest link in the network and therefore appropriate investments must be made to acquire the requisite competencies for each entity at the desired stage of maturity.

5. **Intellectual capital:** Intellectual capital is defined in terms of the firm's knowledge assets: structural capital, human capital, and abortive capacity. At lower levels of

integration, the form of intellectual capital will be more structural (e.g., codified and embedded in routines, processes, and systems). Advancement in integration requires more business savvy people with not only technical acumen, but also who are able to deal with increasingly complex and unstructured environments. Thus, the efficacy of management and technical talent will vary greatly from each stage of maturity. In order to gain what Roth (1996) coined as 'economies of knowledge' from integration, the firm must be willing and able to make the requisite investments in human capital and in the organization's ability to learn and adapt.

6. **Innovative capability:** Innovation is the ability to create something new that will be demanded by customers. Clearly, the organization's collective creativity and agility are important drivers of innovation. Proactiveness and anticipation are other facets of innovation. Increasing richness of the interactive tools, collaborative, and e-business applications that are afforded by integration must be leveraged. Investment in higher levels of innovation requires increasing levels of innovative capability.

Importantly, the ability of the entity network to function in a seamless manner will be limited by the weakest link. For example, if one partner in the network has incomplete or inadequate data, this lack of data integrity has a multiplicative impact through the network that effectively brings all other entities to the same level. Arguably, relative maturity on interconnectivity, interoperability, and information integrity are more tangible and technical elements. As a result, an entity's relative maturity stage on these elements is easier to detect than its maturity on softer, intangible elements of organizational competence, intellectual capital, and innovative capability.

In our experience, most companies emphasize alignment on the tangibles, and only give lip service, or even totally neglect the intangible maturity elements that are more difficult and timely to gauge. Take Toyota, for example. Toyota's organizational competence is set up to manage the entire value stream for each product family, rather than leaving each supply network entity to optimize its own activities. Consequently, Toyota spends considerable effort on understanding and improving the organizational competencies of its suppliers and distribution entities, and working on joint process analyses. Similarly, getting a better grasp of a partner's innovative capability maturity, for example, will allow for a more realistic assessment of potential benefits of integration for accelerating time to volume ramp up for new product and services. Thus, getting the tangible elements in sync is not enough. All entities must be aligned at the same maturity stage across all six key factors in order to reap the *full* benefits of further progression.

STRATEGIC INTEGRATION: IT'S MORE THAN SYSTEMS INTEGRATION

Challenges of Implementing and Integrating CRM and SCM Solutions

Choosing the right path for any organization requires making short-term and long-term trade-offs. As companies move toward higher levels of integration, most will be hard pressed to keep their home grown or bolt-on solutions current. The pace of technological change is dizzying. On the other hand, the full integrating vendors will need to become more flexible and agile as their customers' needs for flexibility, best-of-breed, and customized solutions are rising. The marketplace dynamics will not be kind to those vendors that cannot swiftly adapt.

Though the potential benefits of fully integrated CRM and SCM solutions are great, the challenges can be formidable and success is not automatic. Despite the promise, statistics show that many CRM-SCM implementations failed to achieve their business goals. Beyond the matching of maturity elements, we found some common pitfalls among the failures - nonintegrated business and technology strategy, inconsistent top management support, lack of trust, and inadequate understanding of technology. Turn these pitfalls into promise by:

- **Building a strong business case.** The system is only as good as the business strategy that it supports. Successful SCM and CRM solutions require a sound underlying business case coupled with metrics to measure and monitor the results. This business strategy must be clearly articulated and communicated to all stakeholders.

- **Securing management support and commitment.** SCM and CRM solutions reflect a business approach that extends far beyond mere technology tools. Successful implementation requires the involvement of and commitment from personnel spanning sales and marketing, operations, and information technology. Support and commitment from the top help ensure that all are aligned and working towards the same objectives. The CEO and the team should 'own' the implementation. Once implemented, the integration is a key strategic tool around which critical business decisions are to be made - and this should not be relegated to technical experts.

- **Building communication and trust.** In corporate politics, information is power and this can result in an environment in which information is not shared. Successful integration of SCM and CRM solutions requires the sharing of information across the organization, and potentially with partner organizations as well. Build teams and constantly share expectations and lessons learned.

- **Developing an understanding of the technologies.** Although technology is just one component of the solution, it is vital to its overall success. Factors such as scalability, integration, and functionality need to be considered up-front. Inherent capabilities of the technologies should be understood in advance.

Millennium Chemicals

AMR Research reported that many companies are accelerating their integration efforts to make way for e-business interactions. Large chemical companies spent at least $10 million on systems integration and say that their ROI can even be higher (Fattah and D'Amico, 2003). The benefits of an integrated customer relationship management and supply chain management solution are evident at Millennium Chemicals, a major international chemical company, with leading market positions in a broad range of commodity, industrial, performance, and specialty chemicals. With $1.6 billion in annual sales and an employee network spanning five continents, Millennium Chemicals is the world's second-largest producer of titanium dioxide (TiO_2); a leading producer of fragrance chemicals; the second-largest producer of acetic acid and vinyl acetate monomer in North America; and a 29.5 percent owner of Equistar Chemicals, LP, the second-largest producer of ethylene and third-largest producer of polyethylene in North America.

The goal of Millennium Chemicals is to use the internet to increase business and reduce costs. To date, they have seen more on the cost side through their implementation of ERP. To garner added revenues, Millennium opened its online store front, called Millennium Direct, in 2000 and is using CRM to implement it. The advantage of a good integrated information system

with the online storefront is to get a competitive edge on service. Since titanium dioxide is a commodity, Millennium's online storefront is a service differentiator to its customers. Providing a competitive edge, its supply chain module has been implemented in 95 percent of the business in 1999 and is stable. Millennium sees SCM-CRM as the backbone of their e-business. Their highly integrated SCM-CRM gives customers not only the ability to display product catalogs and select products online, but also provides real-time feedback with available-to-promise information and adjusted delivery dates based on production schedules and on-hand inventory. The customers can review their order with the delivery information and either modify the order or submit it. The system then confirms the order and provides the order number for tracking purposes. Customers have real time access to all aspects of their order, including reviewing order status, checking account balances, and dynamic invoicing. All other processes around creating delivery and collecting receivables remained stable; however, the order-to-cash process improved significantly.

Millennium Chemical's SCM-CRM integration illustrates their relative maturity on the key factors. The internet provided a high level of *interconnectivity* with customers. *Interoperability* was handled through features and functionality built into the portal; *information integrity* was quite high since the CRM module was integrated with a stable supply chain module implementation, so customers received correct information in a timely fashion. Millennium is attacking *interorganizational competencies* by segmenting its customer base. It is unrealistic to expect all customers to use Millennium Direct at once. Consequently, they prioritized the vendor managed inventory (VMI) segment, which represents 25 percent of the business. As a result, Millennium could eliminate a redundant order entry system. In addition, they built organizational competence with the assistance of highly skilled technology vendors, who had a keen understanding of business processes. Millennium found that the *intellectual capital base* had to be revamped in order to reap the benefits of the newly integrated systems. For example, the customer service representatives' (CSRs) roles changed from being reactive 'order takers' to proactive 'order makers.' This transition required added investments in training, changes in the reward systems, and continuous communications and team building. Finally, Millennium has demonstrated innovative capabilities, as it is now using the integrated system for fine tuning its package type planning and interregional shipment planning.

Millennium found that customers valued the additional information. Orders were processed more quickly. The system helps their customer service representatives work more efficiently. Cost savings resulted from providing the same level of service with fewer CSRs and real time information was available to customers. They estimated a 5-10 percent inventory costs savings from visibility. The internal business processes around production planning and interregional shipments benefited from having a better grip on customer demand, resulting in significantly less global transfer of products.

In summary, Millennium benefited from its SCM-CRM integration. It lowered costs – reduced inventory and headcount - and improved its customer service by providing its customers with real time data and making conducting business with itself easier. The CRM applications managed the customer interaction, and the SCM solutions manage the transactions on the backend. Some lessons learned in their SCM-CRM implementation journey were:

1. Design the system with features and functionality before you go shopping for software.
2. Top management support is critical.
3. Find good technology implementation partners, if in-house capabilities are not sufficient, and be sure they understand business processes.
4. Build the use of new systems into employee objectives.
5. Have a phased rollout.
6. Develop a strategy with lots of reinforcement and communications internally with employees and externally with supply chain partners.
7. Tie CRM in with a stable SCM system
8. Learn by sharing experiences

REFERENCES

Baljko, J. (2003). At Risk Of Losing Its Grip, Palm Improves Demand Management. *EBN,* Feb. 17, 2003, 1.

Bartholomew, D. (2004). Making Ends Meet: Manufacturers seek to connect supply chain with customer systems. *IndustryWeek.com*, April 1. Retrieved July 3, 2007, from http://www.industry-week.com/ReadArticle.aspx?ArticleID=1420

Chan, J. O. (2005). Towards a Unified View of Customer Relationship Management. *The Journal of American Academy of Business, 6*(1), 32-38.

Cook, M., & Hagey, R. (2003). Why Companies flunk supply supply-chain 101: Only 33 percent correctly measure supply-chain performance; few use the right incentives. *Journal of Business Strategy, 24*(4), 35-42.

Fattah, H., & D'Amico, E. (2003). Tying IT all together; the push for systems integration is on. *Chemical Week, 165*(5), 15-18.

Frohlich, M. T., & Westbrook, R. (2001). Arcs of integration: an international study of supply chain strategies. *Journal of Operations Management, 19*, 185-200.

Heikkilä, J. (2002). From supply to demand chain management: Efficiency and customer satisfaction. *Journal of Operations Management, 20*, 747-767.

IBM. (2004). The Consumer Driven Supply Chain. *IBM Retail and Consumer Products Industry Solutions.*

Johnson, J. (2004). Making CRM Technology Work. *British Journal of Administrative Management, 39,* 22-23.

Koudal, P., & Lavieri, T. (2003). Profits in the Balance: When costs and customer and supplier relationships are balanced evenly, profitability increases. *Optimize, 22*(June), 81.

Masini, A., & Van Wasshenove, L. N. (2008). ERP Competence-Building Mechanisms: An Exploratory Investigation of Configurations of ERP Adopters in the European and US Manufacturing Sectors. *Manufacturing & Service Operations Management,* in press.

McAfee, A. (2002). The impact of enterprise information technology adoption on operational performance: An empirical investigation. *Production and Operations Management, 11*(1), 33-53.

Min, S., & Mentzer, J.T. (2000). The role of marketing in supply chain management. *International Journal of Physical Distribution & Logistics, 30*(9), 765-787.

Mithas, S., Krishan, M. S., & Fornell, C. (2005). Why Do Customer Relationship Management Applications Affect Customer Satisfaction? *Journal of Marketing, 69*(October), 201-209.

Morphy, E. (2003). CEO Survey: Fast-Track Firms Chasing Customers. *CRMDaily.com,* January.

Oliveira, P., & Roth, A.V. (2008). The Influence of Service Orientation on B2B e-Service Capabilities. *FCEE-Catolica, Lisbon Portugal and Clemson University Working Paper.*

Ramaswami, S. N., Bhargava, M., & Srivastava, R. (2004). Market-based Assets and Capabilities, Business Processes and Financial Performance. *Marketing Science Institute Working Paper Series No. 04-102.*

Robey, D., Ross, J. W., & Boudreau, M. (2002). Learning to implement enterprise systems: an exploratory study of the dialectics of change. *Journal of Management Information Systems, 19*(1), 17-46.

Rosenzweig, E. D., & Roth, A.V. (2007). B2B Seller Competence: Construct Development and Measurement Using an Operations Strategy Lens. *Journal of Operations Management, 25*(6), 1311-1331.

Rosenzweig, E. D., Roth A. V., & Dean, J. (2003). The Influence of Integration Intensity on Competitive Capabilities and Business Performance: An Exploratory Investigation of Consumer Products Manufacturers. *Journal of Operations Management, 21*(4), 437-456.

Ross, D. F. (2005). E-CRM from a Supply Chain Management Perspective. *Information Systems Management, 22*(1), 37-44.

Roth, A.V. (1996). Achieving Strategic Agility through Economies of Knowledge. *Strategy and Leadership* (formerly *Planning Review), 24*(2), 30-3.

Roth, A.V., Cattani, K., & Froehle, C. (2008). Antecedents and Performance Outcomes of Global Competence: An Empirical Investigation. *Journal of Engineering & Technology Management--Special issue on Research of Technology and Innovation in a Global Context,* in press.

Roth, A.V., Tsay, A., Pullman, M., & Gray, J. (2008). Reaping What You Sow? *International Consumer Research,* in press.

Schultz, G. J. (2002). Data that flows in context: Workflow and other new tools weave data collection into a better business context. *MSI, Oak Brook, 20*(10), 71-76.

Smith, T. (2002). Deloitte Study: Linking CRM, Supply Chain Boosts Profits. *Internetweek.com.* Retrieved February 12, 2002.

Standish Group. (1995). *Chaos Report,* Standish Research Paper. Retrieved July 5, 2007, from http://www.projectsmart.co.uk/docs/chaos-report.pdf.

Stratman, J. K., & Roth, A. V. (2002a). Enterprise Resource Planning (ERP) Competence Constructs: Two-Stage Multi-Item Scale Development and Validation. *Decision Sciences, 33*(4), 601-628.

Stratman, J. K., & Roth, A.V. (2002b). Beyond ERP Implementation: Critical Success Factors for North American Manufacturing Firms. *Supply Chain & Logistics Journal, 5*(1), 5-8.

Stratman, J. K., & Roth, A.V. (2008). Towards a Theory of Enterprise Resource Planning Competence: An Empirical Model of the Post-Installation Success Factors on Financial Performance. *University of Utah and Clemson University Working Paper.*

Westervelt, R. (2004). Finding value in edge-of-enterprise apps. *SearchSAP.com,* February 19. Retrieved July 5, 2007, from http://searchsap.techtarget.com/originalContent/0,289142,sid21_gci951397,00.html

Young, L. (1999). The best buy: Dupont Canada saves millions with network purchasing. *Micromedia Limited, Canadian Business and Current Affairs, 44*(8), 51.

Zhao, X., Flynn, B., & Roth, A.V. (2007). Decision Science Research in China: Current Status, Opportunities and Propositions for Research in Supply Chain Management, Logistics, and Quality Management. *Decision Sciences, 38*(1), 39-80.

KEY TERMS

360° View of the Customer: Having all customer related data consolidated into one location, in order to provide the most complete and thorough view of the customer's information and preferences.

Customer Relationship Management (CRM): The strategic process of selecting and managing interactions with customers to optimize the value of the customer to the organization as well as satisfaction for the customer.

Enterprise Resource Planning (ERP): An integrated information system that serves all departments and functions within an enterprise

Materials Requirement Planning (MRP): Computerized ordering and scheduling system for manufacturing or production process

Marketing Automation: The use of software to automate marketing processes such as customer segmentation, customer data integration, and campaign management.

Sales Force Automation (SFA): Software that automates an organization's sales activities such as lead distribution and tracking, contact management, sales process management pipeline management, sales forecasting tools, and automated generation of quotes and orders.

Supply Chain: The sequence of organizations and functions that mine, make, or assemble materials and products from suppliers to manufacturers to distributors to customers.

Supply Chain Management (SCM): The planning, scheduling and control of the supply chain.

Chapter XII
Enterprise Systems Strategic Alignment and Business Value

Euripidis Loukis
University of the Aegean, Greece

Ioakim Sapounas
University of the Aegean, Greece

Konstantinos Aivalis
ICAP, Greece

ABSTRACT

This chapter is dealing with the alignment of enterprise systems with business strategy and its impact on the business value that enterprise systems generate. Initially the research on the strategic potential of ICT, which constitutes the basic theoretical foundation of the need for strategic alignment of enterprise systems, is analyzed. Then the previous research that has been conducted concerning enterprise systems strategic alignment is critically reviewed. It is grouped into three basic streams. The first of them is dealing with the conceptualization and basic understanding of enterprise systems strategic alignment. The second research stream aims at the development of models and frameworks for directing and assessing enterprise systems strategic alignment. The third research stream examines the impact of enterprise systems strategic alignment on business performance. Finally, an empirical investigation that has been conducted by the authors concerning the impact of enterprise systems strategic alignment on business performance as a guidance for future research on this topic is described. We expect that this chapter will sufficiently inform on strategic alignment, both researchers and practitioners in the area of enterprise systems, so that they can incorporate this highly important concept in their research and practice respectively.

INTRODUCTION

The strategic alignment of information systems (IS) has been ranked as the most important issue that IS managers face in the two most recent formal surveys conducted by the Society for Information Management (SIM) of USA (www.simnet.org) concerning the key IS management issues (Luftman & McLean, 2004; Luftman, 2005). Also, the strategic alignment of IS has been ranked in very high positions in most of the surveys of the key IS management issues that have been conducted in various countries (e.g. Palvia et al, 2002). Several definitions of IS strategic alignment have been proposed by the relevant literature. According to Broadbent & Weil (1993) as IS strategic alignment is defined the extent to which business strategies are enabled, supported and stimulated by information strategies. Luftman (2000) provides a more detailed definition stating that 'Business-IT alignment refers to applying Information Technology in an appropriate and timely way, in harmony with business strategies, goals and needs. This definition of alignment addresses: 1. how IT is aligned with the business and 2. how the business should or could be aligned with IT' (p.3). Duffy (2002) in an IDC Report states that IT technical people have criticized corporate general management for a lack of interest in the IS function; at the same time general management people have criticized the IT technical people for not understanding the business and for not being profit-oriented, being interested mainly in solving technical problems and not business problems. However, at the same time he remarks that 'However valid both of these criticisms may have been, there is evidence that the gap between the two groups is now narrowing" (p.2), and defines 'IT/Business Alignment' as 'the process and goal of achieving competitive advantage through developing and sustaining a symbiotic relationship between IT and Business' (p.4).

The strategic alignment of enterprise systems consists in the establishment of a bilateral rela-tionship between the enterprise systems planning process and the business/strategy planning processes, which allows:

- The mission, goals, competitive strategy, future directions and action plan of the enterprise, and also the analysis of its external environment (e.g. competition, opportunities, threats) and the analysis of its internal environment (e.g. resources, capabilities, strengths, weaknesses), which are basic elements of its business/strategy plan, to be taken into account for the formulation of its enterprise systems plan,
- And also the capabilities, strengths and weaknesses of existing enterprise systems, the planned enterprise systems, the forms and the extent of information and communication technologies (ICT) usage in the industry and the capabilities offered by existing and emerging ICTs that may interest and influence the enterprise, which are basic elements of the enterprise systems plan, to be taken into account for the formulation of the business/strategy plan.

The basic objective of this bilateral relationship is to exploit ICT in the enterprise in the best possible manner for both supporting and enriching its business strategy, and to take advantage to the highest possible extent of the significant strategic potential of ICT.

This chapter is dealing with the alignment of enterprise systems with business strategy and its impact on the business value that enterprise systems generate. It aims to inform on this highly important issue both researchers and practitioners in the area of enterprise systems, so that they take it into account and incorporate it in their research and practice respectively. In this direction in the following second section of this chapter is reviewed briefly the research that has been conducted on the strategic potential of ICT, which constitutes the basic theoretical foundation of the need for strategic alignment of enterprise systems. Then in the third section the previous research that has been conducted concerning enterprise systems strategic alignment is critically reviewed. In the fourth section is described an empirical investigation that has been conducted by the authors concerning the impact of enterprise systems strategic alignment on business performance, based on the construction of complete econometric models, which are founded on the well-established and validated Cobb-Douglas production function, and using objective measures of business performance and enterprise systems investment, and on. Finally the conclusions and the future trends concerning enterprise systems strategic alignment are discussed.

THE STRATEGIC POTENTIAL OF ICT

There has been for more than two decades a high level of interest of both researchers and practitioners in the alignment between enterprise systems and business strategy, which is founded on the recognition that ICT have a significant strategic potential, i.e. if properly exploited they can have a significant strategic impact on the enterprise and provide valuable competitive advantages. The initial research on this strategic potential of ICT has been based on the work of M. Porter (1980) on competitive strategy, which identifies three generic business strategies: differentiation, cost leadership and focus; also it concludes that organizations use these generic strategies in order to control five basic industry forces, which determine their competitive position and profitability: rivalry among existing competitors, bargaining power of suppliers, bargaining power of buyers, threat of substitute products/services and threat of new entrants. Parsons (1983) applied the above work of M. Porter to the ICT and reached the conclusion that IS can have a significant strategic impact if the are used to change the products,

services, markets or production economics of an industry, to affect the buyers and suppliers of the enterprise, to prevent customers from buying products and services from competitors, to preclude new competitors, to alter the degree of rivalry, or to support one of the abovementioned M. Porter's generic strategies. McFarlan (1984) applied the above work of M. Porter to the ICT and concluded that they can have a strategic impact, if they are used in order to build barriers against new entrants, build switching costs, change the basis of the competition, generate new products and services and change the balance of power in supplier relationships. Building on these conclusions Benjamin et al (1984) enriched the perspective of the strategic potential of ICT by concluding that it is not only IS affecting customers or supporting new products and services that can have a strategic impact, but also IS affecting internal operations and supporting traditional products and services can be of high strategic importance as well and provide competitive advantages. Ives and Learnmonth (1984) applied the concept of value chain to the interaction of a customer with an enterprise and concluded that an IS that fits into customer lifecycle and differentiates products or services from those of the competitors can be of high strategic importance. Wiseman (1985) concludes that IS supporting the internal operations or the traditional products and services of an enterprise can have strategic impact if they support its 'strategic thrusts', such as M. Porter's generic strategies, innovation, growth or alliances, in a manner that influences relationships with customers, suppliers or competitors. Important is the contribution of Porter & Millar (1985) on this topic, who identify three basic ways that ICT can affect competition: by altering industry structures, supporting differentiation and cost leadership strategies, and also by spawning entirely new businesses; they also argue that ICT have strategic potential if they can add value to a product or service in at least one of the primary activities (inbound logistics, operations, outbound logistics, marketing and sales, after-sales support and services) or one of the support activities (human resources management, technology development, infrastructure management, procurement) of the value chain. At the same time been many case studies have been published on this topic describing and analyzing 'real-life' IS that have provided valuable competitive advantage (e.g. Earl, 1989; Hopper, 1990; Robson, 1997; Pemberton et al, 2001; Picolli & Applegate, 2003), which validate and prove the practical applicability of the above research conclusions.

Subsequent research on this topic emphasizes the need for combining ICT with other resources of the enterprise in order to have a strategic impact. In this direction Carr (2003) argues that a narrow and exclusively technological focus cannot result in competitive advantages ('IT Doesn't Matter'). Powell and Dent-Micallef (1997) from an empirical study in the retail industry found that ICT alone cannot produce sustainable performance advantages, but such advantages can be gained only by using ICT in order to leverage intangible, complementary human and business resources. Miller (2003) found that sometimes these complimentary resources can be of low value, or even considered as liabilities, until they are they are incorporated in a new ICT-based 'engine of value creation'; therefore ICT can be instrumental in leveraging existing enterprise resources of low value, or even liabilities, into valuable resources that offer (in combination with other resources and ICT) competitive advantage. Another important dimension of the strategic potential of ICT as enablers of 'strategic agility' is proposed by Sambamurthy et al (2003), who argue that the capabilities of ICT can create new strategic 'digital options' for the enterprise and enable it to launch new competitive initiatives and respond quickly and effectively to changes in its environment.

Also, research has been conducted concerning the sustainability of the competitive advantages provided by ICT. Mata et al (1995), based on a resource-based view of the firm, conclude that 'managerial ICT skills' (defined as the ability of ICT management to understand the business needs of other functional units, customers and suppliers, and in cooperation with them to develop IS that cover these needs) is the only ICT attribute of an enterprise that can provide a sustainable competitive advantage. Bharadwaj (2000) adopting also a resource-based perspective and using a matched-sample comparison group methodology found that superior firm-specific ICT resources (ICT infrastructure, human ICT resources and ICT-enabled intangibles) result in superior financial performance. Picolli & Ives (2005) from an extensive literature review identified four basic barriers to the erosion of the competitive advantages provided by 'IT-dependent strategic initiatives': IT resources barrier, complementary resources barrier, IT project barrier and preemption barrier; they conclude that the existence of one or more of these barriers can make the competitive advantages offered by 'IT-dependent strategic initiatives' sustainable for long time.

In conclusion, from the above research considerable theoretical support and empirical evidence has been produced that ICT can provide (usually in combination with other resources of the enterprise) significant competitive advantages, which under specific conditions can be sustainable; it has also been concluded that the realization of this strategic potential is not an easy task and necessitates the establishment of a connection between ICT and the overall strategy of the enterprise.

REVIEW OF RESEARCH ON ENTERPRISE SYSTEMS STRATEGIC ALIGNMENT

The above conclusions gave rise to considerable research in the last twenty years concerning various dimensions of enterprise systems strategic alignment. This research can be grouped into three basic streams: i) conceptualization and basic understanding of enterprise systems strategic alignment, ii) development of models and frameworks for assessing and directing enterprise systems strategic alignment, and iii) investigation of the impact of enterprise systems strategic alignment on the business performance. These three research streams are briefly reviewed next.

Conceptualization and Basic Understanding of Enterprise Systems Strategic Alignment

The main objective of this research stream is to conceptualize and understand the strategic alignment of enterprise systems, focusing on the identification of its basic processes, barriers, critical success factors and benefits (King, 1978; Lederer & Mendelow, 1988; Earl, 1989; Jarvenpaa & Ives, 1990; Zviran, 1990; Chan, 1992; Earl, 1993; Luftman, 1996; Reich & Benbasat, 1996; Armstrong & Sambamurthy, 1999; Luftman, Papp & Brier 1999; Luftman & Brier, 1999; Kearns & Lederer, 2000; Reich & Benbasat, 2000; Allen & Wilson, 2003; Campbell et al, 2005; Rantham et al, 2005). Due to space limitations we are going to outline briefly only the most representative publications of this research stream. Lederer and Mendelow (1988) argue that one of the most important barriers of enterprise systems strategic alignment is the difficulty of convincing top management of the strategic potential of ICT, because the top management usually lacks sufficient awareness on ICT strategic potential, regards the use of computers as a strictly operational support tool, perceives a credibility gap, does not view information as a resource, demands financial justification and also is action-oriented; for overcoming these difficulties the authors propose a number of techniques: educate top management, market IS department accomplishments to the top management, have users to do this 'selling', promote the business image of the IS department, respond to 'outside forces' influencing top managers, capitalize on changes in management and perform highly sophisticated

IS planning that necessitate top management involvement. Jarvenpaa & Ives (1991) conclude that the 'involvement' of executives in IS activities (i.e. the 'psychological state') is more strongly associated with the progressive use of ICT in the enterprise than the 'participation' of executives in IS activities (i.e. their 'actual behaviors'); also executive involvement is influenced by a CEO's participation, prevailing organizational conditions, and the executive's functional background. Earl (1993) identified five basic approaches that are adopted by businesses for achieving enterprise systems strategic alignment: the business-led approach, the method-led approach, the administrative approach, the technological approach and the organizational approach; each of these approaches has different characteristics and therefore different likelihood of success, the organizational approach appearing to be more effective. Luftman, Papp and Brier (1999) identified a number of enablers of alignment between business and ICT strategies: senior-executive support for IT, IT involvement in strategy development, IT understanding the business, partnership between IT and non-IT units, well-prioritized IT projects and IT demonstrating leadership). Reich & Benbasat (2000) investigated the influence of four factors on the 'social dimension' of enterprise systems strategic alignment (defined as the extent to which business and IT executives mutually understand and are committed to both the business and the IT mission, objectives, and plans): shared domain knowledge between business and IT executives, IT implementation success, communication between business and IT executives, and connections between business and IT planning processes; they found that all these four factors influence 'short-term alignment', while only the shared domain knowledge influences 'long-term alignment'. Campbell et al (2005), based on a review of the previous research on enterprise systems strategic alignment, identify two basic approaches in it: the 'social' (focusing primarily on the people involved in achieving alignment) and the 'intellectual' (investigating mainly the relevant plans and planning methodologies); also, they remark that most of the research on enterprise systems strategic alignment adopts the intellectual approach, and recommend a combination of these two approaches as the optimal approach. Also adopting such a combined approach and based on the analysis of the content from a number of interviews with senior ICT managers they concluded that all of them believed that strategic alignment generally depends upon communication, collaboration, development of trust and shared domain knowledge, as suggested in the relevant literature; however, it was practically problematic to achieve these prerequisites, due to the prevalent culture in their organizations that promoted competition between departments.

This research stream has provided a basic conceptualization and understanding of the strategic alignment of enterprise systems, concerning mainly its basic processes, barriers, critical success factors and benefits. However, more in-depth research is required on these topics, in various types and sizes of enterprises, in various industries and national and cultural contexts, and for various types of ICT, in order to get a deeper and more complete understanding of them.

Development of Models/Frameworks for Directing/assessing Enterprise Systems Strategic Alignment

This research stream aims to support the practical application in 'real-life' of the ICT strategic alignment concept by developing models/frameworks for assisting the technical and the business management in directing and assessing enterprise systems strategic alignment. The most widely used of the models/frameworks that have been developed for directing strategic alignment is the 'Strategic Alignment Model' (SAM) developed by Henderson and Venkatraman (1999). As we can see in Figure 1 it is based on two basic dimensions of required linkage: i) the 'strategic

fit' (=linkage between 'external components' (concerning the external environment of the enterprise) and 'internal components' (concerning the internal environment of the enterprise)) and ii) the 'functional integration' (=linkage between the 'business domain' and the 'IS domain'). In the strategic fit dimension the model views strategy as consisting of two components, the 'external' and the 'internal' one, which should be well integrated. In particular, it views ICT strategy as consisting of one component concerning the 'external domain' (=decisions on how the enterprise is positioned in the ICT marketplace, e.g. which of the existing ICT in the marketplace it is going to use, which are their required performance and cost attributes, what kind of relations it has with their vendors, such as outsourcing, strategic alliances, etc.) and one component concerning the 'internal domain' (=decisions on how the internal ICT infrastructure of the enterprise will be configured and managed: ICT architecture, processes and skills), which should be well integrated. Similarly it views business strategy as consisting of two components which should be also well integrated: one component concerning the 'external domain' (= decisions about business scope, distinctive competencies and business relations with other organizations) and one component concerning the 'internal domain' (= decisions about its administrative infrastructure/architecture, business processes and human resources skills). In the functional integration dimension the model views two domains, the business domain and the IS/ICT domain, and proposes integration between them at two levels: 'strategic integration' (=integration between their external domain components) and 'operational integration' (=integration between their internal domain components).

Based on the above dimensions the SAM proposes that the complete enterprise systems strategic alignment consists in the integration between these four domains of strategic choice: business external strategy, ICT external strategy, business internal strategy and ICT internal

Figure 1. The 'Strategic Alignment Model' (SAM)

		External Business Strategy	External ICT Strategy
STRATEGIC FIT	External		
	Internal	Internal Business Strategy	Internal ICT Strategy

Business   ICT

FUNCTIONAL INTEGRATION

strategy. Also using this model the authors propose and describe four alignment perspectives: business strategy execution (external business strategy → internal business strategy → internal ICT strategy), technology-based transformation (external business strategy → external ICT strategy → internal ICT strategy), exploitation of ICT competitive potential (external ICT strategy → external business strategy → internal business strategy) and service level improvement (external ICT strategy → internal ICT strategy → internal business strategy).

Smaczny (2001) argues that a major disadvantage of the SAM is that its basic alignment approach is the sequential development of strategies; he states that this approach was the appropriate one for the period in which SAM was developed (characterized by a more stable business environment), but latter, due to major market changes and also due to the increased reliance of organizations on ICT, it has become slow and insufficient (at least for some industries and business contexts). For this reason he proposes a 'fusion' approach instead, which allows business and ICT strategies to be developed and implemented simultaneously. On the contrary Avison et al (2004) used successfully and validated this SAM in a financial services firm, and finally concluded that it has a good conceptual and practical value; also they developed

a framework for its practical application, which enables the technology and business management to determine the current level of alignment and to monitor and change it in the future as required. Furthermore, it is worth mentioning another approach that developed by Van Der Zee & De Jong (1999) for planning and setting goals for ICT and evaluating its results based on the business context, which is founded on the concepts of the Balanced Business Scorecard.

Also, a number of models/frameworks have been developed for assisting technical and business management in assessing the level of enterprise systems strategic alignment in their organization. The most widely used of them is the 'Strategic Alignment Maturity Model' (SAMM) developed by Luftman (2000); it is based on six criteria of ICT strategic alignment maturity (Communications Maturity, Competency/Value Measurement Maturity, Governance Maturity, Partnership Maturity, Scope & Architecture Maturity, Skills Maturity), each of them consisting of a number of attributes (sub-criteria), which are evaluated in a five-levels scale (Initial/Ad-hoc Process, Committed Process, Established Focused Process, Improved/Managed Process, Optimised Process). The SAMM enables the evaluation of ICT alignment practices in an organization and also the design of improvements of them. Another

IT alignment maturity model has been developed by the IT Governance Institute (ITGI) (www.itgi. org) as part of the CobiT (Control objectives for IT and related Technologies) framework (ITGI, 2005). In particular, CobiT includes a process named 'Define a Strategic Information Technology Plan', which aims to satisfy 'the business requirement to strike an optimum balance of Information Technology opportunities and IT business requirements'; this process includes a strategic alignment maturity model consisting of six levels (0:Non-existent, 1:Initial/AdHoc, 2:Repeatable and Intuitive, 3:Defined Process, 4:Managed and Measurable, 5:Optimized) and also guidance for using it in order to assess the maturity level of an organization. Bleistein et al (2006a, 2006b) argue that ICT strategic alignment is necessary not only at the executive level, but also at the level of the individual IT projects as well; in this direction they propose a requirements engineering framework that addresses the business strategy and the alignment of IT projects' requirements with business strategy.

In conclusion, the research of this stream has produced some first 'high-level' models/frameworks for directing and assessing enterprise systems strategic alignment, which offer some basic guidance, but in general they require further elaboration, evolution and adaptation to the new ICT that are continuously emerging and the new models of their exploitation by modern organizations. Therefore further research is required for the development of 'lower-level' and more practically applicable models/frameworks, which offer a more specific and complete guidance for directing and assessing enterprise systems strategic alignment, and also are adapted to the technological advances and the new globalized and highly competitive business environment; moreover, further research is required for validating such models/frameworks in 'real-life' conditions and situations.

Impact of Enterprise Systems Strategic Alignment on the Business Performance

This third research stream aims to investigate the impact of enterprise systems strategic alignment on business performance or on the contribution of enterprise systems to business performance. In this stream, despite its significance, has been conducted less research work that in the other two. In the following we review the main empirical studies that have been conducted in this direction. King & Teo examined empirically the impact of four types of integration between the business plan (BP) and the information systems plan (ISP) (administrative, sequential, reciprocal and full integration) on the perceived contribution of enterprise systems to various measures of organizational performance and on the perceived extent of various types of ISP problems (organization problems, implementation problems, database problems, hardware problems and cost problems) (Teo and King, 1996; King and Teo, 2000); using data from 157 large USA firms from the Corporate 1000 Book and performing independent sample t-tests and calculating correlations they found that the extent of BP-ISP integration and also its proactive orientation has a statistically significant positive relation with the perceived enterprise systems contribution to organizational performance, and also a statistically significant negative relation with the perceived extent of ISP problems. Chan et al (1997) investigated empirically the impact of enterprise systems strategic alignment on perceived enterprise systems effectiveness and perceived business performance; using data from 164 North-American financial services and manufacturing firms (from USA and Canada) with more than 100 employees from the Dun and Bradstreet directories they constructed a structural equations model (SEM), from which it was concluded that enterprise systems strategic alignment has statistically significant positive contributions to both perceived enterprise systems effectiveness and perceived business performance. Using the same data Sabherwal and Chan (2001) addressed the same research question, but in regard to the business strategy the enterprise follows; they considered three different business strategies: 'defenders', 'prospectors' and 'analyzers' and found that the strategic alignment of enterprise systems affects perceived business performance, only in enterprises following a 'prospector' or 'analyzer' business strategy, but not in the ones following a 'defender' business strategy. Cragg et al (2002) examined the link between enterprise systems strategic alignment and four measures of perceived firm performance (long term profitability, sales growth, financial resources availability and public image & customer loyalty) in the context of small firms; using data from 250 small UK manufacturing firms and performing analysis of variance (ANOVA) they found that the subgroup of firms having higher levels of alignment had also higher levels of all these four measures of perceived firm performance than the ones with lower levels of alignment. Bergeron et al (2003), based on data collected through a mail survey from 110 Canadian small and medium firms, and using cluster analysis found that low-performance firms exhibited a conflictual coalignment pattern of business strategy, business structure, IT strategy and IT structure.

It should be mentioned that all the above empirical studies have used subjective (perceived) measures of business performance and/or enterprise systems contribution to business performance. The only empirical investigation of the impact of enterprise systems alignment on business performance that uses objective measures of business performance has been the one conducted by Byrd et al (2005); based on data from 275 fabricated metal products manufacturing companies from South-eastern USA they constructed econometric models with sales revenue per employee and profit per employee as dependent variables, while as independent variables they used the IT expenditure per employee, a measure of enterprise systems strategic alignment and an interaction term equal to the product of the above two variables. In these econometric models the coefficient of this interaction term was found to be positive and statistically significant, so it is concluded that there is a synergistic coupling (positive interaction) between IT strategic alignment and IT investment with respect to both these measures of firm performance. However, the econometric models constructed in this study did not include some fundamental independent variables, such as non-IT capital and labour, which constitute basic determinants of firm output according to production economics (Nicholson, 2004).

In conclusion, from the research of this stream has been produced some first evidence of a positive contribution of enterprise systems strategic alignment to business performance. However, further research is required in order to understand better the contribution of different types of strategic alignment of enterprise systems to various dimensions of business performance, in various types and sizes of enterprises and in various sectoral, national and cultural contexts, based on objective business performance measures and also on sound theoretical foundations from the area of production economics. Also it is necessary to investigate the dependence of the contribution of enterprise systems strategic alignment to business performance on various external and internal environment factors (e.g. business strategy, competition, etc.) and to identify its main moderators.

AN EMPIRICAL INVESTIGATION

In this section are presented briefly the main results of an empirical study conducted by the authors, which contributes to the third of the above research streams, investigating the effect of enterprise systems strategic alignment on the contribution of enterprise systems investment to business performance. It aims to overcome the two main deficiencies of the previous research on this issue, which have been mentioned in the previous section: use of subjective (perceived) measures of business performance and/or enterprise systems contribution to business performance, and construction of models that do not include all fundamental independent variables.

In this direction our study is based on two objective measures of business performance as basic dependent variables, the value added (=yearly sales revenue minus yearly expenses for buying materials and services) and the labour productivity (=value added per employee), and also on an objective measure of enterprise systems investment. We constructed theoretically sound econometric models for both these business performance measures, which are based on the theory developed in the area of production economics, and in particular on the Cobb-Douglas production function (Nicholson, 2004), and include all fundamental variables. The Cobb-Douglas production function has been successfully used in the past for estimating the contribution to firm output of various firm inputs, including ICT investment (e.g. Brynjolfsson & Hitt, 1996; Stolarick, 1999; OECD, 2003; OECD, 2004). As recommended by this literature we used an extended form of the Cobb-Douglas production function, in which the capital is divided into ICT capital and non-ICT capital:

$$VA = e^{\beta_0} L^{\beta_1} K^{\beta_2} ICK^{\beta_3} \qquad (1)$$

where VA is the yearly firm value added, and L, K and ICK are the yearly labour expenses, the non-ICT capital and the ICT capital respectively, while the $\beta_1 - \beta_3$ are the corresponding output elasticities with respect to these inputs. By log-transforming equation (1) we obtain the following linear model:

$$\qquad (2)$$
$$ln\,VA = \beta_0 + \beta_1\,ln(L) + \beta_2\,ln(K) + \beta_3\,ln(ICK)$$

In order to investigate the effect of enterprise systems strategic alignment on the contribution of the ICT capital to firm value added we added to this model one 'interaction term' (Greene, 2003; Gujarati, 2003), which is equal to the product of a 'strategic alignment factor' F (=degree of bilateral relationship between the ICT Plan and the Overall Business/Strategy Plan) and the ln(ICK):

$$ln\,VA = \beta_0 + \beta_1\,ln(L) + \beta_2\,ln(K) +$$
$$\beta_3\,ln(ICK) + \beta_4\,ln(ICK)\cdot F \qquad (3)$$

Similar models have been also been constructed for the second business performance measure (dependent variable), the value added per employee, but with all the above independent variables (L, K, ICK) normalised (divided by the number of firm employees N).

For constructing the above econometric models we used data that have been collected through a survey among Greek companies, which has been conducted in cooperation with ICAP, one of the largest business information and consulting companies of Greece. This survey was based on a structured questionnaire, which included questions about the basic financial data of the company (yearly sales revenue, expenses for materials and services, labour expenses, value of capital, value of ICT capital, etc.) and also about enterprise systems strategic alignment. We received completed questionnaires from 281 companies (99 small, 98 medium and 84 large ones) from the 27 most important sectors of Greek economy. Their average yearly sales revenue was 183.7 million Euro and their average number of employees was 493.

Initially for the value added (VA) we estimated the two models of the above equations (2) (basic model) and (3) (model with interaction term) and the results are shown in Tables 1 and 2 respectively.

In the estimated basic model of Table 1 we remark that the coefficients of labour, non-ICT capital and ICT capital are all positive and statistically significant, so we conclude that all these

Table 1. Regression model for the impact of labour, non-ICT capital and ICT capital on firm value added

Dependent variable : ln (VA)			
Independent variable	Coefficient	Standardized Coefficient	Significance
constant	2.313		0.000
ln (L)	0.608	0.581	0.000
ln (K)	0.122	0.140	0.002
ln (ICK)	0.235	0.233	0.000
R-squared : 0.723			

Table 2. Regression model for the impact of labour, non-ICT capital, ICT capital and interaction between ICT capital and strategic alignment factor on firm value added

Dependent variable : ln (VA)			
Independent variable	Coefficient	Standardized Coefficient	Significance
constant	2.739		0.000
ln (L)	0.607	0.580	0.000
ln (K)	0.122	0.128	0.004
ln (ICK)	0.196	0.195	0.000
ln(ICT)* STR_ALIGN	0.113	0.112	0.003
R-squared : 0.733			

three inputs make a positive contribution to firm value added. These results confirm the conclusion of our previous study (Loukis & Sapounas, 2005), which had been based on a different data set, that ICT investments of Greek companies make a positive and statistically significant contribution to their output, so there is no evidence for 'ICT Productivity Paradox' in the Greek context. Also, we can see that the standardised coefficient of the ICT capital is higher than the one of the non-ICT capital, so we can conclude that the investment on enterprise systems contributes to value added more than the investment on 'traditional capital'. In the model of Table 2 we can see that the coefficients of labour, non-ICT capital and ICT capital remain all positive and statistically significant, and that the coefficient of the interaction term is positive and statistically significant as well and

also of considerable magnitude; therefore it is concluded the strategic alignment of enterprise systems increases considerably their contribution to value added.

Next we estimated similar models for the labour productivity (=VA/N), but with all the independent variables divided by the number of firm employees N, and the results are shown in Tables 3 (basic model) and 4 (model with interaction term) respectively.

In the model of Table 3 we can see that the coefficients of normalised labour, non-ICT capital and ICT capital are all positive and statistically significant, so we conclude that all these three inputs make a positive contribution to labour productivity as well. The comparison of their standardised coefficient leads to a conclusion similar to the one drawn from the model of Table 1: the

Table 3. Regression model for the impact of normalised labour, non-ICT capital and ICT capital on labour productivity

Dependent variable : ln (LP=VA/N)			
Independent variable	Coefficient	Standardized Coefficient	Significance
constant	3.194		0.000
ln (L/N)	0.551	0.495	0.000
ln (K/N)	0.097	0.126	0.018
ln (ICK/N)	0.201	0.208	0.000
R-squared : 0.376			

Table 4. Regression model for the impact of normalised labour, non-ICT capital, ICT capital and interaction between normalised ICT capital and strategic alignment factor on labour productivity

Dependent variable : ln (LP=VA/N)			
Independent variable	Coefficient	Standardized Coefficient	Significance
constant	3.339		0.000
ln (L/N)	0.551	0.494	0.000
ln (K/N)	0.088	0.113	0.030
ln (CK/N)	0.170	0.176	0.001
ln (CK/N)*STR_ALIGN	0.101	0.151	0.004
R-squared : 0.398			

investment per employee on enterprise systems contributes to labour productivity more than the investment per employee on 'traditional capital'. Finally from the model of Table 4 we can see that the coefficients of normalised labour, non-ICT capital and ICT capital remain all positive and statistically significant and also that the coefficient of the interaction term is positive, statistically significant and also of considerable magnitude; therefore it is concluded that the strategic alignment of enterprise systems increases considerably their contribution to labour productivity.

In conclusion, this empirical investigation contributes to the third of the research streams mentioned in the third section of this chapter and provides sound evidence that the strategic alignment of enterprise systems increases considerably their contribution to both these objective measures of business performance (value added and labour productivity). This evidence is theoretically sound and reliable, since it has been produced based on the construction of econometric models including all fundamental variables founded on the production economics theory (Cobb-Douglas production function), and also using objective measures of business performance and enterprise systems investment. Further research is in progress by the authors for investigating the impact of various types of enterprise systems strategic alignment at different hierarchical levels on the contribution of enterprise systems to business performance, and also on its dependence from various external and internal environment factors.

CONCLUSION AND FUTURE TRENDS

This chapter dealt with the alignment of enterprise systems with business strategy and its impact on the business value that enterprise systems generate. The research that has been conducted on the strategic potential of ICT (reviewed in the second section of this chapter), has generated considerable theoretical support and empirical evidence that ICT can provide (usually in combination with other enterprise resources) competitive advantages, which under specific conditions can be sustainable. This strategic potential of ICT has given rise to considerable research in the last twenty years concerning the strategic alignment of enterprise systems. This research (reviewed in the third section of this chapter) has produced a basic body of knowledge concerning various dimensions of the strategic alignment of enterprise systems, which can be quite useful for both researchers and practitioners in the area of enterprise systems. In particular, it has produced a basic conceptualization and understanding of enterprise systems strategic alignment, and some first 'high-level' models/frameworks for directing and assessing enterprise systems strategic alignment; also it has been produced some first evidence of a positive contribution of enterprise systems strategic alignment to business performance.

However, further research is required in this area and also further practical exploitation by practitioners of the knowledge produced in this research. In particular, further research should be conducted first concerning the strategic potential of ICT and ways of exploiting them strategically in enterprises and combining them with other enterprise resources for achieving sustainable ICT-based competitive advantages. Also, further research is required for understanding better and in more depth the basic processes, barriers, critical success factors and benefits of enterprise systems strategic alignment, and for developing practically applicable models/frameworks, which can offer clear and complete guidance for directing and assessing the strategic alignment of enterprise systems. Finally, extensive research should be conducted concerning the 'value' generated by the strategic alignment of enterprise systems, in order to understand better the contribution of different types of strategic alignment of enterprise systems at different hierarchical levels to various dimensions of business performance; this research, in order to give reliable and practically useful results, and also to allow meaningful comparisons between different types of strategic alignment applied in different in various sectoral, national and cultural contexts, etc., should be based on objective business performance measures and also on sound theoretical foundations from the domain of production economics, such as the Cobb-Douglas production function. In the fourth section of this chapter is described an empirical investigation conducted by the authors that follows these principles, as a guidance for future research on this topic. Also it is necessary to investigate the dependence of the value generated by strategic alignment of the enterprise systems from various external and internal environment factors (e.g. business strategy, competition, etc.) and to identify its main moderators.

At the same time it is highly important that this knowledge on the basic concepts, methods and value of enterprise systems strategic alignment be practically exploited to a larger extent and be incorporated much more in the practice and processes of enterprises.

REFERENCES

Allen, D., & Wilson, T. (2003). Vertical trust/mistrust during information strategy formation. *International Journal of Information Management, 23,* 223-237.

Avison, D., Jones, J., Powell, P., & Wilson, D. (2004). Using and validating the strategic alignment model. *Journal of Strategic Information Systems, 13,* 223-246.

Armstrong, C. P., & Sambamurthy, V. (1999). Information technology assimilation in firms: the influence of senior leadership and IT infrastructures. *Information Systems Research, 10(4),* 304-327.

Benjamin, R. J., Rockart, J. F., Scott Morton, M. S., & Wyman, J. (1984). Information Technology: A Strategic Opportunity. *Sloan Management Review, 25(3),* 3-10.

Bharadwaj, A. S. (2000). A Resource-Based Perspective of Information Technology Capability and Firm Performance: An Empirical Investigation. *MIS Quarterly, 24(1),* 169-196.

Bleistein, S. J., Cox, K., & Verner, J. (2006a). Validating strategic alignment of organizational IT requirements using goal modeling and problem diagrams. *Journal of Systems and Software, 79,* 362-378.

Bleistein, S. J., Cox, K., Verner, J., & Phalp, K. T. (2006b). B-SCP: A requirements analysis framework for validating strategic alignment of organizational IT based on strategy, context and process. *Information and Software Technology, 48,* 846-868.

Broadbent, M., Weill, P. (1993). Improving business and information strategy alignment: learning from the banking industry. *IBM Systems Journal, 32 (1),* 162–179.

Brynjolfsson, E., & Hitt., L. M. (1996). Paradox lost? Firm level evidence on the returns to information systems spending. *Management Science, 42(4),* 541–558.

Byrd, T. A., Lewis, R. B., & Bryan, R. W. (2006). The leveraging influence of strategic alignment on IT investment: An empirical examination. *Information & Management, 43,* 308-321.

Campbell, B., Kay, R., & Avison, D. (2005). Strategic alignment: a practitioner's perspective. *Journal of Enterprise Information Management,* 18(6), 653-664.

Carr, N. G. (2003). IT Doesn't Matter. *Harvard Business Review, 81(5),* 41-49.

Chan, Y. E., & Huff, S. L. (1992). Strategy: An information systems research perspective. *Journal of Strategic Information Systems, 1(4),* 191-201.

Chan, Y. E., Huff, S. L., Barclay, D. W., & Copeland, D. G. (1997). Business strategic orientation, information systems strategic orientation, and strategic alignment. *Information Systems Research, 8(2),* 125–150.

Cragg, P., King, M., & Hussin, H. (2002). IT alignment and firm performance in small manufacturing firms. *Journal of Strategic Information Systems, 11,* 109-132.

Duffy, J. (2002). *IT/Business Alignment: Is it an option or is it mandatory?* IDC Document 26831.

Earl, M. J. (1989). *Management Strategies for Information Technology.* Great Britain: Prentice-Hall International.

Earl, M. J. (1993). Experiences in strategic information systems planning. *MIS Quarterly, 17(1),* 1–24.

Greene, W. H. (2003). *Econometric Analysis- 5e edition.* Prentice Hall Inc.

Gujarati, D. N. (2003). *Basic Econometrics - 4e edition.* Mc-Graw Hill Higher Education.

Henderson, J. C., & Venkatraman, H. (1999). Strategic alignment: Leveraging information technology for transforming organizations. *IBM Systems Journal, 38(2),* 472 -484.

Hopper, M. D. (1990). Ratting SABRE – New Ways to Compete on Information. *Harvard Business Review, 68(3),* 118-126.

Jarvenpaa, S. P., Ives, B. (1990). Information technology and corporate strategy: a view from the top. *Information Systems Research, 1(4),* 352–376.

Johnson, G., Scholes, K. (2005). Exploring Corporate Strategy– Text and Cases, 7th edition. London, UK: Prentice Hall.

IT Governance Institute (ITGI) (2005). *Control objectives for IT and related Technologies (CO-BIT) 4.0.* Accessed from www.itgi.org.

Ives, B., Learmonth, G. P. (1984). The Information System as a Competitive Weapon. *Communications of the ACM, 27(12),* 1193-1201.

Kearns, G.S., & Lederer, A.L, (2000). The effect of strategic alignment on the use of IS-based

Resources for competitive advantage. *The Journal of Strategic Information Systems, 9(4),* 265-293.

King, W. R. (1978). Strategic Planning for Management Information Systems. *MIS Quarterly, 2(1),* 27-37.

King, W. R., & Teo, T. S. H. (2000). Assessing the impact of proactive versus reactive modes of strategic information systems planning. *Omega – The International Journal of Management Science, 28,* 667 – 679.

Lederer, A. L., & Mendelow, A. L, (1988). Convincing top management of the strategic potential of information systems. *MIS Quarterly, 12(4),* 525-534.

Luftman, J. N. (1996). *Competing in the information age: strategic alignment in practice.* New York, USA: Oxford University Press.

Luftman, J. N., Papp, R., & Brier, T. (1999). Enablers and Inhibitors of Business-IT Alignment. *Communications of the Association for Information Systems, 11(3),* 1-33.

Luftman, J., & Brier, T, (1999). Achieving and sustaining business-IT alignment. *California Management Review, 42*(1), 109.

Luftman, J. (2000). Assessing Business-IT Alignment Maturity. *Communications of the Association for Information Systems, 4(14),* 1-51.

Luftman, J., McLean, E. R. (2004). Key Issues for IT Executives. *MIS Quarterly Executive, 3(2),* 89-104.

Luftman, J. (2005). Key Issues for IT Executives 204. *MIS Quarterly Executive, 4(2),* 269-285.

Mata, F. J., Fuerst, W. L., & Barney, J. B. (1995). Information Technology and Sustained Competitive Advantage: A Resource-Based Analysis. *MIS Quarterly, 19(4),* 487-505.

McFarlan, F. W. (1984, May-June). Information Technology Changes the Way you Compete. *Harvard Business Review, 62(3),* 98-103.

Melville, N., Kraemer, K., & Gurbaxani, V. (2004). Information technology and organizational performance: An integrative model of IT business value. *MIS Quarterly, 28(2),* 283-322.

Miller, D. (2003). An Asymmetry-Based View of Advantage: Towards and Attainable Sustainability. *Strategic Management Journal, 24(10),* 961-976.

Nicholson, W. (2004). *Microeconomic Theory: Basic Principles and Extensions - 9th edition.* USA: South-Western College Publications.

Organisation for Economic Co-operation and Development (OECD) (2003). *ICT and Economic Growth – Evidence from OECD Countries, Industries and Firms.* Paris, France.

Organisation for Economic Co-operation and Development (OECD) (2004). *The Economic Impact of ICT – Measurement, Evidence and Implications.* Paris, France.

Palvia, P. C., Palvia, S. C. J., & Whitworth, J. E. (2002). Global information technology: A meta analysis of key issues. *Information & Management, 39,* 403-414.

Parsons, G. L. (1983). Information Technology: A New Competitive Weapon. *Sloan Management Review, 25(1),* 4-14.

Pemberton, J. D., Stonehouse, G. H., & Barber, C. E. (2001). Competing with CRS-Generated Information in the Airline Industry. *Journal of Strategic Information Systems, 10(1),* 59-75.

Picolli, G., & Applegate, L. M. (2003). Wyndham International: Fostering High-Touch with High-tech. *Harvard Business School Publishing,* Case # 9-803-092.

Piccoli, G., & Ives, B. (2005). Review: IT-Dependent Strategic Initiatives and Sustained Competitive Advantage: A Review and Synthesis of the Literature. *MIS Quarterly, 29(4),* 746-775.

Porter, M. E. (1980). *Competitive strategy: Techniques for Analyzing Industries and Competitors.* New York, USA: The Free Press.

Porter, M. E., & Millar, V. E. (1985). How Information Gives You Competitive Advantage. *Harvard Business Review, 63(4),* 149-160.

Powell, T. C., & Dent-Micallef., A. (1997). Information Technology as Competitive Advantage: The Role of Human, Business, and Technology Resources. *Strategic Management Journal, (18)5,* 375-405.

Rantham, R. G., Johnsten, J., & Wen, H. J. (2005). Alignment of business strategy and IT strategy: A case study of a Fortune 50 financial services company. *Journal of Computer Information Systems, Winter 2004-2005,* 1-8.

Reich, B. H., & Benbasat, I. (1996). Measuring the linkage between business and information technology objectives. *MIS Quarterly, 20(1),* 55–81.

Reich, B. H., & Benbasat, I, (2000). Factors that influence the social dimension of alignment between business and information technology objectives. *MIS Quarterly, 24(1),* 81-113.

Robson, W, (1997). *Strategic management and information systems: An integrated approach - 2nd edition.* Great Britain: Pitman Publishing.

Ross, J. W., Beath, C. M., & Goodhye, D. L. (1996). Develop Long-Term Competitiveness Through IT-Assets. *Sloan Management Review, 38(1),* 31-42.

Sabherwal, R., & Chan, Y. E. (2001). Alignment between Business and IS Strategies: A Study of Prospectors, Analyzers, and Defenders. *Information Systems Research, 12(1),* 11-33.

Sambamurthy, V., Bharadwaj, A. & Grover, V. (2003). Shaping Agility Through Digital Options: Reconceptualizing the Role of Information Technology in Contemporary Firms. *MIS Quarterly, 27(2),* 237-263.

Loukis, E., & Sapounas I. (2005). The Impact of Information Systems Investment and Management on Business Performance in Greece. In the Proceedings of the *13th European Conference on Information Systems 2005 (ECIS 2005)*, May 26-28, 2005, Regensburg, Germany.

Smaczny, T. (2001). Is an alignment between business and information technology the appropriate paradigm to manage IT in today's organisations? *Management Decision, 39(10),* 797-802

Stolarick, K. (1999). IT Spending and Firm Productivity: Additional Evidence from the Manufacturing Sector. *Center for Economic Studies, U.S. Census Bureau, Working Paper 99-10.*

Teo, T. S. H., & King, W. R. (1996). Assessing the impact of integrating business planning and IS planning. *Information & Management, 30,* 309-321.

Van Der Zee, J. T. M., & De Jong , B. (1999). Alignment is not enough: Integrating business and Information Technology management with the balanced business scorecard. *Journal of Management Information Systems, 16(2),* 137-156.

Wiseman, C. (1985). *Strategy and Computers: Information Systems as Competitive Weapons.*, Homewood, USA: Dow-Jones-Irwin.

Zviran, M. (1990). Relationships between organizational and information systems objectives: some empirical evidence. *Journal of Management Information Systems, 7(1),* 65-84.

KEY TERMS

Business/Strategy Plan: A document describing the mission, goals, competitive strategy, future directions and action plan of the enterprise, which are based on the analysis of its external environment (e.g. competition, opportunities, threats) and its internal environment (e.g. resources, capabilities, strengths, weaknesses).

Cobb-Douglas Production Function: A particular widely used form of production function, which posits that firm output in a particular time period is an exponential function of the capital and the labour employed in this period.

Enterprise Systems Plan: A document with the capabilities, strengths and weaknesses of existing enterprise systems, the forms and the extent of information and communication technologies (ICT) usage in the industry, the capabilities offered by existing and emerging ICTs that may interest and influence the enterprise and also the planned enterprise systems.

ICT Strategic Potential: Capability of ICT to provide valuable competitive advantages and make a significant strategic impact on the enterprise, if properly exploited.

Information Systems Strategic Alignment: The extent to which business strategies are enabled, supported and stimulated by information strategies

Production Function: A function that connects the output produced by an enterprise during a particular time period (dependent variable) with the quantities of the inputs it has used in the same period (independent variables).

Strategic Alignment Maturity Model: A model that aims at assisting technical and business management in assessing the level of enterprise systems strategic alignment in their organization, based on a number of proposed criteria/sub-criteria.

Strategic Alignment Model: A model that aims at directing and assisting strategic alignment in an organization by proposing and describing required steps.

Section III
Enterprise Systems:
Small, Medium, and Large Organizations

Chapter XIII
Enterprise Systems in Small and Medium–Sized Enterprises

Sanjay Mathrani
Massey University, New Zealand

Mohammad A. Rashid
Massey University, New Zealand

Dennis Viehland
Massey University, New Zealand

ABSTRACT

The market for enterprise systems (ES), continues to grow in the post millennium era as businesses become increasingly global, highly competitive, and severely challenged. Although the large enterprise space for ES implementation is quite stagnated, now all of the ES vendors are focusing on the small to medium-sized enterprise (SME) sector for implementations. This study looks at the current ES implementation scenario in the SME sector. The purpose of the study is to gain insights into what is a typical case of ES implementation and to understand how current implementations in the SME sector differ from the earlier implementations in the large enterprise sector through a perspective of ES vendors, ES consultants, and IT research firms in a NZ context. Implications for practice in implementation processes, implementation models, and organizational contexts are discussed.

INTRODUCTION

Enterprise systems (ES), also known as enterprise resource planning (ERP) systems, are large, complex, highly integrated information systems designed to meet the information needs of organizations and are, in most cases, implemented to improve organizational effectiveness (Davenport, 2000; Hedman & Borell, 2002; Markus & Tanis, 2000). These are comprehensive, fully integrated software packages supporting automation of most standard business processes in organizations including extended modules such as supply chain management (SCM) or customer relationship management (CRM) systems. ES applications connect and manage information flows across complex organizations, allowing managers to make decisions based on information that accurately reflects the current state of their business (Davenport & Harris, 2005; Davenport, Harris, & Cantrell, 2002). In a more integrated and global market, extended ES offers new functions and new ways of configuring systems, as well as web-based technology to establish the integrated, extended business enterprise (Shanks, Seddon, & Wilcocks, 2003). The market for ES continues to grow despite much speculation on its future in the post millennium era. Although most large enterprises have completed their ES implementations by now, the ES market continues to grow in the small and medium-sized enterprises (SME) sector. A number of research studies have been conducted to establish and understand the critical success factors for ES implementations (e.g., Allen, Kern, & Havenhand, 2002; Bancroft, Sep, & Sprengel, 1998; Holland & Light, 1999; Parr & Shanks, 2000; Plant & Willcocks, 2006; Sarker & Lee, 2000; Scott & Vessey, 2002; Skok & Legge, 2001; Sumner, 1999; Yang & Seddon, 2004). However, there has been little research that examines ES implementation at the strategic decision-making process level (Viehland & Shakir, 2005) and compares current implementations in the SME sector with earlier implementations in the large organizations. The purpose of this study is to examine the current ES implementations scenario in New Zealand. The main objectives of this study are to explore what is a typical case of ES implementation and to understand how current implementations in the SME sector differ from the earlier implementations in the large enterprise sector. The study does so through a practitioners' perspective, with interview data collected from ES vendors, ES consultants, and IT research firms who are actively engaged in ES implementation. This approach differs from

the organizational approach usually found in the literature. This is a replication study following a similar approach used by Shakir (2002), who also investigated aspects of ES implementation in the NZ vendor-and-consultant community. The focus of that study was to identify key drivers influencing ES adoption and implementation (e.g., Shakir and Viehland, 2004) whereas the focus of the current study is to understand how current implementations in the SME sector differ from the earlier implementations in the large enterprise sector. The current study extends and builds upon existing ES research.

Semi-structured interviews were conducted with key players of ES implementations in New Zealand including ES vendors, ES consultants, and IT research firms to explore the current ES implementation scenario. Several measures such as the number of users, modules implemented, cost of implementation, number of sites/locations where implemented, industry type, organization size, implementation phases, time to implement, implementation partners, and levels of customization were discussed to understand a typical case of ES implementation and current implementation practices. The empirical findings are analyzed and reported in this paper. This study has been conducted in a New Zealand (NZ) context which can be extended to show current trends worldwide.

RESEARCH METHODOLOGY

Using a qualitative research methodology, data were collected by way of semi-structured interviews with ten key respondents in the ES implementation industry. The interviews were carried out between February and August 2006. The key respondents were senior ES consultants or senior managers in the organizations which are key players in the field of ES in New Zealand, principally major ES vendors, ES consultants, and IT research organizations (see Table 1). The positions of the respondents included: director professional services, consulting manager, managing director, consulting practice director, partner group manager, vice president, consulting partner, general manager, and business consultant.

The purpose of the interviews was to seek insights from experienced ES stakeholders and professionals in answering what is a typical ES implementation in New Zealand and what are the current ES implementation practices? Questions were asked to extract information such as the number of users, the modules implemented, cost of implementation, number of sites where ES were implemented, type of industry and the size of the organizations in terms of number of employees and revenue.

Contact was first established with the respondents through email and by phone. An introductory letter explaining the study briefly and seeking appointment for an interview was then sent to the respondents. On receipt of confirmation, the research information sheet along with the questions was sent prior to the interview. The answers were then discussed during the interview.

The respondents discussed ES implementations based upon their perspective and experience in terms of their ES applications, their clients, and their implementation methodologies. Ten face-to-face meetings took place at the respondent's organizations with one interview from each firm. The interviews lasted between 60 and 90 minutes each. The interviews were tape recorded and transcribed immediately after each interview. The empirical findings were analyzed using the Nvivo 7.0 qualitative software tool and the inferences reported.

TYPICAL ES IMPLEMENTATIONS IN NZ

Findings in this study reveal that the ES market is based on three different size segments -- the large enterprise segment, the medium-sized enterprise and the small firm. Most respondents used the number of employees as a measure for organizational size, however some respondents used revenue. Until recently, the focus of implementations was on the large enterprise – businesses and government agencies with more than 500 employees and revenue greater than $250M. But now the focus for new implementations has shifted to the SME sector. The higher end of medium-sized organizations in NZ employ between 100 to 299 staff and have revenue between $50M to $200M. At the lower end of this segment, employees are between 20 to 100 and revenue is between $10M to $50M. In the small organization segment in NZ, employees are less than 20 and revenue less than $10M.

Findings revealed that the large enterprises in NZ could have 200 or more users in a typical implementation. SME-based implementations could be between 20 and 200 users. A classification by consultancy firm IDC, provided as part of the current study, shows the sizes of companies in terms of number of users where ES is implemented as a percentage of companies in NZ. A small organization with less than 20 users are 26% in a NZ context, a medium-sized organization with 20 – 200 users at 49%, and any organization above 200 users are large at 25% in the NZ market, as shown in Table 2. In another study by

Table 1. Key respondents for the study

ES Vendors (Flagship ES products)	ES Consultants	IT Research
SAP NZ (SAP)	PricewaterhouseCoopers NZ	Gartner Limited NZ
Oracle NZ (Oracle, J.D. Edwards, PeopleSoft)	Ernst & Young NZ	IDC NZ
Microsoft NZ (Dynamics (earlier Navision))	KPMG Consulting NZ	
Infor NZ (Mapics, SSA Global (earlier BaaN))	EMDA NZ	

Parr and Shanks (2000), in an Australian context, the number of users reported for small organizations is less than 100, medium less than 200, and large more than 200.

Most respondents agreed that typical implementations in NZ currently are predominantly in the medium-sized enterprise category with 20 - 200 users whereas the range used to be 200 – 500 users a few years ago. These findings also confirm the Shakir (2002) study where the numbers of users for majority implementations in NZ were found to be 100 in medium-sized organizations with revenue between $50M- $250M.

Many small businesses below 100 users in NZ are companies that are basically part of multinational corporations that implement solutions "but are more governed out of the regional or global office and the NZ office really has no control". There are also many small businesses in NZ, the usual 20 – 25 user organizations that find it hard to justify an ES investment from a cost perspective, and typically do not implement expensive enterprise solutions from large vendors. These businesses prefer smaller inexpensive fragmented solutions. The big players like SAP and Oracle have also moved their business model and are now targeting smaller sites.

Microsoft revealed that there are about 3,500 medium-sized companies in NZ with employees from 100 to 200, which have not used one of the traditional ES as their core technology and a large proportion of these businesses did not have any technological solution to help them with their business problems. Microsoft believes they have 400 of these as their current customer base. The growth market in NZ is in the medium-sized market segment. The declining markets include large companies which have already made their $10M investment and are not looking to make another investment. "These companies might make a million or half a million dollar investment but they are not the growth area for software companies."

It was evident from vendors' perspective that the large enterprise space is quite stagnated now and all of the ES vendors are focusing on SME's. Once an implementation is completed in an organization it goes out for a recycle every 7-8 years, so these software vendors need to look for new customers. A general consensus among the software vendors was that more opportunities exist in the SME space or even at the lower end of the SME space. There are many small companies using home grown PC-based systems where their usage has outgrown their original requirements, but they have not been replaced. Or a hodgepodge of several different types of disparate systems exist which are expensive to integrate and maintain. The software vendors are trying to push into this space, although there are many challenges within that space such as limited resources, lack of infrastructure or lack of necessary in-house skills to cope with changing requirements associated with implementing an ES. The challenge facing software vendors is to figure out how they take the learning acquired in the large enterprise implementations down to a smaller enterprise. And it is a fallacy to believe that large organizations require different information as compared to smaller organizations. They actually require quite the same information. It is a different degree of how much they require. Since

Table 2. Number of users in NZ companies where ES is implemented

Size of Organization	Number of Users	Percent in NZ
Large	>200	25%
Medium	20-200	49%
Small	<20	26%

the SME space offered most opportunity, therefore larger players like SAP and Oracle are focusing on the SME sector which was overlooked earlier. "Whenever any new technology evolves there are leaders, followers, and the laggards. Typically the large enterprise organizations are the leaders but now they are beyond the leader category and it's the SME now which are going up in that curve." Traditionally SAP customers were the large enterprises, companies like Fonterra, Telecom, and Carter Holt Harvey in NZ. However, in the last 5 years due to shift in focus on the SME's, SAP is now moving to smaller companies with annual revenues $5M or more and are offering two different types of solutions. One is similar to a Microsoft based type solution called "Business One". The other is "All-in-One" and is the traditional SAP solution. The large enterprises are probably old SAP or one of the Oracle family member customers having implemented either PeopleSoft, JD Edwards, or Oracle systems. Now the focus of the software vendors is to compete for winning upgrade or add-on contracts from such large enterprises. SAP recently bagged such a contract from Fonterra which is an old loyal customer of SAP. But the main battlefield for new implementations is in the SME sector.

The Microsoft respondent, who had earlier worked with other vendors (i.e. JD Edwards, PeopleSoft, and Oracle), remarked "there's no such thing as a typical enterprise solution implementation in NZ". According to him, the size of enterprises ranges from large with 500 or more users through to SME with 5 to 10 users at the lower end and hence there is no typical organization. He suggested however, the size of an organization that may drive business intelligence (BI) and knowledge capital as information tools are the medium to large organizations. Organizations that employ 100 plus staff and have an ES with a user base of more than 40 are more mature in the context of using information for business benefit. Microsoft's largest customer in NZ has a user base of 130 while their smallest customer has just two with majority of customers in the

range of 15 to 50 users in NZ.

From an Oracle perspective, Oracle has three ES product lines - Oracle E-Business Suite, PeopleSoft and JD Edwards (JDE) from their acquisitions. The E-Business Suite and PeopleSoft are generally implemented in the larger enterprises and JDE in the SME's. "Unfortunately, some of these lines are blurred because while a company may be a SME in NZ it may have some large offshore subsidiaries and therefore the group may not necessarily be tiny. For example, Fisher and Paykel might not be considered one of the largest companies in NZ but if you consider its holdings and offshore organizations, it is quite substantial from the NZ perspective of a large company category that runs JDE. But typically, we apply the rule, an SME will be putting in JDE and if it is a large enterprise it will be putting E-Business Suite or PeopleSoft."

Most informants suggested that the ES implementations are typically divided into two "waves" or phases. The first wave or phase 1 is the implementation of core ES modules such as finance; materials management including purchasing, warehousing and inventory; and operational modules including production management, production planning, logistics, sales, and distribution. Some companies also include HR and payroll in the first phase. In the second wave or phase 2, the companies implement supplementary modules (also called ERP II by Gartner (Zrimsek, 2002)), which include collaborative scenarios such as customer relationship management (CRM), supply chain management (SCM), supplier relationship management (SRM), and management services applications such as business intelligence (BI). Companies consider extending applications to satellite businesses or international operations in the second phase. These findings differed to the Shakir (2002) study which noted that phase 1 implementations would always include the core modules of financials plus one or two other modules that may include SCM and CRM. This change can be attributed to the larger number of modules that ES vendors have put into the market in the last five years and SME owners being more ambitious in phase 2 implementations. Findings from the current study revealed that about 75% organizations are still in phase 1 and comprise mostly of new implementations in the SME sector. Balance 25% organizations are large that have moved into phase 2.

Traditionally, the time for implementation used to be more. However, since the focus is now towards SME's, the implementation time has decreased. Earlier, processes such as modelling the organization and configuring the design used to take time. Now, using accelerators such as preconfigured business processes, the time to implement has been slashed, and so has the cost of implementation, which has made these systems much more affordable for the small businesses. In the Shakir (2002) study the length of time to the first phase implementations varied from 2.5 months to 2 years. However, in the current study although the time for implementation varied between different informants, the general consensus was that currently large projects take around 12 to 24 months and SME's 3 to 12 months to complete.

The cost of implementation is related to the number of modules, their types, the software package size and brand, the number of user licenses issued, consulting costs, customization levels, along with the vendor or third party implementation cost. The hardware cost, and the cost of training and change management may be additional. According to informants in this study, in the SME sector, cost is the most important factor in selecting an ES for implementation. This was attributed by them, due to the smaller size of organizations and their limited funds for investment.

One vendor explained the reason for the high costs in large organizations compared to smaller ones is because large organizations have more complex operations and require more customizations. Their decision making processes may not be as efficient, and require a lot of change management procedures. On the other hand, smaller companies are more agile, more decisive, and especially more inclined to adopt a best practices implementation, greatly reducing customization and change management costs.

Table 3 summarizes the time and costs estimates for ES implementations as suggested by various participants in the current study based on the size of the project. The costs include software,

Table 3. Time and cost for ES implementations

Key Participants	Time for Implementation (Months)	Cost Based on Project Size (NZ$)
SAP	Large – 18 to 36 SME – 6 to 18	Very large > $10 M Large - $2 M to 10 M SME - $0.5 M to 2 M
Microsoft	Large – 18 to 24 Medium – 9 to 12 Small – 3 to 6	Very large – Multi-million $ Mid-market – $0.5 M to 2 M Small – $0.1 M to 0.5 M
Oracle	Large – 18 to 24 SME – 6 to 12	Not answered in figures
EMDA Consulting	Large – 10 to 12 SME – 3 to 6	Large > $1 M SME – $0.2 M to 1 M
PricewaterhouseCoopers	Large – 24 to 48 SME – 4 to 12	Very large – $10 M to 50 M Large – $2 M to 10 M SME – $0.5 M to 2 M
IDC	Large – 9 to 18 SME – 3 to 9	Not answered in figures

number of licenses, hardware, consultancy, implementation, customization, and training costs.

Locations are the one or more sites where the ES is implemented. Findings in this study show that currently more implementations are multi-site while in the earlier years implementations were more single site. This represents a continuing trend to more multi-site implementations in NZ, first observed by Shakir (2002). Traditionally, in large organization implementations, each location had its own implementation. However, companies in the SME sector are now optimizing by using one implementation at multi-locations because they are finding it too hard to manage and maintain separate implementations at all these locations. "Organizations are realizing its no use having IT administrators in all the locations doing a similar task." The growth in export markets of NZ companies coupled with availability of Internet-capable technology is also driving multi-site ES implementations in NZ. These implementations now are single instance which as explained by SAP meant that only one installation of the software is made to run on one server but the software is used at multiple locations. This environment is different to the earlier multi-instance where multiple installations of the software were made to run across the company in one or more locations. Typical implementations today are single instance multi-site implementations. Organizations are now implementing ES into one site which is their main manufacturing or business centre and this single instance is used by all other subsidiary sites, distribution warehouses, and sales offices.

An implementation partner is mostly used for managing the ES project. Findings revealed that while a third party or a consultant implementer was popular in the past for large organization implementations, SME customers now prefer the software vendor's direct involvement. This finding again confirms the Shakir (2002) study which also noted that vendor driven implementations were on the increase. A majority of the participants in the current study suggested that

there has been a shift over the last five years. Customers traditionally preferring to work with the big 5 consulting companies for implementation are now more inclined to work with the software vendor directly so that they have a one-stop shop. Customers are starting to realize that the technical skills a software vendor provides may not be possible from consultants. One vendor explained what customers feel is that unless they actually talk to the software owners, they may not get the best value from a price perspective and from the perspective of having the best experts involved in the project.

The post implementation and after sales support from the software vendor or the implementer to the customer organization normally includes three levels of support (see Figure 1). The first level is at the customers' end where the customers' super user (i.e. ES champion), determines whether it is a "how to" question -- where the user does not know how to use the system -- or something else. If the problem is related to the user or an organizational issue it is resolved at the first level. If not an end-user problem, then is it a general business requirement issue? If so, it is referred to the second level support which is the local vendor implementer or the implementation partner. The second level support determines whether it is a functionality or software performance setting issue that requires additional configuration to make it work and meet the business requirement. Finally, if the local implementation partner determines that the problem is a software bug or a product-related issue it is raised to level three which is the support channel inside the software vendor. So it is a typically a three tier support model as shown in Figure 1.

Customization is the process in which changes are made to the ES software during the implementation phase to suit the needs of the organization where it is being implemented. This happens when the best business practices embedded in the ES software do not satisfy the needs of the business, and the software is changed to meet the require-

Figure 1. Three tier post implementation support model

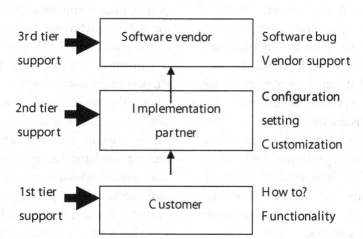

ments of the organization (Davenport & Prusak, 1998; Kumar & Van Hillegersberg, 2000).

There are two implementation strategies or models. The first is the "comprehensive customization" type when many and sometimes major changes to the software are performed during the implementation to satisfy business requirement. The second is "vanilla" or "out-of-the-box" when the ES software application is implemented without any changes to the software and the business processes within the organization are changed to suit the functionality of the software. SAP explained that there is a potential source of confusion about the extent of customization as every project needs some form of customer specific reports, customer specific interfaces, and customer specific data conversion programs. ES software is designed to meet most customization requirements by adjusting parameter settings. All modern software vendors now have a software architecture that does not require modification to the core software statements to achieve results. The user access can be built through parameter settings to accommodate specific requirements. However, this should not be confused with what is called true customization in which the core software is actually modified.

Findings in this study revealed that organizations now view the ES software not as a bunch of statements but as pre-defined business processes. These organizations prefer to adhere to the pre-defined business processes in the software and change their own processes to the software's requirements. The companies doing this are more likely to be successful in capturing the benefits and controlling the cost of the implementation as this also helps in future upgrades, and the overall cost of ownership gets reduced. These findings also confirm the Brehm, Heinzl, and Markus (2001) study in which they have estimated that greater the customization, the more will the implementation encounter difficulties, suffer on cost, schedule and performance metrics. The company will also experience difficulties when attempting to upgrade to a later package release. But on the other hand the organizational adaptation to the ES will be easy and the system will meet the needs of the business. The current study revealed that vanilla implementations are more common in the SME category whereas the large organizations are more likely to have comprehensive implementations. Shakir and Viehland (2004) noted cost as a driver towards vanilla implementations as the two approaches has major implications on the change management strategy. When the best practice is chosen, people issues become top priorities whereas when the implementation strategy is geared towards customization, it is more of a technical challenge. Parr and Shanks (2000) have reported in their study on different ES implementation approaches that vanilla implementations are usually single site and comprehensive multi-site. However, the current study suggests that vanilla implementations could be single or even multi-site and currently more implementations are multi-site.

An implementation is considered new when it is implemented in an organization for the first time. An upgrade is when a revised version of the software with some additional functionality is implemented to upgrade the existing software in the current implementation (Dalal, Kamath, Kolarik, & Sivaraman, 2004). Add-ons, also called bolt-ons, include adding new modules to the existing implementation. Replace means change the existing implementation with a different vendor's software. The Shakir (2002) study observed that while new implementations were happening in SME's, large organizations were focusing only on upgrades and add-ons comprising of 10-15% of the total implementations. However, findings in this study suggest an equal split between new implementations vs. upgrades, add-ons, and replacements in NZ organizations.

In the current study, SAP suggested a 50-50 split. "We're definitely focusing on new implementations because that's where our goal is. However, we have to look after our existing customer base and as their requirements change, the presentation of our software in their business may also need change." In the case of replacements, Oracle noted that an organization will replace an ES only if there is a need to satisfy some major benefit which remains unsatisfied in their existing system, because it is expensive to replace. It is not just the cost of the software, but it is the huge organizational change that the organization has to go through to replace an enterprise system. Oracle also revealed that in the past this cost was underestimated, but "replacement cost is three times the cost of upgrade". Oracle also revealed the maintenance aspect which included the cost

of up-grading the ES. "Typically in every five-year period, companies spend up to four times the initial purchasing implementation cost, just to maintain the ES. That is why IT budgets in organizations allocate substantially for upgrade support as opposed to new requirements."

Another model used during ES implementation is the best-of-breed, as opposed to a single vendor implementation. The best-of-breed model includes implementation of a mix of different vendor modules which the vendor specializes in, to have the best of everything (James & Wolf, 2000; Pender, 2000). A single vendor implementation includes all the modules from a single vendor as an integrated package. Findings in this study revealed that typically best-of-breed model was adopted by many organizations in the past. For example, an organization might install HRM module from PeopleSoft, financials from Oracle and manufacturing from SAP in the first phase. Then subsequently install bolt-on modules such as CRM from Microsoft, SCM from SAP or Oracle, or BI from Cognos in the second phase.

However, both customers and vendors are now moving towards single vendor implementation. This is because the additional benefit received from a best-of-breed implementation is vastly outweighed by the cost of implementing, maintaining, and managing those disparate systems. Organizations have realized that although there are really good benefits in PeopleSoft, SAP, and Oracle for the different modules, the cost to implement and maintain is enormous. While they may only get 85% to 90% of the best-of-breed benefit in a single vendor implementation that is preferable especially since it can save three times the cost of implementation and maintenance. Vendors also do not release new versions of the software exactly at the same time, therefore managing the upgrade path becomes difficult, the investment depreciates faster than expected, and organizations are unable to take advantage of the new features of the software. This aspect differed from the findings of the Shakir (2002) study which noted that while traditional ERP implementations still dominate new implementations, upgrades, add-ons, and replacements appear to favor the best-of-breed model. The best-of-breed model is also a consideration for new implementations, especially for organizations that operate in niche industries.

The application service provider (ASP) implementation model is one in which a service provider provides an ES application software as a service or hosting to organizations at a fixed cost for a specific period (Malcolm, 2002; Pamatatau, 2002). There was a mixed response from respondents on this model. One vendor noted, "ASP pops up every 5 years and was a bit like an economy that came and went and nothing really happened. I'm not too sure it is addressing a real market requirement need". Another vendor responded "I don't think this model has picked up at all". However, yet another vendor confirmed that the ASP model is used in NZ. "We use it. Customers are happy with it. We have time and resources for providing the service. There's a huge market there. These are small companies that do want an ES and they don't mind paying sixty to seventy thousand dollars a year but are not able to spend half a million to one million dollars for buying the software. It is not too difficult for these companies to put up a few servers each with the latest operating system of windows. We've got the people and it's not much of their time, so we can provide this service. There is no trend, but there is a huge market out there if marketed properly." Except for this one vendor, the overall response was not very positive for the use of the ASP implementation model, either in the current ES environment or in the recent past (Shakir, 2002).

Another model referred to as the business process outsourcing (BPO) or the managed service model was cited by respondents as a growing implementation model in a NZ context. In this model outsourcers run a customized managed service of ES implementation for customers where effectively a single solution is sold to a customer. One consultant explained that this is a low cost commodity solution where the customer prefers not to manage the ES. This model positions itself very much in the SME market for example, in outsourcing transaction services or specific functions like finance, or payroll, or a similar function to a third party supplier. "An organization may have implemented Oracle financials or SAP finance for example, but may be paying, say to IBM, to run the technology and specific functions for them".

Despite its risks, ES implementation is pervasive in many different types of industries (Kumar & Van Hillegersberg, 2000; Mabert, Soni, & Venkataraman, 2000). A majority of the respondents noted that ES implementations are covered in most industry sectors in NZ; however, some respondents provided specific examples in highlighting trends. SAP explained that traditionally, over the last 10 years, there have been many implementations in the consumer packaging goods, manufacturing, forestry, and pulp and paper industries. However, in the last two years there has been a slight shift in the ES market in NZ with several implementations in the retail and utilities industry, and this trend is likely to continue for the next two years.

ES maturity in an organization depends upon the number of year's experience the organization has had with ES and the stage of ES implementation (Hawking, Stein, & Foster, 2004). This concept of ES maturity and the different stage of ES implementation is reinforced by the Nolan and Norton Institute (2000) classification that groups implementations into levels of maturity such as beginning where ES is implemented in the past 12 months, consolidating where ES is implemented between 1 and 3 years, and mature where ES is implemented for more than 3 years.

Findings revealed that most NZ organizations are reasonably mature with ES technology and IT in general. Most large organizations and many SMEs in NZ have been using some form of ES technology for more than a decade and are at a fairly advanced level of maturity. This also confirms the Shakir (2002) study which noted that although NZ is a small country, technology is mature and on par with what's happening in the U.S.

However, as per the respondents, there are a couple of issues in managing ES projects which do highlight the slower pace of ES maturity within the NZ industry. First, many NZ organizations do not conduct a proper business justification of their implementation. Although some improvement has been seen in the last couple of years, most NZ organizations produce little or no value assessments that often lead to weak business cases and insufficient benefit models which cannot be used for benefit tracking. Plant and Willcocks (2006) in their study on critical success factors for ES implementations have also found an increased emphasis upon the determination of clear goals and objectives at the project outset as one of the important factors for ES implementation success. Second, many organizations in NZ believe implementation of ES is a technology challenge. However, according to most respondents, it is more about change management, people, and processes and less about technology. With better business case development, these are two areas in which many NZ companies are struggling.

Respondents also revealed that typically when a new system is implemented, productivity drops for a period and then goes up again. Oracle suggested the depth of the drop depends upon how well the system is implemented, how well the change is managed, how well the business case is defined, and how well the managers are measuring and managing benefits before the organization starts seeing the benefits starting to flow through.

Until a few years ago the majority of organizations did not use the ES in its true capacity. ES was used as a financial system, as a central repository for HRM records, or as a method for raising purchase orders. This was because the organizations had not thought about what they were trying to optimize, what benefits they were trying to bring into the organization, what they were trying to change, how they were trying to

manage the business, and whether they could actually get the information to manage the business. However, recently the software vendors have started to see several companies trying to find ways to get more value out of their investment. Companies have recently started asking how to establish analytical processes to optimize and realize business value from their ES investment. Many NZ organizations have already completed their first phase of ES needs and are now extending into the second phase with CRM, SCM, or BI. Most respondents agreed that the slower pace of ES maturity within the NZ organizations is due to the limited spending power, which is attributable to the comparatively small NZ economy. However, this trend is now changing. NZ organizations have now started realizing the value of technology and its use to stay ahead of competition.

Findings revealed that the mix between national and international ES implementations is a 50-50 split in NZ. Respondents noted that on several occasions the implementations started as a national implementation but quite quickly reached out to countries like Fiji, Australia, Europe, Singapore or wherever the sales and distribution offices are located. Although many NZ companies are based in NZ and the reach is national, there is a growing trend in NZ organizations to expand to global markets therefore now the reach is becoming global. This is also supported by the growing export-oriented market of NZ organizations.

Global implementations are also part of multinational organizations that implement ES within their NZ companies. These implementations are normally "roll-outs" based on a global template that includes standard business processes. The "roll-out", as explained by one consultant, is an implementation generated from a template customized for an overseas location. The roll-out starts with a massive data set prepared by the first implementation followed by the addition of country specific and localized data. For example, GST or VAT percentages are different, the states as part of the addresses are different, and therefore a couple of master files which are country specific are implemented on top of the local customer and vendor base that is created. The data-set roll-out is established using country specific data where new country settings override the template settings. A separate dedicated warehouse for these locations is also included for tracking transactions. However, many NZ companies are governed by their parent organizations; hence all the decision making for the ES implementation is done offshore by the parent company, without much control from the NZ businesses. This is nothing new. Implementations based on global templates and critical decision-making being made offshore were observed in Shakir's 2002 study. In summary, ES implementations in NZ organizations are moving from national towards a global reach either by expansion into overseas markets or offshore ownership.

CONCLUSION AND FURTHER RESEARCH

The main objective of this study was to understand typical ES implementations and practices in NZ and how current implementations in the SME sector differ from the earlier implementations in the large enterprise sector. The findings are analyzed and summarized in table 4, based on different organizational size segments of the ES market. Table 4 suggests the different ES implementation determinants for both large and SME organizations and explains the relationships between the organization size and the implementation process variables.

It is evident from the table that typical cases of ES implementation in NZ exist in both large and SME organization segments. Typical implementations in the large organization segment with revenues more than $250M are currently in phase 2 and the organizations are fairly mature

Table 4. Determinants for describing typical ES implementation based on organizational size segment

Organizational Characteristics	Organization Size Revenue in Million ($NZ)	Large 250M and Over	SME Small 10-50 M SME 50-250 M
ES implementation process variables	Phases of ES implementation	Phase 2	Phase 1
	Modules	Supplementary modules (HR, SCM, CRM, data warehousing and BI)	Core modules (Finance, manufacturing, distribution)
	Time for implementation	12 to 24 months	3 to 12 months
	Locations	Single or multi-site	Multi-site
	Cost of implementation	Above $NZ 2 M	$NZ 100,000 – $NZ 1 M $NZ 1 M – $NZ 2 M
	Number of users	Above 200	Below 20 20 – 200
ES implementation models	Implementation partners - Vendor vs. Third party	Third party	Vendor
	Customization - Vanilla vs. Comprehensive	Comprehensive	Vanilla
	Implementation - New vs. Upgrades/add-ons/replace	Upgrades/add-ons/replace	New
	Implementation - Single vendor vs. Best-of-breed	Best-of-breed	Single vendor

with their ES. These organizations are likely to be in the phase of acquiring collaborative scenarios like SCM or CRM, or management services applications such as BI. These can be single or multi-site implementations. The number of users is estimated to be 200 or above and the cost of the project is likely to be more than $2M. In the SME segment, typical implementations are in organizations with revenue between $50 - 200M. These implementations are likely to be new with two or more core ES modules. These can be single or multi-site implementations with number of users in the range of 20 – 200 and the cost of the implementation between $100,000 – 1M.

Many ES implementations in New Zealand are several years old now however, these companies have only recently started asking how to actually optimize processes and realize business value from their ES investments. Organizations are establishing analytical processes for tracking benefits continuously improving in taking advantage of the technology.

The findings of this study are limited to the views of professionals from different ES vendors, ES consultants, and IT research organizations and are limited by a small sample size. There may also have been some influence on the responses by the commercial interests of the firm the participant worked for. However, the study has achieved its objectives. This is achieved due to the seniority and experience of the respondents within the organizations interviewed, and the position of these organizations as key players in the ES industry in New Zealand. Further research is in progress to analyze the current practices and the critical effectiveness constructs of ES in New Zealand from the practitioners' perspectives identified by this study.

REFERENCES

Allen, D., Kern, T., & Havenhand, M. (2002). ERP Critical Success Factors: An Exploration of the Contextual Factors in Public Sector Institutions. *Paper presented at the Proceedings of the 35th Annual Hawaii International Conference on System Sciences*, 9/02, Hawaii.

Bancroft, N. H., Sep, H., & Sprengel, A. (1998). *Implementing SAP R/3* (2nd Edition ed.). Greenwich, USA: Manning Publications.

Brehm, L., Heinzl, A., & Markus, M. L. (2001). *Tailoring ERP systems: A spectrum of choices and their implications.* Paper presented at the 34th Hawaii International Conference on System Sciences, Hawaii.

Dalal, N. P., Kamath, M., Kolarik, W. J., & Sivaraman, E. (2004). Toward an integrated approach for modeling Enterprise processes. *Communications of the ACM, 47*, 83-87.

Davenport, T. H. (2000). Transforming the Practice of Management with Enterprise Systems. In *Mission Critical* (p. 203-235). Boston, MA: Harvard Business School Press.

Davenport, T. H., & Harris, J. G. (2005). Automated Decision Making Comes of Age. *MIT Sloan Management Review, Summer 2005 46(4)*, 83-89.

Davenport, T. H., Harris, J. G., & Cantrell, S. (2002). *The Return of Enterprise Systems: The Director's Cut.* Accenture Institute for Strategic Change.

Davenport, T. H., & Prusak, L. (1998). Working Knowledge. *Boston, Harvard Business School Press.*

Hawking, P., Stein, A., & Foster, S. (2004). Revisiting ERP systems: Benefit Realisation. *Paper presented at the Proceedings of the 37th Hawaii International Conference on System Sciences*, Hawaii.

Hedman, J., & Borell, A. (2002). *The impact of Enterprise Resource Planning Systems on Organi-*

zational Effectiveness: An Artifact Evaluation. In F. F.-H. Nah (Ed.), *Enterprise Resource Planning Solutions & Management* (p. 125-142). Hershey, London: IRM Press.

Holland, C., & Light, B. (1999). A critical success factors model for ERP implementation. *IEEE software, May/June*, 30-36.

James, D., & Wolf, M. L. (2000). A Second Wind for ERP. *McKinsey Quarterly, Issue 2*, 100-107.

Kumar, K., & Van Hillegersberg, J. (2000). ERP Experiences and Evolution. *Communications of the ACM, 43*(4), 23-26.

Mabert, A. M., Soni, A., & Venkataraman, M. A. (2000). Enterprise Resource Planning Survey of US Manufacturing Firms. *Production and Inventory Management Journal, 41(2)*, 52-58.

Malcolm, A. (2002). Fonterra Rents its Accounting Application. *Computerworld IDG Communication Ltd., 11 July, 2002,* Web page: http://www.idg.net.nz/webhome.nsf/UNID/8433B6BCB6BE15FECC256BF1007BF560

Markus, M., & Tanis, C. (2000). The Enterprise Systems Experience - From Adoption to Success. In R. W. Zmud (Ed.), *In Framing the Domains of IT Research Glimpsing the Future Through the Past* (p. 173-207). Cincinnati: Pinnaflex Educational Resources, Cincinnati, USA.

Nolan and Norton Institute. (2000). *SAP Benchmarking Report 2000.* Melbourne.

Pamatatau, R. (2002). The Warehouse outsources Oracle Management. *NZ Infotech Weekly, 24 June, 2002, p. 3.*

Parr, A., & Shanks, G. (2000). A Model of ERP Project Management. *Journal of Information Technology, 15*(4).

Pender, L. (2000). *Damned If You Do: Will Integration Tools Patch the Holes Left By An Unsatisfactory ERP Implementation? CIO Magazine,*

September 15, 2000. Retrieved from http://www.cio.com/archive/091500_erp.html

Plant, R., & Willcocks, L. (2006). *Critical Success Factors in International ERP Implementations: A Case Research Approach.* Working Paper Series - 145, London: Department of Information Systems, London School of Economics and Political Science.

Sarker, S., & Lee, A. S. (2000, 13 November 2000). Using a case study to test the role of three key social enabales in ERP implementation. *Paper presented at the ICIS 2000,* 13 November 2000 http://www.commerce.uq.edu.au/icis/ICIS2000.html

Scott, J. E., & Vessey, I. (2002). Managing Risks in Enterprise Systems Implementations. *Communications of ACM, April 2002, 45*(4).

Shanks, G., Seddon, P. B., & Wilcocks, L. P. (2003). *Second-Wave Enterprise Resource Planning Systems: Implementing for Effectiveness.* Cambridge University Press.

Shakir, M. (2002). Current Issues of ERP Implementations in New Zealand. *Research Letters in Information and Mathematical Science, 4*(1), 151-172. Massey University, Auckland, New Zealand.

Shakir, M., & Viehland, D. (2004). Business Drivers in Contemporary Enterprise System Implementations. *Proceedings of the Tenth Americas Conference on Information Systems,* New York, 103-112.

Skok, W., & Legge, M. (2001). Evaluating Enterprise Resource Planning (ERP) Systems Using an Interpretive Approach. *Paper presented at the Proceedings of The 2001 ACM SIGCPR Conference on Computer Personnel Research,* April, p. 189-197.

Sumner, M. (1999). Critical Success Factors in Enterprisewide Information Management Systems Projects. *Paper presented at the 5th America's Conference on Information Systems,* Milwaukee, Wisconsin, USA.

Viehland, D., & Shakir, M. (2005). Making Sense of Enterprise Systems Implementation. *Business Review, University of Auckland,* 7(2), 28-36.

Yang, S., & Seddon, P. B. (2004). Benefits and Key Success Factors from Enterprise Systems Implementations: Lessons from Sapphire 2003. *Paper presented at the 35th Australasian Conference in Information Systems.* Hobart, Australia.

Zrimsek, B. (2002). *ERPII: The Boxed Set.* Retrieved Mar. 4, 2002, from www3.gartner.com/pages/story.php.id.2376.s.8.jsp

KEY TERMS

Application Service Provider (ASP): An ASP is a business that provides computer-based services of specialized software to customers over a network.

Business Intelligence (BI): Software tools that use the ERP database to generate customizable reports and provide meaningful information and analysis to employees, customers, suppliers, and partners for more effective decision making at the organization.

Business Process Outsourcing (BPO): Contracting of specific business task (s), such as payroll, marketing, billing etc, to a third party service provider as a cost saving measure

Enterprise Resource Planning (ERP): Software systems for business management that integrates functional areas such as planning, manufacturing, sales, marketing, distribution, accounting, finances, human resource management, project management, inventory management, service and maintenance, transportation, and e-business.

Customer Relationship Management (CRM): Software systems that help companies to acquire knowledge about customers and deploy strategic information systems to optimize revenue, profitability and customer satisfaction.

Critical Success Factors (CSF): Are the factors which are critical for an organisation or a project and which must go right to achieve the defined mission.

Customization: Altering a system's software code to include functionality specifically wanted by an organization, although not originally included in the package itself.

Extended ERP: Extends the foundation ERP system's functionalities such as finances, distribution, manufacturing, human resources, and payroll to customer relationship management, supply chain management, sales-force automation, and Internet-enabled integrated e-commerce and e-business

Small and Medium-Size Enterprise (SME): A business enterprise independently owned by contributing most of the operating capital and managed by the owners or managers, having fewer than 250 employees and a small-to-medium market share. This number differs in different regions or countries (in some countries it is less than 500 while in others the number may be less than 100). The number may also vary depending on the type of business.

Supply Chain Management (SCM): Software systems for procurement of materials, transformation of the materials into products, and distribution of products to customers, allowing the enterprise to anticipate demand and deliver the right product to the right place at the right time at the lowest possible cost to satisfy its customers.

Chapter XIV
Integration Concept for Knowledge Processes, Methods, and Software for SMEs

Kerstin Fink
University of Innsbruck, Austria

Christian Ploder
University of Innsbruck, Austria

ABSTRACT

Small and medium-sized enterprises (SMEs) are a vital and growing part of any national economy. Like most large businesses, SMEs have recognized the importance of knowledge management. This Chapter investigates the use of knowledge processes and knowledge methods for SMEs. The learning objectives of this Chapter are to assess the role of knowledge management and knowledge processes in SMEs. Furthermore, the reader should be able to describe major knowledge management programs in SMEs and assess how they provide value for organizations. Empirical studies conducted by the authors show that for SMEs, only four knowledge processes are important: (1) knowledge identification, (2) knowledge acquisition, (3) knowledge distribution and (4) knowledge preservation. Based on the research result of several empirical studies, an integration concept for knowledge processes, knowledge methods, and knowledge software tools for SMEs is introduced and discussed.

INTRODUCTION

The academic literature on knowledge management has become a major research field in different disciplines in the last decade (Davenport & Prusak, 1998). Through knowledge management, organizations are enabled to create, identify and renew the company's knowledge base and to deliver innovative products and services to the customer. Knowledge management is a process of systematically managed and leveraged knowledge in an organization. For Mockler and Dologite (2002, p. 18) knowledge management "refers to the process of identifying and generating, systematically gathering and providing access to, and putting in use anything and everything which might be useful to know when performing some specified business activity. The knowledge management process is designed to increase profitability and competitive advantage in the marketplace". Before implementing a knowledge integration concept, there must be a common understanding of the term knowledge, its characteristics, and its impact on knowledge management. The multi-faceted nature of the term knowledge is reflected in a variety of definitions (Kakabadse, Kouzmin, & Kakabadse, 2001, p. 138). Davenport and Prusak (1998) use the term *"knowledge in action"* to express the characteristics of the term knowledge management in a way it is valuable for the company and to capture it in words because it resists in the minds of the humans and their action. Davenport and Prusak (1998, pp. 6) identify five key components that describe the term knowledge management:

1. The first component is *experience*. Knowledge develops over time, and it builds on the lifelong learning and training practice of an employee. Experience has a historical perspective, and it is based on the skills the knowledge-worker applies to familiar patterns to make connections between these links.

2. The second component of the term knowledge is *"ground truth"* (Davenport & Prusak, 1998) which is a term used by the U.S. Army's Center for Army Lessons Learned (CALL). CALL used the term "ground truth" to express experiences that come from the ground rather than from theories and generalizations. "Ground truth" refers to the way that the people involved know what works and what does not. CALL experts'

take part in real military situations, and they pass their observations to the troops through videotapes or photos. The success of this knowledge management approach lies in "After Action Review" programs which try to cover the gap between what happened during an action and what was supposed to happen. This reflection process helps uncover disparities and differences

3. The third component is *complexity*. The skill to solve complex problems and the ability to know how to deal with uncertainties distinguish an expert from a normal employee.

4. A forth characteristic of knowledge is *judgment*. An expert can judge new situations based on experience gained over time. Furthermore, they have the ability to refine them through reflection. Knowledge, in this sense, is a living system that interacts with the environment.

5. Finally, knowledge is about heuristics and *intuition*. An expert acts based on their intuitive knowledge.

Knowledge is tacit, action-oriented, supported by rules, and it is constantly changing. In a global and interconnected society, it is more difficult for companies to know where the best and most valuable knowledge is, thus it becomes more difficult to know what the knowledge is. A successful implementation of knowledge management only can be achieved in a culture that supports knowledge sharing and transfer. An appropriate organizational culture can empower effective knowledge management. The organizational culture of a company consists of its shared values or norms which are transmitted through common beliefs and feelings, regularities of behavior, and historical processes. Trompenaars and Hampden-Turner (2006, p. 6) define culture as a group of people concerned with problem solving processes and reconciliation dilemmas. Culture itself has three different levels. The first, and highest level, is *national culture* or regional society; the second level describes *organizational culture*, and, finally, *professional culture* focuses on the knowledge of specific groups. A knowledge culture is the most important value for the implementation of knowledge management, because organizational knowledge resides in the culture, structure and individuals who make up the organization.

Besides culture and networking, the objective for knowledge management technology is the creation of a connected environment for the exchange of knowledge (Mentzas, Apostolou, Young, & Abecker, 2001). These new software products facilitate communication and interaction among people as well as among people and systems. Mentzas et al. (2001, p. 95) discuss two key components that are required to support the sharing of information and knowledge:

- *Collaboration facilities* for knowledge workers are mainly the domain of groupware products. Other technology examples in this group are email systems, workflow automation, discussion groups, document management, shared databases, scheduling and calendar functions.
- *Discovery facilities* are required for searching and retrieval purposes. Knowledge workers are in constant need of finding and accessing information and knowledge from other experts. A wide variety of information sources support the finding of expertise, and they include the Internet, corporate Intranets, legacy systems and corporate local area networks (LANs).

Knowledge management is more than the technological solutions provided to give people access to better and more relevant information (Wang & Plaskoff, 2002, p. 113). It is important that the design of the knowledge management systems reflects the mindset of the knowledge workers and their way of offering highly qualitative knowledge solutions with quick solution processes. An effective knowledge management system must integrate people, processes, technology and the organizational structure.

Historically, knowledge management focused on the domain of larger organizations. Consequently issues of culture, networking, organizational structure and technological infrastructure have been examined upon the implementation of knowledge management initiatives in large multi-national organizations and seem to give little relevance (Delahaye, 2003) to small and medium enterprises (SMEs). However, the success and growth of SMEs depends on how well they manage the knowledge of their knowledge workers. Managers in SMEs have to recognize that the uniqueness and creativity of each knowledge worker will lead to customer satisfaction and the success of the SMEs. Dezouza & Awazu (2006) point out that SMEs have to compete with know-how in order to gain competitive advantages. As SMEs do not have much money to spend on knowledge management initiatives, knowledge must be leveraged so that goals can be achieved in an effective and efficient manner. There are several research articles dealing with knowledge management in SMEs (2001), but only a few empirical studies have been conducted to see the impact of knowledge processes in them. McAdam & Reid (2005) concluded that the time is right for knowledge management within the SME-sector. The results of their comparative study of large organizations and SMEs showed that both have much to gain from the development of knowledge management systems. Salojärvi, Furu & Sveiby (Dunkelberg & Wade, 2007) concluded that SMEs should be able to enhance their performance and competitive advantages by a more conscious and systematic approach to knowledge management.

There are several quantitative (2007, p. 240) and qualitative definitions of the term SME depending on regional and national differences. Street & Cameron (Fink & Ploder, 2007a, 2007b) conducted a literature review from 1990 until

2002 to analyze the current status of SMEs and found a variety of definitions of SMEs with the following clustering: individual characteristics of the entrepreneur, organizational characteristics of the SME, relationship characteristics, performance characteristics, strategic planning characteristics or relationship characteristics. In 2000, the European Council set the clear strategic goal for the European Union (EU) of becoming "the most competitive and dynamic economy in the world, capable of sustaining economic growth with more and better jobs and greater social cohesion" by the year 2010 (ec.europa.eu/growthandjobs). SMEs are playing a key role in European economic performance because they account for a high proportion of the Gross Domestic Product (GDP) and employ some two thirds of the European workforce. According to the OECD Small and Medium Enterprise Outlook 2005 (www.oecd.org) SMEs are very important for strengthening economic performances. They represent over 95 percent of enterprises in most OECD countries, and generate over half of private sector development. Looking at the European countries of Austria and Switzerland including Liechtenstein a similar SME landscape can be found. According to the Austrian Statistical Year Book (www.statistik.at) and the Austrian Institute for SMEs Research (www.kmuforschung.ac.at) in the year 2006, 99.7 percent of companies in Austria, or 297,800, were SMEs. According to the data from CHSME (www.kmu.admin.ch), 99.7 percent of the companies in Switzerland are SMEs.

In the United States (US), the definition of small business is set by a government department called the Small Business Administration (SBA) Size Standards Office. The SBA uses the term "size standards" to indicate the largest a concern can be in order to still be considered a small business. It must also be independently owned and operated. Unlike the European Union, which has simple definitions applied to all industries, the United States has chosen to set size standards for each individual industry. This distinction is intended

to better reflect industry differences. SMEs are also of high importance for in the US Economy. Similar to Europe, more than 97 percent of the firms in the US can be defined as SME.

A comparable influence of SMEs on economic value can be found in the report of the Asia-Pacific Economic Cooperation (www.apec.com), where about 90 percent of enterprises are SMEs. During their 2006 meeting in Beijing the members agreed to strengthen SME's competitiveness for trade and investment. For example, SMEs account for more than 95 percent of companies in Australia. Of the 624,010 SMEs in Australia, more than two thirds employ between one and four people. A further 180,880 SMEs employ between five and 19 people meaning that 93.5 percent of people employed by SMEs in Australia are employed by what can be described as 'micro-SMEs', namely companies with fewer than 20 employees.

In section two the authors introduce an integration concept for the implementation of knowledge management systems in SMEs by taking the knowledge processes, knowledge methods and supporting knowledge software tools into consideration. Section three discusses future research and describes objectives.

INTEGRATION CONCEPT FOR KNOWLEDGE MANAGEMENT IN SMES

Research Framework and SME Definition

This section focuses on discussing the integration concept for SMEs. Our research findings (2006) indicate that SMEs need only four key knowledge processes (1) Knowledge Identification, (2) Knowledge Acquisition, (3) Knowledge Distribution and (4) Knowledge Preservation and therefore the authors propose a knowledge layer concept designed specifically for implementing knowledge management in SMEs. The empirical studies conducted by the authors combine the concepts of knowledge processes as well as knowledge methods for SMEs in a single study. The key objective of this section is the matching of knowledge methods to knowledge processes in these companies. Figure 1 illustrates the research process for modeling knowledge processes in SMEs and assigning knowledge methods to each of the four key processes with supporting software tools. The basic research model is the "building block" approach by Probst, Raub & Romhardt (Laudon & Laudon, 2006) with their description of the knowledge processes (Figure 1, layer 1). Involved are eight components that

form two cycles, one inner cycle and one outer cycle. Among other knowledge process models (2006), the building block approach of Probst, Raub & Romhardt (Edwards & Kidd, 2003) has the advantage that it is well known in European companies, including SMEs, and furthermore it has a unique and complete design.

The authors use the definition of SMEs of the European Commission 2006 for their research design. The European Commission analyzes SMEs by using the following three characteristics: (1) number of employees, (2) annual turnover and (3) total assets. Characterized through these three factors, the European Commission differenti-

Figure 1. Knowledge integration layer concept for SMEs

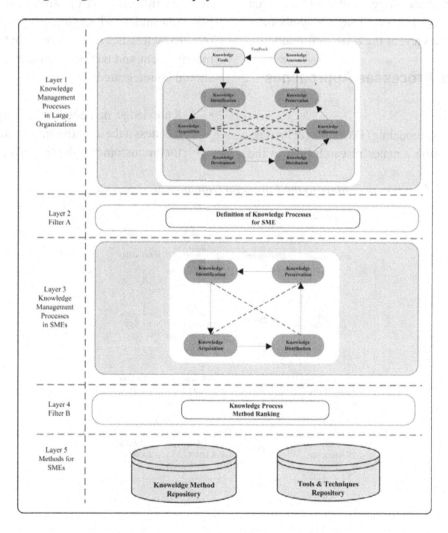

ates between (1) middle enterprises [fewer than 250 employees and less than EURO 50 million annual turnover or less than EURO 43 million total assets], (2) small enterprises [fewer than 50 employees and less than EURO 10 million annual turnover or less than EURO 10 million total assets] and (3) micro enterprises [fewer than 10 employees and less than EURO 2 million annual turnover or less than EURO 2 million total assets]. Figure 2 illustrates the European Commission's definition of SMEs. Focusing on this definition, the authors follow the research view of a quantitative perspective of SMEs. This means, that all enterprises with fewer than 250 employees and less than EURO 50 million annual turnover or less than EURO 43 million total assets in Austria and Switzerland including Liechtenstein are the target population. In figure 1 layer 2 symbolizes the quantitative view of the SME definition.

Knowledge Processes Approaches (Layer 1)

Business process modeling (Davenport & Prusak, 1998) has become a major research field in the information systems discipline in the last ten years. Davenport sees the term business process as "a structured, measured set of activities designed to produce a specified output from a particular customer or market" (Probst et al., 2006; Rao, 2004). However, in recent years, not only business process management, but also knowledge management has been developing into a new research field (2003, p. 124). The term knowledge process modeling comes from the linking of these two research fields. Key features of knowledge intensive processes can be described as follows: diversity of sources and media, variance and dynamic development of the process organization, plentiful process participants with different expertise, use of creativity, high level of innovation and influence on the area of the decision. Edwards and Kidd (2000) used the following five characteristics to emphasize that knowledge management and business process management should be integrated:

- Knowledge management is important for business if the initiative implies an advantage for the customers. The idea of implementing

Figure 2. SME definition according to the European Commission definition

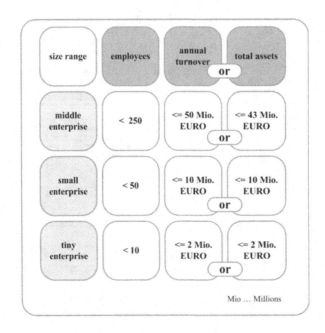

the customer's requests – may be internal or external – is the basis for including the customer.

- Knowledge doesn't follow business borders. Business processes also model activities carried out by global trading companies and lay the foundations for modeling knowledge intensive processes.
- Knowledge management can only be efficient if it follows a structured model. Business processes are modeled by structured actions and they are necessary to deduce knowledge intensive processes.
- The success of knowledge management depends on the measurement of knowledge. There is a similarity to the measurement of business processes. The measurement of the knowledge potential provides a central position and biases the success.
- Knowledge management is affected by a holistic approach. Every part of the business process modeling is important for success but every aspect should be considered.

In addition, knowledge management and business process modeling initially focused on large companies. The knowledge economy has to shift from focusing on large companies to small and medium-sized enterprises (SME) because of their importance for industrial economies. The main reason behind today's change of focus is that all businesses depend on methods and tools of knowledge management in order to gain competitive advantages and to deal with the knowledge potential of their employees.

The basic research model is the "building block" approach by Probst, Raub & Romhardt (2006) with their description of the knowledge processes (Figure 1, layer 1). Involved are eight components that form two cycles, one inner cycle and the other outer cycle. The inner cycle is composed of six key knowledge processes:

- *Knowledge Identification* is the process of identifying external knowledge for analyzing and describing the company's knowledge environment.
- *Knowledge Acquisition* refers to what forms of expertise the company should acquire from outside through relationships with customers, suppliers, competitors and partners in co-operative ventures.
- *Knowledge Development* is a building block which complements Knowledge Acquisition. It focuses on generating new skills, new products, better ideas and more efficient processes. Knowledge Development includes all management actions consciously aimed at producing capabilities.
- *Knowledge Distribution* is the process of sharing and spreading knowledge which is already present within the organization.
- *Knowledge Utilization* consists of carrying out activities to ensure that the knowledge present in the organization is applied productively for its benefit.
- *Knowledge Preservation* is the process where the selective retention of information, documents and experience required by management takes place.

In addition, there are two other processes in the outer cycle, Knowledge Assessment and Knowledge Goals, which provide the direction to the whole knowledge management cycle:

- *Knowledge Assessment* completes the cycle, providing the essential data for strategic control of knowledge management.
- *Knowledge Goals* determine which capabilities should be built on which level.

Knowledge Processes in SMEs (Layer 2 and 3)

The research method for the identification of knowledge processes in SMEs were expert interviews or what Gillham (Gillham, 2000, p. 64) referred to as "elite interviewing". This kind of interviewing is chosen to address someone in a special position or an expert. Gillham lists several characteristics of open-ended interviews (Davenport & Prusak, 1998; Ruggels, 1997):

- The respondents will know more about the topic and the setting than the interviewer. Sometimes they can even tell the interviewer what questions to ask.
- By virtue of their authority and experience, they will have their own structuring of their knowledge. They will not allow an interview for which they have to answer a series of questions addressed at them.
- The best thing the interviewer can hope for is a response to a topic raised.
- The experts can be particularly informative about the location of documents, records, or other experts.
- The experts will expect some control over the interviewer, and they also will demand a level of accountability and feedback.

These five characteristics of elite interviews also apply to the interview situation for the knowledge processes in SMEs. The managers or company owners were highly motivated to articulate their view of knowledge processes and wanted to share their personal position about the key knowledge processes. The first interview session was conducted in 2004 and was limited to Austrian SME managers. This study was the proving ground for the future procedure of the empirical studies in 2005/2006/2007. The research hypothesis was:

Hypothesis: SMEs need a simple knowledge process model in order to implement knowledge management successfully.

The second interview session was conducted from December 2005 to February 2006 (Figure 1,

layer 2). The research method was the elite interview. The data sample ranged from all industry sectors in which SMEs could be found in Austria at this time with a special focus on enterprises in the of consulting and information technology sector. The survey subjects were CIOs (Chief information officer) and CEOs (Chief executive officer) in Austrian and Swiss SMEs as these are recognized as proficient in answering questions concerning knowledge management (1980, p. 21). The data sample of 36 interviewees was the proving ground for asking open ended questions. The data was analyzed by content analysis defined by Krippendorf (Davenport & Prusak, 1998) as "a research technique for making replicable and valid inferences to the content". The interview sessions lasted approximately one hour and the authors were the interviewers. The result of the Austrian and Swiss research showed clearly that in both countries only four knowledge processes identified in the Probst, Raub & Romhardt (2006) model are ranked as important for the implementation of knowledge management in SMEs (see Figure 1, layer 3):

- **Knowledge identification:** In SMEs it is highly important to identify the key sources of knowledge, experiences and know-how in order to stay competitive on the market.
- **Knowledge Acquisition:** The know-how of SMEs resides in many cases in the head of the experts or knowledge worker.
- **Knowledge distribution:** This process focuses on the sharing of explicit and implicit knowledge between knowledge workers in SMEs. As SMEs are characterized by smaller groups, a knowledge sharing culture which facilitates the exchange of knowledge with other groups and utilizes knowledge tools and mechanisms is especially important.
- **Knowledge preservation:** It is well recognized that the most critical asset of any company are the sum of its collective knowl-

edge and intellectual property (Laudon & Laudon, 2006; Schwartz, 2006). Knowledge preservation and growth of this asset requires effective knowledge management throughout SMEs, so as to make sure that the right information is available to the right people when they need it. In addition, the managers of the SMEs in our study pointed out that the process of *knowledge disposal* is also relevant for SMEs with the objective of not overloading the information flow between the individuals. From the content analysis of the expert interviews with Austrian and Swiss managers, knowledge disposal can be identified as an integrated part of knowledge preservation.

There were no significant differences in the answers given by the managers of SMEs in Austria and Switzerland. In general, it can be stated that SMEs are satisfied with only four knowledge processes instead of the original framework with eight building blocks. This implies that hypothesis 1 is verified. These four key knowledge processes and the basic framework they provide for assigning knowledge methods in SMEs will be part of our future research.

Knowledge Methods (Layer 4)

Based on a literature review (Fink & Ploder, 2007b) a list of existing knowledge methods which support one of the four key knowledge processes was developed (Figure 1, layer 4). The objective of this empirical study was to find out which of the methods are most relevant for SMEs. The data sample of 587 enterprises was stochastically appointed from the target population. It was average allocated across the federal states of Austria, Switzerland to get a representative result. In Austria there are 535,031 SMEs and in Switzerland/Liechtenstein there are 308,819. The online questionnaire was carried out in summer 2006 after a pre-test with 30 respondents. The

respondents were divided into seven industry sectors. 60 percent were from the three key industries: industry, information & consulting and trade & handcraft, with the remaining 40 percent dispersed over various other industries. Figure 3 lists the key methods for the four knowledge management processes, which are stored in the knowledge method repository (Figure 1, layer 5) and can be extended to new knowledge methods.

Knowledge Software-Support (Layer 5)

In a next step, the objective was to match a cost-efficient software product to each knowledge method which is usable in practice. In the research design the focus was on Freeware and Shareware software tools in order to fulfill the presetting of cost-efficient software support. An online research method was used which resulted in a list of evaluated cost-efficient software products. The evaluation of each software product was conducted by applying the ISO/IEC 9126 norm. The Quality Model of the norm is divided into two parts which are important for the evaluation of the software products to support knowledge methods:

- the internal and the external quality of the software as well as
- the quality for use.

The ISO norm (see Figure 4) lists five characteristics to evaluate software products: (1) functionality, (2) reliability, (3) usability, (4) efficiency and (5) assignability. For each characteristic a different number of items were assessed by a likert scale from -2 up to +2. The process used by the authors to make the assessment is shown in the appendix. The data sample of the Quality Model included more than 200 different software products. A key research finding was that some of the software products cannot be used in practice because their quality is inadequate. Finally there were 45 software products which are suitable for use in SMEs.

Figure 3. List of knowledge methods

PROCESS 1 Knowledge Identification	PROCESS 2 Knowledge Acquisition	PROCESS 3 Knowledge Distribution	PROCESS 4 Knowledge Preservation
Balanced Scorecard	Brainstorming	Knowledge Maps	Document Management
	Synektik	Story Telling	Conceptualization
Tobin`s q	Mind Mapping	Lessons Learned	Checklist
	System Simulation	Communities of Practice	
Market- Asset Value - Method	eMail System	Questionnaire	Mind Mapping
		eMail System	Content Management
	Scenario Technique	Cheklist	
Knowledge Balance	Business Games	Best Practice	Neural Network
		Handbook	
Skandia Navigator	Knowledge Network	Micro Article	Database
	Search Engines	Groupware	Project Review
Morphological Box	Yellow Pages	Chatroom	Expert System
Synektik	Micro Article	FAQs	

Figure 4. Example of ISO 9126-1

Functionality	ISO Ranking	Reliability	ISO Ranking	Usability	ISO Ranking	Efficiency	ISO Ranking
Accuracy	2	Maturity	2	Comprehensibility	1	Time Responsibility	1
Adequacy	2	Fault Tolerance	1	Learnability and Usability	2	Resource Respon-sibility	1
Interoperability	1						
Subtotal	5		3		3		2

Assignability	ISO Ranking			Process	Knowledge Acquisition		
Installation	1			Method	Brainstorming		
Conformance	1			Software	Concept X7		
Compatibility	2						
Subtotal	4	Ranking	17				

Costs	149 EURO
Disk Space	74,7 MB
License	License for 1 User
Annotation	supporting tablet computers, great functional range

Table 1 gives an overview of all methods supporting the four knowledge processes for SMEs and the corresponding cost-efficient software tools. Table 1 also lists the absolute number of each method in the likert scale. The ranking of each method is the calculated value based on the likert scale. The "ISO Ranking" illustrates the assessment of the software based on the Quality Model. The absolute frequency with which the software was named by the respondents can be seen in the last column.

Knowledge Balance (92) was ranked highest among the methods for the first process of the *identification of knowledge*. 56% of SMEs think that this is the best method. Further methods are the Balanced Scorecard (89) and the Skandia Navigator (74). The methods Market-Asset Value-Method (-5) and Tobin's q (-15) were rated by less than 30% to be of good use in SMEs.

Brainstorming (225) and Knowledge Network (203) are popular methods for the *acquisition of knowledge*. Mind Mapping (195), eMail Systems (134), Scenario Technique (126) and System Simulation (98) are also suitable methods for this knowledge process, while Business Games (91) are also a possibility. The method of "Synektik" was rated very low because of its complexity. The absolute star for the acquisition of knowledge was the Search Engine (232) with over 70% for efficient use in SMEs. In this case the Google Desktop Search Engine was the prior selection software. 60% of the respondents chose eMail-Systems which can be supported by the software Thunderbird1.5. For Brainstorming a good tool is Concept X7, while for Mind Mapping the tools Free Mind (42%) and Think Graph (41%) were rated highly. As support software to a Business Game 64% rated Gamma was well

As illustrated in Table 1 the methods eMail-System (185), Handbook FAQs (159), Communities of Practice (152), Groupware (139), Questionnaire (110) and Best Practice (108) are the favorites for the *distribution of knowledge*. It has to be pointed out that the methods Micro Article

(2) and Chatroom (29) are rated not as well in the survey. The software products for the methods of transferring knowledge are InfoRapid supporting Knowledge Maps, EasySurvey supporting Questionnaire, Skype and MSN supporting Chatroom, eGroupware1.2 and AlphaAgent1.6.0 supporting Groupware, CUCards 2000 supporting Checklists and Pegasus Mail, Thunderbird1.5 and Amicron Mailoffice 2.0 for the support of eMail-Systems.

Databases (242) are a recognized method of *the knowledge preservation process*. 80% of the SMEs think that they will organize their knowledge with databases. Mind Mapping (200), Document Management System (195) and Checklists (164) are further efficient methods. Content Management Systems (126), Project Review (122), Expert Systems (74) and Conceptualization (40) are methods which can be chosen but are not the favorite choice. Neural Network (-10) is not an adequate method for preserving knowledge in an SME. There were many different software products to support this process. MySQL is the favorite database software followed by the MSDE from Microsoft. Document management can be done by the Office Manager, the UDEX dotNETContact or the QVTutto. There are also software tools for the other methods which are described in Table 1.

CONCLUSION AND SECTION OBJECTIVES

In the future the research area will be expanded from Austria, Germany and Switzerland to other key members of the European Union as well as to the U.S. and Asia-Pacific area. Furthermore, in future research work the authors will focus on knowledge diffusion to the dissemination of explicit knowledge captioned in SMEs from many sources. The diffusion of knowledge through an effective SME website creates benefits not only to the enterprise itself but also to customers and

Table 1. Ranking of cost-efficient software products (2006, p. 50ff)

	Ranking	Supporting cost-efficient software products	ISO Ranking	Ranking Survey
Knowledge Identification				
Knowledge Balance	92	no cost-efficient software product, Office similar products		
Balanced Scorecard	89	no cost-efficient software product, Office similar products		
Skandia Navigator	74	no cost-efficient software product, commercial Software		
Market - Asset Value - Method	-5	no cost-efficient software product, Office similar products		
Tobin's q	-15	no cost-efficient software product, Office similar products		
Knowledge Acquisition				
Search Engine	232	Google Desktop Search; MSN Toolbar; Yahoo Dektop Suche	not possible	25; 12; 10
Brainstorming	225	Brainstorming Toolbox; Concept X7	6;17	44; 88
Knowledge Network	203	no cost-efficient software product		
Mind Mapping	195	Free Mind; Think Graph, Tee Tree Office	16; 12; 8	69; 53; 28
eMail System	134	Pegasus Mail; Thunderbird Mail; Amicron Mailoffice 2.0	21; 21; 12	63; 165; 26
Scenario Technique	126	no cost-efficient software product, Office similar products		
System Simulation	98	no cost-efficient software product, commercial Software		
Business Game	91	Gamma	15	75
Synektik	-17	no cost-efficient software product, commercial Software		
Knowledge Distribution				
eMail System	185	Pegasus Mail; Thunderbird Mail; Amicron Mailoffice 2.0	16; 12; 8	63; 165; 26
Handbook FAQs	159	no cost-efficient software product, Office similar products		
Communities of Practice	152	no cost-efficient software product, Office similar products		
Groupware	139	eGRoupware1.2; AlphaAgent 1.6.0; Tiki CMS - Groupware	15; 14; 16	40; 26; 24
Questionnaire	110	Easy Survey	10	61
Best Practice	108	no cost-efficient software product, Office similar products		
Checklist	103	CUEcards 2000	8	128
Lessons Learned	103	no cost-efficient software product, Office similar products		
Knowledge Maps	82	InfoRapid KnowledgeMap	13	69
Story Telling	42	no cost-efficient software product, Office similar products		
Chatroom	29	Skype; MSN, ICQ	not possible	71; 33; 25
Microarticle	2	no cost-efficient software product, Office similar products		
Knowledge Preservation				
Database	242	MySQL; MSDE		86; 44
Mind Mapping	200	Free Mind; Think Graph, Tee Tree Office	16; 12; 8	69; 53; 28
Document Management System	195	Office Manager; UDEX dotNETContact; QVTutto	15; 15; 14	74; 35; 22
Checklist	164	CUEcards 2000	8	128
Content Management	126	CONTEX; ContentKit; VIO MATRIX	16; 13; 13	0; 47; 13

continued on following page

Table 1. continued

Project Review	122	no cost-efficient software product, Office similar products		
Experts System	74	KnowIT; KnowME	10; 7	38; 52
Conceptualization	40	no cost-efficient software product		
Neural Network	-10	no cost-efficient software product, commercial Software		

suppliers as well as to new alliances. Empirical studies conducted by Ordanini show that the website is the only solution which has been used by the majority of SMEs, while the adoption of a highly-sophisticated website is a relevant matter for only 10 percent or 20 percent of SMEs. The use of information technology, especially websites, is recognized as a critical success factor for knowledge management initiatives in the SME sector (Wong & Aspinwall, 2005). Wong (2005) sees information technologies as a key enabler for the implementation of knowledge management and considers factors such as the simplicity of technology, ease of use, suitability for users' needs, relevancy of knowledge content, and standardization of a knowledge structure as key factors for knowledge diffusion in the development of a knowledge management systems. Knowledge diffusion through websites is a dominant factor for successful knowledge initiatives. The central research question of this section can be described as follows: How can SMEs spread their knowledge competencies through their websites? For successful knowledge diffusion (Fink & Ploder, 2007a) in SMEs the authors propose a three-dimensional theoretical framework as shown in figure 5: (1) Data/Information/Knowledge Dimension, (2) Technical-oriented Dimension and (3) Social-cognitive Dimension.

The major learning objectives of this chapter are:

- Identification and description of contemporary approaches to knowledge management in SMEs.

- Assessing contemporary knowledge processes that are required for successful implementation of knowledge management in SMEs.
- Identification of major knowledge methods supporting the key knowledge processes in SMEs: identification, acquisition, dissemination, preservation referring to the layer concept
- Discussion of the impact of cost-efficient software support for knowledge initiatives.
- Analyzing the relationship of knowledge transfer through SME websites.

In summary, it can be stated that the use of an integration concept can help SMEs leverage their core competencies by promoting the sharing of information and knowledge inside and outside their organization. The impact of cost-efficient software products for knowledge management facilitates business models based on simple knowledge processes. The knowledge process model highlights specific processes in the business where competitive advantages can be achieved and knowledge management systems will have a greater impact. The integration concepts view knowledge management in SMEs as a holistic approach where primary knowledge processes are directly related to knowledge methods and software tools.

Figure 5. Three-dimensional framework for knowledge diffusion

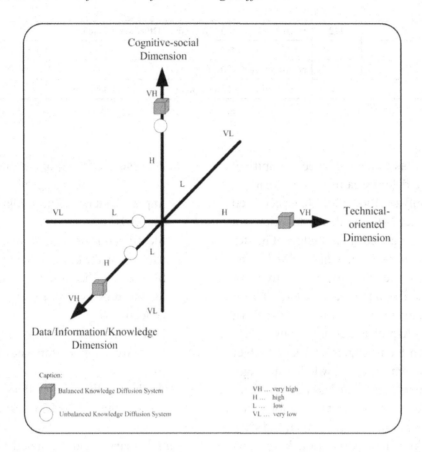

REFERENCES

Davenport, T., & Prusak, L. (1998). *Working knowledge: how organizations manage what they know.* Boston, MA: Harvard Business School Press.

Delahaye, D. (2003). Knowledge Management in a SME. *International Journal of Organisational Behaviour, 9*(3), 604-614.

Dezouza, K., & Awazu, Y. (2006). Knowledge Management at SMEs: Five peculiarities. *Journal of Knowledge Management, 10*(1), 32-43.

Dunkelberg, W., & Wade, H. (2007). Overview: Small Business Optimism. *NFIB Small Business Economic Trends,* 1-12.

Edwards, J., & Kidd, J. (2003). Bridging the Gap from the General to the Specific by Linking Knowledge Management to Business Process Management. In V. Hlupic (Ed.), *Knowledge and Business Process Management.* Hershey: Idea Group Publishing.

Fink, K., & Ploder, C. (2007a). A comparative Study of Knowledge Processes and Methods in Austrian and Swiss SMEs. In H. Österle, J. Schelp & R. Winter (Eds.), *Proceedings of the 15th European Conference on Information Systems (ECIS2007).* St. Gallen.

Fink, K., & Ploder, C. (2007b). Knowledge Process Modeling in SME and Cost-Efficient Software Support: Theoretical Framework and Empirical Studies. In M. Khosrow-Pour (Ed.), *Managing Worldwide Operations and Commu-*

nications with Information Technology. Hershey: IGI Publishing.

Gillham, B. (2000). *Case Study Research Methods.* London/New York: Continuum.

Kakabadse, N., Kouzmin, A., & Kakabadse, A. (2001). From Tacit Knowledge to Knowledge Management: Leveraging Invisible Assets. *Knowledge and Process Management, 8*(3), 137-154.

Krippendorf, K. (1980). *Content Analysis,* 5. Beverly Hills: Sage Publication.

Laudon, K. C., & Laudon, J. P. (2006). *Management information systems: managing the digital firm* (9th ed.). Upper Saddle River, NJ: Pearson/Prentice Hall.

McAdam, R., & Reid, R. (2001). SME and large Organization Perception of Knowledge Management: Comparison and Contrast. *Journal of Knowledge Management, 5*(3), 231-241.

Mentzas, G., Apostolou, D., Young, R., & Abecker, A. (2001). Knowledge Networking: a Holistic Solution for Leveraging Corporate Knowledge. *Journal of Knowledge Management, 5*(1), 94-106.

Mockler, R., & Dologite, D. (2002). Strategically-Focused Enterprise Knowledge Management. In D. White (Ed.), *Knowledge Mapping & Management* (pp. 14-22). Hershey: IRM Press.

Ordanini, A. (2006). *Information Technology and Small Businesses: Antecedents and Consequences of Technology Adoption.* Massachusetts: Edward Elgar Publishing.

Probst, G., Raub, S., & Romhardt, K. (2006). *Wissen Managen,* 5. Wiesbaden: Gabler Verlag.

Rao, M. (2004). *Knowledge Management: Tools and Techniques.* Oxford: Elsevier.

Ruggels, R. (1997). *Knowledge Management Tools.* Boston: Butterworth-Heinemann.

Salojärvi, S., Furu, P., & Sveiby, K. (2005). Knowledge management and growth in Finnish SMEs. *Journal of Knowledge Management, 9*(2), 103-122.

Schwartz, D. (2006). *Encyclopedia of Knowledge Management.* Hershey: Idea Group Publishing.

Street, C., & Cameron, A. (2007). External Relationships and the Small Business: A Review of Small Business Alliance and Network Research. *Journal of Small Business Management, 45*(2).

Trompenaars, F., & Hampden-Turner, C. (2006). *Riding the waves of culture: understanding cultural diversity in business* (2. reprint. with corr. ed.). London: Brealey.

Wang, F., & Plaskoff, J. (2002). An Integrated Development Model for KM. In R. Bellaver & J. Lusa (Eds.), *Knowledge Management Strategy and Technology* (pp. 113-134). Boston: Artech House.

Wong, K. (2005). Critical success factors for implementing knowledge management in small and medium enterprises *Industrial Management & Data Systems, 105*(3), 261-279.

Wong, K., & Aspinwall, E. (2005). An empirical study of the important factors for knowledge-management adoption in the SME sector. *Journal of Knowledge Management, 9*(3), 64-82.

KEY TERMS

Enterprise: Considered to be any entity engaged in an economic activity, irrespective of its legal form. This includes, in particular, self-employed persons and family businesses engaged in craft or other activities, along with partnerships or associations regularly engaged in economic activities. The category of micro, small and medium-sized enterprises (SME) is made up of enterprises which employ fewer than 250 persons and which have an annual turnover not exceeding EURO 50 million, and/or an annual balance sheet total not exceeding EURO 43 million. Within the SME category, a small enterprise is defined as an enterprise which employs fewer than 50 persons and whose annual turnover and/or annual balance sheet total does not exceed EURO 10 million. Within the SME category, a micro enterprise is defined as an enterprise which employs fewer than 10 persons and whose annual turnover and/or annual balance sheet total does not exceed EURO 2 million.

Knowledge Distribution: Can be defined as the transfer of knowledge within and across settings, with the expectation that the knowledge will be "used" conceptually (as learning, enlightenment, or the acquisition of new perspectives or attitudes) or instrumentally (in the form of modified or new practices.). There are those who see distribution as having other legitimate outcomes. Some of these outcomes include: (1) increased awareness; (2) ability to make informed choices among alternatives and (3) the exchange of information, materials or perspectives.

Knowledge Integration Concepts: Aim to customize knowledge processes and knowledge methods for SMEs in a single enterprise solution platform. Enterprise application such as knowledge management systems are designed to support the SME orientation of business and knowledge processes to that the SMEs can operate efficiently.

Knowledge Management: Can be seen as the overall dealing with knowledge. Knowledge is a fluid mix of framed experience, values, contextual information, and expert insight that provides a framework for evaluating and incorporating new experiences and information. It originates and is applied in the minds of those who know. In organizations, it often becomes embedded not only in documents or repositories but also in organizational routines, processes, practices and norms (Davenport & Prusak, 1998).

Knowledge Management Systems: A fast growing area of corporate software investment. Contemporary technologies such as Portals, Content Management Systems, Search engines, ontologies help managers and employees in their daily decisions and processes. At each level of the organization, knowledge management systems support the major knowledge processes of the business.

Knowledge Methods: Support knowledge processes and are designed to add value to these within organizations. Depending on the identification of industry specific knowledge processes, SMEs have to choose from a knowledge method repository the corresponding knowledge method.

Knowledge Processes: Accelerate the company's business processes while ensuring compliance with the knowledge of the employees. Knowledge processes concentrate on the identification, acquisition, dissemination and preservation of knowledge in order to gain competitive advantages and enhance the value of the company. Organizations have to use the ability to incorporate their knowledge into their business processes.

Chapter XV
Enterprise System in the German Manufacturing Mittelstand

Tobias Schoenherr
Michigan State University, USA

Ditmar Hilpert
Reutlingen University, Germany

Ashok K. Soni
Indiana University, USA

M.A. Venkataramanan
Indiana University, USA

Vincent A. Mabert
Indiana University, USA

ABSTRACT

Although the research on integrated enterprise systems (ES) is proliferating, the knowledge base about ES implementations, usage and experiences outside the United States is still small. This is also true for Germany, despite the crucial importance of ES in the country, and the potential uniqueness of its ES environment. Most ES research to date has also been focusing on larger corporations, neglecting the challenges and issues that small and medium sized enterprises (SMEs) have been experiencing. Collectively often referred to as the Mittelstand, German SMEs form the backbone of the German economy. This chapter brings attention to these areas by describing observations obtained from eight SMEs in the German manufacturing sector. These findings about ES implementation, usage, and experiences are reported and summarized along nine points of interest.

INTRODUCTION

Enterprise systems (ES) promise seamless integration of processes and information flows throughout an organization, streamlining operations and increasing their efficiency. These systems, often also referred to as Enterprise Resource Planning (ERP) systems, enable companies to compete in the global marketplace and expand their reach. Having evolved via materials requirements planning (MRP) and manufacturing resource planning (MRP II) systems, they are nowadays often an integral part of and a competitive necessity for companies worldwide.

Most ES research to date has focused on large organizations operating in North America, neglecting company experiences with ES in other parts of the world. Some exceptions exist, for example studies conducted in Ireland (Adam and O'Doherty, 2000), Singapore (Soh, Kien and Tay-Yap, 2000), China (Davison, 2002), and some European countries (van Everdingen, van Hillegersberg and Waarts, 2000). It is our objective with this chapter to expand the body of knowledge about ES implementation, usage and experiences in Europe, specifically in Germany. Crucial components preceding the implementation and usage phases are the decision and planning phases, for which we also provide insight. We focus on small and medium sized enterprises (SMEs) who have been following their larger counterparts in ES implementation and usage. Their often constrained environment (cf. Quiescenti et al., 2006) makes them a particularly interesting subject of investigation. SMEs are usually slower in adopting new concepts, and while an ES may be present, they often still operate in functional silos (Billet, 2008). However, the ES market for SMEs is booming (Bell and Orzen, 2007), which is also illustrated by more targeted and tailored offerings from ES providers, such as SAP's Business One solution.

This chapter reports additional findings from a larger study carried out by the international author team. Related results were already reported in Schoenherr, Venkataramanan, Soni, Mabert and Hilpert (2005), whose focus was a comparison of experiences by German and U.S. companies. The present chapter provides some very interesting insights of issues not already reported. More specifically, we explore the impetus for the system, the power of the final decision, the system and system provider selection, the time spent in system selection, planning and implementation, the order of implementation, the issue of standard packages, modifications and in-house developed applications, the involvement of employees and training, the implementation success and satisfaction, and the topic of upgrades after implementation. The remainder of this chapter is structured into four sections. The next section provides an overview of related literature, followed by a section describing our methodology and sample characteristics. The subsequent section reports the results, with the final section providing a brief summary and conclusion.

LITERATURE REVIEW

Experiences with integrated ES (ERP systems) were first published in practitioner journals (Mecham, 1998) and the popular press (Kirkpatrick, 1998; Diederich, 1998). Shortly afterwards first academic research reports appeared (Davenport, 1998), fuelling interest and excitement among academics. Up to date a multitude of articles have appeared dealing with both the positive (Bradford, Mayfield, and Toney, 2001) and negative (Sumner, 2000) effects of ES implementations, as well as their associated considerable cost (Mabert, Soni, and Venkataramanan, 2000). Mabert (2007) and Jacobs and Weston (2007) provide a comprehensive chronology of the historical development and evolution of these systems.

Most of the early research in ES dealt with the experiences made by large corporations, which also represented the early adopters of this new integrated technology. Small and medium enterprises (SMEs) however followed quickly. Soon it was also realized that SMEs differ significantly from their larger counterparts, for example in terms of motivation factors, types of systems implemented, implementation strategies, implementation costs, and the degree of customization (Mabert, Soni and Venkataramanan, 2003). Differences between SMEs and large firms in regards to their ES adoption were also described by Buonanno et al. (2005). Other studies chronicled how SMEs are coping with their ES (Olson and Sætre, 2007) and how they managed uncertainty in ERP-controlled manufacturing environments (Koh and Saad, 2006). Additional manuscripts investigated the impact of an ES on their productivity (Shin, 2006) and cautioned that disadvantages associated with an implementation can be exaggerated for SMEs (Brehm and Gómez, 2005). It was also reported that SMEs take a more cautious approach toward extended ES (de Búrca, Fynes and Marshall, 2005), but that they can become a competitive weapon (Koh and Simpson, 2005, 2007). These studies illustrate that there are key differences between large and small companies, and that ES issues are approached differently. Since research on large corporations and their experiences with ES is proliferating, we decided to focus on small and medium sized enterprises.

While most ES research has concentrated on the North American environment, some studies exist that examine these issues in an international or country-specific context. For example, Soh, Kien and Tay-Yap (2000) report the ES implementation experiences made by seven Singaporean hospitals. The researchers stress to recognize the unique Asian context when implementing an ES, which is generally based on Western practices. Davison (2002) lists further examples how Western ES can lead to complications in Asian cultures. Akkermans et al. (2003) present results from a Delphi study involving Dutch supply chain executives, investigating the future impact of ES on supply chain management. Wang et al. (2005) provided an overview of ERP research in China.

A few of these international studies also focused on SMEs. For instance, Adam and O'Doherty (2000) report results from 14 ERP implementation projects in Irish organizations, concentrating on the relationships between the firms and their implementation partners. Van Everdingen, Van Hillegersberg and Waarts (2000) observe the increasing interest of European SMEs in ES, as well as the associated implications for vendors targeting this market segment. Morabito, Pace and Previtali (2005) focus on the marketing of ERP systems to Italian SMEs. More recently, Chien et al. (2007) report implementation experiences made by SMEs in China and Taiwan, highlighting factors for project success.

The present book chapter focuses on the experiences of German SMEs with the implementation and use of integrated ES. Collectively often referred to as the *Mittelstand*, German SMEs form the backbone of the German economy. Over one million firms employ more than 20 million individuals, are responsible for almost 40 percent of total German gross investments, and account for 30 percent of the exports (Hauser, 2000). These businesses are often characterized by their innovative and entrepreneurial nature, their competitive position in the international marketplace, and their focus on highly customized and engineered products. Against this background ES become an inevitable competitive weapon (Taylor, 1999; Voigt, 2001). Germany's exceptional vocational training system provides these firms with an educated and skilled workforce, which is usually very loyal and stable. Overall, this setting of German SMEs provides a unique opportunity to study their experiences with integrated ES.

METHODOLOGY AND SAMPLE

A series of eight case studies was conducted to obtain insight into ES implementation and usage among German *Mittelstand* companies. Case study methodology was deemed to be the most promising approach since insight into this particular topic and setting is limited. The case study approach is an excellent tool to acquire detailed information (Yin, 1994), is becoming increasingly popular (Eisenhardt and Graebner, 2007), and has a long tradition of being employed in the information systems literature (Orlikowski, 1992; Robey and Sahay, 1996). The primary objective for conducting the case studies was to obtain reliable and detailed information on ES practice among German SMEs.

Companies were chosen so that a broad insight in the German manufacturing industry could be obtained. Special care was taken to select true German *Mittelstand* companies that are, despite their size, global market leaders. All companies started out as small family businesses, and most of them are still family owned in their fifth or sixth generation. The firms may have subsidiaries overseas; however, they may not be a subsidiary of a foreign company. Four companies were located in the Main-Tauber region, whereas four were in the Reutlingen area, both in the south of Germany. These companies were chosen to give us a nice overview of the state of ES implementations in the German manufacturing industry. It was also hoped to detect some regional peculiarities, given the southern countrified mentality in these regions.

Interviews were exploratory in nature and were conducted with key business managers and IT professionals in 2002, with a follow-up in 2004. The interviews lasted between two and four hours and involved as many as four employees. Four interviewers of the research team were present at all times, leading the interview in a semi-structured fashion asking open-ended questions. The interview team consisted of two U.S.-American professors, a German professor and a German graduate student working towards his doctorate in the U.S. The interviews were conducted either in English or German, depending on the preference of the interviewees. All conversations were tape-recorded and meticulously transcribed in English.

Our chosen companies were judged to be an appropriate sample for our study. While the firms were all in the manufacturing industry, their products ranged from textiles to elevators, including medical technology, furniture, complete workstations and home appliances (Table 1). Their size was between 593 and 1,200 employees and annual turnover varied between 64 and 378 million Euros. While these firms do not fall into the defined categories by for example the European Union, which classifies SMEs as firms having 250 or fewer employees (European Commission, 2008) or the German Institute for SME Research, which classifies SMEs as firms having fewer than 500 employees (Institute für Mittelstandsforschung, 2008), they fall in the SME category as it was defined by prior academic research (e.g., Mabert et al., 2003; Muscatello et al., 2003). However, an even more important selection criterion was that the firms represented true characteristics of the *Mittelstand* in Germany, as described above, with size only being a secondary consideration.

Firms in our sample were at all stages in regard to their ES implementations, thus giving us a representative account of experiences at different points in time. We distinguish between the decision phase, the planning phase, the implementation phase and the usage phase. The location of each firm on this timeline, along with timeline designs of other researchers, is graphed in Figure 1. Table 2 provides an overview of the firms' past, current and future ES, as well as the current stage on the ES implementation and usage timeline.

RESULTS AND DISCUSSION

This section reports the experiences of our sample with ES implementation and usage, and can provide useful insight for firms in similar situations and contexts, contemplating the adoption of an ES.

Table 1. Company characteristics

	Business Type	**Industry**	**Size (# Employees)**	**Turnover (Million €)**
Company A	family business	scales, food processing equipment	1,000	378
Company B	family business	mixing and grinding technology	600	120
Company C	family business	textile	900	64
Company D	family business	food technology, home appliances	770	90
Company E	family business until 1991, then bought by holding	material handling (forklifts)	593	~100
Company F	family business	furniture	1,200	140
Company G	family business	machines for woodworking, tooling, grinding	1,100	320
Company H	family owned stock corporation	elevators, medical technology, gear technology	700+	80-85

Figure 1. ES implementation and usage timeline

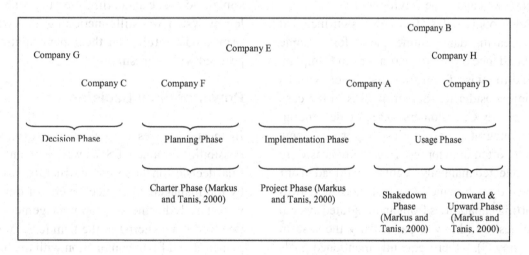

Impetus for a New System

One point of interest for us was to investigate what impetus led the company to consider a new system, or which functions in a firm were driving forces. Literature suggests that the desire to go to a new system is often initiated by finance, accounting and controlling (Adam and O'Doherty, 2000; Mabert, Soni and Venkataramanan, 2002a).

We were able to confirm this in our case studies, both for companies that had already made the implementation decision, and for firms that were still in the contemplation phase. For example, the financial department in Company C required more detailed and sophisticated reporting tools, which the legacy system could not provide. In other companies, such as Company D, the present system in finance could not be linked with other

Table 2. Past, current and future main system, stage

	Past Main System	**Current Main System**	**Future Main System**	**Stage**
Company A	various (IBM, in-house developed)	SAP, in-house developed systems	n/a	Usage / Implementation
Company B	various island solutions	IBM MAS90	n/a	Usage
Company C	n/a	various (IBM, in-house developed)	Walter + Partner	Decision
Company D	IBM, Honeywell-Bull	SAP	n/a	Usage
Company E	n/a	Brain	SAP	Planning / Implementation
Company F	n/a	obsolete standard software, in-house developed PPS	SAP	Planning
Company G	n/a	various island solutions (in-house developed)	SAP, upgrade of old standard system (GBA), keeping of in-house developments	Decision
Company H	PPS system	Baan	n/a	Usage

systems, thus making true integration impossible. Finance was again the driving force.

Additional catalysts for a new system included an increasing data volume due to for example an abundance of product variations in Company G, and the wish for greater integration with its foreign subsidiaries. Sometimes, as in the case of Company C, customers were also demanding more integrated capabilities, requiring a new system; often data for reports and invoices were still collected manually. A common thread in our case study companies was that more statistical reporting capabilities from an integrated system were desired (this was particularly the case in Company G). Other frequently mentioned goals included the desire to make processes and operations more efficient, reduce costs and improve planning.

In all cases the decision was made to implement a new system rather than to upgrade the old one, which would have been much more expensive and time-consuming. This option was chosen even in instances where the old system, which was partly developed in-house and tailored very carefully to the firm's internal processes, would have been working fine for the next couple of years. In that particular case the firm, Company D, had the advantage to not be under time pressure, since their legacy system was still functioning. This way the firm could carefully plan the implementation and proceed without rushing.

Power of Final Decision

In most instances the decision to explore the possibility for a new ES, as well as the ultimate final decision on the software structure was made by top management. Since several of our firms were family businesses, top management often involved the owner(s) of the firm (e.g., in Companies H and F), in conjunction with the head of the IT department. As much as owners can be a catalyst for ideas, they can also have the role of an inhibitor, being conservative and reluctant to change something "old, valuable and still well functioning." Interesting scenarios evolve when the owner is against a new system implementation, whereas the son is in favor of it, which was the case in one of our companies.

Although the decision is made in an autocratic way in many family businesses, quite frequently the department heads were consulted and involved into the decision process (e.g., in Company C). In a few cases input was also solicited from lower levels of authority. This recognizes the need that everyone in the company must support the decision, especially since in a lean environment the execution of such a project would mean more work for everyone. In one instance, the entire implementation team was heavily involved in the selection. On another occasion, where the firm was part of a large holding company, the decision to move from one ES package to another was indoctrinated by headquarters (Company E). The firm had to follow the order, although they knew that they would not see any improvements with the new system. In yet a different case, Company A, the decision was made entirely by the head of IT, whose vision determined the entire company IT infrastructure.

System and Provider Selection

Once the decision has been made *that* a new system is needed, the question arises *what* system is best for the company. For some firms this choice was not given since they were so early with their implementation decision; they had to take whatever the market was offering at that time. Most often, these solutions were rather generic and could not satisfy the specific industry context and requirements of many firms. However, as the ES market was developing, more sophisticated, tailored and customized providers and offerings emerged, and firms were given a considerable choice. It now becomes a challenge to choose the best provider, and compromises between functions may have to be made to avoid internal conflicts. In the following we report insight into who influenced the decision in our case companies, followed by criteria used to choose a provider and system.

Although accounting and finance are often the impetus behind the wish for an integrated ES, their processes follow standards across most organizations. Thus, these areas will be satisfied with most integrated software packages, whereas

production and material management might not. Our case companies provided good illustration that material-flow processes can differ quite significantly, and are frequently associated with unique process capabilities leading to competitive advantage. For example, Company B's production, which is essentially a job shop, is very complex; customers may fully customize and modify their product from the base model, increasing the possible product variations exponentially. The desire to keep the proven production structure and processes is therefore often the winning argument for or against a particular ES. This was also true for Company C, which had some very unique and patented manufacturing process steps. Nevertheless, depending on the significance individual departments have in the company, finance can be the deciding force as well, as was the case in Companies D and E. Since they are a strong advocate for a new system they may also possess enough clout to determine what new system should be implemented.

When considering ES providers, their history and traditional strengths were assessed. As such, SAP has traditionally been very strong on the financial side, whereas Baan, coming from the manufacturing industry, has more strengths in production planning, logistics and material management. Besides, at the time of our research, Baan was known to be able to cater more to medium sized companies whereas SAP primarily satisfied the requirements of big enterprises. Depending now on which department has more influence in the decision process or which capabilities are regarded as being more important, the respective system is chosen.

Important aspects considered were also the price of the ES, data warehousing capabilities, and the functionality of the system. For example, SAP was chosen by Company F because of its ability to deal with their many product variations effectively, whereas Baan was chosen by Company H because it supported more reporting abilities on all levels. Further criteria considered in the decision were the reputation of the provider and its likelihood to survive the next years (Company F), industry fit (Company C), outside studies assessing the proficiency of certain ES along several dimensions (Company H), as well as the sales pitch of ES representatives at our case study companies (Company H). It turned out that there were significant differences in knowledge and proficiency of representatives.

Time Spent in System Selection, Planning and Implementation

Our sample companies recognized the importance of carefully selecting a system, which could decide on the success or failure of an implementation. Therefore most companies allowed themselves ample time for the selection of an ES provider. For example, Company D considered exhaustive documentation processes examining system fit, and consulted research reports and rankings of system providers. Extensive workshops with potential providers were conducted by Company F, which then had to demonstrate how their system could represent the companies' processes.

The planning process can also be quite lengthy and deliberate. For our companies the planning process began up to three years before the scheduled implementation, and the core planning group involved as many as five percent of the total workforce, which was the case for Company H. Business models and elaborate requirement catalogues were developed in these planning teams. Company G hired a consulting group to examine the entire present IT infrastructure and identify improvement potential, which then lead the way to selecting the optimal system. Time spent planning and outlining the future IT infrastructure pays off. In one of our sample firms, Company A, an IT master-plan was developed in 1999 with very meticulous planning and did not have to be changed since.

Similar to selection and planning, the implementation period can also be quite long, lasting up to two-and-a-half years among our sample firms, as was the case for Company D. Reasons for such lengthy implementation periods may include the complexity of the business and the need to undertake certain modifications. Also, firms wanted to make sure that an implemented module functioned perfectly before they started the introduction of the next module. In the case of a big bang or an implementation involving several modules introduced at once, firms were more comfortable going live with these systems in a time when the whole company was down, which was usually only the case over the Christmas holidays (Company D), and in some instances during vacation close-downs in the summer. This constraint sometimes forced a further extension of the implementation period.

A significant amount of time is spent in selecting, planning and implementing the ES. Companies were in no rush since most of the time since the old system was still working fine, as was the case for Companies C and D. Firms also recognized the deliberate process as a chance to build a sound and solid basis for their IT infrastructure, upon which other applications could be built and future systems could rely on. This very careful and meticulous procedure is in line with Hofstede's (1991) findings. He classified Germany as being very high on his scale of uncertainty avoidance, as compared for example to the U.S. High uncertainty avoidance is likely to result in high risk avoidance, for which all of our observations stand for. Risk is mitigated by careful and deliberate system selection, planning and implementation.

Order of Implementation

ES are often multi-module systems, which can be implemented either module-by-module (phased in approach) or all at once (big bang approach). Three companies in our sample (B, F and H) considered or had already conducted a big bang to go live, which is generally regarded to be more risky. All other firms opted for the phased-in approach due to complex and unique internal processes that had to be accommodated. It was thus easier and safer to go step-by-step, leaving time for potential delays or complications. Further substantiations for this strategy included high degree of customization in terms of products produced (Company G), and the presence of sophisticated in-house developed programs, which could not easily be replaced by standard package software (Company A). Therefore, areas that were easier to be mapped by the package application were introduced first, while other more demanding functions were added as need arose, or as new releases became available that were able to accommodate the firm's specific processes. However, Company H wanted to modify their processes to accommodate the standard ES, instead of waiting until better and more suitable solutions were available. This firm relied on future benefits accrued by the ES.

As reported above, finance frequently initiated the move to a new system, which led to the financial modules also often being among the first to be implemented. This approach ensured that all organizational components were mapped out correctly in the system, upon which other modules could then rely on. Having a common integrated financial system is frequently also mandated by a mother firm, as was the case for our Company E. Functional areas that followed with the implementation of their respective modules included production, materials management and logistics. A third wave of implemented modules consisted of quality management and human resources, if

they were implemented at all. Nevertheless, not all companies follow this scheme. One firm in our sample, Company H, implemented the logistic modules first due to this function's superior position in the company. This particular firm also selected Baan over SAP, since the former has traditionally been strong in the logistics area.

Standard Packages, Modifications, and In-house Developed Applications

When looking at the final system architecture in some of our firms it was interesting to see that many still kept some of their legacy systems in addition to the new ES package. This can be problematic, and it has been suggested that firms keep not more than 20 percent of their previous applications (Rowe, 1999). Considering the spectrum of enterprise systems illustrated in Figure 2, most of our firms fall in between the two extremes, i.e. the majority of the companies had either a standard ES with some modifications, or they had in-house developed programs linked with a standard ES.

Some firms in our sample, for example Company A, opted to integrate various legacy applications rather than implementing a new ES package. This option enabled the firms to accommodate unique processes and requirements, which would not have been possible with a standard ES. In-house developed applications are sometimes highly sophisticated and technically advanced, representing a superior value to the business. Hav-

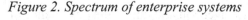

Figure 2. Spectrum of enterprise systems

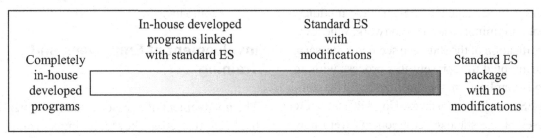

ing such a system can be an important competitive advantage. For one of our firms, Company G, the ES packages available at that time were also too broad in scope and would be much more than what was actually needed by the firm.

In-house developed systems are frequently complemented by standard software components. This was especially done when the technical status of the applications was low, when there were standard processes in place that were easily representable in a standard ES, or when the advantages of in-house developed applications do not outweigh the advantages of the standard software package. The standard software components then linked via interfaces to in-house developed applications. Company G developed a comprehensive matrix along some of these dimensions for their systems to facilitate the decision. Company A had a particularly elaborate IT infrastructure, whose backbone was a central data-warehouse on which both the standard ERP package and internally-developed legacy systems replied.

Oftentimes, in order to accommodate unique company processes or due to a reluctance to change, standard systems are modified to fit the operations (instead of changing the processes to fit the system). This can be an expensive undertaking; one of our firms, Company D, expended as much as 25 man-days from outside consultants to implement these changes. However, the ability of a firm to represent their internal processes in the system can be a crucial necessity to remain competitive, which was stressed by Company B. Modifications make also future upgrades and maintenance more challenging. One of our case studies, Company A, accommodated this concern by a unique approach. The firm did not modify anything in the standard ES package modules, except some minor customization work. Whenever a modification of the standard seemed necessary, the firm opted to represent this process with an in-house application, synchronized with the standard ES via clean interfaces. Upgrades and new releases of the standard components were now

executable very easily with a minimum amount of work.

As expected, financial processes in our case studies were usually accommodated very easily via standard software components, due to the similarity of these processes mandated by regulatory and governmental reporting requirements (e.g., Companies C and G). For logistic and supply chain activities, such as sales and order entry, an in-house developed application was often better able to represent the sometimes very unique and specific processes, as was the case for Company A. If a standard package was employed, modifications needed to be undertaken or add-ons to be purchased, which was reported by Company H.

It is clear that one size does not fit all. A firm must assess its unique situation and decide whether the advantages of a standard package outweigh the advantages of in-house developed software, or vice versa. Considerations can include, but are not limited to, the following issues:

- unique requirements on system capabilities, caused by multifarious product characteristics, elaborate processes, or other company-specific complexities, which are not representable by a standard software package;
- in-house developed system as a source of a competitive advantage;
- tradeoff between luxury of having modifications to fit processes now and resulting difficulties later on in upgrades;
- tradeoff between changing the system and changing the firm's processes and operations;
- risk aversion and uncertainty avoidance of a company.

Involvement of Employees and Training

The involvement of everyone in an organization has been stressed as a key for ES implementations (e.g., Mabert, Soni and Venkataramanan, 2001a). We saw this involvement in all companies we visited. The implementation team members were usually released from their normal duties, so they could focus solely on the implementation project. Often the actual implementation was conducted by a combination of in-house personnel and outside consultants, which was the case for Company H. In very few instances top management was directly involved, but always gave direction and monitored the progress of the project. Input was also sought from every department, most often from the department heads, as was illustrated by Company C.

In terms of training companies took different approaches. Some firms, for example Company B, went with a service partner, who sometimes also had project management responsibilities. Associated costs varied widely. Company D invested 1,000 man-days of education upfront; for their 340 users they needed 20 to 30 teachers at times, so it became very expensive. For Company H it was relatively inexpensive since they relied on internal training and education. In addition to a little training in-house by consultants from the system provider, the implementation team merely took a two-day preparation course. Everything else was accomplished in self-training, which team members regarded as more beneficial than a course.

Implementation Success and Satisfaction

The success of an ES implementation can objectively be measured by parameters such as under/on/over budget and whether the project was completed on time, before or after the scheduled date (Mabert, Soni and Venkataramanan, 2001b). Although some companies could confirm that they exceeded their budget and time deadlines, most companies were not able to give us any objective measures by which they gauged their success. The difficulty of this assessment was associated with the lack of benchmarks to which they could compare the performance of the company before and after implementation. Furthermore, one of our firms, Company H, grew so fast in other areas, so that an identification of monetary or operational benefits attributable to ES implementation alone was not possible.

Nevertheless, judging from the subjective comments almost all ES implementations were a big success, reaping improvements in controlling, logistics and distribution due to the presence of an integrated and consolidated system. For example, Company H realized 99 percent on-time delivery with the new ES. An interviewee at the same company mentioned that it was clear to management that the company could not have gone any other way; the old system would have come to an end, sooner or later. At another firm, Company B, transparency achieved throughout the whole workflow and less tedious central planning and controlling was appreciated; among other things it resulted in reduced safety stock and more efficient purchasing capabilities.

The voices of management are sometimes not as unanimous as the examples just described. Often there were internal conflicts among management. In most instances we dealt with family businesses, where the father and son or the son-in-law were part of top management. It then usually was the case that the younger management was more open to change and to the introduction of an integrated system, however hitting on resistance from senior management. Generally this opposition was overcome, however with leaving negative sentiments behind. Companies A and B made such experiences.

Problems that caused an over budget or beyond deadline implementation were seen in a constructive manner, and as an opportunity to learn. Company B attributed a delay in time to internal personal problems and disagreements, whereas Company H experienced an over-budget implementation because particular add-ons were not considered in the original calculation and the consulting company they used for the project went out of business. Nevertheless, although we did not have objective figures in most instances gauging the implementation success, the experiences were positive across the board. None of our case study companies regretted the implementation, even when problems occurred; all saw the benefits associated with a new integrated system.

The often meticulous and detailed preparation for implementation phase frequently had nice side-benefits for our companies. For example, firms usually mapped and analyzed all internal processes before an ES implementation very carefully, thus gaining a thorough understanding of the intricate nature of their business procedures, enabling them to make considerable improvements. Often process maps and work plans were nonexistent and had to be created as a basis for a solid system. Moreover, data were frequently missing or were available in an incompatible format. Several man-years of past data thus had to be collected and entered to provide a sound foundation for the decision making tools of the enterprise system, as was the case in Company A. All these efforts not only created a solid groundwork for the system and its applications to rely on, it also eliminated existing process and product inefficiencies, many of which resulted from the multitude of non-integrated stand-alone island solutions. In one instance a firm was able to reduce its present 285,000 part and material masters to a mere 12,000 (Company A). This illustrates that ES implementations entail both product and process benefits (Bendoly and Schoenherr, 2005).

Upgrades after Implementation

The issue of upgrades is an interesting topic, since often considerable work and effort is involved, not to mention potential complications when certain parts of the system were modified earlier to fit company-specific processes. Depending on the extent of changes and modifications undertaken and the complexities and processes of the system,

time needed for upgrades ranged from one to several months among our case studies. This makes it impossible to implement every new release. Company H spent even more time for a major upgrade than it spent on the implementation of the original system, partly also because of the absence of time pressure. This was the case even though the employees from the original implementation team were now responsible for the upgrade.

In general, our case study companies do not upgrade their system regularly. Most firms were happy with their systems and did not want to undergo another potentially hazardous implementation experience with an upgrade or new release. Companies have become more careful, also because of market developments, where the lesson was learned that following the latest hype is not always the best. Even one of the most proactive firms in our sample, Company D, which uses upgrades frequently to enhance the system, does not go with every upgrade or new addition. The particular company was one of the first to introduce CRM capabilities to their integrated system. Since the firm made unfavorable experiences with it, they were waiting with the implementation of APO until it was further developed.

SUMMARY AND CONCLUSION

Although the research on integrated enterprise systems is proliferating, the knowledge base for ES implementations and usage outside the U.S. is still small. This is also true for Germany, despite the crucial importance of ES in the country, and the potential uniqueness of its ES environment. Most ES research to date has also been focusing on larger corporations, neglecting the challenges and issues that small and medium sized enterprises have been experiencing. This chapter brought light into both of these areas by describing observations obtained from eight *Mittelstand* companies in the German manufacturing sector. Findings were reported along the following dimensions:

impetus for the system; power of the final decision; system and system provider selection; time spent in system selection, planning and implementation; order of implementation; standard packages, modifications and in-house developed applications; involvement of employees and training; implementation success and satisfaction; and upgrades after implementation. Overall results are summarized in Exhibit 1.

An ES implementation is a large project, posing many challenges, but also offering many benefits in return. Considered to be important success factors were excellent data integrity planning and technical infrastructure in system

Exhibit 1. Summary of experiences

- ES systems are also in Germany implemented in companies of all sizes
- The decision to implement an ES is generally made by the owner where applicable, otherwise top management makes the decision with input from department heads
- Whether or not to invest in ES was not the question, it was merely a matter of when
- The impetus to go to a new integrated system often came from finance, accounting and controlling
- The type of new ES is determined by the department with the biggest clout and importance; usually it is either a financial or a logistics department
- When selecting an ES provider, issues considered consist of history, traditional strengths, reputation, long-term survivability, and capabilities of the provider, as well as price and functionality of the system
- Companies are not afraid to go to smaller ES providers
- Time spent to select the ES, as well as to plan and implement can be quite considerable, emphasizing the careful and meticulous approach our sample companies took
- Financial modules were generally implemented first, followed by logistic modules; exceptions exist
- It depends on the company and the structure of its internal, and to a lesser extent, external processes, whether a firm prefers a systems environment made up of completely in-house developed components, a standard software with a few modifications undertaken, a complete acceptance of a standard package with only minor customization, or a mixture of these; we suggested some considerations influencing this decision
- A one-size-fits-all ES does not fit the enterprise in most instances; almost all firms keep other in-house developed systems for specialized functionalities or unique processes
- Often the actual implementation was conducted by a combination of in-house personnel, spanning various departments, and consultants
- User training approaches and associated costs varied widely
- Almost all of our case studies prefer the phased-in implementation approach over the big bang approach
- All companies that had implemented an ES were satisfied with it, even when complications had occurred
- Companies were not able to provide objective figures gauging implementation success
- ES systems improve data availability, quality and transparency significantly, enabling faster and better informed decisions
- The ES implementation frequently had some nice side-benefits associated with it, such as better understanding of processes, and more complete, consolidated and clean data
- Depending on the extent of changes and modifications undertaken and the complexities and processes of the system, time needed for upgrades ranged from one to several months; most companies do not upgrade their system regularly, avoiding potentially hazardous implementation experiences
- Smaller companies may have an easier time implementing and modifying ES due to the better manageable and less complex inter-organizational network
- Companies have reached a mature stage where they do not follow blindly the ES hype of the late 1990s, nowadays they think twice about the implications, both positive and negative, of an ES

administration and implementation, as well as how the company was organized organizationally. A suggested approach was to structure the organization in a way how tax authorities would arrange it, i.e. from an accounting point of view. It is also crucial that during an implementation the right resources are available at the right time and at the right place. Every step in the process must be analyzed carefully, taking into account complexities and potential hang-ups, and must be given appropriate and sufficient amount of time and resource to complete. Employees further commented that it is critical for success to have a group of people who are enthusiastic and motivated about the cause, since overtime is often necessary. Moreover, persuasion work is needed in many areas because some employees are often strongly opposed to the moves and do not understand the change. Besides, it is important that the group is at one with each other.

This study provided valuable insights towards understanding ES implementations and their peculiarities in the German manufacturing sector. Every company we visited made some unique experiences and learned in their own way. For some companies an advanced IT infrastructure posed a competitive advantage, whereas it was a necessity for others. The area of enterprise systems continues to remain an exciting area for research. It is hoped that this chapter will serve as a motivation to further explore these topics, preferably also reporting experiences of companies in regions and countries other than North America and Germany.

REFERENCES

Adam, F., & O'Doherty, P. (2000). Lessons from enterprise resource planning implementations in Ireland – Towards smaller and shorter ERP projects. *Journal of Information Technology, 15*(4), 305-316.

Akkermans, H. A., Bogerd, P., Yücesan, E., & van Wassenhove, L. N. (2003). The impact of ERP on supply chain management: Exploratory findings from a European Delphi study. *European Journal of Operational Research, 146*(2), 284-301.

Bell, S., & Orzen, M. (2007, May 15). Jumping on the ERP bandwagon. *APICS e-News*, 7.

Bendoly, E., & Schoenherr, T. (2005). ERP system and implementation-process benefits: implications for B2B e-procurement. *International Journal of Operations and Production Management, 25*(4), 304-319.

Billet, D. L. (2008). Focus on small- and medium-sized companies: Challenges and opportunities. *APICS e-News, 8*(6), April 1, 2008.

Bradford, M., Mayfield, T., & Toney, C. (2001). Does ERP fit in a lean world? *Strategic Finance, 82*(11), 28-34.

Brehm, N., & Gómez, J.M. (2005). Secure web service-based resource sharing in ERP networks. *Journal of Information Privacy & Security, 1*(2), 29-48.

Buonanno, G., Faverio, P., Pigni, F., Ravarini, A., Sciuto, D., & Tagliavini, M. (2005). Factors affecting ERP system adoption: A comparative analysis between SMEs and large companies. *Journal of Enterprise Information Management, 18*(4), 384-426.

Chien, S.-W., Hu, C., Reimers, K., & Lin, J.-S. (2007).The influence of centrifugal and centripetal forces on ERP project success in small and medium-sized enterprises in China and Taiwan. *International Journal of Production Economics, 107*(2), 380-396.

Davenport, T. (1998). Putting the enterprise into the enterprise system. *Harvard Business Review, 76*(4), 121-131.

Davison, R. (2002). Cultural complications of ERP. *Communications of the ACM, 45*(7), 109-111.

De Búrca, S., Fynes, B., & Marshall, D. (2005). Strategic technology adoption: Extending ERP across the supply chain. *Journal of Enterprise Information Management, 18*(4), 427-440.

Diederich, T. (1998). Bankrupt firm blames SAP for failure. *ComputerWorld*, (August 28, 1998).

Eisenhardt, K. M., & Graebner, M. E. (2007). Theory building from cases: opportunities and challenges. *Academy of Management Journal, 50*(1), 25-32.

European Commission (2008). SME definition. Retrieved May 12, 2008, from http://ec.europa. eu/enterprise/enterprise_policy/sme_definition/ index_en.htm.

Institute für Mittelstandsforschung (2008). KMU Definition des IfM Bonn. Retrieved May 12, 2008, from http://www.ifm-bonn.org/index. php?id=89.

Hauser, H.-E. (2000). *SMEs in Germany – Facts and figures.* Bonn, Germany: Institut für Mittelstandsforschung.

Hofstede, G. H. (1991). *Cultures and organizations: Software of the mind.* London, UK: McGraw-Hill.

Jacobs, F. R., & Weston, F. C. T., Jr. (2007). Enterprise resource planning (ERP) - A brief history. *Journal of Operations Management, 25*(2), 357-363.

Kirkpatrick, D. (1998). The E-Ware war: Competition comes to enterprise software. *Fortune, 138*(11), 103-112.

Koh, S. C. L., & Saad, S. M. (2006). Managing uncertainty in ERP-controlled manufacturing environments in SMEs. *International Journal of Production Economics, 101*(1), 109-127.

Koh, S. C. L., & Simpson, M. (2005). Change and uncertainty in SME manufacturing environments using ERP. *Journal of Manufacturing Technology Management, 16*(6), 629-653.

Koh, S. C. L., & Simpson, M. (2007). Could enterprise resource planning create a competitive advantage for small businesses? *Benchmarking, 14*(1), 59-76.

Mabert, M. A. (2007). The early road to material requirements planning. *Journal of Operations Management, 25*(2), 346-356.

Mabert, V. A., Soni, A. K., & Venkataramanan, M. A. (2000). Enterprise resource planning survey of U.S. manufacturing firms. *Production and Inventory Management Journal, 41*(2), 52-58.

Mabert, V. A., Soni, A. K., & Venkataramanan, M. A. (2001a). Enterprise resource planning: Common myths versus evolving reality. *Business Horizons, 44*(3), 69-76.

Mabert, V. A., Soni, A. K., & Venkataramanan, M. A. (2001b). Enterprise resource planning: Measuring value. *Production and Inventory Management Journal, 42*(3/4), 46-51.

Mabert, V. A., Soni, A. K., & Venkataramanan, M. A. (2003). The impact of organization size on enterprise resource planning (ERP) implementations in the U.S. manufacturing sector. *Omega – The International Journal of Management Science, 31*(3), 235-246.

Markus, M. L., & Tanis, C. (2000). The enterprise system experience - From adoption to success. In: M. F. Price (Ed.), *Framing the domains of IT management* (pp. 173-207). Cincinnati, OH: Pinnaflex.

Mecham, M. (1998). Get started very early. *Aviation Week and Space Technology, 149*(21), 17.

Morabito, V., Pace, S., & Previtali, P. (2005). ERP marketing and Italian SMEs. *European Management Journal, 23*(5), 590-598.

Muscatello, J. R., Small, M. H., & Chen, I. J. (2003). Implementing enterprise resource planning (ERP) systems in small and midsize manufacturing firms. *International Journal of Operations and Production Management, 23*(8), 850-871.

Olsen, K.A., & Sætre, P. (2007). IT for niche companies: Is an ERP system the solution? *Information Systems Journal, 17*(1), 37-58.

Orlikowski, W. J. (1992). The duality of technology: Rethinking the concept of technology in organizations. *Organization Science, 3*(3), 398-427.

Quiescenti, M., Bruccoleri, M., La Commare, U., Noto La Diega, S., & Perrone, G. (2006). Business process-oriented design of Enterprise Resource Planning (ERP) systems for small and medium enterprises. *International Journal of Production Research, 44*(18/19), 3797-3811.

Robey, D., & Sahay, S. (1996). Transforming work through information technology: A comparative case study of geographic information systems in county government. *Information Systems Research, 7*(1), 93-110.

Rowe, F. (1999). Cohérence, intégration informationnelle et changement: Esquisse d'un programme de recherche à partir des Progiciels Intégrés de Gestion. *Systèmes d'Information et Management, 4*(4), 3-20.

Schoenherr, T., Venkataramanan, M. A., Soni, A. K., Mabert, V. A., & Hilpert, D. (2005). The 'new' users: Manufacturing SMEs and the Mittelstand experience. In: by E. Bendoly, & F. R. Jacobs (Eds.), *Strategic ERP extension and use* (pp. 36-51). Stanford, CA: Stanford University Press.

Shin, I. (2006). Adoption of enterprise application software and firm performance. *Small Business Economics, 26*(3), 241-256.

Soh, C., Kien, S. S., & Tay-Yap, J. (2000). Cultural fits and misfits: Is ERP a universal solution? *Communications of the ACM, 43*(4), 47-51.

Sumner, M. (2000). Risk factors in enterprise-wide/ERP projects. *Journal of Information Technology, 15*(4), 317-327.

Taylor, J. (1999). Fitting enterprise software in smaller companies. *Management Accounting, 80*(February), 36-39.

Van Everdingen, Y., Van Hillegersberg, J., & Waarts, E. (2000). ERP adoption by European midsize companies. *Communications of the ACM, 43*(4), 27-31.

Voigt, T. (2001). *mind 02 – Mittelstand in Deutschland*. Köln, Germany: Gruner + Jahr.

Wang, C., Xu, L., Liu, X., & Qin, X. (2005). ERP research, development and implementation in China: An overview. *International Journal of Production Research, 43*(18), 3915-3932.

Yin, R. K. (1994). *Case study research: Design and methods*. Thousand Oaks, CA: Sage Publications.

KEY TERMS

German *Mittelstand* (German SMEs): The German *Mittelstand* refers to small and medium sized enterprises (SMEs) in Germany, which form the backbone of the country's economy. Numbering over one million companies, the *Mittelstand* employs over 20 million people, is responsible for almost 40 percent of total German gross investments and accounts for 30 percent of the exports (Hauser 2000). These enterprises are often highly innovative and entrepreneurial, and are frequently very competitive international market leaders. The primary focus of these German SMEs is usually on highly customized and specialized products and services, resulting in information systems becoming a key competitive weapon (Taylor, 1999; Voigt, 2001). The companies can rely on a highly skilled and flexible work force, which is supplied by Germany's exceptional vocational training system. This leads to a very loyal and stable workforce, with a turnover rate of only about 3 percent. Overall, German SMEs provide a unique setting to study the design and complexity of enterprise systems. The *Mittelstand* companies in our sample ranged in size between 593 and 1,200 employees, with annual revenues between 64 and 378 million Euros.

ES Implementation and Usage: In our chapter we describe the experiences companies made when implementing and using enterprise systems. Four of our case study firms were in either of these two phases. Crucial preceding stages include the decision and planning phase. Without those two additional phases implementation and usage would not be possible, or only in a very haphazard way. In our chapter we therefore describe experiences of our companies in all of these stages, as illustrated in Figure 1 of the paper. A similar implementation and usage timeline was suggested by Markus and Tanis (2000).

Impetus for a New System: One of our nine areas of investigation reported in the chapter. Here we explore who or what was the driving force behind the ES implementation, i.e. what ultimately led the company to their current or future system. This can include functional departments, but also changes in the marketplace, increased competition, changing demands by customers, etc.

Implementation Success and Satisfaction: In this eighth issue we investigate in our chapter we describe the success and satisfaction companies reported with their ES planning, implementation and usage. While it can be difficult to quantify hard performance measures, also intangible benefits are realized.

Involvement of Employees and Training: With this seventh area of investigation we examine the level of employee involvement and training, and how these tasks were approached. Costs associated were also discussed.

Order of Implementation: The fifth of our nine areas we focus on in the chapter. Here we deal with the order in which the different mod-

ules or components of the ES were implemented in the company, and the rationale behind the sequence.

Power of Final Decision: This is the second of our nine issues that we focus on, which deals with who was responsible for the final decision to modify or replace the current ES infrastructure. Change agents can include top management, the owner of the firm, or IT personnel.

Standard Packages, modifications, and In-house Developed Applications: This sixth focus area in our chapter reports on whether standard packages supplied by providers were chosen, and if yes, whether and to what extent modifications were carried out. If in-house developed applications were preferred, benefits and challenges, as well as integration possibilities, were discussed. Rationales behind each choice were explored.

System and Provider Selection: The third of our nine focus areas deals with the process or approach taken to select the system and its provider(s). Possible influencing factors include the availability of solutions with good fit, the sustainability of the provider, the capabilities of the system, the preferences of the company, and its internal processes.

Time Spent in System Selection, Planning and Implementation: In this fourth area of investigation we report on the time spent for selecting the system, planning the implementation, and then finally implementing the ES. The time taken and required can be quite long at times, which however often ensures a sound and thorough process.

Upgrades After Implementation: This final area of investigation in our chapter deals with how upgrades and new releases after the implementation were handled. These upgrades can be quite time-consuming, and usually not every new release is implemented.

Chapter XVI
Size Matters!
Enterprise System Success in Medium and Large Organizations

Darshana Sedera
Queensland University of Technology, Australia

ABSTRACT

Organizations invest substantial resources in acquiring Enterprise Systems, presumably expecting positive impacts to the organization and its functions. Despite the optimistic motives, some Enterprise System projects have reported nil or detrimental impacts. This chapter explores the proposition that the size of the organization (e.g. medium, large) may contribute to the differences in benefits received. The alleged differences in organizational performance are empirically measured using a prior validated model, using four dimensions employing data gathered from 310 respondents representing 27 organizations.

INTRODUCTION

Enterprise System (ES) is an ideology of planning and managing the resources of an entire organization in an efficient, productive, and profitable manner, and is manifested in the form of configurable information system packages (Laukkanen, Sarpola et al. 2007). The Enterprise System vendors promote a fully integrated core business processes through the organization where seamless integration of the information flowing from one functional area to the other. Amongst the myriad of benefits, Enterprise Systems said to deliver key benefits like: cost reduction, productivity improvement, quality improvement, customer service improvement, better resource management, improved decision-making and planning, and organizational empowerment (Shang and Seddon 2002).

Organizations devote substantial resources and time on acquiring an Enterprise System, presumably expecting positive impacts to the organization and its functions. These extensive ES implementations are typically measured in millions of dollars Pan et al (2001), and for many organizations they represent the largest single IT investment. The substantial resource requirements for Enterprise Systems have restricted Enterprise System market to the Medium-Large organizations with many suggesting that ES are best suited for Large Corporations (Hillegersberg and Kumar 2000). Recent changes in market place, wherein the demand for Enterprise Systems from large organizations has plateau, vendors are attempting to shift their emphasis into the Small-Medium Enterprises (SMEs) with scaled-down ES products (Piturro 1999; Everdingen, Hillegersberg et al. 2000).

Measuring the impacts of Enterprise Systems takes on special importance since the costs and risks of these large technology investments rival their potential payoffs. Often carefully rationalized in advance, ES investments are too seldom systematically evaluated post-implementation (Thatcher and Oliver 2001). Welsh and White (1981) differentiated the small and large organizations using such aspects like time, skills, and resources – where the medium organizations lacking all three compared to their counterparts. D'Amboise and Muldowney (1988) argue that the lack of resources has made smaller organizations more vulnerable to the environmental effects and misjudgments forcing them to allocate more time to adjusting to, rather than devoting time on predicting and controlling. The resource lack of constraints has been found to hinder IT adoption (Baker 1987; Cragg and Zinatelli 1995; Iacovou, Benbasat et al. 1995; Proudlock, Phelps et al. 1999), and to negatively affect IS implementation success (Thong 2001) and IT growth (Cragg and King 1993) in SMEs.

With the aforementioned background – where organizations devote huge resources acquiring ES and many not receiving anticipated benefits, where the traditional market leveling with ES vendors moving into the SME market segment

– this chapter discusses whether the organization size has an influence over the benefits brought-to-bear by the Enterprise System. This study aims to contribute to the encyclopedia by investigating the relationship of organizational size with the performance of the system (commonly referred to as System Success). Although prior research (Raymond 1985; DeLone 1988; Raymond 1992; Lai 1994) has contributed to our understanding of IS and organization size, few have empirically assessed influence of organizational size for contemporary IS success. More importantly, instead of resorting to the customary approach of considering large and medium-sized organizations as one homogenous group receiving equal benefits, this study aims to bring forth the differences between these two groups using four system related dimensions. This study presented herein investigates the influence of organization size on ES performance. ES impacts are empirically measured using information received from 310 responses representing 27 organizations that had implemented a market leading Enterprise System solutions in the second half of 1990.

The chapter begins with a historical overview of literature on size as an important determinant. The broad contextual overview begins by differentiating characteristics of the medium vs. large organizations and demonstrating the impact of such contextual factors on System success. The research context is introduced next followed by discussions on the research methodology and data collection instrument. The final section demonstrates the observed differences between the two organizational sizes and research implications.

BACKGROUND

Prior research suggests that organizational context is a determinant of Information System (IS) success. Researchers have concluded that medium organizations have distinctive and unique needs compared to large organizations (Raymond 1985;

DeLone 1988; Lai 1994) and therefore, the research findings of large organizations cannot be generalized to small to mid-sized firms.

Schultz and Slevin (1975) and Ein-Dor and Segev (1978) were among the very first point out the importance of organizational factors in managing Information Systems. In their early work, Ein-Dor and Segev (1978) proposed a framework after studying Management Information System (MIS) in which they identified organization size as a critical variable. Ein-Dor and Segev (1978) identified ten (10) organizational variables with direct or indirect influence on the impact of an IS. The identified variables are: (1) organization size, (2) maturity, (3) structure, (4) time frame, (5) psychological climate towards [CB] IS, (6) organizational situation, (7) rank of responsible executives, (8) location of responsible executives, (9) steering committee location and rank and (10) resources. They found that the organization size had special importance because of its influence on resource availability, requirements necessary for integration of professional units within an organization, degree of formalization of organizational systems, and lead time for planning and implementation. Furthermore, Ein-Dor and Segev (1978) recognized organization size as an uncontrollable variable and stated that [CB] IS projects are less likely to succeed in smaller organizations compared to larger organizations.

Bilili and Raymond (1993) described SME decision making process as reactive, informal, and intuitive. (Doukidis, Lybereas et al. 1996; Proudlock, Phelps et al. 1999) asserted the opportunistic, day-to-day focus of the small to mid-sized organizations in relation to Information Systems. Whisler (1970) studied nineteen insurance companies and reputed that firm size was directly related to performance of IS. Cheney (1983) identified various factors that would affect a small business firm's success or failure in using information systems and found three areas of difficulty associated in small businesses information systems: (1) software problems, (2) hardware problems and (3) implementation problems.

DeLone (1981) studied the relationship between the size of a manufacturing firm and IS usage and concluded that firm size is: (1) directly related to the age of the firm's computer operations, (2) inversely related to the amount of external programming that is used, (3) directly related to the portion of revenues allocated to Electronic Data Processing (EDP), and (4) inversely related to the percentage of EDP costs that are used for computer equipment. He also explained that smaller firms experience more computer related problems than their larger counterparts. Melone (1985) found that managers in small to mid-sized organizations rate accounting and inventory control as the most frequently used and important applications, and reported that inventory control was the most problematic aspect of computer usage in such organizations. Nickel and Seado (1986) reputed similar findings using 121 small businesses stating that budgeting and inventory control were the primary uses of IS in small organizations. Farhoomand and Hrycyk (1985) reported lack of technical staff as a substantial issue for the small to mid-sized companies.

A study by Cooley et al. (1987) identified the importance of user-friendly interfaces and lower implementation costs as key factors affecting end users in small to mid-sized organizations. Montazemi (1988) investigating the aforementioned preposition, confirmed the impact of organization size on end user satisfaction.

An organization has two basic options when it decides to implement a computerized application; (1) to have its own staff develop the software, or (2) to acquire packaged software from a vendor (Raymond, 1985). Turner (1992) stated that as a firm increases in size, it would demand more sophisticated software. Even though that this argument is intuitive, it suggests a correlation between organization size and the adoption of package software. Turner (1992) specifically emphasized the importance of small to mid-tier organizations obtaining assistance from external sources rather than developing applications in house. To the contrary, Raymond (1985) found that small firms are capable of developing, implementing and administering their own applications in-house, compared to their larger counterparts, specifying that small organizations could maintain an IS with minimal financial, technical and personnel requirements. The resource constraints has lead SMEs to follow an incremental approach to IT investments, which, in turn, may result in isolated and incompatible systems, as well as decreased flexibility (Levy and Powell 1998). Raymond (1992) emphasized on the advantages of small to mid-sized firms in developing in-house applications rather than adopting packaged software from commercial vendors. They further added that *end user computing,* (where the user have direct control over their computing needs) is more appropriate to such organizations than adopting a packaged software application.

Many researchers have alluded to the skill scarcity for information systems in Small to mid-sized organizations (Bilili and Raymond 1993; Levy and Powell 1998; Mitev and Marsh 1998). Laukkanen et al. (2007) suggest that the resource constraints faced by SMEs may hinder their ability to maintain technology up to date, while at the same time forcing them to consider their investments in IT as something that should last for a long time (Levy and Powell 1998). Soh et al. (1992) investigated the importance of external consultants on computerization success in small businesses, concluding that the level of computer system usage in small businesses with consultants is higher than that of small businesses without consultants. Further, they added that small businesses that engage consultants are less likely to complete there IS project on time and within budget. Harrison (1997) using the Theory of Planned Behaviour (TPB) to explained technology adoption. They found that as business size increased, the importance of expectations from the [social] environment increased. However, they observed a negative correlation with the importance of intra-firm consequences and control over the potential barriers for IS adoption. Hong and Kim (2001) explored the *'fit perspective'* in 34 Enterprise System installations where organizational size was implicitly considered as a critical contingency variable.

In classifying organizations in the small → medium → large spectrum, many authors use the number of employees as the sole classifier. For example in a recent study (Laukkanen, Sarpola et al. 2007), SMEs are defined here as enterprises with fewer than 250 employees, wherein the small organizations defined as companies with less than 50 employees and large organizations are simply classified as those companies that do not meet the definition of SMEs and have more than 250 employees (Chau 1994; Chau 1995). However, it is unrealistic to associate a 50 staff (or less) organizations with a large scaled traditional Enterprise System implementations as such systems are targeted at larger counterparts. Though the number of employees in a company provides some indication to the size of the Enterprise System, at times it can be quite misleading due to not all employees having access to an Enterprise System. For example, in a Health and Pharmaceutical organization – where the majority of the staff is on medical duties (e.g. doctors and nurses) – the actual Enterprise System users will be a small proportion of the total number of employees. In recent years, Sedera et al (2003) suggest the use of *number of user licenses* to determine the size of the organization for Enterprise System discussions. They suggest keeping 1000 (or over) concurrent user licenses as a benchmark for large organizations and anything below classifying as medium enterprises.

THE STUDY CONTEXT

The empirical data collection was conducted across 27 public sector agencies running live the market leading Enterprise System. These 27 agencies were the first Australian state agencies to have implemented common financial management software state-wide namely. In 1995 the state Government commenced implementation of the Financials module across all state Government agencies (later followed by Controlling, Materials Management and in some agencies Human Resources) and soon became one of the largest Enterprise System installations in Australia. The state Government approach was very much focused on using the Enterprise System as a common reporting and financial management tool. The objectives of the new financial system were to provide a financial management system to state Government agencies that would: (1) support the 'Managing for Outcomes' (MFO) framework and financial management improvement activities, (2) encourage best practice resource management across state Government, (3) facilitate the consolidation of state Government financial information, (4) meet the business needs of agencies and (5) achieve economies of scale in main operations.

Despite the claimed benefits by most of the agencies, a relatively smaller agency that provides corporate services to a group of other agencies demonstrated their dissatisfaction with their Enterprise System. Even though the Enterprise System provided rich functionality to this organization, the senior management believed that the system in place was too complex and too expensive to operate in a smaller organization. After three years of using the implemented Enterprise System, the agency decided to replace that with a local, small scaled Enterprise System. The contextual

background further questions the preposition in discussion – whether the organizational size influences the benefits you receive.

THE SURVEY

A survey instrument was designed to operationalize 27 measures of ES-success depicted in Table 1 (See details in (Gable, Sedera et al. 2003; Sedera and Gable 2004). All items were scored on a seven-point Likert scale with the end values (1) 'Strongly disagree' and (7) 'Strongly Agree', and the middle value (4) 'Neutral'. The draft survey instrument was pilot tested with a selected sample of staff of the state Government Treasury Department. Feedback from the pilot round respondents resulted in minor modifications to survey items. The survey gathered additional demographic details on respondents' employment title (e.g. Director, Business Analyst, Application programmer). Furthermore, the respondents were asked to provide a brief description of their involvement with the Enterprise System. Supplementary information on the organizational structure, characteristics of the Enterprise System (i.e. modules in use and hardware in place) and the number of users in each agency was gathered from objective sources.

In addition to the 27 items of Table 3, the questionnaire included two criterion items aimed at gauging the respondent's perception of overall ES-success: (1) 'overall...the impact of [the name

Table 1. The measures of the ES-success measurement model

	System Quality		Information Quality		Individual Impact		Organisational Impact
SQ1	Ease of use	IQ1	Availability	II1	Learning	OI1	Organisational costs
SQ2	Ease of learning	IQ2	Usability	II2	Awareness / Recall	OI2	Staff requirements
SQ3	User requirements	IQ3	Understandability	II3	Decision effectiveness	OI3	Cost reduction
SQ4	System features	IQ4	Relevance	II4	Individual productivity	OI4	Overall productivity
SQ5	System accuracy	IQ5	Format			OI5	Improved outcomes/outputs
SQ6	Flexibility	IQ6	Conciseness			OI6	Increased capacity
SQ7	Sophistication					OI7	e-business
SQ8	Integration					OI8	Business Process Change
SQ9	Customisation						

of the Enterprise System] on the agency has been positive' and (2) 'overall… the impact of [the name of the Enterprise System] on me has been positive'.

RESULTS AND ANALYSIS

A total of three hundred and nineteen (319) responses from twenty-seven (27) public sector agencies were received. Nine responses were removed from the analysis due to missing values and perceived frivolity. Using the number of SAP user licenses, the sample was divided into two mutually exclusive representing the respondents from medium organizations and large organizations. Organizations with more than 1000 SAP user licenses considered as large agencies and the rest were medium agencies. Additional criteria were established (i.e. Number of employees, dispersion of the organization) to be used in the grouping exercise to supplement the principal criterion, where the initial classification was unclear. Table 2(a) shows the break down of organizations, classified into medium and large organizations and Table 2(b) shows the classification of respondents

segregated into the two agency cohorts. All indications suggest that this distribution is representative of users of the Enterprise System in the state Government. All participated agencies having: (1) the same Enterprise System software application, (2) the similar versions of the Enterprise System, (3) in the same phase of the ES life cycle, and (4) installed Financial Accounting and Controlling, Materials Management modules created a unique homogeneous environment increasing the comparability of the data.

The one-way analysis of variance (ANOVA) F-test was chosen as the method for conducting the analysis of the Likert scale data. For each variable measured with Likert scale the statistics reported include the arithmetic mean (mean) and standard deviation (std dev.) of the responses in each company group, the significance of group mean differences (sig.) indicated by F-test, and the group sizes (n). If a significant difference was found in ANOVA at the 0.05 level, paired t-tests comparisons were conducted to see which of the company groups differ from each other. The criterion item (*Overall, the impact of [the name of the Enterprise System] on the agency has been positive*) was used to establish the peripheral

Table 2. Respondent classification

Table 2 (a): Composition of Organizations		
	#	%
MEDIUM	22	81%
LARGE	5	19%
Table 2 (b): Respondents classification		
	#	%
MEDIUM	244	79%
LARGE	66	21%

Table 3. Results of t-test for the criterion measure (alpha = 0.05)

	Mean	St: Dev	P	t-value	Sig. (2-tailed)
Medium	4.41	1.51			
Large	5	1.08	0.00024	-3.58	0.00048

Table 4. Results of t-test for the success dimensions (alpha = 0.05)

Success Dimension		F	Sig.	t	df	Sig. (2-tailed)
System Quality	Equal variances assumed	2.49	0.12	-1.83	308.00	0.05
	Equal variances not assumed			-1.93	111.63	0.06
Information Quality	Equal variances assumed	0.53	0.47	-1.32	308.00	0.19
	Equal variances not assumed			-1.32	103.09	0.19
Individual Impact	Equal variances assumed	8.32	0.00	-3.20	308.00	0.00
	Equal variances not assumed			-3.68	128.24	0.00
Organization Impact	Equal variances assumed	4.53	0.03	-2.37	308.00	0.02
	Equal variances not assumed			-2.69	125.47	0.01

differences between the two cohorts. Analysis of our survey data indicates that significant differences exist between the medium-sized, and large organization with a high F value of 5.22. It is also observed that the large organizations demonstrate a higher mean score for the criterion item over the medium organizations.

Encouraged by the findings above, using the averages of each of the four success dimensions, we conducted an independent sample t-test to further explore the differences between the two organizational sizes with regards to the dimensions.

Results depicted in Table 4 indicate significant differences between the two organizational sizes in three of the four success dimensions. The differences are observed in System Quality, Individual Impacts and Organization Impacts.

Having determined that two organizational sizes demonstrate significant differences in relation to the Enterprise System success dimensions, the chapter now attempts to identify *where* those differences exists and whether an Enterprise System investment favors a particular organizational size. In order to establish this, we now look at the mean scores of each success dimension and their corresponding measures.

SYSTEM QUALITY

The quality of a system under investigation is a multifaceted phenomenon. The system quality construct is designed to capture how the system performs from a technical and design perspective. Nine validated measures have been employed in this study. Results depicted in Figure 1, it is evident that for all 09 measures on Enterprise System Quality, large organizations demonstrate relatively larger mean scores compared to their smaller counterparts. Moreover, the following observations are made in relation to the measures of system quality. All, but two measures (flexibility and customization), have received below scale-median (4) values for the large organizations. To the contrary, for medium organizations, 6 of the 9 measures report below scale-median scores.

The two cohorts demonstrate substantial differences in mean scores across IT-sophistication and the employment of system features. Similarly, the mean scores on Enterprise System meeting the requirements of the organization demonstrate differences between the medium and large cohorts, with large reporting high mean scores. It is noticed with some interest that system centric attributes such as: integration and customization do not demonstrate strong differences between the two cohorts.

INFORMATION QUALITY

Measures of information quality focus on the output – both *on-screen and reports* – produced by the system, and the value, usefulness or relative importance attributed to the output by the users.

Figure 1. Mean scores for system quality

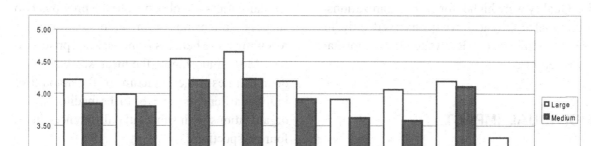

In an early leading study of IS success, Bailey and Pearson (1983) identified nine characteristics of information quality: accuracy, precision, currency, timeliness, reliability, completeness, conciseness, format and relevance. Sirinivasan (1985) added 'understandability' of information as another important sub-construct; while Saaksjarvi and Talvinen (1993) employed content, availability, accuracy as sub-construct measures of information quality in their study of marketing information systems. Rainer (1995) found accuracy, timeliness, conciseness, convenience and relevance as being key aspects of Executive Information Systems information quality. Results of the exploratory survey and expert workshops revealed context-specific measures of information quality and thus significant changes have been made to the sub-constructs of information quality. The study employs the six validated measures from the ES-Success of Gable Sedera et at 2003; Sedera Gable 2004. The Figure 2 depicts the mean scores for the six measures of Information Quality. Similar to System Quality dimension discussed above, large organizations demonstrate a higher mean score for all six measures.

Figure 2. Mean scores for information quality

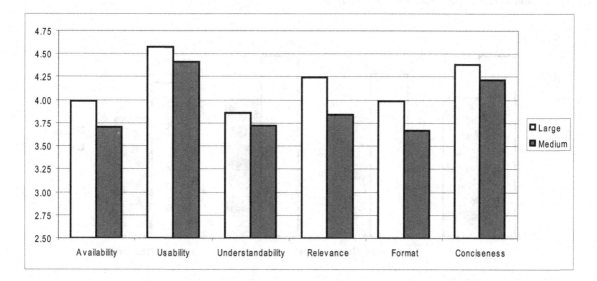

Though all mean-scores reported for Information Quality were higher for large organizations, substantial differences were observed only in relation to Information Relevance and the format of the reports.

INDIVIDUAL IMPACT

Individual impact is concerned with how the Enterprise System influences the performance of the individual user. Individual impact tends to encompass a broad range of subjective measures such as: confidence in decisions made, improvements in decision-making, and the time to reach a decision (Ein-Dor, Segev et al. 1981; Sirinivasan 1985; Kim and Lee 1986). Dickson et al. (1977) provided early insights into Individual Impact citing decision quality, decision time, decision confidence, and estimated outcomes. Though individual productivity and decision making effectiveness have been mentioned in prior studies as impacts from the system, the potential benefits from the Enterprise System exceeds those and includes aspects such as – facilitating organizational learning and information recall and awareness through organizational transparency.

Observing mean scores reported in Figure 3, similar patters are observed to the previous two success dimensions with large organizations receiving more benefits from the Enterprise System. More importantly, the mean score analysis demonstrates a bleak picture of the amount of individual benefits received to the medium scaled organizations with substantial differences in all four perspectives.

ORGANIZATIONAL IMPACTS

The impact of an Enterprise System on organizational performance is some-what difficult to isolate from the general organizational performance indicators. The eight measures of the ES-success measurement model purportedly isolate the impact of the system with the one of the organization. The analyses of the mean scores for the 08 measures support all observations above favoring the large organizations.

It is also observed that the medium organizations report substantially lower mean scores for five out of the eight measures. The biggest differences were seen in facilitation of e-business through Enterprise Systems and the introduction

Figure 3. Mean scores for individual impacts

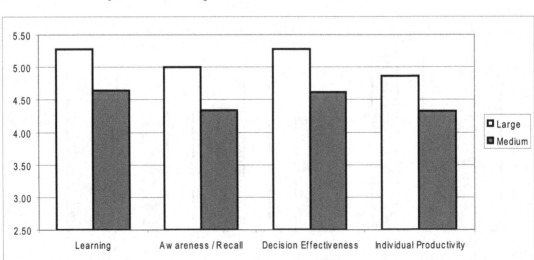

Figure 4. Mean scores for organization impacts

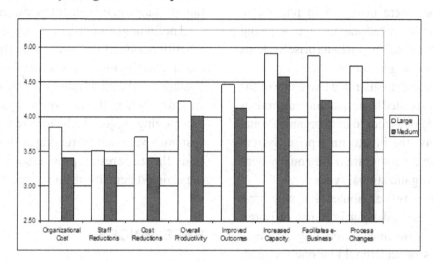

of optimal business process changes. The three cost related aspects: (1) reduction of organization costs, (2) reduction of staff and (3) operational costs reductions have received below median scores for both organizational cohorts (See figure 4 for details).

CONCLUSION

This chapter explored whether there are significant differences exist between medium-sized and large enterprises regarding the success of the Enterprise System. In doing so, it gathered data from 310 respondents from 27 organizations that had implemented a market leading Enterprise System in the second half of 1990. The impact of the Enterprise System was empirically measured using validated constructs measures of the Enterprise System Success Measurement Model (Gable, Sedera et al. 2003; Sedera and Gable 2004).

The findings indicate that organization size undoubtedly has a strong influence over the benefits received from the system. Though there have been other studies investigating various aspects of Enterprise System (e.g. differences between small, medium and large organizations on Enterprise System initial objectives and con-

straints of adoption (Laukkanen, Sarpola et al. 2007), implementation issues (Mabert, Soni et al. 2003), this is one of the first to demonstrate the differences in relation to the outcomes of the system.

The homogeneity in the study context – where all the sampled organization having implemented the same Enterprise System, similar modules and are at the same phase of the lifecycle – provided a distinct strength to the study, where the results are less vulnerable to extraneous factors. The study employed the number of Enterprise System User Licenses to classify the organizations in to the two organizational sizes. The authors argued the bias and the influence that other factors (e.g. number of employees and budget) may bring forth in a study of this nature.

The results empirically provide evidence to a well-known anecdote that traditional Enterprise Systems are better suited for the Large Organizations. The results demonstrated significant differences between the medium and large organizations in relation to Enterprise System Quality, Impacts to the Individuals, and Impacts to the Organization. No differences were observed in relation to the Quality of Information derived from the system.

Substantial differences between the two types of organizations were observed in relation to Individual and Organizational impacts – raising concerns over the suitability of Enterprise Systems for medium sized organizations.

The result also demonstrated that some of the common system related issues, such as customization, are equally deterrent to both organizational types. Similarly, the innate Enterprise System advantages like the integration are equally beneficial to both organizational types.

We recognize two attributes that may have contributed to the under-performance of Enterprise System in medium tiered organizations. The economies of scale could be one the leading factors that hamper the results of medium tiered organizations. From the study findings it is evident that medium sized organizations have received reasonable benefits through System and Information Quality dimensions. However, the stark differences observed in Individual and Organization Impacts suggests that though the system and information quality were adequate, mid-sized companies have failed to attain cost, productivity and resource benefits. Specifically, in resource-demanding ERP investments, the larger enterprises have been found to be able to take advantage of economies of scale and, hence, compared to their larger counterparts, smaller companies are faced with a relatively bigger commitment when adopting Enterprise Systems (Mabert, Soni et al. 2000).

Secondly, the resource limitations characterized in medium organizations is identified as another probable contributor to the poorer success reported by the medium-sized companies. Akin to a popular view where practitioners argue that 'implementing an Enterprise System is just the beginning', organizations are required to make continuous investments into optimizing an Enterprise System. The resource scarcity of mid-sized organizations may not allow further investments into the Enterprise System on training, upgrades, business process improvements and organizational change management practices.

The findings are particularly important to the IT practitioners (and academics alike) to understand the diversity of impacts received from Enterprise System and the importance of contextual factors. At a time where the Enterprise System vendors are moving aggressively towards scaled-down systems specifically targeting at small organizations, the study results provide some caution over the claimed benefits of Enterprise Systems.

REFERENCES

Bailey, J. E., & Pearson, S. W. (1983). Development Of A Tool For Measuring And Analyzing Computer User Satisfaction. *Management Science, 29*(5), 530-545.

Baker, W. H. (1987). Status of information management in small businesses. *Journal of Systems Management, 38*(4), 10-15.

Bilili, S., & Raymond, L. (1993). Information technology: Threats and opportunities for small and medium-sized enterprises. *International Journal of Information Management 13*(6). 439-48.

Chau, P. Y. K. (1994). Selection of packaged software in small businesses. *European Journal of Information Systems, 3*(4), 292-302.

Chau, P. Y. K. (1995). Factors used in the selection of packaged software in small businesses: views of owners and managers. I*nformation and Management, 29*(2), 71-8.

Cheney, P. H. (1983). Getting The Most Out Of Your First Computer System. *American Journal of Small Business, 7*(4), 476-485.

Cooley, P. L., Walz, D. T., et al. (1987). A Research Agenda For Computers And Small Business. *American Journal of Small Business, 11*(3), 31-42.

Cragg, P. B., & King, M. (1993). Small-firm computing: motivators and inhibitors. *MIS Quarterly 17*(1), 47-60.

Cragg, P. B., & Zinatelli, N. (1995). The evolution of information systems in small firms. *Information and Management, 29*(1), 1-8.

d'Amboise, G., & Muldowney, M. (1988). "Management theory for small business: attempts and requirements." The Academy of Management Review 13(2): 226-40.

DeLone, W. H. (1981). Firm Size And The Characteristics Of Computer Use. *MIS Quarterly 5*(4), 65-77.

DeLone, W. H. (1988). Determinants Of Success For Computer Usage In Small Business. *MIS Quarterly, 12*(1), 50-61.

Dickson, G., Senn, J. et al. (1977). Research In Management Information Systems: The Minnesota Experiments. *Management Science, 23*(9), 913-923.

Doukidis, G. I., Lybereas, P. et al. (1996). Information systems planning in small businesses: A stage of growth analysis. *Journal of Systems and Software, 33*(2), 189-201.

Ein-Dor, P., & Segev, E. (1978). Organizational Context And The Success Of Management Information Systems. *Management Science, 24*(10), 1064-1077.

Ein-Dor, P., Segev, E. et al. (1981). Use Of Management Information Systems: An Empirical Study. *Proceedings of the 2ⁿᵈ International Conference on Information Systems*, Cambridge, Massachusetts, Association for Information Systems.

Everdingen, Y., Hillegersberg, J. et al. (2000). ERP adoption by European midsize companies. *Communications of the ACM, 43*(4), 27-31.

Farhoomand, F., & Hrycyk, G. P. (1985). The Feasibility Of Computers In The Small Business Environment. *American Journal of Small Business, 9*(4),15-22.

Gable, G., Sedera, D. et al. (2003). Enterprise Systems Success: A Measurement Model. *Proceedings of the 24ᵗʰ International Conference on Information Systems*, Seattle, Washington, Association for Information Systems.

Harrison, D. A., Mykytyn, J. P. P., & Riemenschneider, C. K. (1997). Executive Decisions about Adoption of Information Technology in Small Business: Theory and Empirical Tests. *Information Systems Research, 8*(2), 171-196.

Hillegersberg, J. V., & Kumar, K. (2000). ERP experience and evolution. *Communications of the ACM, 43*(4), 23-26.

Hong, K.-K., & Kim, Y.-G. (2001). The Critical Success Factors For ERP Implementation: An Organizational Fit Perspective. *Information and Management, 40*(1), 25-40.

Iacovou, C. L., Benbasat, I. et al. (1995). Electronic data interchange and small organizations, adoption and impact of technology. *MIS Quarterly, 19*(4), 465-85.

Kim, E., & Lee, J. (1986). An Exploratory Contingency Model Of User Participation And MIS Use. *Information & Management, 11*(2), 87-97.

Lai, V. S. (1994). A Survey Of Rural Small Business Computer Use: Success Factors And Decision Support. *Information & Management, 26*(6), 297-304.

Laukkanen, S., Sarpola, S. et al. (2007). Enterprise size matters: objectives and constraints of ERP adoption. *Journal of Enterprise Information Management, 20*(3), 319-334.

Levy, M., & Powell, P. (1998). SME flexibility and the role of information systems. *Small Business Economics, 11*(2), 183-96.

Mabert, V. A., Soni, A. et al. (2000). Enterprise Resource Planning Survey Of U.S. Manufacturing Firms. *Production and Inventory Management Journal, 41*(2), 52-58.

Mabert, V. A., Soni, A. et al. (2003). The impact of organization size on enterprise resource planning (ERP) implementations in the US manufacturing sector. *Omega, 31*, 235-246.

Melone, S. C. (1985). Computerising small business information systems. *Journal of small business management* April: 10-16.

Montazemi, A. R. (1988). Factors Affecting Information Satisfaction In The Context Of The Small Business Environment. *MIS Quarterly, 12*(2), 238-256.

Nickell, G. S., & Seado, P. C. (1986). The Impact Of Attitudes And Experience On Small Business. *American Journal of Small Business, 10*(1), 37-48.

Pan, S. L., Newell, S. et al. (2001). Knowledge Integration As A Key Problem In An ERP Implementation. *Proceedings of the 22nd International Conference on Information Systems*, New Orleans, Louisiana, Association for Information Systems.

Piturro, M. (1999). How midsize companies are buying ERP. *Journal of accountancy, 188*(3), 41-48.

Proudlock, M. J., Phelps, B. et al. (1999). IT adoption strategies: Best practice guidelines for professional SMEs. *Journal of Small Business and Enterprise Development, 6*(4), 240-52.

Rainer, J. K. R., & Watson, H.J. (1995). The Keys to Executive Information System Success. *Journal of Management Information Systems, 12*(2), 83-99.

Raymond, L. (1985). Organizational Characteristics And MIS Success In The Context Of Small Business. *MIS Quarterly, 9*(1), 37-52.

Raymond, L., & Bergeron, F. (1992). Personal DSS success in small enterprises. *Information & Management, 22*(5), 301-308.

Saaksjarvi, M. T. V., & Talvinen, J. M. (1993). Integration And Effectiveness Of Marketing Information Systems. *European Journal of Marketing, 27*(1), 64-79.

Schultz, R. L., & Slevin, D. P. (1975). Implementation and organisational validity: An empirical investigation. *Implementing operational research / management science*. R. L. Shultz and D. P. Slevin. New York, Elsevier, North-Holland: 153-182.

Sedera, D., & Gable, G. (2004). A Factor and Structural Equation Analysis of the Enterprise Systems Success Measurement Model. *International Conference of Information Systems*, Washington, D.C.

Sedera, D., Gable, G. et al. (2003). ERP Success: Does Organization Size Matter? *Proceedings of the 7th Pacific Asia Conference on Information Systems*, Association for Information Systems.

Shang, S., & Seddon, P. B. (2002). Assessing And Managing The Benefits Of Enterprise Systems: The Business Manager's Perspective. *Information Systems Journal, 12*(4), 271-299.

Sirinivasan, A. (1985). Alternative Measures Of System Effectiveness: Associations And Implications. *MIS Quarterly, 9*(3), 243-253.

Soh, C. P. P., Yap, C. S. et al. (1992). Impact of consultants on computerisation success in small businesses. *Information and Management, 22*, 309-319.

Thatcher, M. E., & Oliver, J. R. (2001). The impact of technology investments on a firm's production efficiency, product quality, and productivity. *Journal of Management Information Systems, 18*(2), 17-45.

Thong, J. Y. L. (2001). Resource constraints and information systems implementation in Singaporean small business. *Omega, 29*(2), 143-56.

Turner, J. S. (1992). Personal DSS success in small business. *Information and Management, 22*, 301-308.

Welsh, J. A., & White, J. F. (1981). A amall business is not a little big business. *Harvard Business Review, 59*(4), 18-32.

Whisler, T. (1970). *The Impact Of Computers On Organizations*. New York, NY, Praeger Publishers.

KEY TERMS

Enterprise System: Customizable, standard software solutions that have the potential to link and automate all aspects of the business, incorporating core processes and main administrative functions into a single information and technology architecture.

Individual-Impact: A measure of the extent to which [the IS] has influenced the capabilities and effectiveness, on behalf of the organization, of key-users.

Information-Quality: A measure of the quality of [the IS] outputs: namely, the quality of the information the system produces in reports and on-screen.

Organizational-Impact: A measure of the extent to which [the IS] has promoted improvement in organizational results and capabilities.

Public Sector: The public sector is the part of economic, administrative and Governance process that deals with the delivery of goods and services by and for the government.

SAP: SAP [used to denote SAP R/3 software] is a market leading Enterprise System software.

System-Quality: A measure of the performance of [the IS] from a technical and design perspective.

Section IV
Enterprise Systems:
Implementations and Applications

Chapter XVII
Implementing Best of Breed ERP Systems

Joseph Bradley
University of Idaho, USA

ABSTRACT

ERP implementation projects normally involve a single vendor providing the packaged software for the entire system. Although most companies follow this practice, a significant number of firms employ an alternate strategy of "best of breed" ERP. This strategy involves selecting software that best matches the current or desired business practices of the company from a variety of vendors. This strategy reduces the need for the firm to customize the software or to significantly reengineer its business practices. Best of Breed offers firms the opportunity to maintain or create competitive advantage based on unique business processes. "Vanilla" ERP implementations may result in competitors all adopting the same business processes leaving no firm with an advantage.

INTRODUCTION

In an increasingly competitive global environment, firms are using information technology to increase their competitiveness and gain better information for decision making. Many firms have implemented enterprise resource planning (ERP) systems to further these goals. Enterprise resource planning systems are off-the-shelf software systems, which claim to meet the information needs of organizations. These systems are usually adopted to replace hard to maintain legacy systems developed by IS departments or older off-the-shelf packages that often provided only piecemeal solutions to the organization's information needs. ERP systems evolved in the 1990s from material requirements planning systems (MRP), which was developed in the 1970s, and manufacturing resources planning systems (MRPII), which was developed in the 1980s. ERP systems serve the entire organization, not just material or manufacturing planning. A major advantage of ERP is that it integrates all the information for the entire organization into a single database, thus reducing repetitive data entry and the number of errors.

ERP systems have proven expensive and time consuming to implement. Failed and abandoned projects have been well publicized in the business press. Muscatello and Parente (2006) cite ERP failure rates to be as high as 50%. ERP systems are "expensive and difficult to implement, often imposing their own logic on a company's strategy and existing culture (Pozzebon, 2000, p. 1015)." Hershey Foods, for example, was unable to fill Halloween candy orders after spending $112 million on an ERP project resulting in a drop in its stock price and lost market share (Severance & Passino, 2002). Davenport (1998) identifies other unsuccessful projects such as Fox-Meyer Drug that claimed an ERP systems led to its bankruptcy, Mobil Europe that spent hundreds of millions on ERP but abandoned the project when a merger partner objected and Applied Material that gave up on its ERP project when it became overwhelmed with organizational change issues. Nike's ERP implementation is included in a listing of "infamous failures in IT project management" (Nelson, 2007). Major ERP related inventory problems at Nike resulted in a profit drop of $100 million in the 3rd quarter of 2000.

Most firms utilize a single software vendor for the complete ERP system throughout their organizations. The integrated nature of ERP software favors this single vendor approach. An alternative strategy adopted by some firms is the best of breed approach, where the adopting organization picks and chooses ERP functional modules from the vendor whose software best supports their business processes. Organizations adopting a best of breed believe that this approach will create a better "fit" with existing or required

business processes; reduce or eliminate the need to customize a single vendor solution; and reduce user resistance. Jones and Young (2006) found that 18% of companies surveyed used a best of breed approach to select ERP software packages.

This article examines what ERP implementation projects involve, what the best of breed strategy is, when it is used, what advantage adopting companies seek, examples of best of breed implementations, differences in critical success factors in "vanilla" and best of breed projects, and future trends in the best of breed strategy.

BACKGROUND

ERP implementation projects can be distinguished from other IT projects by three characteristics (Somers, Ragowsky, Nelson, & Stern, 2001). First, ERP systems are "profoundly complex pieces of software, and installing them requires large investments in money, time and expertise (Davenport, 1998, p. 122)." Second, software packages may require the user to change business processes and procedures, may require customization, and leave the firm dependent on a vendor for support and updates (Lucas, Walton, & Ginsberg, 1988). Finally, adopting firms are usually required to reengineer their business processes. Implementation projects must be managed as broad programs of organizational change rather than a software implementation (Markus & Tanis, 2000; Somers et al, 2001)

ERP systems include functionality for basic business processes based on the vendor's interpretation of best practices. However, the selected functionalities do not generally match the existing business processes of all organizations.

Typical ERP functions from SAP R/3, a major ERP vendor, are shown in Table 1. SAP R/3 modules provide a wide range of functional solutions, however, with the wide range of potential ERP customers, some organizations may not be a good fit. With the best of breed strategy, organizations can pick and choose the ERP modules from which ever vendor provides the best fit with its business processes and possibly reduce the amount of reengineering of business processes required, hence reducing the level of employee resistance. The better fit will also reduce or eliminate customizing the software to meet firm requirements.

BEST OF BREED IN INFORMATION SYSTEMS

The term "best of breed" was originally used in information systems literature to describe a situation where individual departments are allowed to install systems which best met their needs rather than a corporate standard.

Software acquisition costs are lower when all departments use the same software systems

because of joint purchase benefits such as volume discounts and other economies of scale. But other costs may offset these savings. Unit document costs may be higher on a single vendor approach compared with best of breed. Cost to translate and reformat data may be excessive. Switching costs may differ depending on the system chosen (Dewan, Seidmann, & Sunderesan, 1995).

BEST OF BREED ERP

ERP vendors design systems, which are "purported to represent best practice and a more competitive business model (Light & Holland, 2001, p. 217)." However, organizations interested in adopting ERP argue that "ERP software functionality is often lacking, the implicit business model does not represent their own and therefore

Table 1. Some functions available in SAP R/3 (Source: Davenport, 1998)

Financials	Operations and Logistics
Accounts receivable and payable	Inventory management
Asset accounting	Material requirements planning
Cash management and forecasting	Plant maintenance
Cost-element and cost-center accounting	Production planning
Executive information systems	Project management
Financial consolidations	Purchasing
General ledger	Quality management
Product-cost accounting	Routing management
Profitability analysis	Shipping
Profit-center accounting	Vendor evaluation
Standard and period-related costing	
Human Resources	**Sales and Marketing**
Human-resources time accounting	Order management
Payroll	Pricing
Personnel planning	Sales management
Travel expenses	Sales planning

reengineering business processes in line with this presents major difficulties (Light & Holland, 2001, p. 217)."

Single vendor packages seem to have strengths in a particular functional area. PeopleSoft is known for exceptional human resource modules and Oracle has a reputation for exceptional financial modules (Light & Holland, 2001).

Best of breed solutions provide an alternative strategy to enable organizations to implement ERP when a single vendor may not provide the functionality that the adopter requires or when modules from different vendors may provide a better match with existing or required business processes than a single vendor solution. Lack of feature-function fit may be due to the design of most ERP for discrete manufacturing. Many organizations have specialized business processes common to their industry that may not be solved by the best practices embedded into single vendor ERP systems. Various modules may not support process manufacturing industries, such as food processing and paper manufacturing, project industries, such as aerospace, or industries that manufacture products with dimensionality, such a clothing or footwear (Markus & Tanis, 2000).

While providing the additional needed functionalities, the best of breed approach complicates integration. With a single vendor ERP system, "the whole package is designed for data compatibility (Grant & Tu, 2005)." With best of breed implementations middleware is usually needed to link the various modules and databases. "The chance of being able to arrive at the same levels of integration as with an ERP system is very low, but this may be worth accepting as a means of saving the cost and pain associated with ERP implementation (Payne, 2002)."

Although most firms select a single vendor, a survey of Fortune 1000 firms found that 18% of the respondents chose ERP packages based on best of breed criteria. 32% of respondents used a combination of packages, such as SAP, People-Soft, Oracle, Baan, JD Edwards, Lawson, Adage, SSA/CT (Jones & Young, 2006).

Although little empirical research has been done on best of breed ERP implementations, the information shown in Table 2 is the result of a single case study of a business referred to as Global Entertainment (Light & Holland, 2001). The best of breed approach clearly gives the adopting organization the ability to determine functionality, rather than accepting a single vendor's determination of best practices. The adopting organization can select packages that best support their existing or desired business processes.

The adoption of a single vendor ERP may cause the loss of competitive advantage. The single vendor software may require the adopting organization to abandon its existing business processes, which may have created competitive advantage for the organization in favor of ERP vendor defined "best practices." The organization's competitors may have also adopted these vendor defined best practices, leaving the organization without a competitive advantage.

The best of breed approach may also spread the risk of the failure of an ERP vendor. If a vendor drops out of the ERP market for any reason, only a part of the system will be affected, not the entire system.

On the negative side, the best of breed approach requires more knowledge and skills in the adopting firm's IT department to support multiple packages. IT staff must be trained to support software from multiple vendors and maintain integration software as packages are upgraded.

Integration of modules from more than one vendor may be time consuming and costly. Upgrades to any of the vendor packages can cause complexities not encountered with a single vendor approach.

EXAMPLES OF BEST OF BREED

Examples of best of breed selection and implementation projects may provide insight into the reasons best of breed remains a viable option for firms selecting ERP systems. Example 1 is a

Table 2. Best of breed vs. single vendor ERP (Source: Adapted from Light, Holland, Wills, 2001)

BEST OF BREED	SINGLE VENDOR ERP
Organization requirements determine functionality	Vendor determines functionality
Context approach to business process reengineering	Clean slate approach to BPR
Good flexibility in process redesign due to choice of components	Limited flexibility on process redesign
Reliance on numerous vendors distributes risk	Single vendor may increase risks
IT department requires multiple skills sets to deal with multiple software sources	Single skills set required in IT
Capabilities may be retained or enhanced with unique combinations of vendor packages and custom components	Distinctive capabilities may be impacted in common business processes throughout industry
Need for flexibility and competitiveness is acknowledged up front	Flexibility and competitiveness may be constrained
Integration of applications may be time consuming, upgrades can be complicated	Integration of applications is pre-coded into system and maintained in upgrades

simple best of breed project with only two vendors. Example 2 represents a more complex best of breed project involving five different vendor packages.

Example 1

This example presents a relatively simple use of a best of breed solution. In 1995, a Houston-based energy services company embarked on a major systems effort. Legacy systems were accounting oriented and provided little operating information. Y2K problems were the catalyst for proceeding with the project.

With extensive help from the consultants on the project, Oracle was selected for the financial part of the new system. Oracle was considerably less expensive than other systems the company considered and the majority owner of the company implemented Oracle several years earlier. The decision was complicated by the lack of an Oracle module to support process manufacturing.

To resolve Oracle's inability at the time to support process manufacturing, the company adopted a process manufacturing package from Datalogix called Global Enterprise Manufacturing Management Systems (GEMMS). The interface

software between Oracle and GEMMS presented many technical implementation problems, which were resolved by the vendors and implementation consultants. While these technical integration problems caused some minor delays, the problems were not a major implementation issue from the point of view of the company.

During the course of the implementation project a risk of the best of breed strategy occurred. Oracle acquired Datalogix in the midst of the project. Instead of helping resolve any problems by consolidating the software in one vendor, the acquisition exacerbated the problem because of a post-acquisition exodus of Datalogix personnel.

The best of breed approach did not significantly contribute to cost over-runs or delays in implementation. Overall, the project is regarded as a success. The problems caused in the integration of the two vendor solutions impacted mainly the software vendors and consultants, although company personnel had to coordinate the parties in reaching solutions. Project success can be attributed to the existence of project champions, extensive training, and use of a project manager with both ERP and project management experience and co-managers with extensive business experience with the company (Bradley, 2005).

Example 2

This example involves three divisions of a major defense contractor based in Southern California. A series of acquisitions had left it with several non-integrated mainframe systems supplemented by PC based point solutions. Prior to the ERP project each division was pursuing different approaches to their information systems needs. One division was in the process of implementing an out of the box Baan ERP system, the second division was using a heavily customized WDS system and the third division had no IT infrastructure. The corporate parent of these divisions wanted a single solution to control costs and leverage its purchasing power on the purchase of the software. This goal was complicated because the divisions had been highly independent of parent control and no single vendor offered a solution, which met the needs of all three divisions. Standard packages failed to meet the needs of the bulk of its business. The parent was faced with balancing the benefits and cost savings of standardization with the flexibility and independence of the divisions.

In 1996, when the project started, no single vendor provided a solution to the company's needs. A joint oversight team from the three divisions selected WDS (now Manugistics) as the core, but incorporated best of breed solutions including PeopleSoft for human resource management, Oracle for financials, TIP QA for quality control, and Matrix One for product data management.

The best of breed approach did not cause significant problems according to the project manager, however, this project was his first ERP implementation, so he had little basis for comparison. The project exceeded the original cost estimate and original time estimate, but was completed within contingency factor allowed in these estimates. The original budget was $14 million with $2 million as a contingency factor. The cost totaled $15.7. The time budget was 24 months with a 6 month contingency. The project was completed in 30 months. The management was satisfied that systems quality and information quality were improved by the project. Users were satisfied that they had better tools to do their jobs (Bradley, 2005).

Example 3

Dell Computer selected a best of breed ERP strategy after struggling for two years implementing SAP R/3 2.2. Dell's strategy change from a worldwide focus to a segmented regional focus demanded more flexibility than the current version of SAP R/3 provided. Dell selected i2 Technologies to manage raw materials throughout the company, Oracle for order management, and Glovia for manufacturing tasks (Stein, 1998).

CRITICAL SUCCESS FACTORS

Identifying and utilizing critical success factors in major IT projects can enhance the probability of success of an implementation project. Bradley (2005) identified and tested ten proposed critical success factors in eight case studies. Sumner and Bradley (2007) examined these same ten proposed critical success factors in ERP implementation in "vanilla" ERP projects and Best of Breed ERP projects. The proposed factors examined in both studies included:

1. IT and business planning integration
2. Full time project manager
3. Reporting level of project manager
4. Experience of the project manager
5. Quality and quantity of training
6. Use of consultants
7. CEO Involvement
8. Champion
9. Management's effectiveness in reducing change resistance
10. Steering committee

Sumner and Bradley (2007) found little difference in these factors between the two strategies. Best of breed projects shared CSFs with vanilla implementations in all areas. The strongest relationship to project success was found in choosing the right full-time project manager, the quality and quantity of employee training and the existence of effective champions.

Sumner and Bradley (2007) identified critical success factors unique to best of breed ERP implementations in a case study of two best of breed implementation projects. These success factors involved building interfaces between the different vendor packages, managing upgrades from different vendors, and managing the cost implications to justify the project in terms of business results. While vendor management is important in all implementation projects, the existence of multiple vendors further complicates this issue and increases its importance in best of breed projects (Bradley, 2005).

ERP ADD-ONS

Practitioners have extended the term best of breed to include add-on applications not included in typical transaction processing ERP systems. These applications include (Leahy, 2004):

- Business performance management tools,
- Sarbanes-Oxley compliance tools,
- Human resource connection tools which provide linkage between performance and compensation,
- Expense management tools to control travel and entertainment expenses
- Portfolio management tools to view IT project risks and returns, and
- Receivables collection/cash flow management tools, many of which are industry specific.

Leahy (2004) predicts that "best-of-breed products will continue to evolve at a rapid clip over the next few years." Although vendor consolidations will continue at a rapid pace, new partnerships and alliances will continue to be formed to develop new applications.

FUTURE TRENDS

The Gartner Group coined the term "ERP II" to describe the shift in ERP from an enterprise information base focusing on back office transaction processing within one organization to moving information across the supply chain ("Taking the Pulse of ERP," 2001). Others refer to this process as "extended" enterprise systems. ERP II or extended enterprise systems include:

- customer relationship management (CRM) applications, which accumulate information to better serve customers,
- supply chain management (SCM) applications which manage materials and services from acquisition to delivery to the customer, and
- e-business applications to enable the organization to reach customers and suppliers over the Internet.

Davenport and Brooks (2004) refer to basic ERP as infrastructural and SCM modules as strategic capabilities, raising the question of "whether to implement the infrastructural capabilities first, strategic capabilities first, or both simultaneously." They believe that while the infrastructural capabilities of ERP "provide very little in the way of real business value...they are critical to long-term internal and external integration." What they lack are short term cost savings and competitive advantage. SCM and other extended enterprise systems modules is where the pay off is in terms of competitive advantage.

Best of breed terminology, while originally used for ERP software, is also applied to ERP II software. Major ERP vendors have concentrated on the transaction processing or back office procedures in ERP. Independent vendors have concentrated on the add-ons that constitute ERP II. Davenport and Brooks (2004) point out that this situation is changing. Mainstream ERP vendors are adding SCM and other functionalities to their packages, avoiding some of the integration issues. But smaller vendors "have the edge in state-of-the-art functionality (Davenport et al, 2004)." These smaller vendors are willing to explore clients' needs and find markets. Van Decker of the Meta Group believes that stand-alone software providers "can develop new products and bring those products to market faster than ERPs" (Leahy, 2004, p. 1). Greenbaum, a consultant with Enterprise Applications Consulting, observes that "vendors have been forced by customers to open up their technology to allow easier integration…as a result they've actually expanded the best-of-breed market. (Westervelt, 2003, p. 1)." These observations seem to predict that the best of breed strategy will continue to be a viable strategy choice for both ERP and ERP II.

Service-oriented architecture (SOA) may add some of the features of best of breed with the concept of modularity and can be web-based. SOA builds a set of business processes from smaller modules called services. A service may be as simple as viewing an online account statement or more complex like "check credit" (Koch, 2005). Services are strung together to create business process functionality. Services may include legacy systems or other vendor's ERP processes in almost any programming language.

The SOAs add complexity to enterprise software. SOAs become additional layers of code superimposed on the existing layers of software. The concept of reusable code may work for small tasks, but as the services performed become more complex, the concept of reusability becomes more difficult. When processes fail, the recovery task

may become more difficult with multiple software layers (Rettig, 2007).

CONCLUSION

Both single vendor and best of breed enterprise systems are complex and present a wide range of implementation problems. The single vendor approach provides high levels of integration, but may require high levels of business process reengineering. Adopting the best practices for business processes defined by a single vendor may lead to competitors adopting the same business practices. With all firms employing the same business processes, no firm would enjoy a competitive advantage by providing superior business processes. Competitive advantage can stem from the application of business processes that are superior to competitors.

The best of breed strategy will continue to be a viable option in both ERP and ERP II for organizations which attempt to create competitive advantage by assembling a "custom" ERP system to support their business processes rather than adopting the same off-the-shelf, "vanilla" ERP systems adopted by their competitors. While most adopting organizations will stick with the full integration of a single vendor package, firms willing to take risks to obtain competitive advantage will assemble a best of breed solution which enhances their ability to serve their customers.

Example 1 demonstrates how a best of breed strategy can compensate for the lack of a desired functionality in one vendor's package by supplementing it with a second package. Example 2 shows how the strategy can blend together the diverse needs of three operating divisions to arrive at a solution acceptable to all parties using software from five different vendors. Example 3 demonstrates that changes in business strategy may require more flexibility than can be provided in standard ERP packages. The technical challenges presented by the best of breed option did not seriously hamper any of these implementation projects.

Both implementation strategies will continue to be complex and costly. Best of breed may provide an avenue to reduce the reengineering required at the cost of increased integration problems. The single vendor approach may result in more reengineering of business processes but avoids the integration issues.

The best of breed implementation strategy is an area of ERP systems that has not been fully explored. More research of this promising alternative implementation strategy is needed. Future research is needed in the best of breed area:

- What will be the effect of vendor consolidation? Oracle has purchased PeopleSoft and J. D. Edwards. Will this consolidation continue, limiting the choices for companies seeking the best of breed option? Will new stand alone vendors continue to develop leading edge products? How fast will major ERP suppliers move into niche markets enjoyed by the stand-alone vendors?
- Can best of breed be more effective in providing competitive advantage than vanilla ERP? If every competitor adopts business processes from vanilla ERP packages, can any firm have a competitive advantage?
- How will ERP II change the best of breed market?
- Does best of breed reduce user resistance?
- What is the return on investment of best of breed ERP versus vanilla ERP?
- Does standardization of processes globally make sense in light of cultural differences, economic differences, and business practice differences?
- Will service-oriented architecture become the method of choice to serve unique business processes in ERP environments?

REFERENCES

Bradley, J. (2005). Are All Critical Success Factors Created Equal? *Proceedings of Eleventh Americas' Conference on Information Systems*, Omaha, NE, August 11-14, 2005, pp. 2152-2159

Davenport, T. H. (1998). Putting the Enterprise into the Enterprise System. *Harvard Business Review, 76*(4, July-August), 121-131.

Davenport, T. H., & Brooks, J. D. (2004). Enterprise Systems and the Supply Chain. *Journal of Enterprise Information Management, 17*(1), 8-19.

Dewan, R., Seidmann, A., & Sunderesan, S. (1995). *Strategic Choices in IS Infrastructure: Corporate Standards versus "Best of breed" Systems.* Paper presented at the ICIS, Amsterdam.

Gelinas, S., & Fedorowicz (2004). Business Processes and Information Technology. USA : Thomson-South-western.

Goodhue, D. L., Wixon, B. H., & Watson, H. J. (2002, June). Realizing business benefits through CRM: Hitting the right target in the right way. *MIS Quarterly Executive*, 1(2), 79-94

Grant, D., & Tu, Q. (2005). Levels of Enterprise Integration: Study Using Case Analysis. *International Journal of Enterprise Information Systems, 1*(1), 1-22.

Jones, M. C., & Young, R. (2006). ERP Usage in Practice. *Information Resources Management Journal, 19*(1), 23-42.

Koch, C. (2005). A New Blueprint for the Enterprise, CIO Magazine, 18(10), 1-7.

Kos, A. J., Sockel, H. M., & Falk, L. K. (2001, Jan-Mar). Customer relationship management opportunities. *The Ohio CPA Journal*, 55-57.

Leahy, T. (2004). Best-of-Breed Software, Business Finance, July 2004. Downloaded from http://www.businessfinancemag.com/magazine/archives/article.html?articleID=14251

Light, B., & Holland, C. P. (2001). ERP and best of breed: A comparative analysis. *Business Process Management Journal, 7*(3), 216-224.

Lucas Jr., H. C., Walton, E. J., & Ginsberg, M. J. (1988). Implementing Packaged Software. *MIS Quarterly*(December 1988), 537-549.

MacLeod, M. (2002). ERP or best of breed? *Fulfulment & e-Logistics Magazine*, June 2002.

Markus, M. L., & Tanis, C. (2000). The Enterprise Experience - From Adoption to Success. In R. W. Zmud (Ed.), *Framing the Domains of IT Research: Projecting the Future Through the Past*. Cincinnati, OH: Pinnaflex Educational Resources, Inc.

Muscatello, J. R., & Parente, D. H. (2006). Enterprise Resource Planning (ERP): A Postimplementation Cross-Case Analysis. *Information Resources Management Journal, 19*(3), 61-80.

Nelson, R.R. (2007). IT Project Management: Infamous Failures, Classic Mistakes and Best Practices. *MIS Quarterly Executive, 6*(2), 67-78.

OASIS (2008). OASIS Committees by Category: SOA, downloaded from http://www.oasis-open.org/committees/tc_cat.php?cat=soa on 2/12/08.

Palaniswamy, R. & Frank, T. (2000). Enhancing Manufacturing Performance with ERP Systems. *Information Systems Management*, Summer, 43-55.

Pan, S. L. (2005). Customer Perspective of CRM Systems: A Focus Group Study. *International Journal of Enterprise Information Systems, 1*(1), 65-88.

Payne, W. (2002). The time for ERP? *Work Study, 51*(2/3), 91-93.

Peppers, D. & Rogers, M. (1993). The one to one future. New York: Doubleday.

Pozzebon, M. (2000). *Combining a Structuration Approach with a Behavioral-Based Model to Investigate ERP Usage*. Paper presented at the AMCIS 2000, Long Beach, CA.

Parvatiyar, A., & Sheth, J. N. (2001). Conceptual Framework of Customer Relationship Management. In Customer Relationship Management-Emerging Concepts, Tools and Publications. Sheth, J.N., Parvatiyar, A. and Shainesh, G., eds. New Delhi, India, Tata/McGraw-Hill, 3-25.

Rettig, C. (2007). The Trouble with Enterprise Software. *MIT Sloan Management Review, 49*(1), 21-27.

Severance, D. G., & Passino, J. (2002). *Making I/T Work*. San Francisco: Jossey-Bass

Somers, T. M., Ragowsky, A. A., Nelson, K. G., & Stern, M. (2001). *Exploring Critical Success Factors across the Enterprise Systems Experience Cycle: An Empirical Study* (Working Paper). Detroit, Michigan: Wayne State University.

Sumner, M., & Bradley, J. (2007). Critical Success Factors in Best of Breed ERP Implementation. In M. Khosrow-Pour (ed.), *Managing Worldwide Operations and Communications with Information Technology*, (pp. 526-529). Hershey, PA: IGI Global.

Stein, T. (1998), Dell Takes 'Best-of-Breed' Approach in ERP Strategy. Information Week on Line, News in Review, May 11, 1998. Downloaded 6/6/2007 from http://www.informationweek.com/681/81iuerp.htm

Taking the Pulse of ERP. (2001, February 2001). *Modern Materials Handling*, 44-51.

Westervelt, R., (2003, August 20). Debating ERP and best-of-breed, SAP News. Downloaded 6/6/08 from http://searchsap.techtarget.com/originalContent/0,289142,sid21_gci920428,00.html

Winer, R. S. (2001). A framework for customer relationship management. *California Management Review*, 43(4), 89-105.

KEY TERMS

Best of Breed: Combination of ERP software provided by more than one vendor and legacy systems designed to meet the needs of an organization in a manner superior to the single vendor ERP approach.

Business Processes: "A business process is a set of business events that together enable the creation and delivery of an organization's products or services to its customers (Gelinas et al, 2004)."

Customer Relationship Management (CRM): These are software packages that enable a business to develop knowledge of their customer's needs and buying patterns. These systems "focus on the integration of externally based customer data for the organization to pursue more customer-oriented activities like targeted advertising, one-on-one marketing (Peppers et al., 1993), customer retention and building a real-time integrated view of the customer (Goodhue et al., 2002; Kos et al., 2001; Winer, 2001)" (Pan, 2005, p. 66). Another definition is "a comprehensive strategy and process of acquiring, retaining and partnering with selective customers to create superior value for the company and customers" (Parvatiyar and Sheth, 2001, p. 5).

Enterprise Resource Planning Systems (ERP): An off-the-shelf accounting-oriented information system that is designed to meet the information needs of most organizations. ERP systems enable organization to procure, process and deliver customer goods or services in a timely, predictable manner. These systems are complex and expensive information tools, which have proven difficult and time consuming to implement.

ERP II or Extended Enterprise Systems: ERP II opens ERP systems beyond the enterprise level to exchange information with supply chain partners and customers. ERP II extends beyond the four-walls of the business to trading partners. Typically, ERP II includes customer relationship management (CRM) packages, supply chain management (SCM) packages and e-business packages.

Integration: Integration is generally defined as "the bringing together of related components to form a unified whole...The primary concern of integration is 'oneness' and 'harmony' between user, technology, and the environment (Grant & Tu, 2005, p.8)." Grant & Tu propose a taxonomy of ERP integration ranging from the lowest level, system-specification integration, to global integration which deals with "issues of language, time difference, culture, politics, customs, management style." Their proposed level-II deals with system-user integration at both the ergonomic and cognitive level. Level-III deals with integration of islands of technology throughout the firm.

Legacy Systems: Transaction processing systems designed to perform specific tasks. Systems that have become outdated as business needs change and the hardware and software available in the market place have improved.

Material Requirements Planning Systems (MRP). Processes that use bills of materials, inventory data and a master productions schedule to time phase material requirement, releasing inventory purchases in a manner that reduces inventory investment yet meets customer requirements.

Manufacturing Resources Planning (MRPII): MRPII extends MRP by addressing all resources in addition to inventory. MRPII links material requirements planning with capacity requirements planning avoiding the over and under shop loading typical with MRP. MRPII includes more business functionality than MRP, dealing with sales, production, inventory, schedules, and cash flows (Palaniswamy & Frank, 2000)

Service-Oriented Architecture (SOA):
Service Oriented Architecture (SOA) represents a collection of best practices principles and patterns related to service-aware, enterprise-level, distributed computing (OASIS, 2008).

Supply Chain Management (SCM): These software packages exchange information with supply chain partners to order and track the procurement of goods and services. SCM can be viewed in four basic categories (Davenport & Brooks, 2004): supply planning tools; demand planning tools; plant scheduling tools; and logistics systems. A newer functionality in SCM is collaborative planning, forecasting, and replenishment (CPFR). In CPFR, "supply chain partners exchange not only orders and shipment notices, but sales plans and production forecasts with each other, so that they can synchronize their respective processes more fully (p. 12)."

Chapter XVIII
Enterprise Resource Systems Software Implementation

Ganesh Vaidyanathan
Indiana University, USA

ABSTRACT

Enterprise resource planning systems are complex yet single, integrated software programs that runs off a single database so that the various departments can easily share information and communicate with each other. The integrated approach can have a tremendous payback if companies implement the software correctly. This chapter illustrates the implementation steps as followed by major corporations in the United States, and provide an insight into the practical implementation issues. A business case for such systems is introduced in this chapter as well. The chapter provides seven ERP issues and elaborates these issues in the context of implementation. The implementation details during conceptualization, design, implementation, go-live, and operation stages are provided with a note to practitioners on ERP implementation.

INTRODUCTION

Enterprise resource planning (ERP) software attempts to integrate all departments and functions across a company onto a single computer system that can serve all those different departments' particular needs (Koch 2002). Each of those departments typically has its own computer system optimized for the particular way that the department does its work. But ERP combines them all together into a single, integrated software program that runs off a single database so that the various departments can more easily share information and communicate with each other. That integrated approach can have a tremendous payback if companies install the software correctly.

Typically, when a customer places an order, that order begins a mostly paper-based journey from in-basket to in-basket around the company, often being keyed and re-keyed into different departments' computer systems along the way. These activities cause delays and errors. Meanwhile, no one in the company truly knows what the status of the order is at any given point because there is no way for the finance department, for example, to get into the warehouse's computer system to see whether the item has been shipped. ERP can replace the old standalone computer systems in accounting, human resources, manufacturing, and warehouse with single unified software. This results in integrated software that is linked together so that someone in finance can look into the warehouse module to see if an order has been shipped. Most vendors' ERP software is flexible enough to install certain modules without buying the whole package.

Enterprise systems that encompass all departmental processes can often be complex and interdependent. Highly interdependent technology solutions such as ERP are used by firms to enhance the efficiency and ease of in-house capabilities. The use of ERP is characterized by high levels of task interdependence (Sharma and Yetton 2003). To implement such highly complex and interdependent systems is often a daunting process. Implementing an enterprise-wide application like an ERP system to help run a business is a costly and complex process and is like implementing a civil engineering endeavor or sizable construction project (Hawksworth 2007). A certain amount of planning, discipline and wisdom are required to complete implementation on schedule to meet the requirements of a firm.

Many of the current ERP literature share implementation experiences from various companies. While some of them attempt to explain why the ERP implementation is difficult and what needs to be done to achieve desirable results, others present various models of implementation stages and different implementation methodologies (Moon, 2007). The contributions of this chapter to researchers and practitioners include:

a. Illustration of the implementation steps as followed by major corporations in the United States, and
b. Provision of an insight into the practical implementation issues, and
c. Introduction to a business case for ERP systems.

This chapter details the implementation issues of ERP systems and provides an insight into the practical aspects of such implementation. The next section provides seven ERP issues and elaborates these issues in the context of implementation. The following section describes ERP software and the ERP implementation scheme during conceptualization, design, implementation, go-live, and operation stages of implementation. The chapter concludes with a note to practitioners on ERP implementation.

WHAT CAN ERP DO?

ERP is an enterprise software package. With ERP, it is possible to keep track any transaction in an enterprise in real-time. ERP allows managers to process business information more effectively to support sound decision making. ERP solutions cover all of the core operations necessary to run successful small and midsize businesses, including accounting and banking, customer and vendor management, purchasing and sales, logistics and production, as well as reporting and analysis.

The benefits of ERP systems have been researched extensively in literature. Gefen and Ragowsky (2007) examined associations between the business characteristics of manufacturing firms and their perceived benefits from ERP system investments at both enterprise and a specific IT module level and found that the perceived value for ERP investments was consistently better explained at the specific IT module level. Ranganathan and Brown (2006) found that ERP projects with greater functional scope (two or more value-chain modules) or greater physical scope (multiple sites) result in positive, higher shareholder returns. ERP systems replace complex and sometimes manual interfaces between different systems with standardized, cross-functional transaction automation (Hendricks et al., 2005). Information integration using ERP can replace functionally oriented and often poorly connected legacy software, resulting in savings in infrastructure support costs (Hendricks et al., 2005). Other business benefits include:

- **Improved productivity:** ERP engages and connects users within and beyond the enterprise, including customers, suppliers, and partners. An intuitive, role-based portal environment gives the system wide access to a single, consistent view of the business. Higher levels of efficiency and collaboration may be achieved and as a result firms can respond to new competitive threats, and proactively meet customer needs.
- **Increased insight:** ERP improves decision-making by giving managers a clear understanding of activities across functions. They can retrieve the right information at the right time to address problems and pursue new opportunities.
- **Enhanced governance:** ERP provides comprehensive functionality for corporate governance, enabling the firm to comply with Sarbanes-Oxley and International Accounting Standards. ERP also integrates corporate reporting, analysis, and compliance with underlying business processes and transaction systems.
- **Improved flexibility:** ERP provides a scalable and adaptable solution that seamlessly integrates end-to-end processes with the ability to add other external solutions that may include customer relationship management, supply chain management, and product life-cycle management.

- **Reduced costs:** ERP enables firms to manage IT costs by leveraging the investments they have already made.
- **Increased visibility:** ERP solutions provide real-time visibility across the entire enterprise, so firms can streamline their supply chain, bring products to market faster, get more out of procurement, and eliminate duplication of effort.

ERP IMPLEMENTATION ISSUES

Companies that install ERP do not have an easy time of it. To implement ERP right, the ways that they do business need to change and the ways people do their jobs need to change too. And that kind of change does not come without pain. The important thing is not to focus on how long it will take but rather to understand why the firms need ERP and how they will use it to improve their business.

Cost

Meta Group recently did a study looking at the total cost of ownership (TCO) of ERP, including hardware, software, professional services and internal staff costs. The TCO numbers include getting the software installed and the two years afterward, which is when the real costs of maintaining, upgrading and optimizing the system for business are felt. Among the 63 companies surveyed (Ketbi et al. 2002)—including small, medium and large companies in a range of industries—the average TCO was $15 million (the highest was $300 million and lowest was $400,000). The nature of ERP implementations are such that there are usually unforeseen and unexpected occurrences that increase the overall costs (Al-Mudimigh et al., 2001). In summary, the cost of implementing ERP remains quite high (Wu et al., 2007).

Schedule

The criticality of schedule and budget overruns as risk factors in ERP implementation projects has been rated to be high by all companies regardless of their size (Laukkanen, 2007). The time and effort to implement is likely to be underestimated in the case of implementing ERP systems. ERP systems come in modules and do not have to be implemented entirely at one time; many companies follow a phase-in approach in which one module is implemented at a time. Some of the most commonly installed modules are sales and distribution (SD), materials management (MM), production and planning, (PP), and finance and controlling (FI) modules. The average length of time for a "typical" implementation is more than a year and can use more than 150 consultants. Corning, Inc. rolled out ERP in ten of its diversified manufacturing divisions in five to eight years (Stedman 1998). The length of implementation is affected to a great extent by the number of modules being implemented, the scope of the implementation (different functional units or across multiple units spread out globally), the extent of customization, and the number of interfaces with other applications.

Customization

ERP packages are very general in nature and need to be configured to a specific type of business. The customization is very tedious and takes a long time, depending on the specific requirements of the business. Customized development can provide a better fit with the operational procedures of a firm, yet often results in a system that is more risky to implement and more complicated to maintain and upgrade (Gebauer and Lee, 2008). An ERP system like SAP is so complex and general that there are more than 8000 switches that need to be set properly to make it handle the business processes in a way a company needs. The more customization needed, the longer it will take to roll

out the software and the more it will cost to keep it up-to-date. The length of implementation time could be cut down by keeping the system "plain vanilla" and reducing the number of "bolt-on" application packages that require custom interfaces with the ERP system. However, the downside to this "plain vanilla" approach may or may not completely match business requirements.

Some companies undertake costly customizations to automate its processes on its ERP system—only to learn that the "plain-vanilla" version of the software performed certain functions much better. Companies even pull the plug partway into an ERP project because of functional or even philosophical problems. A technological mistake often made in SAP implementations, says Graham McFarlane, director of Western Management Consultants, is that organizations modify the software more than they should, rather than modifying their business processes (Hilson, 2001). The Military Sealift Command (MSC) successfully implemented Oracle's ERP solution. One rule they cite for achieving ERP success is that agencies must find an ERP package that mirrors their business practices as closely as possible, then resolve to implement the package without significant modifications. MSC managers made a key decision to minimize the risk of ERP implementation by taking a "vanilla" approach. They committed to installing the software as it was packaged, without any modifications. The MSC put together 1,000 requirements the optimal software would fulfill. There were only 11 areas where their processes didn't match the software and the commander made the decision to modify MSC processes to fit the Oracle software (Dean, 2001).

Management Commitment

Management commitment for information systems (IS) projects has been researched extensively (Aloini et al., 2007, Aladwani 2002, Ravichandran and Rai 2000). They found empirically that management commitment this work can make human, monetary, and other important resources available for the IS project leading to a conducive and superior problem solving environment as well as increase the likelihood of IS product quality and efficiency. Top management must consider the strategic implications of implementing an ERP solution (Davenport 1998). Management must also ask several questions before embarking on the project. Does the ERP system strengthen the company's competitive position? How might it erode the company's competitive position? How does ERP affect the organizational structure and the culture? What is the scope of the ERP implementation -- only a few functional units or the entire organization? Are there any alternatives that meet the company's needs better than an ERP system? If it is a multinational corporation, the management should be concerned about whether it would be better to roll the system out globally or restrict it to certain regional units? Management must be involved in every step of the ERP implementation. Handing over the ERP project to the IS department may result as a risk to the entire company's survival because of the ERP system's profound business implications. The top management must not only fund the project but also take an active role in leading the change. The success of a major project like an ERP implementation completely hinges on the strong, sustained commitment of top management. This commitment when percolated down through the organizational levels results in an overall organizational commitment. An overall organizational commitment that is very visible, well defined, and felt is a sure way to ensure a successful implementation (Bingi et al., 1999).

Integration

The system integration between existing information systems and ERP system is a technical problem which might complicate the entire ERP project (Liang and Lien, 2007). Firms have amassed multiple software that are either legacy systems or current add-ons. Different functions of the company have bought or developed different applications and are used to the software. Figure 1 illustrates before and after ERP implementation software integration in a business. Various functions of the firm and possible software associated with each one of the functions and how ERP can be integrated with some of the software are shown in the figure. Some of this software can be replaced by the newly proposed system and some of them can be integrated into the software. The databases (DB) of individual software, for instance product data management (PDM) database, can be integrated with ERP database as well. In this case, ERP serves as a backbone, and all the different software are bolted on to the ERP software. There is third-party software, middleware, which can be used to integrate software applications from several vendors to the ERP backbone. Middleware vendors concentrate only on the most popular packaged applications and tend to focus on the technical aspects of application interoperability rather than linking business processes. Many times, organizations have to develop their own interfaces for commercial software applications and the homegrown applications. Integration software also poses other kinds of problems when it comes to maintenance. It is a nightmare for information systems group to manage this software whenever there are changes and upgrades to either ERP software or other software that is integrated with the ERP system.

Until the end of 1996, for example, Dell Computer Corp. planned to roll out SAP's full R/3 suite, but it stopped after implementing only the HR modules. Jerry Gregoire, who joined the company as CIO that year, saw that a single software monolith would not be able to keep pace with Dell's extraordinary corporate growth—the company grows by a billion dollars every six to eight weeks. Instead Gregoire designed a flexible middleware architecture to allow the company to add or subtract applications quickly and selected software from a variety of vendors, including Glovia International LLC, to handle finance and manufacturing functions (Slater, 1999).

Reengineering

Reengineering existing business processes to the best business process standard is one of the activities in ERP implementation. ERP systems are process oriented; therefore only in a process-based organization they can completely express their integration potentiality (Guido and Pierluigi, 2008). ERP systems are built on best practices that are followed in the industry. One major benefit of ERP comes from reengineering the company's existing way of doing business. In this case, all the processes in a company conform to the ERP software and as a result the cost and benefits of aligning these processes with an ERP model could be very high. Since ERP systems such as SAP were built on a foundation of process best practices, it is probably easier and less expensive to change processes to adapt to SAP than the other way around. Many companies have reported good success from combining a SAP implementation with a reengineering project (Bingi et al., 1999).

The concept of reengineering traces its origins back to management theories developed as early as the nineteenth century. The purpose of reen-

gineering is to make all of a firm's processes the best-in-class. In reengineering, there is one best way to conduct tasks.

Initiatives like Business Process Reengineering (BPR) and ERP promise radical improvements in relatively short periods of time. Processes, organization, structure and information technologies are the key components of reengineering. In implementing ERP, both business processes and information technology are combined into integrated software. This automates business processes across the enterprise and provides an organization with a well designed and managed information system. Companies like IBM, Texas Instruments, American Express, Johnson & Johnson, Chrysler, Ford, Shell oil and many others have achieved major reengineering successes. Many organizations have successfully implemented ERP systems and reported huge benefits. Yet many research studies estimate that at least 90 % of ERP implementations end up late or over budget and several failure stories are cited (Jarrar et al., 2000).

Consultants and Other Resources

Consultants are most often used as implementation partners at two to ten times the cost of the ERP software for the initial implementation (Karimi

Figure 1. Integrated ERP software in a firm

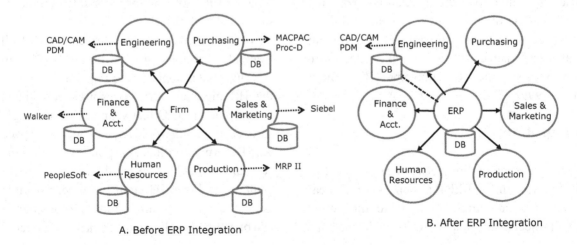

et al., 2007). The client, the management, must be involved in the consulting recruitment process. Simply trusting the consulting firm or not understanding what the consultants know is a risk. The more layers between the project manager and consulting company, the more the consultant's rates are reduced means that the consultants are willing to work for the lower rate and are usually the least knowledgeable.

SAP: ERP SOFTWARE

SAP the company was founded in Germany in 1972 by five ex-IBM engineers. SAP stands *for Systeme, Andwendungen, Produkte in der Daten- verarbeitung* which - translated to English - means *Systems, Applications, Products in Data Process- ing*. SAP AG is now the third largest software maker in the world, with over 17,500 customers (including more than half of the world's 500 top companies). There are more than 50,000 instal- lations of SAP, in over 120 countries, with more then 10 million users! SAP today is available in 46 country-specific versions, incorporating 28 languages including Kanji and other double-byte character languages. SAP R/3 is delivered to a customer with selected standard process turned on, and many other optional processes and features

turned off. At the heart of SAP are about 10,000 tables which control the way the processes are executed. Configuration is the process of adjusting the settings of these tables to get SAP to run the way companies want it to. Functionality included is truly enterprise wide including: Financial Ac- counting (e.g. general ledger, accounts receivable etc), Management Accounting (e.g. cost centers, profitability analysis etc), Sales, Distribution, Manufacturing, Production Planning, Purchasing, Human Resources, Payroll, etc.

SAP is an integrated client/server software ap- plication. The features of SAP are as follows:

- Centralized database (ORACLE)
- Planning functions like Material Resource Planning
- Reporting functions
- Business workflow to simulate the busi- ness
- Development workbench that uses a lan- guage called ABAP (Advanced Business Application Programming)
- Implement Management Guide (IMG) used to configure the system
- An integration of finance, accounting, pro- duction planning, logistics, sales, material management, plant maintenance, human resources, etc.

Figure 2. SAP table structure

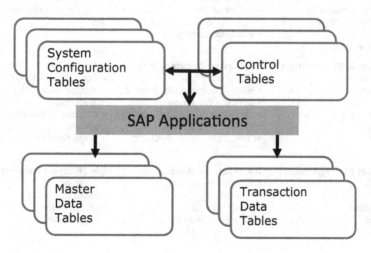

SAP Database

The SAP repository or the data dictionary serves primarily as a tool to enter, manage, delete and evaluate company information. The rules for structuring this information are consistent with the concepts of the relational data model using tables and fields. The data repository is active at all times and therefore the information is always up-to-date and available to all authorized users at all times. The SAP repository is built on a table structure. A database most often contains one or more tables. Each table is identified by a name (e.g. "Customers" or "Orders"). Tables contain records (rows) with data. As shown the Figure 2, there are four different tables for configuration, control, master data and transaction data. System configuration tables are tables that define the structure of a system. An example of this type of table is one that defines the peripherals such as printers. To customize the system, the other three tables are used. Control tables define functions that guide the users their activities. For example, a control table might be designed such that a material master data is entered before a

purchase order is accepted. Control tables contain the structure or the process of the company. These tables contain data such as which plants are related which products, which sales organizations are related which products, etc. Master data tables define customers, vendors, materials, equipment, etc. Customer master data might include customer name, address, contact information, etc. This table might also be related to other tables that represent the location of warehouse or repair shops that support the customer. Transaction data table represents the daily operations data such as sales orders, invoices and shipments. SAP modules are shown in Figure 3.

Business Case for ERP Implementation: IT Strategy

Companies implement ERP for many reasons. Y2K (Year 2000) was a costly fix for many companies and many of them resorted to ERP as a strategy as an easy, less costly to fix the Y2K problem. However, these companies found out that the reality was that ERP takes more time, more difficult to install, and cost as much if not

Figure 3. SAP modules

FI (Financial Accounting)	CO (Controlling)	MM (Materials Management)
• General ledger	• Cost elements	• Requisitions
• Book close	• Cost centers	• Purchase orders
• Tax	• Profit centers	• Goods receipts
• Accounts receivable	• Internal orders	• Inventory management
• Accounts payable	• Activity based costing	• BOMs
• Consolidation	• Product costing	
• Special ledgers		
SD (Sales & Distribution)	**CA (Cross Applications)**	**PP (Production Planning)**
• RFQ	• WF – workflow	• Capacity planning
• Sales orders	• BW – business warehouse	• Master production
• Pricing	• Office – for email	scheduling
• Picking	• Workplace	• Material requirements
• Packing	• Industry solutions	planning
• Shipping	•CRM, PLM, SRM, APO etc	• Shop floor
AM (Asset Management)	**HR (Human Resources)**	**QM (Human Resources)**
• Purchase	• Employment history	• Planning
•Sale	• Payroll	• Execution
•Depreciation	• Training	• Inspections
•Tracking	• Career management	• Certificates
	• Succession planning	

more. As a result of the cost and time involved with the ERP implementation, a business case is needed. The thought process of IT department in many of the organizations can be generalized as below in Figure 4 (Norris et al. 1998). Figure 4 shows the four main components in this thought process. Information is gathered to be consumed and this information is managed by applications. The applications have to be created and managed by technology. Technology has to be managed by IT organization with its roles and responsibilities, and governance. As Norris et al. (1998) points out IT organizations need to answer the following questions on information:

1. What is the information?
2. Where does this information come from?
3. How do we create information from data?
4. How does information get distributed?
5. How does information get consumed?

The answers the above questions lead to the software applications. This is the level that users of IT and developers of IT deal with most of the time. Here the following questions need to be answered:

1. What applications does the company currently use to collect, collate, compute, and transform to useful information, store,

distribute, and retrieve data?
2. Is there a better application software available to carry out these tasks in a more efficient, less time-consuming, less resource-consuming and less expensive way?
3. Is there software available as Complete-Off-The-Shelf (COTS)?
4. By using this software, could the company redirect resources into other areas of the business in which it can establish and maintain competitive advantage?

Then the decision on hardware begins especially on technology platforms, techniques, servers, tools, etc. Each company has a different perspective on each one of these objects. For example, SAP is platform independent and has as a company provided an open-architecture presence which is an advantage for corporations. Finally, the questions to be answered for the IT organization are as follows:

1. What management principles will govern IT organization?
2. What processes for system development, operations, support and maintenance are used?
3. What are the roles and responsibilities of all the individuals in the organization?

Figure 4. IT thought process in a company (Adapted from Norris et al., 1998)

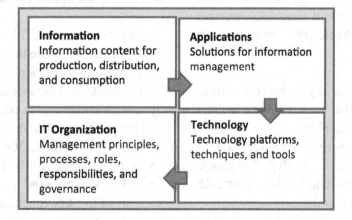

4. What is the relationship as in power structure between the IT organization and the business units?

This thought process need to be followed before the implementation of SAP which will ensure smooth implementation. Once an IT strategy has been developed, and once an ERP solution is determined to be right, a company is ready to build a business case. Business case involves analysis of cost and benefits and determining the payback period for the expenses incurred for the implementation and getting the approvals from leadership.

Norris et al. (1998) shows how the complexity of the implementation, as well as the project risk and cost, increases as a company moves out on the continuum of the degree of business process change and up along the continuum of organizational change. As the level of business process change is increased, the level of organizational change necessary to carry it out must also increase. The key to successful implementation is assertive control over the project's scope and over the degree of business process changes to be undertaken. Clear objectives and justification (Weston, 2001), evaluation and selection (Van Everdingen et al., 2000), alignment between the ERP package and business strategies and requirements (Somers and Nelson, 2003) as part of the business case are critical to the success of implementation. To build a cost-based business case for ERP, firms need to extract savings that depend on ERP alone from the total savings to be had from ERP together with other sources. Wagle (1998) proposed five steps that include:

1. Create a base case of year-by-year savings from cost cuts that could be made without the ERP system in place.
2. Create an ERP case of year-by-year savings that could be made with ERP. This should include savings that do not depend on ERP as well as those that do.

3. Subtract the base-case savings (step 1) from the ERP-case savings (step 2) on a year-by-year basis, and calculate the net present value (NPV) of the residual cash flow. A positive NPV will indicate that the firm should probably proceed with the deployment of ERP.
4. If step 3 produces a positive NPV, conduct a sensitivity analysis to ensure that the business case is strong enough to withstand slippage and cost overruns.
5. Back-allocate all ERP system deployment costs to individual business units so that they can factor them into their planning. Ensure each unit is held responsible for producing the promised savings.

To summarize, the following factors need to be considered for the business case:

1. The decision must be driven by the business considerations, not merely the desire for new technology
2. Firms need to extract savings that depend on ERP alone from the total savings to be had from ERP together with other sources
3. ERP system will not solve business process and organizational dynamic problems.
4. ERP implementation cannot be delayed until the company is able to use to its fullest ability.

SAP IMPLEMENTATION STEPS

Botta-Genoulaz et al. (2005) in their survey of research literature note that recent research is on ERP post-implementation issues, customization of ERP projects, and the sociological issues of ERP systems, and return on investment of ERP systems. Implementation should depend on the size of the company (Mabert et al., 2003) and industrial sector (Wu and Wang, 2003). The roadmap to ERP or SAP is shown in the figure 5. The roadmap consists of five key functions that include:

- Project Preparation
- Business Blueprint
- Realization
- Final Preparation
- Go Live and Support

Each one of these functionalities has various steps. The following figure shows the implementation steps for enterprise software. The design and implementation phase consists of the following functionalities:

- Establishing hardware and SAP settings
- Establishing the key master data
- Establishing the processes and functions inside the organization
- Implementing Reports, Interfaces, Conversions and Enhancements (RICE)
- Testing the system
- Training the users
- Go-Live
- Post production maintenance and support

The reason that ERP system implementations are time-consuming and costly is because of the complex nature of the implementation and the dynamics of the implementation involving with the organization. The basic functionalities described above may be expanded and is shown in Table 1.

Project Preparation

The purpose of this activity is to start detailed planning for the project. There are many basic issues to resolve at this early stage to ensure the project's success. The principal elements that determine how the ERP project is accomplished will be established in this phase. These activities set the groundwork for project kickoff, and provide a baseline of information to be referenced throughout the implementation. For all project team members to operate in an effective manner, it is necessary that project standards and procedures are established at the beginning of the project, and then communicated to all team members. Project planning is an ongoing cycle and should be constantly refined. Even when the project plan is created, it must be made clear that

Figure 5. SAP implementation roadmap

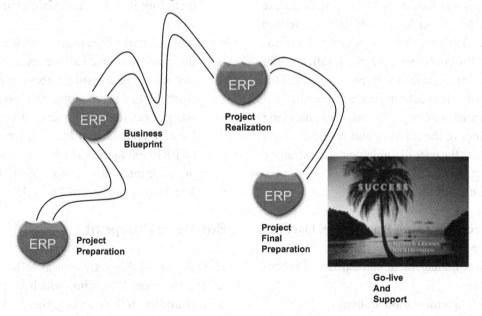

Figure 6. SAP implementation model

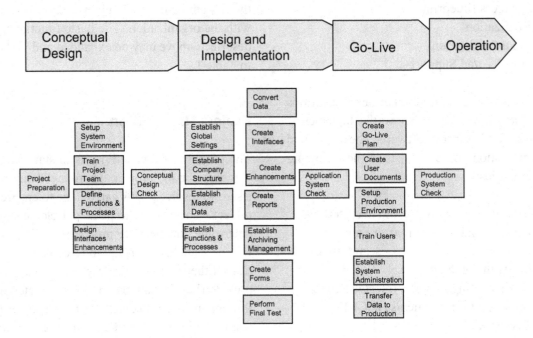

project planning is a continual, rolling process. As the project progresses, fewer revisions are necessary. In the SAP Business-to-Business Procurement system, requirement coverage requests for non-production materials or services are directly processed further, and purchase orders are placed. If data is missing for purchase orders, the Materials Management functions are used to complete them. The follow-on documents for the purchase orders are also created in the SAP Business-to-Business Procurement system (confirmation, goods receipt / service entry and invoice). This phase also includes defining end user training and documentation strategy. This includes analyzing and developing the training and documentation strategy with the overall implementation strategy and project plan.

The results of this activity are:

- Project Plan (Work Plan, Budget Plan, Resource Plan).
- Project management standards and procedures.
- ERP implementation strategy.

- Approved project organization
- Configuration standards
- End user training and documentation strategy
- Testing strategy
- Post-implementation support strategy
- Design of the company's system landscape, including its setup and maintenance strategy
- Official start of the project, presentation of the input mentioned above, explanation for any issues or questions about the project from the kickoff meeting participants.
- All project team members have attended Level 1 courses and have an introduction to ERP, navigation skills, and knowledge of major integration points of the system.
- The formal sign-off of Phase 1.

Business Blueprint

The purpose of this activity is as follows to create the Business Blueprint, which is a detailed documentation of the results gathered during re-

Table 1. Basic functionalities in SAP implementation

Project Preparation	Business Blueprint
Initial Project Planning	Project Management Business Blueprint Phase
Project Procedures	Organizational Change Management Blueprint
Create Training Plans	Technical Design Planning
Project Kickoff	Establish Development System Environment
Quality Management Project Preparation Phase	Design Training Plans
	Organizational Structure Definition
Realization	Business Process Definition
Project Management Realization	Business Process Definition - Final
Organizational Change Management Realization	Quality Management Business Blueprint Phase
Create Training Materials	
Baseline Configuration and Confirmation	
Develop System Test Plans	**Final Preparation**
Establish Quality Assurance Environment	Project Management Final Preparation Phase
Establish Production Environment	Deliver End User Training
Final Configuration and Confirmation	System Management
Prepare and Coordinate ABAP Development	Conduct System Tests
Develop Conversion Programs	Detailed Project Planning
Develop Application Interface Programs	Cutover
Develop Enhancements	Quality Management Final Preparation Phase
Create Reports	
Create Forms	
Establish User Role and Authorization Concept	**Go Live and Support**
Establish Data Archiving	Production Support
Final Integration Test	Ongoing KPI Management
Quality Management Realization Phase	Project End

quirements workshops. Furthermore, the Business Blueprint documents the business process requirements of the company. This phase also establishes a proper cycle of project management activities to ensure that the implementation project is on target. It determines all project planning, controlling and updating activities. It also identifies where changes in the relationship between business processes and the organizational structure need to be managed, in consultation with departmental management. The same work package is also in the subsequent phases. It is also defined now what content the customer needs, what user populations and needs that content will serve, and how the content will be structured. Also, definitions of enhancement contexts that customers need to create and maintain their own materials are completed. In general, the idea is to start with a single context and then create additional contexts based on the first one. The relationships between enhancement contexts are called enhancement chains. Description of processes and sub-processes that are particular to the following business processes such as training management, performance assessment, and web content management are also completed in this phase. At this time, all user master records with roles and responsibilities along with authorizations for the project team members are also created.

The business process definitions create the Business Blueprint. In case of a rollout most of the company requirements should already be determined and mapped to the corresponding ERP software settings. The Business Blueprint serves as the conceptual master plan, and eventually becomes a detailed written document. This document shows the business requirements in detail, and serves as the basis for organization, configuration and, if necessary, development activities. End User Requirements Document, Current Data Warehouse and Information Access Environment Document, Master Data/Transaction Data Requirements Document, Data Mapping Document, Data Access Recommendations Document, and Data Management Requirements Document are also completed.

The outputs of this activity are:

- Regularly scheduled project status meetings
- Updated Project Plan
- Definition of end user roles and responsibilities

- Quality Reviews
- Content Requirements document, which identifies user populations, existing information, and new information requirements.
- A business blueprint
- The technical infrastructure (network, system, and front-end environment) is documented
- A signed Business Requirements Analysis Document to include Completed business process questions, Completed CI template, Completed KPI template

Realization

The purpose of this phase is to implement business and process requirements based on the Business Blueprint. The objectives are final implementation in the system, an overall test, and the release of the system for production (live) operation. The project team also receives relevant knowledge. All testing is completed in order to implement the completely functional system

RESULT

The outputs of this activity are:

- Implementation of all necessary enhancement contexts, enhancement releases, and enhancement context chains
- The data extraction is configured.
- Configured and tested ERP system.
- Tested programs to migrate into the QA environment
- ERP system meets the business application requirements as defined in the Business Blueprint.

Project Final Preparation

The purpose of this phase is to perform the established cycle of project management activities to keep the implementation project on target. This determines all project planning, controlling and updating activities, and identifies changes between business processes and the organizational structure. Project management and consulting management must work closely together to guarantee that the project stays on schedule. Also, technical and performance tests will be conducted to verify that the production environment is ready and can be supported for productive operation. These tests should be performed in the actual production environment or in an environment that closely represents the actual environment. At this time, the move from a pre-production environment to live production operation will be done. In addition, it is important to monitor system transactions and overall performance. During the process of going live, there are two critical periods. In the first few days, the team must execute the production support plan and check the results. Any issues or problems that occur in this period must be resolved as quickly as possible. Following the first few days of live operation, monitoring issues for the long term, particularly with reference to system performance, capacity and functions should be addressed.

The results of this activity are:

- All roles and responsibilities defined with proper backups in place
- All procedures and responsibilities documented and signed off
- The entire technical infrastructure is tested and validated, including failure scenarios and disaster recovery.
- The configuration of the system and the procedures defined for the technical environment are tested and validated.
- A stress test is carried out successfully. Its result determines the validity of the planned go-live date.
- All ERP system aspects and support organization is approved, and the production system is released.

- The output of this activity is the formal sign-off of Phase 4.

CONCLUSION

A brief ERP implementation procedure using the SAP implementation documentation as well as issues regarding ERP implementations are detailed in this chapter. ERP implementations in the recent years have raised a number of questions regarding its success. Many companies regard ERP as their one and only savior and many others despise that ERP as a single system has brought them to their knees. Regardless, many more companies, small to medium size companies in particular, are beginning to invest in ERP. An industrial practitioner from such small to medium companies needs to understand how to implement ERP. This study provides the necessary tools and background for the industrial practitioner to implement not only ERP systems but implement the next generation of enterprise applications as well.

REFERENCES

Aladwani, A. M. (2002). An Integrated Performance Model of Information Systems Projects. *Journal of Management Information Systems, 19* (1), 185-210.

Al-Mudimigh, A., Zairi, M., & Al-Mashari, M. (2001). ERP software implementation: an integrative framework. *European Journal of Information Systems, 10*(4), 216-226.

Aloini, D., Dulmin, R., & Mininno, V. (2007). Risk management in ERP project introduction: Review of the literature. *Information & Management, 44*(6), 547-567.

Bingi, P., Sharma, M., & Godla, J. 1999. Critical issues affecting an ERP implementation. *Information Systems Management, 16*(3), 7-14.

Capaldo, G., & Pierluigi, R. (2008). A methodological proposal to assess the feasibility of ERP systems implementation strategies. *Proceedings of the 41ˢᵗ Hawaii International Conference on System Sciences*, Waikoloa, Hawaii, January 7-10, 401-401.

Davenport, T. (1998). Putting the Enterprise into the Enterprise System. *Harvard Business Review, 74*(4), 121-131.

Dean, J. (2001). Weathering the ERP Storm. *Government Executive*, July 1, 2001

Gebauer, J., & Lee, F. (2008). Enterprise system flexibility and implementation strategies – Aligning theory with evidence from a case study. *Information Systems Management, 25*(1), 71 – 82.

Gefen, D., & Ragowsky, A. (2005). A multi-level approach to measuring the benefits of an ERP system in manufacturing firms. *Information Systems Management, 22*(1), 18–25.

Hawksworth, M. (2007). *Six steps to ERP implementation*. IFS White Paper, IFS.

Hendricks, K. B., Singhal, V. R., & Stratman, J. K. (2007). The impact of enterprise systems on corporate performance: A study of ERP, SCM, and CRM system implementations. *Journal of Operations Management, 25*(1), 65-82.

Hilson, G. (2001). Human factor plays big role in IT failures. *Computing Canada, 27*(6).

Jarrar, Y. F., Al-Mudimigh, A., & Zairi, M. (2000). ERP implementation critical success factors-the role and impact of business process management. *Proceedings of the 2000 IEEE International Conference on Management of Innovation and Technology, 1,* 122 – 127.

Karim, J., Somers, T. M., & Bhattacherjee, A. (2007). The impact of ERP implementation on business process outcomes: A factor-based study. *Journal of Management Information Systems, 24*(1),101–134.

Ketbi, O. A., Azaizeh, A., Carrico, W., Cook, R., & Cooke, D. (2002). 2002 Industry Studies: Advanced Manufacturing. Report Number: A105624, Industrial Coll of the Armed Forces, Washington, D.C.

Botta-Genoulaz, V., Millet, P. A., & Grabot, B. (2005). A survey on the recent research literature on ERP systems. *Computers in Industry, 56,* 510–522.

Koch, C. (2002). The ABCs of ERP. *CIO Magazine*, March 7, 2002.

Laukkanen, S., Sarpola, S., & Hallikainen, P. (2007). Enterprise size matters: objectives and constraints of ERP adoption. *Journal of Enterprise Information Management, 20*(3), 319–334.

Liang, S., & Lien, C. (2007). Selecting the optimal ERP software by combining the ISO 9126 standard and fuzzy AHP approach. *Contemporary Management Research, 3*(1), 23-44.

Mabert, V. A., Soni, A. K., & Venkataramanan, M. A. (2003). The impact of organization size on enterprise resource planning (ERP) implementations in the U.S. manufacturing sector. *Omega , 31,* 235-246.

Moon, Y. B. (2007). Enterprise resource planning (ERP): A review of the literature. *International Journal of Management and Enterprise Development, 4*(3), 235-264.

Norris, G., Wright, I., Hurley, J., Dunleavy, J., & Gibson, A. (1998). *SAP: An Executive's Comprehensive Guide*. John Wiley & Sons, Inc., New York, NY.

Ranganathan, C., & Brown, C. V. (2006). ERP investments and the market value of firms: Toward an understanding of influential ERP project variables. *Information Systems Research, 17*(2), 145-161.

Ravichandran. T., & Rai. A. (2000). Quality management in systems development: An organizational system perspective. *MIS Quarterly, 24*(3), 381-416.

Sharma, R., & Yetton, P. (2003). The contingent effects of management support and task interdependence on successful information systems implementation. *MIS Quarterly, 27*(4), 533-555.

Slater, D. (1999). How to choose the right ERP software package. *CIO*, February 16, 1999.

Somers, T. M., & Nelson, K. G. (2003). The impact of strategy and integration mechanisms on enterprises system value: empirical evidence from manufacturing firms. *European Journal of Operational Research, 146,* 315-38.

Stedman, C. (1998). Global ERP rollouts present cross-border problems. *Computerworld, 32* (47), 10.

Van Everdingen, Y., Van Hillegersberg, J., & Waarts, E. (2000). ERP adoption by European midsize companies. *Communications of the ACM, 43*(4), 27-31.

Wagle, D. (1998). The case for ERP systems. *The McKinsey Quarterly, 2*, 130-138.

Weston, F. C. (2001). ERP implementation and project management. *Production and Inventory Management Journal, 42*(3/4), 75-80.

Wu, J. H., & Wang, Y. M. (2003). Enterprise resource planning experience in Taiwan: An empirical study and comparative analysis. 30th *Annual Hawaii International Conference on System Science (HICCS '03)*, Big Island, Hawaii, January 6-9.

Wu, L., Ong, C., & Hsu, Y. (2008). Active ERP implementation management: A Real Options perspective. *Journal of Systems and Software, 81*(6), 1039-1050.

KEY TERMS

Customization: Customization refers to modifications to the original software that is typically not supported by the software vendor and those needed by the customer because of their unique business processes.

Enterprise Resource Planning (ERP): Software systems for business management that integrates functional areas such as planning, manufacturing, sales, marketing, distribution, accounting, finances, human resource management, project management, inventory management, service and maintenance, transportation, and e-business.

Enterprise Systems: Enterprise systems are software that provides solutions to an integrated business organization.

Implementation: Implementation consists of defining a project, putting together project teams, reengineering of existing business processes, customizing the software to reflect new business processes, testing the software in organizational environment such that the software is usable for the organizational users.

Integration: ERP software integration is the process of integrating ERP systems with other enterprise information resources or systems within an enterprise.

Management Commitment: Management commitment is direct participation by the highest level executives in a specific and critically important aspect or program of an organization.

Chapter XIX
Restructuring the Marketing Information System for eCRM:
An Application of the Eriksson–Penker Method

Călin Gurău

GSCM – Montpellier Business School, France

ABSTRACT

This chapter considers the importance of business modelling for implementing e-CRM systems. The introduction of e-business models requires the adaptation of the Marketing Information System the specific characteristics of the online environment. The representation of various components of the Marketing Information System, and of the flows of information among various organizational departments, represents an essential step for the successful implementation of e-CRM systems. Considering the specific requirements of this restructuring process, chapter presents the advantages of the Eriksson-Penker Business Extensions of the Unifying Modeling Language (UML), and exemplifies their use for modeling the Marketing Information System during the implementation of an interactive e-CRM approach.

INTRODUCTION

The development and introduction of new information technology applications and marketing paradigms are forcing business organisations to continuously evaluate and restructure their *Marketing Information System (MIS)*. However, the complexity of the *MIS* and its connections with various organisational departments, functions and processes, creates important challenges for the restructuring process. From this perspective, the application of a *business modeling* approach represents an essential pre-requisite for identifying the *MIS* components that need to be adapted to the new competitive conditions and for representing their future integration in the organisational architecture. This chapter presents the advantages of the *Eriksson-Penker Business Extensions* of the *Unified Modeling Language (UML)*, and exemplifies their use for modeling the *Marketing*

Information System during the implementation of an interactive *eCRM* approach.

BACKGROUND

The opportunities provided by the rapidly evolving online markets have determined many firms to initiate e-business operations. However, the success of these initiatives is determined by capacity of enterprises to properly understand the specificity of the Internet, and to restructure their *Marketing Information Systems* in order to develop a competitive advantage. In this context, the *eCRM* systems represent interesting solutions for adopting a customer-centric approach and for increasing the online value propositions (Jayachandran, Sharma, Kaufman, & Raman 2005; Payne, & Frow 2005; Srinivasan, & Moorman 2005). Value maximisation happens when firms and customers engage in long-term relationships (Vargo, & Lusch 2004), co-creating personalised value (Prahalad, & Ramaswamy 2004), based on information exchange and close collaboration in all the stages of product R&D, manufacturing and commercialisation.

The *eCRM* system comprises a number of business processes, inter-linked in a logical succession:

- Market segmentation: the collection of historical data, complemented with information provided by third parties (such as marketing research agencies), is segmented on the basis of *customer life-time value (CLV)* criteria, using data mining applications.
- Capturing the customer: the potential customer is attracted to the web site of the firm through targeted promotional messages, diffused through various communication channels.
- Customer information retrieval: The information retrieval process can be either implicit or explicit. When implicit, the information retrieval process registers the web behaviour of customers, using specialized software

applications, such as 'cookies'. On the other hand, explicit information can be gathered through direct input of demographic data by the customer (using online registration forms or questionnaires). Often, these two categories of information are connected at database level.

- Customer Profile definition: the customer information collected is analyzed in relation with the target market segments identified through data mining, and a particular customer profile is defined. The profile can be enriched with additional data, e.g. external information from marketing information providers. This combination creates a holistic view of the customer, its needs, wants, interests and behaviors (Pan, & Lee, 2003).
- Personalization of firm-customer interaction: the customer profile is used to identify the best customer management campaign (CMC), which is applied to personalize the company-customer online interaction.
- Resource management: the company-customer transaction require complex resource management operations, which are partially managed automatically, through specialized IT-applications such as Enterprise Resource Planning (ERP) or Supply Chain Management (SCM), and partly through the direct involvement and co-ordination of operational managers.

BUSINESS MODELING IN THE DIGITAL ENVIRONMENT

The effective functioning of the *eCRM* system requires a gradual process of planning, design and implementation, which can be greatly enhanced through *business modeling*. The selection of an appropriate *business modeling* language is essential for the successful implementation of the eCRM system, and consequently, for evaluating and improving its performance (Kotorov, 2002). The starting point for this selection is an analysis of the specific characteristics and requirements of the eCRM system (Opdahl, & Henderson-Sellers, 2004; Chen, & Chen, 2004):

- *eCRM* is an Internet-based system, therefore the modeling language should be able to represent web processes and applications;
- the interactive nature of *eCRM* systems requires a clear representation of the interaction between customers and web applications, as well as between various business processes within the organisation;
- *eCRM* systems are using databases which interact with software applications; the modeling language should support data modeling profiles and database representation;
- the necessity for resource planning and control requires a clear representation of each business process with its inputs, outputs, resources and control mechanisms;
- the implementation and management of an *eCRM* system requires the long-term collaboration of various specialists, such as business and operational managers, programmers and web designers, which are sometimes working from distant locations; the modeling language should provide a standard, intuitive representation of the *eCRM* system and business processes, in order to facilitate cross-discipline interaction and collaboration;
- the complexity of the *eCRM* system requires a modeling language capable to present both the organisational and the functional architecture, at the level of system, process, software applications and resources; this will facilitate a multi-user, multi-purpose use of the same business model, although the detail of representation might differ depending on the required perspective.

The *Unified Modeling Language (UML)* is well suited to the demands of the online environment. It has an object-oriented approach, and was designed to support distributed, concurrent, and connected models (Bennett, McRobb, & Farmer,

2005; Rumbaugh, Jacobson, & Booch, 2004). The UML extension for representing business processes, proposed by Eriksson and Penker (2000), is the notation presented in this paper to support the *business process modeling* activity.

THE UNIFIED MODELING LANGUAGE (UML)

The *UML* was developed in 1995 by Grady Booch, Ivar Jacobson, and Jim Rumbaugh at Rational Corporation (Rittgen, 2006; Rumbaugh et al., 2004), with contributions from other leading methodologists, software vendors, and users. Rational Corporation chose to develop UML as a standard through the Object Management Group (OMG). The resulting co-operative effort with numerous companies led to a specification adopted by OMG in 1997.

UML has a number of specific advantages:

- **Simplicity of notation:** The notation set is simple and intuitive.
- Standard: The UML standard achieved through the OMG gives confidence to modellers.
- **Support:** A significant level of support is available to modellers in using the UML:
  - ° text books that describe the UML notation and consider specific application areas.
  - ° papers in journals and publications/ resources on the Internet spread knowledge of the UML (e.g. Rational Resource Center and UML Zone).
  - ° software tools, often referred to as Computer Aided Software Engineering (CASE) tools are available.
- **Uptake:** The UML notation answers a real need, favorising its adoption by specialists. The more the UML is used, the wider the knowledge pool becomes, which leads to a wider dissemination of information concerning the benefits of its use.

- **Methodologies:** The development of methods or methodologies that provide support and guidelines of how to use the UML in a particular situation is widespread. A prime example is the Rational Unified Process (Jonkers, Lankhorst, Van Buuren, Hoppenbrouwers, Bonsangue, & Van der Torre, 2004).
- **Extensibility:** The UML has a number of standard extension mechanisms to make the notation flexible: stereotypes, tagged values and constraints (Kulak, & Guiney, 2003).
- **Living Language:** The UML notations and standards is constantly developing, though in a controlled manner. The OMG works with representatives from various companies to clarify and address problems in the UML specification as well as considering recommendations for extensions to the language.

The *UML* is used to model a broad range of systems (software systems, hardware systems, databases, real-time systems and real-world organisations). By sharing a common notation across system and business boundaries, business and system analysts can better communicate their needs, being able to build a system that effectively solves customers' problems. For modelling purposes, *UML* proposes nine types of diagrams: class diagrams, object diagrams, state chart diagrams, activity diagrams, sequence diagrams, collaboration diagrams, *use case* diagrams, component diagrams and deployment diagrams

In addition, *UML* is developing in three main directions that are of interest for this paper:

- **Data Modeling:** Databases represent an essential component of almost all e-business applications, including CRM. Programming databases is often a difficult part of complex system development, because each database may use a different method to declare data structure. UML has addressed this problem by introducing a Data Modeling profile, which includes an additional set of notations to capture the data modeling and database connectivity aspects (Naiburg, & Maksimchuk, 2003; Bennett et al., 2005).
- **WWW System Modeling:** The development of Internet business systems has lead to an extension of UML for modeling web based systems. This capability is provided as an UML profile that enables modellers to represent various elements that compose a Web application – client pages, server pages, forms, frames, etc. (Zanoni, & Audy, 2004).
- **Business Process Modeling:** Important extensions to UML notations describe the processes, goals, and rules of business (Eriksson and Penker, 2000; Rittgen, 2006).

USING ERIKSON-PENKER EXTENSION FOR BUSINESS MODELING

Extension mechanisms—stereotypes, tagged values and constraints—are provided by the UML, allowing users to customise and extend the language in order to suit their particular needs. The UML specification also contains an UML extension for *business modeling*, which briefly describes possible extensions for business modelling, although no clear rules are provided regarding their application. Because of this lack of support for business modeling, a number of propositions have been made in order to provide additional *UML* extensions (Kim, 2004). The *Eriksson-Penker Business Extensions* are one of these propositions, which merge the UML with processes modeling, adapting the basic UML activity diagram and introducing a so-called process diagram (Noran, 2001). Table 1 describes the notation used in this section.

An example of an *Eriksson-Penker method* for representing a process is shown in Figure 1. The diagram represents a process and the objects involved in that process. The process is triggered by an event and outputs a further resource. The use of the *UML* stereotype notation clarifies the role of each object (e.g. <<goal>>, <<infor-

mation>>) and association (e.g. <<achieve>>, <<supply>>), as necessary. The direction of associations clearly show the input and output relationship that objects have with the given process symbol.

Using the Eriksson-Penker method, the implementation of an *eCRM* system will be further presented and analysed. The process is common for every type of e-business, and the diagrams presented can be used as ***business modeling*** frameworks by any Internet-based organisation. On the other hand, in order to keep the model simple and easy to understand, the diagrams only

show the major business processes involved in the system. The development of these diagrams to include more specific and detailed processes can be done by every business organisation, depending on its specific goals, structure and strategy.

The business process diagram also allows a detailed representation of the way in which a given business process is implemented in a system. Using an implementation diagram, ***use cases***, packages, and other model artefacts may be linked back to the business process with <<implementation>> links to signify a dependent relationship (Kulak, & Guiney, 2003). The example provided

Table 1. Summary of UML Notation used in this paper

Modeling icon	Name	UML Definition
<<text here>>	Stereotype	The text shown in chevron brackets is used for extra clarification.
<<process>> Name	Business process	A process, takes input resources from its left-hand side and indicates its output resources on its right-hand side (shown as dependencies to and from the process, according to standard UML syntax). The process symbol may also include the stereotype <<process>>, which is a textual description of the process.
Name	Business object	An object which is input to or output from an object. A stereotype may be added to clarify process goals (<<goal>>), physical resource (<<resource>>), or people (<<people>>).
<<information>> Name	Information object	An object, which is specifically identified as information. The alternative icon is used for clarity.
<<event>> Name	Event	An event is the receipt of some object, a time or date reached, a notification or some other trigger that initiates the business process. The event may be consumed and transformed (for example a customer order) or simply act as a catalyst.
	Dependency	Connecting line with arrow shows dependencies between model components. Direction of arrow indicates direction of dependency. This can also be annotated with a stereotype to clarify the nature of dependency.

Figure 1. Eriksson-Penker method

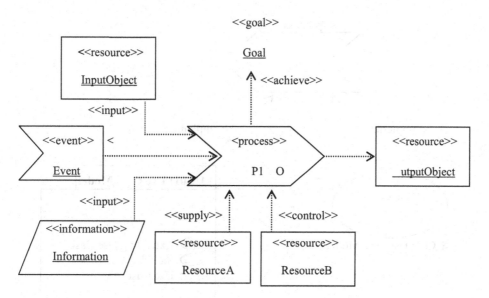

in Figure 2 illustrates how a Business Process is implemented by a *Use Case* and a package. As the model develops and the functional software components are built and linked to *Use Cases*, the business justification for each element can be derived from this representation.

To increase the accuracy of the representation, the model presented in Figure 2 also implies what is not being delivered. As the Business Process will typically include a wide range of manual and automated procedures, this model illustrates exactly what functionality (*Use Cases*) needs to be provided to service a particular business process; on the other hand, any missing functionality must be outsourced from other systems and/or procedures.

Using *UML* notations, the main business processes involved in eCRM systems can be represented as follows:

eCRM Process 1: Segmenting the Market

In order to segment the market, the firm needs to collect data about its customers. This can be done either through online automated systems that register the history of customer-firm interaction

(historical data) and/or buying the necessary data from a third party (usually a specialised market research agency). These data will be usually located in databases. Applying the *CLV* method, and using the segmentation criteria established by marketing managers, the collected data can be automatically processed using data mining applications such as pattern recognition and clustering. The output will represent a database of various customer segments, which have different lifetime values (value segmentation) and therefore present different levels of priority for the firm (Rosset, Neumann, Eick, & Vatnik, 2003).

eCRM Process 2: Capturing the Customer (Figure 3)

This process is not represented in this paper since it implies a multiple channel strategy and interaction. The customers can be attracted to the company's web site either through promotional messages, or through word-of-mouth referrals. The access to the company web site will be made using various intermediaries (such as search engines or company directories) and web applications (such as hiperlinks).

Figure 2. Example of implementation diagram

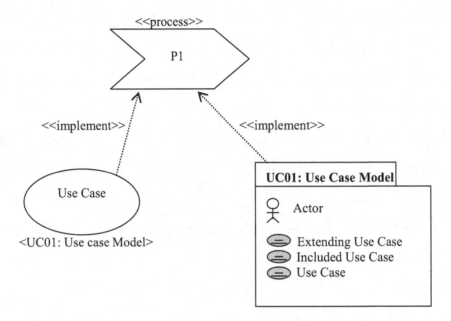

Figure 3. Market segmentation

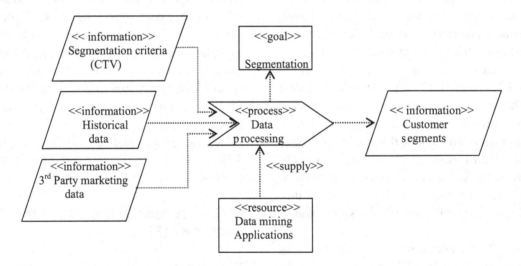

eCRM Process 3: Customer Information Retrieval (Figure 4)

The customer information retrieval process will be usually initiated by the customer's request for a product or service (<<event>>). The information retrieval can be implicit (using web tracking applications), or explicit (using 'information request' web pages). The retrieved information is collected into a specific customer database account.

eCRM Process 4: Customer Profile Definition (Figure 5)

The information contained in the customer data account is analysed and compared with the customer segments identified in the market segmentation stage, and a specific customer profile is defined. In order to refine this profile, additional information can be outsourced from specialised marketing agencies.

eCRM Process: Personalised Customer-Firm Transaction (Figure 6)

To increase the loyalty of the most profitable customers, the company needs to design and implement customised e-marketing strategies (Tan, Yen, & Fang, 2002).

The customer profile defined in the previous stage will be matched with the most effective customer campaign applications, determining the personalization of company-customer interactions. The completed transaction results in profits for the firm, increased satisfaction for customer, as well as information, which is integrated in the transaction history of that particular customer.

eCRM Process 6: Resource Management

This particular process involves complex interactions between operational managers, the company, and the firm's network of suppliers. The modeling of this business process requires advanced network modeling procedures. *UML* can be used efficiently to represent the networked interactions between the firm and external suppliers, being a distributed and highly standardized modeling language.

The Integration of Business Processes in the eCRM System (Figure 7)

Figure 7 presents four main business processes integrated into the *eCRM* system. The model shows how the outputs of one stage represent the inputs for the next stage. The resulting historical data at the end of the process closes the loop, and restarts the process for a better tuning of company's activities to customers' needs.

Although only two of the represented business processes are visible to the online customer, the whole *eCRM* system uses software programmes and applications, which are either Internet-based or are interacting closely with web processes. Additional representation details can be included in the model, depending on the end-user orientation.

CONCLUDING REMARKS

Because of its complexity, the successful restructuring of the *Marketing Information System* for

Figure 4. Customer information retrieval

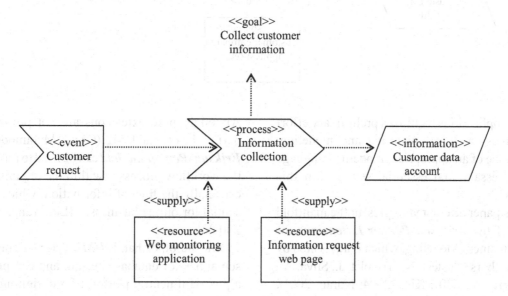

269

Figure 5. Customer profile definition

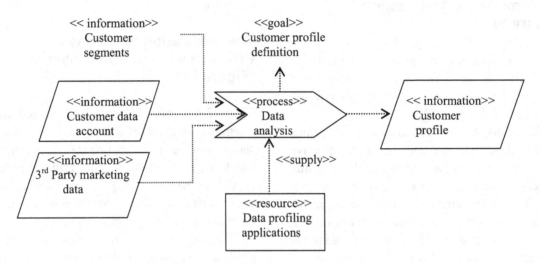

Figure 6. The personalisation of Customer-Firm transaction

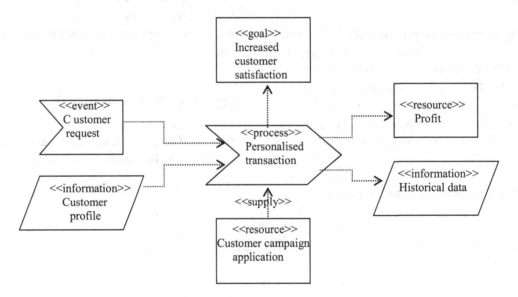

eCRM applications requires a preliminary effort of business analysis, planning and modeling. The choice of an appropriate modeling language is a necessary and essential step within this process.

This paper attempted to present the manifold utility of the **Eriksson-Penker Extensions** for UML Business Modeling, which is advocated by many authors (Castela, N., Tribolet, J., Silva, A., & Guerra, A., 2001; Kim, 2004; Noran, 2001).

Although these extensions are not presently a part of the official UML (OMG) Metamodel, the **Erikson-Penker method** can be used to represent the workflow processes within the organisation, especially the flow of information, which is essential for online businesses (Lin, Yang, & Pai, 2002).

On the other hand, **UML** offers a complete semantics for database design, and can provide a powerful neutral platform for designing data-

Figure 7. The integration of business processes in the eCRM system

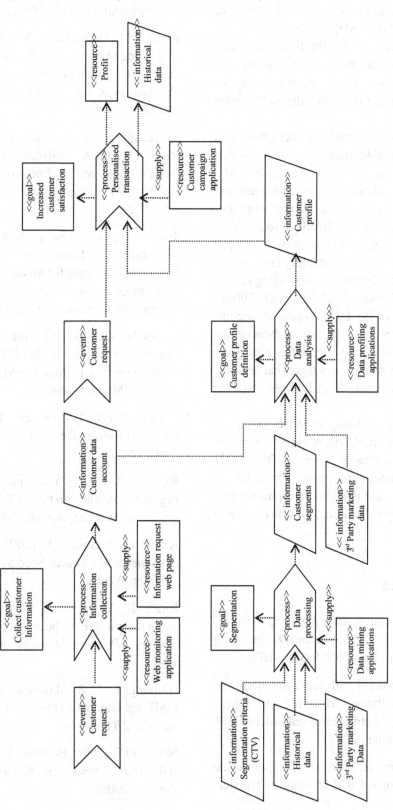

base architecture and data profiling, especially in the case of multi-user databases (Naiburg, & Maksimchuk, 2003). UML can be used to represent the interaction between the digital company and different types of customers, helping the operational managers to identify the areas/activities of value creation and those of value destruction (Kim, 2004).

UML provides the basis for designing and implementing suitable information systems that support the business operations. The use of UML both for software description and for *business modeling* offers the possibility to map large sections of the business model directly into software objects (Field, Heim, & Sinha, 2004). UML can provide a protocol neutral modeling language to design the interface between co-operating virtual organisations (Kotorov, 2002; Tan et al., 2002).

The capacity of the *UML* to provide a common platform for representing both web processes and organisational architecture, offers a unifying tool for the multi-disciplinary team that designs, implements and controls the eCRM system (Bennett et al., 2005).

The *business modeling* exercise should be based on an analytical and modular approach. The implementation and functioning of the *eCRM* system must be represented stage by stage, taking however into account the final integration into a complete, functional system, as it was presented in this paper.

REFERENCES

Bennett, S., McRobb, S., & Farmer, R. (2005). *Object-Oriented Systems Analysis and Design Using UML*. 3rd edition, London: McGraw-Hill.

Castela, N., Tribolet, J., Silva, A., & Guerra, A. (2001). Business Process Modeling with UML. http://www.inesc-id.pt/ficheiros/publicacoes/689.pdf [accessed January 2008].

Chen, Q., & Chen, H.-M. (2004). Exploring the success factors of E-CRM strategy in practice.

Journal of Database Marketing & Consumer Strategy Management, 11(4), 333-343.

Field, J. M., Heim, G. R., & Sinha, K. K. (2004) Managing Quality in the E-Service System: Development and Application of a Process Model. *Production & Operations Management, 13*(4), 291-306.

Jayachandran, S., Sharma, S., Kaufman, P., & Raman, P. (2005). The Role of Relational Information Processes and Technology Use in Customer Relationship Management. *Journal of Marketing, 69*, 117-192.

Jonkers, H., Lankhorst, M., Van Buuren, R., Hoppenbrouwers, S., Bonsangue, M., & Van der Torre, L. (2004). Concepts for Modeling Enterprise Architectures. *International Journal of Cooperative Information Systems, 13*(3), 257-287.

Kennedy, A. (2006). Electronic Customer Relationship Management (eCRM): Opportunities and Challenges in a Digital World. *Irish Marketing Review, 18*(1/2), 58-68.

Kim, H.-W. (2004). A Process Model for Successful CRM System Development. *Software IEEE, 21*(4), 22-28.

Kotorov, R. P. (2002). Ubiquitous organization: organizational design for e-CRM Business. *Process Management Journal, 8*(3), 218-232.

Kulak, D., & Guiney, E. (2003). Use *Cases: Requirements in Context*. Second Edition. Harlow: Addison Wesley.

Lin, F.-R., Yang, M.-C., & Pai, Y.-H. (2002). A generic structure for business process modeling. *Business Process Management Journal, 8*(1), 19-41.

Naiburg, E. J., & Maksimchuk, R. A. (2003). UML for Database Design. *Online Information Review, 27*(1), 66-67.

Noran, O.S. (2001). Business Modeling: UML vs IDEF. http://www.cit.gu.edu.au/~noran [accessed January 2008].

Opdahl, A. L., & Henderson-Sellers, B. (2004). A Template for Defining Enterprise Modeling Constructs. *Journal of Database Management, 15*(2), 39-74.

Pan, S. L., & Lee, J.-N. (2003). Using e-CRM for a unified view of the customer *Communications of the ACM, 46*(4), 95-99.

Payne, A., & Frow, P. (2005). A Strategic Framework for Customer Relationship Management. *Journal of Marketing, 69*, 167-176.

Prahalad, C. K., & Ramaswamy, V. (2004). *The Future of Competition: Co-Creating Unique Value with Customers*. Boston: Harvard Business School Press.

Rittgen, P. (2006) *Enterprise Modeling and Computing with UML*. Hershey: Idea Group.

Rosset, S., Neumann, E., Eick, U., & Vatnik, N. (2003). Customer Lifetime Value Models for Decision Support. *Data Mining and Knowledge Discovery, 7*(3), 321–339.

Rumbaugh, J., Jacobson, I., & Booch, G. (2004). *Unified Modeling Language Reference Manual*. The Second Edition. Harlow: Addison-Wesley.

Srinivasan, R., & Moorman, C. (2005). Strategic Firm Commitments and Rewards for Customer Relationship Management in Online Retailing. *Journal of Marketing, 69*, 193-200.

Tan, X., Yen, D. C., & Fang, X. (2002). Internet integrated customer relationship management - A key success factor for companies in the e-commerce arena. *Journal of Computer Information Systems, 42*(3), 77-86.

Vargo, S. L., & Lusch, R. F. (2004). Evolving to a New Dominant Logic for Marketing. *Journal of Marketing, 68*(1), 1-17.

Zanoni, R., & Audy, J.L.N. (2004). Project Management Model: Proposal for Performance in a Physically Distributed Software Development Environment. *Engineering Management Journal, 16*(2), 28-34.

KEY TERMS

Electronic Customer Relationship Management (eCRM): CRM comprises the methods, systems and procedures that facilitate the interaction between the firm and its customers. The development of new technologies, especially the proliferation of self-service channels like the web and wap phones, has changed consumer buying behaviour and forced the companies to manage electronically the relationships with customers. The new CRM systems are using electronic devices and software applications that attempt to personalize and add value to customer-company interactions.

Customer Lifetime Value (CLV): Consists in taking into account the total financial contribution - i.e. revenues minus costs - of a customer over his or her entire life of a business relationship with the company.

Enterprise Resource Planning (ERP): A business management system based on specialised software systems that manage various information flows, integrating all business facets, including planning, manufacturing, sales, and marketing.

Supply Chain Management (SCM): A management system that coordinates, integrates and controls the move of materials, information, and finances from supplier to manufacturer to wholesaler to retailer to consumer, in order to reduce inventory and increase the efficiency of the supply process.

UML Constraints: Extensions to the semantics of an UML element. These allow the inclusion of rules that indicate permitted ranges or conditions on an element.

UML Stereotypes: Extensions to the UML vocabulary, allowing additional text descriptions to be applied to the notation. The stereotype is shown between chevron brackets <<>>.

UML Tagged Value: Extensions to the properties of an UML element.

Chapter XX
Analyzing an ES Implementation in a Health Care Environment

Albert Boonstra
University of Groningen, The Netherlands

ABSTRACT

At the present moment, many hospitals are going through a process of change directed at the integrated delivery of health care. Enterprise Systems (ES) are increasingly used to support this process and to manage hospitals on a coherent basis. We also know, however, that ES implementation itself, can be viewed as an organizational change process that affects many stakeholders. For that reason it is relevant to study how ES implementation takes place within hospitals and how it tends to impact the existing organizational arrangements. The purpose of this chapter is therefore to describe and analyze how ES implementation within a hospital affects the interests of stakeholders and which specific problems may arise as a result. This chapter uses the evidence of a case study to reveal some important dimensions of the organizational change issues related to ES implementation within hospitals.

INTRODUCTION

Many hospitals are going through a process in which they are changing from loosely coupled units into more integrated entities. Hospital managers are increasingly accountable for the cost-effectiveness and the quality of their organizations, which explains their need for more integration and control. To achieve this, the managers are look- ing for information systems that can help them to manage their hospitals on an integrated basis (Merode, van et al, 2004). This is why in recent years many hospitals have started to implement enterprise systems (Jossie et al., 2005). Enterprise systems are software packages that facilitate the integration of transactions-oriented data and business processes throughout an organization (Klaus et al., 2000). Traditionally, enterprise systems are used in manufacturing, which differs in many respects from a hospital context. It is therefore relevant to describe and analyze how ES implementation within hospitals takes place and which specific problems are faced by the implementers and managers.

In this chapter we will describe and analyze the implementation of an enterprise system in a medium-sized hospital in The Netherlands. We will analyze this implementation by focusing on the roles of the various stakeholders involved, the meaning that they attach to the system, and the actions they take throughout the project. We have chosen this perspective because stakeholders involved in hospitals differ significantly from those involved in other industries. This chapter aims to provide insight into the role that the different stakeholders involved in hospitals may play during ES-implementations. Understanding the possible impact of ES on particular stakeholder interests may help project managers and others to manage ES implementation within hospitals in a more effective way.

There are only few descriptive accounts of how groups and individuals related to hospitals interpret IS proposals in general and ES systems in particular, and how they respond subsequently (Levine et al., 1995). Especially empirical case studies that focus on the role of politics and stakeholders in relation to ES implementation within hospitals are scarce. As a result, our insight into the role of stakeholders in the implementation of IS applications within hospitals in general and that of ES applications in particular is limited. This means that we have a lack of understanding of why groups and individuals act in the way they do. Knowledge of barriers to implementation and approaches to analyze them is of importance to practitioners, such as project managers, who are involved in implementing ES within hospitals, and hospital managers, who have to decide whether to implement ES.

The chapter is organized as follows. In the next section we will explain the distinctive features of enterprise systems and describe theory and models that the research has been based on, which may help us understand the relevance of studying enterprise systems in health care environments. After that, we will describe the methodological background of the research. The following section presents the case study and then an interpretation will be given of this case study on the basis of the model. In the final section we will put the study in a broader perspective and put forward some views about the practical implications for managers responsible for ES implementations within hospitals.

BACKGROUND

Enterprise systems are software applications aimed at integrating a range of business functions in order to acquire an overview of the business based on a single information architecture (Merode, van., 2004). Starting from manufacturing and financial systems, enterprise systems may eventually allow the integration of inter-organizational supply chains (Markus et al., 2000; Fowler et al., 2003). Enterprise systems are multi-functional and cover a range of activities, such as logistics, human resources and finance. These functions are integrated in such a way that whenever data are entered into one of these functions, they become available to all related functions. Enterprise systems are modular and can be used in many combinations of modules. They link the different organizational units by coordinating the business processes.

Because these systems affect so many aspects of an organization's internal and external operations, their successful deployment and use are critical to organizational performance and survival. In the case of ES successful implementation is important, since the costs and risks of these technology investments rival their potential payoffs. Failure of enterprise system implementation projects may lead to bankruptcy (Markus et al.,

2000; Davenport, 1998; McAfee, 2003). The ES implementation as described in this chapter also brought the hospital into severe problems, which almost led to bankruptcy.

This illustrates that implementing enterprise systems is a complicated enterprise, not only from a technical point of view but also from many other perspectives, including strategic, organizational, political, and cultural viewpoints. One very important issue is that a large number of stakeholders from different organizational units are involved. Since as a result the decisions are no longer taken on a local or departmental level, the question of who participates in the analysis, development and implementation of ES becomes more difficult.

We already mentioned that many hospitals are in a process of transformation, directed at the integrated delivery of health care through a more homogeneous range of health care products. Motives behind this change are a higher level of cost control, the need for organizational procedures for patients, and an increasing accountability of the hospital managers for the way in which the hospital operates. This process toward integration can be stimulated by information systems that help managers organize the central planning and control (Haux, 2006). Since enterprise systems have helped organizations in various industries to integrate and organize the real time information delivery, they are now also applied in many hospitals. Suppliers of enterprise systems have developed modules that are specifically customized for hospitals, such as patient management modules and electronic patient files. Modules used in other industries have been slightly adapted to fulfill hospital requirements (Paré et al., 2001).

The empirical research conducted for this chapter is based on interpretive (Walsham, 1993), processual (Boonstra, 2003) and integrationist (Orlikowksi, 1992) models of change. These models emphasize how various groups of people in organizations may have different interpretations of information systems, which may shape

their actions and influence the implementation and evolution of such systems. The change view is rooted in social constructivism, which is focused on the meaning that people attach to a particular technology (Pinch et al., 1992). Social constructivism found its way to IS research by the so-called interpretive approaches (Walsham, 1993, Orlikowski, 1992) and emphasizes the subjective meaning that an actor ascribes to an information system, which is based on particular interests, preferences, history and so on. From this perspective, system implementation can be explained by studying the interplay of attitudes and actions of various stakeholders, which may be subject to change over time (Dawson, 1994).

Pettigrew (1988) argues that organizational change can be understood by considering the interactions among the substance, context and process of change within the organization and their continuous interplay. The implementation of change is an 'iterative, cumulative and reformulation-in-use process'. Successful change is a result of the interaction among the content or 'what' of change, the process or 'how' of change (implementation) and the organizational context or 'where' of change (the internal and external environment). He also suggests that the change agent must be willing to intervene in the political systems of the organization, and to legitimate the change in the face of competing proposals and ideas. Bennis (1984) suggests that management of change is 'management of meaning', involving the attempt to convince others of the credibility and legitimacy of particular definitions of problems and solutions, and to gain consent and compliance (Boddy, 2002).

It is well documented that the development of information systems requires the participation of the parties interested and that the willingness and the effectiveness of this participation influences the success of the resulting system. Normally these participants include developers, intended users and managers. However, in the case of enterprise systems within hospitals, this range of people and parties is much broader and crosses organizational functions, which means that the stakeholders are more loosely coupled. Identifying these stakeholders and exploring their perspectives in terms of their interests in the system and their power to 'make or break' the system is essential.

When the stakeholders are identified, their interests can be related to the enterprise system. This means that part of the analysis consists of the assessment of the stakeholders' perception of the ES. How do they interpret the ES and to what extent do they believe that it will be instrumental in attaining their objectives and that it will fit in with their values? In other words: what are their perceived interests in the system?

However, an enterprise systems does not depend solely on the interests of stakeholders but also on the power relations among the parties involved. A powerful party with a clear interest in a particular ES can apply its power to force less powerful parties to use it, regardless of their perceived interest in the system (Standifera, 2003). At the same time, it might be rather difficult for parties with a great deal of interest in a particular enterprise system, but with a lack of power to implement it successfully, if the other parties are not really interested. In this chapter, we will define power as the capacity to exert one's will over others in order to realize certain intended goals (Boddy, 2002). Since power is a capacity to exert one's will, it is possible to indicate the source of this capacity, or in relation to ES: parties may possess different sources of power to force others to cooperate and use (or not use) an ES. The power and interests of stakeholders may change during the course of a project and may affect the role they play.

To characterize this role during a certain phase we have used the stakeholder typology of Mitchell et al. (1997). They identify seven types of stakeholders: dormant, discretionary, demanding, dominant, dependent, dangerous, and definitive stakeholders. *Dormant stakeholders* have the power to influence, but this power remains unused for a certain period of time. *Discretionary stakeholders* possess legitimacy, but have no power to influence the project. *Demanding stakeholders* have urgent claims, but neither possess the legitimacy nor the power to materialize these claims. *Dominant stakeholders* are both powerful and legitimate. Their influence in the relationship is assured, since as a result of this power and legitimacy they form the dominant coalition. *Dependent stakeholders* are characterized by a lack of power, but have urgent and legitimate claims. These kinds of stakeholders depend on others to carry out their will. *Dangerous stakeholders* possess urgency and power but no legitimacy and may be coercive or even dangerous. *Definitive stakeholders* possess power, legitimacy and urgency.

METHOD

To conduct this case study, we used a diverse set of qualitative methods, including in-depth interviews, participant observation and documentary research (Ammenwerth, 2003). The initial access to stakeholders was negotiated with a staff member of the IS department. We focused the research on what we regarded as the most immediate stakeholders in the ES project. During a period of six months the authors visited the hospital five times. They conducted interviews, which lasted approximately 1- 2 hours, with members of the general management, IT, the administrative staff, the medical staff, and with external consultants. A snowball sampling strategy was used to identify the subsequent respondents. This means that later on, discussions were held with other members of staff, who were either working with or affected by the enterprise system. The interviews began with a generic question that allowed the interviewees to express how they experienced the ES implementation process. After that, more specific questions were asked about critical incidents, the specific stakeholders' interests, and the meaning they attached to the system. Handwritten notes were taken and individual reports of the interviews were made. The accounts based on these notes were presented to the interviewees and revised slightly on points of detail, if necessary. The data were analyzed by reviewing the respondents' comments, placing them on a time line and dividing them into categories based on their attitudes to the enterprise system. The data are presented in the following sections.

CASE HISTORY

The hospital studied is a medium-sized general hospital located in the western part of The Netherlands. It has 375 beds and 1250 employees. The hospital is divided into six main units: 1) clinical care, 2) ambulant care, 3) physicians, 4) facilities, 5) personnel, and 6) IT and Finance. The physicians are largely remunerated through a service-based fee, and they normally use information systems that function separately from the hospital systems to manage their practices and support their medical treatments.

Episode 1. Preparation

The initial motive to implement an enterprise system was the conclusion of a contract with the former vendor of the Hospital Information System (HIS). HIS was actually a set of separate systems that were loosely linked. The system was not being maintained appropriately and the contacts with the vendor were not very good. This is why the board of management as well as the IT department were interested in a modern product that could help them to establish an integrated, modular and adaptive hospital system. Management also had the ambition to be the first in combining the billing process of the hospital with that of the physicians. At that time, medical treatments involved two separate types of invoices: one from the hospital and one from each relevant physician. A member of the board of management argued:

We were struggling with a set of outdated systems that only supported some business functions separately. We lacked the proper management information and were in need of a system that had the potential to support all hospital processes in an integrated manner.

The hospital aimed at a system that could be adapted to the operational processes of the hospital, and not vice versa. Based on these requirements, a long list of potential vendors was reduced to a shortlist, and a multidisciplinary team selected a number of SAP modules to be implemented by an external consultancy. This consultancy claimed to be experienced in implementing SAP in hospitals. An internal IT manager said:

The consultancy convinced us that it was an expert in adapting and implementing SAP within hospital environments. The company claimed that SAP was very flexible and could be easily adapted to the specific requirements of any hospital.

Another consultancy delivered an external project leader, responsible for the implementation project. One member of the multidisciplinary team (a representative from the nurses) said about the start of the process:

We were invited by the project management to celebrate the start of the project. We all got champagne and everyone seemed to be in agreement. Management and the external consultants promised that the new system would solve all the problems caused by the old and isolated hospital systems. The organization would become a unity with one single information base for all main processes.

However, the actual participation of the hospital's administrators and physicians was quite passive. They were in fact merely bystanders or passive recipients of information about the project. Moreover, the promoters were very confident about the benefits of the system and others did not have the expertise or experience to challenge that.

Episode 2. Start

After the selection of this particular software package, four working groups were formed to prepare the implementation in more detail and to adjust the system to the organization. Technical, administrative, policlinic and billing issues were the focus points of these four groups. They were chaired by the department heads. The board of management and the project leader put a great deal of pressure on them to work fast, whereas all members, including the chairmen, had to combine the preparation of the implementation with their regular tasks. The time pressure was so high, because the hospital was no longer allowed to use its former system. Because of this time pressure, the company's communication with the prospective users was very limited. One chairman of a working group said:

The real objectives of the system did no longer seem relevant, and the only objective that remained was to get it implemented. We were all working very hard, but we could not explain why we were doing so much work only to replace one system with another. Through all of this work we lost track of the initial motives to implement the system.

In actual fact, the mutual adjustment of the various modules and the adaptation to the organization was limited. All energy was put into the technical and organizational complexities. It became clear that the external consultancy was not as experienced in implementing SAP as they had claimed to be. In other hospitals they had adjusted processes to SAP rather than the other way around. Due to the time pressure, the project manager decided to follow the same strategy here.

One member of a working group who had been involved right from the start said:

During the preparation phase, the inherent flexibility and the potential functionalities of the system were emphasized. However, when it came to implementation, we were forced to rush and make sure that the system was installed in time.

A member of the medical staff could recall about this phase:

We attended some of the meetings, but we got the impression that the system was merely a toy for the managers, and not suitable for actual use. However, we did emphasize how complex some of the processes, including the billing processes, are. But the implementers did not seem to be impressed by these remarks.

After implementation of the system, a number of problems arose. Both at the policlinic and at various other clinics, the administrative staff did not know how to use the system, since no formal opportunities had been offered for training. In addition, there was a lack of motivation to use the system, because the staff was not properly informed about the motives behind the SAP implementation. Many people also felt that the degree of user friendliness of the system was lower than that of the old system. And a few of the more conscientious employees even discovered that some output of the system was erroneous.

Episode 3. Crisis

As already mentioned, the hospital followed two billing procedures, one of the hospital and one of the medical staff. Both procedures had to be integrated into one system. Since the income of the medical staff depends directly on a well-functioning billing process, a successful change-over was crucial to them. Up to then, the medical staff had not really been involved and was hardly interested in the ES implementation. However, after a few days of system use, some people discovered that some treatments were not invoiced at all, whereas other treatments were invoiced incorrectly or double. A representative of the medical staff said about this phase:

The implementers totally underestimated the complexity of this crucial process. They assumed that by means of their so-called efficient flow charts each treatment could be invoiced in the same way. However, the reality of our practices is very different from their world of schemes, charts and systems.

A few ingenious administrators tried to keep the system working by so-called 'work arounds', which means that, only after having checked each invoice manually, they were sent away. These work arounds led to new problems; the medical staff as well as the patients and insurers started to complain. They believed that the hospital was no longer in control of its main financial processes. A real crisis developed when the regional press became aware of the problems. The medical staff became convinced that they were missing out on revenues. They informed the board of management that they did not have any confidence in the system and that they refused to use it any longer. The representative of the medical staff said:

Both the implementers and management were clearly not in control. They panicked.

The board of management was forced to intervene and agreed that a separate billing system was acquired beside the SAP system. This separate invoicing system was already used by some groups of the medical staff. From that moment on, all invoices were checked manually and compared with the new shadow system. At the same time, the SAP system was gradually adapted. All these problems led to the immediate retirement of the CFO. In addition, the hospital decided to sue the external consultancy for having failed to meet the main terms of the agreement. After six months, all the adaptations and extra attention seemed

to have some effect. However, due to this crisis, some people think that the hospital missed out on at least 10% of its annual revenues and was very near to bankruptcy because of the implementation of this system. Various people commented that the lower administrative staff had 'saved' the implementation by using redundant systems and checking all financial flows manually. An observer said:

This project was initiated by the top and by externals, but it was realized by the loyalty of the lower administrative staff.

The crisis was overcome by using additional and redundant systems and by gradually adapting the enterprise system to the old working practices. This took approximately six months, during which the administrative staff, nurses and physicians actually adapted and succeeded in managing the operation of the system. At that time, the in-house IT department, which had been left out the preparation and implementation phase, recaptured its tasks. Externals stepped back and the normal operations were once again continued.

Episode 4. Use

After some time, the system was assimilated and the organization became used to it. However, management did not feel that it stimulated the improvement of the management information or led to a more integrated organizational structure. Because its implementation had been rushed, little attention was paid to the further possibilities of the system. For this reason a new project was started, which aimed at generating management information and reports. Only a few clinics have used the SAP system in an optimal way, and many other clinics still use only a limited number of functions. Management is not convinced that the system has helped to achieve the objectives on which the project was based.

ANALYSIS

In this section the roles and interests of the different stakeholders during this process and the meaning they attached to the system will be discussed. After that, we will interpret some successive actions that affected the process. Then we will list what went wrong during this implementation and what lessons can be learned from that. This analysis will be conducted on the basis of the theoretical backgrounds as presented in the third section.

Positions of Stakeholders

The most important stakeholders involved in this implementation project were the board of management, the external consultancy, the external project leader, the physicians, the administrators and the IT staff. Many of these stakeholders are groups with many internal varieties, but also with a relatively high level of consistency with regard to their perceptions of interests, problems, solutions and meaning in relation to this project.

The board of management had a clear interest in a successful and efficient implementation of the enterprise system. They strongly felt that one integrated system would provide them with the management information the needed. The system was intended to replace many local and outdated operational systems, which did not deliver any useful information to the board. The board of management clearly acted as a definitive stakeholder, possessing power, legitimacy and acting from a sense of urgency. After the first stages, however, they delegated a number of their responsibilities to external parties, which means that they became a dormant stakeholder.

The external consultancy had accepted the project on a fixed price basis and obviously had a clear interest in a fast and smooth implementation process. The company was hoping that it could use its previous experiences to realize an effective implementation in this case. But it underestimated the power and roles of the medical practices, which required a system that would comply with the established processes and medical practices. The external project leader, who was from another consultancy, had similar views on the interests, problems and their meaning. Both can be characterized as dependent stakeholders. They both felt a clear urgency, and they both had been given authorization by the board, but they did not really have the power to force other stakeholders to comply.

The administrators can be regarded as users of both the old and the new system. They did not have a clear interest in the new system, since they were used to the current working practices. The external implementers did not really involve the administrators in the implementation process. This was due to time pressures but also because the implementers tried to adapt the hospital processes to the system rather than the other way around. Physicians and administrators argued that the external parties underestimated the hospital's internal complexities and that they lacked a clear interest in its current processes.

The IT staff and the board of management agreed upon the desirability of a single compact and modern IT package for the whole organization. The IT department, however, lacked sufficient knowledge about such systems, and for the time being it had to be busy with maintaining the old set of systems. This is why during the implementation process IT played a background role.

In general, the medical staff want to do their work with some degree of autonomy and without too much managerial interference. In addition, they tend to seek systems that reduce their non-medical workload as much as possible. One member argued that it would be in the interest of the doctors to have loosely-coupled systems, which are tightly adapted to their own specific medical practices. This was not in line with the interests of the board of management, who wished to have an overview of all main processes. The physicians were mainly bystanders during the early stages of the project. They felt that it was an issue to be dealt with by the managers but not by them. This is why they can be characterized as dormant stakeholders; they possessed the power but neither felt the urgency nor had the legitimacy to interfere. This changed dramatically once they became aware that there were serious problems with the billing processes. They then instantly became definitive stakeholders, who clashed with the only other definitive stakeholder: the board of management.

What Went Wrong?

A number of things went wrong during the implementation of this ERP-system. The most important ones are the following:

Management and consultants showed a lack of attention for organizational change issues. In this case history, hospital management attempted to implement an integrated system in a loosely coupled organization without paying much attention to organizational change issues. Management mainly focused on their own goals, namely the replacement of the old hospital system and the implementation of a modern integrated product. They did not consider the consequences of this product for other powerful stakeholders. The external consultancy argued that it was possible to use this ERP solution not only as a replacement, but also as a solution of a number of other management problems. By doing so, they adopted an exclusive 'management rationalism' approach (Heeks, 2006), while ignoring process complexity and diversity and power of the workforce (see section 3).

The project was characterized by the rush to implement and the ambition to innovate, which led to ignorance of problems and complications. Management and implementers were in a rush since the hospital was not longer allowed to use the old hospital system. Besides, management expressed the ambition of 'being the first in combining the billing process'. This limited

timeframe led to 'hard design'(Heeks, 2006) and also to sloppy thinking with regard to process details. The billing process was also much more complex than the consultancy expected and was actually too complicated to capture into the new system. The underestimation of this complexity led to errors and a decreasing confidence in the system by staff and physicians.

There was a low degree of real participation and a lack of attention to the interests of important stakeholders. Physicians and administrators reported that participation during the initiation and start phase was limited. This low degree of participation caused a lack of co-ownership and explained that physicians did feel the responsibility to co-operate in replacing their own billing systems by the new ERP-system. Physicians argued that this was a project of management and consultants so they did not feel a reason to spend time to the realization of this new system. When the actual billing procedure proved to be unreliable, physicians, as being powerful bystanders, could enter the arena and blame others for the installation of an unreliable new system.

Communications about project objectives were ambivalent and sometimes incorrect. On the one hand, management and the consultancy argued that the hospital needed a software product that would help the hospital to become integrated and to deliver consistent and up to date management information. On the other hand, they told the administrators and physicians that the system would be adapted, in order to adjust the system to the organization. This ambivalence caused misunderstanding among members of working groups and physicians. In case of adjustment, experts had to study hospital processes and to modify the system. In case of change, physicians and administrators would be more affected.

Competencies of external consultancy were not adequate. The consultancy claimed to have expertise in implementing in ERP in hospitals, but this expertise was mainly in adjusting hospital processes to systems, rather than the other way around. They also lacked expertise in dealing with organizational change processes, since they had a technical focus.

Lessons

Based on this case history, the following lessons can be learned that are relevant for vendors/consultants of hospital ERP and senior management of hospitals.

1. ERP implementation in hospitals is a combination of technology change and organizational change and should be managed accordingly. This means that project management should use expertise from both fields to implement such change successfully. Markus (2004) provides a number of useful principles for adequate project management in case of the implementation of technology combined with organizational change.
2. In case of a high time pressure or a short time frame, the objectives and ambitions of ERP implementation in hospitals should be brought back to realistic levels. After the initial implementation other projects can be started to make further steps. Since process complexity in hospitals is often high, close attention and time is needed to translate them into the system in adequate ways.
3. Active participation of key stakeholders leads to co-ownership and a responsible attitude during the various stages of implementation. Especially in case of highly affected and powerful stakeholders, such as physicians in hospitals, it is essential to secure active roles and responsibility of physicians or their representatives. Principles of 'soft design' (Heeks, 2006) should be applied in such cases.
4. Management has to be very clear and consistent to anyone affected about the objectives of ERP implementation. Especially about the choice to adjust the system to the organization or to change hospital processes to the system is very crucial. This decision determines how the project has to be managed and how participation of stakeholders has to be organized.
5. In case of process change, adequate change managers have to be in charge. In case of the use of external consultancies, management has to make sure that these consultancies have relevant expertise in realizing such change in hospitals.

CONCLUSION

Enterprise systems are not only technical artifacts, but also a reflection of management philosophies, which may or may not fit in with existing organizational arrangements. This implies that ES implementations may challenge vested interests, and may lead to opposing views of various players. Especially in hospitals, where physicians possess discretionary power to organize their processes and to manage their practices, ES may clash with their interests and viewpoints. Enterprise systems are designed to integrate functions and to standardize business processes, which were previously dispersed and diverse. The physicians affected do have the power to choose whether they wish to adopt or to reject such systems.

For these reasons it is essential for managers of ES implementations within hospitals to be aware of the ways in which ES affects the established institutional settings (Yi et al., 2006). During the initial stages of the implementation process, decisions have to be made about necessary changes in either the system or the organization, or in both. These changes can be required to meet certain needs of stakeholders in order to make sure that they cooperate and participate in effective ways. It is not acceptable if potential influential players remain passive until the actual use phase starts. This case illustrates that aggressive resistance after implementation can lead to a counter-productive crisis, which could have been prevented by a thorough analysis of the interests of the key players right from the start. Such an analysis could be followed by a discussion that leads to an agreement among the most important stakeholders upon how to implement the system and how to adapt the relevant processes. Such an agreement could be a compromise of various contrasting interests.

The chapter also shows that ES implementation within hospitals is a dynamic process. This means that certain views, which are held by stakeholders at one point in time, may change during the project. There may be various reasons why views change, including cognitive, political and opportunistic ones. In this case the physicians and administrators remained relatively passive, until problems arose during the use phase. It indicates that implementing ES within hospitals is a complex venture, in which the opportunities and limitations of the system have to be aligned with the existing and always changing organizational arrangements, including various perceptions, quests for power, leadership and subtle processes to gain support for further continuation of the project.

In this case a power vacuum (caused by the board of management) stimulated behavior that was more politically-oriented, and resulted in a lack of agreement on the direction and use of the system. Through this lack of agreement, the various stakeholders mainly followed mainly their own goals and undermined to some extent the hospital-wide explicit objectives of the project. The chapter shows that the promoters of the hospital-wide enterprise system took a too optimistic view of the power of such a system to improve the operation of the hospital's processes. In the rush to implement, no careful attention was paid to the complexities of the internal processes, the stakeholders' interests and their mutual relations. The rational image of system implementation could not conceal its poor understanding of the deeper organizational realities, such as history, culture and power.

REFERENCES

Ammenwerth, E., Iller, C., & Mansmann, U. (2003). Can evaluation studies benefit from triangulation? A case study. *International Journal of Medical Informatics, 70*(2), 237-248.

Bennis, W. G. (1984). Transformative power and leadership. In: TJ. Sergiovanni and JE Corbally (eds), *Leadership and Organizational Culture*. Urbana, University of Illinois Press; 1984.

Boddy, D. (2002). *Managing Projects*. London: Prentice Hall.

Boonstra, A. (2003). Structure and Analysis of IS decision making processes. European *Journal of Information Systems, 12*(3), 195-209.

Davenport, T. H. (1998). Putting the Enterprise into the Enterprise System, *Harvard Business Review, 76*(4), 121-132.

Dawson, P. (1994). *Organisational Change: A Processual Approach*. London: Chapman.

Fowler, A., & Gilfillan, M. (2003). A Framework for Stakeholder Integration in Higher Education Information Systems Projects. *Technology Analysis & Strategic Management, 15*(4), 467-489.

Haux, R. (2006). Health information systems - past, present, future. *International Journal of Medical Informatics, 75*(3), 268-281.

Jossi, F. (2005). ERP on the Rise. Some hospitals see the advantages in a single system. Healthcare Informatics, 2005, www.healthcare-informatics. com/issues/2005/06_05/jossi.htm 79-80, accessed on March 21st 2006.

Klaus, H., Rosemann, M., & Gable, G. G. (2000). What is ERP? *Information Systems Frontiers, 2*(3), 141-162.

Levine, H. G., & Rossmoore, D. (1995). Politics and the Function of Power in a Case Study of IT Implementation. *Journal of Management Information Systems, 11*(3), 115-133.

Markus, M. L., & Tanis, C. (2000). Multisite ERP implementations. *Communications of the ACM, 43*(4), 42-26.

Markus, M. L., Axline, S., Petrie, D., & Tanis, C. (2000). Learning from adopters' experiences with ERP: problems encountered and success achieved. *Journal of Information Technology, 15*(4), 245-265.

Markus, M. L. (2004). Technochange Management: Using IT to drive organizational change. *Journal of Information Technology, 20*(1), 4-20.

McAfee, A. (2003). When too much IT knowledge is a dangerous thing. *Sloan Management Review, 44*(2), 83-89.

Merode, G. G. van, Groothuis, S. van, & Hasman, A. (2004). Enterprise Resource Planning for Hospitals. *International Journal of Medical Informatics, 73*, 6, 493-501.

Mitchell, R. K., Agle, B. R., & Wood, D. J. (1997). Toward a Theory of Stakeholder Identifiction and Salience: Defining the Principle of who and what really counts. *Academy of Management Review, 22*(4), 853-886.

Orlikowski, W. J. (1992). The Duality of Technology: Rethinking the Concept of Technology in Organisations. *Organisation Science, 3*(1), 398-427.

Paré, G., & Sikotte, C. (2001). Information technology sophistication in health care: an instrument validation study among Canadian hospitals. *International Journal of Medical Informatics, 63*(2), 205-223.

Pettigrew, A. M. (1988). *The Management of Strategic Change*. Basil Blackwell, Oxford.

Pinch, T. J., & Bijker, W. E. (1992). The Social Construction of Facts and Artifacts: Or How the Sociology of Science and the Sociology of Technology Might Benefit Each Other. In W.E. Bijker, T.P. Hughes and T.J. Pinch (eds.) *The Social Construction of Technological Systems*, MIT Press, Cambridge, Ma, 1992.

Standifera, R. L., & Wall, J. A. (2003). Managing Conflict in B2B E-Commerce. *Business Horizons, 46*(2), 65-70.

Walsham, G. (1993). *Interpreting Information Systems in Organizations*. Chichester, Wiley.

Yi, M.Y., Jackson, J. D., Park, J. S. & Probst, J. C. (2006). Understanding information technology acceptance by individual professionals: Toward an integrative view. *Information & Management, 43*(3), 350-363.

KEY TERMS

Enterprise System: Enterprise systems are software applications aimed at integrating a range of business functions in order to acquire an overview of the business based on a single information architecture

Power: Power is the capacity to exert the will over others in order to realize certain intended benefits.

Power (Re)distribution: Power (re)distribution is the degree to which power is distributed within and between organizations and the extent that an enterprise system changes that division of power.

Stakeholder of an Enterprise System: An individual or group who can affect or can be affected by the implementation of an enterprise system.

Stakeholder Salience Theory: Divides stakeholders in seven types depending on their degree of power, urgency and legitimacy. These types are: dormant, discretionary, demanding, dominant, dependent, dangerous and definitive.

Interest of Stakeholders: The interest of a stakeholder reflects the perception that an IOS contributes to the overall goals of the stakeholder.

Chapter XXI
Designing to Deploying Customisable ERP Cost Effectively

S. Padmanaban
Pune, India

ABSTRACT

ERP systems have become key enablers of businesses today. While many organizations wish to adopt ERP for competitive advantage, they find choosing, using, and realizing expected benefits from, appropriate ERP extremely daunting, given the multitude of factors and options along technologies, vendors, people, and customisation cost and time. It is in this context that the experience presented in this chapter from two Indian projects on designing to deploying ERP systems—for two different organizations engaged in education and construction—becomes very relevant. Reporting on the various processes, practices, techniques, and methods employed through the projects, and the lessons learnt therefrom, the paper argues that time has come for designing and deploying industry-neutral generic ERP systems cost effectively. It proposes that through a combination of appropriate technologies, innovative tools, techniques and strategies, highly adoptive and customisable ERP systems can be designed and deployed at affordable costs and within reasonable timeframes.

INTRODUCTION

Enterprise systems [ES] in general and Enterprise Resource Planning systems [ERP][1] in particular have become the most important enablers of business today. The emerging trend is that a number of business enterprises as well as not-for-profit organisations like universities and hospitals--regardless of their size, market, products, services, industry, location--have now started looking at ERP as an effective facilitator of, and a powerful tool for, managing the organisation better. Most of them believe that they can create and sustain cost and competitive advantages by adopting ERP. We must note here that even for universities, hospitals, NGO's, and charitable institutions running a variety of socially relevant programs, cost is a major concern and, with globalisation and opening of up of economies, competition real and important. Even small and medium size enterprises opt for [or would like to adopt] ERP more as a strategic initiative to combat competition than merely as part of information system. Consider, for example, the case of a small textile firm in Tiruppur, Tamil Nadu, India which had to go for on-line hook-up with the supply chain management system of Wall Mart, USA, in order to win and execute supply contract. (Surajeet Gupta, 2004)[1]

However, when it comes to choosing and adopting an ERP most appropriate for the enterprise, the exercise is neither easy nor straight forward. A number of key questions and challenges arise when an enterprise considers adopting ES/ERP. Ranging from relevance, cost-benefit justification, appropriateness, to choice of source [licensing, renting, owning], architecture, designing, developing, and finally deploying the very system 'successfully', these questions and challenges are big and complex, and encompass a number of considerations and options in terms of 'economics', 'technology', 'human resource', 'organisational culture', and 'environmental issues'. Going by example is not feasible either, as published real life cases are limited in number and inconclusive on key issues, presenting more of successes and understandably less of failures. Even fewer are reported in detail about the experiences through-- and more importantly the lessons learnt from--the Software/System Development Life Cycle [SDLC] phases and processes.

Given this scenario, it is no wonder that while the number of enterprises wishing to adopt ERP is growing, the rate of such adoption is not phenomenal. Major restraints appear to be in terms of high cost, long time, and uncertain benefits.

More specifically, enterprises hesitate to adopt ES/ERP because:

- of high total cost of ownership [TCO] and total cost of operations [TCOP]; let us call these and underlying factors collectively, the COST;
- of unduly long time to reach 'full adoption' stage; let us call these and related factors collectively, the TIME; and
- the anticipated benefits are not cognizable and realizable; let us call these and related factors collectively, the QUALITY.

In other words, concerns around three dimensions, viz., COST, TIME, and QUALITY [CTQ] seem to act as 'barriers' for enterprises adopting ERP. Of course, there are a number of other indirect factors as well, like 'people being not ready', 'business process re-engineering [BPR] not properly done' and so on. While 'people' and 'processes' are certainly important, we note that their impact gets reflected in CTQ [people not being ready delays adoption; delay costs time and money; bad processes cause delay and damage which in turn affect cost, time and quality]. Obviously, COST and TIME are more easily quantifiable than QUALITY.

While the foregoing illustrates issues from the enterprise perspective, there is an equally challenging and complex set of issues for the 'designer, developer, vendor' to consider and resolve. Some of the key questions and challenges here are:

- Why should ES/ERP [the software part] continue to be costly, even after several years of designing and developing [including re-designing] by a number of players in the field?
- What is happening on the 're-usability of code [components]', 'avoidance of re-inventing of the wheel' front, leading to reduction in cost/time for re-design and re-development?

- Why should ES/ERP be industry-specific, and thereby the cost of customisation adding to TCO and TCOP? Can the degree of 'abstraction' in design be increased, so that the resultant application architecture becomes industry-neutral, and is more easily customizable and maintainable?
- How much of Open Source Standards [OSS] and Object Oriented Analysis and Design [OOAD] approach and tools can be used in simplifying the design, architecture, and thus improving reliability, maintainability, and upgradeability?

In other words, the 'designer, developer, vendor' perspective and concern should ideally be to meet and match the CTQ concerns of the enterprise, via technological options, methodologies, techniques which include/exploit: 'reusability of code'; 'OSS'; 'industry-neutrality', 'OOAD approach'; all leading to 'designing to deployment of ERP effectively'. But they aren't, as things stand today.

Juxtaposing the eagerness and concerns of enterprises in terms of CTQ on adopting ERP on the one side, with the issues and challenges before designers, developers and vendors, on the other, this Chapter proposes to show that it is possible to address many of the issues mentioned and break the 'barriers to ERP adoption by enterprise', through a presentation and detailed discussion of experience from two software development projects in India. Beginning with working definitions for some contextually relevant terms, key details of the projects as Background [the next section], the Chapter proceeds to discuss [in the subsequent sections] the projects in detail, in terms of objectives, critical issues faced and responses given by the sponsoring-organisations, and presents the experiences drawn from the projects along with learning gained. It concludes [in the last section], in the light of the limited empirical evidence drawn and recorded from the projects, that

- it is possible to design highly customisable [and therefore very flexible and user-centric] and generic [i.e., industry-neutral] ERP by using a combination of innovative ideas of design, technology options and sources available today; and
- also to deploy it effectively through a judicious combination of people and process factors, with CTQ advantages for the enterprise.

BACKGROUND

Some Definitions

Before getting into the details of the projects, let us place some contextually relevant acronyms and terms, and discuss their broad working definitions and meanings as we use them here. These terms are: ERP, TCO, TCOP, CTQ, BPR, OSS, and OOAD.

We look at ERP both as a system and as software package. ERP, as a system, is an enterprise-wide, orderly, and cohesive arrangement of computers, people, information flows and processes, procedures and control mechanisms, and communication facilities, in such a manner that the business of the enterprise can be carried out effectively and efficiently. It encompasses and integrates synergistically through information processes and flows, at on-line and real time, all typical and key functional areas of business: viz., marketing/ sales/ distribution, materials/purchase/ stores, production/qc/maintenance, accounting/ finance, and human resource development, at operations, tactical, and strategic levels of management. Ideally, it should focus on and facilitate customer servicing, competitiveness, and growth with surplus from the operations of business.

ERP as a custom-built or vendor-supplied off-the-shelf-shrink-wrapped customisable package, is a set of software [computer] programs, capable of running on and linking computers and computing devices [PCs, PDAs, mobile phones, bar code readers, POS machines, CNC machines], regardless of their make, model, and numbers; across offices, production floors, plants, warehouses, regardless of their location; in real time and on-line mode; integrating all 'business processes' [BPs] across functional areas like marketing, sales, logistics, production, quality assurance, materials, stores, maintenance, accounting and finance, human resource, automating as many 'BPs' as feasible; through a common data base; for the unified purposes of optimised enterprise wide resource usage. We are of course excluding patented, protected, and secretly guarded 'production and conversion' processes from the purview. What, however, is included is the 'information part'.

Extensions to ERP covering inter-enterprise operations and processes include software categorized as CRM [customer relation management] and SCM [supply chain management] systems, and often may be treated as part of ERP itself.

Note the definition is industry-neutral, and implies that not only planning of 'resources'--but also their effective and integrative management--through information and communication technology [ICT] is central to ERP. Resources for this purpose mean and include: men [people], machines, materials, money, and mouse [meaning information!], along time and quality dimensions. Note the omission of 'land' [the first factor of production in Economics] from the list of resources, and addition of 'information' to it. In the words of Turban et. al. (2004), "Managing information resources, new technologies, and communications networks is becoming a – or even *the* – critical success factor in the operations of many organisations, private and public, and will be essential to the survival of organisations in the digital economy." [2] Information is a key factor leading to knowledge, both at individual and corporate levels, and enterprises thus regard both information and knowledge as valuable resource. Indeed, as Ruggles (1998) [3][3] notes, quoting Peter Drucker, "knowledge has become

the key economic resource and the dominant - and perhaps even the only - source of comparative advantage". (p.80)

We also note that because of the close links among 'information', 'knowledge' and CTQ advantages that can arise from adopting ERP, its applicability and usefulness extend beyond business enterprise, to even not-for-profit and governmental organisations and institutions.

We define TCO as the sum of investments made up to the current time on ERP-assets [e.g., hardware, software licence/media, security and so on, all attributable to ERP and all of a long-lasting nature] acquired/developed/ replaced/upgraded over time by the enterprise, adjusted for accumulated depreciation and tax concessions on such assets up to that time. All expenses including costs of procurement, installation and commissioning of all ERP-assets of amortizable nature would be included in TCO, duly amortized. Invariably, TCO is treated as 'cumulative investment net of depreciation' and so shown in the books of accounts as 'assets' as on the time of ascertainment.

TCOP is defined as the sum of expenditure incurred periodically [usually per annum] and measured during any point in time in such period, on maintenance of ERP-assets and supportive resources/services. These include: hardware, software licence/media maintenance/upgrade fees, salaries to IT staff, ongoing training to staff, consultants fee, security drills and upkeep, and so forth, all of 'recurring' nature, non-amortizable, and attributable to ERP. Invariably, TCOP is treated as 'recurring expenditure' and written off in the books of accounts pertaining to the period to which it belongs by a charge on the surplus [or income] earned. If there is no surplus, then it would appear as 'cash loss' or 'accumulated loss' and effectively reduce the capital. In other words, TCOP would be 0 at the beginning and at its highest at the end of the period of ascertainment.

CTQ stands for Cost-Time-Quality, the key dimensions along which enterprises aspire to have control, to gain and sustain competitive advantage and growth with surplus. Every organisation tries to establish and sustain its comparative and competitive advantages by having better control on its cost of production/services, reducing time to market/service, and in the process improve [and not compromise] the quality of its products/services. In these days of Internet and ICT, it has realized that by effectively and innovatively using ICT, it can turn CTQ in its favour. It has been reported in a survey that intelligent enterprises establish their effectiveness in their markets and environments via CTQ control, by using and exploiting ICT (Anil Patrick R, 2005).[4]

A question often raised at this juncture, but rarely fully answered in the literature, is: at what TCO, TCOP should an enterprise regard ERP-adoption as justified? While applying cost benefit analysis is sticky, given the difficulties in quantifying many of the intangible benefits, it has also been argued that there are genuine strategic compulsions for adopting--and other methods of justifying investment in--ERP (Padmanaban, 2006).[5] In any case, justifying investment in ERP, or leveraging it to gain the anticipated benefits by the enterprise is beyond our purview. Our focus is on establishing that there are empirical evidences to bring down both TCO and TCOP considerably, which leads to CTQ advantage via adopting ERP by the enterprise. Suffice is to say that relating TCO to capital [corpus in case of not-for-profit organisations], and TCOP to turnover [or outlay in case of not-for-profit organisations] on an ongoing basis across industry verticals would be one of the good measures.

BPR for our discussion means and includes an organisation's willingness and propensity to critically and continually evaluate the manner in which it handles [processes] its business functions, and its ability to drop, modify, and even introduce new, ways of handling such functions, all leading to greater customer satisfaction, better quality, higher productivity, and shorter cycle time to market/serve customer. Here again the implications are in terms of CTQ.

We recognize OSS as an important emerging trend not to be ignored. It signifies a major paradigm shift giving newer meaning for ownership and usage of intellectual property rights. If properly explored, it could lead to considerable savings in cost, thus yielding CTQ advantage to the enterprise. For the 'designer, developer, vendor' it offers tremendous intellectual challenge, scope, as well as satisfaction, in terms of creating, improving, and sharing of: operating systems, communication protocols, databases, development frameworks, utilities, and toolkits.

OOAD includes incorporating innovative design ideas, exploiting its principles of abstraction, and guidelines on creating and improving 're-usable code', all leading to designing of industry-neutral ERP.

Having defined and discussed the relevant terms, let us now discuss the projects in detail, beginning with some key data about the projects themselves.

Some Key Data about the Projects

The two projects involved three organisations in India, falling into three totally different lines of business/industry, viz., education, construction, and IT products/services. Both the projects were conceived to design, develop, and deploy homegrown [meaning in-house and custom-built] ERP capable of running across a number of institutions/enterprises. The entire discussion that follows is based on the experience and some learning by the author, a key and the only common member between the two project teams, playing mainly the role of advisor/consultant.

The first project, nicknamed EERPMS [Educational Enterprises Resources Planning and Management System], commenced in September 2004 as an in-house ERP software development initiative at/by a charitable trust named Sreekshethra Dharmasthala Manjunatheswara Educational Society [SDMES], Ujire, Karnataka, India. EERPMS aims at integrating all functional aspects of about 45+ educational institutions located in different cities and towns in the state of Karnataka, offering education and training services at different levels, in various fields, including medical, dental, engineering, and management. The project went through testing in March 2007, and is expected to go live in July 2007, in respect of FIVE modules [Accounts & Inventory, Academics & Admissions, Human Resource, and Library] at three locations as initial phase. Using a combination of Open Source resources and web technologies including Java and JSP, and at one fifth the normal market costs, EERPMS has given a number of insights useful to both ERP adaptors and designers.

The second project, nicknamed URCIS [URC Information System], commenced in September 2006, also as an in-house effort, with the help of an external software developing company [to be called SDC], meant to integrate the business processes of a leading construction company [to be called CC] in Tamil Nadu, a state in South India, connecting five branches and about 40 project sites on-line real-time.[2] The project is expected to go live in phases beginning July 2007. Using a combination of .NET resources and also home-grown tools and utilities, URCIS has established that ERP can be made not only at cost almost one sixth of what vendors of off-the-shelf packages quoted, but also with flexibility to make it almost industry-neutral.

The following sections narrate how both EERPMS and URCIS provided challenges and opportunities to try and experiment with some bold and innovative initiatives in: design and development of an ERP system capable of meeting the varying needs of enterprises in different industries/sectors; its deployment among institutions with differing levels of autonomy; and above all in accomplishing goals of integration and consolidation of information about resources at the management level at optimum cost.

The discussion would be common across both the projects, noting significant differences

as and when applicable. Table 1 lists a number of important aspects of both the projects.

Let us now discuss the entire project experience, in terms of key objectives, issues and concerns, responses, and learning.

THE PROJECT EXPERIENCE AND LEARNING

Key Objectives, Issues, Concerns and Responses

Although the projects commenced at different times, they both had some common objectives, issues, and concerns before them. One could see that many of these are almost generic and applicable to any ERP initiative, regardless of the industry or line of business. We discuss what we consider were critical, and also present the response/choice made by the organisations along with reasons:

• How/why is an educational institution [SDMES] similar to, or different from, a business enterprise [CC]? What are the compulsions to consider using an ERP? Can a generic ERP be designed to address several differences between not only SDMES and CC, but also among the constituents of SDMES?

These implied not only clearly identifying anticipated benefits [objectives] in advance as a means to justify ERP investment, but also exploring possibilities of designing generic ERP, with the desired levels of 'customisability' and also 'security'. For instance, SDMES has pharmacy colleges and hospitals with medicine production facilities, and therefore the ERP should ideally include production, packing, sales and distribution modules as well. Even among its several constituent institutions, special differences existed in terms of admission procedures [government controlled], functional autonomy [some were

Table 1. Comparative features of EERPMS and URCIS

Parameters	EERPMS	URCIS
Commenced in	Sep-2004	Sep-2006
Going live from [in phases]	Jul-2007	Jul-2007
Number of modules; List	14; admission, academics, library, accounts & inventory, production & sales, assets management, estate management, HR	6; business development, tendering-bidding, project management & execution, finance & accounts, inventory+centering materials, machinery, HR
Software development team; Size range over time	in-house; 9-15-4	in-house + SDC team; 3-20-7
OS, technology, RDBMS, development environment/ tools; deployment architecture	Windows/IE + Mozilla + Suse Linux + MySQL+ Java+ JSP	Windows/IE+VB .NET+ MySQL plus some other open source toolkits for 'report generation'.
Software development cost *	INR 2.5 million	INR 2.2 million
Outlay/Turnover	INR 1 billion	INR 2.5 billion
Commercial Quote Range	INR 5-10 million	INR 10-20 million
Shortest Commercial Time Indicated for Deployment	24 months	12 months
Perception about % of match between requirements specified and vendor offer	5%	15%

* Approximate figure, comprising mainly of salaries and fees paid to team members, including consultant fees; ascertained as on 31 March 2007;

affiliated to University, some were autonomous], curriculum design, placement and so on. CC, on the other hand, has some educational institutions run under its indirect supervision via some trusts created for the purpose.

Both, in this sense, looked for synergistic benefits from a common initiative. The main objective of the ERP initiative was 'to integrate the various departments, divisions, constituents through an information system which would automate a number of clerical functions at the operations level, help in making and improving decisions by middle management, and also yield strategic control and consolidated information for the top management'. With these objectives and concerns forming the backdrop of their require-

ments, the organisations then began looking at the next two important issues, i.e., the design for 'generic' ERP, and the source of such ERP. On the fist issue, some bold and innovative tools and techniques were introduced both by SDMES and CC. More about these in the next section. On the second issue of 'source', the options ranged from 'buying/licensing to renting to in-house development'. The choice was 'in-house'. The rationale follows.

• What is the option for sourcing ERP? Why in-house development? How does one justify the cost and time involved? How about project management and mobilization of resources?

It became apparent from the beginning itself that the option of 'buying/licensing off-the-shelf package offered by vendors' was going to cost way beyond the 'affordable' points. For instance, the quotes ranged from INR [Indian rupees] 10 to 20 million, inclusive of customisation and training.[3] The timeframe indicated also ranged from 12 to 24 months from the date of signing of contract. Note that these figures did not include hardware and software components like the operating system, data base management system, and communication ware.

One can of course argue that the so called 'affordable' points and the perception of timeframes as too long are subjective and may vary depending upon the risk-preference profile of the investing organisation. Nevertheless the point is that any organisation considering the ERP initiative for the first time would have its own yardsticks on these, and they are normally inclined to accept the lowest TCO and the shortest timeframe, if and when they consider procuring 'shrink-wrapped' package. The 'renting' option, offered by some vendors also implied that their products were not meeting even 20% of the requirements. The choice therefore was 'in-house development' with whatever support one could get from outside, after detailed estimates and discussion convinced the management that this would be the least risky option with better control on cost and time. While SDMES went ahead with in-house team building, roping in consultants from within to form the project team, CC went in for in-house team supplemented by services from SDC and an external consultant [the author] to direct and manage the project. The next question was about development platform and environment.

- What software platform, including data base management system? Which source: open or proprietary? What type of architecture: simple client server on LAN/WAN or web-based Internet technologies?

While open source was the favoured choice because it meant 'readily available tools, Operating Systems [OS, e.g. Linux], database management systems [MySql], language and frameworks [Java and J2EE], web browsers [Mozilla] and servers [Tomcat/Apache] at minimum/no cost from the Internet', it also posed some challenges. These included: unfamiliarity; lack of accountable support; need for protecting [or continuing to use] the existing OS, database systems and so on. A combination therefore of proprietary and open source was inevitable. While SDMES's choice drew more from OSS, CC chose more from proprietary, mainly because of strong familiarity considerations. On the question of architecture, simple LAN/WAN based client/server vs. web-based n-tiered, both favoured the latter mainly because of low cost communication and networking options via Internet. See Table 1 for details.

Next key issue was about the project management itself, through the SDLC cycle, through phases like analysis, design, development, testing, and deploying.

- How about the project management, per se, taking into account analysis, design, development, testing, user acceptance, and deployment?

While detailed software requirement specifications [SRS] were drawn up in consultation with user groups, it was becoming obvious that there were conflicting interests and aspirations from a few departments/divisions/constituents, sometimes negating the very objectives the management had. For instance, two of the institutions of SDMES felt threatened about losing their independence, while some others felt they did not need an ERP at all, or a 'differently designed ERP'. One of the departmental heads of CC opined that his requirements were so complex that they could not be met by ERP. A tactical response from the team was that adequate 'configurability' would take care of difference in the requirements, while autonomy/independence would be affected to the minimum.

For the designers, these signals of resistance and hesitation meant that the design should yield a high degree of 'customisability' without much loss of time, while ensuring that the original objectives could still be met. They realized that while users in general would be limited in specifying their expectations or requirements, intensive involvement of a few selective more knowledgeable users would lead to better design and larger scope. For instance, one of the librarians took a lot more interest than others [there were at least 20 representing different colleges/institutions] in demanding the best and current features like OPAC [open public access catalogue].

It became obvious through the SDLC phases that both people and process related issues like the ones mentioned above would have to be handled carefully and tactfully. Periodic formal meetings and communication by the top management representative [the Secretary of SDMES, and the Executive Director of CC] with the user groups, heads of institutions/departments helped in tackling these issues. In the case of CC, an additional 'ambassador' group comprising of 1-2 staff members from each department was created, and charged with authority and accountability to ensure smooth transition to the deployment phase. We shall discuss more on these in the next section.

While SDMES project team suffered from attrition and multi-location coordination problems resulting considerable loss of productive time, accompanied by part-time team leaders, the CC team had its own difficulties in terms of working from two different locations, delay in hiring people, and re-training of staff in the technologies chosen. EERPMS took almost more than two years to reach deployment, while URCIS took just about nine months.

The only inference we could draw for this major difference is that while SDMES environment allowed a 'laid-back' attitude and 'persuasive

and democratic' approach with only part-time involvement from team-leaders, typical of educational/charitable institutions, the URCIS environment could manage to create and maintain a 'business-like' attitude and 'more compelling and demanding' approach, typical of business enterprises.

Both projects reached the stage of deployment roughly 9 [CC] to 30 [SDMES] months after commencement. As at the time of writing, SDMES has launched 5 modules at one location, while CC has completed beta testing using 'real life' data, and is in the process of going live on all the modules with basic functionalities in five locations.

Three Important Challenges and Learning

We now discuss what we consider to be the three most important points of challenges and learning revealed through the various aspects of the projects:

- Designing for Industry-neutrality & Genericity;
- Automating and improving degree of 'customisability'; and
- Strategic People and Process factors to ensure quick and smooth deployment.

At the core, ERP is meant for effective planning and management of resources through integration of various business functions. A design which aims at building industry-neutrality and genericity should therefore begin with an understanding of similarities [if any] across functional processes among different industries for this purpose, and also provide for dissimilarities [if any]. It is obvious that similarities occur naturally if the functional process remains same. For instance, an educational system may have some production systems as well [as in the case of SDMES], having procurement, production, storing, dispatch, and receivables typical of a manufacturing system. In such cases, one could easily provide for 'modules' dealing with these processes as 'add-ons'.

However, if there is no natural commonality across functions, then what should the designer do? Here, the principle of 'abstraction' comes to help, and we try and visualize commonalities in an abstract manner. For instance, can the 'admission' process of an educational system be likened to the 'procurement [buying]' process of a manufacturing system, treating the 'object of procurement' to be 'natural individual person [say, student]' in the first case, and 'material [say, iron ore]' for the second case, assuming that both the systems treat the resources as 'inputs' to be processed to yield some 'outputs'. One can argue that this is height of 'abstraction' and it is absurd to treat 'student' the same as 'iron ore', and much weirder to treat 'admission' process as equivalent to 'buying' process. *The idea is not to treat them as same but similar, and take advantage of such similarities into coding of the core part of ERP.* Indeed, this is the essence of OOAD approach, exploiting the concepts of encapsulation, inheritance, and polymorphism. Going further, we can recognize and account for 'procurement costs' [all costs incurred to bring in the best student; all costs incurred to bring in the best iron ore], 'conversion costs' [costs incurred in training the student; costs incurred in converting iron ore into steel], measuring costs against standards and reporting variances and so on. Note these cover other functional processes as well, such as 'production', 'costing', and 'accounting'.

If we are able to capture, in this particular example, the steps and sequences of the processes as *input to output conversion specifications*, and have code to execute such specifications, then we have 'neutrality' built into the code. Of course, externally, as part of user interface we have to provide for 'aliases', and also internally, as part of database management system, we have to build appropriate querying and manipulating code. *In other words, we are designing and building code,*

to accept and act according to specifications of the modules in a generic manner around what are internally known as resources, and not processes as defined or understood by analysts,. The responsibility to specify rests with the user, while the responsibility for proper design and code to implement rests with the designer/ developer. A strategic implication here is that knowledgeable key users become part of designer/developer group. The SDC team was able to evolve a utility featuring these capabilities, and use it in 'creating the architecture'.

Essentially, the above methodology implies that the user, or a small group of users, well informed on the processes, will be helped to define/specify both visually and textually, the functionalities in terms of inputs, processes, and outputs, and a utility created for this purpose enables building/assembly of the ERP as the specification proceeds. Known as 'meta specification' or 'architecture specification', this concept is not new, but its application is, and not widely reported. Indeed, service oriented architecture [SOA] (Wikipedia, 2007)[6] emphasizes this approach, and a few companies have come up with their own approaches, tools and techniques, e.g., EnterpriseTenFold2007® from TenFold Corporation, USA, featuring Ajax [another emerging technology component to expedite creation and deployment of rich user interface] capabilities (TenFold, 2007)[7]. Another example is IBM's Rational Rose® (TechRepublic, 2007).[8] Some CASE [computer aided software engineering] tools and OOAD approaches using Unified Modeling Language (Tsang et al, 2005)[9] have also been mentioned in literature, claiming not only quicker development of robust software, but also superiority in approach and results over others.

The main difference in our experience is that we tried to apply these ideas in creating a utility in-house to facilitate 'industry-neutral' ERP, and any interested designer/developer can try, develop and adopt similar approach and utilities. Once tested and tried well over time, such utilities and tools can help expedite the process of building [or assembling as it were] an enterprise-appropriate ERP much faster and with fewer doubts about its capabilities. The only hitch as of now is such tools may be specific to the integrated development environment [IDE], and even then the one we built applied very well for CC. SDMES adopted another variation and came up with an add-in named 'Info Store' which enables the user to create even data types, and therefore data stores [tables in the database] of their choice.

One word of caution is called for here. It is possible, and inevitable, that some specific core processes [especially the technical processes as applicable to manufacturing systems] may call for special interfaces to be in place and therefore require specific extra coding. Subject to this rider, the advantages of building such a utility in the applicable environment first yields certainly CTQ advantages for the designer/developer, and by extension to the enterprise.

The reader may have observed that the foregoing also implies a degree of 'customisability'. However, we differentiate 'customisability' from 'genericity' in that the latter *stands for 'architecture' that incorporates some fundamental abstract core code capable of accepting and acting as per specifications about functional modules/processes that make up that architecture' while the former stands for 'module behavior at all sub levels of user interface, including formatting of inputs and outputs, procedure specification' as desired by the user.*

Using a tool combined into the utility referred to earlier, CC could improve the 'customisability' of URCIS, and expedite the process of building and releasing it. This tool essentially captures user interfaces for every input-output-process of every module incorporated into the ERP, and automates the generation of functional code. A quick comparison of time and effort pre- and post-tool scenario convinced us that developer productivity increased at least by 5-7 times. For instance, as against 1-2 days taken by a coder for coding

one complex user interface comprising one input form and one output document, referring to two tables, the tool enabled the same coder to finish three such sets in a day. More over, a number of cosmetic features and preferences could be set by the user himself.

Key Learning

The first and most important lesson learnt that the people and process related factors are very important, not only pre-ERP but also during ERP phases. Both top management involvement and critical user group involvement from the beginning matter a great deal. As noted earlier, top management involvement accompanied by a 'business like' attitude and 'demanding' approach quickened the deliverables from one project.

The second is that the 'customisability' at the hands of the user shifts the responsibility for 'successful adoption' to the user from the designer/developer. This has some strategic implications as well in expediting adoption.

The third point learnt is that bold and innovative ideas must be encouraged and the environment should support trials and failures. Although such trials and failures may cause initially delay and doubts about outcome, persistence guided by proper professional advice will yield positive results. The utility and tool created from the projects, yielding 'industry-neutrality' at the core module level, and 'customisability' at the user-interface levels, stand testimony to this. These are also helping the organisations concerned to gain and secure CTQ advantage.

Finally, BPR as a process pre or during ERP to bring about CTQ advantage did not have much applicability in compliance and statutory functional processes. Again, educational institutions bound by external agencies [like university or government] had much less scope than business organisations to apply BPR.

LIMITATIONS AND FUTURE TRENDS

Our empirical study has put much less emphasis on certain other aspects of information system per se. These include: security both in Intra- and Internet environments, processing power of servers and the application overhead on them, disaster recovery & business continuity planning [DRBCP], and BPR. This is not to say that these are any less important, but the point is that limited attention has been so far paid to these because of the priority and pressures attached to the building the basic bloc of ERP. Plans are afoot to take security and DRBCP issues into the software.

The second aspect is that further empirical evidence and follow up research as well as survey on similar experiments are needed to validate our conclusions. Some key questions are:

- Are there factors/barriers beyond CTQ? For instance, does size matter?
- How can organisations ensure continuous CTQ advantage?
- How can organisations deal with knowledge, the emerging differentiator, and its management?

While current literature has covered some aspects of these questions, the newer technologies and innovations [virtual organisations, nano technologies, and knowledge society] pose enormous scope for work and better understanding of their implications on running businesses and organisations effectively.

CONCLUSION

While ERP, as an enterprise-wide integrative information system, has been well recognized as the most important business enabler by business enterprises and even by not-for-profit organisations, its adoption by the latter has been restricted mainly by cost, time, and quality concerns. Although these concerns dominate both pre and during ERP phases, we have mainly focused on the cost and time aspects in pre-ERP phase, on the premise that cost and time for acquiring [or custom-building] an appropriate ERP have been high.

Based on the experiences gained and lessons learnt from two ERP software development projects in India, we conclude that:

- It is possible to build and re-build ERP in timeframes much shorter and at costs significantly lower than what 'packages' market offers today;
- It is also possible to incorporate 'industry-neutrality' and high degree of 'customisability' into ERP;

We also believe that:

- The experiments conducted and experiences recorded would be useful for both organisations contemplating adoption of ERP, and also for designer/developer/ vendor groups working in this area.
- It should now be possible for a large number of enterprises and organisations to build and adopt appropriate-ERP at much shorter timeframes and lower costs, by using a combination of current tools and technologies available from Open Source, innovatively applied OOAD approach and automation utilities, and fully exploiting Internet and Web technologies;
- Top management support and commitment, manifesting in formal and informal communications to users about the need for and importance of adopting ERP, is a critical factor in improving the quality dimension.
- Preparing the people is also an equally important factor in ensuring smooth and quick adoption of ERP.

- BPR has a limited role and application when it comes to compliance adherence and reporting functions.

Further follow up research and surveys to assess the validity of some of the conclusions presented here, would be of immense value to business enterprises and organisations aspiring to acquire/adopt ERP, as well as designer/developer groups.

REFERENCES

Gupta, D. S. (2004). Small is big business, news item from *e-biz newsletter* dated December 1, 2004. Retrieved December 2, 2004 from http://www.zdnetindia.com/biztech/ebusiness/sme/stories/nsl, 13331.html;

Padmanaban, S. (2005). Justifying ERP as Strategic Business Initiative: A multi-dimensional Analytical Framework. *Paradigm, the Journal of IMT,* 9(1), 1-8.

Patrick, R. A. (2005). Celebrating Innovation. *Network Magazine*, issue of November 2005, 26-56.

Ruggles, R. (1998). The State of the Notion: Knowledge Management in Practice. *California Management Review*, 40(3), 80-89.

TechRepublic (2007). *IBM® Rational Rose*. Retrieved 25 June 2007 http://search.techrepublic.com.com/search/IBM+Rational+Rose.html

TenFold Corporation. (2007). *EnterpriseTenFold-2007PersonalEdition.pdf* Retrieved 25 June 2007, www.tenfold.com

Tsang, C. H. K., Lau, C. S. W., & Leung, Y. K. (2005). *Object-Oriented Technology From Diagram to Code with Visual Paradigm for UML.* New Delhi: Tata McGraw-Hill

Turban, E., Mclean, E., & Wetherbe, J. (2004). *Information Technology for Management Transforming Organisations in the Digital Economy*, (4th edition). New Delhi: Wiley-India. (p. 5).

Wikipedia (2007). *SOA Practitioners Guide: Why Services-Oriented Architecture?* Retrieved 25 June 2007 from http://en.wikipedia.org/wiki/Service-oriented_architecture

KEY TERMS

Enterprise Resource Planning (ERP): A set of software [computer] programs, capable of running on and linking computers and computing devices [PCs, PDAs, mobile phones, bar code readers, POS machines, CNC machines], regardless of their make, model, and numbers; across offices, production floors, plants, warehouses, regardless of their location; in real time and online mode; integrating all 'business processes' [BPs] across functional areas like marketing, sales, logistics, production, quality assurance, materials, stores, maintenance, accounting and finance, human resource… automating as many 'BPs' as feasible; through a common data base; for the unified purposes of… optimised enterprise wide resource usage.

Total Cost of Ownership (TCO): The sum of investments made up to the current time on ERP-assets [e.g., hardware, software licence/media, security and so on, all attributable to ERP and all of a long-lasting nature] acquired/developed/replaced/upgraded over time by the enterprise, adjusted for accumulated depreciation and tax concessions on such assets up to that time. All expenses including costs of procurement, installation and commissioning of all ERP-assets of amortizable nature would be included in TCO, duly amortized. Invariably, TCO is treated as 'cumulative investment net of depreciation' and so shown in the books of accounts as 'assets' as on the time of ascertainment.

Symbolically,

$$TCO_t = \sum_{i=0}^{t} (TCO_i - Depreciation_i)$$

where

TCO_t = Total Cost of Ownership [ERP-assets] at current time 't';

TCO_i = Total Cost of Ownership [ERP-assets] at time 'i' preceding current time; [$i <= t$]. i.e.,

ERP assets = Cost of (hardware + software licence/media + security +...acquired/ replaced/ upgraded) at time 'i'; $Depreciation_i$ = Depreciation applicable to time 'i'.

All expenses including costs of procurement, installation and commissioning of all ERP-assets of amortizable nature would be included in TCO, duly amortized. By rearranging the 'time' part, one can derive TCO values both as 'projected' to be part of initial evaluation of ERP- investment, and as 'actual' to be used for monitoring the ERP-usage.

Total Cost of Operations (TCOP): Defined as the sum of expenditure incurred periodically [usually per annum] and measured during any point in time in such period, on maintenance of ERP-assets and supportive resources/services. These include: hardware, software licence/media maintenance/upgrade fees, salaries to IT staff, ongoing training to staff, consultants fee, security drills and upkeep, and so forth, all of 'recurring' nature, non-amortizable, and attributable to ERP. Invariably, TCOP is treated as 'recurring expenditure' and written off in the books of accounts pertaining to the period to which it belongs by a charge on the surplus [or income] earned. If there is no surplus, then it would appear as 'cash loss' or 'accumulated loss' and effectively reduce the capital. In other words, TCOP would be 0 at

the beginning and at its highest at the end of the period of ascertainment.

Defined as follows:

Symbolically,

$TCOP_t$ = Total Cost of Operations [ERP-related] at current time 't';

Cost of (maintenance of hardware + software licence/media, salaries to IT staff + ongoing training to staff + consultants fee + security drills and upkeep...and so forth, all of 'revenue' nature, attributable to ERP)

System/Software Development Life Cycle (SDLC): Refers to the apparently cyclical phases of analysis, design, development, testing, and deployment of an information system and/or software thereof. There are some variations in literature in the nomenclature and also the very cyclic nature of these phases, referred to as models [waterfall, spiral] and approaches [rapid development, joint development] and so on.

Cost, Time, and Quality (CTQ): Stands for three key dimensions along which enterprises measure their competence and effectiveness in their environments by the impact they can create on customer, product, service, and other stake holders.

Open Source Standards (OSS): Inclusively refer to the large number of software ideas, programs, utilities, tools, systems, applications, packages, and so on, including standards, available mainly via Internet, almost for no or low cost on the terms and conditions of GPL [general public license] intended to guarantee freedom to share and change free software in its 'source' [human readable and understandable] format.

Object Oriented Analysis and Design (OOAD): refers to the approach and orientation employed in SDLC for analysis, design, and development of software, treating the software more as a collection of classes and objects [anything and everything] and the running of software as the manifestation of exchange of messages among objects and responses by objects in behavioral changes [methods]

Service Oriented Architecture (SOA): A reference to the emerging paradigm shift in the way software is available on/from the Internet, incorporating features of inter-operability among operating systems, data base management systems and browsers, treating and serving incoming demands as 'request for service' on some formats commercially viable to all the parties concerned.

ENDNOTES

[1] The terms ES and ERP are used interchangeably in the literature. Indeed, Wikipedia, the World Wide Web encyclopedia, [accessed 15 June 2007], redirects definition requests for 'ES' to 'ERP', using 'integration' as one of the key common threads. For a similar consideration of cost being a key common concern, we regard 'enterprise' and 'organisation' as interchangeable.

[2] Names of both these companies have been changed to protect confidentiality conditions. SDMES is, however, real. Both SDMES and CC became the owner/user of their respective ERP. SDC played the role of extended/contracted service provider giving software development, testing, and release support, entirely under the control of CC. We will henceforth collectively refer to them as organisations.

[3] All monetary figures are in Indian currency denoted by INR.

Chapter XXII
ERP Systems in Higher Education from Regional Perspective

Mateja Podlogar
University of Maribor, Slovenia

Katalin Ternai
Corvinus University of Budapest, Hungary

ABSTRACT

This chapter introduces the ERP systems, their complexity, and especially their integration in higher education as a significant challenge for many institutions. Information society paradigm, globalization, and the rapidly changing environment affect the contents and organization of higher education. In the always-conservative academic world, the organizational structure is very hierarchical and the knowledge transfer is fragmented. The real-world requirements are just the opposite; there is a vast demand for students and professionals having the ability of integration, cooperation, and knowledge absorption. During the last years, European Countries went through an intensive development and changing phase in which the experiences of transition and coping with the information society requirements mixed up. A way to develop training programs in the higher education on an integrated ERP platform from regional perspective is also illustrated in the chapter.

INTRODUCTION

Integrating ERP systems in higher education has been a major challenge for nearly ten years now. The tremendous complexity of ERP systems posed a significant challenge for many institutions. As Roseman (2004) said, from 1997 a wider integration of ERP systems in the curricula of Business, Information Technology/Information Systems and Engineering schools could be globally observed.

ERP systems education is an area demanding special attention for a number of reasons. Students have a strong interest in this subject hoping to gain market driven skills. While this often ensures high attendance, student perceptions and expectations must be managed carefully, in that it is not the objective of such initiatives strictly to enhance student skills via training activities. Managing ERP systems is typically comprehensive and complex. The frequency of upgrades and innovations from one software release to the next characterizes the rapidly evolving nature of these IS solutions. It is often difficult for the lecturer to stay abreast of these changes and to understand the implications of these changes to business practice, and to research and education, in general. By the time current textbooks of satisfying quality are available, there are new systems' upgrades and innovation cycles to deal with (Roseman, 2004).

Most of the market-leading Enterprise Systems vendors established University Alliances with regional relationship managers. These alliance programs have enabled curriculum innovations at the undergraduate and postgraduate levels often under a certain subject, such as Information Systems (IS). A number of academics contributed to the area of ERP systems education with case studies (Roseman, 2004).

While implementing these new technologies a lot of changes in business processes have to be made; ERP implementation is impossible without process reengineering and BPM (Business Process Management). ERP will support or even automate the whole supply chain. Geographical differences will be reduced and enterprises will procure/sell goods from suppliers/buyers located anywhere in the world. From this point of view regional perspective is very important.

THE EVOLUTION OF ERP SYSTEMS

An enterprise's success is related to the speed with which it can respond to changes in its business environment and create value for its chosen market space. Today it is almost impossible to run a competitive business without a computerized information system. The rapidly increasing use of the web has changed the manner in which business is done in almost all organizations. Computer-based information systems in conjunction with web applications are enhancing competitiveness and creating strategic advantage to organizations.

Providing a computerized solution to a business problem may require integrating a lot of information systems. ERP (Enterprise Resources Planning) systems are one of the most popular enterprise applications, and present a new model of enterprisewide computing. (Figure 1) They allow enterprises to replace their legacy systems with a single, integrated system, in which it is possible to plan and manage the use of the resources of an entire enterprise. We can say that ERP is a structured approach to optimizing an enterprise's internal value chain (Norris *et al.*, 2000). What ERP really does is organize, codify, and standardize an enterprise's business processes and data. The software transforms transactional data into useful information and collates the data so that it can be analyzed. In this way, all of the collected transactional data becomes information that enterprises can use to support business decision-making (Norris *et al.*, 2000). The main benefits are the increased efficiency, the improved quality, productivity, and profitability and they require major changes to organizational, cultural, and business processes.

ERP systems cover the core activities of the firm (e.g., accounting, finance, manufacturing, human resources). In these traditional functional areas repetitive tasks exist that are essential to the operation of the organization. ERP solutions are centered on business transactions. The information system that automates manual computations is called the transaction processing system (TPS) (Claybrook, 1992; Subrahmanyam, 1999; Wallace & Kremzar, 2001).

The more powerful ERP developments improve decision making. These systems support access, organize, summarize and display information for repetitive decision making and managers in the functional areas. Such applications are called functional management information systems (MIS) (Koory, 1987; McLeod ,1990).

Some ERP systems also support office workers (office automation system - OAS), people working in groups in different locations (group support system – GSS), robotics and computer-aided design and manufacturing (CAD/CAM) (Palaniswamy, 2000).

Most ERP vendors add business intelligence functionalities to their applications. Computerized support to complex, no routine decision (decision support system – DSS) and all managers in the enterprise (executive information system – EIS) are built into these systems (Dutta, 1997; Turban, 1990).

The new generation of ERP systems are the ERP II systems - the integration of ERP, customer relationship management (CRM) , knowledge management (KM) and data warehousing (DW) and data mining (DM) with e-business. This is of a great importance. In this new model e-commerce not only refers to buying and selling, but is also about enhanced productivity, reaching new customers, and sharing knowledge across institutions for competitive advantage (Davenport & Prusak, 1998; Gray, 2001).

To handle such a large and complex application ERP vendors started to break up their systems into individual components. Componentization helps the vendors to enhance their solutions and the customers to customize and upgrade the software (Johnson, 2000).

ERP KNOWLEDGE TRANSMISSION FROM PRACTICE TO TEACHING

ERP complexity knowledge transmission as a part of educational process is a critical activity. Nowadays enterprises are not willing to wait the typical one to three years time needed for the implementation of a new information technology

Figure 1, ERP evolution (Turban et al., 2002)

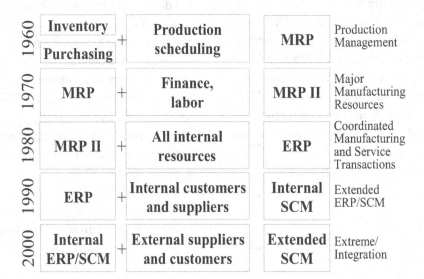

1960	Inventory / Purchasing	+	Production scheduling	**MRP**	Production Management
1970	**MRP**	+	Finance, labor	**MRP II**	Major Manufacturing Resources
1980	**MRP II**	+	All internal resources	**ERP**	Coordinated Manufacturing and Service Transactions
1990	**ERP**	+	Internal customers and suppliers	**Internal SCM**	Extended ERP/SCM
2000	**Internal ERP/SCM**	+	External suppliers and customers	**Extended SCM**	Extreme/ Integration

as in the past. To meet rapidly changing business needs, enterprises have to find ways to implement most or parts of ERP systems in a matter of months, not years. Knowledge sharing is a critical activity for a rapid implementation (Shields, 2001).

ERP complexity knowledge transmission combines two fields of knowledge. The first part deals with ERP Systems adoption and the second one captures business process knowledge. This leads us to the conclusion that we can not educate our students without their direct connection with practical work in enterprises (Figure 2) (Roseman, 2004). The students regard gaining practical experience as a key success factor for learning ERP systems.

The benefit of incorporating ERP systems into curricula through process analysis is to expose students to important concepts of ERP systems and their business process focus. ERP systems enable today's enterprises to transform themselves from a functional orientation towards a business process orientation. Therefore, one of the main reasons to introduce ERP systems into curricula is to expose students to how business processes extend across the enterprise and the enterprise's information value chain. Students need to gain a broader understanding of the strategic goals of an enterprise and the business processes that sup-

port these goals. Students should be aware of the problems enterprises experience as they undertake a major ERP system implementation and how, as a business or systems professional, they can help minimize threats to successful projects. As students interact with the vendor-provided database (IDES in Sap is such system) that serves as a hypothetical enterprise, they can see first-hand how complex and truly integrated these systems are (Bradford *et al.*, 2003 pp.437-456).

In this kind of teaching we are talking about the LivingLab concept (Bjørn-Andersen et al 2007; Boutellier et al. 2007, p. 10; Frößler et al. 2007)). The objective of the Living Lab is to develop a multi-disciplinary research and testing platform concentrating on the immediate environment from the user point of view. The Living Lab aims at addressing two questions: What do the users want? How it can be produced? Research activities include developing design-on-demand, mass-customization and co-configuration solutions for generating individual domestic environments. Furthermore, the challenge is to create an operational model of cooperation between enterprises, government agencies, and universities. With the Living Lab concept we can arrange a strong connection between practice, research and education. Living Labs are open to enterprises

Figure 2. ERP complexity knowledge transmission: ERP Systems adoption and business process knowledge

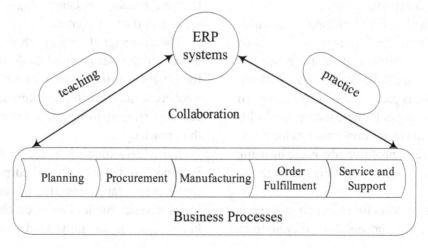

and universities in the neighboring countries creating an emerging eRegion (http://www.elivinglab.org/Objectives.htm) and are open to participate in an international network of several corresponding laboratories in order to support the European diversity better. In these days the European Union launched Living Lab Open Innovation Community. This is the open forum for development of Living Lab services towards a new European Innovation Infrastructure and the first step towards a new innovation system. We can talk about creating a network of Living Labs around Europe (www.cdt.ltu.se/~zcorelabs). Based on this Living Lab concept also the following ERP and e-commerce teaching case is presented.

ERP AND E-COMMERCE TEACHING CASE

At the Faculty of Organizational Sciences, University of Maribor, we transfer the knowledge of ERP systems through the following subjects: Information Systems, Organizational Process Design, eCommerce and Information System Project. We are trying to connect strongly all our teaching process to the real life problems inside and between enterprises (Podlogar & Basl, 2006). It is also important to have most of the new information technology (MySAP ERP, Oracle EBS, MS Navision, RFID technology and others) in our labs for students experimenting.

At our faculty, ERP teaching is executed by use of different ERP systems for hands-on experiences and through students' prototype development projects for use in interested enterprises. Students present results from seminar papers and prototypes to these enterprises. This new information creates opportunities for enterprises to achieve competitive advantage by using ERP systems and their integration through the supply chain.

In all cases students first form project teams that consist of three students. Then they go to an enterprise and investigate a problem inside the process, which is proposed by their subscriber from an enterprise.

In our ERP teaching case students analyze the real life process. Usually a procurement and/or selling process as one of the key business processes in each enterprise. This is a reason that have been usually used these two processes for our teaching cases (Podlogar 2007). Problems inside the process and then try to find suggestions/solutions, how to implement ERP system successfully into the chosen process in practical environment. Students work out different prototypes as a result of the seminar. Parallel with work at the enterprise and prototype developing, students also have lectures, where they get theoretical knowledge about the understanding of IS development methods, IS elements and the use of information technology for better organizational effectiveness (Figure 3).

KNOWLEDGE INTEGRATION ON AN INTEGRATED PLATFORM

The departmental organization of teaching in the higher education is fairly atomized. Controlling professor teaches controlling, accounting professor teaches accounting, etc. The students learn different terminology, different concepts, they get different practical assignments. There is always a challenge to see the interconnections among logistics, accounting, controlling and many other aspects of the management.

The advantage of using an advanced integrated information system behind the formal academic teaching is inevitable. The main goal is to provide a coherent and consistent background to the several departments to integrate the education and the knowledge.

It is widely known how the SAP core system is composed. For educational purposes not only the implementation but also the complex business reference model has to be observed. This knowledge can be transferred to the academic

Figure 3. Concept of ERP and e-commerce knowledge acquiring in the procurement-selling process

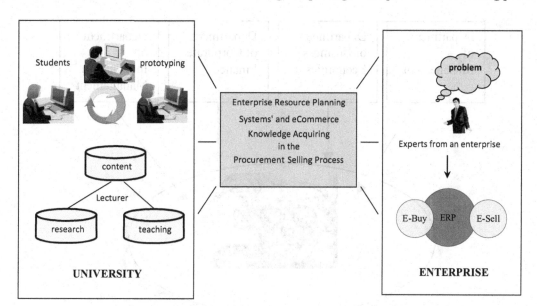

environment, so it could confront with theories. The complexity and the integrity of the system make the SAP capable of helping the education in every field of the corporate management. Students get familiar with the state-of-the art information technology, architecture and business solution. SAP establishes the opportunity for students to enrich and enlarge their knowledge - acquainted during lectures - in practical seminars. It also allows them to conduct practical experiments in different economy related fields.

The application of modern techniques, technologies and theories, the continuous development of the system raises SAP to one of the leaders of the corporate information system market. In accordance with it, another advantage of applying SAP in education is, that as a consequence of software upgrading, the contents of subjects - taught at the university - also have to be updated, therefore they are more likely to keep up with the newest achievements. As the result of the synthesis of theoretical and practical education, SAP raises the education indisputably to a higher level.

If the curricula are different the practical assignments will help the students to integrate the knowledge with the help of the common platform. (Figure 4) Students like the idea to learn different subjects in the same environment (not mentioning the fact, that they learn only once how to navigate in the system and they can use that "many" times.) The advantages of the co-operation are indisputable.

It is also an issue what type of practical assignment would serve the educational purposes best on this complex platform. We offer the three-layer application:

- Demonstration
- Problem solving application
- Major case study

Demonstration aims mainly illustration. The students' participation is passive, the teacher shows/demonstrates functions – in a fully operational environment. Sometimes the explanation of the environment is longer and more complicated than the illustrated function itself. Therefore it assumes well-trained teachers, and effective support.

Figure 4. Knowledge integration in students' minds

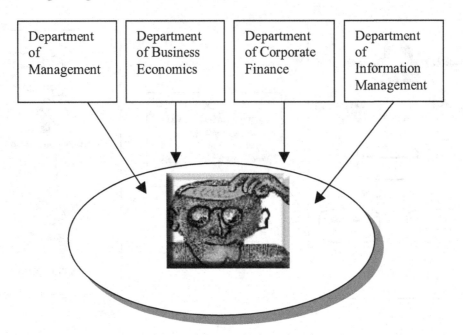

Problem solving application: Smaller assignments to the students, but the students work independently and actively. Part of the course is in-group; part of it needs individual efforts. Students usually apply their knowledge and it is not a goal to modify or develop the system.

Major case studies usually lead to the thesis work and they can be equivalent with an elective subject as well. There are a big variety of topics, as quality management, workflow management, and project management. A deeper understanding of the system is assumed and the creative application is a core requirement. Implementing a case study also goes with a major help of the system administrator. It is the responsibility of the departments to assign any kind of assignment; the only "plus" is a slight horizontal co-ordination.

The real added value comes from the opportunity of development of new courses. The already running courses can be upgraded from the process-oriented view to the more complex problem-solving view. New areas can also be investigated such as IT audit, which is a nice and interesting combination of management ac-

counting, controlling, information technology and information management. The other new features of the development lead to real executive programs.

The focus in BCE (Corvinus University of Budapest) is on providing knowledge on finance, accounting, controlling and information management in order to facilitate executives (students) to give a solid foundation of their decisions. The Information Manager postgraduate course should be a good example.

Besides ERP knowledge transmission from practice to teaching, the knowledge integration on an integrated platform also has to be achieved. The following knowledge integration on an integrated platform is described on the basis of the case that is taken from the ten years practice at the Corvinus University of Budapest, Hungary. Courses are being held on controlling, corporate finance, information management, workflow management, and recently we are dealing with business objects and services created from SAP functions (these business functions could be anything from transaction processing to decision support analysis to resource planning) in order to facilitate SOA integration. At the faculty also new courses on BPM are executed. ARIS methods and solutions are preferred because of ARIS integration into the Netweaver Platform.

AN INNOVATIVE INTERNATIONAL EDUCATION COLLABORATION

The next step further is that this common platform supplies integrated education not only in co-operation with the different departments, but with other universities as well. The inter-organizational co-operation cannot be restricted to the Hungarian or Slovenian higher education, but this is the frame for an international co-operation as well. In the US the SAP Alliance program is an option. In Europe there are plenty of opportunities under the frame of SAP support activities and other European programs (e.g. LLP/ERASMUS). Two further types of international collaboration: Excellence Center and International Network - "eBusiness ALADIN" are described.

Excellence Center

Officially the SAP Excellence Center was announced on 27th of August 1999, during the most important IT conference in higher education, in Debrecen. Professionals, responsible for IT education got acquainted with the Excellence Center idea and services, and from that moment they could join an open platform for co-operation. Technical universities, colleges, (the actual number of the participants is more than ten) agreed in joint development of curricula, joint development and exchange of teaching material, also in joint teaching activities. The latter mentioned is a great challenge itself, since the combination of a web based technology with a web based on line teaching is not a trivial task.

Of course, on the one hand every university would like to have its own system. On the other hand the maintenance and administration of a complete system is very costly. Therefore the partners like the idea of the virtual university SAP center. (Figure 5). Costs could be saved, while through the academic network the participants reach the server and many of the services (help

Figure 5. BUES-SAP Excellence Center

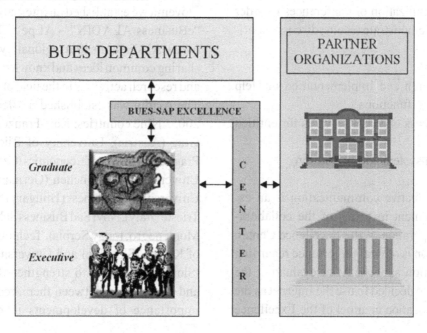

desk, promotion campaign, upgrades, not talking about the advantages of knowledge sharing).

Main task groups of the Excellence Center:

1. Implementation and maintenance of the modules of the SAP system.
2. Educational support:
   - Design and operate the "Teach-the-Teacher" program. The courses prepare the applicant teachers to be able to insert the SAP modules into the curriculum of their academic course. In the first period the program consists of a few one-day intro-courses, later three-day standard-courses per modules
   - Invitation and co-ordination of SAP thesis topics. Providing and organizing continuous consultation
   - Composing curriculum and/or establishing connection to existing curriculum, that are needed for self-training and help deepening SAP knowledge
3. Establishing the Higher Education Club (HEC)
   - Organization of workshops with invited guests
   - Organization of conferences in order to demonstrate results, discuss experiences
4. Help Desk
   - Design and implementation of Help Desk functions
   - Access of WEB services for entitled users
5. User and system administration

Fast and effective communication is an essential requirement in terms of the collaboration and the operation of the Excellence Center. Communication is of vital importance regarding to the integration as well. After evaluating the possibilities, we decided to use the Internet as the main communication channel of the Excellence Center. Advantages: fast, cheap, widely used in the academic world, flexible. The communication system, as the part of the whole Excellence Center, has to be developed in conjunction with the whole system. As the system gets more complex and more integrated, the communication subsystem has to become more complex and integrated as well.

According to this, now the Corvinus University of Budapest, Hungary, and the Faculty of Organizational Sciences, University of Maribor, Slovenia, have set up the newest Netweaver Platform. For both universities also, the actual SAP IDES version is in use. The IDES is an already installed and parameterized training system.

International Network - "eBusiness ALADIN"

To achieve successful education on the field of ERP systems implementation we need to assure teaching and practice collaboration and knowledge integration.

To succeed this goal we need to cooperate with other universities all around the world. The idea is to make an innovative international collaboration on the field of e-Integration Research & Teaching in the Region. Based on this idea in Slovenia we established an international network "eBusiness ALADIN" – ALpe ADria Initiative (www.Aladin.units.it) at regional level, that means sharing common ideas and knowledge in teaching and research activities in the field of e-commerce. The Aladin was established in Bled on June 5th 2005. Nine countries: Karl-Franzens University Graz (Austria), University of Rijeka (Croatia), Prague University of Economics (Czech Republic), University BW München (Germany), Corvinus University of Budapest (Hungary), University of Trieste (Italy), Novi Sad Business School (Serbia & Montenegro, today Serbia), Technical University of Košice (Slovakia) and University of Maribor (Slovenia) desiring to strengthen the friendship and cooperation between them, recognizing the importance of developments in e-Integration, particularly in e-Business, e-Geomatics, e-Government, e-Health, e-Learning and e-Logistics, and in all the applications of the Information & Communication Technology (ICT) for the benefits of the European Citizens. As already successfully experimented in the ALADIN network, common ideas and knowledge in teaching and research activities have been shared, cooperating to create mobility of students and professors, offering common lectures and educational programs, creating virtual teams of students from different Universities and professors lecturing at different Universities, promoting research cooperation with SMEs and Governments, in order to harmonize with global and international activities of ICT in the Enlarged Europe.

Through joint teaching at different universities and strong connections with practice, the teaching of ERP and e-commerce systems will become more effective and more understandable to students, lecturers and business.

FUTURE TRENDS

As IT systems have grown exponentially, traditional architectures have reached the limit of their capabilities; enterprises have been left to handle increasingly complex software architectures. But corporate management still needs to respond quickly to new business requirements, continually reduce the cost of IT to the business, and absorb and integrate new business partners and customers. The software industry has improved multiple computing architectures designed to allow fully distributed processing. Programming languages are designed to run on any platform and greatly reduce implementation schedules. And it has developed a huge amount of connectivity architectures designed to allow better and faster integration of applications.

Now, service oriented architecture (SOA) is the next evolutionary step. Just as the object-oriented development paradigms forced the power of code reuse, SOA allows business analysts and

IT architects to access the power of reusing automated business services (Carter, 2007). Once process designers have direct access to reusable automated business services, their focus can shift to making more sophisticated use of process architectures and continuous improvement of those processes.

Software development as a whole has been evolving to improve the flexibility of business applications. The new standards and application platforms dramatically simplified the development of applications. Instead of designing an entire monolithic application these platforms provided the basic application structures in a pre-built fashion, giving opportunity to focus on the value-added portions of the applications.

A competitive enterprise has to adapt core value-added processes with unprecedented speed, to act appropriately regardless of the situation (Sprott, 2004). For this perfectly designed and continuously improved process models must be implemented in the real world with real employees interacting with real software applications which must be integrated with real integration platforms. Modern BPM suites are evolving to automate the modeling, monitoring and redesign of complex, collaborative processes to achieve these goals (Carter, 2007).

BPM and SOA together mean the next phase of business process evolution from merely automating repeatable processes to flexible automation of dynamic processes (Noel, 2005).

SAP is active participant in SOA and BPM world following the leading philosophy and technology. The Netveawer platform links SAP to the e-business platform components as the business models of ARIS for SAP connect SAP functionalities into e-business processes. With these capabilities we can develop not only our courses but our collaborative level. We can connect our business processes from SAP on a higher technical level.

CONCLUSION

Being learning institutions, the mission of our universities is to identify, to create and to transfer the business need, the collaborative environment, knowledge sharing schemas, to our customers – students and enterprises, as effectively and as much as we can. We need to transfer knowledge from practice to teaching as applicable as we can, taking into consideration the knowledge integration on an integrated platform.

From our point of view ERP systems afford a unique opportunity to learn concepts through process analysis. In an ideal situation, when ERP is implemented and integrated across courses, students are able to visualize the business process view of enterprise, identify and eliminate non-value added activities, and enrich value added processes better.

Universities have to achieve an innovative international collaboration. Running an Excellence Center and being a part of the international group "eBusiness Aladin" are great challenges for both universities: Corvinus University of Budapest, Hungary, and Faculty of Organizational Sciences, University of Maribor, Slovenia.

The newest technology, which is in line with enterprises demand, is needed. Our universities logically follow the leading technology of software enterprises, however the business processes are significantly differing from a manufacturing or commercial enterprise, and even from a service enterprise, not mentioning the differences between the corporate/organizational cultures. Therefore many cases, development issues should be handled in a unique way. Gaining and utilizing these experiments keep us on track and add value to our higher education.

REFERENCES

Bjørn-Andersen, N., Flügge, B., Ipenburg, F. v., Klein, S., & Tan, Y.-H. (2007). ICT Challenges in Cross-border trade: The Itaide perspective. *Paper presented at the European Conference on Information Systems (ECIS 2007)*, St. Gallen.

Boutellier, R., Flügge, B., & Raus, M. (2007). Challenges of Global Trade and the transfer to enabled Business models in the Swiss Socks Market, *Proceedings of 20th Bled E-Conference eMergence: Merging and Emerging Technologies, Processes, and Institutions*, Bled, Slovenia, Markus, L. et al, Editors, Moderna organizacija, Kranj, June 4 - 6.

Bradford, M., & Vijayaraman, B. S., & Chandra, A. (2003). The Status of ERP Integration in Business School Curricula: Results of a Survey of Business School. *Communications of the Association for Information Systems, 12*, 437 - 456.

Carter, S. (2007). The New Language of Business. *SOA & Web 2.0, IBM Press.*

Claybrook, B. (1992). *OLTP Online Transaction Processing.* John Wiley & Sons.

Davenport, T. H., & Prusak, L. (1998). Working Knowledge: How Organizations Manage What They Know, Boston: *Harvard Business School Press.*

Dutta, S. et al. (1997). Designing Management Support Systems. *Communications of the ACM.*

Gray, P., & Byun, J. (2001). *Customer Relationship Management.* University of California, Irvine, www.crmassist.com/documents.

Johnson, R. A. (2000). The Ups and Downs of Object-Oriented Systems Development. *Communications of the ACM.*

Koory, J. L., & Medley, D. B. (1987). *Management Information Systems: Planning and Decision Making*, South-Western Publishing Co.

McLeod Jr., R. (1990). *Management Information Systems.* New York: McMillan, 4th ed.

Noel, J. (2005). BPM and SOA: Better Together. *IBM Corporation.*

Norris, G., Hurley, J. R., Hartley, K. M., Dunleavy, J. R., & Balls, J. D. (2000*). E-Business and ERP, Transforming the Enterprise.* Canada: John Wiley & Sons, Inc.

Palaniswamy, R., & Frank, T. (2000). Enhancing Manufacturing Performance with ERP Systems. *Information Management Journal.*

Podlogar, M. (2007). E-procurement success factors: Challenges and opportunities for a small developing country, E-procurement in emerging economies. *Theory and cases.* Hershey, PA: Idea Group, Pani, A. K. & Agrahari, A. 42-75.

Podlogar, M., & Basl., J. (2006). SAP ERP case study at the University of Maribor, Slovenia and at the University of Economics, Prague, Czech Republic. *Journal of Management, Informatics and Human Resources, 39*(3), 184-191.

Roseman, M. (2004). The Integration of SAP Solutions in the Curricula – Outcomes of a Global Survey, white paper and submitted to the *Journal of IS Education*, Quesland University of Technology, Brisbane.

Shields, M. G. (2001). *E-Business and ERP. Rapid Implementation and Project Planning.* Canada: John Wiley & Sons, Inc.

Sprott, D. (2004). Service Oriented Architecture: An introduction for managers. *CBDI Report.* www.cbdiforum.com

Subrahmanyam, A. (1999). *Nuts and Bolts of Transaction Processing,* www.subrahmanyam.com/articles/transactions/NutsAndBoltsOfTP.html

Turban, E. (1990). *Decision Support and Expert Systems: Management Support Systems.* New York, London: Macmillan, second edition.

Wallace, T. F., & Kremzar, M. H. (2001). *ERP: Making It Happen. The Implementer's Guide to Success with Enterprise Resource Planning,* Canada: John Wiley & Sons, Inc.

Other Internet Sources

www.Aladin.units.it

www.cdt.ltu.se/~zcorelabs

www.elivinglab.org/Objectives.htm

KEY TERMS

Enterprise Resource Planning (ERP): The information pipeline system within a company, which allows the company to move internal information efficiently so that it may be used for decision support inside the company and communicated via e-business technology to business partners throughout the supply chain. It is an enterprise-wide set of forecasting, planning, and scheduling tool, which:

- Links customers and suppliers into a complete supply chain,
- Employs proven processes for decision-making, and
- Coordinates sales, marketing, operations, logistics, purchasing, finance, product development, and human resources.

Excellence Center: An open platform for co-operation of universities, colleges which agreed in joint development of curricula, joint development and exchange of teaching material, also in joint teaching activities.

Internet Demonstration and Evaluation System (IDES): Represents a model company in the SAP system. It consists of an international group with subsidiaries in several countries. IDES contains application data for various business scenarios. The business processes in the IDES system are designed to reflect real-life business requirements, and have access to many realistic characteristics. The focal point of IDES is not the functionality itself, but the business processes and their integration.

Knowledge Integration: Means the networking of knowledge from different fields/departments (management, business economics, corporate finance, information management …), processes, human resources, their tasks and the information and communication technology used.

University Alliance: It is an alliance program for enabling curriculum innovations at the undergraduate and postgraduate levels often under a certain subject, such as Information Systems (IS).

Section V
Enterprise Systems:
ERP and Beyond

Chapter XXIII
From ERP to Enterprise Service–Oriented Architecture

Valentin Nicolescu
Technische Universität München, Germany

Holger Wittges
Technische Universität München, Germany

Helmut Krcmar
Technische Universität München, Germany

ABSTRACT

This chapter provides an overview of past and present development in technical platforms of ERP systems and its use in enterprises. Taking into consideration the two layers of application and technology, we present the classical scenario of an ERP system as a monolithic application block. As the demands of modern enterprise software cannot be met by this concept, the shift to a more flexible architecture like the service-oriented architecture (SOA) is the current status quo of modern companies. Keeping in mind the administrative complexity of such structures, we will discuss the new idea of business Webs. The purpose of our chapter is, on the one hand, to show the historical development of ERP system landscapes and, on the other hand, to show the comparison of the presented concepts with respect to application and technology view.

INTRODUCTION

With the emergence of the SOA concept, the classical architecture of ERP system has started to change and is in a constant flux towards new structures. We want to show these changes, starting with the architecture of ERP systems and describing the different parts of this concept. To exemplify it, we will present the most important aspects of concrete implementations of these principles. As one of the most important ERP systems, we will focus on the structure of the SAP ERP system and will describe the changes of this platform.

Our analysis will comprise of an application-centered and a technical view, considering changes in business paradigms and new technologies that enabled new kinds of business and process management. Starting at classical ERP systems and their implementation in SAP R/3, we will move on to the current concept of SOA and Enterprise SOA. This goes along with a change in technical architectures as well. The SAP NetWeaver platform will be presented as an example of complete Enterprise SOA platforms. Its most important functions will be pointed out and utilizing this example, components that are necessary to realize Enterprise SOA are identified. The light in which SAP NetWeaver is seen has changed in the last years as not the technical components are in the spotlight anymore but the applications that are made possible by such a platform. Finally, we will show the future concept of business webs which will base on Enterprise SOA and conclude our chapter with an outlook to the further development in this area of topic. The structure of our chapter is illustrated in Figure 1.

CLASSICAL ERP SYSTEMS

Classical ERP system can be described as commercial software products that are adaptable to company-specific demands. Their typical functional modules include: purchasing, manufacturing, sales, finances, human resources, service and in general reporting. Classical ERP systems focus on data integration and also support process integration within one company.

The technical basis of an ERP system today is usually a Client/Server architecture, where often more than one application server is connected to the central database server. The user of a classical ERP system most time works with basic business transactions like "create order", "update customer contact data", "print invoice", "execute report xy" etc. Changes within such a system due to business transactions are usually propagated in "business" realtime meaning a few seconds or minutes.

The following figure from Davenport visualizes the architecture of a classical ERP system. In addition to the facts mentioned before, there is usually a wide range of reporting functionality for management and stakeholders, based on the central ERP data.

There are a lot of advantages that unfold with the use of ERP Systems (Vogel and Kimbell 2005; N.N. 2007) In the following a few of them are spotlighted:

Figure 1. Structure of this chapter

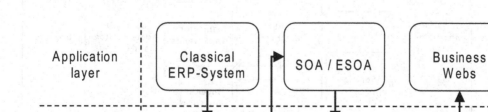

- Standardisation
- Integrated "best practice" business knowledge
- Data quality
- Data- and process integration
- Central authorisation, authentication

However, there are also a lot of potential risks related with the use of ERP-Systems.

- Possible single point of failure
- Problems integrating different ERP-Systems
- Tracking of complex processes – even if they are handled by only one ERP-System
- operated by personnel with inadequate education in ERP in general

Additional, considerable risks that need to be especially emphasized arise from *deficiencies in the ERP introduction project*. Example thereof could be:

- mistakes in the selection of the ERP System,
- misunderstandings/mistakes in the system customizing
- failures in the business / IT alignment

Despite the possible problems that served as exampales, ERP systems can be seen as something that Carr calls ubiquity information systems power (Carr 2003). Nowadays it is not the question of using an ERP System in your company, but how. There is also research available describing the value of ERP Systems more concretely. See for example (Martin, Mauterer et al., 2002).

SAP R/3 BASIS

For the discussion of the technology of classical ERP systems, we will take a closer look at SAP R/3 and the underlying technological platform SAP Basis. Since SAP's application was the first enterprise software fulfilling the characteristics

Figure 2. Anatomy of an enterprise system (Davenport, 1998)

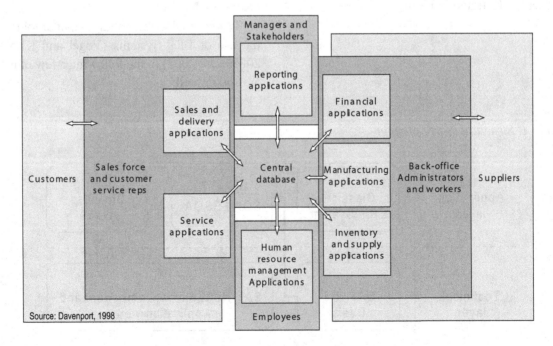

of an ERP system and still represents the leading edge in ERP technology, analyzing this product provides a complete outline of the past and present development in ERP system technology.

SAP R/2 was the first enterprise application integrating functions of different enterprise divisions in one piece of software and thus representing the first ERP system. It provided functions for finance, accounting, human resources, sales, procurement, and manufacturing. The system ran on mainframe architectures, while its successor, R/3, relies on a client server architecture and also includes a whole set of new functions. (Vogel and Kimbell 2005). Because SAP R/3 for a long time was *the* ERP system, it shall serve as our starting point for the detailed analysis of the technology layer

Moving from a mainframe structure to the client server architecture the technical part of the SAP application was divided in a 3-tier landscape consisting of the front end tier typically running on the user's desktop, the application tier and the database tier. The front end tier is a fat client that displays all kinds of screens based on small information packages exchanged with the application tier. The application tier resides on high performance servers and represents the application logic and enterprise functionality as well as the connection to the database layer. The databases used for R/3 have been provided by different manufacturers and, with their database product SAPDB, also by SAP itself. By dividing the technical architecture into these three tiers, it became scalable and could be enhanced by adding more desktop computers or servers to the tier that lacks computational power.

The technical layer of the application tier and thus of SAP R/3 systems is called SAP Basis. This layer's characteristics of capital importance indclude platform and database independence with respect to the interpretation of application source code. The code is written in SAP's programming language called Advanced Business Application Programming (ABAP). All of SAP's

out of the box functions can be viewed in plain text, edited (with some limitations) and hence also be enhanced. The integrated development environment called ABAP workbench can be used for these tasks. Providing these possibilities, the platform can be adopted in a very flexible way to individual needs. In practice however, only few modifications are made to the source code delivered by SAP because the algorithms represent the know-how of many business experts. Framed in other words, the implemented algorithms are procedures cast into best practices such as how to support a specific process at best.

When using SAP R/3 for crucial functions, enterprises have a data centralization spanning the whole company. Nonetheless SAP R/3 turned out to be insufficient for the integration of suppliers and customers as well as for performing in-depth analysis of business data. Thus new applications like SAP Customer Relationship Management (CRM), Supplier Relationship Management (SCM) or the Business Warehouse (BW) were created to meet the growing demands. All these new products were based on SAP Basis. This is why a highly integrated system landscape could be implemented despite the different systems. By using the same technical layer, all systems can communicate and exchange data very easily utilizing the same functions. These functions are arranged in a hierarchical structure defined by business areas and this way facilitate changes and enhancements of business processes. Furthermore, most functions are encapsulated in so called function modules which can be called remotely by another application like another SAP system or a third party product. Therefore communication with applications of third party vendors can be established within limitations. This packaging of functions is also an important step towards a service oriented architecture as will be shown later (Buck-Emden 1998).

Although the SAP Basis of SAP R/3, as shortly presented above, was already quite flexible and enabled the communication to other applications to and from SAP or third party vendors, the degree of integration was limited. There was no complete integration of functions and data of different applications to create completely new business processes across system boundaries. Additionally, changing or enhancing crucial functions or processes was very difficult as the dependencies between systems and function modules were not clearly documented. A fundamental problem of this technical layer was also its integration into the application layer: SAP Basis could not be used without SAP R/3 or other products based on this very platform. These issues forced a fundamental change to provide a much more flexible technical layer for future business applications.

SOA and Enterprise SOA

We will rely on the following definition of a SOA: "SOA is an architectural style whose goal is to achieve loose coupling among interacting software agents. A service is a unit of work done by a service provider to achieve desired end results for a service consumer. Both provider and consumer are roles played by software agents on behalf of their owners." (He 2003) In addition to this definition, SOA is characterized by intensive use of standards (like SOAP, UDDI, etc.) to implement services. But the concept of SOA itself is not connected to a technical or business domain. It is a concept of how functions can be implemented on distributed entities, just like the client-server concept or the idea of object orientation (OO). Both of the mentioned actually can be related to SOA. Services within a SOA could for example be implemented using an OO programming language. The result could be run technically in an environment that follows the client server concept. The central components of a SOA are shown in Figure 3.

The central element within a SOA is the service. Whenever an application wants to use a service, it communicates with the service repository (for example via UDDI) using the (enterprise) service bus as technical backbone. Examples for service busses include IBM WebSphere ESB, Microsoft biztalk, Oracle ESB and SAP XI.. The application front end is used to access the network of services.

A service itself consists of an implementation describing the business logic and data. Also it is formalized by a service contract (i.e. IDL, WSDL) and a service interface (i.e. SOAP) (Booth, Haas et al., 2004).

Figure 3. The key abstractions of a SOA (Krafzig, Blanke et al., 2004)

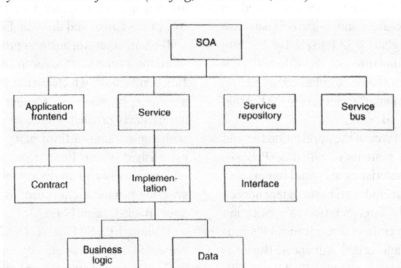

Key features of SOA as described by Erl (Erl 2005) are:

- **Self-describing:** The service can be fully described on a formal level; that is, what operations are available and which data types can be exchanged. Formal self-description is the basis for automatically generating proxies. Note that in this context the word "description" does not refer to the semantic description.
- **Locatable:** Potential consumers can locate and contact the service. There is a registry for this purpose that operates as a "Yellow Pages" of services and allows users to search for services.
- **Roughly structured:** Services are roughly structured when they return comprehensive data (for example, a sales order) in response to a service call instead of delivering individual attributes (such as an order quantity).
- **Loosely linked:** Services are said to be loosely linked if potential functional changes within the services have no effect on the availability of operations. Services are considered to be independent if they have no dependencies on other services i.e. if the availability of a service is not affected by a potential unavailability or improper functioning of any other service.
- **Reusable:** Reusability is one of the most important and longest-standing requirements in software technology. It aims at ensuring that components are reused as often as possible without modification to the functional core or interfaces.

Enterprise SOA extends the features of the SOA concept with a business view on services. Therefore services additionally have the following key features:

- Services represent business services instead of technical services

- Support of inter-organizational collaboration on a business level

The technical basis of an Enterprise SOA today is usually a client-server architecture, where many application server and many database servers are part of the - often regionally distributed - IT-landscape. In contrast to a list of basic ERP Transactions, Enterprise SOA offers access to high level business processes like "hire employee", "produce good", "distribute good" etc. Seen in this light one might define Enterprise SOA as the *business glue* connecting isolated business tasks, such as the previously mentioned examples, to comprehensive business processes. Working that way, Enterprise SOA opens the door to realtime business processes instead of realtime transactions.

DIFFERENT VIEWS ON SAP NETWEAVER

The presented idea of service oriented architectures and its use in an enterprise domain forces the need for a technical platform that can enable the interaction of the different services. SAP developed the currently most complete technical layer for Enterprise SOA called SAP NetWeaver. NetWeaver is comparable to the SAP R/3 Basis, however doess not itself provide any business functions but is the technical basis for enterprise applications like SAP Enterprise Resource Planning (ERP) (Woods and Word 2004). Since the components of this layer are already a few years old, the view on this platform has changed. First we will present the classical component based view covering the specific technical systems that are part of this platform. Afterwards we will show the shift from the component based to an application based view that does not care anymore about technical systems but focuses on the application of a set of systems for business purposes.

Component Based View on NetWeaver

The component based view on SAP NetWeaver is also called the "NetWeaver Fridge" because you can use specific components of the NetWeaver platform just as you can take ingredients from your fridge for lunch. This technical fridge consists of four layers representing different aspects of an enterprise system landscape as well as two cross-functional areas that are used for all other products. We can distinguish the layers for application platform, process integration, information integration and people integration. The general areas are life cycle management and SAP's Composite Application Framework (CAF). The specific layers combine different software products of the SAP portfolio. Thus this view on NetWeaver is a rather technical one (Karch, Heilig et al., 2005). In Figure 4 you find an overview of all layers and their elements at which we want to have a closer look.

The **application platform** consists of three elements whereas the DB and OS abstraction is an integral part of the two other elements. These two elements are the ABAP and the Java core of all SAP applications. They are called Web Application Server (Web AS) ABAP and Web AS Java. Depending on the application that is to be executed on the Web AS, either one or both cores are used as a runtime environment. The SAP NetWeaver Portal for example needs only the Java core while SAP Process Integration uses both Java and ABAP. The Web AS can also be used for technical purposes like monitoring without enterprise applications building upon it (Heinemann and Rau 2003).

The **process integration** layer represents the elements of an integration broker and of business process management which are combined in SAP's product called Process Integration (PI, formerly Exchange Infrastructure). The integration broker's task within NetWeaver is the exchange of data using different formats and protocols. It can for example convert messages sent via FTP in an XML format to a message for an SAP function module based on one of SAP's internal protocols. Besides this technical conversion, also changes to

Figure 4. Component based view SAP NetWeaver

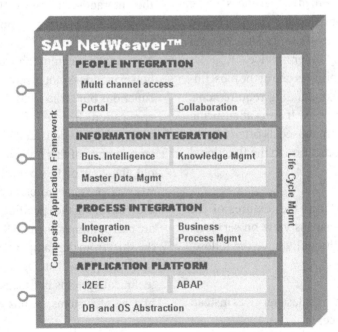

322

the content can be processed such as converting the values of the gender (female, male) to values for a suitable salutation (Ms, Mr.). Business Process Management (BPM), also known as cross-component BPM (ccBPM), provides functions for workflow management across boundaries of single enterprise systems. It can help to implement automated processes by triggering and coordinating data exchange between all kinds of enterprise systems which can be accessed by the integration broker. A business process can therefore automatically manage the selection of the supplier with the best price after receiving all quotations and may subsequently place an order. NetWeaver 's process integration layer and the product of the same name can be regarded as the communication backbone of a modern enterprise system landscape. It provides centralized functions for data exchange within the landscape and with systems in supplier or customer domains.

The **information integration** layer combines three tasks which are arranged in three different applications. Master Data Management (MDM) and Business Intelligence (BI) can be found in the products of the same name while Knowledge Management (KM) is part of the SAP NetWeaver Portal which is part of the subsequent layer. MDM helps to consolidate data within an enterprise across system boundaries. The same data is often saved in different places because of technical reasons. In many cases this redundancy can be changed so that the data is saved only in one place or at least synchronization between different databases can be set up. Thus the same data is available in all connected systems. Using this correct data proper propped business decisions can be made. As the amount of data on which decisions are based on can be vast, SAP's Business Intelligence helps to arrange and visualize data from different points of view. By using SAP's Strategic Enterprise Management (SEM), balanced scorecards can be used as an enterprise dash board or management cockpit. While MDM and BI are used for structured data, KM components help to manage

unstructured data like files containing different kinds of information. As KM is part of the NetWeaver Portal it can easily be integrated in the front end and therefore in daily work.

In the layer of **people integration**, three different tasks are combined in 2 applications. On the one hand one can identify the multi channel access provided by SAP's Mobile Infrastructure (MI). On the other hand there is SAP NetWeaver Portal including the tasks of portal, collaboration and knowledge management which form the information integration layer. This layer hence contains applications for end user communication. The Mobile Infrastructure provides a client server architecture that enables the synchronization of data on mobile devices like PDAs or Notebooks with the enterprise system landscape. This way traveling salesmen have all the data they need to help customers place an order. The portal itself provides a web based framework for arranging and displaying screens and information. Furthermore it integrates business process screens providing a single point of entry to front ends in the enterprise system landscape. It can be used to implement flexible wizards working across system boundaries. These basic functions can be enhanced by synchronous or asynchronous collaboration and knowledge management.

The cross function area of **life cycle management** covers all activities for running an application in an enterprise system landscape. This includes the installation preparation of specific applications, customizing activities, monitoring and maintenance, upgrade and migration tasks. The SAP product supporting these tasks is the SAP Solution Manager which provides part of these functions as a first step towards the implementation of ITIL.

As a SOA consists of many different small services, an integration layer for coordinating the steps within a business process is needed. This layer is the **Composite Application Framework (CAF)** which allows the development of applications based on the underlying services - web services or SAP function modules provided by SAP applications. The implementation of a persistence layer as well as the design of user interfaces are as well part of this development. In order to access backend systems, persistence and user interfaces, the appropriate Java source code can be generated. This code is running within the SAP NetWeaver Portal providing the connectivity of a Web AS Java and the user interface of the portal framework. CAF can be used to have professional developers generate Java-based applications or to quickly implement an adhoc-workflow called guided procedure. By relying on other NetWeaver products, a new CAF application or a guided procedure can take advantage of existing functions like the connection to third party systems or user interface functions.

Application Based View on NetWeaver

As we already pointed out, the component based view on the NetWeaver fridge is dominated by a technical aspect. For most scenarios more than one of these products is necessary to attain the goal. Thus the NetWeaver fridge has been cut into slices to show that the NetWeaver platform does not exist for its own sake, but to enable and support different IT practices (see Figure 5).

The result of cutting the NetWeaver fridge into slices are 10 IT practices which shall be discussed now. Each of the practices itself is divided into IT scenarios describing concrete activities to achieve the target of a scenario, for example implementing single sign-on for an application or in a whole system landscape (Nicolescu, Funk et al., 2006).

1. The first IT practice called **user productivity enablement** aims at improving the daily work of users by providing tools to exchange information between them, any by means of personalization for an easier access to data and business processes. This IT practice mainly builds upon the SAP NetWeaver Portal.

2. The Practice of **data unification** tries to consolidate and harmonize data that is stored in different databases all over the enterprise. As this task is mainly connected in identifying redundancy and keeping data in different places synchronous, the vital application of this task is the Master Data Management (MDM).

3. **Business information management** is an important support task for decision makers in a company. This practice tries to provide structured and unstructured information to

Figure 5. Shift from component based view to application based view on NetWeaver

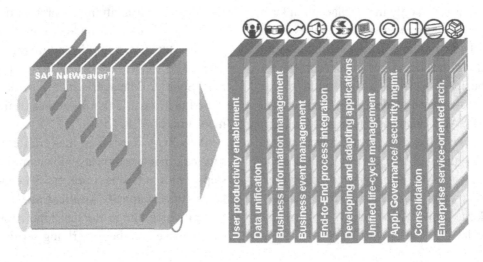

make the right decision based on the given data. As this combines elements of Business Intelligence and Knowledge Management, BI and portal are the main components of this practice.

4. Unlike the business information management that provides functions for proactive work with business data, the **business event management** works by a Push technology. Whenever important events happen in the company the relevant people will be informed and can react. Reacting on events is abstracted to the necessary data and entry to appropriate business transactions for a given situation. Main components of this practice are again SAP Business Intelligence and SAP NetWeaver Portal.

5. **End-to-end process integration** allows the implementation and monitoring of business processes across system boundaries within a company's own system landscape and with systems of business partners. This way, crucial processes can be monitored and adjusted centrally. The component providing these features is SAP Process Integration.

6. **Development and adaptation of enterprise applications** represents the sixth IT practice which includes the creation of completely new software as well as changing and enhancing existing functions. Because development in an enterprise environment poses many challenges, it is supported by components like the Composite Application Framework.

7. The IT Infrastructure Library (ITIL) plays an important role in today's IT management, which is why the IT practice of **unified life cycle management** covers most of its concepts. An important building block for attaining this goal is the use of the SAP Solution Manager.

8. The topic of **application governance and security management** is covered by the eighth IT practice. It deals with the holistic management of applications within a system landscape, addressing issues like communication and security of the systems. The Concept of implementing single sign-on is just one example. As this task affects all systems in an enterprise, there is no specific component to point out.

9. While the presented IT practice of data unification aims at the consolidation of data, the IT practice of **consolidation** deals with all approaches to simplify the whole system landscape. Examples of these approaches are service oriented architecture or server virtualization.

10. The last IT practice **enterprise service-oriented architecture design and deployment** covers the areas of planning, developing, reusing und maintaining SOA applications. By separating the formerly monolithic applications into smaller services the administrative effort to keep track of these modules and to wisely reuse them is a major issue for development.

BUSINESS WEBS

"Low-Cost Information and communication technologies, global markets, and global competition have forced enterprises to rethink their traditional, vertically integrated structure. As the cost of collaboration plummets, it increasingly makes sense for companies to focus on core competencies and partners for all other functions. As a result, corporations are transforming into flatter and more specialized enterprises, linking with suppliers and other businesses to form a larger, more open, value-creation entity" (Tapscott 2007) – the business web.

The innovation potential and practical relevance of the business web is a recent topic for ERP Software providers. SAP (Karch, Heilig et al., 2005; Tapscott 2007) and salesforce.com (Gilbert 2006) described it as an important shift in the future similar to the migration from the classical world wide web to Web 2.0.

The business web can only be realized if an adequate ecosystem has been set up. The following figure illustrates such an ecosystem.

In addition to the well know eCommerce or supply chain models this ecosystem not only focuses on special partners but instead on a whole community. The idea of integrating virtually everything is not a new one, but it often failed due to high complexity. Enterprise SOA now offers a concept and appendant tools that allow to manage complexity by partitioning and linking the emerging parts (partner processes) together.

CONCLUSION

Companies try to save investments in old applications by wrapping old code into web services.

This can be described as a three step approach: Legacy to SOA is the first step to go. The idea is to make your business transactions accessible, independent of the platform they run on and to abstract from the programming language they were implemented in. The second step is to map these services onto different business processes by focusing on your internal processes and your immediate business partners, i.e. customers and suppliers. The consequential third step is to extend the reach of your services – and along with it the reach of your business – by integrating them into a business web.

This demonstrated the power of implementing (Enterprise) SOA. As a first benefit value is generated by reducing the effort for integrating your internal IT-Systems. Then additional value is generated by offering your direct partners access to your (Enterprise) SOA implementation. Finally value is generated by your community if they use

Figure 6. Line 56 – ecosystem (56 o.D.)

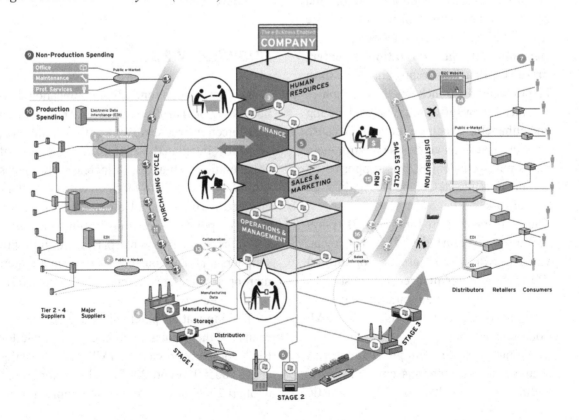

your enterprises services within the business web to enable their own business processes.

REFERENCES

56, L. (n/a). *SOA Ecosystem.* from http://www2. sims.berkeley.edu/academics/courses/is290-4/ s02/readings/line56ecosystem.gif.

Booth, D., H. Haas, et al., (2004). *Web Services Architecture.* W3C.

Buck-Emden, R. (1998). *Die Technologie des SAP-Systems R/3.* München, Addison-Wesley.

Carr, N. G. (2003). IT doesn't matter. *Harvard Business Review, 81*(5), 41-49.

Davenport, T. H. (1998). Putting the Enterprise into the Enterprise System. *Harvard Business Review, 76*(4), 121-131.

Erl, T. (2005). *Service-Oriented Architecture - Concepts, Technology, and Design.* Upper Saddle River NJ: Prentice Hall.

Gilbert, A. (2006). *Salesforce CEO's vision for 'business Web'.* www.news.com. DOI

He, H. (2003). *What Is Service-Oriented Architecture.* www.xml.org Retrieved 14.06.2007, 2007, from http://www.xml.com/lpt/a/1292.

Heinemann, F., & Rau, C. (2003). *SAP Web Aplication Server.* Bonn: Galileo Press.

Karch, S., Heilig, L. et al., (2005). *SAP NetWeaver.* Bonn: Galileo Press.

Krafzig, D., Blanke, K. et al., (2004). *Enterprise SOA - Service-Oriented Architecture Best Practise.* Upper Saddle River, NJ: Prentice Hall.

Martin, R., Mauterer, H. et al., (2002). Systematisierung des Nutzens von ERP-Systemen in der Fertigungsindustrie. *Wirtschaftsinformatik, 44*(2), 109-116.

N. N. (2007). Enterprise resource planning. Retrieved 8.06.2007, 2007, from http://en.wikipedia. org/wiki/Enterprise_resource_planning.

Nicolescu, V., Funk, B. et al., (2006). *SAP Exchange Infrastructure for Developers.* Bonn: Galileo Press.

Tapscott, D. (2007) Rethinking Enterprise Boundaries: Business Webs in the IT Industry. *NEWPARADIGM, DOI:*

Vogel, A., & Kimbell, I. (2005). mySAP ERP For Dummies. Indianapolis: Wiley Publishing, Inc.

Woods, D., & Word, J. (2004). *SAP NetWeaver For Dummies.* Wiley Publishing, Inc.

KEY TERMS

Business Web: Corporations are transforming into flatter and more specialized enterprises, linking with suppliers and other businesses to form a larger, more open, value-creation entity – the business web.

IT Practice: The application based view on SAP NetWeaver identifies different main use cases within an enterprise system landscape which are called IT Practices. In different abstraction levels, they describe the activities necessary to achieve the implementation of a specific technical task in a company.

SAP R/3: SAP R/3 has been released 1992 as the first ERP system for very large businesses based on a client-server architecture. It was divided in different functional modules and was the central point of enterprise system landscapes.

SAP NetWeaver: Moving from SAP R/3 to SAP ERP, the technical foundation of SAP R/3 SAP Basis was separated from the business functions and enhanced by many other technical features. This new technical basis that enables SOA is called NetWeaver.

SOA: SOA is an architectural style whose goal is to achieve loose coupling among interacting software agents. A service is a unit of work done by a service provider to achieve desired end results for a service consumer. Both, provider and consumer are roles played by software agents on behalf of their owners.

Chapter XXIV
ERP and Beyond

Suresh Subramoniam
Prince Sultan University, Saudi Arabia

Mohamed Tounsi
Prince Sultan University, Saudi Arabia

Shehzad Khalid Ghani
Prince Sultan University, Saudi Arabia

K. V. Krishnankutty
College of Engineering, Trivandrum, India

ABSTRACT

Enterprise-wide automation has already transformed the relations among suppliers, purchasers, producers, and customers. Conventional ERP helps only to automate individual departments. It could neither integrate its back-office benefits into the front-office, nor could it establish consistent control of all business processes. Competitive pressures and globalization stresses the need for more effective, total enterprise solutions. The world class competition, modern business environment, and the availability of the Internet are the premises which stress the need for ERP. The salient features of ERP II are presented in addition to describing some of the disruptive technologies which will help reengineer ERP systems rapidly. The results of an international survey pertaining to the embedding of intelligence in the modern day ERP shows an evolutionary trend. The order placement over the Internet by a sales clerk from a remote location forms a part of this chapter to benefit the readers in understanding the functioning of an ERP system.

INTRODUCTION

Enterprise is a group of people and associated resources to achieve a common goal. Enterprise Resource Planning (ERP) System is an enterprise wide system which encompasses corporate mission, objectives, attitudes, beliefs, values, operating style and people who make the organization. It is a software solution that addresses the Enterprise needs, taking a process view of the overall organization to meet the goals, by tightly integrating all functions under a common software platform. In other words, ERP systems are computer based systems designed to process an organization's transactions. It facilitates integrated and real-time planning, production and customer response. ERP has multilingual capability, multi-currency handling ability, and can recognize legal and tax reporting needs of various nations across the world.

The real need for such an integrated system has emerged with the onset of Supply Chain Management, e-business and global operations which calls for exchange of information with other companies and customers directly (Krajewski et al., 2000). A world-class competitor means being successful against any competitor on quality, lead time, flexibility, cost/price, customer service and innovation (Table 1). It needs transforming relations among suppliers, purchasers, producers and customers. This can be achieved only through enterprise automation which assists innovators to achieve their market share and at the same time operate at peak efficiency to satisfy customer needs. The world in which we do business is shrinking, and virtually every enterprise is either marketing or selling to customers in other countries, or simply using parts or materials that are produced elsewhere. Internet has overcome time and distance to a great extent. It has become the need of the hour to think globally and to include the same in plans, processes and strategies.

Globalization and Web commerce riding on the development of the Internet have changed traditional business behaviors and practices. Leveraging the Internet by the business has become a need to quickly establish a virtual presence. They must use collaborative technology in order to respond to customer's requirements better and faster. When the operations are scattered through multiple locations around the world, the need is to gain visibility across all sites. This enhanced visibility can lead to more negotiating power for purchasing parts and more efficient centralized accounts payable and receivable thereby improving overall performance. Solutions like ERP, supply chain management or CRM solutions provide tools to manage the information that is essential to growing business value.

The need to achieve world class status, rapid development in Internet and related technologies, and the evolving business trends are the premises which accelerates the evolution of ERP systems. Virtually every enterprise is either marketing or selling to customers in other countries, or simply buying parts or materials that are produced else-

Table 1. Key success factors for achieving World-Class status

> ➤ Reduce lead time;
> ➤ Speed in time-to-market;
> ➤ Operation cost reduction;
> ➤ Exceed customer expectation;
> ➤ Manage global enterprise;
> ➤ Streamline outsourcing processes;
> ➤ Improve business performance visibility.   **Adapted from www.mapics.com**

where. It has become a necessity for businesses to embrace Internet to quickly establish virtual presence through web commerce.

Enterprise wide automation alone can address transforming relations among suppliers, purchasers, producers and customers. ERP has fallen short in the following areas that are critical to today's business needs (www.exactamerica.com): Scope of conventional ERP is limited; conventional ERP helps automate individual departments and did not integrate its back-office benefits into the front-office to help businesses manage people, workloads and supply-chain issues; it could not establish consistent control of all the processes of the business. Competitive pressures and globalization have made it clear that the business world is still in need of more effective, total enterprise solutions. Figure 1 shows the typical ERP architecture.

EVOLUTION OF ERP

In the 1960s, computers were used only to automate routine business tasks like payroll which is simple multiplication of number of hours worked with hourly rate and subtracting from the result taxes and deductions. Subsequently, financial applications like the general ledger, accounts payable, accounts receivable and fixed assets were automated. This is the reason why IS/IT department reported to Vice President of Finance in the past (Shields, 2001). The computer programmers of olden times were disadvantaged by lack of high level languages, relational databases management systems, abundant memory in the computer, graphical user interfaces and real time dialog handlers.

Material Requirements Planning (MRP) was used in 1970s for raw material ordering based on order at hand. It is a computerized inventory control and production planning system responsible for scheduling the production of all items in the main assembly (Khalid, 2001). Joseph Orlicky, George Plossl and Oliver Wight of the American Production and Inventory Control Society (APICS) get the credit for implementing MRP. The basic functions of MRP could be carried out by Electronic Data Interchange (EDI) using sequential file processing. Supply Chain Management Systems evolved much later with the sharing of long range production schedules

Figure 1. ERP Architecture

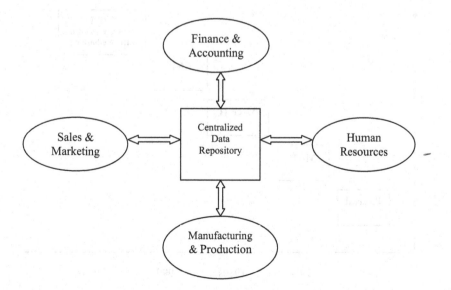

among manufacturers and their suppliers. This was called simply MRP or MRP I. Manufacturing Resources Planning widely known as MRP II evolved later. The ultimate aim of MRP I is to maintain lowest level of inventory. It simply expedites or delays inventory ordering depending on the situation. Whenever there is lack of inventory which will delay the overall production, MRP I expedites inventory. MRP I delay the inventory whenever material need is postponed due to unexpected schedule changes. Both these rules jointly optimize the level of inventory available in the organization at any point of time. The idea of working with different sets of numbers for financial people and manufacturing people became more acceptable which made MRP II more popular than MRP I (Brady et al., 2003). MRP II incorporated financial accounting, human resource management and distribution. It provides information regarding staffing levels and overtime needs through detailed capacity requirements planning. Till this point of evolution, information systems provided insight only regarding internal operations of the organization and could not exchange information directly with custom-

ers or with other companies (Krajewski, 2000). This evolving need for exchanging information between companies and own customers resulted in the emergence of a new breed of information system called ERP System. The Figure 2 shows the evolution of Information System over the years from simple payroll computation in the 1960s to complicated Internet enabled ERP systems or ERP II in the 2000s.

On the other side of the coin, development of business applications individually by various companies was viewed as reinventing the same wheel in the 1970s and 1980s by computer consultants and programmers (Shields, 2001). This resulted in the creation of standard software which could save lots of money for individual companies without sacrificing quality of the software used as these were generated, tested and evaluated by best in the field. In 1972, five IBM employees left their job to start a company which created standard financial software for corporations. Revenue from this venture grew to $5 Billion in 1999. The idea of standard software for payroll, HR applications and similar management functions to cater to the needs of several organizations in one shot, with

Figure 2. Evolution of ERP

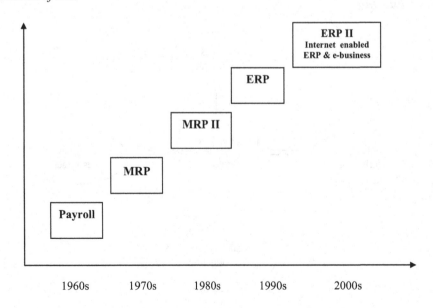

minor changes here or there, became a huge business arena for the IS/IT business. Most of these standard packages ran on mainframes without common databases and real time interfaces between the packages. Any interface development which shared information between application packages had to be internally developed by the company or firm and the same became obsolete as soon as new versions of standard packages were released by the vendors of these application packages.

The idea of application suites emerged in 1990s. Rapidly changing markets, top-heavy/over-staffed organizations incapable of reacting quickly to change and the idea of business processes mooted by Michael Hammer (Hammer et al., 1993) culminated in the idea developing an enterprise wide system. Business managers started viewing business as a set of cross functional processes (Brady et al., 2003). The problems faced by standard package users of the 1980s were overcome by the development of package which could share information in real time and could use centralized database. These became a reality because of the rapid development in hardware, database and operating system technologies. Some such suites developed even had multi-platform compatibility. The evolution of such ERP systems are viewed either as embodiment of reengineering or forced reengineering (Gendron, 1996; O'Leary, 2000).

There exist differences between ERP systems and application packages as shown in the Table 2. ERP is process based whereas an application package is function based. A process has to cut across boundaries of many functional departments to achieve the result whereas an application package remains within the needs of a particular functional department. ERP systems are scalable and have distributed database support with a centralized database repository. The client-server architecture is the commonly used technology for implementing ERP systems, which aids scalability at ease. ERP supports going global by handling multi-location facilities, multiple languages and multiple currency thereby bringing geographically distributed operations closer and manageable.

Earlier ERP products were just extensions of Material Requirements Planning of the past and did not have functionalities like, advanced planning, call centers, business analytics and data warehousing to name a few. Financial, Manufacturing, Human Resources and Distribution were the only four primary areas which were addressed by ERP vendors in the 1990s and the rest were addressed by vertical market and industry solutions.

Table 2. Primary differences between ERP and Application packages

ERP
➤ Process based;
➤ Scalable;
➤ Helps going global and handles multi currency and language.
Application Packages
➤ Function based;
➤ Usually for fixed number of users;
➤ Caters only functional needs within the department.

KEY CHARACTERISTIC FEATURES OF AN ERP SYSTEM

ERP systems integrate business processes. It is a single database repository for various functional departments of the organization without replication in storing and facilitates real time data access. It helps integrate geographically distributed plant locations by supporting multi language and multi currency handling ability. Multitude of industries is supported by ERP by having separate version to aid each industry work flow. The ease of external access to information systems of other companies has resulted in widespread acceptance of such a system in the business arena. The web readiness of the integrated data repository with its ability to run on client-server architecture makes it an indispensable tool in the Internet era. Table 3 shows characteristic features of an ERP system.

ERP is not for manufacturing organizations alone and can also be very well used for the service organizations. It facilitates fast communication of information within the company (Davenport, 1998). It provides consistent information through out the organization by the use of a centralized data repository and improves efficiency through single data entry for all the organizational needs (David, 2004). ERP systems strive for optimization of company's overall operational effectiveness and profitability rather than eyeing at local optimal efficiency aimed by individual departments due to compartmentalized thinking. This enterprise wide thinking towards the common objective of profit maximization at the organizational level by sacrificing local optima at departmental level has become a reality only with the advent of such a system which will cut across the boundaries of various functional departments within the organization.

Though ERP systems provide better system/data integration and offer best practices at lesser computational cost, it is not without disadvantages. Some of the cons are less flexibility, difficult to make corrections, lesser freedom to enhance creativity and heavy training expense and other hidden costs (David, 2004).

NEED FOR ERP

If various functional departments work in isolation, one department may not know what the other does. Each department generates conflicting interests which will lead to too much deviation from organizational goals. If all the departments consult a centralized data repository prior to making their own departmental decisions, only those activities which will make the firm's operation profitable only are encouraged. The idea of ERP is to generate such a centralized information system which

Table 3. Characteristic features of an ERP system

> ➤ Ability to integrate business processes;
> ➤ Provides scalability to expand;
> ➤ Data repository/Enterprise wide database without replication in storing;
> ➤ Facilitates real time data access;
> ➤ Helps integrate multi location activity which are geographically separated;
> ➤ Supports multi languages and multi currencies;
> ➤ Possible to customize without programming;
> ➤ It fosters speedy intra and extra organizational communication;
> ➤ Written based on a specific industry work flow;
> ➤ Designed for client-server architecture and is either web based or traditional software based.

will allow seamless flow of information cutting across various functional departmental barriers and automate business processes concentrating on the profitability of the enterprise.

Information system comprises of people, hardware, software, network communication and data which collects, processes and disseminates data. Management Information System (MIS) produces only specific reports which are predefined and cannot produce anything more than that. Accurate, timely and right data at the right point of time are signs of good information system. Production information is required for stores, raw material procurement and finance department, for earmarking funds for the purchase of the same. Table 4 shows the need for ERP in the e-business era.

The integrated management of information leads to Integrated Data Model which supports a centralized data repository. This data repository gives up to date status of the organization at any point of time without data redundancy and assuring total integrity.

Better integration cutting across various functional departments in an organization is ensured which helps make real time decisions in the quickest possible. Compartmentalized thinking is no more encouraged and process based thinking has already set in. This ensures optimal decisions for the firm at all times. Even the work flow redesign is performed to generate the most optimal path to achieve the end result of the process with the minimum usage of resources. Most processes end up in the generation of too many reports and long process map comprising of many non value added activities when designed for the first time. ERP system with the optimal workflow for the industry is the trend of the day and saves resources from being wasted. As the ERP system has the flexibility to accommodate different currencies and languages including different accounting standards and multi location activity, it is a true integrator cutting across organizational and geographical boundaries. ERP system helps locate plants in various parts of the world giving due consideration to various factors without loosing the power of centralized control and decentralized decision making. This is in line with Federalism advocated by the famous management guru Peter Drucker. Irrespective of the location of the various plants, business communication on real-time basis is established between the Corporate Office and plants to achieve uninterrupted exchange of data or information made possible through the Internet infrastructure in a secure way. Business to business connection is a typical example of establishing a secure connection using Internet infrastructure, as in Virtually Private Network, without having dedicated lines installed by each business separately. Better analysis and planning using decision support systems and simulation resulting in better decision making. Data warehousing helps store past data which are useful only for trend analysis and retrieve them using data mining

Table 4. Need for ERP

> ➢ Better integration to provide real time decision capability;
> ➢ Flexibility to accommodate multi-currency, language and accounting standards;
> ➢ Better analysis and planning using decision support systems and simulation resulting in better decision making;
> ➢ Technology demonstrator;
> ➢ Dramatically reduced data entry, paper trails, and administrative tasks;
> ➢ Improved data visibility and decision support, resulting in better performance.
>
> Adapted from Leon, 2002

as and when required. This helps optimization of database searches in the ERP. Only current data which really useful immediately are kept online and the rest are judiciously warehoused. ERP can be thought of as a product which uses hardware and software in a balanced way and responds quickly to emerging trends in both to tap the potential further. It is really an avenue for demonstrating and using developments in information technology. World class competition, modern business scenario and the Internet have transformed the way business is done in the modern era. A World-Class competitor means being successful against any competitor on quality, lead time, flexibility, cost/price, customer service and innovation for which ERP is definitely inevitable. The world in which we do business is shrinking, and virtually every enterprise is either marketing or selling to customers in other countries, or simply using parts or materials that are produced elsewhere. Internet has overcome time and distance to a great extent. It has become the need of the hour to think globally and to include the same in plans, processes and strategies. Globalization and Web commerce because of Internet have changed traditional business behaviors and practices. Leveraging the Internet by the business has become a need to quickly establish a virtual presence.

ERP II

The need for e-business, Internet readiness in the Internet era and a situation which prevailed to tide over Y2K problems in the late 90s and early 2000s pushed ERP into the market. Average price of setting up a commercial website for a large or midsize organization was kept at $ 1 million by Research agencies like Gartner Research Group (Shields, 2001). Most of the websites developed during this period were not having backend support and could only accept shopping cart details from customers, print them out and do the rest of the processing manually. This means that only

front-end website existed which made it appear as if everything was integrated electronically. Modules in the suite supplied by Oracle and SAP had sufficient functionality to attract a good majority of any business wanting to implement the e-way. Companies had to spent lots of money on maintaining the interfaces among the components after implementing the system during this early stage of e-business proliferation. With the development of the middleware called Enterprise Application integration (EAI), most of the integration issues remained within limits. The differences between ERP, new-generation application packages and e-business started vanishing beyond recognition at the boundaries. ERP of the past can be thought of as fully integrated modules which provided automated support for various functions.

In 1999, ERP by major vendors started incorporating Internet technologies to perform transactions through a browser and these vendors renamed themselves as e-business vendors. By 2000, the market saw the proliferation of e-business suites which could even engulf other functions like Customer Relationship Management (CRM) and Supply Chain Management (SCM) which were not present in traditional ERP. This made the ERP in Internet era really support the e-business wave and the palm top for ERP connectivity from remote locations really changed the way how the business was carried out. Real time connectivity and centralized data repository became features of the ERP system. Moreover, ERP vendors maintained the various versions of the system and its interfaces developed by them thereby relieving the users who go for best-of-the-breed. E-business and ERP integration really boosted the concept of digital firm which was catching the wave during that time. Digital firm in terms has to have a digitally enabled environment for the interaction and processing among customers, employees, employer and the stakeholders alike as shown in Figure 3 (Laudon et al., 2002).

ERP II superseded ERP and its two lesser known iterations called *extended ERP* and *En-*

Figure 3. Digital firm (Adapted from Laudon et al., 2002)

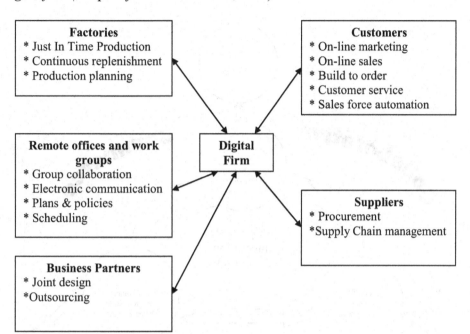

terprise Application Suite (EAS) (www.vendor-showcase.com). The most apparent change from ERP to ERP II is a change in focus from one that is totally enterprise-centric and preoccupied with internal resource optimization and transactional processing to a new focus on process integration and external collaboration. ERP II application deployment strategies relates to information that is exchanged between two or more businesses over the Internet. This exchange information electronically via the Internet is known as collaborative commerce or c-commerce. So it can be concluded that ERP II has c-commerce features. ERP II has also expanded to include areas such as *Supply Chain Management* (SCM), *Customer Relationship Management* (CRM), Knowledge Management (KM), *business intelligence* (BI), and *inventory optimization* (IO). The features in ERP II is very much in line with the Gartner research paper which predicted that ERP II would take ERP foundation and extend it outward to position the enterprise in the supply chain (www.gcis.ca). Figure 4 shows ERP II model which engulfs c-commerce.

The following are the notable differences between ERP and ERP II (www.erpwire.com):

i.   ERP II is web enabled where as ERP was not;

ii.   ERP was giving selected intensive coverage or wide extensive coverage in its modules. But ERP II gives the right mix of the macro and the micro and provides users with remedial measures after detecting the error;

iii.   ERP was targeted more towards manufacturing and the problem is overcome in ERP II by offering solution for all industries and sectors as well;

iv.   ERP could not integrate different functions from different departments but ERP II could integrate different functions across departments as well as from different industries;

v.   ERP II has embraced CRM & SCM functionality in addition to being web and WAP enabled;

vi.   ERP II revolutionalized the function to an external one and facilitated better networks than remaining as internal application.

Figure 4. ERP II which engulfs collaborative commerce

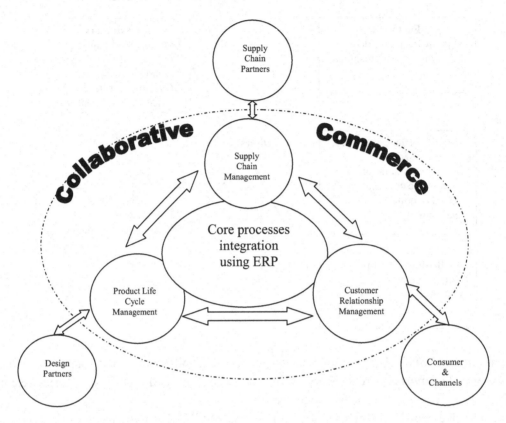

An international survey was floated by the authors to study the status of the use of latest technologies like Artificial Intelligence (AI) and tools in building intelligence in the modern day ERP (Suresh, et al. 2006). The results are as shown in the Table 5. Some of the newer disruptive technologies like managed code, extensible mark-up language and component architecture, born out of Object Oriented programming, are worth studying to establish the level of exploitation in developing and using such technologies in building ERP systems. The survey response analysis based on responses from 92 subjects helps to conclude that 84.8% agreed that ERP requires intelligence for making use of ERP systems in strategic decision making which confirms the existence of a reengineering path through incorporation of AI techniques in ERP. It can be inferred that ERP is already in the path of evolution since 75% disagreed that ERP is good

for transaction processing alone. In the era of web-enabled systems only web-enabled software can survive and the same is depicted in the result since 80.1% agreed that web-enabled ERP helps the evolution of ERP. Though it is found that ERP is in its evolutionary path, it is evident that sufficient scope exists for the application of AI techniques as 71.7% disagreed that widespread use of AI techniques are available in present day ERP. Evolution is inevitable for ERP since 87.5% disagreed that ERP will remain only as a transaction processing system. Majority (79.3%) disagreed that difficulty in building intelligence in ERP is due to lack of availability of web tools which gives a clear indication that technology is ready for building intelligent ERP. Also it may be noted that 75% disagreed that intelligence is not integrated in ERP due to security reasons which implies that no security related issues impedes incorporating intelligence in ERP. About half

Table 5. Results of the International email survey to study the status building more intelligence in ERP (Suresh et al., 2006)

	Hypothesis	Result
1	ERP requires intelligence for strategic decision making	84.8% Agreed
2	Web enabled strategic decision making helps ERP evolution	80.1% Agreed
3	ERP will remain as transaction processing system	87.5% Disagreed
4	ERP is good for transaction processing alone	75% Disagreed
5	Widespread use of AI techniques are available in ERP	71.7% Disagreed
6	Difficulty in building intelligent ERP is due to lack of web tools	79.3% Disagreed
7	Intelligence is not integrated in ERP due to security reasons	75% Disagreed
8	No major vendor wants to risk by developing intelligent ERP	48.9% Disagreed
9	ERP being mission critical, intelligence should not be integrated	85.9% Disagreed
10	AI techniques & web tools are not mature for integrating in ERP	59.8% Disagreed

the respondents (48.9%) disagreed that major ERP vendors does not want to risk by developing intelligent ERP in the market. The real reason for lack interest of ERP vendors in developing intelligent ERP can be attributed to some other reason other than financial risk since 36.96% were unsure of this cause. Majority (85.9%) disagreed that ERP being a mission critical real time system, intelligence should not be integrated which means mission criticality of the real time ERP system does not stand in the way of making intelligent ERP. Relatively good percentage of respondents (59.8%) disagreed that AI techniques and web tools are not ripe enough for integration in ERP indicating that AI techniques and web tools are ripe enough for integration in ERP.

REASONS FOR THE GROWTH IN ERP

ERP integrates firm's activities and improves business performance by reducing cycle time and helps deliver order in time. The time taken between start of the conversion of raw materials and completion of manufacturing of the product can be compressed to optimally low levels without sacrificing quality by the use of completely integrated departmental databases provided in the ERP system It also achieves drastic reduction in inventory by keeping the inventory level at the optimal level. Reduction in lead time is achieved through efficient inventory management system integrated with sales, marketing, purchasing, production planning and control departments. Keeping track of lead times of several thousands of items manually is practically impossible. As soon as the order is received through the sales module in the front-end, triggering of various related action starts taking place simultaneously. Computation for the generation of bill of materials to support the new order is one among them and availability of various components for the fulfillment of the new order is checked. As a result of this process, a list of items for which order is to be placed is generated after cross checking the availability of the same in the inventory. ERP systems also take care of invoice management, vendor selection and other required activities up to the release of purchase order. This computerized system compresses the time taken for such a process from many days to few seconds and with better accuracy than manual system.

Various strategies like make-to-stock or make-to-order or a combination of the above can be beneficial to each product manufactured throughout its product life cycle. ERP gives the flexibility which most suits the product under consideration. Engineering changes can be effectively handled in limited time with appropriate approvals received at specified levels or authority for the smooth implementation of engineering changes.

Multiple keying of the same information for the use of different departments in the same company is avoided by adopting integrated data model approach and centralized data repository. This reduces time taken and chances of human error which might creep in at the time of subsequent keying in of the same information at the departmental levels. As ERP is written based on the workflow followed in the top few companies in the industry, it captures the best practices in the industry. Any company in the industry following the ERP workflow will induct the best, optimal and proven work flow for the industry thereby resulting in enhanced profits and optimal functioning. This also results in organizational standardization among various plants of the same organization located in different places. Substandard processes are eliminated with standardized processes unifying the common view to the outside world. New product and new customers are best supported by ERP which fosters business growth.

Improved resource utilization is achieved through proper capacity planning. Modern ERP systems support both rough-cut and detailed capacity planning. Inputs for resource requirements for production comes from Master Production Schedule like which product, how many and when. Capacity definitions are sourced from work centers based on machine records. This helps identify resources which become constraints from time to time and is automatically pinpointed by the ERP system. To a certain extent such systems

also support simulation to evaluate scenarios to arrive at the best option.

The changing customer needs are immediately reflected in the product line without taking much time due to tighter integration between front-end and back-end operation. The input received from sales, which is front-end, is immediately processed by the engineering design and production at the back-end through the incorporation engineering changes needed from time to time. As this is almost like a closed loop activity carried out on a real-time mode, wastage is minimized to the lowest level possible. Better service levels achieved through ERP systems is another factor which satisfies the customer better. Better flexibility in supporting new product designs in addition to engineering change management of existing designs with minimum disruption is a key feature of such systems.

Its multi-language and multi-currency handling ability embraces different locations of the same organization cutting across geographical boundaries with ease. Unlike in legacy system, here the data or information once is available on line and need not be re-keyed to make it available in another part of the organization and is available 24X7 on real-time basis. Integrated and flexible real-time support achieved in ERP helps manage an organization by gathering information once and at source eliminating multiple hierarchies of personnel exclusively posted for upward/downward communication. It really flattens an organization to a certain extent. As the data is stored in a centralized data repository, which will not allow multiple values for the same variable making it inconsistent, polices data inconsistencies and information asymmetries. Right information at right place at the right time is the key feature which makes the ERP system unique. This improved data/information accuracy substantially improves decision making ability. ERP became the most accepted solution for the new millennium which only could convince the business world that it is much superior to modified legacy systems in solving the Y2K problem.

The present day growth in ERP business is mainly due to spread of ERP solution to mid-sized organizations as shown in Table 5. One organization can be efficient and fast only as much as its weakest supplier or partner in business is a universal truth. So the need of the hour for any organization is to bring in their suppliers within the ERP net. This helps establish B2B connection among the geographically distributed company and its suppliers in the Internet era by integrating the two. Thus ERP solutions not only improve intra organizational communication but also inter organizational communication. Integration achieved helps simultaneous sharing of the same database among business partners as well as production planning and control within the same organization. This really helps manage supplier/partner performance better as they deliver quality products for lower prices. Modules in the ERP systems in a web enabled environment, helps negotiate, monitor and control procurement costs/schedule in addition to routine processes like vendor selection. Just-In-Time which is explained later in this book becomes a reality only with such systems leading to integration beyond organizational boundaries.

REASONS FOR THE FAILURE OF ERP

It is risky to implement a system in a company without proper advice from experienced consultants. As there are many vendors in the market offering ERP solutions, only a consultant based on his/her experience in the field only will know which is the right product to be used for the situation under consideration. Only experienced consultants in the particular industry may prove to be the right choice. This insists that product and competency of the consultants are important in ERP system implementation.

Implementation has to take place at a rapid pace but not in a haphazard fashion without giving sufficient importance to factors which are very critical in the selection and implementation of ERP systems. Sudden transformation, in the jobs of many in the organization, from clerical jobs

Table 5. Reasons for the growth in ERP market

> Integrates firm's activities:
>   • Reduces lead time;
>   • On time shipment;
>   • Reduces cycle time.
> Employs "Best practices" in the industry:
>   • Improves resource utilization;
>   • Increased flexibility;
>   • Ensures better customer satisfaction.
> Enables organizational standardization;
> Eliminates information asymmetries;
> Provides real-time information on-line;
> Avoids data inconsistency between production and planning:
>   • Better & faster decision making.
> Fosters inter and intra-organizational communication:
>   • Improved supplier performance.

Source: Adapted from O'Leary, 2000

Table 6. Reasons for the failure of ERP system implementation

> ➤ Wrong ERP solution chosen for implementation;
> ➤ Incompetent consultants;
> ➤ Haphazard implementation;
> ➤ Sudden transformation of employees from clerical to decision making jobs;
> ➤ Lack of training;
> ➤ Fear of unemployment.
>
> Source: Adapted from Leon, 2002

to computer assisted real-time decision making makes it difficult for the employees to adjust to the new environment for a while. An simple key press on the enter button of a computer by a sales clerk triggers many actions like releasing of purchase orders for raw materials, changes schedules in the shop floor, alerts HR manager for the release of advertisement for recruiting people to fill the voids in skill levels and the like to support the order committed by the sales clerk. The lack of knowledge of the sales clerk in other areas of operation like production, which is a back-end operation, develops stress in the clerk as he is not completely aware of all the operations which will follow order commitment over his computer. Training is definitely useful in driving the fear away the fear in employees regarding clicks and their effects on the system. No individual likes change except a baby with wet diaper and the same is true to this situation. Training helps alleviate resistance to change.

Computer and its use in automation are often thought of as method for down-sizing by the employees. Fear of unemployment in employees due to ERP implementation can be eliminated by building awareness in them regarding the changing needs of the industry and the transformation from manual jobs to computerized jobs which only is taking place to meet the extremely high levels of demand in market at short notices. Table 6 enumerates some of the common causes for the failure of ERP implementation.

WORKING OF AN ERP SYSTEM

In order to demonstrate the working of an ERP system, SAP R/3 system is used here. The example discussed is adapted from Edmundson et al., 1997 and O'Leary, 2001. Assume that for a company located in Bangalore, sales representative is taking order from a retailer in London. The sales representative is taking order in her lap top, with connectivity to her back-end at Bangalore where the production is taking place, using the sales module of SAP R/3. The system checks retailer's credit history to decide whether the sale can take place. If allowed to proceed with the sale, the system module checks for probable price and corresponding discounts that the retailer is eligible for.

Next check by the R/3 system is the availability of inventory in the nearest warehouse. Assume that the company is having a warehouse at Frankfurt. The system checks for the availability of the product ex-stock as per order in the Frankfurt warehouse which is the nearest one. If it is found that only a portion of the order is available, the rest has to come from factory at Bangalore. Inventory module of the R/3 system immediately alerts the warehouse to ship the quantity available ex-stock at the warehouse and simultaneously, back-end is informed of the shortage to complete the order.

R/3's Production module at the back-end schedules the production of the quantity of product not available ex-stock at the warehouse. An invoice

Figure 5. Order placement over Internet using an ERP system

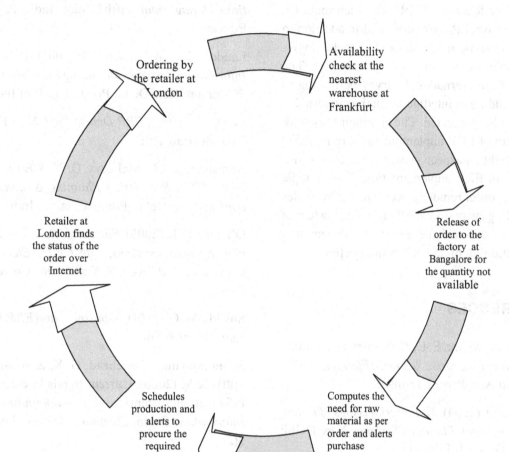

is printed in English and Euro as currency by the sales clerk and the same is handed over to the retailer.

If the Human Resources module of the R/3 system finds shortage of workers to meet the order on schedule, the personnel manager is immediately alerted to procure additional temporary manpower in corresponding areas.

R3's material planning module alerts the purchasing manager to release orders for raw materials. The quantity computation is automatically done by the ERP system.

The retailer at London can log on to R3's Front end through the Internet and find that a portion of the order is completed. It also gives the retailer to place order for more quantity, if needed. Figure 5

shows how the interaction with R/3 software by a sales clerk sitting remotely from its factory at London triggers a chain of action to the extent of changing schedules at the factory floor by merely confirming an order over Internet.

CONCLUSION

An attempt has been made in this chapter to define ERP and to explain the meaning of the same in the e-business era. The world class competition, modern business environment and the availability of the Internet are the premises which stress the need for ERP. The evolution of ERP is presented briefly starting with Pay roll and Bill of Materials in the 1960s to Web enabled ERP in the 2000s. The salient features of ERP II which makes it different from ERP are presented in addition to presenting some of the disruptive technologies which help reengineer ERP systems fast. The results of an international survey pertaining to the embedding of intelligence in the modern day ERP are also presented. The common causes for the failure of ERP implementation are included to shed light on aspects which are of utmost importance to ERP implementation. The example of placing order remotely over Internet by a sales clerk sitting away from the factory forms a part of this chapter to benefit the readers in understanding the functioning of an ERP system better.

REFERENCES

Brady, J. A., Monk, E. F., & Wagner, B. J. (2003). *Concepts in Enterprise Resource Planning*, India: Thomson Asia Private Limited.

David, L. O. (2004). *Managerial issues of Enterprise Resources Planning Systems*. New Delhi: Tata McGraw-Hill Edition.

Davenport, T. H. (1998). Putting the enterprise into the enterprise system. *Harvard Business Review, July-August*, 121-131.

Edmundson, G., Baker, S., & Cortese, A. (1997). Silicon valley on the Rhine. *Business Week, November 3*, 162-166.

Gendron, M. (1996). Learning to live with electronic embodiment of reengineering. *Harvard Management Update, November*.

Hammer, M., & Champy, J. (1993). *Reengineering the corporation*. USA: Free Press.

Khalid, S. (2001). *Manufacturing Resource Planning with introduction to ERP, SCM and CRM*. Tata McGraw Hill.

Krajewski, L. J., & Ritzman, P. (2000). *Operations Management*. Fifth Edition, India: Pearson Education.

Laudon, K. C., & Laudon, J. P. (2002). *Managing Information Systems: Managing the digital firm*, 7th Edition, New Delhi: Prentice Hall of India.

Leon, A. (2002). *ERP Demystified*. New Delhi: Tata McGraw Hill.

Narasimhan, S. L., McLeavy, D. W., & Billington, P. J. (1997). *Production Planning & inventory control*. New Delhi: Prentice Hall of India.

O'Leary, D. E. (2000). *Enterprise Resource Planning Systems: Systems, Life Cycle, Electronic Commerce and Risk*. UK: Cambridge University Press.

Shields, M. G. (2001). *E-business and ERP*. USA: John Wiley & Sons.

Subramoniam, S., Shehzad, G. K. & Krishnankutty, K V. (2006). Current trends in enterprise information systems, *Applied Computing and Informatics, Saudi Computer Society Journal, 5(2)*.

Web Sites

www.erpwire.com/erp-articles/erpII-vs-erp.htm

www.erpworld.com

www.exactamerica.com

www.gcis.ca/english/cdne-077-aug-16-2001.html

www.informationweek.com

www.mapics.com

www.vendor-showcase.com/Research/ResearchHighlights/Erp/2004/06/research_notes/TU_ER_XSW_06_18_04_15.asp

KEY TERMS

c-Commerce: The B2B exchange of information electronically via the Internet for enabling ERP II is known as collaborative commerce or c-commerce.

Digital Firm: Digital firm is a digitally enabled environment for the interaction and processing of information among customers, employees, employer and the stakeholders.

Enterprise: Enterprise is a group of people and associated resources to achieve a common goal.

Enterprise Resource Planning (ERP) System: ERP system is an enterprise wide system which encompasses corporate mission, objectives, attitudes, beliefs, values, operating style and people who make the organization.

ERP II: The most apparent change from ERP to ERP II is a change in focus from one that is totally enterprise-centric and preoccupied with internal resource optimization and transactional processing to a new focus on process integration and external collaboration. ERP II application deployment strategies relates to information that is exchanged between two or more businesses over the Internet.

Integrated Data Model: The integrated management of information leads to Integrated Data Model which supports a centralized data repository. This data repository gives up to date status of the organization at any point of time without data redundancy and assuring total integrity.

Material Requirements Planning (MRP) System: MRP was used in the 1970s for raw material ordering based on order at hand.

Manufacturing Resources Planning (MRP II) System: MRP II incorporated financial accounting, human resource management and distribution in addition to material requirements planning. It provides information regarding staffing levels and overtime needs through detailed capacity requirements planning.

Chapter XXV
E–Government and ERP:
Challenges and Strategies

Gita A. Kumta

SVKM's NMIMS University, School of Business Management, Mumbai, India

ABSTRACT

*The chapter introduces the essence of ERP in government as a tool for integration of government functions which provides the basis for citizen services. It discusses the challenges faced in modernization of **government** "businesses" and discusses strategies for implementation. The basis of **Enterprise Resource Planning** (ERP) solutions is integration of functions which capture basic data through transactions to support critical administrative functions such as budgeting and financial management, revenue management, supply chain management and human resources management. Today, **Enterprise solutions** (ES) go beyond ERP to automate citizen-facing processes. The integration of data sources with each contact point is essential to ensure a consistent level of service. The author expects that researchers, governments and solution providers will be able to appreciate the underlying constraints and issues in implementation of ERP and hopes that the learning from industry would be useful to plan implementation of ES in government using emerging technologies.*

INTRODUCTION

ERP provides an enterprise-wide view of an organization and **integrates various silos of activity.** Such an **integrated** approach has a tremendous payback if **implemented** properly. Most ERP systems were designed to be used by manufacturing companies to track men, machines and material so as to improve productivity and reduce inventory. Viewing it from a business perspective, ERP systems are now known as **Enterprise Solutions** (ES) which takes a customer order and provides a software road map for automating the different steps along the path to fulfilling the order. The major reasons why companies look at ES can be summarized as:

- Integrate financial information
- Integrate customer order information
- Standardize and speed up operational processes
- Reduce inventory
- Standardize HR information

Governments worldwide have been making efforts to use **information and communications technologies** (ICT) as an instrument of change to provide better services to citizens, facilitate work flow, and provide better governance and transparency. Popularly known as **E-Government**, the focus has initially been on information dissemination which has now moved on to **transactions**. What is required is a **transformation of the public administration** which takes a citizen service request and provides a software road map for automating the different steps along the path to fulfilling the request. This cuts across various departments and it is therefore critical to lay down suitable policies, guidelines and specifications and also **redefine processes to facilitate faster proliferation of ICT applications.**

E-government does not happen with more computers or a website. While online service delivery can be more efficient and less costly than other channels, cost savings and service improvements are not automatic. **E-government** has therefore to focus on planning, sustained allocation of budgets, dedication of manpower resources and above all, the political will. The **e-government** field, like most young fields, lacks a strong body of well-developed theory. One strategy for coping with theoretical immaturity is to import and adapt theories from other, more mature fields. (Flak, Rose, 2005)

Literature survey on **implementations** of **e-governance** has brought out the following observations which would help us in **redefining** the use of **Information & Communication Technology** (ICT) in the right perspective.

- Most **governments** have not changed their processes in any way, and instead have automated flawed **processes**.
- Government budgets and **administration** tends to be in departmental silos, but e-governance cuts across departments.
- Too much attention to "citizen portals" has taken attention away from **internal government functioning.** There is a big gap between a web site and **integrated service delivery.**
- **Governments** often underestimate the security, **infrastructure,** and scalability requirements of their applications which impact the quality of service. (Khalil, Lanvin, Chaudhry, 2002)

Learning from the experiences of the corporates, **governments** today understand the need for a consistent and **flexible information infrastructure** that can **support organizational change,** cost-effective service delivery and regulatory compliance. ERP is therefore needed to meet organizational objectives and outcomes by better allocating resources - its people, finances, capital, materials, and facilities. **Modernization** programs however involve a broad range of activities and require a wide array of skills and experiences, as these programs affect everything from computers to culture. The objective is to reduce administrative overhead and **improve core product/service delivery**.

ESSENCE OF ERP IN GOVERNMENT

Before moving on to the ERP discussion it is necessary to dwell a little on various aspects of **E-government** which is about **transforming the way government interacts** with the governed.

The **E-Government handbook** for developing countries identifies three major phases –Publish,

Interact and Transact. These however are not sequential phases and hence can be considered as
major aspects of e-government. In short, e-government utilizes **technology to accomplish reform**
by fostering transparency, eliminating distance
and other divides, and empowering people to participate in the political processes that affect their
lives. (Khalil, Lanvin, Chaudhry, 2002). Each of
the phases is briefly summarized below.

- **Publish:** Governments generate and also
  publish in print large amount of information
  which can be disseminated to the public
  using ICT. Some of these cases are
  ◦ E-Government Portal of Canada is
    considered as one of the best govern-
    ment portals in the world. http://www.
    canada.gc.ca.
  ◦ The JUDIS (Judgment Information
    System) in India posts court records,
    case information and judicial deci-
    sions. http://indiancourts.nic.in/itin-
    jud.htm
- **Interact:** Interactive **e-government** involves two-way communications, starting
  with basic functions like email contact
  information for **government** officials or
  feedback forms that allow users to submit
  comments on legislative or policy proposals.
  Some of the cases are
  ◦ Citizen Space. A section of the British
    Government's web portal allowing
    citizens to comment on government
    policy. http://www.ukonline.gov.uk
  ◦ The Central Vigilance Commission
    in India allows citizens to file online
    complaints about corruption. http://
    www.cvc.nic.in/vscvc/htm
- **Transact:** Just as the private sector in developing countries is beginning to make use of
  the Internet to offer e-commerce services,
  governments will be expected to do the same
  with their services. A transact website will
  offer a direct link to government services,

available at any time. Some of the cases
are
  ◦ The Bhoomi Project. Delivery of
    land titles online in Karnataka, In-
    dia...http://www.revdept-01.kar.nic.
    in/Bhoomi/Home.htm
  ◦ The Government E-Procurement
    System in Chile...http://www.com-
    praschile.cl/Publico/entrada_publico.
    asp

To achieve this it is essential to look at the
internal processes of the government, the **relationships between various departments**, sharing
of information between departments and the IT
infrastructure required to support these aspects.
The following section indicates the characteristics of content, process, people and technology
required by **government** to implement the various
initiatives, thereby identifying the essence of ERP
in government (refer to Table 1).

The **E-Government handbook** for developing countries has many more case studies listed
which highlight these phases. (Khalil, Lanvin,
Chaudhry, 2002).

Enterprise **modernization** is therefore a complex, **ongoing evolutionary process** that involves
the **integrated transformation** of strategies,
policies, organization and governance structures,
business processes and systems, and underlying
technologies. Only by aligning these elements
with its business goals can an agency achieve a
successful **modernization** program. (Kirwan,
Sawyer, and Sparrow, 2003).

The very essence of enterprise **modernization**
is integration of processes and connectivity of
stakeholders. It therefore involves connecting:

- Government to government (G2G):Depart-
  mental integration of processes ERP
- Government to businesses (G2B): Information to suppliers and procurement SCM
- Government to citizens (G2C): information
  and service to citizens CRM

Table 1. Requirements for e-government initiatives

Phase	Content	Process	People	Technology
Publish Focus: centralization of content	Existing documents in terms of rules and regulations, documents, and forms	Simple process of capture and monitoring.	Small project team with skill focus on IT. Involvement of department staff minimal. Minimal technical support for usage.	Basic IT infrastructure, storage and web services – Portal. Batch mode. Can be totally outsourced.
Interact Focus: Involvement of citizens	Grievances, suggestions, feedback	Process of coordination with departments and communication on status of content.	Small internal teams with skill focus on communication and people management. Moderate technical support for usage.	E-mail facility and collaborative systems. On-line and batch mode Can be partially outsourced.
Transact Focus: Direct link of citizens to government services.	Integration of functional processes Service flow from application to service delivery. Covers forms, logic of computation, controls, operational and legal policies.	Process of data capture through transaction, validation, processing using defined logic. Focus on managing business processes.	Large Project teams. Skills in communication, people management. And functional knowledge. Extensive technical support for usage.	Large and robust IT infrastructure. Storage, internal network, ERP solution, web services and e-commerce. Online, real-time mode. Cannot be outsourced. Requires technology partnerships ICT policies.

- Government to employees (G2E): information and service to employees ERP

As citizens grow in awareness, **governments** today are under increasing pressure to deliver a range of services – from ration cards, motor licenses and land records to health, education and municipal services – in a manner that is timely, efficient, economical, equitable, transparent and corruption-free. For any government that is keen to respond to this demand and to hasten the pace of development –**information technology** comes as an **excellent tool**. However technocratic responses in themselves are not a solution. They are a tool. A solution is one that is holistic and describes how the tool can be feasibly deployed. (Carter, 2005).

ERP solutions in government should therefore provide horizontal components, which are relevant to every part of a government and should support vertical **integration** needed for the delivery of specific services. Such solutions would facilitate governments to offer cross-functional services to citizens which no longer need to be restricted to the structure of the government.

Tremendous potential exists for **rethinking of the business of government** to reduce cost and improve the quality of government/constituent interactions. Most so-called "e-governance" initiatives have been simply **focused on internet-enabling old processes** and systems which have resulted in a series of costly, overlapping, and uncoordinated projects. **Transformation** is possible only when one examines the inter-relationships between government agencies – both processes and systems which would result in true efficiencies of E-Business.

"The benefits come from changing your **business processes**, not from installing ERP," says Bill Swanton, a vice president at AMR Research in Boston. Adds Buzz Adams, president of Peak Value Consulting that specializes in process improvement, "The technology will work the way you implement it, so what's important is how you improve the processes — the way you do things." (Bartholomew, 2004).

FUNCTIONAL MODEL OF PUBLIC ADMINISTRATION

Enterprise resource planning (ERP) systems are becoming pervasive throughout the public sector for their support of critical administrative functions such as budgeting and financial management, procurement, human resources (HR), business process, and customer relationship management (CRM).

ERP solutions for financial management cover accounts payable, accounts receivable, fixed asset accounting, cash management, activity-based and project accounting, cost-centre planning and analysis, financial consolidation, financial reporting, and legal compliance and reporting. Budget management solutions support economic policy, collection and analysis of budget and economic

data, economic forecasting, revenue allocation to government agencies, budget approval, and budget monitoring.

The **Public Administration Functional Model** can be diagrammatically depicted as shown in Figure 1.

Tax and revenue management also fall under the financial and budget management umbrella. This includes both tax filing and tax case management. Tax filing covers taxpayer identification and registration, tax assessment, management of online or offline revenue collection and reimbursements, secure processing, and payment. Tax case management involves investigation and enforcement, revenue auditing, and analysis.

Supply chain management (SCM) functions cover cataloguing, bidding and negotiation, and tendering with workflow support for preparation of tender requests, invoicing and payment, purchasing and reporting. Logistics support in the areas of material and equipment planning, inventory, warehouse management, transportation and distribution, and the maintenance, repair, and disposal of assets is another major area of public administration.

Figure 1. Public Administration Functional Model

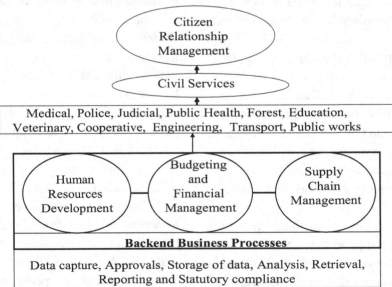

350

Human resource management covers civil service recruitment, individual and collective training, performance assessment, career development, payroll and benefits, and travel and the movement of public employees.

Finally citizen-facing processes within an organization through Web-portals and call centers as well as traditional over-the-counter services require integration of data sources with each contact point to ensure a consistent level of service.

Traditionally processes were people driven and the emphasis of ERP was on automation. Having achieved the basic requirements, organizations expected to achieve efficiency and control. Today the expectation from an ERP system is strategic support adding value to business. Collectively, all the functionalities of publishing, interacting and transacting now need to be aligned to manage the entire government business. ERP combines them all together into a single, **integrated software solution** that operates on a **single database** so that the various departments can more easily **share information**, communicate with each other and provide end-to-end service to its stakeholders.

CHALLENGES IN IMPLEMENTATION OF ICT SOLUTIONS

E-governance initiatives are common in most countries as they promise a more citizen-centric government and reduce operational cost. Unfortunately most of these initiatives have not been able to achieve the benefits claimed. Often the reason for this failure is a techno-centric focus rather than a governance-centric focus (Saxena, 2005). The following challenges faced by organizations are equally applicable to governments.

Acquisition Process

All government ICT and modernization programs face major challenges, one of which is the acquisition process. This process requires a holistic view of the public administration for identifying and evaluating the right solution, taking decisions regarding outsourcing and managing the whole implementation as a project. It's not very difficult to buy software and hardware that fulfill the needs of a single division without considering the needs of the entire organization. However, if each division of an organization develops its own business processes and IT infrastructure, the result will be lack of interoperability, duplicated components, functional gaps, and inability to share information.

Though external consultants do provide support, the challenging task is creating an IT organization structure to support this process within the government structure.

High Expectation from Citizens

Citizens themselves are becoming increasingly demanding as they compare government services with other services like banking. Citizens do not want to be transferred from department to department for an answer to a simple telephone query and be forced to queue at public offices to make a straightforward transaction. They demand facilities to be offered round the clock. They expect high standards of service, instant access to information, efficient **transactions,** and support, whenever and wherever they need it.

Integration of Various Functions

Today it is the era of packaged software which in most cases is exhaustively comprehensive. The organization therefore needs to change its processes to align it to 'best practices' incorporated in the software package. However in the excitement to implement such solutions one often loses sight of the fact that each department has its own policies and rules that make it unique. "For **integration** to work, your internal systems must be working properly," says Mary Kay DeVillier, director/c-business and information resources at Albemarle (Mullin, 2000).

Requirement of Clean Data

Organizations embarking on an ERP initiative must take care not to underestimate the amount of work needed to develop a clean set of master data. The chart of accounts, **citizen data**, policies & norms and other mission-critical information has to be accurate from the start or mistakes will multiply exponentially throughout the system. Many an ERP project has been scuttled or gone south altogether because companies failed to do this kind of basic blocking and tackling early on (Bartholomew, 2004).

Standards for Interoperability

In order to support these demands the internal functions of supply chain management assume greater importance. There is tremendous importance for **rules and procedures in the government**. Unless the records are kept properly, accessing information and tracing the precedents becomes time consuming and this is one of the reasons for the delays in government administration. The rules and procedures can be made transparent to the citizens, and traceability can be incorporated which would improve the pace of effectiveness of governance by using Information Technology (Budhiraja, 2003).

With multiple players and departments increasingly becoming involved in the e-Government initiatives, **standards for e-Government** have become an urgent imperative for **interoperability**. **Enterprise solutions** would therefore help in **streamlining operations**, be flexible and agile enough to respond to the demands of public sector reforms.

Information Security

Managing a secure environment in an era of integrated and seamless service delivery presents an increasing challenge for governments as it can be overwhelming and costly without the right infrastructure. While processing sensitive data such as citizen and financial information stored on ERP systems, government organizations want to ensure they take every possible measure to maximize security.

Project Management

To get the most from the software, the people inside the government have to adopt the work methods outlined in the software. Getting people inside the government to use the software to improve the ways they do their jobs is by far the most critical challenge. Most ERP implementations fail due to **resistance to change** and poor **project management** (Koch). The whole **implementation** has to be taken up as a **project** clearly identifying the scope, cost, time and resource requirements with clear definition of milestones.

Hidden Costs

Certain costs which are more commonly overlooked or underestimated than others are training, integration, customization, testing, data conversion and data analysis which are not adequately factored into the budgets. This leads to delay in implementation which results in apathy and dissatisfaction.

IMPLEMENTATION STRATEGIES

An ERP system helps the different parts of the organization share data and **knowledge**, reduce costs, and improve management of **business processes**. In spite of their benefits, many ERP systems fail (Stratman and Roth, 1999). Many ERP systems face **implementation** difficulties because of workers' resistance (Aladwani, 2001). Effective implementation of ERP requires establishing five core competencies, among which is the use of change management strategies to promote the infusion of ERP in the workplace (Al-Mashari and Zairi, 2000).

During the last few years there have been major initiatives among different Governments towards ushering in ICT and its tools in the functioning of Government. The emphasis has been on providing better services to citizens and in improving the internal productivity. Cases listed in the Report for the President's Management Council in December 2005 is testimony to this fact (Evans, 2005).

The strategies get more focused when we view the organization as an open system composed of interdependent components that include Strategy, Processes, Structure, Technology and Culture as mapped by Scott-Morton in the Management of the 1990s equilibrium model (Scott-Morton, 1991). This model is depicted in Figure 2. The salient aspect of this open systems model is that an impact of change on one component is immediately felt on the other components either directly or indirectly.

The **ERP implementation strategies** can therefore be classified into organizational, technical, and people strategies. Organizational strategies would cover **strategic planning**, business alignment, **project management** and change management. The technology strategies would cover **enterprise architecture**, business process mapping, data capture and information security. **People strategies** would cover communication, **managing resistance to change** and ongoing support.

Strategic Planning

The state of Missouri in USA was the first to implement one of the largest government ERP systems which was implemented in phases and operational by 2001. The finance, budgeting and purchasing functions serve 6,000 end users, and its human resources and payroll modules serve 9,000. One of the most important keys to success for the **implementation** was that all state agencies had a say in the project from its earliest stages. (Douglas, 2002).

Developing a **strategic plan** and **bringing all stakeholders on board** are crucial early steps in **implementing** ERP", said Ken Munson, senior principal in the State and Local Solutions Division of AMS Inc., Missouri's ERP vendor. "The plan has to be well communicated and well bought in, not just by the different branches of government, but by all levels of each of the branches," he said. (Douglas, 2002).

The Department of Information Technology, Government of India, has felt it necessary to create a rational framework for assessing e-Governance projects on various dimensions. It is desirable that a set of instruments is available to the administrators of those projects to appreciate the various attributes of a good e-governance project, apply midcourse corrections, where needed, and steer these projects in the right direction.(Rao, etal, 2004).

Many problems related to ERP **implementation** are related to a misfit of the system with the characteristics of the organization. (Markus et al., 2000). ERP 'tends to impose its own logic on a company's strategy, culture, and organization' which may or may not fit with the existing organizational arrangements. (Davenport, 1998),

Effective Project Management

Success depends on a well designed implementation plan. An ERP system is the information backbone and reaches into all areas of the business and value-chain. It is necessary to consider implementation as a **project** and **plan the activities involving people, processes and technology.**

SAP's Accelerated SAP Implementation Methodology provides a guideline for implementation. (Dejpongsarn, 2005). It focuses on five broad phases covering

- Project Preparation: This covers the requirement of resources- people, technology and budget

- Business Blueprint: This covers the documentation of **current processes** (As is) **and comparison to the solution which has best practices. A gap analysis** provides a starting point to identify the changes required by the departments and new development.

- Realization: Set-up (configuration), testing, data migration and development
- Final Preparation: Training, final functional testing
- Go-live & Support: Different approaches are followed for going live (all modules / related modules), support through internal or external teams.

Management of Change

Governments are using organizational **change management** techniques that have worked in the commercial world within their own **modernization** programs. (Kauzlarich, 2003).

Modernization strategies, such as ERP **implementation**, commonly involve change. Hence, **responsiveness to internal customers** is critical for an organization to avoid the difficulties associated with this change (Al-Mashari and Zairi, 2000; Aladwani, 1999; Aladwani, 1998).

ERP **implementation** should be viewed as **an organizational change process,** rather than as the replacement of a piece of technology. (Boonstra, 2005). Though change management strategies facilitate the success of ERP **implementation,** many ERP systems still face resistance, and ultimately, failure. (Aladwani, 2001).

For the **reform** to succeed, governments need to be culturally and technically prepared to understand and implement change. Procedural and legal **changes in the decision making and delivery processes** as well as internal functioning are required to make a success of ERP implementation.

Business Process Mapping

Administrative reforms will have to precede attempts at implementation of an ERP. The emphasis will have to be on **simplifying procedures**, rationalizing **processes** and **restructuring Government functions.** However, this is an ideal situation but in practice changes and ERP implementation go on parallel as one cannot expect reforms to take place in a short period.

The whole government reform agenda has a profound effect on government financial management. A shift of emphasis from inputs to

Figure 2. Management of the 1990s Equilibrium Model

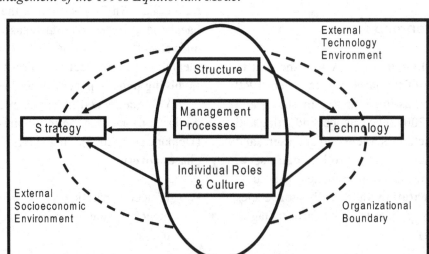

outcomes is a key driver behind many reform initiatives.(Microsoft). These include public / private partnerships, contracting, and decentralization of service delivery to semi-autonomous agencies, competition between service providers, cost-recovery, revenue generation, and the many other alternatives for service provision.

Data Capture

The **basis of an ERP** system is the **data captured through transactions** which integrates the business processes to achieve a task. It is therefore necessary to have data standards for use across government to enable easier, more efficient exchanging and processing of data. It will also remove ambiguities and inconsistencies in the use of data. The United States Government is one of the largest users and acquirers of data, information and supporting technology systems in the world. The E-Government program continuously identifies IT opportunities for collaboration and consolidation using the Federal **Enterprise Architecture** (FEA) framework. The framework is a comprehensive business-driven blueprint to enable the federal government to identify opportunities to leverage technology to:

- Reduce redundancy;
- **Facilitate horizontal** (cross-federal) **and vertical** (federal, state and local) **information sharing;**
- Establish a direct relationship between IT and mission/program performance to support citizen-centered, customer-focused government; and
- Maximize IT investments to better achieve mission outcomes.

The FEA framework and its five supporting reference models (Performance, Business, Service, Technical and Data) are now used by departments and agencies in developing their budgets and setting strategic goals. **Data forms the base of a**

transactional system and hence **data integrity is essential for inter-operability**. The FEA **Data Reference Model** (DRM) defined by the Office of Management and Budget, US, provides a "common language" for diverse agencies to use while communicating with each other and with state and local governments seeking to collaborate on common solutions and sharing information for improved services (Evans, 2005).

The potential uses of the model have been summarized as:

- Provides a FEA mechanism for identifying what data the Federal government has and how it can be shared in response to a business/mission requirement
- Defines a **frame of reference to facilitate Communities of Interest** (which will be aligned with the Lines of Business) toward common ground and common language to facilitate **improved information sharing**
- Provides guidance for implementing repeatable processes for sharing data Government-wide

Enterprise Architecture

If each division of an organization develops its own **business processes** and **IT infrastructure,** the end result may be lack of interoperability, duplicated **Enterprise architecture** components, functional gaps, and inability to share information. is required. (Tucker and Debrosse, 2003).

To avoid these problems, the federal government now mandates the use of enterprise architectures (EAs) by federal agencies seeking to obtain funding for any significant IT investment. Enterprise architectures act as a kind of roadmap for the design, development, and acquisition of complex, mission-oriented information systems. **Creating enterprise architecture** requires participation from many areas of the organization and a great deal of communication to plan and implement each stage of the process. The result is a roadmap that guides an organization through the **modernization** process and enables it to achieve its goals (Tucker and Debrosse, 2003).

Managing People and Communication

Managing the **implementation** requires a dedicated team with adequate skills and a clear plan and agenda. It needs to be managed as any large project with clear milestones and deliverables. The migration to an **enterprise resource planning (ERP)** system is often fraught with peril. Research and experience show that communication is a key mechanism for breaking down barriers to change. Employees are better able to tolerate change if they **understand why the change is important** and if they feel the changes are being handled with fairness and transparency. **Good communication** throughout the enterprise builds **trust and understanding**. People must see how the changes will affect the organization, the citizens and themselves (Kauzlarich, 2003). The success of **implementation** of ICT **projects** depends on **attitudinal readiness of the beneficiaries** for accepting change (Bowonder, Mastakar, Sharma, 2005).

Knowledge Management

Knowledge Management is a **combination of culture and technology**. Culture drives knowledge management while technology enables it. The following characteristics of government based on its structure and functions drive its knowledge management needs.

- Knowledge which is **actionable information** (also known as knowledge assets) is a central resource of the government. Effective functioning of government rests on effective **acquisition and dissemination of knowledge.**

- Similar knowledge requirements spread across the states, districts, and other local governments.
- Transfer of people across government departments calls for a **repository of knowledge** which can be used wherever they move.
- Proactive action is required if governments want to **transform** themselves into "anticipatory governments" to meet the challenges of the emerging E-governance era (Misra, Hariharan, Khaneja, 2003).

EMERGING TRENDS

While ERP is concerned with the use of IT for efficient functioning of government departments, attempts are on to morph the customer relationship management concepts for creating effective service for the citizens which has given birth to a new field of knowledge called Citizen Relationship Management. (Kannabiran, Xavier, Anantharaaj, 2005). It is about **making better use of the considerable amounts of information** that government already collects (Smith, 2003). CzRM is about becoming "citizen-centric" (Nowlan, 2001; Hunter & Shine, 2001).

A citizen can be defined as a consumer of public goods and services (Nowlan, 2001). In the emerging e-Governance scenario, citizens should be treated as customers of business organizations, where serving citizens is the sole purpose of governments. Citizen Relationship Management (CzRM) is a division of customer relationship management that focuses specifically on how governmental bodies relate to their constituents (Xavier, 2002; Jha & Bokad, 2003).

Post-ERP trends are geared towards increasing customer relationships and analysis of the market place for maximum profit. Data mining and Business Intelligence now are not only supporters of growth but also act as initiators of growth. Today's organizations are looking for applications to inspire and lead the way. IT is no more an internal system of automation but is now an external means of customer communication and market analysis (Tucker and Debrosse, 2003).

The services strategy entails building an **integration layer** that is separate and distinct from any of the software applications, including ERP. **Services extract pieces of data** and business logic from systems and databases and bundle them together into units that are expressed in 'business' terms. Implementing a **service-oriented architecture** can involve developing **applications that use services**, making applications available as services so that other applications can use those services, or both. (Ort, 2005).

Service-oriented architecture (SOA) is the emerging trend in enterprise computing because it holds promise of IT becoming **more agile in responding to changing business needs.** Gartner reports that "By 2008, SOA will be a prevailing software engineering practice, ending the 40-year domination of monolithic **software architecture**" A service-oriented architecture is an information technology approach or strategy in which applications make use of **services** available in a network such as the World Wide Web.

The **Internet** aids good governance by increasing transparency and customer-oriented service delivery. (Torres, Pina, Acerete, 2006) .By taking advantage of Internet protocols and technologies, one can minimize the need for ad hoc links between your company and your service supplier. Moreover, because the new **service-based applications** run inside Web browsers, your staff can connect to the service provider from various locations. Another bonus of **Web-based ERP applications** is that the server location is transparent. (Apicella, 2000).

CONCLUSION

In the ultimate analysis, we find that the electronic governance wave has started worldwide. With the technologies to implement electronic governance

already available/understood by the government, managerial issues are of key importance. Change in the mindset of the people particularly at the top levels in the bureaucracy and policy making is important because it is they who provide the leadership.

It is important to think beyond automation, and towards redesign of the basic workflow within the government. The next generation of e- Governance will not be mere automation, but will require a reengineering of the government structurally and functionally.

Enterprise **modernization** involves changes to all dimensions of an organization. It affects. (Kirwan, Sawyer, Sparrow, 2003).

- Organizational structure
- Policies, processes, and procedures
- Business and technical architectures
- Investment management practices
- Governance
- Culture

Government agencies have the advantage of applying lessons learned from the commercial business world, based on the analysis of both failures and successes of ERP **implementations.** Governments today understand the need for a consistent and **flexible information infrastructure** that can support organizational **change** and meet regulatory compliance. However, one cannot expect to revolutionize the government operations with **ERP as it affects mostly the existing "back office" processes**. This helps in optimizing the way things are done internally which is essential for building relationships with citizens, suppliers or partners.

If ERP is the focus of an effort to bring dramatic improvements to the way government functions, it will bring with it some **post-ERP depression too.** The most common reason for the performance problems is that people see a change in the way **processes** were executed earlier. When people can't do their jobs in the familiar way and haven't yet mastered the new way, they panic, and the operations go into spasms.

A **government** that plans to implement ERP should expect "to be **very committed**, because it's a long process," advised Jan Heckemeyer, administrator of Statewide Advantage for Missouri (SAM) II. It is especially important to involve every agency and resolve policy questions before configuring the system. "It drags out the process a bit, trying to build **consensus** and work out those issues," she said. "But it's time very well spent." (Douglas, 2002).

REFERENCES

Aladwani, A. (1998). Coping with users resistance to new technology implementation: an interdisciplinary perspective. *Proceedings of the 9th IRMA Conference*, Boston, MA, 17-20 May, pp. 54-9.

Aladwani, A. (1999). Implications of some of the recent improvement philosophies for the management of the information systems organization. *Industrial Management & Data Systems*, 99(1), 33-9.

Aladwani, A. M. (2001). Change management strategies for successful ERP implementation. *Business Process Management Journal,* 7(3), 2001 Technical paper

Al-Mashari, M., & Zairi, M. (2000). Information and business process equality: The case of SAP R/3 implementation. *Electronic Journal on Information Systems in Developing Countries*, 2 (http://www.unimas.my/fit/roger/EJISDC/EJISDC.htm)

AMR Research, (2002). *The Multibillion-Dollar Enterprise Performance Planning Market,*16 August 2002.

Apicella, M. (2000). The hand that moves your business - ERP software moves to the Web, presenting both pitfalls and opportunities.*(enterprise resource planning), Info World June 26, 2000*

Bartholomew, D. (2004). The ABC's of ERP. *CFO IT*, October 5, 2004. http://www.cfo.com/article.cfm/3171508/c_2984786?f=Technology_topstories

Boonstra, A. (2005). *Information Systems as Redistributors of Power Interpreting an ERP implementation from a stakeholder perspective.* som.eldoc.ub.rug.nl/FILES/reports/themeA/2005/05A06/05A06.pdf

Bowonder, B., Mastakar, N.,& Sharma, K. J. (2005). Innovatiive ICT platforms: The Indian Experience. *International Journal of Services Technology & Management,* 6(3/4/5), 1-1.

Budhiraja, R. (2003). Electronic Governance – A key issue in the 21st century. *A paper by Additional Director Electronic Governance Division Ministry of Information Technology Govt. of India).*

Carter, M. (2004). Key note address on E-governance – Transforming India. *National summit – India: The Knowledge Capital* February 17, 2004

Davenport, T. H. (1998). Putting the Enterprise into the Enterprise System. *Harvard Business Review*, 76(4), 121-132.

Dejpongsarn, N. (2005). *ERP Framework with mySAP Solution.* A presentation.

Douglas, M. (2002). *Planning for the Enterprise.* New York. April 16, 2002

Evans, K. S. (2005). Expanding E-Government: Improved Service Delivery for the American People Using Information Technology. *A Report for the President's Management Council* Dec 2005

Flak, L. S., & Rose, J. (2005). Stakeholder Governance: Adapting Stakeholder Theory To E-Government. *Communications of AIS*, 2005, *16*, 642-664, 23

Gartner's Four Phases of E-Government Model (2001) USA, Gartner Group. Europa (2001) "E-government - Electronic access to public services. (online)(cited on 20th December, 2003). Available from <URL: http://europa.eu.int/>

Hunter, D. R., & Shine, S. (2001). Customer Relationship Management- A Blueprint for Government. *White Paper , Australia, Accenture.*

Jha, B., & Bokad, P. (2003).Managing Multiplicity of Citizens' identity -A Taluka level case study. *International Conference on E-Governance*, 1(5), 24-31

Kannabiran, G. Xavier, M. J., & Anantharaaj, A. (2005). Enabling E-Governance Through Citizen Relationship Management-Concept, Model And Applications. *Journal of Services Research,* 4(2) (October 2004 - March 2005).

Kauzlarich, V. (2003). Organizational Change Management is Key to Program's Success. *Enterprise Modernization Issue, fall 2003, 7(2).*

Khalil, M. A., Lanvin, B. D., & Chaudhry, V. (2002). The E-government Handbook for Developing countries. *infoDev Program The World Bank Group.*

Kirwan, K., Sawyer, D., & Sparrow, D. (2003). Transforming Government Through Enterprise Modernization. *Enterprise Modernization Issue, Fall 2003 7(2).*

Koch , C. (n/a). ABC: An Introduction to ERP Getting started with Enterprise Resource Planning (ERP). http://www.cio.com/article/40323/ABC_An_Introduction_to_ERP

Markus, M. L., Axline, S., Petrie, D., & Tanis, C. (2000). Learning from adopters' experiences with ERP: Problems encountered and success achieved. *Journal of Information Technology,* 15, 245-265.

Microsoft. Enterprise Resource Planning- Managing the Lifecycle of Government Business. lead feature from the *Tourism and Travel edition of Microsoft in Government, Worldwide.*

Misra, D.C., Hariharan, R., & Khaneja, M. (2003, March). E-Knowledge Management Framework For Government Organizations" *Information Systems Management,* 20(2), 38 - 48

Mullin, R. (2000). *ERP-2-ERP:* "Forging a Proprietary Link" (Brief Article), *Chemical Week,* June 28, 2000.

Nowlan, S., (2001). Citizen Relationship Management E-CRM in the Public Sector,USA. Pricewaterhouse-Coopers.

Ort, E.E. (2005). Service-Oriented Architecture and Web Services: Concepts, Technologies, and Tools. *Sun Developers Network.* http://java.sun.com/developer/technicalArticles/WebServices/soa2/SOATerms.html#soaterms

Rao, T. P., Rama, R., Venkata. V., Bhatnagar, S. C., & Satyanarayana, J. (2004). "E-Governance Assessment Frameworks (EAF Version 2.0)" *Report for Department of Information Technology,* Government of India May 2004

Saxena, K. B. C. (2005). Towards excellence in e-governance. *International Journal of Public Sector Management,* 18(6), 498-513, 16

Scott-Morton, M. (Ed). (1991). The corporation of the 90s. Information technology and organizational transformation. *Oxford: Oxford University Press.*

Smith, A., Opinion (2003). Citizen Relationship Management. (online) (cited June 12, 2003). Available from <URL:http://www.crm-forum.com>.

Stratman, J., & Roth, A. (1999), Enterprise resource planning competence: A model, propositions and pre-test, design-stage scale development. *30th DSI Proceedings*, 20-23 November, pp. 1199-201.

Torres, L., Pina, V., & Acerete, B. (2006). E-Governance Developments in European Union

Cities: Reshaping Government's Relationship with Citizens. *Governance*, Apr2006, 19(2), 277.

Tucker, R., & Debrosse, D. (2003). Enterprise Architecture: Roadmap for modernization" *Enterprise Modernization Issue, fall 2003,* 7(2)

Xavier,M.J,(2002, April-June). Citizen Relationship Management- Concepts, Tools and Applications. *South Asian Journal of Management,* 9(2), 23-31.

KEY TERMS

Clean Data: For an organization to function effectively, data needs to be easily accessible both to customer sand internal users. Data is dispersed as governments like business organizations work in silos. To make this data accessible to others **data conversion** is a necessity as multiple sources and input formats, inconsistent styles and complexity of data structures. For any new system to get started it is necessary to convert the existing data from legacy systems or manual records to fit into the new data structures. This is a critical factor in ERP implementation projects. By clean data it is meant that there are no duplicates definitions of data which cause inconsistency.

Customization: In an attempt to deal with the potential problems presented by existing information systems, there is a shift towards the implementation of ERP packages. Generally it is felt that ERP packages are most successfully implemented when the standard model is adopted. Yet, despite this, customisation activity still occurs reportedly due to misalignment of the functionality of the package and the requirements of those in the implementing organisation. In such a situation the first thought that comes to a layman's mind is to modify the software to provide the necessary report or layout.

Most ERP products are generic. Hence, some customisation is needed to suit the company's

needs. But optimal customisation in most cases is subjective with no definite rules as end-users are not always technically equipped to understand the far-reaching implications of the changes that they are demanding. There is always a risk of destabilising the core application. Customisation can make or break the implementation of an ERP. It is therefore necessary to strike the right balance.

E-Government: Government's foremost job is to focus on safeguarding the nation / state and providing services to society as custodian of the nation's / state's assets. E-Government can therefore be defined as a technology-mediated process of reform in the way Governments work, share information, engage citizens and deliver services to external and internal clients for the benefit of both government and the clients that they serve.

Enterprise Architecture: An organisation has assigned roles and responsibilities, and established plans for developing products and services. The scope of Enterprise Architecture can be defined as encompassing the whole enterprise with confirmed institutional commitment to deliver products and services, both current and planned with clear transition plans. This in fact would define the organisation structure, functions and the relationships that would facilitate the organisation to meet its desired goals. This is extremely essential for enterprise modernisation.

Development of the enterprise architecture will typically involve:

- Analysing the current architecture which will be a process of description, documenting the architecture "as-is" or "baseline" architecture;
- Moving on to a definition of the architecture as it is planned to develop in the future - the architecture as it should be or "target" architecture which would align with the vision of the organisation.

Enterprise Resource Planning (ERP): It is an integrated information system that integrates all departments within an enterprise. Evolving out of the manufacturing industry, ERP implies the use of packaged software rather than proprietary software. ERP modules may be able to interface with an organization's own software with varying degrees of effort, and, depending on the software, ERP modules may be alterable via the vendor's proprietary tools as well as proprietary or standard programming languages.

An ERP system can include software for manufacturing, order entry, accounts receivable and payable, general ledger, purchasing, warehousing, transportation and human resources. The major ERP vendors are SAP and Oracle specialising in transaction processing that integrates various departments.

Information infrastructure: It is the technology infrastructure required to manage information in an organisation. It consists of the computers, software, data structures and communication lines underlying critical services that society has come to depend on. It consists of information systems which cover critical aspects such as financial networks, the power grid, transportation, emergency services and government services. This is required to implement an ERP system.

Inter-Operability: Various departments organize work in silos and tend to work independently. Data forms the basis of a transaction processing system like ERP which integrates these departments so that basic data entered once can be used by many. More efficient exchanging and processing of data is required to provide a seamless execution of a service. Inter-operability therefore means the capability of different departments working together to provide a service.

Public Administration: Every facet of our daily lives is impacted in some way by the actions of the federal, state, or local bureaucracies that manage and organize the public life of the country and its citizens. Public administration is the study of public entities and their relationships with each other and with the larger world. It addresses issues such as:

- How public sector organizations are organized and managed;
- How public policy structures the design of government programs that we rely upon;
- How our states, cities, and towns work with the federal government to realize their goals and plan for their futures;
- How our national government creates and changes public policy programs to respond to the needs and interests of our nation.

Service-Oriented Architecture: Service-oriented architecture (SOA) is the emerging trend in enterprise computing because it holds promise of IT becoming more agile in responding to changing business needs. Implementing a service-oriented architecture can involve developing applications that use services, making applications available as services. A service-oriented architecture is an information technology approach or strategy in which applications make use of services available in a network such as the World Wide Web.

Chapter XXVI
Emerging Frameworks in User–Focused Identity Management

Manish Gupta
State University of New York, USA

Raj Sharman
State University of New York, USA

ABSTRACT

A paradigm shift is occurring in identity management philosophy. User-focused identity management is one the emerging and most promising paradigms. One of the fundamental principles of the user-focused identity management frameworks is that the users control their identity formations, revelations, and interactions. This means that users must be given the choice of which identities to use at which services; they have choice to decide what identity information will be disclosed to services and how those services will use their identity information. User-focused identity management frameworks are posed to make users' online interactions easier and safer. In this chapter, we survey 11 of the most common user-focused identity management frameworks that are emerging, and their associated technologies. First, the chapter discusses issues and challenges with domain-centric identity management paradigm and presents unique value propositions of user-focused frameworks. Secondly, this chapter provides a comprehensive and cohesive coverage of common user-focused identity management frameworks. Users, technologists, businesses; and systems and security managers will gain a comprehensive understanding of the concepts, frameworks and associated technologies relating to user-focused identity management.

1. INTRODUCTION

Digital identities come in all shapes and sizes. Usually people use different digital identities in different contexts depending on association of different information with each identity. For example, an identity that we use with a online retailer will allow access to personal information such as credit card information, shipping information, purchasing history and personalized recommendations, the one used with social networking sites such as orkut.com does not. There are different methods and protocols to create new identities depending on context and user preferences. Insecure identity management has led to severe consequences. Recent research (Javelin, 2007) shows that the number of US is 8.4 million in 2007 and total one-year fraud amount is $49.3 billion in 2007.

Identity is a collection of unique characteristics of an entity which are either inherent or are assigned by another entity (Pfitzmann and Waidner, 2004). A digital identity comprises electronic records that represent network principals, including people, machines, and services (Windley, 2005; March, 2003). To be able to create, maintain and use digital identities the deployment of a digital identity management system is required. The term "identity management" (Casassa, 2003) is currently associated with technologies and solutions, mainly deployed within enterprises, to deal with the storage, processing, disclosure and disposal of users' identities, their profiles and related sensitive information. This infrastructure uses identities in the process of authentication and maps identifiers to the information needed for identification and authorization (Buell and Sandhu, 2003; Pfitzmann and Waidner, 2004). Identity Management covers the spectrum of tools and processes that are used to represent and administer digital identities and manage access for those identities (Allan et al., 2008). The three main business drivers for identity management solutions are security efficiency (lower costs and improved service), security effectiveness (including regulatory compliance) and business agility and performance (including workforce effectiveness and customer convenience) (Allan et al., 2008).

Identity Management is a means to reduce such risks, representing a vital part of a company's security and auditing infrastructure ((Buell and Sandhu, 2003). The secure and efficient administration of numerous personal attributes that make up digital identities is one of the key requirements in open and closed networks. Especially in respect to confidentiality and integrity, the users themselves, rather than popular external threads like viruses, phishing, or pharming attacks represent the main risk (Stanton et al, 2005). As a result of incorrect account management and inadequately enforced security policies users accumulate a number of excessive rights within the organizations' IT systems over time, violating the principle of the least privilege (Ferraiolo et al., 2003). Moreover, people have a hectic life and cannot spend their time administering their digital identities (El Maliki and Seigneur, 2007). Identity Management in open networks like the Internet has received tremendous attention throughout the last years with researchers. Although considered important, Identity Management in closed networks, however, has not gained comparable significance within the research community.

In this paper, we survey eleven of the most common user-focused identity management frameworks that have evolved and their associated technologies. Contributions of the paper are two-fold. First, the paper discusses issues and challenges with domain-centric identity management paradigm and presents unique value propositions of user-focused frameworks. Secondly, the paper provides a very comprehensive and cohesive coverage of most common user-focused identity management frameworks. Users, technologists, companies and systems and security managers will gain a comprehensive understanding of the concepts, frameworks and associated technologies relating to user-focused identity management. The paper is organized as follows. In Section 2, we discuss motivation and background for the user-focused identity management philosophy and frameworks. Section 3 briefly touches upon basic concepts and preliminaries that will be helpful in understanding discussions on the frameworks in Section 4. In Section 4, we discuss architecture and functioning of eleven user-focused identity management frameworks. Section 5 will present discussions and conclusions.

2. BACKGROUND

While availability of plethora of information systems coupled with Internet's dynamic evolution has provided users tremendous advantages such as shopping, banking, trading, socializing online, it has also put significant burden on them to maintain and provide credentials to all the online service providers. Users have different login-password combinations for each online service, or even different credentials for different roles within a service. As a result they tend to make password choices that are easy to remember, or even repeat the same login-password information on different services, which poses interesting and challenging security and privacy risks for both the users and the service providers. Identity Management solutions have been around and in use for a longtime now. The solution is to shift to identity management systems that are user-focused. Such a system will issue a digital identity for every user and will be able to control the complete lifecycle of the identity, including managing different contexts. An important requirement for such a system will be the single sign-on mechanism, whereby a single action of user authentication and authorization can permit the user to access multiple services. The benefits are improved convenience, security, accountability and privacy protection.

Identity management is often considered a service providers' area of work i.e. it is consid-

ered an activity to be managed by the service provider. Service providers often design identity management systems to be cost effective, easily manageable and scalable. Focus on user's convenience and privacy concerns has not been primary requirements for such systems. This has resulted in poor usability. Users often have to remember multiple passwords for accessing different services, which is a minor inconvenience if users only access a few online services. However, with the growth in availability and usefulness of various online services, the traditional approach to identity management is already showing serious negative effects on the user experience. The industry has responded by proposing new identity management models to improve the user experience, but in our view these proposals give little relief to users at the cost of relatively high increase in server system complexity. A federated identity management system consists of software components and protocols that handle the identity of individuals in a decentralized manner throughout their identity life cycle (Jøsang, 2007). There are several innovative user-focused identity management frameworks that are emerging from different collaborative efforts, with mixed results though. In next section we discuss some of the common terms and philosophy behind these frameworks. In Section 4, we discuss eleven of these frameworks in detail.

3. USER-FOCUSED IDENTITY MANAGEMENT: PRELIMINARIES

Lately, the term "user-focused" and "user-centric" identity management are being talked about a lot. Strong emergence of some of the frameworks is testament to the growing importance of user-focused identity management frameworks in personal and business applications alike. It is generally understood to be an innovative and different way of expressing the identity management philosophy as opposed to what we know as "domain-specific" or "enterprise-centric" approach that are widely used within provisioning, federation and even simplified sign-on situations.

There are other terms used to refer to the same user-focused philosophy, including Identity 2.0 and "Personal Identity Framework". However, underlying theme and approach of all these are towards resolving the same set of issues that are characterized by "domain-specific" approach. User-focused frameworks are gaining tremendous support and momentum. This is clearly reflected in the support by large companies like Yahoo, Google, Microsoft, OASIS and IBM, amongst others. A model of identity can be seen as follows (Spantzel et al., 2006):

- User who wants to have access to a service
- Identity Provider (IdP): is the issuer of user identity
- Service Provider (SP): is the relay party imposing identity check
- Identity (Id): is a set of user's attributes Id management systems are elaborated to deal

When making services and resources available through computer networks, issues of access management such as users, roles, access privileges and policies. In this context, identity management has two main parts, where the first consists of issuing users with credentials and unique identifiers during the initial registration phase (Role of Identity Provider – IdP) and the second consists of authenticating users and controlling their access to services and resources based on their identifiers and credentials during the access stage (Role of Service Provider – SP). A problem with many identity management systems is that they are designed to be effective from the perspective of the identity providers(IdP) and service providers (SP), which creates inconvenience, security risks and poor usability. One basic shortcoming in traditional identity management systems is that

they have largely ignored that it is often equally critical for users to identify service providers, as it is for service providers to authenticate users. Currently each SP provides its own user interface and methods which means the user has to learn new techniques for each SP. Sometimes it can be only for one time use (e.g. site registration). By separating the identity component from the rest of the application, the user will be able to identity the SP, which also helps thwart phishing.

The basic premise of user-centric or user-focused frameworks is that the users should be able to have more control over their identity and shared data during interactions with resources (web sites, vendors, government entities etc). In words of Dick Hardt, the user-focused identity would mean that (Hardt, 2006):

- The user is in the middle of a data transaction. This does not mean the user has to approve every transaction, but that the data always flows through the user's identity agent. This does have user control and consent advantages that others point out, but I think more importantly, it provides huge scale advantages, as the Identity Provider does not have to have any prior knowledge of the Service Provider. The network of sites can build up ad-hoc, just like SMTP servers do today.
- The user has a consistent user experience. That does not mean that all users have the same user experience, but that a specific user is using the same identity agent over and over for each identity transaction, similar to the interfaces we all see for saving and printing files regardless of the application. Currently each SP provides its own user interface which means the user is learning a new interface, sometime for onetime use (eg. site registration) By separating the identity component from the rest of the application, the user also has more certainty on who the SP is which helps resolve phishing.

Today, we have several types of systems that either demonstrate or are evolving to similar types of functionalities but with a twist. Among them we have services such as OpenID, Microsoft's CardSpace, Sxip, YADIS, and so on. In next section, we discuss functioning and architecture of eleven of most common ones in detail. However, to some extent, all are based on the idea that the identity verifier must be a third-party organization, (the identity provider) and that the users should in full control of their online selves. In other words, they provide users the mechanisms to authenticate only once, while having the ability to identify who they are depending on the context and their preferences. These frameworks are architectural constructs and technical product components that augment rather than replace existing IAM architectures and are intended to provide users with control of their identity attributes when registering and accessing online services (Kreizman and Wagner, 2007). Client identity selectors, Web site integration components, and service definition and discovery components are common among different developers' framework implementations (Kreizman and Wagner, 2007). We next discuss these frameworks in detail.

4. USER-FOCUSED IDENTITY MANAGEMENT FRAMEWORKS

User-focused Identity Management frameworks are architectural constructs and technical product components that augment the existing identity management architectures and are intended to provide users with control of their identity attributes when registering and accessing online services (Kreizman and Wagner, 2007). All of them have common philosophy that the identity verifier must be a third-party organization (the identity provider) and that the users should in full control of their online selves. In other words, these frameworks should provide users the mechanisms to authenticate only once, while having the ability to identify who they are depending on the context and their preferences. Table 1 lists the frameworks that are discussed next in this section. There are varying levels of success, thus far, that these frameworks have achieved. For example, OpenID developers can claim the most implementations; however, OpenID currently has rudimentary functionality and some security weaknesses. Microsoft recently released CardSpace, a full-featured user-focused framework, along with Vista; however, it will be several years before

Table 1. Frameworks

Section	Framework	Collaborator(s) / Supporters
4.1	Bandit	Open Source
4.2	Concordia	Open Source
4.3	Higgins	Open Source, IBM, Novell
4.4	Cardspace	Microsoft
4.5	OpenID	OpenID foundation, several major supporters
4.6	SASSO	NTT Lab
4.7	Shibboleth	Open Source, Internet2
4.8	SXIP	SXIP
4.9	WSF/Liberty	Liberty Alliance / OASIS
4.10	XRI/DRI	OASIS
4.11	YADIS	Yadis, OASIS

Vista adoption is commonplace. IBM, Novell and others have created Higgins, but component developments are predominantly prototypes (Kreizman and Wagner, 2007). It is obvious that these frameworks will have to be elaborated, also with respect to interoperability amongst themselves. This area is not only attracting the technology companies and experts, but it is also starting to catch the interest of millions of users. The website providers are getting engaged early on to catch the user-focused identity management wave to best meet the changing expectations of their users.

4.1 Bandit

Bandit is a set of components that provide consistent identity services for Authentication, Authorization, and Auditing (Bandit Project, 2008). The Bandit project manages communities that organizes and standardizes identity-related technologies in an open way, promoting both interoperability and collaboration. Bandit implements open standard protocols and specifications such that identity services can be constructed, accessed, and integrated from multiple identity sources (Bandit Project, 2008). Bandit components support different authentication methods and provide user-focused credential management. Using a common identity model, it is building additional services needed for Role Based Access Control (RBAC) and other controls to verify compliance with organizational policies. All components of Bandit are Open Source and work with industry standards and other open source projects to provide open, interoperable, decentralized, identity services. The Bandit project is based on open source philosophy and fosters a secure enterprise-computing environment on its own strengths. Bandit's current emphasis is in the following areas (Bandit Project, 2008):

- Provide simple application access to multiple identity stores

- Support multiple and pluggable authentication methods to provide consistent application access
- Provide a simple application interface to unify system access based on roles
- Allow applications to easily participate in a common compliance system

4.2 Project Concordia

Project Concordia is a global initiative designed to drive interoperability across identity protocols by soliciting and defining real-world use cases and requirements for the usage of multiple identity protocols together in various deployment scenarios, and encouraging and facilitating the creation of protocol solutions in the appropriate homes for those technologies (Concordia, 2008). The way this project works is that they solicit issues and challenges in integrating multiple identity protocols and derive and design a solution for it, which then is documented as use cases, requirements, and inter-op scenarios by project members who then work with a wide swath of the Internet community for documentation. All Concordia output is recorded on the wiki. Concordia welcomes participation by representatives of all identity-related initiatives as well as the wider Internet community with an interest in the areas of work the project is undertaking. While members of the Liberty Alliance conceived of Concordia, it is organizationally independent and run as an open and self-regulating community.

As expressed by the name (Roman goddess of agreement, understanding, and harmony), the goal of this group is to help drive the development of use-case scenarios where multiple identity specifications, standards and/or other initiatives might co-exist, recognizing heterogeneous deployment environments of the marketplace. Based on this open knowledge gathering process, the group recognizes that additional specifications, profiles and/or services may need to be defined (Concordia, 2008). The group's goals are as follows (Concordia, 2008):

- Drive development of a ubiquitous, interoperable, privacy-respecting layer for identity in order to:
- Help drive deployment costs down
- Assure implementers and deployers of better success and greater productivity
- Lead to more commercial products and open source offerings, in turn leading to a healthy market
- Facilitate new service offerings
- Assure interoperability across this layer
- Deliver confidence to implementers and deployers in implementing today with successful interoperability tomorrow
- Encourage strong, cross-sector, cross-geography participation through an open development process

4.3 Higgins

Higgins is also, like Bandit, an open source framework that to enable users and systems to integrate identity, profile, and relationship information from across multiple heterogeneous systems (Higgins, 2007). It enables enterprises to adopt, share across multiple systems and integrate to new or existing applications, digital identities and profiles. Higgins unifies all identity interactions (regardless of protocol/format) under a common user interface metaphor called i-cards (Higgins, 2007). Higgins enables developers to write to a common API for Identity management, rather than needing to support multiple identity management systems individually. Software applications written to Higgins will allow people to store their digital identities and profile information in places of their choice and to share the stored information with companies and other parties in a controlled fashion. Higgins relieves the developers from knowing all the details of multiple identity systems, thanks to one API that supports many protocols and technologies: MS CardSpace, OpenID, XRI, Bandit, etc. The Higgins Project is supported by IBM and Novell and competes with Microsoft's

Cardspace project. IBM and Novell's participation in the project was announced in early 2006. The first code for the Higgins Project was written by Paul Trevithick in the summer of 2003 (IBM Press Release, 2006).

Higgins is being managed by the Eclipse open source foundation enables individuals to actively manage and control their online personal information, such as bank account, telephone and credit card numbers, or medical and employment records -- rather than institutions managing that information as they do today. People will decide what information they want shared with trusted online websites that use the software (IBM Press Release, 2006).

4.4 Microsoft Cardspace

Microsoft CardSpace is the name for a new technology in Microsoft .NET Framework 3.0 that simplifies and improves the safety of accessing resources and sharing personal information on the Internet. It helps developers build Web sites and software that are less susceptible to the most commonly deployed identity-related attacks such as phishing. By helping users better manage their personal information and control how it is released and to whom, Windows CardSpace can facilitate more secure online experiences such as online shopping, banking, and bill payment (Microsoft, 2008).

Microsoft CardSpace allows users to manage their digital identities from various identity providers and employ them in different contexts where they are accepted to access online services, where identities are represented to users as "Information Cards" (or "InfoCards"). One important class of applications where Information Card-based authentication can be used is applications hosted on web sites and accessed through web browsers (Chappell, 2006). CardSpace provides a consistent UI that enables people to easily use these identities in applications and web sites where they are accepted. By providing users with a way to select identities and more, CardSpace plays an important role in using open standard protocols to negotiate, request and broker identity information between trusted IdPs and SPs.

When an Info-card-enabled application or website wishes to obtain information about the user, the application or website requests specific user details. The CardSpace UI, using the CardSpace service, displays the user's stored identities as visual Information Cards. The user picks the InfoCard to use and the CardSpace software contacts the issuer of the identity to obtain a digitally signed XML token that contains the requested information (Wiki-Cardspace, 2008). CardSpace allows users to create personal (also known as self-issued) Information Cards, which can contain one or more of 14 fields of telephone book-quality identity information. Other transactions may require a managed InfoCard; these are issued by a third party identity provider that makes the claims on the person's behalf, such as a bank, employer, or a government agency. Microsoft CardSpace is built on top of the Web Services Protocol Stack, an open set of XML-based protocols, including WS-Security, WS-Trust, WS-MetadataExchange and WS-SecurityPolicy. This means that any technology or platform that supports WS-* protocols can integrate with CardSpace (Wiki-Cardspace, 2008).

4.5 OpenID

OpenID is a shared identity service, which allows Internet users to log on to different web sites using a single digital identity, eliminating the need for a multiple user names and passwords. OpenID is a decentralized and open standard allowing lets users to control types and the amount of personal information they provide to web sites. Using OpenID-enabled sites, web users do not need to remember traditional authentication tokens such as username and password. Instead, they only need to be registered with any OpenID "identity provider" (IdP). Since OpenID is decentralized,

any website can use OpenID as a way to allow users to sign in without requiring a centralized authority to confirm a user's digital identity. OpenID is increasingly gaining adoption among large sites, with organizations like AOL, BBC, Google, IBM, Microsoft, Orange, VeriSign, Yandex and Yahoo acting as providers (OpenID Foundation, 2008; Riley, 2008; Krebs, 2008; IBM Press (2), 2007 & Bergman, 2007). In addition, integrated OpenID support has been made a high priority in Firefox 3 and also Microsoft CardSpace.

The OpenID framework version 1.0 dealt only with http-based URL authentication protocols. OpenID 2.0, however, supports both URL and XRI user identifiers. A URL uses an IP or DNS resolution and is unique and is widely supported. OpenID can identify a user based on an URL or an XRI address. Light-Weight Identity (LID), the original URL-based identity protocol, is a set of protocols to represent digital identities on the Internet without relying on any central authority. LID is now a part of OpenID. LID supports digital identities for humans, human organizations and non-humans (e.g. software agents, things, websites, etc.). It implements Yadis, a meta-data discovery service, for identity service discovery for URLs and XRI resolution protocol. Since, OpenID does not need a centralized authority for enrollment and it is can be considered as a form of federated identity management. Besides, IdP can randomly generate a digital address used specially for any SP to provide anonymity.

The original OpenID authentication protocol was developed in May 2005 (Fitzpatrick, 2005 & Fitzpatrick[2], 2005) by Brad Fitzpatrick, creator of popular community website LiveJournal. Since then many leading software companies have announced their support to OpenID initiatives and to interoperability with their identity management products. The roster includes Symantec (Symantec press, 2007), Microsoft, JanRain, Sxip, VeriSign (Graves, 2007), AOL (Panzer, 2007) and Sun Microsystems. In June 2007, the OpenID Foundation was officially formed in Oregon (OpenID doc, 2007) and OpenID Europe Foundation was officially incorporated in Belgium. In early December 2007, Non-Assertion Agreements were collected by the major contributors to the protocol, and the final OpenID Authentication 2.0 and OpenID Attribute Exchange 1.0 specfications were ratified.

4.6 NTT Labs' SASSO

NTT Labs - NTT Labs has developed SASSO, a personal Identity Provider that enables users to single-sign-on to a PC and leverage the strong authentication capabilities of the mobile phone to conduct a wide range of secure identity-based transactions. SASSO uses the increasingly ubiquitous mobile phone as an Identity Provider (IdP) to allow users to access a Service Provider (SP) (Liberty Press, 2007). Once authenticated by their own mobile phone, the IdP on the mobile phone issues a SAML assertion signed by a private key and sends that assertion to SPs. The application drives strong authentication into online transactions and leverages the convenience and privacy capabilities of the mobile phone to allow users to better control their own identity information (Liberty Press, 2007).

The application is currently targeted to the mobile industry by leveraging the FirstPass Digital Authentication Service of NTT DoCoMo, but the solution can be applied to any segment and region where strong authentication is required. SASSO is easy to use, leverages the mobile phone many people already have and does away with "token necklace" problems currently associated with many strong authentication solutions. SASSO helps mitigate security risks and increases opportunities for deploying security sensitive services by easily implementing strong authentication (Liberty Press, 2007). The solution reduces the time and costs of deploying new services and helps reduce customer churn. Interoperable Federation Technologies – To realize a "plug and play" us-

age model, universal interoperability among the implementation of SPs is important. By leveraging the mobile phone as an identity-aware client, SASSO demonstrates a convergence of the OpenID, Cardspace and SAML styles of user-centric identity management (Liberty Press, 2007).

4.7 Shibboleth

The Shibboleth System is a standards based, open source software package for web single sign-on. It allows sites to make informed authorization decisions for individual access of protected online resources in a privacy-preserving manner (Shibboleth, 2008). Shibboleth is an Internet2 Middleware Initiative project and provides architecture and open-source framework for SAML based federated authentication and authorization infrastructure. This allows for cross-domain single sign-on and removes the need for content providers to maintain user names and passwords. Shibboleth is a web-based technology that implements the HTTP/POST, artifact, and attribute push profiles of SAML, including both Identity Provider (IdP) and Service Provider (SP) components. Identity providers (IdPs) supply user information, while service providers (SPs) consume this information and provide access to secure content. Shibboleth also provides extended privacy functionality allowing the browser user and their home site to control the attributes released to each application.

The Shibboleth project was started in 2000 under the MACE working group to address problems in sharing resources between organizations with often wildly different authentication and authorization infrastructures. Shibboleth 2.0 was released on March 19, 2008, which is built upon SAML 2.0 specifications. Shibboleth is developed in an open and participatory environment, is freely available, and is released under the Apache Software License.

4.8 SXIP

SXIP is a platform based on a fully decentralized architecture providing an open and simple set of processes to exchange identity information. Like OpenID, it is an URL-based protocol that allows a seamless user's experience and follows the user-focused paradigm. Users using SXIP for identity management have full control over their identities and have an active role in the exchange of their identity data to different sites. Therefore, user can benefit from the portable authentication to connect with many websites. SXIP 2.0 has resolved many problems that arise from securely exchange identity data across sites. This provides the user with more choices and control over exchange of his/her identity data.

The Simple eXtensible Identity Protocol (SXIP) was designed to provide an Internet-scalable and user centric identity architecture that imitates real-world interactions (El Maliki and Seigneur, 2007). If a SP has integrated SXIP in his Website, which is easily done by using SDKs, it is a Membersite. When a subscriber of SXIP would like to have access to this Membersite (El Maliki and Seigneur, 2007):

a. he types his URL address and clicks on [sxip in],
b. he types his URL identity issued by IdP (called Homesite),
c. the browser is redirected to the Homesite,
d. he enters his username and password, being informed that the Membersite has requested data, selects the related data and verify it and can select to automatically release data for other visit to this Membersite and confirms,
e. the browser is redirected to the Membersite,
f. the user has access to the content of the site.

4.9 WSF/Liberty

In 2001, Liberty Alliance was formed as open standards governance organization for federated identity management standards and specifications. Deployed by organizations around the world, Liberty Federation allows consumers and users of Internet-based services and e-commerce applications to authenticate and sign-on to a network or domain once from any device and then visit or take part in services from multiple Web sites. This federated approach does not require the user to reauthenticate and can support privacy controls established by the user (Wiki-Liberty, 2008). With the deployment of Liberty Federation and Liberty Web Services continuously increasing, the Liberty Alliance has tracked well over one billion Liberty-enabled identities and devices at the end of 2006 (Wiki-Liberty, 2008). Its goals are to guarantee interoperability, support privacy, and promote adoption of its specifications, guidelines and best practices.

Liberty Alliance also offers capabilities for SSO and linking accounts in the set of SPs' in the boundary of the trust circle, which is referred to as Identity Federation Framework (ID-FF). On top of that it offers specifications for enhanced identity federation and interoperable identity-based web services, known as Identity Web Services Framework (ID-WSF). ID-WSF provides support for the new open standards such as WSSecurity developed in OASIS. The Security Assertion Markup Language (SAML) is another OASIS specification that provides guidelines to structure the identity assertions, protocols to exchange assertions, bindings for protocols to typical message transport mechanisms, and profiles. SAML consists of a set of specifications and XML schemas, which together define how to construct, exchange, consume, interpret, and extend security assertions for a variety of purposes. Basically, SAML is a set of XML and Simple Object Access Protocol (SOAP) based services and formats for the exchange of authentication and authorization information between security systems. The Liberty Alliance specifications rely heavily on other standards such as SAML and WS-Security. The WS-* (the Web Services protocol specifications) are a set of specifications from Microsoft and IBM. It is a part of larger efforts to define a security framework for web services, known as WS-*. It includes specifications such as WSPolicy, WS-Security Conversation, WS-Trust, and WS-Federation. WS-Federation has functionality for using pseudonyms and attribute-based interactions. WS-Trust has the ability to ensure security tokens as a means of brokering identity and trust across domain boundaries.

4.10 XRI/XDI

XRI(EXtensible Resource Identifier) is a scheme and resolution protocol for abstract identifiers compatible with Uniform Resource Identifiers and Internationalized Resource Identifiers, developed by the XRI Technical Committee at OASIS. The goal of XRI is to provide a universal format for abstract, structured identifiers that are domain-, location-, application-, and transport-independent, so they can be shared across any number of domains, directories, and interaction protocols (Wiki-XRI, 2008). XRI is a scheme and resolution protocol for abstract identifiers compatible with Uniform Resource Identifiers and Internationalized Resource Identifiers, developed by the XRI Technical Committee at OASIS. The goal of XRI is to provide a universal format for abstract, structured identifiers that are domain-, location-, application-, and transport-independent, so they can be shared across any number of domains, directories, and interaction protocols. Note that the XRI specification and the reasoning supporting it are contended by the W3C Technical Architecture Group which has a draft finding which asserts that the same aims can be achieved with better interoperability using http: scheme URIs (XRI Technical Committee, 2008)

XRIs offer identifiers that can be persistent or transient, which suits security and scalability requirements for SSO systems. For any entity identification, they can support multiple contexts and multiple versions of the same logical resource. XRI data is exchanged using XDI (XRI Data Exchange) - Data Sharing protocol. Both XRI and XDI are being developed under the support of OASIS. I-name and I-number registry services for privacy-protected digital addressing use XRI. It can be used as an identifier for persons, machines and agents. URIs are very widely used as identifiers over the Internet. However there are limitations of the standard URI syntax that is not able to accommodate the growth of the Internet technologies, protocols and users that has led to new requirements for resource identifiers. With the growth of XML, Web services, and other ways of leveraging the Internet to automated, machine-to-machine communications, new set of requirements emerged. One of such requirements was internationalization which was taken care of by developing a new form of URI called an Internationalized Resource Identifier (IRI) jointly by the W3C and IETF. The IRI specifications are built on the URI standards. The XRI TC has also developed a resolution protocol based on HTTP(S) and simple XML documents called Extensible Resource Descriptor Sequence (XRDS).

4.11 YADIS

Yadis is a Communications protocol for discovery of digital identity authentication services, such as OpenID, and related data sharing services. This allows digital identities to be composed from several different services, and lets Internet users define what information they expose to third parties (Wiki-Yadis, 2008). Yadis sites identify people and services from traditional URLs (web site addresses) or "addresses" for the Yadis documents. The basic assumption is that identities can be addressed with URLs, or with other identifiers (such as i-names) that can be resolved to URLs.

For example, a user called Joe Smith might have his Yadis home page at <*www.joesmith.net*>, or perhaps <*www.webitesforall.com/joesmith*>. Yadis follows the REST-ful, "small pieces loosely joined" paradigm that has proven to be successful in the development of the web (Yadis Site, 2008). The owner of any Yadis URL can choose which protocols to support. Similarly, a Relying Party such as a website accepting Yadis URLs as identifiers can select an appropriate protocol to use for authentication (Wiki-Yadis, 2008). This can allow existing web sites, like blogs, to easily implement basic Yadis functionality (for instance, redirecting users who arrive at the blog to relevant information about the person the blog belongs to) while also making it possible to build many more advanced applications (for example, allowing complex queries of a site-owner's information to be submitted directly to the Yadis site as an extension of the URL itself) (Miller, 2008).

Yadis was initiated by developers of the Light-Weight Identity (LID) and OpenID protocols; and then furthered with collaboration from members of the OASIS XRI Technical Committee, particularly those working on i-names (Miller, 2008). However, as Yadis is an open initiative, it is hoped that other developers will start using Yadis lightweight capabilities description, making possible a "mix and match" approach to building Yadis-enabled applications, enabling application developers to choose their own balance between ease of implementation on one hand, and range of features on the other (Miller, 2008).

The Yadis specification provides (Miller, 2008):

- A general-purpose identifier for persons and any other entities, which can be used in a variety of services.

- A syntax for a resource description document identifying services available using that identifier and an interpretation of the elements of that document.

- A protocol for obtaining that resource description do*cument, given that identifier.*

5. DISCUSSION AND CONCLUSION

Identity management has turned into a double-edged sword over the past few years. Users have to manage their identities by registering different subsets of their personal information at service providers and subsequently selecting and using these different profiles appropriately (Pfitzmann and Kohntopp, 2009; Bonatti and Samarati, 2000). There are many research projects that focus some of shortcomings of identity management (Camenisch et al., 2005; Bhargav-Spantzel et al., 2005).

One of the fundamental principles of the user-focused identity management frameworks is that the users must be in control of their identity formations, revelations and interactions. This implies that users must be given the choice of which identities to use at which services, they must know what identity information will be disclosed to those services if they use them, and they must be informed how those services will use the information disclosed. User-focused identity management frameworks are posed to makes it easier and safer for users the when accessing resources on the Internet. It lets users select from among a portfolio of their digital identities and use them at Internet services of their choice where they are accepted. User-focused identity management frameworks require that a site prove its identity to a user before the user ever supplies any information to the site. Not only users, but businesses will also benefit from User-focused identity management frameworks. User-focused identity management frameworks will have the following business impact (Kreizman and Wagner, 2007):

- Reduced data entry burden when registering and revisiting service providers, and a hopefully increased willingness to provide personal information because it is more convenient to do so

- Reduced sign-on for business contexts (sets of related services) where credentials can be shared
- Common user experience for selecting the appropriate digital identities (sets of attributes) and providing them to service providers — an electronic analogy for wallets, purses and remotely managed vaults that hold a combination of context-specific identity
- Credentials and attributes or claims similar to driver's licenses, library cards, credit cards and store-brand loyalty cards
- A standard development framework for developers that can be abstracted from and can make use of disparate identity protocols and identity repositories

User-focused identity management frameworks such as OpenID, Microsoft's CardSpace, Sxip, YADIS, and others are here to improve the way we identify ourselves online and eliminate the necessity to register for every single service (Petkov, 2007). These frameworks deal with the problems of digital identity by managing and disclosing identity information in an open and standard way (El Maliki and Seigneur, 2007). All identity systems will coexist and they will all offer sufficient unique capabilities that will allow them to grow independently to some extent. In spite of the unique capabilities, there is a significant degree of duplication of functionality between the various systems. A convergence between the systems would eliminate such duplications and result in a simpler identity landscape (El Maliki and Seigneur, 2007).

User centricity is a significant concept in user-focused identity management frameworks that provides for stronger user control and privacy. We discussed development of requirements, architectures, and technologies for user-focused identity

managements in the chapter. We believe that many of the threats, usability issues, uncertainties and compliance concerns can be managed well by wide adoption of user-focused identity management frameworks. Widespread deployment of the user-focused identity management frameworks have the potential to solve several problems engendering from domain-centric models of identity management and to foster the long-term growth of the Internet by making the online world more trustworthy, and easier to use. In conclusion, we believe a user-focused approach to identity management is a very promising way to improve the user experience and the security of online interactions. This has the potential to stimulate increased adoption of online services.

REFERENCES

Allan, A., Perkins, E., Carpenter, P., & Wagner, R. (2008). What is Identity 2.0? *Key Issues for Identity and Access Management, 2008*, 7 April 2008, Gartner Research Report, ID Number: G00157012

Bandit Project. (2008). Retrieved on April 12, 2008 from http://www.bandit-project.org/index. php/Project_overview

Bergman, A. (2008). OpenID Foundation - Google, IBM, Microsoft, VeriSign and Yahoo", O'Reilly Media, 2008-02-07. Retrieved on 2008-03-19 from http://radar.oreilly.com/archives/2008/02/openid-foundation-google-ibm-m.html

Bhargav-Spantzel, A., Squicciarini, A., & Bertino, E. (2005). *Establishing and protecting digital identity in federation systems*. TR 2005-48, Purdue University (2005)

Bonatti, P. A., & Samarati, P. (2000) Regulating Service Access and Information Release on the Web. In: *Proceedings of CCS 2000*, Athens, ACM Press (2000)

Buell, A. D., & Sandhu, R. (2003, Noevmber). Identity Management. *IEEE Internet Computing, 7*(6), 26-28.

Camenisch, J., Shelat, A., Sommer, D., Fischer-H¨ubner, S., Hansen, M., Krasemann, H., Lacoste, G., Leenes, R., & Tseng, J. (2005). Privacy and identity management for everyone. In: *1st conference on Digital IdentityManagement*, ACM Press (2005)

Casassa, M., Bramhall, P., & Pato, J. (2003). *On Adaptive Identity Management: The next generation of Identity Management Technolgies*, HP Labs Technical Report, HPL-2003-149, 2003

Chappell, D. (2006). Introducing Windows CardSpace, *Windows Vista Technical Articles*. April 2006

Concordia. (2008) Retrieved on April 13, 2008 from (http://projectconcordia.org/index.php/Purpose_and_Principles)

El Maliki, T., & Seigneur, J-M. (2007).A Survey of User-centric Identity Management Technologies. *Emerging Security Information, Systems, and Technologies, 2007*. SecureWare 2007. The International Conference on 14-20 Oct. 2007 (pp. 12-17).

Ferraiolo, D. F., Kuhn, R. D., & Chandramouli, R. (2003). *Role-Based Access Control*. Artech House computer security series, ISBN 1-58053-370-1 (2003).

Fitzpatrick, B. (2005). Distributed Identity: Yadis. *LiveJournal*. Retrieved on April 19, 2008 from http://community.livejournal.com/lj_dev/683939.html

Fitzpatrick, B. (2005). OpenID. *LiveJournal*. Retrieved on April 19, 2008 from http://community.livejournal.com/lj_dev/684200.html

Graves, M. (2007). VeriSign, Microsoft & Partners to Work together on OpenID + Cardspace. *VeriSign*. Retrieved on April 19, 2008 from

http://blogs.verisign.com/infrablog/2007/02/verisign_microsoft_partners_to_1.php

Hardt, D. (2006). *What is user-centric identity?* June 26, 2006 Retrieved on April 11, 2008 from http://www.windley.com/archives/2006/12/introducing_usercentric_identity.shtml

Higgins. (2007). Project Web site. October 22, 2007 Retrieved online on April 21, 2008 from http://www.eclipse.org/higgins/index.php

IBM Press release. (2006). Open Source Initiative to Give People More Control Over Their Personal Online Information: IBM, Novell, and Parity Communications to Drive New Generation of Security Software Based on Framework., ARMONK, NY - 27 Feb 2006:

IBM Press (2). (2007). Technology Leaders Join OpenID Foundation to Promote Open Identity Management on the Web (008-02-07) from http://www-03.ibm.com/press/us/en/pressrelease/23461.wss

Javelin. (2007). *2007 Identity Fraud Survey Report: Identity Fraud Is Dropping, Continued Vigilance Necessary*, February 2007. Retrieved online on April 20, 2008 from http://www.javelinstrategy.com

Jøsang, A., AlZomai, M., & Suriadi, S. (2007). *Usability and Privacy in Identity Management Architectures*. (AISW2007), Ballarat, Australia, 2007.

Krebs, B. (2007). *Microsoft to Support OpenID*. Retrieved on 2008-03-01 from http://blog.washingtonpost.com/securityfix/2007/02/microsoft_to_support_openid.html

Kreizman, G., & Wagner, R. (2007). *Personal Identity Frameworks*. Gartner Research Report

Liberty Press. (2007). Liberty Alliance Announces Winners of the 2007 IDDY Award eBIZ. mobility, Tuesday, September 25, 2007, SAN FRANCISCO, Retrieved online on April 20, 2008 from http://www.projectliberty.org/news_events/ press_releases/liberty_alliance_announces_winners_of_the_2007_iddy_award

Marsh S. (2003). Identity and Authentication in the E-Economy. *Information Security, Elsevier Science Press, 7.3*(2003), 12-19.

Microsoft Web site. (2008). Microsoft Cardspace. Retrieved on April 21, 2008 from http://www. microsoft.com/net/cardspace.aspx

Miller, J. (2008).*Yadis Specification. Version 1.0.* 18 March 2006. Retrieved online in April 2, 2008 from yadis.org/papers/yadis-v1.0.pdf,

OpenID doc. (2008). OpenID Board of Directors (2007-06-01). OpenID Foundation. OpenID Foundation. Retrieved on April 19, 2008 from http://openid.net/foundation/

OpenID Foundation. (2008). How do I get an OpenID?. OpenID Foundation. Retrieved on 2008-03-20 from http://openid.net/get/

Petkov, P. D. (2007). *Identity 2.0: How Attackers Break into Identity-centric Services*, Aug 17, 2007. Retrieved online on April 21, 2008 from http://www.informit.com/articles/article. aspx?p=787262

Pfitzmann, A., & Kohntopp, M. (2000). Anonymity, unobservability, pseudonymity, and identity management – A proposal for terminology. In: *Lecture Notes in Computer Science, 2009*, 1-9. Springer.

Pfitzmann B., & Waidner M. (2004). *Anonymity, Unobservability, Pseudonymity, and Identity Management - A proposal for terminology.* Tu Dresden, Department of Computer Science Technical report, 2004

Riley, D. (2008). Google Offers OpenID Logins Via Blogger. *TechCrunch*. Retrieved on 2008-03-20 from http://www.techcrunch.com/2008/01/18/ google-offers-openid-logins-via-blogger/

Shibboleth. (2008). Retrieved online on April 21, 2008 from http://shibboleth.internet2.edu/about. html

Spantzel, A. Bhargav, C., J., Gross, T., & Sommer, D. (2006). *User Centricity: A Taxonomy and Open Issues.* IBM Zurich Research Laboratory, 2006.

Stanton, J. M., Stam, K. R., Mastrangelo, P., & Jolton, J. (2005). Analysis of end user security behaviors. *Computers & Security 24*(2), 124-133.

Symantec Press. (2008). *Symantec Unveils Security 2.0 Identity Initiative at DEMO 07 Conference.* Symantec (2007-01-31). Retrieved on April 19, 2008 from http://www.symantec.com/about/ news/release/article.jsp?prid=20070131_01

Wiki-Cardspace. (2008). Retrieved online on April 20, 2008 from http://en.wikipedia.org/wiki/ Windows_CardSpace

Wiki-Liberty. (2008). Wikipedia article retrieved online on April 5, 2008 from http://en.wikipedia. org/wiki/Liberty_Alliance

Wiki-XRI. (2008). Retrieved online on April 20, 2008 from http://en.wikipedia.org/wiki/XRI

Wiki-Yadis. (2008). Retrieved online on April 20, 2008 from http://en.wikipedia.org/wiki/Yadis

Windley P.(2005). "Digital Identity". Sebastopol, California: O'Reilly, 2005

XRI technical committee. (2008). Retrieved online on April 20, 2008 from http://www.oasis- open. org/committees/tc_home.php?wg_abbrev=xri

Yadis Site. (2008). Retrieved online on April 20, 2008 from http://yadis.org/wiki/Main_Page

KEY TERMS

EXtensible Resource Identifier (XRI): is a scheme and resolution protocol for abstract identifiers compatible with Uniform Resource Identifiers and Internationalized Resource Identifiers, developed by the XRI Technical Committee at OASIS.

Identity Management (IDM): Identity Management comprises technologies and solutions employed for provisioning, maintaining and terminating users' identities, their profiles and related sensitive information.

Microsoft Cardspace: Microsoft CardSpace is the name for a new technology in Microsoft .NET Framework 3.0 that simplifies and improves the safety of accessing resources and sharing personal information on the Internet.

OpenID: OpenID is a shared identity service, which allows Internet users to log on to different web sites using a single digital identity, eliminating the need for a multiple user names and passwords.

Shibboleth: The Shibboleth System is a standards-based, open source software package for web single sign-on.

SXIP: SXIP is a platform based on a fully decentralized architecture providing an open and simple set of processes to exchange identity information.

User-Focused IDM: User-focused Identity Management frameworks are architectural constructs and technical components that are intended to provide users with control of their identity attributes when registering and accessing online services.

Yadis: Yadis is a Communications protocol for discovery of digital identity authentication services, such as OpenID, and related data sharing services.

Chapter XXVII
Next–Generation IT for Knowledge Distribution in Enterprises

Ramón Brena
Tecnologico de Monterrey, Mexico

Gabriel Valerio
Tecnologico de Monterrey, Mexico

Jose-Luis Aguirre
Tecnologico de Monterrey, Mexico

ABSTRACT

From the Knowledge Management perspective, Knowledge distribution is a critical process in organizations. As many of the other Knowledge-related processes, it has received basic support from Information Technologies in the form of databases and repositories, client-server systems and other standard IT. Nevertheless, most basic IT tools fail to provide the flexible environment Knowledge distribution needs to be effective in many organizations. In this chapter we review some very advanced IT that are being proposed for supporting Knowledge distribution processes. Even though they are not mainstream technologies nowadays, they show actual trends that are expected to materialize in future generations of IT for Knowledge distribution.

INTRODUCTION

The key factors that determine success in companies and national economies rely on effectiveness in gathering and managing knowledge nowadays (United Nations, 2000). In economies based on knowledge, creation, distribution, and use of information to generate knowledge increases opportunities for development. In this context of increasing economic importance of knowledge, Knowledge Management (KM, Beckman, 1999) has emerged with the goal of taking advantage of information and knowledge every company owns. Most authors in KM agree with the need for executing the processes of generating, storing and distributing knowledge.

The process of generating knowledge encourages continuous improvement and growth through innovation, generation of new ideas, pattern recognition and development of new processes (Ruggles, 1997). Storing process implies keeping information in the organization repository; this is the organizational memory of the company. Finally, distribution has the goal of making available useful information to the members of the company in the shortest time. This fact allows users to access the information no matter where they are.

One of the strongest catalysts of KM has been the necessity for managing large amounts of information efficiently (Carrillo, 1999). Aside from the importance of generating and storing the necessary information in order to generate knowledge, the efficient distribution of such information has become a relevant subject last years. In companies, sharing knowledge resources via distribution is essential for two reasons: first, because it avoids duplicating efforts to obtain and maintain knowledge. Second, because it encourages consistent decision-making since all employees have access to the same knowledge (Probst, Raub & Romhardt, 1999).

In spite of its importance, most of the information stored in a company repository is never used since it is not distributed efficiently. Nowadays, one of the most challenging issues is the time spent by employees searching for information already stored in their repositories (Dalkir, 2005). Introduction of IT in every aspects of society has allowed storing and generating gigabytes of information, however, it hardly reaches relevant people at the right time. According to Sarnikar (2007), in order to accomplish an efficient information flow, proactive KM technologies are required; these technologies should automate and control distribution of information. Although many techniques

of distribution and filtering have been developed last years, providing the right knowledge to users in the right context, continues being a complex issue (Sarnikar, 2007).

We can safely conclude that IT has not supported in a satisfactory way Knowledge Distribution (KD) processes. In this situation, solutions could come from several fronts:

- Develop and refine KM strategies that could improve KM processes efficiency with the current IT sophistication level;
- Introduce more flexible and sophisticated IT tools that could provide a more flexible and better support to KM processes.

In this chapter we investigate the second possibility, though having in mind that KM strategies refinement is also an essential issue, which is being explored by researchers and practitioners (Liebowitz, 2005).

BACKGROUND

Many IT tools and strategies have been used for supporting KD. For the sake of classifying them, we could identify two "pure" strategies for sharing knowledge that they support (Albino, 2004)

1. *Codification*: Tries to "encode" that is, make explicit knowledge. This could take the form of manuals, guides, filled forms eventually stored in a database, or any symbolic information that encodes knowledge available to all or some individuals in the organization.
2. *Socialization*: Leaves knowledge in people instead of expressing it with symbols. This kind of knowledge is sometimes called "tacit" knowledge. The associated way of transferring it is by meetings or any other form of people interaction.

Current support for socialization strategies is very limited. It is restricted to manage the conditions required for people's interaction, such as calendar or schedule management. Nevertheless, even schedule management could be very complex when it is necessary to take into account multiple criteria, such as, for instance, that some meetings could be moved or cancelled but not others, or that not every participant is equally important, and some have special rights about the meeting, etc. We will go back to these issues when discussing advanced IT.

Most IT support is for codification-based processes, such as message distribution or repository storage and access. This is of course no surprise: computers handle symbolic information, and codification strategies are aligned with symbolic representation of information and knowledge.

There are many stages or aspects of codification-based knowledge distribution that could be IT-supported, but we will consider *capture*, *storing*, and actual *distribution*.

Knowledge Capture Support

Usually symbolic information is typed, not anymore in a typewriter, but in a computer text editor. Text editors could be a general purpose editor, like Microsoft Word, of they could be specialized editors for a specific task or context, so that they guide users at filling in information. Further, text editors could be stand-alone -running on the user's computer- or web-based -controlled by a server, typically in an intranet. Normally web-based capture interfaces are better suited for guiding the user through a form-filling task.

Knowledge Storage Support

Symbolic knowledge and data, just as any information, could be stored for sharing purposes either in paper or on a computer-based system. Of course, having explicit knowledge on a computer system could, at least potentially, make it amenable to more efficient search processes, as well as less expensive distribution: indeed generating information copies is almost a free process ("free" as in "free beer"), given the ever declining prices of computer storage.

Knowledge Actual Distribution Support

Knowledge text-based distribution could consist of a direct user-to-user communication, or it could consist of a more elaborate process involving first storing knowledge in a computer-based system. Direct user-to-user communication has been supported for a longtime by basic IT in the form of text messages: users generate messages composed by text that are distributed to other users. This can be classified in synchronous and asynchronous message distribution, meaning that, in the first case, messages are delivered "in the moment" they are sent, like in the instant messages software (for instance, Microsoft IM, AIM or other "chat" system). Asynchronous messages are delivered to be read at any later time by the recipient, like in the email messages; the user does not have to be "connected" at the moment the message is sent. A particularly important form of asynchronous knowledge distribution is computer-based access of digital repositories: knowledge is put in by a user, with no explicit recipient in mind, and eventually another user reads that knowledge. These repositories could be databases, or websites, or any combination of them, and are accessed in modern systems though a web browser.

Knowledge and information in repositories could be distributed to the user either by user's initiative ("pull" mode) or system's initiative ("push" mode). Push modality means that a system delivers information to a user without the user initiative (like the email delivery) whereas pull modality means that a user actively gets information from an electronic resource, typically the Web. We can identify push modality with Negroponte idea of changing human-computer interaction from a "point-and-click" style (that is, user clicks and selects an object as well as a function to be performed to the object) to a "delegation" style, where the computer takes care of a complex task over a period of time, finding the appropriate moments to accomplish it (Negroponte, 1996).

Typical "push technologies" (also called "Webcasting", "Netcasting" and other names) were proposed in the 90s as an alternative way to distribute Information and Knowledge to users (Chin, 2003). In this type of systems, the user selects information "channels," and/or fills a "user profile" and gets updated information from these selected channels. Push systems sounded promising, because the user could be relieved from getting information updated, which is for sure a boring and repetitive task. Advocators of push systems claimed that users would be poured with a wealth of useful information by just staying "plugged" to their information sources. Though push systems have made their way since the 90's, their application as a general information distribution paradigm is nowadays fairly restricted, mainly due to problems related to the bandwidth efficiency, and the flooding of information to users. Nevertheless, the idea of distributing information by the system's initiative –that is, Negroponte's *delegation*- remains valid, and could be put into practice using other technologies, as we will se later in this chapter.

TECHNOLOGICAL ELEMENTS OF NEXT-GENERATION KD SYSTEMS

Many modern IT-based systems give support to processes combining knowledge capture, knowledge storage and knowledge distribution or access, in many forms. On this subject, there are tools as common as e-mails clients, as there are solutions that incorporate, in a single package, a set of different solutions that were developed separately, such as documents managers, collaborative work platforms and knowledge portals, among others.

E-mail clients allow users to share their knowledge through text editors; how well the captured text represents useful knowledge is of course another question. At the same time, they allow users to store and organize the information captured through folders organized by the user owner of the information. Finally, these tools allow distributing information to other e-mail users. On the other hand, documents management's tools, in addition of the typical text editors functions, incorporate functionalities that allow them to store and organize all the information generated in a document repository that only the managers administrate and give the right to the other users to subscribe to folders so that the information could be distributed with a minimal intervention from those users. Collaborative work platforms provide virtual spaces where users can use asynchronous tools such as e-mail, forums and boards; and synchronous tools such as chats, web conferences and videoconferences. All of these are used to capture, store and distribute knowledge on a daily basis. Finally, in many big enterprises, portals are the single door to multiple services where e-mail clients, documents management's tools, collaborative work spaces and many other services are accessed.

Nevertheless, most current IT systems supporting KD fall short at linking the *right knowledge to the right user*. As it has been mentioned at the introduction section, many users spent hours looking for the knowledge they need, while most stored knowledge never gets actually consulted. This is of course a profoundly unsatisfactory situation.

We do not pretend that IT support is the only critical issue for advancing the state of KD, but we do claim that more sophisticated IT systems could make KD systems much more useful. In this section we review some of the most relevant very advanced technologies that could support future KD systems.

Support for Socialization Strategies

Here we discuss ways of supporting direct people interaction. Of course, one of the main issues here is *how to know with who to interact*. As trivial as it could sound, in large organizations it is actually very difficult to pinpoint the expert we need to consult. In real organizations, informal reputation networks are formed, through a "mouth to mouth" word spread. This process can be supported by the presence of "Social Networks" IT tools.

There are some proposals for automatically calculating the "reputation" of human experts, meaning by reputation the reliability, or the degree of expertise. Social networks exist in any company and can be used to interpret the way in which people are interacting. With the help of social network analysis (SNA) and the network visualization tools, the information of the organization's knowledge map can be analyzed. This map allows you to see how the knowledge flows inside such organizations (Liebowitz, 2005). SNA consists of mapping and measuring the relationship between people, organizations and other information processing entities (Hanneman, 2002, cited by Liebowitz, 2005). When you combine SNA tools and the network visualization software you can make analysis in distinct areas such as sociology, organizational behavior and many other disciplines (Liebowitz, 2005).

Semantic Support for Accessing Repositories

Many digital repositories are so large that users get lost when navigating them, undermining then the possibility of linking the right knowledge to the right user. Of course, one low-technology issue is how to well-structure the repository, but there are other options as well.

There have been some recent proposals for automatically taking into account the meaning of documents within an IT environment, so the system could better guide the user to the knowl-edge he/she is looking for in a digital repository, which could be internal to the organization or even the entire internet. With the title of "Semantic Web" (Berners-Lee, 2001) a set of technologies and standards have been proposed, such as XML and RDF. In the Semantic Web (SW) initiative, documents are self-described, and there is the possibility of automatically reason about the knowledge it contains. The SW markup languages allow to declare knowledge in "ontologies", which are a form of declarative definition of classes and objects. Berners-Lee sees the collection of inter-related web pages written in the SW standards as a huge knowledge base, which can be consulted from anywhere. Of course, restricted collections within a given organization can be formed using the SW technologies, taking the role of knowledge repositories.

The SW initiative has been considered as a very solid trend; The Gartner group recently reported that Semantic Web (with related technologies such as ontologies, metadata management, and taxonomies) is one of the top strategic technologies for 2005 (Gartner, 2005). Nevertheless, the current Semantic Web is marginal (an estimated ten millions semantic documents, compared to some 11.5 billion documents indexed in the main search services (the actual internet size is much larger). Though the Semantic Web is growing faster that the regular web, it cannot get a comparable size in the near future. But of course this argument does not undermine the possibility of writing internal enterprise-level digital repositories using SW technologies, and actually we believe this could be beneficial.

Other initiatives for considering meaning of items in a repository rely on quantitative methods. For instance (Martinez, 1998) proposed a way of automatically finding the topic of a given text, from a predefined set of topics. Of course, having the topic of each item as a metadata in a repository would be extremely helpful for users, as they would be able to restrict searches to specific topic, without the need of thoroughly classifying the repository in topics. This could be particularly useful for existing repositories with tons of poorly classified information.

In this line, (Ramirez, 2006) proposed a fully automatic mechanism for building a semantic "map" of a given repository, where main topics are identified, and their relative semantic distances are calculated. Such a mechanism, called "Semantic Contexts" by its authors, could be applied to search knowledge in a repository, but not only using keywords, like in current "Google style" search technology, but using topics or "knowledge areas" to guide the search, without any need of a prior thematic classification of information and knowledge. For instance, assume a user is trying to find information items about how to display pictures on a Palm PDA device. Let us assume that the intranet has a "Google style" search facility. This could bring results about, for instance, items about pictures of palm trees, about pictures of Palm devices, about pictures of Palm beach in California, and so on. A state-of-the-art search service is just unaware of what the information items are about. But with Semantic Context-enhanced search, the user could be presented a choice of related topics, like the ones we just mentioned. Once the user selects one topic, all the retrieved items would belong to that topic. This, of course, would help very much to focus the search and give to the user more relevant results.

Recommendation Systems

To "recommend" a repository item to a user implies that some other user, or the system, considers that item contains relevant knowledge for that user. IT support for recommendations could consist of helping humans to recommend to other humans, or automated systems, which provide recommendations to humans with no direct human intervention.

Recommender systems have been classified into *content-based* and *social* systems (Basu, 1998). In a content-based system, also called "intrinsic" or "item-based", recommendations are based on the characteristic of the item to recommend. Typically, users are classified according to their preferences, as well as the items, so when an item's characteristics matches a user interests, then that item is recommended to the user. For instance, in a movie recommendation application, users would be asked to give their preferences, according to genres, preferred actors and so on, and the system would recommend movies matching those characteristics. Of course, intrinsic recommender systems suffer from the difficulties in classifying both users and items, though automatic learning techniques have been applied to this (Al Mamunur Rashid, 2002).

Social recommender systems, in contrast to "intrinsic" ones, do not analyze item's characteristics, but instead try to identify groups of users with similar sets of preferred items. For instance, if you share more than 90% of preferred movies with some other users, there are many chances that you will like *any* new film recommended by those users; this conclusion does not rely on the movie intrinsic characteristics. A very successful form of social recommendation is collaborative filtering; it is applied on a daily basis in online stores like Amazon (Linden, 2003).

Now let us consider the application of recommender systems to information distribution from digital repositories. In this area we do find some works, both "intrinsic" and "social", but we cannot say they have become mainstream.

JITIK (Brena, 2001) is a Knowledge and Information distribution system which could also be viewed as an "intrinsic" recommendation system. In JITIK, users are classified according to their interests and position in the organization (that is, their roles and responsibilities, their department or division, etc.), and information to be distributed is also classified. Then the matching between information and users is done by means of "rules" of the form "if-then-do…". Conditions in the "if" part of rules can include users and items classifications, but also conditions currently prevailing in the system, such as the date or hour, or some event that just has occurred. Some internal processes in the organization could generate events. For example, in a university library, when a book is added to the catalog, professors interested in an area related to the one of that book should be notified. Of course, we are assuming that internal processes are "computerized" or leave some sort of "trace" in the information systems environment of the organization, so that the corresponding event in JITIK could be generated. Further, processes external to the organization can be periodically and automatically monitored in search for some specific condition, such as the modification of a web page, a value of some variable in a database, and so on.

Consideration of events in JITIK makes it an "opportune" information recommendation system, because JITIK tries to distribute information "when it is needed". Of course, the logic of when to distribute which information to who, is encoded in its conditional rules.

"Opportune" or "just-in-time" information distribution systems face the challenge of determining what the user is doing at a point in time, and even what are their goals and information needs; this has been called "user modeling" (Horvitz, 1998). In some cases this could be easily inferred detecting a very particular event. Imagine, for instance that a new student in a university gets a registration at the library; then, we can assume this is a good moment to send him/her the information about library policies. But there are much more complicated situations, that combine several conditions, some of them could not be registered in the information system, such like exact user location.

User modeling from detection of events in the physical world is a recent and very challenging area (Heckmann, 2006). It is a kind of investigator work, where detected events in the physical world as taken as clues for determining the user activity. Of course, some prior knowledge about the user is necessary for taking advantage of clues. For instance, if it is detected (for instance, using a radio-frequency RFID chip) that the user is in a meeting room, it is likely that he/she is in a meeting, belief that would be reinforced if we know other people are at the same room. Prior knowledge about a user could include his/her usual schedule, people he/she meets or talks to, his/her duties and roles in the organization and so on.

Other advanced technology proposed for recommender systems is *argumentation*, which is a form of automated reasoning (Amgoud, 2000). In an argumentation system, a kind of dialog is constructed between several participants. In contrast with centralized automated reasoning systems, in argumentation each participant could have private information and interests. A specific proposal for using argumentation applied to information distribution (which is indeed a form of recommendation) is given by Chesnevar (2005). In this proposal, the question of whether or not to distribute a specific information item to a given user is calculated using a special form of argumentation called "defeasible logic programming" (DeLP). In DeLP, a distinction is made between strict rules, that are always valid, like "if X is an elephant, then X is a mammal", and defeasible rules, that are tentative, like "if X is an elephant, X does not fly". When this last rule is applied to an individual "dumbo" gives the conclusion that dumbo does not fly; but if we know dumbo does fly, we "defeat" the defeasible rule. A valid argument is a chain of defeasible and strict rules which has no defeaters.

So, the task of a DeLP argumentation-based information distribution system is to find a valid argument, using strict and defeasible rules, of *why* a certain information item should or should not be distributed. In such a context, defeasible rules express general preferences of users or the organization as a whole. Argumentation proved to be an extremely flexible method for taking information distribution decisions, as it is presented in Chesnevar (2005).

Intelligent Agents

Another relevant advanced IT for Knowledge and Information distribution is the *Intelligent Agents* technology (Wooldridge, 2001). In fact it is not a single technology, but a family of related technologies; they encompass many aspects, which relate to the delegation paradigm (such as communication, coordination techniques, cooperation, autonomy, competition, distribution, mobility, among other issues). Agents are long-life autonomous computational processes which thrive to achieve their goals (eventually goals delegated by a user or another agent), and which interact with the external world and with other agents. Intelligent Agents offer the promise of much more modularity, flexibility and adaptability when building complex systems, particularly the so-called "multiagent" systems, consisting of several interacting agents.

Intelligent agents can be delegated Knowledge and Information distribution tasks, as shown in Brena (2001). The JITIK system –mentioned before in this chapter- is a multiagent-based system for disseminating pieces of IK among the members of a large or distributed organization, thus

supporting a Knowledge-management function. It is aimed to deliver the right IK to the adequate people just-in-time.

The JITIK agent model is shown in Figure 1. Personal Agents work on behalf of the members of the organization. They filter and deliver useful content according to user preferences. The Site Agent provides of Information and Knowledge to the Personal Agents, acting as a broker between them and Service agents. Service agents collect and detect IK pieces that are supposed to be relevant for someone in the organization. Examples of service agents are the Web Service agents, which receive and process external requests, as well as monitor agents, which are continuously monitoring sources of Information and Knowledge (web pages, databases, etc.). Other Service agents monitor at time intervals the state of an information resource, like a web page, data in an enterprise's database, etc. The Ontology agent contains knowledge about the interest areas for the members of the organization and about its structure. That knowledge is hierarchically described in the form of taxonomies, usually one for interest areas and one describing the structure

Figure 1. JITIK agent architecture

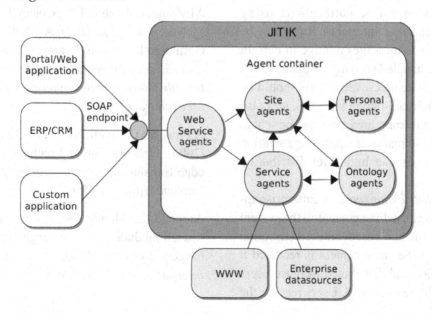

of the organization. For example, in an academic institution, the interest areas could be the science domains in which the institution is specialized, and the organizational chart of the institution gives the structure of the organization. Site agents are the heart of a "cluster" composed by one site agent and several personal agents served by the former. In an organization, clusters would be associated to departments, divisions, etc., depending on the size of them. Networks can be made up connecting several site agents. Distributed organizations like multinational companies would have a web of many connected site agents.

Among the services provided by JITIK we have the following:

- *Recommendation services*: A user's profile is represented by a set of points in the taxonomies, as each user could have many interests and could be located at different parts of the organizational structure. As JITIK keeps track of user interests and preferences it is able to recommend content to users on demand. Recommended content may be used in Portals or Web applications.

- *Subscription services*: JITIK allows users to subscribe to changes in specific areas. Also, users may customize the media and frequency of JITIK notifications using simple web-based interfaces. Rules may be defined so as messages relative to certain topics are handled with higher priorities. A rule may state that several alerts should be sent to their cell-phone via SMS, and also define that interest-area messages be sent in a weekly summary via email. Organization managers may set high-level distribution rules.

- *Content distribution services*: Enterprise applications can deliver content to the system using its semantic-based content distribution services. When new content is received it is classified and distributed to those users who could be interested. Users receive the notifications of new content as specified by their own rules.

CONCLUSION

As we can see from the set of technological trends we just presented for supporting information and knowledge distribution in organizations, there is at the same time the possibility of combining several technologies, as if they were independent (for instance, agent-based recommender systems for social networks), and also almost every single technology is related to the other ones; for instance, the delegation paradigm relates "push" modality to agent systems; semantic web can help agents to relate to each other in open markets, and so on.

It is difficult to foresee which of the advanced technologies we just presented will become mainstream in the near future, but we are certain that many of the technological elements we reviewed are going to actively participate in the information and knowledge distribution systems of the years to come.

REFERENCES

Al Mamunur Rashid, I. A., Cosley, D., Lam, S. K., McNee, S. M., Konstan, J. A., & Riedl, J. (2002). Getting to know you: Learning new user preferences in recommender systems. *Proceedings of the 7th international conference on Intelligent user interfaces*, pp. 13-16.

Albino, V., Garavelli, A. C., & Gorgoglione, M. (2004). Organization and technology in knowledge transfer. *Benchmarking: An International Journal 11*(6), 584-600.

Amgoud, L., Maudet, N., & Parsons, S. (2000). Modelling dialogues using argumentation. MultiAgent Systems, 2000. *Proceedings. Fourth International Conference on*, pp. 31-38.

Basu, C., Hirsh, H., & Cohen, W. (1998). Recommendation as classification: Using social and content-based information in recommendation. *Proceedings of the Fifteenth National Conference on Artificial Intelligence*, pp. 714-720.

Beckman (1999). Knowledge Management Handbook (Jay Liebowitz, ed.). *NASA Goddard Space Flight Center*, Greenbelt, Maryland, CRC Press.

Berners-Lee, T., Hendler, J., & Lassila, O. (2001). The Semantic Web. *Scientific American Magazine, 284*(5), 34-43.

Brena, R., Aguirre, J. L., & Trevino, A. C. (2001). Just-in-time information and knowledge: Agent technology for KM business process. *Systems, Man, and Cybernetics*, 2001 IEEE International Conference on.

Carrillo, J. (1999). The Knowledge Management Movement: Current Drives and Future Scenarios, 3dr. *International Conference on Technology, Policy and Innovation: Global Knowledge Partnerships: Creating Value for the 21st century*. Austin, Texas.

Chesnevar, C., Brena, R., & Aguirre, J. (2005). Knowledge distribution in large organizations using defeasible logic programming. *Proc. 18th Canadian Conf. on AI (in LNCS 3501*, Springer, pp. 244-256.

Chin, P. (2003). Push technology: Still relevant after all these years? *Intranet Journal*, http://www.intranetjournal.com, July.

Gartner Group (2004). Top 10 Strategic Technologies for 2005. *Gartner Symposium ITXPO*, March 28 - April 1, San Diego Convention Center, San Diego, California.

Heckmann, D. (2005) *Ubiquitous User Modeling PhD thesis*, Department of Computer Science, Saarland University, Germany.

Horvitz, E., Breese, J., Heckerman, D., Hovel, D., & Rommelse, K. (1998). The Lumiere Project: Bayesian User Modeling for Inferring the Goals and Needs of Software Users. *Proceedings of the Fourteenth Conference on Uncertainty in Artificial Intelligence*, pp. 256-265.

Liebowitz, J. (2005). Linking social network analysis with the analytic hierarchy process for knowledge mapping in organizations. *Journal of Knowledge Management, 9*(1) 76-86.

Linden, G., Smith, B., & York, J. (2003). Amazon.com recommendations: Item-to-item collaborative filtering. *Internet Computing, IEEE, 7*(1), 76-80.

Martinez, J., Martinez, B., & Arenas, A. (1998). CLASITEX: A tool for knowledge discovery from texts. Principles of Data Mining and Knowledge Discovery. *Proceedings of the 2nd European Symposium*, pp. 459-467.

Negroponte, N. (1996). *Being digital*. Random House Inc., New York, NY, USA.

Probst, G., Raub, S., & Romhardt, K. (1999). *Managing Knowledge: Building Blocks for Success*. Wiley, pp. 218-241.

Ramirez, E., & Brena, R. (2007). Semantically Mapping the Web. *Research in Computer Science, 27*, 125-136.

Ruggles, R. (1997). *Knowledge Tools: Using Technology to Manage Knowledge Better*. Retrieved on 2001, from http://www.cs.toronto.edu/~mkolp/lis2103/kmtools.pdf

Sarnikar, S. (2007). *Automating knowledge flows by extending conventional information retrieval and workflow technologies*. Ph.D. dissertation, The University of Arizona, United States -- Arizona. Retrieved June 1, 2007, from ProQuest Digital Dissertations database.

Satyanarayanan, M. (2001). Pervasive computing: Vision and challenges. *IEEE Wireless Communications, 8*(4), 10-17.

Wooldridge, M. (2001). *An Introduction to MultiAgent Systems*. John Wiley and sons, LTD, Baffins Lane, England.

KEY TERMS

Asynchronous Tools: Information tools where it is not necessary the participation of several involved parties at the same time.

Collaborative Work Platforms: Computer-based systems which help users to interact so they can collaborate to perform tasks in an organization.

Digital Repository: Set of interrelated electronic documents, stored in files or a database, usually classified in categories and other criteria, that stores knowledge useful to an enterprise or other organization.

Enterprise Portals: Specialized websites, common in big enterprises, where a logged-in user can access a wealth of information services.

Forums and Boards: Electronic discussion lists, where participants can "post" a new comment, respond to a previous post, etc.

Information Filtering: Process that eliminates (filters out) part of a given information, leaving just what is believed to be useful.

IT (Information Technologies): Set of technologies related to electronic information processing.

Knowledge Management: Discipline that studies the efficient use of knowledge in enterprises and other organizations.

Negroponte's Delegation: A human user can delegate a task to a synthetic agent, meaning that the latter is going to carry it out on behalf of the former.

Ontologies: Definition of classes of objects, attributes, properties and relations to other objects, expressed in Semantic Web markup languages such as OWL.

Semantic Web: A set of technologies aiming to allow machines to reason about the content of internet documents.

Social Networks: The set of human relations in an organization, which exist independently of whether or not they are analyzed; as a discipline, social networks is the study of those interrelations.

Symbolic Information: Information written as sequences of symbols, which is normally text, as opposed to images, sound, etc.

Taxonomies: Tree-like classifications.

Virtual Spaces: A simulated place in an information system, like a working group. Some virtual spaces incorporate virtual reality concepts, but in enterprises it is not common practice

Compilation of References

Accelerated SAP (ASAP). Implementation Roadmap Version 3.0. (2005, September). SAP Service Marketplace, SAP Solution Manager, Downloads. Retrieved June 26, 2006, from <http://service.sap.com/solutionmanager>

Adam, F., & O'Doherty, P. (2000). Lessons from enterprise resource planning implementations in Ireland – Towards smaller and shorter ERP projects. *Journal of Information Technology, 15*(4), 305-316.

Adhikari, R. (2002, May). 10 Rules For Modeling Business Processes. *DMReview.* Retrieved From Http://Adtmag.Com/Article.Asp?Id=6300

Adhikari, R. (2002, May). Putting The Business In Business Process Modeling. *DMReview.* Retrieved From Http://Adtmag.Com/Article.Asp?Id=6323

Akkermans, H. A., Bogerd, P., Yücesan, E., & van Wassenhove, L. N. (2003). The impact of ERP on supply chain management: Exploratory findings from a European Delphi study. *European Journal of Operational Research, 146*(2), 284-301.

Al Mamunur Rashid, I. A., Cosley, D., Lam, S. K., McNee, S. M., Konstan, J. A., & Riedl, J. (2002). Getting to know you: Learning new user preferences in recommender systems. *Proceedings of the 7th international conference on Intelligent user interfaces*, pp. 13-16.

Aladwani, A. (1998). Coping with users resistance to new technology implementation: an interdisciplinary perspective. *Proceedings of the 9th IRMA Conference*, Boston, MA, 17-20 May, pp. 54-9.

Aladwani, A. (1999). Implications of some of the recent improvement philosophies for the management of the information systems organization. *Industrial Management & Data Systems*, 99(1), 33-9.

Aladwani, A. M. (2001). Change management strategies for successful ERP implementation. *Business Process Management Journal,* 7(3), 2001 Technical paper

Aladwani, A. M. (2002). An Integrated Performance Model of Information Systems Projects. *Journal of Management Information Systems, 19* (1), 185-210.

Albino, V., Garavelli, A. C., & Gorgoglione, M. (2004). Organization and technology in knowledge transfer. *Benchmarking: An International Journal 11*(6), 584-600.

Allan, A., Perkins, E., Carpenter, P., & Wagner, R. (2008). What is Identity 2.0? *Key Issues for Identity and Access Management, 2008,* 7 April 2008, Gartner Research Report, ID Number: G00157012

Allen, D., & Wilson, T. (2003). Vertical trust/mistrust during information strategy formation. *International Journal of Information Management, 23,* 223-237.

Allen, D., Kern, T., & Havenhand, M. (2002). ERP Critical Success Factors: An Exploration of the Contextual Factors in Public Sector Institutions. *Paper presented at the Proceedings of the 35th Annual Hawaii International Conference on System Sciences*, 9/02, Hawaii.

Alliance for Enterprise Security Risk Management (2006). *Convergent security risks in physical security systems and it infrastructures.* Alexandria, VA.

Al-Mashari, M., & Zairi, M. (2000). Information and business process equality: The case of SAP R/3 implementation. *Electronic Journal on Information Systems in Developing Countries, 2* (http://www.unimas.my/fit/roger/EJISDC/EJISDC.htm)

Al-Mudimigh, A., Zairi, M., & Al-Mashari, M. (2001). ERP software implementation: an integrative framework. *European Journal of Information Systems, 10*(4), 216-226.

Aloini, D., Dulmin, R., & Mininno, V. (2007). Risk management in ERP project introduction: Review of the literature. *Information & Management, 44*(6), 547-567.

Alshawi, S., Themistocleous, M., & Almadani, R. (2004). Integrating diverse ERP systems: A case study. *The Journal of Enterprise Information Management*, 17(6). Emerald Group Publishing Limited, pp.454-462.

Alter, S. (2002). *Information Systems: Foundation of E-Business* (4th ed.). Upper Saddle River, NJ: Prentice Hall.

Amgoud, L., Maudet, N., & Parsons, S. (2000). Modelling dialogues using argumentation. MultiAgent Systems, 2000. *Proceedings. Fourth International Conference on*, pp. 31-38.

Ammenwerth, E., Iller, C., & Mansmann, U. (2003). Can evaluation studies benefit from triangulation? A case study. *International Journal of Medical Informatics*, 70(2), 237-248.

AMR Research, (2002). AMR Research predicts enterprise applications market will reach $ 70 billion in 2006. *AMR Research*. Online available at www. amrresearch. com

AMR Research, (2002). *The Multibillion-Dollar Enterprise Performance Planning Market*, 16 August 2002.

Anderson, A. (2003). *When Closeness Counts*. Retrieved Dec. 23, 2003, from http://www.datasweep.com/ds/2003/article_2003.asp?page_id=newsln_002print

Apicella, M. (2000). The hand that moves your business - ERP software moves to the Web, presenting both pitfalls and opportunities. *(enterprise resource planning), Info World June 26, 2000*

Armstrong, C. P., & Sambamurthy, V. (1999). Information technology assimilation in firms: the influence of senior leadership and IT infrastructures. *Information Systems Research, 10(4)*, 304-327.

Aversano, L., & Canfora, G. (2002). Process and Workflow Management: Introducing Eservices in Business Process Models. *Proceedings of the 14th International Conference on Software Engineering And Knowledge Engineering.*

Avison, D., Jones, J., Powell, P., & Wilson, D. (2004). Using and validating the strategic alignment model. *Journal of Strategic Information Systems, 13*, 223-246.

Bailey, J. E., & Pearson, S. W. (1983). Development Of A Tool For Measuring And Analyzing Computer User Satisfaction. *Management Science, 29*(5), 530-545.

Baker, W. H. (1987). Status of information management in small businesses. *Journal of Systems Management, 38*(4), 10-15.

Baljko, J. (2003). At Risk Of Losing Its Grip, Palm Improves Demand Management. *EBN,* Feb. 17, 2003, 1.

Bancroft, N. H., Sep, H., & Sprengel, A. (1998). *Implementing SAP R/3* (2nd Edition ed.). Greenwich, USA: Manning Publications.

Bandit Project. (2008). Retrieved on April 12, 2008 from http://www.bandit-project.org/index.php/Project_overview

Barney, J. (1991). Firm resources and sustained competitive advantage. *Journal of Management, 17*(1), 99-120.

Bartholomew, D. (2004). Making Ends Meet: Manufacturers seek to connect supply chain with customer systems. *IndustryWeek.com*, April 1. Retrieved July 3, 2007, from http://www.industryweek.com/ReadArticle.aspx?ArticleID=1420

Bartholomew, D. (2004). The ABC's of ERP. *CFO IT*, October 5, 2004. http://www.cfo.com/article.cfm/3171508/c_2984786?f=Technology_topstories

Baskerville, R., Pawlowski, S., & McLean, E. (2000). Enterprise resource planning and organizational knowledge: patterns of convergence and divergence. *Paper presented at the International Conference on Information Systems, Proceedings of the 21st International Conference on Information Systems*, Brisbane, Australia, p. 396-406.

Basu, C., Hirsh, H., & Cohen, W. (1998). Recommendation as classification: Using social and content-based information in recommendation. *Proceedings of the Fifteenth National Conference on Artificial Intelligence*, pp. 714-720.

Beal, B. (2003). The priority that persists. Retrieved November, 2003, from SearchCIO.com Web site: http://searchcio.techtarget.com/originalContent/0,29142,sid19_gci932246;00.html

Beard, J. W., & Sumner, M. (2004). Seeking strategic advantage in the post-net era: viewing ERP systems from the resource based perspective. *Journal of strategic Information Systems, 13*(2004), 129-150.

Beckman (1999). Knowledge Management Handbook (Jay Liebowitz, ed.). *NASA Goddard Space Flight Center*, Greenbelt, Maryland, CRC Press.

Belcher, L. W., & Watson, H. J. (1993). Assessing the value of Conoco's EIS. *MIS Quarterly. 17*(9), 239-253.

Bell, S., & Orzen, M. (2007, May 15). Jumping on the ERP bandwagon. *APICS e-News*, 7.

Bendoly, E., & Schoenherr, T. (2005). ERP system and implementation-process benefits: implications for B2B e-procurement. *International Journal of Operations and Production Management, 25*(4), 304-319.

Bendoly. (2002). Theory and Support for Process Frameworks of Knowledge Discovery and Data Mining from ERP Systems. *Information and Management, 40*(7), August 2002.

Benjamin, R. J., Rockart, J. F., Scott Morton, M. S., & Wyman, J. (1984). Information Technology: A Strategic Opportunity. *Sloan Management Review, 25(3),* 3-10.

Bennett, S., McRobb, S., & Farmer, R. (2005). *Object-Oriented Systems Analysis and Design Using UML.* 3rd edition, London: McGraw-Hill.

Bennis, W. G. (1984). Transformative power and leadership. In: TJ. Sergiovanni and JE Corbally (eds), *Leadership and Organizational Culture.* Urbana, University of Illinois Press; 1984.

Bergman, A. (2008). OpenID Foundation - Google, IBM, Microsoft, VeriSign and Yahoo", O'Reilly Media, 2008-02-07. Retrieved on 2008-03-19 from http://radar.oreilly.com/archives/2008/02/openid-foundation-google-ibmm.html

Berners-Lee, T., Hendler, J., & Lassila, O. (2001). The Semantic Web. *Scientific American Magazine, 284*(5), 34-43.

Bharadwaj, A. S. (2000). A Resource-Based Perspective of Information Technology Capability and Firm Performance: An Empirical Investigation. *MIS Quarterly, 24(1),* 169-196.

Bhargav-Spantzel, A., Squicciarini, A., & Bertino, E. (2005). *Establishing and protecting digital identity in federation systems.* TR 2005-48, Purdue University (2005)

Bhat, M. J., & Deshmukh, N. (2005). Methods for Modeling Flexibility in Business Processes. *Sixth Workshop on Business Process Modeling, Development, and Support (BPMDS'05).* Porto, Portugal June 13-14.

Bhattacherjee, A. (2000). Beginning SAP R/3 Implementation at Geneva Pharmaceuticals. *Communications of the Association for Information Systems, 4*(2).

Bilili, S., & Raymond, L. (1993). Information technology: Threats and opportunities for small and medium-sized enterprises. *International Journal of Information Management 13*(6). 439-48.

Billet, D. L. (2008). Focus on small- and medium-sized companies: Challenges and opportunities. *APICS e-News, 8*(6), April 1, 2008.

Bingi, P., Sharma, M., & Godla, J. (1999). Critical issues affecting ERP implementation. *Information System Management, 16*(3), 7-14.

Bjørn-Andersen, N., Flügge, B., Ipenburg, F. v., Klein, S., & Tan, Y.-H. (2007). ICT Challenges in Cross-border trade: The Itaide perspective. *Paper presented at the European Conference on Information Systems (ECIS 2007),* St. Gallen.

Bleistein, S. J., Cox, K., & Verner, J. (2006a). Validating strategic alignment of organizational IT requirements using goal modeling and problem diagrams. *Journal of Systems and Software, 79,* 362-378.

Bleistein, S. J., Cox, K., Verner, J., & Phalp, K. T. (2006b). B-SCP: A requirements analysis framework for validating strategic alignment of organizational IT based on strategy, context and process. *Information and Software Technology, 48,* 846-868.

Boddy, D. (2002). *Managing Projects.* London: Prentice Hall.

Bonatti, P. A., & Samarati, P. (2000) Regulating Service Access and Information Release on the Web. In: *Proceedings of CCS 2000,* Athens, ACM Press (2000)

Boonstra, A. (2003). Structure and Analysis of IS decision making processes. European *Journal of Information Systems, 12*(3), 195-209.

Boonstra, A. (2005). *Information Systems as Redistributors of Power Interpreting an ERP implementation from a stakeholder perspective.* som.eldoc.ub.rug.nl/FILES/reports/themeA/2005/05A06/05A06.pdf

Booth, D., H. Haas, et al., (2004). *Web Services Architecture.* W3C.

Bose, R. (2006). Understanding management data systems for enterprise performance management. *Information Management and Data Systems, 106*(1), 43-54.

Botta-Genoulaz, V., Millet, P.-A., & Grabot, B. A. (2005). Survey on the recent research literature on ERP systems. *Computers in Industry, 56,* 510-522.

Boutellier, R., Flügge, B., & Raus, M. (2007). Challenges of Global Trade and the transfer to enabled Business models in the Swiss Socks Market, *Proceedings of 20th Bled E-Conference eMergence: Merging and Emerging Technologies, Processes, and Institutions,* Bled, Slovenia, Markus, L. et al, Editors, Moderna organizacija, Kranj, June 4-6.

Bowonder, B., Mastakar, N., & Sharma, K. J. (2005). Innovatiive ICT platforms: The Indian Experience.

International Journal of Services Technology & Management, 6(3/4/5), 1-1.

BPMI.Org. Releases Business Process Modeling Notation (BPMN) Version 1.0. Retrieved April 5, 2005 from Http://Xml.Coverpages.Org/Ni2003-08-29-A.Html

Bradford, M., & Mayfield, T. (2001). Does ERP Fit in a LEAN World? *Strategic Finance, 82*(11), 28-34.

Bradford, M., & Vijayaraman, B. S., & Chandra, A. (2003). The Status of ERP Integration in Business School Curricula: Results of a Survey of Business School. *Communications of the Association for Information Systems, 12,* 437 - 456.

Bradford, M., Mayfield, T., & Toney, C. (2001). Does ERP fit in a lean world? *Strategic Finance, 82*(11), 28-34.

Bradley, J (2004). *Enterprise Resource Planning Success: A Management Theory Approach to Critical Success Factors.* Doctoral Dissertation, Claremont Graduate University, UMI No. 3139266.

Bradley, J. (2005). Are all critical success factors created equal? In *Proceedings of the 11th Americas' Conference on Information Systems,* Atlanta (pp. 2152-2159). Omaha, NE: Association for Information Systems.

Brady, J. A., Monk, E. F., & Wagner, B. J. (2003). *Concepts in Enterprise Resource Planning,* India: Thomson Asia Private Limited.

Brancheau, J. C., Janz, B. D., & Wetherbe, J. C. (1996). Key issues in information system management: 1994-95 SIM Delphi results. *MIS Quarterly, 20*(2), 225-242.

Brancheau, J. C., Janz, B. D., & Wetherbe, J. C. (1996). Key Issues in Information Systems Management: 1994-95 SIM Delphi Results. *MIS Quarterly, 20*(2), 225-242.

Brehm, L., Heinzl, A., & Markus, M. L. (2001). *Tailoring ERP systems: A spectrum of choices and their implications.* Paper presented at the 34th Hawaii International Conference on System Sciences, Hawaii.

Brehm, N., & Gómez, J.M. (2005). Secure web service-based resource sharing in ERP networks. *Journal of Information Privacy & Security, 1*(2), 29-48.

Brena, R., Aguirre, J. L., & Trevino, A. C. (2001). Just-in-time information and knowledge: Agent technology for KM business process. *Systems, Man, and Cybernetics,* 2001 IEEE International Conference on.

Broadbent, M., & Weill, P. (1993). Improving business and information strategy alignment: learning from the banking industry. *IBM Systems Journal, 32*(1), 162-179.

Broadbent, M., Weill, P., & Clair St., D. (1999). The Implications of Information Technology Infrastructure for Business Process Redesign. *MIS Quarterly, 23*(2), 159-182.

Brown, C. V., & Vessey, I. (2003). Managing the Next Wave of Enterprise Systems: Leveraging Lessons from ERP. *MIS Quarterly Executive, 2*(1), 65-77.

Brynjolfsson, E., & Hitt., L. M. (1996). Paradox lost? Firm level evidence on the returns to information systems spending. *Management Science, 42(4),* 541–558.

Buck-Emden, R. (1998). *Die Technologie des SAP-Systems R/3.* München, Addison-Wesley.

Budhiraja, R. (2003). Electronic Governance – A key issue in the 21st century. *A paper by Additional Director Electronic Governance Division Ministry of Information Technology Govt. of India).*

Buell, A. D., & Sandhu, R. (2003, Noevmber). Identity Management. *IEEE Internet Computing, 7*(6), 26-28.

Bullen, C. V., & Rockart, J. F. (1981, June). Appendix: *A primer on critical success factors.* In Rockart, J. F., & Bullen, C.V. (Eds.), The Rise of Managerial Computing, 383-423. Homewood, IL. Dow-Jones-Irwin.

Buonanno, G., Faverio, P., Pigni, F., Ravarini, A., Sciuto, D., & Tagliavini, M. (2005). Factors affecting ERP system adoption: A comparative analysis between SMEs and large companies. *Journal of Enterprise Information Management, 18*(4), 384-426.

Business Process Modeling with ARIS for SAP NetWeaver. (2006, September 12-15). *Proceedings of SAP TECHED '06 Conference.* Retrieved September 22, 2006 from <http://www.sapteched.com/06/usa/home.htm>

Butler, T., & Pyke, A. (2004). Examining the influence of ERP systems on firm-specific knowledge assets and capabilities. In F. Adam & D. Sammon (Eds.), The enterprise resource planning decade: Lessons learned and issues for the future (pp. 167-206), Hershey, PA: Idea Group Publishing.

Byrd, T. A., Lewis, R. B., & Bryan, R. W. (2006). The leveraging influence of strategic alignment on IT investment: An empirical examination. *Information & Management, 43,* 308-321.

Camenisch, J., Shelat, A., Sommer, D., Fischer-H¨ubner, S., Hansen, M., Krasemann, H., Lacoste, G., Leenes, R., & Tseng, J. (2005). Privacy and identity management for everyone. In: *1st conference on Digital Identity Management,* ACM Press (2005)

Campbell, B., Kay, R., & Avison, D. (2005). Strategic alignment: a practitioner's perspective. *Journal of Enterprise Information Management*, 18(6), 653-664.

Capaldo, G., & Pierluigi, R. (2008). A methodological proposal to assess the feasibility of ERP systems implementation strategies. *Proceedings of the 41st Hawaii International Conference on System Sciences*, Waikoloa, Hawaii, January 7-10, 401-401.

Carlino, J. (1999). AMR Research Unveils Report on Enterprise Application Spending and Penetration, at www.amrresearch.com/press/files/99823.asp accessed July 2001.

Carlis, J., & Maguire, J. (2000). *Mastering Data Modeling: A User Driven Approach (1st Ed.)*. Addison- Wesley.

Carlson, D. (2001). *Modeling XML Applications With UML*. Addison Wesley.

Carlsson, B. (1989). Flexibility and the Theory of the Firm. *International Journal of Industrial Organization*, 7, 179-203.

Carr, N. G. (2003). IT doesn't matter. *Harvard Business Review, 81*(5), 41-49.

Carrillo, J. (1999). The Knowledge Management Movement: Current Drives and Future Scenarios, 3dr. *International Conference on Technology, Policy and Innovation: Global Knowledge Partnerships: Creating Value for the 21st century*. Austin, Texas.

Carter, M. (2004). Key note address on E-governance – Transforming India. *National summit – India: The Knowledge Capital* February 17, 2004

Carter, S. (2007). The New Language of Business. *SOA & Web 2.0, IBM Press*.

Casassa, M., Bramhall, P., & Pato, J. (2003). *On Adaptive Identity Management: The next generation of Identity Management Technolgies*, HP Labs Technical Report, HPL-2003-149, 2003

Castela, N., Tribolet, J., Silva, A., & Guerra, A. (2001). Business Process Modeling with UML. http://www.inesc-id.pt/ficheiros/publicacoes/689.pdf [accessed January 2008].

Caulliraux, H. M., Proença, A., & Prado, C. A. S. (2000). ERP Systems from a Strategic Perspective. *Sixth International Conference on Industrial Engineering and Operations Management*, Niteroi, Brazil.

Chan, J. O. (2005). Towards a Unified View of Customer Relationship Management. *The Journal of American Academy of Business, 6*(1), 32-38.

Chan, Y. E., & Huff, S. L. (1992). Strategy: An information systems research perspective. *Journal of Strategic Information Systems, 1(4)*, 191-201.

Chan, Y. E., Huff, S. L., Barclay, D. W., & Copeland, D. G. (1997). Business strategic orientation, information systems strategic orientation, and strategic alignment. *Information Systems Research, 8(2)*, 125–150.

Chappell, D. (2006). Introducing Windows CardSpace, *Windows Vista Technical Articles*. April 2006

Charfi, A., & Mezini, M. (2004). Service composition: Hybrid Web service composition: Business processes meet business rules. *Proceedings of the 2nd international conference on Service oriented computing*.

Chau, P. Y. K. (1994). Selection of packaged software in small businesses. *European Journal of Information Systems, 3*(4), 292-302.

Chau, P. Y. K. (1995). Factors used in the selection of packaged software in small businesses: views of owners and managers. In*formation and Management, 29*(2), 71-8.

Chen, Q., & Chen, H.-M. (2004). Exploring the success factors of E-CRM strategy in practice. *Journal of Database Marketing & Consumer Strategy Management, 11*(4), 333-343.

Cheney, P. H. (1983). Getting The Most Out Of Your First Computer System. *American Journal of Small Business, 7*(4), 476-485.

Chesnevar, C., Brena, R., & Aguirre, J. (2005). Knowledge distribution in large organizations using defeasible logic programming. *Proc. 18th Canadian Conf. on AI (in LNCS 3501*, Springer, pp. 244-256.

Chien, S.-W., Hu, C., Reimers, K., & Lin, J.-S. (2007).The influence of centrifugal and centripetal forces on ERP project success in small and medium-sized enterprises in China and Taiwan. *International Journal of Production Economics, 107*(2), 380-396.

Chin, P. (2003). Push technology: Still relevant after all these years? *Intranet Journal*, http://www.intranetjournal.com, July.

Clark, M., Fletcher, P., Hanson, J. J., Irani, R., & Thelin, J. (2002). *Web Services Business Strategies and Architectures*. Wrox Press.

Claybrook, B. (1992). *OLTP Online Transaction Processing*. John Wiley & Sons.

Concordia. (2008) Retrieved on April 13, 2008 from (http://projectconcordia.org/index.php/Purpose_and_Principles)

Cook, M., & Hagey, R. (2003). Why Companies flunk supply supply-chain 101: Only 33 percent correctly measure supply-chain performance; few use the right incentives. *Journal of Business Strategy, 24*(4), 35-42.

Cooke, D. P., & Peterson, W. J. (1998). *SAP implementation: Strategies and Results* (No. 1217-98-RR). New York.

Cooley, P. L., Walz, D. T., et al. (1987). A Research Agenda For Computers And Small Business. *American Journal of Small Business, 11*(3), 31-42.

Cotteleer, M. J. (2002). *An Empirical Study of Operational Performance Convergence Following Enterprise-IT Implementation* (Working Paper No. 03-011): Harvard Business School.

Cotteleer, M. J., & E. Bendoly (2006). Order Lead-Time Improvement Following Enterprise Information Technology Implementation: An Empirical Study. *MIS Quarterly* 30(3), 643-660.

Cragg, P. B., & King, M. (1993). Small-firm computing: motivators and inhibitors. *MIS Quarterly 17*(1), 47-60.

Cragg, P. B., & Zinatelli, N. (1995). The evolution of information systems in small firms. *Information and Management, 29*(1), 1-8.

Cragg, P., King, M., & Hussin, H. (2002). IT alignment and firm performance in small manufacturing firms. *Journal of Strategic Information Systems, 11,* 109-132.

Crowston, K., & Howison, J. (2006). Assessing the Health of Open Source Communities. *IEEE Computer,* May, 89-91.

d'Amboise, G., & Muldowney, M. (1988). "Management theory for small business: attempts and requirements." The Academy of Management Review 13(2): 226-40.

Dahlen, C., & Elfsson, J. (1999). *An analysis of the current and future ERP market- with a focus on Sweden.* http://www.pdu.se/xjobb.pdf (accessed April 24, 2003)

Dalal, N. P., Kamath, M., Kolarik, W. J., & Sivaraman, E. (2004). Toward an integrated approach for modeling Enterprise processes. *Communications of the ACM, 47,* 83-87.

Dalal, N. P., Kamath, M., Kolarik, W. J., & Sivaraman, E. (2004). Toward an integrated approach for modeling Enterprise processes. *Communications of the ACM, 47,* 83-87.

Davenport, T. (1998). Putting the enterprise into the enterprise system. *Harvard Business Review, 76*(4), 121-131.

Davenport, T. (2000). *Mission Critical – Realizing the Promise of Enterprise Systems.* Boston, MA: Harvard Business School Press

Davenport, T. H. (1995). *SAP: Big Change Comes in Big Packages,* from http://www.cio.com/archive/101595_davenpor.html

Davenport, T. H. (1998). Putting the Enterprise into the Enterprise System. *Harvard Business Review, 76*(4), 121-131.

Davenport, T. H. (2000). *Mission Critical: Realizing the Promise of Enterprise Systems.* Harvard Business School Press, Cambridge, MA.

Davenport, T. H. (2000). Transforming the Practice of Management with Enterprise Systems. In *Mission Critical* (p. 203-235). Boston: Harvard Business School Press.

Davenport, T. H. (2000). Transforming the Practice of Management with Enterprise Systems. In *Mission Critical* (p. 203-235). Boston, MA: Harvard Business School Press.

Davenport, T. H., & Brooks, J. D. (2004). Enterprise Systems and the Supply Chain. *Journal of Enterprise Information Management, 17*(1), 8-19.

Davenport, T. H., & Harris, J. G. (2005). Automated Decision Making Comes of Age. *MIT Sloan Management Review, Summer 2005 46*(4), 83-89.

Davenport, T. H., & Prusak, L. (1998). Working Knowledge: How Organizations Manage What They Know, Boston: *Harvard Business School Press.*

Davenport, T. H., Harris, J. G., & Cantrell, S. (2002). *The Return of Enterprise Systems: The Director's Cut*: Accenture Institute for Strategic Change.

Davenport, T., & Linder, J. (1994). Information Management Infrastructure: The New Competitive Weapon. *Proceedings of the 27th Annual Hawaii International Conference on Systems Sciences, IEEE,* 1994, 885-899.

Davenport, T., & Prusak, L. (1998). *Working knowledge: how organizations manage what they know.* Boston, MA: Harvard Business School Press.

Davenport, T., Harris, J., & Cantrell, S. (2003). *Enterprise Systems Revisited: The Director's Cut.* Accenture.

Davenport, T.H. (1993). *Process Innovation Reengineering Work Through Information Technology.* Boston, MA: Harvard Business School Press.

David, L. O. (2004). *Managerial issues of Enterprise Resources Planning Systems*. New Delhi: Tata McGraw-Hill Edition.

Davison, R. (2002). Cultural complications of ERP. *Communications of the ACM, 45*(7), 109-111.

Dawson, P. (1994). *Organisational Change: A Processual Approach*. London: Chapman.

De Búrca, S., Fynes, B., & Marshall, D. (2005). Strategic technology adoption: Extending ERP across the supply chain. *Journal of Enterprise Information Management, 18*(4), 427-440.

De Carvalho, R. A. (2006). Issues on Evaluating Free/Open Source ERP Systems. *Research and Practical Issues of Enterprise Information Systems, 667-676.* Springer-Verlag

Dean, J. (2001). Weathering the ERP Storm. *Government Executive*, July 1, 2001

Dejpongsarn, N. (2005). *ERP Framework with mySAP Solution* . a presentation.

Delahaye, D. (2003). Knowledge Management in a SME. *International Journal of Organisational Behaviour, 9*(3), 604-614.

Delic, A. K., & Dayal, U. (2003). The Rise of the Intelligent Enterprise. *Virtual Strategist, 3*(45).

Deloitte, C. (1998). *ERP's Second Wave-Maximizing the Value of ERP-Enabled Processes*. New York: Deloitte Consulting, ISBN 1-892383-42-X.

DeLone, W. H. (1981). Firm Size And The Characteristics Of Computer Use. *MIS Quarterly 5*(4), 65-77.

DeLone, W. H. (1988). Determinants Of Success For Computer Usage In Small Business. *MIS Quarterly, 12*(1), 50-61.

Delphi. (2001). *In Process: The Changing Role of Business Process Management in Today's Economy*. Retrieved From Http://Www.Ie.Psu.Edu/Advisoryboards/Sse/Articles/A4bd42eb1.Delphi-Ip-Oct2001.Pdf

Desai, A. (2005). Adaptive Complex Enterprises. *Communications of the ACM, 48*(5), 32-35.

Dess, G. G., & Beard, D. W. (1984). Dimensions of Organizational Task Environments. *Administrative Science Quarterly, 29*(1), 52-73.

Dewan, R., Seidmann, A., & Sunderesan, S. (1995). *Strategic Choices in IS Infrastructure: Corporate Standards versus "Best of breed" Systems*. Paper presented at the ICIS, Amsterdam.

Dezouza, K., & Awazu, Y. (2006). Knowledge Management at SMEs: Five peculiarities. *Journal of Knowledge Management, 10*(1), 32-43.

Dickson, G., Senn, J. et al. (1977). Research In Management Information Systems: The Minnesota Experiments. *Management Science, 23*(9), 913-923.

Diederich, T. (1998). Bankrupt firm blames SAP for failure. *ComputerWorld*, (August 28, 1998).

Dillard, J. F., & Yuthas, K. (2006) Enterprise Resource Planning Systems and Communicative Actions. *Critical Perspectives on Accounting, 17*, (2-3), 202-223.

Donovan, M. (1998). *There is no magic in ERP software: It's in preparation of the process and people*. Retrieved September 8, 2/7/2002, from http://wwwrmdonovan.com/pdf/perfor_98_9.pdf

Donovan, M. (2001). *Successful ERP Implementation the first time*. Retrieved July 25, 2001, from www.mdonovan.com/pdf/perfor8.pdf

Donovan, M. (2003). *Why the Controversy over ROI from ERP?*, from www.refresher.com/archives19.html

Douglas, M. (2002). *Planning for the Enterprise*. New York. April 16, 2002

Doukidis, G. I., Lybereas, P. et al. (1996). Information systems planning in small businesses: A stage of growth analysis. *Journal of Systems and Software, 33*(2), 189-201.

Dove, R. (2005). Agile Enterprise Cornerstones: Knowledge, Values and Response Ability. *IFIP 8.6 Keynote*, Atlanta, May 2005.

Dove, R. (2005). Fundamental Principles for Agile Systems Engineering. *2005 Conference on Systems Engineering Research (CSER)*, Stevens Institute of Technology, Hoboken, NJ, March 2005.

Dove, R., Benson, S., & Hartman, S. (1996). A Structured Assessment System for Groups Analyzing Agility. *Fifth National Agility Conference*, Agility Forum, Boston, March 1996.

Dreiling, A., Klaus, H., Rosemann, M., & Wyssusek, B. (2005). Open Source Enterprise Systems: Towards a Viable Alternative. *38th Annual Hawaii International Conference on System Sciences*, Hawaii.

Drucker, P. F. (1973). Management: Tasks, Responsibilities, Practices (Harper Colophon 1985 Ed.). New York: Harper Row.

Duffy, J. (2002). *IT/Business Alignment: Is it an option or is it mandatory?* IDC Document 26831.

Duncan & Bogucki, N. (1995). Capturing Flexibility of Information Technology Infrastructure: A Study of Resource Characteristics and Their Measure. *Journal of Management Information Systems, 12*(2), 37-57.

Dunkelberg, W., & Wade, H. (2007). Overview: Small Business Optimism. *NFIB Small Business Economic Trends,* 1-12.

Dutta, S. et al. (1997). Designing Management Support Systems. *Communications of the ACM.*

Earl, M. J. (1989). *Management Strategies for Information Technology.* Great Britain: Prentice-Hall International.

Earl, M. J. (1993). Experiences in strategic information systems planning. *MIS Quarterly, 17(1),* 1–24.

Edmundson, G., Baker, S., & Cortese, A. (1997). Silicon valley on the Rhine. *Business Week, November 3,* 162-166.

Edwards, J., & Kidd, J. (2003). Bridging the Gap from the General to the Specific by Linking Knowledge Management to Business Process Management. In V. Hlupic (Ed.), *Knowledge and Business Process Management.* Hershey: Idea Group Publishing.

Ein-Dor, P., & Segev, E. (1978). Organizational Context And The Success Of Management Information Systems. *Management Science, 24*(10), 1064-1077.

Ein-Dor, P., Segev, E. et al. (1981). Use Of Management Information Systems: An Empirical Study. *Proceedings of the 2nd International Conference on Information Systems,* Cambridge, Massachusetts, Association for Information Systems.

Eisenhardt, K. M., & Graebner, M. E. (2007). Theory building from cases: opportunities and challenges. *Academy of Management Journal, 50*(1), 25-32.

El Maliki, T., & Seigneur, J-M. (2007). A Survey of User-centric Identity Management Technologies. *Emerging Security Information, Systems, and Technologies, 2007.* SecureWare 2007. The International Conference on 14-20 Oct. 2007 (pp. 12-17).

Enterprise Service Wiki. (2007, June (Last Edited)) SAP Developer Network (SDN). Website <https://www.sdn.sap.com/irj/sdn/wiki?path=/display/ESpackages/Home>

Enterprise Service-Oriented Architecture, Sales Order Processing, mySAP SRM 2005 (SRM Server 5.5). (2005).

SAP Developer Network (SDN). Enterprise Services Documentation, Download. Retrieved May 2006 from <https://www.sdn.sap.com/irj/sdn/go/portal/prtroot/docs/webcontent/uuid/c0cd8360-3b74-2910-0fae-dc-ceed7328e7>

Enterprise Services Design Guide. (2005). *SAP Developer Network (SDN).* Retrieved May 2007 from <https://www.sdn.sap.com/irj/servlet/prt/portal/prtroot/docs/library/uuid/943e83e5-0601-0010-acb5-b16258f5f20a >

Enterprise SOA and Business Process Platform FAQ. (n.d.). *SAP Developer Network (SDN).* Retrieved February 19, 2007 from <https://www.sdn.sap.com/irj/sdn/go/portal/prtroot/docs/library/uuid/3071ab59-8faa-2910-cd81-da9e20b629ed>

Erder, M., & Pureur, P. (2006). Transitional architectures for enterprise evolution. *IT Professional, 8*(3), 10-17.

Erl, T. (2005). *Service-Oriented Architecture - Concepts, Technology, and Design.* Upper Saddle River NJ: Prentice Hall.

ERP Implementation Disappoints Companies. (2000, August 31). *Australian Banking & Finance, 9,* 8.

Ettlie, J. E., Perotti, V. J., Joseph, D. A., & Cotteleer, M. J. (2005). Strategic Predictors of Successful Enterprise System Deployment. *International Journal of Operations & Production Management,* 25(9/10), 953.

Ettlinger, B. (2002, March 5). The Future of Data Modeling. *DMReview.* Retrieved From Http://Www.Dmreview.Com/Article_Sub.Cfm?Articleid=4840

European Commission (2008). SME definition. Retrieved May 12, 2008, from http://ec.europa.eu/enterprise/enterprise_policy/sme_definition/index_en.htm.

Evans, J. S. (1991). Strategic Flexibility for High Technology Manoeuvres: A Conceptual Framework. *Journal of Management Studies, 28*(1), 69-89.

Evans, K. S. (2005). Expanding E-Government: Improved Service Delivery for the American People Using Information Technology. *A Report for the President's Management Council* Dec 2005

Everdingen, Y., Hillegersberg, J. et al. (2000). ERP adoption by European midsize companies. *Communications of the ACM, 43*(4), 27-31.

Evgeniou, T. (2002). Building the Adaptive Enterprise. *Information Strategies For Successful Management of Complex, Global Corporations in Times of Change.* INSEAD June 2002.

Ewalt, D. W., (2002, December 12). *BPML Promises Business Revolution*. Retrieved From Http://Www.Computing.Co.Uk/Analysis/1137556

Farhoomand, F., & Hrycyk, G. P. (1985). The Feasibility Of Computers In The Small Business Environment. *American Journal of Small Business, 9*(4),15-22.

Fattah, H., & D'Amico, E. (2003). Tying IT all together; the push for systems integration is on. *Chemical Week, 165*(5), 15-18.

Fernandes, M. J., & Duarte, J. F. (2005). A reference framework for process-oriented software development organizations. *Software Systems Model, 4*, 94-105.

Ferraiolo, D. F., Kuhn, R. D., & Chandramouli, R. (2003). *Role-Based Access Control*. Artech House computer security series, ISBN 1-58053-370-1 (2003).

Feuring, N. & Streibert, T. (2005, November 3-4). *Proceedings of SAP Skills Conference, Business-Process Oriented Life-Cycle Management with the SAP Solution Manager*. Walldorf, Germany. Website <http://www.sap.com/community/pub/events/2005_11_SAP_Skills/index.epx>

Field, J. M., Heim, G. R., & Sinha, K. K. (2004) Managing Quality in the E-Service System: Development and Application of a Process Model. *Production & Operations Management, 13*(4), 291-306.

Fink, K., & Ploder, C. (2007a). A comparative Study of Knowledge Processes and Methods in Austrian and Swiss SMEs. In H. Österle, J. Schelp & R. Winter (Eds.), *Proceedings of the 15th European Conference on Information Systems (ECIS2007)*. St. Gallen.

Fink, K., & Ploder, C. (2007b). Knowledge Process Modeling in SME and Cost-Efficient Software Support: Theoretical Framework and Empirical Studies. In M. Khosrow-Pour (Ed.), *Managing Worldwide Operations and Communications with Information Technology*. Hershey: IGI Publishing.

Fitzpatrick, B. (2005). Distributed Identity: Yadis. *LiveJournal*. Retrieved on April 19, 2008 from http://community.livejournal.com/lj_dev/683939.html

Fitzpatrick, B. (2005). OpenID. *LiveJournal*. Retrieved on April 19, 2008 from http://community.livejournal.com/lj_dev/684200.html

Flak, L. S., & Rose, J. (2005). Stakeholder Governance: Adapting Stakeholder Theory To E-Government. *Communications of AIS*, 2005, *16*, 642-664, 23

Fowler, A., & Gilfillan, M. (2003). A Framework for Stakeholder Integration in Higher Education Information Systems Projects. *Technology Analysis & Strategic Management, 15*(4), 467-489.

Frankel, D. S. (2003). *Model Driven Architecture: Applying MDA To Enterprise Computing*. Wiley.

Frohlich, M. T., & Westbrook, R. (2001). Arcs of integration: an international study of supply chain strategies. *Journal of Operations Management, 19*, 185-200.

Gable, G., Sedera, D. et al. (2003). Enterprise Systems Success: A Measurement Model. *Proceedings of the 24th International Conference on Information Systems*, Seattle, Washington, Association for Information Systems.

Gartner Group (2004). Top 10 Strategic Technologies for 2005. *Gartner Symposium ITXPO*, March 28 - April 1, San Diego Convention Center, San Diego, California.

Gartner's Four Phases of E-Government Model (2001) USA, Gartner Group. Europa (2001) "E-government - Electronic access to public services. (online)(cited on 20th December, 2003). Available from <URL: http://europa.eu.int/>

Gebauer, J., & Lee, F. (2008). Enterprise system flexibility and implementation strategies – Aligning theory with evidence from a case study. *Information Systems Management, 25*(1), 71–82.

Gefen, D., & Ragowsky, A. (2005). A multi-level approach to measuring the benefits of an ERP system in manufacturing firms. *Information Systems Management, 22*(1), 18–25.

Gelinas, S., & Fedorowicz (2004). Business Processes and Information Technology. USA : Thomson-Southwestern.

Gendron, M. (1996). Learning to live with electronic embodiment of reengineering. *Harvard Management Update, November*.

Gilbert, A. (2006). *Salesforce CEO's vision for 'business Web'*. www.news.com. DOI

Gillham, B. (2000). *Case Study Research Methods*. London/New York: Continuum.

Golden, W., & Powel, P. (2004). Inter-organizational Information Systems as Enablers of Organizational Flexibility. *Technology Analysis & Strategic Management, 16*(3), 299-325.

Goldman, S. L., Nagel, R. N., & Preiss, K. (1995). *Agile Competitors and Virtual Organizations.* New York:Van Nostrand Reinhold.

Goodhue, D. L., Wixon, B. H., & Watson, H. J. (2002, June). Realizing business benefits through CRM: Hitting the right target in the right way. *MIS Quarterly Executive,* 1(2), 79-94

Goth, G. (2005). Open Source Business Models: Ready for Prime Time. *IEEE Software,* November/December, pp 98-100.

Grant, D., & Tu, Q. (2005). Levels of Enterprise Integration: Study Using Case Analysis. *International Journal of Enterprise Information Systems,* 1(1), 1-22.

Graves, M. (2007). VeriSign, Microsoft & Partners to Work together on OpenID + Cardspace. *VeriSign.* Retrieved on April 19, 2008 from http://blogs.verisign.com/infrablog/2007/02/verisign_microsoft_partners_to_1.php

Gray, P., & Byun, J. (2001). *Customer Relationship Management.* University of California, Irvine, www.crmassist.com/documents.

Greene, W. H. (2003). *Econometric Analysis- 5e edition.* Prentice Hall Inc.

Grover, V., Teng, J. T. C., & Fiedler, K. D. (1993). Information Technology Enabled Business Process Redesign: An Integrated Planning Framework. *OMEGA International Journal of Management Science, 21*(4), 433-447.

Gujarati, D. N. (2003). *Basic Econometrics - 4e edition.* Mc-Graw Hill Higher Education.

Gupta, D. S. (2004). Small is big business, news item from *e-biz newsletter* dated December 1, 2004. Retrieved December 2, 2004 from http://www.zdnetindia.com/biztech/ ebusiness/sme/stories/nsl, 13331.html;

Gupta, M., & Kohli, A. (2006). Enterprise resource planning systems and its implications for operations function. *Technovation, 26,* 687-696.

Hackney, R., Burn, J., & Dhillon, G. (2000). Challenging Assumptions for Strategic Informations Systems Planning: Theoretical Perspectives. *Communications of the Association for Information Systems, 3*(9).

Haeckel, S. H. (1995). Adaptive Enterprise Design: The Sense-and-Respond Model. *Planning Review, 23*(3), pp. 6-42.

Haeckel, S. H. (1999). *Adaptive Enterprise: Creating and Leading Sense-and-Respond Organizations.* Harvard Business School Press, Boston 1999.

Hall, D., & Hulett, D. (2002). *Universal Risk Project: Final Report, February 2002.* Milford, NH: PMI Risk SIG.

Hamerman, P., & Wang, R. (2006). ERP: Still a Challenge after All These Years, Enterprise Applications, Jan 29, 2006, p. 1-2 Downloaded on Sept. 25, 2006 from http://www.networkcomputing.com/gswelcome/showArticle.jhtml?article ID=177104905.

Hammer, M. (1990). Reengineering Work. Don't Automate, Obliterate. *Harvard Business Review,* 104-112.

Hammer, M. (1996). *Beyond Reengineering: How the Process-Centered Organization Is Changing Our Work and Our Lives.* Harper Collins.

Hammer, M., & Champy, J. (1993). *Reengineering the corporation.* USA:Free Press.

Hardt, D. (2006). *What is user-centric identity?* June 26, 2006 Retrieved on April 11, 2008 from http://www.windley.com/archives/2006/12/introducing_usercentric_identity.shtml

Harrison, D. A., Mykytyn, J. P. P., & Riemenschneider, C. K. (1997). Executive Decisions about Adoption of Information Technology in Small Business: Theory and Empirical Tests. *Information Systems Research, 8*(2), 171-196.

Hauser, H.-E. (2000). *SMEs in Germany – Facts and figures.* Bonn, Germany: Institut für Mittelstandsforschung.

Haux, R. (2006). Health information systems - past, present, future. *International Journal of Medical Informatics, 75*(3), 268-281.

Hawking, P., Stein, A., & Foster, S. (2004). Revisiting ERP systems: Benefit Realisation. *Paper presented at the Proceedings of the 37th Hawaii International Conference on System Sciences,* Hawaii.

Hawksworth, M. (2007). *Six steps to ERP implementation.* IFS White Paper, IFS.

Hayes, D. C., Hunton, J. E., & Reck, J. L. (2001). Market Reactions to ERP Implementation Announcements. Journal *of Information Systems, 15*(1), 3-18.

Hayman, L. (2000). ERP in the Internet economy. *Information System Frontiers, 2,* 137-139.

He, H. (2003). *What Is Service-Oriented Architecture.* www.xml.org Retrieved 14.06.2007, 2007, from http://www.xml.com/lpt/a/1292.

Heckmann, D. (2005) *Ubiquitous User Modeling PhD thesis,* Department of Computer Science, Saarland University, Germany.

Hedman, J., & Borell, A. (2002). The impact of Enterprise Resource Planning Systems on Organizational Effectiveness: An Artifact Evaluation. In F. F.-H. Nah (Ed.), *Enterprise Resource Planning Solutions & Management* (p. 125-142). Hershey, London: IRM Press.

Hedman, J., & Borell, A. (2002). *The impact of Enterprise Resource Planning Systems on Organizational Effectiveness: An Artifact Evaluation.* In F. F.-H. Nah (Ed.), *Enterprise Resource Planning Solutions & Management* (p. 125-142). Hershey, London: IRM Press.

Heikkilä, J. (2002). From supply to demand chain management: Efficiency and customer satisfaction. *Journal of Operations Management, 20,* 747-767.

Heinemann, F., & Rau, C. (2003). *SAP Web Aplication Server.* Bonn: Galileo Press.

Henbury, C. (1996). *Agile Enterprise/Next Generation Manufacturing Enterprise.* http://ourworld.compuserve.com/homepages/chesire_henbury/agility.htm

Henderson, J. C., & Venkatraman, H. (1999). Strategic alignment: Leveraging information technology for transforming organizations. *IBM Systems Journal, 38(2),* 472 -484.

Hendricks, K. B., Singhal, V. R., & Stratman, J. K. (2007). The impact of enterprise systems on corporate performance: A study of ERP, SCM, and CRM system implementations. *Journal of Operations Management, 25*(1), 65-82.

Herzog, T. (2006). *A Comparison of Open Source ERP Systems.* Master thesis, Vienna University of Economics and Business Administration, Vienna, Austria.

Higgins. (2007). Project Web site. October 22, 2007 Retrieved online on April 21, 2008 from http://www.eclipse.org/higgins/index.php

Hillegersberg, J. V., & Kumar, K. (2000). ERP experience and evolution. *Communications of the ACM, 43*(4), 23-26.

Hilson, G. (2001). Human factor plays big role in IT failures. *Computing Canada, 27*(6).

Hitt, L. M., & Brynjolfsson, E. (1996). Productivity, business profitability, and consumer surplus: Three different measures of information technology value. *MIS Quarterly* 20(2), 121-142.

Hitt, L. M., Wu, D. J., & Xiaoge, Z. (2002). Investment in Enterprise Resource Planning: Business Impact and Productivity Measures. *Journal of Management Information Systems, 19*(1), 71-98.

Hofstede, G. H. (1991). *Cultures and organizations: Software of the mind.* London, UK: McGraw-Hill.

Holland, C., & Light, B. (1999). A critical success factors model for ERP implementation. *IEEE software, May/June,* 30-36.

Holland, C., & Light, B. (2001) A Stage maturity model for enterprise resource planning use. *Databse for Advances in Information Systems, 35*(2), 34-45.

Hong, K.-K., & Kim, Y.-G. (2001). The Critical Success Factors For ERP Implementation: An Organizational Fit Perspective. *Information and Management, 40*(1), 25-40.

Hopper, M. D. (1990). Ratting SABRE – New Ways to Compete on Information. *Harvard Business Review, 68(3),* 118-126.

Horvitz, E., Breese, J., Heckerman, D., Hovel, D., & Rommelse, K. (1998). The Lumiere Project: Bayesian User Modeling for Inferring the Goals and Needs of Software Users. *Proceedings of the Fourteenth Conference on Uncertainty in Artificial Intelligence,* pp. 256-265.

Huang, S.-M., Chang, I.-C., Li, S.-H., & Lin, M.-T. (2004). Assessing risk in ERP projects: identify and prioritize the factors. *Industrial Management & Data Systems, 104*(8/9), 681-688.

Hunter, D. R., & Shine, S. (2001). Customer Relationship Management- A Blueprint for Government. *White Paper, Australia, Accenture.*

Hunter, M. G., & Lippert, S. K. (2007). *Critical Success Factors of ERP Implementation.* Paper presented at the Information Resources Management Conference, Vancouver, BC, Canada.

Hunton, J. E., Lippincott, B., & Reck, J. L. (2003). Enterprise resource planning systems: comparing firm performance of adopters and nonadopters. *International Journal of Enterprise Information Systems, 4*(2003), 165-184.

Iacovou, C. L., Benbasat, I. et al. (1995). Electronic data interchange and small organizations, adoption and impact of technology. *MIS Quarterly, 19*(4), 465-85.

IBM Press (2). (2007). Technology Leaders Join OpenID Foundation to Promote Open Identity Management on the Web (008-02-07) from http://www-03.ibm.com/press/us/en/pressrelease/23461.wss

IBM Press release. (2006). Open Source Initiative to Give People More Control Over Their Personal Online Information: IBM, Novell, and Parity Communications to Drive New Generation of Security Software Based on Framework., ARMONK, NY - 27 Feb 2006:

IBM. (2004). The Consumer Driven Supply Chain. *IBM Retail and Consumer Products Industry Solutions.*

IFEAD (Institute for Enterprise Architecture Developments) (2007). *EA & Services Oriented Enterprise (SOE) / Service Oriented Architecture (SOA) and Service Oriented Computing (SOC) IFEAD.* http://www.enterprise-architecture.info/EA_Services-Oriented-Enterprise.htm

IFIP – IFAC Task Force on Architectures for Enterprise Integration. (1999). *GERAM: Generalized Enterprise Reference Architecture and Methodology, 31*

Ikavalko, H., & Aaltonen, P. (2001). Middle Managers' Role in Strategy Implementation – Middle Managers View. *In the proceedings of 17th EGOS Colloquium,* Lyon France.

Institute für Mittelstandsforschung (2008). KMU Definition des IfM Bonn. Retrieved May 12, 2008, from http://www.ifm-bonn.org/index.php?id=89.

Internet Engineering Task Force (IETF). (1997). Request for comment (RFC) 2251, the lightweight directory access protocol, v3. Retrieved January 7, 2007 from http://www.ietf.org/rfc/rfc2251.txt

Internet Engineering Task Force (IETF). (1999). Request for comment (RFC) 2459, Internet x.509 public key infrastructure certificate and CRL profile. Retrieved January 7, 2007, from http://www.ietf.org/rfc/rfc2459.txt

ISO/IEC & ITU-T: Information technology – Open Distributed Processing – Part 1 – Overview – ISO/IEC 10746-1 | ITU-T Recommendation X.901

IT Governance Institute (ITGI) (2005). *Control objectives for IT and related Technologies (COBIT) 4.0.* Accessed from www.itgi.org.

Ittner, C. D., & Larcker, D. F. (2003). Coming Up Short on Nonfinancial Performance Measurement. *Harvard Business Review, 81*(11), 88-95.

Ives, B., Learmonth, G. P. (1984). The Information System as a Competitive Weapon. *Communications of the ACM, 27*(12), 1193-1201.

Jacobs, F. R., & Weston, F. C. T., Jr. (2007). Enterprise resource planning (ERP) - A brief history. *Journal of Operations Management, 25*(2), 357-363.

James, D., & Wolf, M. L. (2000). A Second Wind for ERP. *McKinsey Quarterly, Issue 2,* 100-107.

Jarra, Y. F., Al-Mudimigh, A., & Zairi, M. (2000). ERP Implementation Critical Success Factors - The Role and Impact of Business Process Management. *IEEE & ICMIT, 02/2000,* 122-127.

Jarrar, Y. F., Al-Mudimigh, A., & Zairi, M. (2000). ERP implementation critical success factors-the role and impact of business process management. *Proceedings of the 2000 IEEE International Conference on Management of Innovation and Technology, 1,* 122 – 127.

Jarvenpaa, S. P., Ives, B. (1990). Information technology and corporate strategy: a view from the top. *Information Systems Research, 1(4),* 352–376.

Javelin. (2007). *2007 Identity Fraud Survey Report: Identity Fraud Is Dropping, Continued Vigilance Necessary,* February 2007. Retrieved online on April 20, 2008 from http://www.javelinstrategy.com

Jayachandran, S., Sharma, S., Kaufman, P., & Raman, P. (2005). The Role of Relational Information Processes and Technology Use in Customer Relationship Management. *Journal of Marketing, 69,* 117-192.

Jeng, J-J., Chang, H., & Bhaskaran, K. (2005). On Architecting Business Performance Management Grid for Adaptive Enterprises. *Proceedings of the 2005 Symposium on Applications and the Internet (SAINT' 2005),* IEEE.

Jensen, R., & Johnson, R. (1999) The enterprise resource planning system as a strategic solution. *Information Strategy, 15*(4), 28-33.

Jha, B., & Bokad, P. (2003).Managing Multiplicity of Citizens' identity - A Taluka level case study. *International Conference on E-Governance, 1*(5), 24-31

Johnson, G., Scholes, K. (2005). Exploring Corporate Strategy– Text and Cases, 7th edition. London, UK: Prentice Hall.

Johnson, J. (2004). Making CRM Technology Work. *British Journal of Administrative Management, 39,* 22-23.

Johnson, R. A. (2000). The Ups and Downs of Object-Oriented Systems Development. *Communications of the ACM.*

Jones, M. C., & Young, R. (2006). ERP Usage in Practice. *Information Resources Management Journal, 19*(1), 23-42.

Jones, M. C., & Young, R. (2006). ERP Usage in Practice. *Information Resources Management Journal, 19*(1), 23-42.

Jonkers, H., Lankhorst, M., Van Buuren, R., Hoppenbrouwers, S., Bonsangue, M., & Van der Torre, L. (2004). Concepts for Modeling Enterprise Architectures. *International Journal of Cooperative Information Systems, 13*(3), 257-287.

Jøsang, A., AlZomai, M., & Suriadi, S. (2007). *Usability and Privacy in Identity Management Architectures.* (AISW2007), Ballarat, Australia, 2007.

Jossi, F. (2005). ERP on the Rise. Some hospitals see the advantages in a single system. Healthcare Informatics, 2005, www.healthcare-informatics.com/issues/2005/06_05/jossi.htm 79-80, accessed on March 21st 2006.

Jutras, C. (2007) *The Role of ERP in Globalization* available at http://www.aberdeen.com/summary/report/benchmark/RA_ERPRoleinGlobalization_CJ_3906.asp

Kakabadse, N., Kouzmin, A., & Kakabadse, A. (2001). From Tacit Knowledge to Knowledge Management: Leveraging Invisible Assets. *Knowledge and Process Management, 8*(3), 137-154.

Kalling, T. (2003) ERP systems and the strategic management processes that lead to competitive advantage. *Information Resources Management Journal, 16*(4), 46-67.

Kannabiran, G. Xavier, M. J., & Anantharaaj, A. (2005). Enabling E-Governance Through Citizen Relationship Management-Concept, Model And Applications. *Journal of Services Research, 4*(2) (October 2004 - March 2005).

Kaplan, R., & Norton, D. P. (1996) Using the balance score-card as a strategic management system. *Harvard Business Review*, Jan/Feb, 75-85.

Karch, S., Heilig, L. et al., (2005). *SAP NetWeaver.* Bonn: Galileo Press.

Karim, J., Somers, T. M., & Bhattacherjee, A. (2007). The impact of ERP implementation on business process outcomes: A factor-based study. *Journal of Management Information Systems, 24*(1),101–134.

Kauzlarich, V. (2003). Organizational Change Management is Key to Program's Success. *Enterprise Modernization Issue, fall 2003, 7(2).*

Kearns, G.S., & Lederer, A.L, (2000). The effect of strategic alignment on the use of IS-based

Keen, P. G. W. (1991). *Shaping the Future: Business Design through Information Technology.* Boston: Harvard Business School Press, 1991.

Kennedy, A. (2006). Electronic Customer Relationship Management (eCRM): Opportunities and Challenges in a Digital World. *Irish Marketing Review, 18*(1/2), 58-68.

Ketbi, O. A., Azaizeh, A., Carrico, W., Cook, R., & Cooke, D. (2002). 2002 Industry Studies: Advanced Manufacturing. Report Number: A105624, Industrial Coll of the Armed Forces, Washington, D.C.

Khalid, S. (2001). *Manufacturing Resource Planning with introduction to ERP, SCM and CRM.* Tata McGraw Hill.

Khalil, M. A., Lanvin, B. D., & Chaudhry, V. (2002). The E-government Handbook for Developing countries. *infoDev Program The World Bank Group.*

Kim, E., & Lee, J. (1986). An Exploratory Contingency Model Of User Participation And MIS Use. *Information & Management, 11*(2), 87-97.

Kim, H., & Boldyreff, C. (2005). Open Source ERP for SME. *Third International Conference on Manufacturing Research*, Cranfield, U.K.

Kim, H.-W. (2004). A Process Model for Successful CRM System Development. *Software IEEE, 21*(4), 22-28.

King, W. R. (1978). Strategic Planning for Management Information Systems. *MIS Quarterly, 2(1)*, 27-37.

King, W. R., & Teo, T. S. H. (2000). Assessing the impact of proactive versus reactive modes of strategic information systems planning. *Omega – The International Journal of Management Science, 28*, 667 – 679.

Kirkpatrick, D. (1998). The E-Ware war: Competition comes to enterprise software. *Fortune, 138*(11), 103-112.

Kirwan, K., Sawyer, D., & Sparrow, D. (2003). Transforming Government Through Enterprise Modernization. *Enterprise Modernization Issue, Fall 2003 7(2).*

Klaus, H., Rosemann, M., & Gable, G. G. (2000). What is ERP? *Information Systems Frontiers, 2*(3), 141-162.

Koch, C. (n/a). ABC: An Introduction to ERP Getting started with Enterprise Resource Planning (ERP). http://www.cio.com/article/40323/ABC_An_Introduction_to_ERP

Koch, C. (2002). The ABCs of ERP. *CIO Magazine*, March 7, 2002.

Koch, C. (2005). A New Blueprint for the Enterprise, CIO Magazine, 18(10), 1-7.

Koh, S. C. L., & Saad, S. M. (2006). Managing uncertainty in ERP-controlled manufacturing environments in SMEs. *International Journal of Production Economics, 101*(1), 109-127.

Koh, S. C. L., & Simpson, M. (2005). Change and uncertainty in SME manufacturing environments using ERP. *Journal of Manufacturing Technology Management, 16*(6), 629-653.

Koh, S. C. L., & Simpson, M. (2007). Could enterprise resource planning create a competitive advantage for small businesses? *Benchmarking, 14*(1), 59-76.

Kooch, C. (February 01, 2004). *Open-Source ERP Gains Users*; http://www.cio.com/archive/020104/tl_open.html

Koory, J. L., & Medley, D. B. (1987). *Management Information Systems: Planning and Decision Making,* South-Western Publishing Co.

Kos, A. J., Sockel, H. M., & Falk, L. K. (2001, Jan-Mar). Customer relationship management opportunities. *The Ohio CPA Journal,* 55-57.

Kotorov, R. P. (2002). Ubiquitous organization: organizational design for e-CRM Business. *Process Management Journal, 8*(3), 218-232.

Koudal, P., & Lavieri, T. (2003). Profits in the Balance: When costs and customer and supplier relationships are balanced evenly, profitability increases. *Optimize, 22*(June), 81.

Krafzig, D., Blanke, K. et al., (2004). *Enterprise SOA - Service-Oriented Architecture Best Practise.* Upper Saddle River, NJ: Prentice Hall.

Krajewski, L. J., & Ritzman, P. (2000). *Operations Management.* Fifth Edition, India: Pearson Education.

Krebs, B. (2007). *Microsoft to Support OpenID.* Retrieved on 2008-03-01 from http://blog.washingtonpost.com/securityfix/2007/02/microsoft_to_support_openid.html

Kreizman, G., & Wagner, R. (2007). *Personal Identity Frameworks.* Gartner Research Report

Krief, F. (2004). Self-aware management of IP networks with QoS guarantees. *-International Journal of Network Management, 14* (July 2004), 351-364.

Krippendorf, K. (1980). *Content Analysis,* 5. Beverly Hills: Sage Publication.

Kubil Rolf and Nadhan E. G. (2005). Banking on a Service-Oriented Architecture. EDS

Kulak, D., & Guiney, E. (2003). Use *Cases: Requirements in Context.* Second Edition. Harlow: Addison Wesley.

Kumar, K., & Van Hillegersberg, J. (2000). ERP Experiences and Evolution. *Communications of the ACM, 43*(4), 23-26.

Lai, V. S. (1994). A Survey Of Rural Small Business Computer Use: Success Factors And Decision Support. *Information & Management, 26*(6), 297-304.

Laudon, K. C., & Laudon, J. P. (2002). *Managing Information Systems: Managing the digital firm,* 7th Edition, New Delhi: Prentice Hall of India.

Laudon, K. C., & Laudon, J. P. (1998). *Management Information Systems: New Approaches to Organization & Technology (5th ed.)* Upper Saddle River, NJ: Prentice Hall.

Laudon, K. C., & Laudon, J. P. (2006). *Management information systems: managing the digital firm* (9th ed.). Upper Saddle River, NJ: Pearson/Prentice Hall.

Laughlin, S. P. (1999) An ERP game plan. *Journal of Business Strategy, 20*(1), 32-37.

Laukkanen, S., Sarpola, S. et al. (2007). Enterprise size matters: objectives and constraints of ERP adoption. *Journal of Enterprise Information Management, 20*(3), 319-334.

Laukkanen, S., Sarpola, S., & Hallikainen, P. (2007). Enterprise size matters: objectives and constraints of ERP adoption. *Journal of Enterprise Information Management, 20*(3), 319–334.

Leahy, T. (2004). Best-of-Breed Software, Business Finance, July 2004. Downloaded from http://www.businessfinancemag.com/magazine/archives/article.html?articleID=14251

LeClaire, J. (December 30, 2006). *Open Source, BI and ERP: The Perfect Match?*; http://www.linuxinsider.com/story/LjdZlB0x0j04cM/Open-Source-BI-and-ERP-The-Perfect-Match.xhtml

Lederer, A. L., & Mendelow, A. L, (1988). Convincing top management of the strategic potential of information systems. *MIS Quarterly, 12(4),* 525-534.

Lee, J. C., & Myers, M. D. (2004). Dominant actors, political agendas, and strategic shifts over time: a critical ethonography of an enterprise systems implementation. *Journal of Strategic Information Systems, 13*(2004), 355-374.

Lee, Z., & Lee, J. (2000). An ERP implementation case study from a knowledge transfer perspective. *Journal of Information Technology, 15*, 281-288.

Leeuw, A., & Volberda, H. W. (1996). On the Concept of Flexibility: A Dual Control Perspective. Omega. *International Journal of Management Science, 24*(2), 121-139.

Leon, A. (2002). *ERP Demystified.* New Delhi: Tata McGraw Hill.

Levine, H. G., & Rossmoore, D. (1995). Politics and the Function of Power in a Case Study of IT Implementation. *Journal of Management Information Systems, 11*(3), 115-133.

Levy, M., & Powell, P. (1998). SME flexibility and the role of information systems. *Small Business Economics, 11*(2), 183-96.

Liang, H., Saraf, N., Hu, Q., & Xue, Y. (2007). Assimilation of enterprise systems: The effect of institutional pressures and the mediating role of top management, *MIS Quarterly*, 31(1), 59-87.

Liang, L. Y., & Miranda, R. (2001). Dashboards and scorecards: executive information systems for the public sector. *Government Finance Review, 17*(6), 14-19.

Liang, S., & Lien, C. (2007). Selecting the optimal ERP software by combining the ISO 9126 standard and fuzzy AHP approach. *Contemporary Management Research, 3*(1), 23-44.

Liberty Press. (2007). Liberty Alliance Announces Winners of the 2007 IDDY Award eBIZ.mobility, Tuesday, September 25, 2007, SAN FRANCISCO, Retrieved online on April 20, 2008 from http://www.projectliberty. org/news_events/press_releases/liberty_alliance_announces_winners_of_the_2007_iddy_award

Liebowitz, J. (2005). Linking social network analysis with the analytic hierarchy process for knowledge mapping in organizations. *Journal of Knowledge Management, 9*(1) 76-86.

Light, B., & Holland, C. P. (2001). ERP and best of breed: A comparative analysis. *Business Process Management Journal, 7*(3), 216-224.

Lin, F.-R., Yang, M.-C., & Pai, Y.-H. (2002). A generic structure for business process modeling. *Business Process Management Journal, 8*(1), 19-41.

Lin, J. Y. C., & Orlowska, M. E. (2005). Partial completion of activity in business process specification. *Proceedings of IRMA 2005*, San Diego, CA, USA, pp. 186-189.

Linden, G., Smith, B., & York, J. (2003). Amazon.com recommendations: Item-to-item collaborative filtering. *Internet Computing, IEEE, 7*(1), 76-80.

Loukis, E., & Sapounas I. (2005). The Impact of Information Systems Investment and Management on Business Performance in Greece. In the Proceedings of the *13th European Conference on Information Systems 2005 (ECIS 2005)*, May 26-28, 2005, Regensburg, Germany.

Lucas Jr., H. C., Walton, E. J., & Ginsberg, M. J. (1988). Implementing Packaged Software. *MIS Quarterly*(December 1988), 537-549.

Lucas, H. C., Jr., Walton, E. J., & Ginsberg, M. J. (1988). Implementing Packaged Software. *MIS Quarterly*(December 1988), 537-549.

Luftman, J. (2000). Assessing Business-IT Alignment Maturity. *Communications of the Association for Information Systems, 4(14)*, 1-51.

Luftman, J. (2005). Key Issues for IT Executives 204. *MIS Quarterly Executive, 4(2)*, 269-285.

Luftman, J. N. (1996). *Competing in the information age: strategic alignment in practice.* New York, USA: Oxford University Press.

Luftman, J. N., Papp, R., & Brier, T. (1999). Enablers and Inhibitors of Business-IT Alignment. *Communications of the Association for Information Systems, 11(3)*, 1-33.

Luftman, J., & Brier, T, (1999). Achieving and sustaining business-IT alignment. *California Management Review, 42*(1), 109.

Luftman, J., Kempaiah, R., & Nash, E. (2006). Key issues for IT executives 2005. *MIS Quarterly Executive, 5*(2), 81-99.

Luftman, J., McLean, E. R. (2004). Key Issues for IT Executives. *MIS Quarterly Executive, 3(2)*, 89-104.

Luo, W., & Strong, D. M.(2004). A Framework for evaluating ERP implementation choices. *IEEE Transactions on Engineering Management, 51*(3), 3222-333.

Mabert, A. M., Soni, A., & Venkataraman, M. A. (2000). Enterprise Resource Planning Survey of US Manufacturing Firms. *Production and Inventory Management Journal, 41*(2), 52-58.

Mabert, M. A. (2007). The early road to material requirements planning. *Journal of Operations Management, 25*(2), 346-356.

Mabert, V. A., Soni, A. & Venkataramanan, M. A. (2003). Enterprise Resource Planning: Managing the Implementation Process. *European Journal of Operational Research, 146*(2), 302-314.

Mabert, V. A., Soni, A. et al. (2000). Enterprise Resource Planning Survey Of U.S. Manufacturing Firms. *Production and Inventory Management Journal, 41*(2), 52-58.

Mabert, V. A., Soni, A. et al. (2003). The impact of organization size on enterprise resource planning (ERP) implementations in the US manufacturing sector. *Omega, 31*, 235-246.

Mabert, V. A., Soni, A. K., & Venkataramanan, M. A. (2000). Enterprise resource planning survey of U.S. manufacturing firms. *Production and Inventory Management Journal, 41*(2), 52-58.

Mabert, V. A., Soni, A. K., & Venkataramanan, M. A. (2001). Enterprise resource planning: Common myths versus evolving reality. *Business Horizons, 44*(3), 69-76.

Mabert, V. A., Soni, A. K., & Venkataramanan, M. A. (2001). Enterprise resource planning: Measuring value. *Production and Inventory Management Journal, 42*(3/4), 46-51.

Mabert, V. A., Soni, A. K., & Venkataramanan, M. A. (2003). The impact of organization size on enterprise resource planning (ERP) implementations in the U.S. manufacturing sector. *Omega – The International Journal of Management Science, 31*(3), 235-246.

Mabert, V. A., Soni, A., & venkataramanan, M. A. (2001). Enterprise resource planning: Common myths versus evolving reality. *Business Horizons, 44*(3), 69-76.

MacDonald, E. (1999, Nov. 2). W. L. Gore Alleges PeopleSoft, Deloitte Botched a Costly Software Installation. *The Wall Street Journal,* 14.

MacLeod, M. (2002). ERP or best of breed? *Fulfulment & e-Logistics Magazine,* June 2002.

Malcolm, A. (2002). Fonterra Rents its Accounting Application. *Computerworld IDG Communication Ltd., 11 July, 2002,* Web page: http://www.idg.net.nz/webhome.nsf/UNID/8433B6BCB6BE15FECC256BF1007BF560

Mangan, P., & Sadiq, S. (2002). On Building Workflow Models for Flexible Processes. *Australian Computer Science Communications, Proceedings of the Thirteenth Australasian Conference on Database Technologies - 5, 24*(2)

Marketwire (2007). Thinking Global? *Don't Lose Sight of Profitable Growth* available http://www.marketwire.com/mw/release_html_b1?release_id=224493

Markus, L., Petrie, D., & Axline, S., (2001). Bucking The Trends, What the Future May Hold For ERP Packages, in Shanks, Seddon and Willcocks (Eds.) *Enterprise Systems: ERP, Implementation and Effectiveness,* Cambridge University Press.

Markus, M. L. (1999). Keynote address: Conceptual challenges in contemporary IS research. *Proceedings of the Australasian Conference on Information Systems (ACIS),* New Zeland, pp.1-5.

Markus, M. L. (2004). Technochange Management: Using IT to drive organizational change. *Journal of Information Technology, 20*(1), 4-20.

Markus, M. L., & Tanis, C. (1999). The enterprise systems experience- from adoption to success, In: Zmud, R.W., (Ed.), *Framing the Domains of IT Research: Glimpsing the Future Through the Past, Piinaflex Educational Resources,* Cincinnati, OH.

Markus, M. L., & Tanis, C. (2000). Multisite ERP implementations. *Communications of the ACM, 43*(4), 42-26.

Markus, M. L., & Tanis, C. (2000). The Enterprise Experience - From Adoption to Success. In R. W. Zmud (Ed.), *Framing the Domains of IT Research: Projecting the Future through the Past.* Cincinnati, OH: Pinnaflex Educational Resources, Inc.

Markus, M. L., & Tanis, C. (2000). The Enterprise Experience - From Adoption to Success. In R. W. Zmud (Ed.), *Framing the Domains of IT Research: Projecting the Future Through the Past.* Cincinnati, OH: Pinnaflex Educational Resources, Inc.

Markus, M. L., & Tanis, C. (2000). The enterprise system experience - From adoption to success. In: M. F. Price (Ed.), *Framing the domains of IT management* (pp. 173-207). Cincinnati, OH: Pinnaflex.

Markus, M. L., Axline, S., Petrie, D., & Tanis, C. (2000). Learning from adopters' experiences with ERP: problems encountered and success achieved. *Journal of Information Technology, 15*(4), 245-265.

Markus, M. L., Axline, S., Petrie, D., & Tanis, C. (2000). Learning from adopters' experiences with ERP: Problems encountered and success achieved. *Journal of Information Technology, 15,* 245-265.

Markus, M., & Tanis, C. (2000). The Enterprise Systems Experience - From Adoption to Success. In R. W. Zmud (Ed.), *In Framing the Domains of IT Research Glimpsing the Future Through the Past* (pp. 173-207). Cincinnati: Pinnaflex Educational Resources, Cincinnati, USA.

Marsh S. (2003). Identity and Authentication in the E-Economy. *Information Security, Elsevier Science Press, 7.3*(2003), 12-19.

Marteinek, P., & Szikora, B. (2005). Integrated enterprise resource planning system. *In 28th International Seminar on Electronics Technology* (pp. 417-421). IEEE.

Martin, R., Mauterer, H. et al., (2002). Systematisierung des Nutzens von ERP-Systemen in der Fertigungsindustrie. *Wirtschaftsinformatik, 44*(2), 109-116.

Martinez, J., Martinez, B., & Arenas, A. (1998). CLASITEX: A tool for knowledge discovery from texts. Principles of Data Mining and Knowledge Discovery. *Proceedings of the 2nd European Symposium*, pp. 459-467.

Mas-Colell, A. & Whinston, M. D. (1995). *Microeconomic Theory*. New York, Oxford University Press.

Masini, A., & Van Wasshenove, L. N. (2008). ERP Competence-Building Mechanisms: An Exploratory Investigation of Configurations of ERP Adopters in the European and US Manufacturing Sectors. *Manufacturing & Service Operations Management*, in press.

Mata, F. J., Fuerst, W. L., & Barney, J. B. (1995). Information Technology and Sustained Competitive Advantage: A Resource-Based Analysis. *MIS Quarterly, 19(4)*, 487-505.

McAdam, R., & Reid, R. (2001). SME and large Organization Perception of Knowledge Management: Comparison and Contrast. *Journal of Knowledge Management, 5*(3), 231-241.

McAfee, A. (2002). The impact of enterprise technology adoption on operational performance: an empirical investigation. *Production and Operations Management, 11*(1), 33-53.

McAfee, A. (2003). When too much IT knowledge is a dangerous thing. *Sloan Management Review, 44*(2), 83-89.

McFarlan, F. W. (1984, May-June). Information Technology Changes the Way you Compete. *Harvard Business Review, 62(3)*, 98-103.

McLeod Jr., R. (1990). *Management Information Systems*. New York: McMillan, 4th ed.

McLeod, R., & Schell, G. (2002). *Management Information Systems* (8th ed.). Upper Saddle River, NJ: Prentice Hall.

McNurlin, B. C., & Sprague, R. H. (2002). *Information Systems in Practice* (5th ed.). Upper Saddle River, NJ: Prentice Hall.

Mecham, M. (1998). Get started very early. *Aviation Week and Space Technology, 149*(21), 17.

Melone, S. C. (1985). Computerising small business information systems. *Journal of small business management* April: 10-16.

Melville, N., Kraemer, K., & Gurbaxani, V. (2004). Information technology and organizational performance: An integrative model of IT business value. *MIS Quarterly, 28(2)*, 283-322.

Mentzas, G., Apostolou, D., Young, R., & Abecker, A. (2001). Knowledge Networking: a Holistic Solution for Leveraging Corporate Knowledge. *Journal of Knowledge Management, 5*(1), 94-106.

Merode, G. G. van, Groothuis, S. van, & Hasman, A. (2004). Enterprise Resource Planning for Hospitals. *International Journal of Medical Informatics, 73*, 6, 493-501.

Microsoft Web site. (2008). Microsoft Cardspace. Retrieved on April 21, 2008 from http://www.microsoft.com/net/cardspace.aspx

Microsoft. (2003). Encarta dictionary, Microsoft Press.

Microsoft. Enterprise Resource Planning- Managing the Lifecycle of Government Business. lead feature from the *Tourism and Travel edition of Microsoft in Government, Worldwide.*

Miller, D. (2003). An Asymmetry-Based View of Advantage: Towards and Attainable Sustainability. *Strategic Management Journal, 24(10)*, 961-976.

Miller, J. (2008).*Yadis Specification. Version 1.0.* 18 March 2006. Retrieved online in April 2, 2008 from yadis.org/papers/yadis-v1.0.pdf,

Min, S., & Mentzer, J.T. (2000). The role of marketing in supply chain management. *International Journal of Physical Distribution & Logistics, 30*(9), 765-787.

Mintzberg, H. (1992). Five Ps for Strategy. In the Strategy Process, H Mintberg and JB Quinn (eds.). Englewood Cliffs, NJ: Prentice –Hall

Misra, D.C., Hariharan, R., & Khaneja, M. (2003, March). E-Knowledge Management Framework For Government Organizations" *Information Systems Management, 20(2)*, 38 - 48

Mitchell, R. K., Agle, B. R., & Wood, D. J. (1997). Toward a Theory of Stakeholder Identifiction and Salience: Defining the Principle of who and what really counts. *Academy of Management Review, 22*(4), 853-886.

Mithas, S., Krishan, M. S., & Fornell, C. (2005). Why Do Customer Relationship Management Applications Affect Customer Satisfaction? *Journal of Marketing, 69*(October), 201-209.

Mockler, R., & Dologite, D. (2002). Strategically-Focused Enterprise Knowledge Management. In D. White (Ed.), *Knowledge Mapping & Management* (pp. 14-22). Hershey: IRM Press.

Montazemi, A. R. (1988). Factors Affecting Information Satisfaction In The Context Of The Small Business Environment. *MIS Quarterly, 12*(2), 238-256.

Moon, Y. B. (2007). Enterprise resource planning (ERP): A review of the literature. *International Journal of Management and Enterprise Development, 4*(3), 235-264.

Mooney, G. J., Gurbaxani, V., & Kraemer, L. K. (1996). A Process Oriented Framework for Assessing the Business Value of Information Technology. *The DATA BASE for Advances in Information Systems, 27*(2), 68-81.

Morabito, V., Pace, S., & Previtali, P. (2005). ERP marketing and Italian SMEs. *European Management Journal, 23*(5), 590-598.

Morphy, E. (2003). CEO Survey: Fast-Track Firms Chasing Customers. *CRMDaily.com*, January.

Moynihan, G. P. (1993). Development of an executive information system for Marshall Space Flight Center. In B.Y. Kang & J.U. Choi (Eds.) *Proceedings of the Second International Conference of the Decision Sciences Institute, Vol. 2, Managing the Global Economy: A Decision Sciences Perspective* (pp. 606-608), Seoul, Korea: Sungrim Press.

Moynihan, G. P. (1993). An executive information system: Planning for post-implementation at NASA. *Journal of Systems Management, 44*(7), 8-31.

Mullin, R. (2000). *ERP-2-ERP:* "Forging a Proprietary Link" (Brief Article), *Chemical Week*, June 28, 2000.

Muscatello, J. R., & Parente, D. H. (2006). Enterprise Resource Planning (ERP): A Postimplementation Cross-Case Analysis. *Information Resources Management Journal*, 19(3), 61-80.

Muscatello, J. R., & Parente, D. H. (2006). Enterprise Resource Planning (ERP): A Postimplementation Cross-Case Analysis. *Information Resources Management Journal*, 19(3), 61-80.

Muscatello, J. R., Small, M. H., & Chen, I. J. (2003). Implementing enterprise resource planning (ERP) systems in small and midsize manufacturing firms. *International Journal of Operations and Production Management, 23*(8), 850-871.

mySAP Business Suite: Service Provisioning, Enterprise Service-Oriented Architecture, mySAP Business Suite 2004 and 2005, Version 2.0. (2006, December). *SAP Developer Network (SDN)*. Retrieved May 2006 from <https://www.sdn.sap.com/irj/sdn/go/portal/prtroot/docs/webcontent/uuid/c0cd8360-3b74-2910-0fae-dc-ceed7328e7>

N. N. (2007). Enterprise resource planning. Retrieved 8.06.2007, 2007, from http://en.wikipedia.org/wiki/Enterprise_resource_planning.

Nah, F. F.-H., Lau, J. L.-S., & Kuang, J. (2001). Critical Factors for Successful Implementation of Enterprise Systems. *Business Process Management, 7*(3), 285-296.

Naiburg, E. J., & Maksimchuk, R. A. (2003). UML for Database Design. *Online Information Review, 27*(1), 66-67.

Narasimhan, S. L., McLeavy, D. W., & Billington, P. J. (1997). *Production Planning & inventory control*. New Delhi: Prentice Hall of India.

Natarajan, S. (2006, April 24). *Model a Business Process in ARIS for SAP NetWeaver and Import BPEL in Exchange Infrastructure*. Retrieved May 25, 2007 from <https://www.sdn.sap.com/irj/sdn/go/portal/prtroot/docs/library/uuid/3c58e011-0b01-0010-1e88-b42e01bb961a>

Negash, S., & Gray, P. (2003). Business intelligence. In *9th American Conference on Information Systems* (pp. 3190-3199).

Negroponte, N. (1996). *Being digital*. Random House Inc., New York, NY, USA.

Nelson, R.R. (2007). IT Project Management: Infamous Failures, Classic Mistakes and Best Practices. *MIS Quarterly Executive*, 6(2), 67-78.

Newell, S., Huang, J. C., Galliers, R. D., & Pan, S. L. (2003). Implementing enterprise resource planning and knowledge management systems in tandem: fostering efficiency and innovation complementarity. *Information and Organization, 13*, 25-52.

Nicholson, W. (2004). *Microeconomic Theory: Basic Principles and Extensions - 9th edition*. USA: South-Western College Publications.

Nickell, G. S., & Seado, P. C. (1986). The Impact Of Attitudes And Experience On Small Business. *American Journal of Small Business, 10*(1), 37-48.

Nicolaou, A. I. (2004). Quality of postimplementation review for enterprise resource planning systems. *International Journal of Accounting Information Systems, 5*(2004), 25-49.

Nicolescu, V., Funk, B. et al., (2006). *SAP Exchange Infrastructure for Developers.* Bonn: Galileo Press.

Noel, J. (2005). BPM and SOA: Better Together. *IBM Corporation.*

Nolan and Norton Institute. (2000). *SAP Benchmarking Report 2000.* Melbourne.

Noran, O.S. (2001). Business Modeling: UML vs IDEF. http://www.cit.gu.edu.au/~noran [accessed January 2008].

Norris, G., Hurley, J. R., Hartley, K. M., Dunleavy, J. R., & Balls, J. D. (2000*). E-Business and ERP, Transforming the Enterprise.* Canada: John Wiley & Sons, Inc.

Norris, G., Wright, I., Hurley, J., Dunleavy, J., & Gibson, A. (1998). *SAP: An Executive's Comprehensive Guide.* John Wiley & Sons, Inc., New York, NY.

Nowlan, S., (2001). Citizen Relationship Management E-CRM in the Public Sector,USA. Pricewaterhouse-Coopers.

O'Gorman, B. (2004). The road to ERP: Has industry learned or revolved back to the start? In F. Adams & D. Sammon (Eds.), *The enterprise resource planning decade: Lessons learned and issues for the future* (pp. 22-46). Hershey, PA: Idea Group Publishing.

O'Leary, D. E. (2000). *Enterprise Resource Planning Systems: Systems, Life Cycle, Electronic Commerce and Risk.* UK: Cambridge University Press.

O'riordan, D. (2002. April 10). Business Process Standards for Web Services: The Candidates. *Web Services Architect.* Retrieved From Http://Www.Webservicesarchitect.Com/Content/Articles/Oriordan01.Asp

OASIS (2008). OASIS Committees by Category: SOA, downloaded from http://www.oasis-open.org/committees/tc_cat.php?cat=soa on 2/12/08.

Oliveira, P., & Roth, A.V. (2008). The Influence of Service Orientation on B2B e-Service Capabilities. *FCEE-Catolica, Lisbon Portugal and Clemson University Working Paper.*

Oliver, R. (1999). ERP is dead, long live ERP. *Management Review 88*(10), 12-13.

Olsen, K.A., & Saetre, P. (2007). IT for niche companies: Is an ERP system the solution? *Information Systems Journal, 17*(1), 37-58.

OMB A-130: US Office of Management & Budget (1996). *Memorandum for Heads of Executive Departments and Establishments: Management of Federal Information Resources.*

Oosterhout, van M., Waarts, E, & Hillegersberg, van J. (2006). Change factors requiring agility and implications for IT. *European Journal of Information Systems, 15,* 132-145.

Opdahl, A. L., & Henderson-Sellers, B. (2004). A Template for Defining Enterprise Modeling Constructs. *Journal of Database Management, 15*(2), 39-74.

OpenID doc. (2008). OpenID Board of Directors (2007-06-01). OpenID Foundation. OpenID Foundation. Retrieved on April 19, 2008 from http://openid.net/foundation/

OpenID Foundation. (2008). How do I get an OpenID?. OpenID Foundation. Retrieved on 2008-03-20 from http://openid.net/get/

Ordanini, A. (2006). *Information Technology and Small Businesses: Antecedents and Consequences of Technology Adoption.* Massachusetts: Edward Elgar Publishing.

Organisation for Economic Co-operation and Development (OECD) (2003). *ICT and Economic Growth – Evidence from OECD Countries, Industries and Firms.* Paris, France.

Organisation for Economic Co-operation and Development (OECD) (2004). *The Economic Impact of ICT – Measurement, Evidence and Implications.* Paris, France.

Organization for the Advancement of Structured Information Standards (OASIS). (2006). OASIS service provisioning markup language (SPML) v2 -- DSML v2 profile.

Orlikowski, W. J. (1992). The duality of technology: Rethinking the concept of technology in organizations. *Organization Science, 3*(3), 398-427.

Orlikowski, W. J. (1992). The Duality of Technology: Rethinking the Concept of Technology in Organisations. *Organisation Science, 3*(1), 398-427.

Ort, E.E. (2005). Service-Oriented Architecture and Web Services: Concepts, Technologies, and Tools. *Sun Developers Network.* http://java.sun.com/developer/technicalArticles/WebServices/soa2/SOATerms.html#soaterms

Oswald, G. (2002, May 13). *Optimum Life, SAP's Solution Management Strategy.* SAP INFO. Retrieved June 18, 2007, from <http://www.sap.info/INT/int/index/Category-12613c61affe7a5bc-int/0/ >

Ouédraogo, L-D. (2005). *Policies of United Nations System Organizations Towards the Use of Open Source Software (OSS) in the Secretariats.* Geneva, 43p.

Padmanaban, S. (2005). Justifying ERP as Strategic Business Initiative: A multi-dimensional Analytical Framework. *Paradigm, the Journal of IMT,* 9(1), 1-8.

Palaniswami, R., & Frank, T., (2000). Enhancing manufacturing performance with ERP systems. *Information Systems Management, 17*(3), 43-55.

Palaniswamy, R. & Frank, T. (2000). Enhancing Manufacturing Performance with ERP Systems. *Information Systems Management,* Summer, 43-55.

Palaniswamy, R., & Frank, T. (2000). Enhancing Manufacturing Performance with ERP Systems. *Information Management Journal.*

Palvia, P. C., Palvia, S. C. J., & Whitworth, J. E. (2002). Global information technology: A meta analysis of key issues. *Information & Management, 39,* 403-414.

Pamatatau, R. (2002). The Warehouse outsources Oracle Management. *NZ Infotech Weekly, 24 June, 2002, p. 3.*

Pan, S. L. (2005). Customer Perspective of CRM Systems: A Focus Group Study. *International Journal of Enterprise Information Systems, 1*(1), 65-88.

Pan, S. L., & Lee, J.-N. (2003). Using e-CRM for a unified view of the customer *Communications of the ACM, 46*(4), 95-99.

Pan, S. L., Newell, S. et al. (2001). Knowledge Integration As A Key Problem In An ERP Implementation. *Proceedings of the 22nd International Conference on Information Systems,* New Orleans, Louisiana, Association for Information Systems.

Pang, C. & Eschinger, C. (2006). *Forecast: ERP Software, EMEA, 2005-2010 Update.* Gartner Report.

Pant, S., & Hsu, C. (1995) Strategic Information Systems: A Review. *In the proceedings of the 1995 IRMA conference,* Atlanta, Georgia.

Paré, G., & Sikotte, C. (2001). Information technology sophistication in health care: an instrument validation study among Canadian hospitals. *International Journal of Medical Informatics, 63*(2), 205-223.

Parr, A., & Shanks, G. (2000). A Model of ERP Project Management. *Journal of Information Technology, 15*(4).

Parsons, G. L. (1983). Information Technology: A New Competitive Weapon. *Sloan Management Review, 25(1),* 4-14.

Parvatiyar, A., & Sheth, J. N. (2001). Conceptual Framework of Customer Relationship Management. In Customer Relationship Management-Emerging Concepts, Tools and Publications. Sheth, J.N., Parvatiyar, A. and Shainesh, G., eds. New Delhi, India, Tata/McGraw-Hill, 3-25.

Patrick, R. A. (2005). Celebrating Innovation. *Network Magazine,* issue of November 2005, 26-56.

Payne, A., & Frow, P. (2005). A Strategic Framework for Customer Relationship Management. *Journal of Marketing, 69,* 167-176.

Payne, W. (2002). The time for ERP? *Work Study, 51*(2/3), 91-93.

Pemberton, J. D., Stonehouse, G. H., & Barber, C. E. (2001). Competing with CRS-Generated Information in the Airline Industry. *Journal of Strategic Information Systems, 10(1),* 59-75.

Pender, L. (2000). *Damned If You Do: Will Integration Tools Patch the Holes Left By An Unsatisfactory ERP Implementation? CIO Magazine, September 15, 2000.* Retrieved from http://www.cio.com/archive/091500_erp.html

Peppers, D. & Rogers, M. (1993). The one to one future. New York: Doubleday.

Petkov, P. D. (2007). *Identity 2.0: How Attackers Break into Identity-centric Services,* Aug 17, 2007. Retrieved online on April 21, 2008 from http://www.informit.com/articles/article.aspx?p=787262

Pettigrew, A. M. (1988). *The Management of Strategic Change.* Basil Blackwell, Oxford.

Pezzini, M. (2007, April 10). *Q&A: Shedding Light on SAP NetWeaver XI's Road Map and Strategic Role.* [Research ID Number G00147081]. Gartner, p. 3.

Pfitzmann B., & Waidner M. (2004). *Anonymity, Unobservability, Pseudonymity, and Identity Management - A proposal for terminology.* Tu Dresden, Department of Computer Science Technical report, 2004

Pfitzmann, A., & Kohntopp, M. (2000). Anonymity, unobservability, pseudonymity, and identity management – A proposal for terminology. In: *Lecture Notes in Computer Science, 2009,* 1-9. Springer.

Piccoli, G., & Ives, B. (2005). Review: IT-Dependent Strategic Initiatives and Sustained Competitive Advantage: A Review and Synthesis of the Literature. *MIS Quarterly, 29*(4), 746-775.

Picolli, G., & Applegate, L. M. (2003). Wyndham International: Fostering High-Touch with High-tech. *Harvard Business School Publishing,* Case # 9-803-092.

Pikover, Y., &. Drake, J. (2006). *Security provisioning: Managing access in extended enterprises.* Chicago, IL.

Pinch, T. J., & Bijker, W. E. (1992). The Social Construction of Facts and Artifacts: Or How the Sociology of Science and the Sociology of Technology Might Benefit Each Other. In W.E. Bijker, T.P. Hughes and T.J. Pinch (eds.) *The Social Construction of Technological Systems,* MIT Press, Cambridge, Ma, 1992.

Piturro, M. (1999). How midsize companies are buying ERP. *Journal of Accountancy, 188*(3), 41-48.

Piturro, M. (1999). How midsize companies are buying ERP. *Journal of accountancy, 188*(3), 41-48.

Plant, R., & Willcocks, L. (2006). *Critical Success Factors in International ERP Implementations: A Case Research Approach.* Working Paper Series - 145, London: Department of Information Systems, London School of Economics and Political Science.

Plotkin, H. (1999). ERP: How to make them work. *Harvard Management Updat,e* March, 3-4.

Podlogar, M. (2007). E-procurement success factors: Challenges and opportunities for a small developing country, E-procurement in emerging economies. *Theory and cases.* Hershey, PA: Idea Group, Pani, A. K. & Agrahari, A. 42-75.

Podlogar, M., & Basl., J. (2006). SAP ERP case study at the University of Maribor, Slovenia and at the University of Economics, Prague, Czech Republic. *Journal of Management, Informatics and Human Resources, 39*(3), 184-191.

Porter, M. (1985). *Competitive Advantage: Creating and Sustaining Superior Performance.* New York: Free Press,

Porter, M. (1996). What is Strategy? *Harvard Business Review*, November-December.

Porter, M. E. (1980). *Competitive strategy: Techniques for Analyzing Industries and Competitors.* New York, USA: The Free Press.

Porter, M. E., & Millar, V. E. (1985). How Information Gives You Competitive Advantage. *Harvard Business Review, 63(4),* 149-160.

Porter, M., & Miller, V. (1985). How Information Gives You Competitive Advantage. *Harvard Business Review, 63,* 4.

Poston, R. & Grabski, S. (2001). Financial Impacts of Enterprise Resource Planning Implementations. *International Journal of Accounting Information, 2,* 271-294.

Powell, T. C., & Dent-Micallef., A. (1997). Information Technology as Competitive Advantage: The Role of Human, Business, and Technology Resources. *Strategic Management Journal, (18)5,* 375-405.

Pozzebon, M. (2000). *Combining a Structuration Approach with a Behavioral-Based Model to Investigate ERP Usage.* Paper presented at the AMCIS 2000, Long Beach, CA.

Prahalad, C. K., & Ramaswamy, V. (2004). *The Future of Competition: Co-Creating Unique Value with Customers.* Boston: Harvard Business School Press.

Presley, A. R., Huff, B. L., & Liles, D. H. (1993). A Comprehensive Enterprise Model for Small Manufacturers. *Proceedings of the 2nd Industrial Engineering Research Conference,* 430-434. Institute of Industrial Engineers, Atlanta, Georgia.

Prior, Hommel & Vonkarey. (n.d.). *SAP Solution Manager Webcast: Managing System Complexity and End-to-End System Support.* Retrieved on September 26, 2006 from <http://www.sap.com/community/pub/events/2005_06_ 28/index.epx?logonStatusCheck=0>

Probst, G., Raub, S., & Romhardt, K. (1999). *Managing Knowledge: Building Blocks for Success.* Wiley, pp. 218-241.

Probst, G., Raub, S., & Romhardt, K. (2006). *Wissen Managen,* 5. Wiesbaden: Gabler Verlag.

Proudlock, M. J., Phelps, B. et al. (1999). IT adoption strategies: Best practice guidelines for professional SMEs. *Journal of Small Business and Enterprise Development, 6*(4), 240-52.

Pyke, J. (2005). *BPM in Context: Now and in the Future.* The Process Factory Ltd. www.bptrends.com

Quiescenti, M., Bruccoleri, M., La Commare, U., Noto La Diega, S., & Perrone, G. (2006). Business process-oriented design of Enterprise Resource Planning (ERP) systems for small and medium enterprises. *International Journal of Production Research, 44*(18/19), 3797-3811.

Rainer, J. K. R., & Watson, H.J. (1995). The Keys to Executive Information System Success. *Journal of Management Information Systems, 12*(2), 83-99.

Ramanathan, J. (2005). Fractal Architecture for the Adaptive Complex Enterprise. *Communications of the ACM, 48*(5), 51-57.

Ramaswami, S. N., Bhargava, M., & Srivastava, R. (2004). Market-based Assets and Capabilities, Business Processes and Financial Performance. *Marketing Science Institute Working Paper Series No. 04-102.*

Ramirez, E., & Brena, R. (2007). Semantically Mapping the Web. *Research in Computer Science, 27*, 125-136.

Ranganathan, C., & Brown, C. V. (2006). ERP investments and the market value of firms: Toward an understanding of influential ERP project variables. *Information Systems Research, 17*(2), 145-161.

Rantham, R. G., Johnsten, J., & Wen, H. J. (2005). Alignment of business strategy and IT strategy: A case study of a Fortune 50 financial services company. *Journal of Computer Information Systems, Winter 2004-2005,* 1-8.

Rao, M. (2004). *Knowledge Management: Tools and Techniques.* Oxford: Elsevier.

Rao, T. P., Rama, R., Venkata. V., Bhatnagar, S. C., & Satyanarayana, J. (2004). "E-Governance Assessment Frameworks (EAF Version 2.0)" *Report for Department of Information Technology,* Government of India May 2004

Rashid, M. A., Hossain, L., & Patrick, J. D. (2002). The Evolution of ERP Systems: A Historical Perspective. In F. F.-H. Nah (Ed.), *Enterprise Resource Planning Solutions & Management* (pp. 35-50). Hershey, PA: IRM Press.

Ravichandran. T., & Rai. A. (2000). Quality management in systems development: An organizational system perspective. *MIS Quarterly, 24*(3), 381-416.

Raymond, L. (1985). Organizational Characteristics And MIS Success In The Context Of Small Business. *MIS Quarterly, 9*(1), 37-52.

Raymond, L., & Bergeron, F. (1992). Personal DSS success in small enterprises. *Information & Management, 22*(5), 301-308.

Reich, B. H., & Benbasat, I, (2000). Factors that influence the social dimension of alignment between business and information technology objectives. *MIS Quarterly, 24(1),* 81-113.

Reich, B. H., & Benbasat, I. (1996). Measuring the linkage between business and information technology objectives. *MIS Quarterly, 20(1),* 55–81.

Reingruber, M. C., & Gregory, W. W. (1994). *The Data Modeling Handbook: A Best Practice Approach to Building Quality Data Models.* Wiley And Sons.

Resources for competitive advantage. *The Journal of Strategic Information Systems, 9(4),* 265-293.

Retek (2003). *A&P Completes Supply Chain/Business Process Initiative: IBM and Retek Deliver Enterprise Merchandising Solutions.* Retrieved March 13, 2004, from http://www.retek.com/press/press.asp?id/id=507

Rettig, C. (2007). The Trouble with Enterprise Software. *MIT Sloan Management Review,* 49(1), 21-27.

Riehle, D. (2007). The Economic Motivation of Open Source Software: Stakeholder Perspectives. *IEEE Computer, 40*(4), 25-32.

Riley, D. (2008). Google Offers OpenID Logins Via Blogger. *TechCrunch.* Retrieved on 2008-03-20 from http://www.techcrunch.com/2008/01/18/google-offers-openid-logins-via-blogger/

Rittgen, P. (2006) *Enterprise Modeling and Computing with UML.* Hershey: Idea Group.

Robey, D., & Sahay, S. (1996). Transforming work through information technology: A comparative case study of geographic information systems in county government. *Information Systems Research, 7*(1), 93-110.

Robey, D., Ross, J. W., & Boudreau, M. (2002). Learning to implement enterprise systems: an exploratory study of the dialectics of change. *Journal of Management Information Systems, 19*(1), 17-46.

Robson, W, (1997). *Strategic management and information systems: An integrated approach - 2nd edition.* Great Britain: Pitman Publishing.

Rockart, F. J., Earl J. M., & Ross, W. J. (1996). Eight Imperatives for the New IT Organization. *Sloan Management Review, 38*(1), 43-54.

Rockart, J. F., & DeLong, D. W. (1988). *Executive Support Systems: The Emergence of Top Management Computer Use.* Homewood, IL: Down Jones-Irwin.

Rockart, J. F., & Treacy, M. E. (1982). The CEO goes on-line. *Harvard Business Review, 60*(1), 84-88.

Roseman, M. (2004). The Integration of SAP Solutions in the Curricula – Outcomes of a Global Survey, white paper and submitted to the *Journal of IS Education,* Quesland University of Technology, Brisbane.

Rosenzweig, E. D., & Roth, A.V. (2007). B2B Seller Competence: Construct Development and Measurement

Using an Operations Strategy Lens. *Journal of Operations Management, 25*(6), 1311-1331.

Rosenzweig, E. D., Roth A. V., & Dean, J. (2003). The Influence of Integration Intensity on Competitive Capabilities and Business Performance: An Exploratory Investigation of Consumer Products Manufacturers. *Journal of Operations Management, 21*(4), 437-456.

Ross, D. F. (2005). E-CRM from a Supply Chain Management Perspective. *Information Systems Management, 22*(1), 37-44.

Ross, J. W., & Vitale, M. R. (2000). The ERP Revolution: Surviving vs. Thriving. *Information System Frontiers. 2,* 233-241.

Ross, J. W., Beath, C. M., & Goodhye, D. L. (1996). Develop Long-Term Competitiveness Through IT-Assets. *Sloan Management Review, 38(1),* 31-42.

Rosset, S., Neumann, E., Eick, U., & Vatnik, N. (2003). Customer Lifetime Value Models for Decision Support. *Data Mining and Knowledge Discovery, 7*(3), 321–339.

Roth, A.V. (1996). Achieving Strategic Agility through Economies of Knowledge. *Strategy and Leadership* (formerly *Planning Review), 24*(2), 30-3.

Roth, A.V., Cattani, K., & Froehle, C. (2008). Antecedents and Performance Outcomes of Global Competence: An Empirical Investigation. *Journal of Engineering & Technology Management--Special issue on Research of Technology and Innovation in a Global Context,* in press.

Roth, A.V., Tsay, A., Pullman, M., & Gray, J. (2008). Reaping What You Sow? *International Consumer Research*, in press.

Rowe, F. (1999). Cohérence, intégration informationnelle et changement: Esquisse d'un programme de recherche à partir des Progiciels Intégrés de Gestion. *Systèmes d'Information et Management, 4*(4), 3-20.

Ruggels, R. (1997). *Knowledge Management Tools.* Boston: Butterworth-Heinemann.

Ruggles, R. (1997). *Knowledge Tools: Using Technology to Manage Knowledge Better.* Retrieved on 2001, from http://www.cs.toronto.edu/~mkolp/lis2103/kmtools.pdf

Ruggles, R. (1998). The State of the Notion: Knowledge Management in Practice. *California Management Review, 40*(3), 80-89.

Rumbaugh, J., Jacobson, I., & Booch, G. (2004).*Unified Modeling Language Reference Manual.* The Second Edition. Harlow: Addison-Wesley.

Saaksjarvi, M. T. V., & Talvinen, J. M. (1993). Integration And Effectiveness Of Marketing Information Systems. *European Journal of Marketing, 27*(1), 64-79.

Sabherwal, R., & Chan, Y. E. (2001). Alignment between Business and IS Strategies: A Study of Prospectors, Analyzers, and Defenders. *Information Systems Research, 12*(1), 11-33.

Sadiq, S., Orlowska, M., Sadiq, W., & Foulger C. (2004). Data Flow and Validation in Workflow Modeling. *Proceedings of the Fifteenth Conference on Australasian Database, 27.*

Salmela, H. (1997), From information systems quality to sustainable business quality, *Information and Software Technology,* 39, 819-825.

Salojärvi, S., Furu, P., & Sveiby, K. (2005). Knowledge management and growth in Finnish SMEs. *Journal of Knowledge Management, 9*(2), 103-122.

Sambamurthy, V., Bharadwaj, A. & Grover, V. (2003). Shaping Agility Through Digital Options: Reconceptualizing the Role of Information Technology in Contemporary Firms. *MIS Quarterly, 27*(2), 237-263.

Sanjay, G., Arvind, M., & Omar, El S. (2004). Coordinating for Flexibility in e-Business Supply Chains. *Journal of Management Information Systems, 21*(3), 7-45.

SAP Library: SAP Solution Manager 3.2 SP09. (2005, September). SAP Help Portal. Retrieved September 2005 from <https://help.sap.com/>.

SAP Solution Manager, Release 220. (2002). *SAP Service Marketplace, SAP Solution Manager, Downloads.* Retrieved October 2005, from http://service.sap.com/solutionmanager

Sarker, S., & Lee, A. S. (2000, 13 November 2000). Using a case study to test the role of three key social enabales in ERP implementation. *Paper presented at the ICIS 2000,* 13 November 2000 http://www.commerce.uq.edu.au/icis/ICIS2000.html

Sarnikar, S. (2007). *Automating knowledge flows by extending conventional information retrieval and workflow technologies.* Ph.D. dissertation, The University of Arizona, United States -- Arizona. Retrieved June 1, 2007, from ProQuest Digital Dissertations database.

Satyanarayanan, M. (2001). Pervasive computing: Vision and challenges. *IEEE Wireless Communications, 8*(4), 10-17.

Saxena, K. B. C. (2005). Towards excellence in e-governance. *International Journal of Public Sector Management,* 18(6), 498-513, 16

Schoenherr, T., Venkataramanan, M. A., Soni, A. K., Mabert, V. A., & Hilpert, D. (2005). The 'new' users: Manufacturing SMEs and the Mittelstand experience. In: by E. Bendoly, & F. R. Jacobs (Eds.), *Strategic ERP extension and use* (pp. 36-51). Stanford, CA: Stanford University Press.

Schultz, G. J. (2002). Data that flows in context: Workflow and other new tools weave data collection into a better business context. *MSI, Oak Brook, 20*(10), 71-76.

Schultz, R. L., & Slevin, D. P. (1975). Implementation and organisational validity: An empirical investigation. *Implementing operational research / management science*. R. L. Shultz and D. P. Slevin. New York, Elsevier, North-Holland: 153-182.

Schwartz, D. (2006). *Encyclopedia of Knowledge Management*. Hershey: Idea Group Publishing.

Scott, F. & Shepherd, J. (2002). *The Steady Stream of ERP Investments*. AMR Research Outlook, August 26.

Scott, J. (2003). What risks does an organization face from an ERP implementation? In D. R. Laube & R. F. Zammuto (Eds.), *Business Driven Information Technology: Answers to 100 Critical Questions for Every Manager* (pp. 274-278). Stanford: Stanford Business Books.

Scott, J. E., & Vessey, I. (2002). Managing Risks in Enterprise Systems Implementations. *Communications of ACM, April 2002, 45*(4).

Scott, M. (1991). *The Corporation of the 1990s: Information Technology and Organizational Transformation*. Oxford University Press, Cambridge.

Sedera, D., & Gable, G. (2004). A Factor and Structural Equation Analysis of the Enterprise Systems Success Measurement Model. *International Conference of Information Systems*, Washington, D.C.

Sedera, D., Gable, G. et al. (2003). ERP Success: Does Organization Size Matter? *Proceedings of the 7th Pacific Asia Conference on Information Systems*, Association for Information Systems.

Serrano N., & Sarrieri, J. M. (2006). Open Source ERPs: A New Alternative for an Old Need. *IEEE Software*, May/June, 94-97.

Severance, D. G., & Passino, J. (2002). *Making I/T Work*. San Francisco: Jossey-Bass.

Shakir, M. (2002). Current Issues of ERP Implementations in New Zealand. *Research Letters in Information and Mathematical Science*, 4(1), 151-172. Massey University, Auckland, New Zealand.

Shakir, M., & Viehland, D. (2004). Business Drivers in Contemporary Enterprise System Implementations. *Proceedings of the Tenth Americas Conference on Information Systems*, New York, 103-112.

Shang, S., & Seddon, P (2000). A Comprehensive Framework for Classifying the Benefits of ERP Systems. Proceedings of the Americas' Conference for Information Systems. Long Beach, CA, 1005-14.

Shang, S., & Seddon, P. (2000, August 10-13). A Comprehensive Framework for Classifying the Benefits of ERP Systems. *Paper presented at the 6th America's Conference on Information Systems*, Long Beach, California.

Shang, S., & Seddon, P. B. (2002). Assessing And Managing The Benefits Of Enterprise Systems: The Business Manager's Perspective. *Information Systems Journal, 12*(4), 271-299.

Shanks, G., & Seddon, P. (2000). Editorial. *Journal of Information Technology, 15*, 243-244.

Shanks, G., Seddon, P. B., & Wilcocks, L. P. (2003). *Second-Wave Enterprise Resource Planning Systems: Implementing for Effectiveness*. Cambridge University Press.

Sharma, R., & Yetton, P. (2003). The contingent effects of management support and task interdependence on successful information systems implementation. *MIS Quarterly, 27*(4), 533-555.

Sharp, A., & Mcdermott, P. (2001). *Workflow Modeling: Tools for Process Improvement and Application Development*. Norwood,Ma: Artech House.

Shegalov, G., Gillmann, M., & Weikum, M. (2001). XML-Enabled Workflow Management for E-Services Across Heterogeneous Platforms. *The VLDB Journal — The International Journal On Very Large Data Bases, 10*(1).

Shepherd, J., Locke, B., D'Aquila, M., & Carter, K. (2005). *The Enterprise Resource Planning Report, 2004-2009*. AMR Research Report.

Shi, X. (2006). Sharing service semantics using SOAP-based and REST Web services. *IT Professional, 8*(2), 18 - 24.

Shibboleth. (2008). Retrieved online on April 21, 2008 from http://shibboleth.internet2.edu/about.html

Shields, M. G. (2001). *E-Business and ERP. Rapid Implementation and Project Planning*. Canada: John Wiley & Sons, Inc.

Shin, I. (2006). Adoption of enterprise application software and firm performance. *Small Business Economics, 26*(3), 241-256.

ShuiGuang, D., Zhen, Y., ZhaoHui, W., & LiCan, H. (2004). Enhancement of Workflow Flexibility by Composing Activities at Run-time. *Proceedings of the 2004 ACM Symposium on Applied Computing*, 667-673.

Simsion, G. (2000). *Data Modeling Essentials: A Comprehensive Guide to Data Analysis, Design, and Innovation (2ⁿᵈ Ed.)*. Coriolis Group Books.

Sirinivasan, A. (1985). Alternative Measures Of System Effectiveness: Associations And Implications. *MIS Quarterly, 9*(3), 243-253.

Skok, W., & Legge, M. (2001). Evaluating Enterprise Resource Planning (ERP) Systems Using an Interpretive Approach. *Paper presented at the Proceedings of The 2001 ACM SIGCPR Conference on Computer Personnel Research*, April, p. 189-197.

Slater, D. (1999). How to choose the right ERP software package. *CIO*, February 16, 1999.

Smaczny, T. (2001). Is an alignment between business and information technology the appropriate paradigm to manage IT in today's organisations? *Management Decision, 39(10)*, 797-802

Smets-Solanes, J., & De Carvalho, R. A. (2003). ERP5: A Next-Generation, Open-Source ERP Architecture. *IEEE IT Professional*, 5(4), 38–44.

Smith, A., Opinion (2003). Citizen Relationship Management. (online) (cited June 12, 2003). Available from <URL:http://www.crm-forum.com>.

Smith, H. (2003, September 22). *Business Process Management 101*. Retrieved From Http://Www.Ebizq. Net/Topics/Bpm/Features/2830.Html

Smith, H., & Fingar, P. (2003a). *Business Process Management (BPM): The Third Wave (1ˢᵗ Ed.)*. Meghan-Kiffer Press.

Smith, H., & Fingar, P. (2003b). *Workflow Is Just A Pi Process*. Retrieved From Http://Www.Fairdene.Com/ Picalculus/Workflow-Is-Just-A-Pi-Process.Pdf

Smith, H., & Fingar, P. (2004, February 1). *BPM Is Not About People, Culture And Change. It's About Technology*. Retrieved From Http://Www.Avoka.Com/Bpm/ Bpm_Articles_Dynamic.Shtml

Smith, T. (2002). Deloitte Study: Linking CRM, Supply Chain Boosts Profits. *Internetweek.com*. Retrieved February 12, 2002.

Soh, C. P. P., Yap, C. S. et al. (1992). Impact of consultants on computerisation success in small businesses. *Information and Management, 22*, 309-319.

Soh, C., Kien, S. S., & Tay-Yap, J. (2000). Cultural fits and misfits: Is ERP a universal solution? *Communications of the ACM, 43*(4), 47-51.

Somer, T., & Nelson, K. (2001). The impact of Critical Success Factors across the Stages of Enterprise Resource Planning System Implementations. *Proceedings of the 34th Hawaii International Conference on System Sciences*, 2001, HICSS.

Somers, T. M., & Nelson, K. G. (2003). The impact of strategy and integration mechanisms on enterprises system value: empirical evidence from manufacturing firms. *European Journal of Operational Research, 146*, 315-38.

Somers, T. M., Ragowsky, A. A., Nelson, K. G., & Stern, M. (2001). *Exploring Critical Success Factors across the Enterprise Systems Experience Cycle: An Empirical Study* (Working Paper). Detroit, Michigan: Wayne State University.

Somers, T. M., Ragowsky, A. A., Nelson, K. G., & Stern, M. (2001). *Exploring Critical Success Factors across the Enterprise Systems Experience Cycle: An Empirical Study* (Working Paper). Detroit, Michigan: Wayne State University.

Somogyi, E., & Galliers, R. (1987). *Towards Strategic Information Systems*. Cambridge: Abacus Press.

Spantzel, A. Bhargav, C., J., Gross, T., & Sommer, D. (2006). *User Centricity: A Taxonomy and Open Issues*. IBM Zurich Research Laboratory, 2006.

Spinellis, D. (2006). Open Source and Professional Advancement. *IEEE Software*, September/October, 70-71.

Sprott, D. (2004). Service Oriented Architecture: An introduction for managers. *CBDI Report*. www.cbdi-forum.com

Srinivasan, R., & Moorman, C. (2005). Strategic Firm Commitments and Rewards for Customer Relationship Management in Online Retailing. *Journal of Marketing*, 69, 193-200.

Standifera, R. L., & Wall, J. A. (2003). Managing Conflict in B2B E-Commerce. *Business Horizons, 46*(2), 65-70.

Standish Group. (1995). *Chaos Report,* Standish Research Paper. Retrieved July 5, 2007, from http://www. projectsmart.co.uk/docs/chaos-report.pdf.

Stanton, J. M., Stam, K. R., Mastrangelo, P., & Jolton, J. (2005). Analysis of end user security behaviors. *Computers & Security 24*(2), 124-133.

Stedman, C. (1998). Global ERP rollouts present cross-border problems. *Computerworld, 32* (47), 10.

Stedman, C. (1999). What's next for ERP? *Computerworld*, 33(33).

Stedman, C. (1999, November 1). Failed ERP Gamble Haunts Hershey: Candy maker bites off more than it can chew and 'Kisses' big Halloween sales goodbye. *Computer World,* 1.

Stein, T. (1998), Dell Takes 'Best-of-Breed' Approach in ERP Strategy. Information Week on Line, News in Review, May 11, 1998. Downloaded 6/6/2007 from http://www.informationweek.com/681/81iuerp.htm

Stolarick, K. (1999). IT Spending and Firm Productivity: Additional Evidence from the Manufacturing Sector. *Center for Economic Studies, U.S. Census Bureau, Working Paper 99-10.*

Stratman, J. K., & Roth, A. V. (2002). Enterprise Resource Planning (ERP) Competence Constructs: Two-Stage Multi-Item Scale Development and Validation. *Decision Sciences, 33*(4), 601-628.

Stratman, J. K., & Roth, A.V. (2002). Beyond ERP Implementation: Critical Success Factors for North American Manufacturing Firms. *Supply Chain & Logistics Journal, 5*(1), 5-8.

Stratman, J. K., & Roth, A.V. (2008). Towards a Theory of Enterprise Resource Planning Competence: An Empirical Model of the Post-Installation Success Factors on Financial Performance. *University of Utah and Clemson University Working Paper.*

Stratman, J., & Roth, A. (1999), Enterprise resource planning competence: A model, propositions and pre-test, design-stage scale development. *30th DSI Proceedings*, 20-23 November, pp. 1199-201.

Street, C., & Cameron, A. (2007). External Relationships and the Small Business: A Review of Small Business Alliance and Network Research. *Journal of Small Business Management, 45*(2).

Subrahmanyam, A. (1999). *Nuts and Bolts of Transaction Processing*, www.subrahmanyam.com/articles/transactions/NutsAndBoltsOfTP.html

Subramoniam, S., Shehzad, G. K. & Krishnankutty, K V. (2006). Current trends in enterprise information systems, *Applied Computing and Informatics, Saudi Computer Society Journal, 5*(2).

Sumner, M. (1999). Critical Success Factors in Enterprisewide Information Management Systems Projects. *Paper presented at the 5th America's Conference on Information Systems*, Milwaukee, Wisconsin, USA.

Sumner, M. (2000). Risk factors in enterprise-wide/ERP projects. *Journal of Information Technology, 15*(4), 317-327.

Sumner, M., & Bradley, J. (2007). Critical Success Factors in Best of Breed ERP Implementation. In M. Khosrow-Pour (ed.), *Managing Worldwide Operations and Communications with Information Technology*, (pp. 526-529). Hershey, PA: IGI Global.

Sun Microsystems. (2003, 6 October 2003). Java specification request: J2EE client provisioning specification. Retrieved January 7, 2007, 2007, from http://web1.jcp.org/en/jsr/detail?id=124

Sutton, S. (2003). Keynote Address, AIS Educator Meeting. Copper Mountain, CO.

Swart, R.S., Marshall, B.A., Olsen, D.H., & Erbacher, R. (2007). ERP II System Vulnerabilities and Threats: An Exploratory Study. In M. Khosrow-Pour (ed.), Managing Worldwide Operations and Communications with Information Technology, (pp. 925-8). Hershey, PA: IGI Global.

Symantec Press. (2008). *Symantec Unveils Security 2.0 Identity Initiative at DEMO 07 Conference.* Symantec (2007-01-31). Retrieved on April 19, 2008 from http://www.symantec.com/about/news/release/article.jsp?prid=20070131_01

Taking the Pulse of ERP. (2001). *Modern Materials Handling, 56*(2), 44-51.

Taking the Pulse of ERP. (2001, February 2001). *Modern Materials Handling,* 44-51.

Tallon, P., & Kraemer, K. (2003). *Investigating the relationship between Strategic Alignment and IT Business value: The Discovery of a Paradox, Relationship Between Strategic Alignment and IT Business Value.* Idea Group Publishing, Hershey USA.

Tan, X., Yen, D. C., & Fang, X. (2002). Internet integrated customer relationship management - A key success factor for companies in the e-commerce arena. *Journal of Computer Information Systems, 42*(3), 77-86.

Tapscott, D. (2007) Rethinking Enterprise Boundaries: Business Webs in the IT Industry. *NEWPARADIGM, DOI:*

Taylor, J. (1999). Fitting enterprise software in smaller companies. *Management Accounting, 80*(February), 36-39.

TechRepublic (2007). *IBM® Rational Rose*. Retrieved 25 June 2007 http://search.techrepublic.com.com/search/IBM+Rational+Rose.html

TenFold Corporation. (2007). *EnterpriseTenFold-2007PersonalEdition.pdf* Retrieved 25 June 2007, www.tenfold.com

Teo, T. S. H., & King, W. R. (1996). Assessing the impact of integrating business planning and IS planning. *Information & Management, 30*, 309-321.

Teo, T., & King, W. (1997). Integration between business planning and information systems planning: an evolutionary contingency perspective. *Journal of Management Information Systems, 14*.

Thatcher, M. E., & Oliver, J. R. (2001). The impact of technology investments on a firm's production efficiency, product quality, and productivity. *Journal of Management Information Systems, 18*(2), 17-45.

Thong, J. Y. L. (2001). Resource constraints and information systems implementation in Singaporean small business. *Omega, 29*(2), 143-56.

Torchiano, M., & Bruno, G. (2003). Article Abstracts With Full Text Online: Enterprise Modeling By Means Of UML Instance Models. *ACM Sigsoft Software Engineering Notes,* Volume 28 Issue 2.

Torres, L., Pina, V., & Acerete, B. (2006). E-Governance Developments in European Union Cities: Reshaping Government's Relationship with Citizens. *Governance,* Apr2006, 19(2), 277.

Trompenaars, F., & Hampden-Turner, C. (2006). *Riding the waves of culture: understanding cultural diversity in business* (2. reprint. with corr. ed.). London: Brealey.

Tsang, C. H. K., Lau, C. S. W., & Leung, Y. K. (2005). *Object-Oriented Technology From Diagram to Code with Visual Paradigm for UML*. New Delhi: Tata Mc-Graw-Hill

Tucker, R., & Debrosse, D. (2003). Enterprise Architecture: Roadmap for modernization" *Enterprise Modernization Issue, fall 2003, 7(2)*

Turban, E. (1990). *Decision Support and Expert Systems: Management Support Systems*. New York, London: Macmillan, second edition.

Turban, E., & Aronson, J. (2001). *Decision Support Systems and Intelligent Systems*. Upper Saddle River, NJ: Prentice Hall.

Turban, E., Mclean, E., & Wetherbe, J. (2004). *Information Technology for Management Transforming Organisations in the Digital Economy,* (4th edition). New Delhi: Wiley-India. (p. 5).

Turner, J. S. (1992). Personal DSS success in small business. *Information and Management, 22*, 301-308.

Umble, E. J., Haft, R. R. & Umble, M. M. (2003). Enterprise Resource Planning: Implementation Procedures and Critical Success Factors. *European Journal of Operational Research, 146*(2), 241-257.

Van Der Zee, J. T. M., & De Jong, B. (1999). Alignment is not enough: Integrating business and Information Technology management with the balanced business scorecard. *Journal of Management Information Systems, 16*(2), 137-156.

Van Everdingen, Y., Van Hillegersberg, J., & Waarts, E. (2000). ERP adoption by European midsize companies. *Communications of the ACM, 43*(4), 27-31.

Vargo, S. L., & Lusch, R. F. (2004). Evolving to a New Dominant Logic for Marketing. *Journal of Marketing, 68*(1), 1-17.

Vemuri, V. K. & Palvia, S. C. (2006). Improvement in Operational Efficiency Due to ERP Systems Implementation: Truth or Myth? *Information Resources Management Journal, 19*(2), 18-36.

Viehland, D., & Shakir, M. (2005). Making Sense of Enterprise Systems Implementation. *Business Review, University of Auckland, 7*(2), 28-36.

Vogel, A., & Kimbell, I. (2005). mySAP ERP For Dummies. Indianapolis: Wiley Publishing, Inc.

Voigt, T. (2001). *mind 02 – Mittelstand in Deutschland.* Köln, Germany: Gruner + Jahr.

Wagle, D. (1998). The case for ERP systems. *The McKinsey Quarterly, 2*, 130-138.

Wallace, T. F., & Kremzar, M. H. (2001). *ERP: Making It Happen. The Implementer's Guide to Success with Enterprise Resource Planning,* Canada: John Wiley & Sons, Inc.

Walsham, G. (1993). *Interpreting Information Systems in Organizations.* Chichester, Wiley.

Walstrom, K. A., & Wilson, R. L. (1997). An examination of executive information system (EIS) users. *Information and Management, 32*(1), 75-83.

Walters, B. A., Jiang, J. J., & Klein, G. (2003). Strategic information and strategic decision making: the EIS/CEO interface in smaller manufacturing companies. *Information and Management, 40*(6), 487-495.

Wang, C., Xu, L., Liu, X., & Qin, X. (2005). ERP research, development and implementation in China: An overview. *International Journal of Production Research, 43*(18), 3915-3932.

Wang, F., & Plaskoff, J. (2002). An Integrated Development Model for KM. In R. Bellaver & J. Lusa (Eds.), *Knowledge Management Strategy and Technology* (pp. 113-134). Boston: Artech House.

Wang, F-R. He, D., & Chen, J. (2005). Motivations of Individuals and Firms Participating in Open Source Communities. *Fourth International Conference on Machine Learning and Cybernetics*, 309-314.

Watson, E. E., & Schneider, H. (1999). Using ERP in Education. *Communications of the Association for Information Systems, 1*, Article 9.

Watson, H. J., & Carte, T. A. (2000). Executive information systems in government organizations. *Public Productivity and Management Review, 23*(3), 371-382.

Watson, H., Rainer, R. K., & Koh, C. (1993). Executive information systems: a framework for development and a survey of current practices. *MIS Quarterly, 17*(3), 13-29.

Welsh, J. A., & White, J. F. (1981). A amall business is not a little big business. *Harvard Business Review, 59*(4), 18-32.

Weske, M., Goesmann, T., Holten, R., & Striemer, R. (1999) A Reference Model for Workflow Application Development Processes. *ACM Sigsoft Software Engineering Notes , Proceedings of the International Joint Conference on Work Activities Coordination and Collaboration,* Volume 24 Issue 2.

West, J., & O'Mahony, S. (2005). Contrasting Community Building in Sponsored and Community Founded Open Source Projects. *38th Annual Hawaii International Conference on System Sciences*, Hawaii.

Westervelt, R. (2004). Finding value in edge-of-enterprise apps. *SearchSAP.com,* February 19. Retrieved July 5, 2007, from http://searchsap.techtarget.com/originalContent/0,289142,sid21_gci951397,00.html

Westervelt, R., (2003, August 20). Debating ERP and best-of-breed, SAP News. Downloaded 6/6/08 from http://searchsap.techtarget.com/originalContent/0,289142,sid21_gci920428,00.html

Weston, F. C. (2001). ERP implementation and project management. *Production and Inventory Management Journal, 42*(3/4), 75-80.

WFMC (Workflow Management Coalition) (2002). *Workflow: An introduction.*

Whisler, T. (1970). *The Impact Of Computers On Organizations.* New York, NY, Praeger Publishers.

Wieder, B., Booth, P., Matolczy, Z. P., & Ossimitz, M.-L. (2006). The Impact of ERP Systems on Firm and Business Process Performance. *Journal of Enterprise Information Management, 19*(1), 13-29.

Wiki-Cardspace. (2008). Retrieved online on April 20, 2008 from http://en.wikipedia.org/wiki/Windows_CardSpace

Wiki-Liberty. (2008). Wikipedia article retrieved online on April 5, 2008 from http://en.wikipedia.org/wiki/Liberty_Alliance

Wikipedia (2007). *SOA Practitioners Guide: Why Services-Oriented Architecture?* Retrieved 25 June 2007 from http://en.wikipedia.org/wiki/Service-oriented_architecture

Wiki-XRI. (2008). Retrieved online on April 20, 2008 from http://en.wikipedia.org/wiki/XRI

Wiki-Yadis. (2008). Retrieved online on April 20, 2008 from http://en.wikipedia.org/wiki/Yadis

Windley P.(2005). "Digital Identity". Sebastopol, California: O'Reilly.

Winer, R. S. (2001). A framework for customer relationship management. *California Management Review, 43*(4), 89-105.

Wiseman, C. (1985). *Strategy and Computers: Information Systems as Competitive Weapons.*, Homewood, USA: Dow-Jones-Irwin.

Witty, R.. J., Ant, A., & Wagner, R. (2006). *Magic quadrant for user provisioning, 1h06.* Gartner Group, Boston, MA.

Wong, K. (2005). Critical success factors for implementing knowledge management in small and medium enterprises *Industrial Management & Data Systems, 105*(3), 261-279.

Wong, K., & Aspinwall, E. (2005). An empirical study of the important factors for knowledge-management adoption in the SME sector. *Journal of Knowledge Management, 9*(3), 64-82.

Woods, D., & Word, J. (2004). *SAP NetWeaver For Dummies*. Wiley Publishing, Inc.

Wooldridge, M. (2001). *An Introduction to MultiAgent Systems*. John Wiley and sons, LTD, Baffins Lane, England.

Wu, J. H., & Wang, Y. M. (2003). Enterprise resource planning experience in Taiwan: An empirical study and comparative analysis. 30th *Annual Hawaii International Conference on System Science (HICCS '03)*, Big Island, Hawaii, January 6-9.

Wu, L., Ong, C., & Hsu, Y. (2008). Active ERP implementation management: A Real Options perspective. *Journal of Systems and Software, 81*(6), 1039-1050.

Xavier,M.J,(2002, April-June). Citizen Relationship Management- Concepts, Tools and Applications. *South Asian Journal of Management, 9(2),* 23-31.

XRI technical committee. (2008). Retrieved online on April 20, 2008 from http://www.oasis- open.org/committees/tc_home.php?wg_abbrev=xri

Xu, N. (2003). *An Exploratory Study of Open Source Software Based on Public Archives*. Master Thesis, John Molson School of Business, Concordia University, Montreal, Canada.

Xue, Y., Liang, H., Boulton, W.R., & Snyder, C. A. (2005). ERP implementation failures in China: Case studies with implications for ERP vendors. *International Journal of Production Economics*, 97(3), 279-295.

Yadis Site. (2008). Retrieved online on April 20, 2008 from http://yadis.org/wiki/Main_Page

Yang, S., & Seddon, P. B. (2004). Benefits and Key Success Factors from Enterprise Systems Implementations: Lessons from Sapphire 2003. *Paper presented at the 35th Australasian Conference in Information Systems*, Hobart, Australia.

Yi, M.Y., Jackson, J. D., Park, J. S. & Probst, J. C. (2006). Understanding information technology acceptance by individual professionals: Toward an integrative view. *Information & Management, 43*(3), 350-363.

Yin, R. K. (1994). *Case study research: Design and methods*. Thousand Oaks, CA: Sage Publications.

Young, L. (1999). The best buy: Dupont Canada saves millions with network purchasing. *Micromedia Limited, Canadian Business and Current Affairs, 44*(8), 51.

Zachman, A. J. (1999). A Framework for Information Systems Architecture. *IBM Systems Journal, 31*(3), 445 –470.

Zachman, J. (2004). *Enterprise Architecture and Legacy Systems*. http://members.ozemail.com.au/~visible/ papers/zachman1.htm

Zafiropoulos, I., Metaxiotis, K., & Askounis, D. (2005). Dynamic risk management systems for modeling, optimal adaption and implementation of an ERP system. *Information Management & Computer Security, 13*(2/3), 212-234.

Zanoni, R., & Audy, J.L.N. (2004). Project Management Model: Proposal for Performance in a Physically Distributed Software Development Environment. *Engineering Management Journal, 16*(2), 28-34.

Zhao, X., Flynn, B., & Roth, A.V. (2007). Decision Science Research in China: Current Status, Opportunities and Propositions for Research in Supply Chain Management, Logistics, and Quality Management. *Decision Sciences, 38*(1), 39-80.

Zinnov Research and Consulting. (2006). *Penetration of Open Source in US Enterprise software market – An Overview*. 37.

Zrimsek, B. (2002). *ERPII: The Boxed Set*. Retrieved Mar. 4, 2002, from www3.gartner.com/pages/story.php.id.2376.s.8.jsp

Zviran, M. (1990). Relationships between organizational and information systems objectives: some empirical evidence. *Journal of Management Information Systems, 7*(1), 65-84.

About the Contributors

Hossana H. Aberra is a consultant with Enterprise Integration, Inc. in Alexandria, VA. While at EII, she participated as part of an Independent Verification and Validation team for SAP implementation project by reviewing the project deliverables, evaluating the implementation approach, and testing the solution. She also provided executive consulting to an Enterprise Process Analysis and Strategies Group as the resident specialist on Enterprise Architecture in support of policy compliance, portfolio management, and technology research and evaluation. Hossana holds BBA in computer information and systems science, and MS in enterprise engineering and policy.

Jose L. Aguirre holds a bachelors degree in computer systems engineering from the ITESM (Mexico) in 1980; masters in informatics engineering from ENSIMAG (France) in 1986; PhD on Informatics from INPG (France) in 1989. His research area is Artificial Intelligence with emphasis on Knowledge Based Systems. He has been full-time professor at the ITESM Campus Monterrey since 1990 until 2007. During the last years he has conducted research on Knowledge Flow Systems and the integration of AI technologies to enhance the capabilities of those systems.

Konstantinos Aivalis is chief economic advisor to ICAP SA, the leading Greek business services firm, where he supervises all economic research. He earned his BA in economics magna cum laude from the University of Athens. He also holds an MA in economics from Boston University. Mr. Aivalis has worked as an economics researcher and management consultant since 1984 and has a long experience in applied economic research. Since 1990 he follows and analyses the trends in the Greek business sector and has written ex-tensively in specialized publications and in the press. His other research interests are regional economics, technology and the knowledge economy. He has co-authored a book on the knowledge economy in Greece, which will be published soon.

Nancy Alexopoulou is a research associate at Harokopio University of Athens. She holds an MSc in Advanced information systems and a bachelor degree in Informatics from the Department of Informatics and Telecommunication of the University of Athens. Currently, she works on her PhD in agile business process execution. Her research interests include business process modeling, agile process-aware information systems and enterprise architectures.

Albert Boonstra is an associate professor at the Faculty of Management and Organization at the University of Groningen, The Netherlands. He is director of the graduate programs in Business Administration at this university. He specializes in the organizational issues that surround the use of advanced information technologies, especially in health care environments. He conducted extensive research in this field and has served as consultant in numerous IT-management related projects. He published his research in various international journals, including the *International Journal of Project Management, European Journal of Information Systems, Journal of Information Technology, International Journal of Information Management* and *New Technology, Work & Employment.*

Joseph Bradley is an assistant professor of Accounting at the University of Idaho. He received his BA from Claremont McKenna College and his EMBA and PhD from Claremont Graduate University. His research focuses on ERP implementation issues. His research has been published in the *International Journal of Enterprise Information Systems, Issues in Information Systems* and the *International Journal of Accounting Information Systems.* He has presented his research at the Information Resource Management Association International Conference and Americas' Conference on Information Systems. Prior to his academic career he spent 30 years in industry in various accounting and general management positions.

Ramon F. Brena is full professor at the Center of Intelligent Systems, Tecnologico de Monterrey, Mexico, since 1990, where he is head of a research group in distributed knowledge and multiagent systems. Dr. Brena holds a PhD from the INPG, Grenoble, France, where he presented a doctoral Thesis related to Knowledge in Program Synthesis. His current research and publication areas include Intelligent Agents and Multiagent Systems, Knowledge management, representation and distribution, Semantic Web, and Artificial Intelligence in general. He has been visiting professor at the U. of Texas at Dallas and the Université de Montréal. Dr Brena is member of the ACM, and is recognized as an established researcher by the official Mexican research agency, CONACyT.

Brian H. Cameron is professor of practice in the College of Information Sciences and Technology at The Pennsylvania State University. He is a founding member of the Enterprise Informatics and Integration Center at Penn State, an applied research group seeking to actively engage industry and non-profit organizations to solve critical issues in enterprise and supply chain integration. The main focus areas for his teaching efforts are on senior-level capstone enterprise integration, enterprise information architecture, and information technology consulting & project management courses. Dr. Cameron is currently developing new curricular materials for enterprise integration (through funding from NSF) including a textbook to be published by Wiley & Sons Publishing. He has also designed and taught executive education sessions for senior IT executives. Session topics include service oriented architecture (SOA), business process management (BPM), strategic alignment of IT & business strategies, IT governance, and IT portfolio management. Dr. Cameron currently leads corporately funded research efforts in the following areas: service-oriented architecture and business process modeling, risk analysis and management of enterprise systems integration projects, enterprise resource planning (ERP) and customer relationship management (CRM) implementation best practices and enterprise storage & information management architecture design.

Kerstin Fink is university professor at Innsbruck University and head of the Department of Information Systems, Operational Management and Logistics. Kerstin Fink conducts research in the field of knowledge management and measurement with special focus on small and medium-sized enterprises. She was visiting researcher at Stanford University and the University of New Orleans and is currently guest professor at the University of Linz. Kerstin Fink was awarded with the Tyrolean Chamber of Commerce Prize, the Otto-Beisheim Prize and the Innsbruck Scientific Award for excellent research in the field of knowledge management

Shehzad Khalid Ghani is a faculty member of the Department of Computer and Information Systems in Prince Sultan University. He completed his master's degree in information systems from University of Texas at Dallas in 2002. His research interests include: enterprise resource planning, business process reengineering, e-government, IT management, and ethical aspects of computing in society. He is the Editorial Coordinator of *Applied Computing and Informatics* magazine and a member of the Saudi Computer Society.

Manish Gupta is a PhD Candidate at State University of New York at Buffalo and an information security professional at M&T Bank, Buffalo. He obtained an MBA from SUNY-Buffalo in MIS and bachelors degree in mechanical engineering from University of Lucknow, India. He has published 3 books (one is forthcoming) in information assurance area. He has authored or co-authored more than 20 refereed research articles in leading journals, conference proceedings and books. He serves in editorial boards of 8 international journals and has served in program committees of several national and international conferences.

Călin Gurău is associate professor of Marketing at Montpellier Business School, France, since September 2004. He is a junior fellow of the World Academy of Art and Science, Minneapolis, USA. He worked as Marketing Manager in two Romanian companies and he has received degrees and distinctions for studies and research from University of Triest, Italy; University of Vienna, Austria; Duke University, USA; University of Angers, France; Oxford University and Southampton Business School and Heriot-Watt University, United Kingdom. His present research interests are focused on Marketing Strategies for High-Technology Firms and Internet Marketing. He has published more than 25 papers in internationally refereed journals, such as *International Marketing Review, Journal of Consumer Marketing*, and *Journal of Marketing Communications*.

Ronda Henning, CISSP-ISSAP, CISSP-ISSMP, CISM, is a senior scientist at Harris Corporation; a Melbourne, Florida based international communications company. Ms. Henning is the senior strategist for information assurance at Harris. Her past assignments include network security manager for the FAA Telecommunication Infrastructure (FTI) Program and a DARPA principal investigator on vulnerability visualization technologies. Prior to her employment at Harris, Henning worked in information security research at the National Security Agency. Henning holds an MBA from the Florida Institute of Technology, an MS in computer science from Johns Hopkins University, and a BA from the University of Pittsburgh.

Ditmar Hilpert is professor at the European School of Business (ESB), Reutlingen, Germany. He has earned a master's degree both in biotechnology and economics and holds a PhD in pharmacology and toxicology. After more than 10 years in the pharmaceutical industry, he has held the chair in Strategic Management at ESB for the last 15 years. His current research interest is in the comparison of strategic approaches of SME on an international background. Professor Hilpert also served the European Commission, DG XII, and various Business Schools as an advisor. He acts as an business angel for biotech and medtec companies.

Panagiotis Kanellis is currently a program manager with Information Society S.A. in Athens, Greece. Previous to that he held senior consulting positions with Arthur Andersen and Ernst & Young. He was educated at Western International University in Business Administration (BSc), at the University of Ulster in computing and information systems (Post-Graduate Diploma), and at Brunel University in data communication systems (MSc) and information systems (PhD). He is a research associate in the Department of Informatics and Telecommunications at the National and Kapodistrian University of Athens and an adjunct faculty member at the Athens University of Economics and Business having published more than 50 papers in international peer-reviewed journals and conferences.

Helmut Krcmar has held the chair for Information Systems at the Information Technology Department of the Technische Universität München (TUM) since October 1, 2002. He is a member of the Information Technology Department, a secondary member of the Economics Department, and a member of the Carl von Linde Academy. Since 2004, he has been a member of the board of the elite graduate program in finance and information management (FIM) in the elite network of Bavaria, Germany. Between October 2003 and May 2007, he was academic director of the ¡communicate! program, and has been scientific director of the Center for Digital Technology and Management (CDTM) of the Technical University of Munich since January 2004.

K. V. Krishnankutty is doctorate from Indian Institute of Technology, Madras and also holds an M.Tech from the same Institute. He has guided PhDs and has many national and international papers to his credit. He has headed several boards and has successfully carried out consultancy for many organizations. He is a professor at the Department of Business Administration, College of Engineering, Trivandrum. He is a fellow of the Indian Institution of Industrial Engineering.

Gita A. Kumta has around 30 years experience in industry predominantly in the area of business analysis and consultancy in financial systems. Presently Dr. Kumta is head of the Information Systems faculty at School of Business Management, SVKM's NMIMS University, Mumbai, India and specializes in Information Systems and Knowledge Management. She did her Masters in Statistics from Indian Statistical Institute, Calcutta, India, and has a diploma in bank management from National Institute of Bank Management, Mumbai. She completed her doctoral thesis on *Funds Management in District Central Co-operative Banks in Maharashtra* through University of Mumbai, India.

Euripidis Loukis is assistant professor of Information Systems and Decision Support Systems at the Department of Information and Communication Systems of the University of the Aegean. Formerly he has been information systems advisor at the Ministry to the Presidency of the Government and at the Ministry of Culture, and also National Representative of Greece in the 'Interchange of Data between Administration Program' (IDA) and the 'Telematics for Administration Program' of the European Commission. Also he has lectured in the National Technical University of Athens, in the National Academy of Public Administration and in the University of Thessaly. He has participated in many national and international research programs, and authored numerous journal and conference papers; one of them has been honoured with the International Award of the American Society of Mechanical Engineers (ASME) Controls and Diagnostcs Committee.

Vincent A. Mabert is Emeritus Professor of Operations Management in Kelley School of Business, Indiana University. He conducts research and consults in the areas of supply chain management, work force planning, order scheduling, enterprise resource planning systems, new product development, and manufacturing system design. His publications include articles in *Management Science, Decision Sciences, IIE Transactions, Journal of Operations Management, The Accounting Review, and the Academy of Management Journal.* Routinely he consults with the Rand Corporation concerning supply chain management issues for the United States military. He has been active and held officer positions in a number of professional societies including Industrial Engineering, INFORMS, APICS, and Decision Sciences. Professor Mabert is vise president of the Harvey Foundation, a Fellow of the Decision Sciences Institute, and Editor-in-Chief of the *Production & Inventory Management Journal.*

Drakoulis Martakos is an associate professor at the Department of Informatics and Telecommunications at the National and Kapodistrian University of Athens. He received his BSc in Physics, MSc in electronics and radio communications and PhD in real-time computing from the same university. Professor Martakos is a consultant to public and private organizations and a project leader in numerous national and international projects. He serves on the Board of the Hellenic Chapter of the Association of Information Systems (AIS) and he is the author or co-author of more than 70 scientific publications and a number of technical reports and studies.

Andrea Masini is an assistant professor of Operations and Technology Management at the London Business School. Andrea's research focuses on the strategic and organizational impact of information technology innovations. He studies the mechanisms through which IT investments generate adaptive capabilities and become a source of competitive advantage. By assessing the effectiveness of different IT strategies in different organizational and environmental contexts, his research provides useful insights to firms that want to maximize the value of their IT investments. He is author of various articles appeared in international journals and he actively consults for private and public organizations on themes related to ICT and technological innovation.

Charlotte Mason is professor of Marketing at the Terry College of Business at the University of Georgia where she is Head of the Department of Marketing and Distribution and Director of the Coca-Cola Center for Marketing Studies. Formerly she was at the Kenan-Flagler Business School at the University of Chapel Hill. She received BS and MS degrees in industrial engineering, MS in statistics, and Ph.D. in Business from Stanford University. Before joining academia she worked for Procter & Gamble and Booz, Allen and Hamilton. Her current research addresses the use of customer databases and strategic CRM issues. Her research is published in Marketing Science, Journal of Marketing Research, and other leading journals. Charlotte serves on several editorial boards and is co-author of *The Marketing Game!,* a strategic marketing simulation.

Sanjay Mathrani has been a supply chain manager at Navman Wireless New Zealand until recently. He will be joining the School of Engineering and Advanced Technology (SEAT) at Massey University as a Lecturer in Product Development soon. He has more than twenty years of product development, manufacturing, and supply chain experience. He has held senior managerial positions in various multinationals and organizations of repute including Alstom, Ruston & Hornsby, and David Brown. He has been a practitioner and super user of ERP and business intelligence systems. He holds a B Tech in mechanical engineering, masters in management sciences, and a postgraduate diploma in computer management. He is pursuing a PhD study to evaluate the impact of enterprise systems on organizational functions and processes and its link to business benefits. His research interests are in information and knowledge management, project and supply chain management, product development and manufacturing operations, and enterprise service-oriented architectures. He has published several papers in international conferences and journals and is an invited speaker at various international Universities.

Alok Mishra is associate professor of Computer and Software Engineering at Atilim University, Ankara Turkey. He had his PhD in Computer Science (Software Engineering) besides dual Masters in Computer Science & Applications and Human Resource Management. His areas of interest and research are software engineering, information system, information & knowledge management and object oriented analysis & design. He had extensive experience of distance and online education related to computers and management courses. He has published articles, book chapters and book-reviews related to software engineering and information system in refereed journals, books and conferences including International Journal of Information Management, *Government Information Quarterly*, IET-Software, *Behaviour and Information Technology*, Public Personnel Management, European Journal of Engineering Education, International Journal of Information Technology and Management.

Gary P. Moynihan is a professor in the Department of Industrial Engineering, The University of Alabama. He received BS (chemistry) and MBA (operations management) degrees from Rensselaer Polytechnic Institute, and a PhD (industrial engineering) from the University of Central Florida. While at The University of Alabama, he has taught, developed and expanded courses in information systems design, project management, life cycle costing and engineering economics. His primary areas of research specialization are information systems development, economic analysis, project management, and manufacturing operations analysis.

Valentin Nicolescu studied Economics at the University of Hohenheim, Germany. Since 2003, he has been technical head of the SAP Hochschul Competence Center (SAP University Competence Center (SAP HCC)) at the Technische Universität München. His responsibilities in this role include operating SAP training systems for third-level institutions throughout Germany, and providing SAP training to third-level lecturers. His focus areas are the products in the SAP NetWeaver platform and teaching classic ERP with SAP R/3 and mySAP ERP. He is a certified SAP Technology and Development Consultant for SAP XI and a Technology Consultant for Web AS and Enterprise Portal.

Mara Nikolaidou is an assistant professor of Information Technology at Harokopio University of Athens. She holds a PhD and a bachelor degree in computer science from the Department of Informatics and Telecommunication of the University of Athens. She is a member of IEEE and ISCA. Her research interests include software and information system engineering, e-government and digital libraries.

S. Padmanaban, BCom, MBA (Panjab), CISA, is currently professor-Systems at SDM Institute for Management Development, Mysore, India. Mr. Padmanaban has about 30+ years experience in IT (Information Technology) industry, having worked in India and Zambia (CMC Ltd, Zambia State Insurance Corporation Ltd, et al), in capacities ranging from systems analyst to director (Operations). He has directed and coordinated many large IT/IS projects, including Indian Railways Passenger Reservation

System, Kandla Port Trust MIS, ZSIC General Insurance. Audited and advised banks on IS Security, Audit, and Control systems. He has lectured at University of Zambia, Indian Institute of Management, Tata Institute of Social Sciences, State Bank of India, Bank of Baroda Staff Colleges, National Insurance Academy. Co-authored and published articles, case reviews, and cases. Research interests include: integrated information systems (in-house ERP); systems integration, systems audit/security/control; quality assurance; public systems--especially railways/transport; financial and allied services, specifically insurance and banking, and EIS/MIS.

Christian Ploder is a Research Assistant at the Department of Information Systems, Operational Management and Logistics at the University of Innsbruck and Ph.D. student. In his Ph.D. thesis he is developing a model for diagnosing knowledge intensive business processes. Since working at the Department he is a lecturer for Information System Basic Course, Project & Knowledge Management, author of different journals and papers presented on international conferences. His research interests include knowledge management focused on small and medium-sized enterprises as well as the topic of knowledge intensive processes.

Mateja Podlogar is assistant professor of Information Systems, head of eProcurement Laboratory and head of Supply Chain RFID LivingLab at the Faculty of Organizational Sciences, University of Maribor. Her current research includes: eCommerce in supply chain, RFID systems and new eBusiness models in supply chain, web based ERP systems, ERP systems integration of all supply chain participants, business process reengineering, business data and information systems auditing. She intensively cooperates with the industry, other universities and she is involved in several EU projects. She is also a university advocate of ISACA of the Faculty of Organizational Sciences.

Mohammad Abdur Rashid is a senior lecturer of Computer, Information and Communications Engineering at Massey University, New Zealand. He received MScEng degree in electronics engineering specializing in engineering cybernetics systems from the Technical University of Wroclaw in 1978 and PhD from the University of Strathclyde, UK in 1986. Dr. Rashid is a co-author of *Enterprise Resource Planning: Global Opportunities and Challenges*. He has publications in international journals and conferences covering his areas of research. His research interests are multimedia communication networks, embedded systems design, network protocols and performance studies, mobile wireless multimedia communication and ERP systems.

Rogério Atem de Carvalho holds a BSc in computer science and MSc and DSc in industrial engineering, and is a teacher and researcher at the Federal Center for Technological Education of Campos - CEFET Campos, Bazil. He is the Brazilian representative for the IFIP/Unesco Working Group on Enterprise Information Systems, and is a Founder Member of the IEEE SMC Society Technical Committee on EIS. His research on FOS-ERP was awarded by IFIP in 2006 and jointly by IFIP and IEEE in 2007. He is a consultant for government and private sectors and authored many book chapters and research papers on ERP, ECM, decision support systems, production planning and control, and project management.

Aleda V. Roth is the Burlington Industries distinguished professor of Supply Chain Management at Clemson University. She was the principal investigator of Global Supply Chain Management Futures

Initiative, supported by SAP AG; and member of the Supply Chain Management Thought Leaders Roundtable. She is an internationally recognized empirical scholar in service and manufacturing operations strategy. Her research is motivated by theoretical and practical explanations of how firms can best deploy their global supply chains, operations, and technology strategies for competitive advantage. Dr. Roth has more than 150 publications to her credit; and her work has been distinguished by 51 research awards and 27 grants. She holds senior editorial positions for *Management Science*, *Production and Operations Management (POM)*, *Journal of Operations Management (JOM)*, *Decision Sciences (DSJ)*, *Journal of Supply Chain Management* and others. She served as president of the Production and Operations Management Society (POMS); was named the 2006 OM Scholar at the Academy of Management; and is a fellow of the Decision Sciences Institute, POMS, and UK Advanced Institute of Management Research (AIM). Dr. Roth is a member of the Conference Board's Performance Excellence Council has consulted with corporate staff at leading global companies. She worked in top management for a decade before earning her PhD in at Ohio State University, where she also received her BS. She received her MSPH in biostatistics from UNC-Chapel Hill.

Ioakeim Sapounas is research and teaching assistant and PhD Candidate at the Department of Information and Communication Systems of the University of the Aegean. He has graduated from the Economics Department of the University of Piraeus. Also he holds an Msc in total quality management from the same University. Currently he is also a financial management specialist at the Hellenic Telecommunications Organization (OTE S.A.). His research interests include information systems investment, business value and complemenary factors. He has published several journal and conference papers in the above areas.

Tobias Schoenherr is assistant professor of Supply Chain Management at the Eli Broad College of Business, Michigan State University. Dr. Schoenherr holds a PhD in operations management and decision sciences from Indiana University, Bloomington, from where he also obtained his BSc and MB. He also holds a Diplom-Betriebswirt (FH) from the European School of Business, Reutlingen University, Germany, and is an APICS certified supply chain professional (CSCP). Dr. Schoenherr's research focuses on supply chain management, purchasing, ERP systems, and global manufacturing. His work has appeared or is forthcoming in the *Journal of Operations Management*, the *Journal of Supply Chain Management*, the *International Journal of Operations and Production Management*, *OMEGA - The International Journal of Management Science*, *Business Horizons*, the *Journal of Purchasing and Supply Management*, the *International Journal of Procurement Management*, the *International Journal of Integrated Supply Management*, and *PRACTIX*, among others. Dr. Schoenherr has been active in several professional associations, including DSI, ISM and APICS.

Darshana Sedera is a post doctoral fellow with the Australian Research Council (ARC) and a senior lecturer in the Faculty of IT at the Queensland University of Technology (QUT), Brisbane, Australia. He received his doctor of philosophy for the dissertation titled "Enterprise Systems Success Measurement Model" in 2006 from QUT. His research interests include: Enterprise Systems Lifecycle Management, Information Systems evaluations and success, and Knowledge Management. Dr. Sedera has authored / co-authored over 40 refereed publications in reputed journals and conferences including the *Journal of the Association for Information Systems* (JAIS) and the *International Conference on Information Systems* (ICIS).

Raj Sharman is a faculty member in the Management Science and Systems Department at SUNY Buffalo, NY. He received his BTech and MTech degree from IIT Bombay, India and his MS degree in Industrial Engineering and PhD in computer science from Louisiana State University. His research streams include Information Assurance, Extreme Events, and improving performance on the Web. His papers have been published in a number of national and international journals. He is also the recipient of several grants from the university as well as external agencies.

Ashok K. Soni is chairperson and professor of Operations and Decision Technologies and the SAP Faculty Fellow at the Kelley School of Business at Indiana University. He received a BS in aeronautical engineering from Manchester University, an MS in operations research from Strathclyde University, and an MBA and DBA from Indiana University. Professor Soni's teaching and research interests are in the areas of enterprise applications, technology, e-business, and decision support systems. His research interests are in enterprise technologies and decision support systems. His research interests are in enterprise technologies and decision support systems. His research has appeared in *Management Science*, *Naval Logistics Research*, *Omega*, *IIE Transactions*, and *European Journal of Operational Research*.

Suresh Subramoniam is an assistant professor in the College of Business Administration, Prince Sultan University in Saudi Arabia. He had his BTech from Kerala university and MSIE from Louisiana State University in USA. He also holds a PhD in management from Kerala University. He has around twenty five papers to his credit published in both national and international journals as well as conferences. He is a member of APICS, USA and Indian Institution of Industrial Engineering. He is guiding doctoral research in Kerala University.

Katalin Ternai, PhD, associate professor at the Corvinus University of Budapest, Department of Information Systems. She earned her university degree in Budapest, at ELTE, MSc in mathematics and physics (1981). Later she got a doctoral degree in computer science, (1995). Her expertise: Programming languages, application integration, ERP systems (SAP), system development, information management, process management. Foreign experiences: Information Management Course, University of Amsterdam (1992), PHARE/TEMPUS projects (1990-1997), Memberships: John von Neumann Society for Computing Sciences, Professional experiences learnt in research and application projects. Participated and managed several SAP implementation and educational projects.

Mohamed Tounsi received his PhD in computer science speciality in artificial intelligence from University of Nantes, France in 2002. He was assistant professor at Polytechnic University of Nantes, France. He is currently chairman of computer science department and assistant professor at the Department of Computer Science, Prince Sultan University, KSA. His current research interest includes constraint programming, meta-heuristics, bioinformatics, intelligent agent and optimization algorithm.

Ganesh Vaidyanathan is an assistant professor of Decision Sciences at IUSB. He has conducted research in the areas of eCommerce, supply chain management, project management, knowledge management, technological innovation and IT value. He has authored over 25 publications in journals such as *Journal of Operations Management* and *Communications of the ACM*. He has co-invented four patents in various computer science areas. Dr. Vaidyanathan co-founded eReliable Commerce, Inc., and has held various executive positions at Honeywell, General Dynamics, Lockheed Martin Inc., and Click Commerce Inc. Dr. Vaidyanathan launched products that include security, payment processing, procurement, logistics, ERP, SCM, and data warehousing. He has consulted with Fortune 100 companies including United Airlines, Mitsubishi, Motorola, and Honeywell in technology, business and process reengineering. Dr. Vaidyanathan holds a PhD with a focus on artificial intelligence, robotics and computer engineering from Tulane University and an MBA from the University of Chicago.

Gabriel Valerio is professor and consultant at the Center for Knowledge Systems, Tech of Monterrey, Mexico, since 2001. He has been dedicated to the researching on knowledge management tools for eight years. He is mainly interested in technological tools to support the knowledge flow and the organizational memory. He is a member of research group in Distributed Knowledge and Multiagent Systems. He is a doctor degree student of Educative Innovation, at Virtual University, Tech of Monterrey. He has been visiting professor at the Universidad de Externado at Colombia.

M.A. Venkataramanan is Glaubinger professor of Operations and Decision Technologies and Chair of the Undergraduate Program of the Kelley School of Business at Indiana University, Bloomington. He received his PhD in business analysis and research from the Texas A&M University. His research interests include Enterprise Resource Planning, RFID, network modeling, artificial intelligence, high-speed computing and supply chain models. Venkataramanan organized and managed the Computer Information Systems (CIS) major from 1989 to 1995. He then played a key role in developing the Business Process Management program for the Kelley School of Business at Indiana University as chair of the Operations and Decision Technology Department for six years from 1997-2003. From 2005 to present he is Chair of the Undergraduate Program. His teaching interests are in the area of RFID, decision support systems, computer programming, enterprise resource planning (ERP), optimization techniques, and project management. He is one of the principle investigators in ERP research and teaching initiative at Indiana University. He has more than twenty five research articles published in a variety of journals including *Operations Research, Decision Sciences, Annals of Operations Research, Naval Research Logistics, Computers and OR, EJOR*, and *Mathematical Modeling*.

Dennis Viehland is associate professor of Information Systems at Massey University's Auckland campus in New Zealand. His principal research area is mobile business, with secondary research interests in electronic commerce strategy, ubiquitous computing and innovative use of ICT to manage Information Age organizations. He is a co-author of Electronic Commerce 2008: A Managerial Perspective and has published in numerous international journals and conferences.

Holger Wittges obtained his PhD degree from the University of Hohenheim, Germany, under the supervision of professor Krcmar and with the topic *Connecting Business Process Modeling and Workflow Implementation*. He then worked for three years as an IT project leader with debitel AG in Stuttgart, Germany. Since 2004, he has been operations head of the SAP Hochschul Competence Center (SAP University Competence Center (SAP HCC)) at Technische Universität München. His current research areas are standard software, service-oriented architectures, and performance metrics in ERP systems. He is also a certified technology consultant for SAP NetWeaver—Enterprise Portal & Knowledge Management.

Index